THE ROUTLEDGE HANDBOOK
OF THE COMPUTATIONAL MIND

Computational approaches dominate contemporary cognitive science, promising a unified, scientific explanation of how the mind works. However, computational approaches raise major philosophical and scientific questions. In what sense is the mind computational? How do computational approaches explain perception, learning, and decision making? What kinds of challenges should computational approaches overcome to advance our understanding of mind, brain, and behaviour?

The Routledge Handbook of the Computational Mind is an outstanding overview and exploration of these issues and the first philosophical collection of its kind. Comprising thirty-five chapters by an international team of contributors from different disciplines, the *Handbook* is organised into four parts:

- History and future prospects of computational approaches
- Types of computational approach
- Foundations and challenges of computational approaches
- Applications to specific parts of psychology.

Essential reading for students and researchers in philosophy of mind, philosophy of psychology, and philosophy of science, *The Routledge Handbook of the Computational Mind* will also be of interest to those studying computational models in related subjects such as psychology, neuroscience, and computer science.

Mark Sprevak is a Senior Lecturer in Philosophy at the University of Edinburgh, UK. His book *The Computational Mind* is forthcoming from Routledge.

Matteo Colombo is an Assistant Professor at the Tilburg Center for Logic, Ethics, and Philosophy of Science, Tilburg University, the Netherlands; and a Humboldt Research Fellow at the Clinic for Psychiatry and Psychotherapy, Charité University Clinic Berlin, Germany.

ROUTLEDGE HANDBOOKS IN PHILOSOPHY

Routledge Handbooks in Philosophy are state-of-the-art surveys of emerging, newly refreshed, and important fields in philosophy, providing accessible yet thorough assessments of key problems, themes, thinkers, and recent developments in research.

All chapters for each volume are specially commissioned, and written by leading scholars in the field. Carefully edited and organized, *Routledge Handbooks in Philosophy* provide indispensable reference tools for students and researchers seeking a comprehensive overview of new and exciting topics in philosophy. They are also valuable teaching resources as accompaniments to textbooks, anthologies, and research-orientated publications.

Also available:

THE ROUTLEDGE HANDBOOK OF MECHANISMS AND MECHANICAL PHILOSOPHY
Edited by Stuart Glennan and Phyllis Ilari

THE ROUTLEDGE HANDBOOK OF PHILOSOPHY OF ANIMAL MINDS
Edited by Kristin Andrews and Jacob Beck

THE ROUTLEDGE HANDBOOK OF LIBERTARIANISM
Edited by Jason Brennan, Bas van der Vossen, and David Schmidtz

THE ROUTLEDGE HANDBOOK OF METAETHICS
Edited by Tristram McPherson and David Plunkett

THE ROUTLEDGE HANDBOOK OF EVOLUTION AND PHILOSOPHY
Edited by Richard Joyce

THE ROUTLEDGE HANDBOOK OF COLLECTIVE INTENTIONALITY
Edited by Marija Jankovic and Kirk Ludwig

THE ROUTLEDGE HANDBOOK OF SCIENTIFIC REALISM
Edited by Juha Saatsi

THE ROUTLEDGE HANDBOOK OF PACIFISM AND NON-VIOLENCE
Edited by Andrew Fiala

THE ROUTLEDGE HANDBOOK OF CONSCIOUSNESS
Edited by Rocco J. Gennaro

THE ROUTLEDGE HANDBOOK OF PHILOSOPHY AND SCIENCE OF ADDICTION
Edited by Hanna Pickard and Serge Ahmed

THE ROUTLEDGE HANDBOOK OF MORAL EPISTEMOLOGY
Edited by Karen Jones, Mark Timmons, and Aaron Zimmerman

For more information about this series, please visit:
www.routledge.com/Routledge-Handbooks-in-Philosophy/book-series/RHP

THE ROUTLEDGE HANDBOOK OF THE COMPUTATIONAL MIND

Edited by Mark Sprevak and Matteo Colombo

LONDON AND NEW YORK

First published 2019
by Routledge
2 Park Square, Milton Park, Abingdon, Oxon OX14 4RN

and by Routledge
711 Third Avenue, New York, NY 10017

Routledge is an imprint of the Taylor & Francis Group, an informa business

British Library Cataloguing-in-Publication Data
A catalogue record for this book is available from the British Library

Library of Congress Cataloging-in-Publication Data
Names: Sprevak, Mark, 1977– editor.
Title: The Routledge handbook of the computational mind /
edited by Mark Sprevak and Matteo Colombo.
Other titles: Handbook of the computational mind
Description: Milton Park, Abingdon, Oxon ; New York : Routledge, 2019. |
Series: Routledge handbooks in philosophy |
Includes bibliographical references and index.
Identifiers: LCCN 2018015384 | ISBN 9781138186682 (hbk : alk. paper) |
ISBN 9781315643670 (ebk) Subjects: LCSH: Computational intelligence. |
Cognitive science. | Computational neuroscience. | Philosophy of mind.
Classification: LCC Q342 .R68 2019 | DDC 006.301/9–dc23
LC record available at https://lccn.loc.gov/2018015384

ISBN: 978-1-138-18668-2 (hbk)
ISBN: 978-1-315-64367-0 (ebk)

Typeset in Bembo
by Out of House Publishing

Printed and bound in Great Britain by
TJ International Ltd, Padstow, Cornwall

CONTENTS

Contents

CONTRIBUTORS

Tara H. Abraham is Associate Professor in the Department of History at the University of Guelph in Guelph, Ontario, Canada. She is the author of *Rebel Genius: Warren S. McCulloch's Transdisciplinary Life in Science* (MIT Press, 2016), which was nominated for the 2018 Outstanding Book Prize of the International Society for the History of the Neurosciences. She is currently working on a project that examines the entry of psychiatry into American medical education during the first half of the twentieth century.

Kenneth Aizawa received his PhD in History and Philosophy of Science from the University of Pittsburgh in 1989. Before coming to Rutgers, he taught at Central Michigan University and Centenary College of Louisiana. He works primarily in the history and philosophy of psychology and is the author of *The Systematicity Arguments* and, with Fred Adams, *The Bounds of Cognition*. When he is not doing philosophy he dreams of cycling in the Alps.

Matthew Broome is Professor of Psychiatry and Youth Mental Health, and Director of the Institute for Mental Health at the University of Birmingham. He trained in psychiatry at the Maudsley Hospital, Bethlem Royal Hospital, and the National Hospital for Neurology and Neurosurgery. Matthew has a PhD in Psychiatry from the University of London and in Philosophy from the University of Warwick. He is series editor to the Oxford University Press series, *International Perspectives in Philosophy and Psychiatry*. Matthew's research interests include youth mental health, the prodromal phase of psychosis, delusion formation, mood instability, functional neuroimaging, interdisciplinary methods, and the philosophy of psychiatry.

Stefan Brugger is an Academic Clinical Fellow in the Division of Psychiatry at UCL. His research interests include computational and neuroimaging approaches to psychiatric disorders, with a particular focus on the positive symptoms of psychosis – delusions and hallucinations. He is also undertaking clinical training in psychiatry in Camden and Islington, and currently works clinically in the psychiatry of intellectual disability.

Cameron Buckner began studying artificial intelligence at Texas Tech University and completed his PhD in Philosophy at Indiana University, Bloomington. After an Alexander von

Humboldt Fellowship at Ruhr-University, Bochum, he became an Assistant Professor at the University of Houston.

Rosa Cao is Assistant Professor of Philosophy at Stanford University. Her current research focuses on issues at the intersection of the philosophy of mind, neuroscience, and cognitive science, including questions about naturalizing mental content and the explanatory role of computation. In previous work she has studied neurovascular interactions and the role of astrocytes in sensory processing.

Anthony Chemero is Professor of Philosophy and Psychology at the University of Cincinnati. His research is both philosophical and empirical; typically, it tries to be both at the same time. His research is focused on questions related to nonlinear dynamical modeling, ecological psychology, complex systems, phenomenology, and artificial life. He is the author of *Radical Embodied Cognitive Science* (MIT Press, 2009) and, with Stephan Käufer, *Phenomenology* (Polity Press, 2015). He is currently editing the second edition of The MIT *Encyclopedia of the Cognitive Sciences*.

Mazviita Chirimuuta is an Associate Professor of History and Philosophy of Science at the University of Pittsburgh. She received her PhD in visual neuroscience from the University of Cambridge in 2004, and held postdoctoral fellowships in philosophy at Monash University (2005–2008) and Washington University St. Louis (2008–2009). Her principal area of research is in the philosophy of neuroscience and perceptual psychology. Her book *Outside Color: Perceptual Science and the Puzzle of Color in Philosophy* was published by MIT Press in 2015. She is currently working on a new project on abstraction in neuroscience under the working title *How to Simplify the Brain*.

Matteo Colombo is currently an Assistant Professor at the Tilburg Center for Logic, Ethics, and Philosophy of Science, Tilburg University (the Netherlands), and a Humboldt Research Fellow at the Clinic for Psychiatry and Psychotherapy, Charité University Clinic Berlin (Germany). Most of his published work is in the philosophy of cognitive science, philosophy of science, and moral psychology. He is interested in questions about evidence and explanation in the computational, cognitive, and brain sciences, and more generally in how the scientific and manifest images of mind relate to one another.

Jack Copeland FRS NZ is Distinguished Professor in Humanities at the University of Canterbury, New Zealand, where he is Director of the Turing Archive for the History of Computing. He is also Honorary Research Professor of Philosophy at the University of Queensland, Australia, and is currently John Findlay Professor of Philosophy at Boston University in the US. His books include a highly accessible biography *Turing, Pioneer of the Information Age*; also *Colossus: The Secrets of Bletchley Park's Codebreaking Computers*; *The Essential Turing*; *Alan Turing's Electronic Brain*; and most recently *The Turing Guide* (all with Oxford University Press). He has published more than 100 articles on the philosophy, history and foundations of computing, and on mathematical and philosophical logic. Copeland is the recipient of the 2016 Covey Award and the American Philosophical Association's 2017 Barwise Prize, recognizing a substantial record of innovative research in the field of computing and philosophy.

David Danks is the L.L. Thurstone Professor of Philosophy and Psychology, and Head of the Department of Philosophy, at Carnegie Mellon University (as well as a member of the Center for the Neural Basis of Cognition). He works at the intersection of philosophy, cognitive science, and machine learning, integrating ideas, methods, and frameworks from each to advance our understanding of complex, cross-disciplinary problems. His book, *Unifying the Mind: Cognitive Representations as Graphical Models* (MIT Press, 2014) developed an integrated cognitive model of complex human cognition, including causal cognition, concept acquisition and use, and decision making. Danks is the recipient of a James S. McDonnell Foundation Scholar Award (2008), and an Andrew Carnegie Fellowship (2017).

Joe Dewhurst is currently a Postdoctoral Fellow at the Munich Center for Mathematical Philosophy. His main research interests include philosophy of mind and cognition, the history of cognitive science, and foundational issues in philosophy of computation. His doctoral research focused on the relationship between folk psychology and cognitive science, with reference to recent developments in cognitive neuroscience.

Frances Egan is Professor of Philosophy at Rutgers University, New Brunswick. She received her PhD from the University of Western Ontario. She works in philosophy of mind and cognitive science. Her current interests include the nature of psychological explanation, issues in the foundation of cognitive neuroscience, and the philosophy of perception.

Lotem Elber-Dorozko is a PhD student for computational neuroscience in the Edmond and Lily Safra Center for Brain Sciences at the Hebrew University of Jerusalem. She investigates computational models of decision making as well as the philosophy of cognitive and neural sciences. Her research focuses on the ways evidence of neural correlates of computational models is interpreted and on the explanatory role of mechanistic and computational models in the cognitive sciences.

Frank Faries is completing his PhD in philosophy at the University of Cincinnati. He has two streams of research, the first of which concerns data-driven methods in the mind and brain and their intersection with issues of explanation and integration. His second stream investigates the relationship between inner speech and cognition, based primarily on experimental work on people with aphasia.

James Garson is a Professor in the Department of Philosophy at the University of Houston. He received his PhD at the University of Pittsburgh, and has taught at the University of Pennsylvania, the University of Notre Dame, Rice University, and the University of Illinois at Chicago where he was a Visiting Professor in Computer Science. His publications include articles on logic, semantics, linguistics, the philosophy of cognitive science, connectionism, and computerized education. He is the author of *Modal Logic for Philosophers* and *What Logics Mean* (both with Cambridge University Press).

Clark Glymour is Alumni University Professor at Carnegie Mellon University. He has been a Guggenheim Fellow, a Fellow of the Center for Advanced Studies in the Behavioral Sciences, and a Phi Beta Kappa Lecturer. Besides work in philosophy of science he has worked for many years on the development of computerized procedures for extracting causal information from non-experimental data and the applications of those procedures, most recently to the problem of identifying effective neural connections from functional magnetic resonance (fMRI) scans.

Xiaosi Gu is one of the foremost researchers in the area of computational psychiatry. Her research examines the neural and computational mechanisms underlying human beliefs, decision making, and social interaction, in both health and disease, through a synthesis of neuroimaging and computational modeling. Recently, Dr. Gu has been examining the interaction between beliefs and drugs (e.g. nicotine) in addiction. This work suggests that beliefs about nicotine could override the effects of nicotine on neural substrates involved in reinforcement learning. Dr. Gu began her research at the Department of Psychology at Peking University (PKU), Beijing. After receiving a dual degree in Psychology and Economics from PKU, she moved to New York City to pursue a PhD in Neuroscience at the Icahn School of Medicine at Mount Sinai. She then completed her postdoctoral training in Computational Psychiatry and Decision Neuroscience at the Virginia Tech Carilion Research Institute, Roanoke, VA and the Wellcome Trust Centre for Neuroimaging at University College London (UCL), London, UK. During her time in London, she also set up the world's first computational psychiatry course at UCL and has been an advocate for this nascent field. She is currently a Principle Investigator at the Department of Psychiatry and Neuroscience, the Friedman Brain Institute, and the Addiction Institute, and Director of Computational Psychiatry Unit, at Icahn School of Medicine at Mount Sinai.

Jakob Hohwy is Professor of Philosophy at Monash University, Melbourne, Australia. He was trained in Aarhus, Denmark, St Andrews in Scotland, and at the Australian National University. Hohwy has established the Cognition and Philosophy lab in the philosophy department at Monash and conducts interdisciplinary experiments in philosophy, psychiatry, and neuroscience. Hohwy's research focuses on contemporary theories in theoretical neurobiology and their implications for consciousness, self, belief, and value. He is deputy editor of *Neuroscience of Consciousness* and is the author of *The Predictive Mind* (Oxford University Press, 2013).

Bryce Huebner is a Provost's Distinguished Associate Professor of Philosophy at Georgetown University. He completed a PhD at the University of North Carolina, Chapel Hill before doing postdoctoral research in psychology at Harvard University and in the Center for Cognitive Studies at Tufts University. He has published both theoretical and empirical research, in philosophy and the cognitive sciences. His current research focuses on the role of reinforcement learning in social cognition, the relationships between individual and group agency, and the nature of emotional states.

Daniel D. Hutto is Professor of Philosophical Psychology at the University of Wollongong and member of the Australian Research Council College of Experts. He is co-author of the award-winning *Radicalizing Enactivism* (MIT Press, 2013) and its sequel, *Evolving Enactivism* (MIT Press, 2017). His other recent books include: *Folk Psychological Narratives* (MIT Press, 2008) and *Wittgenstein and the End of Philosophy* (Palgrave, 2006). He is editor of *Narrative and Understanding Persons* (Cambridge University Press, 2007) and *Narrative and Folk Psychology* (Imprint Academic, 2009). A special yearbook, *Radical Enactivism*, focusing on his philosophy of intentionality, phenomenology, and narrative, was published in 2006. He is regularly invited to speak not only at philosophy conferences but at expert meetings of anthropologists, clinical psychiatrists/therapists, educationalists, narratologists, neuroscientists, and psychologists.

Liz Irvine is a Lecturer in Philosophy at Cardiff University. Her research interests are primarily in philosophy of cognitive science and psychology, and philosophy of science. She has published in journals such as *Mind and Language*, *Synthese*, and the *British Journal for Philosophy of Science*.

Alistair M. C. Isaac is a Lecturer in Philosophy of Mind and Cognition at the University of Edinburgh. His research is primarily on the history and foundations of psychology, including especially psychophysics and its implications for the philosophy of perception. Descartes used to be his least favorite philosopher, but he has come around to finding him one of the most fascinating.

Joseph Jebari is currently a graduate student and PhD candidate in the Department of Philosophy at Georgetown University. His research builds upon tools from systems biology and systems neuroscience. He is currently writing a dissertation where he develops a biologically and computationally plausible argument for the claim that there are objectively specifiable moral norms.

Colin Klein is an Associate Professor at the Australian National University and an Australian Research Council Future Fellow. His work focuses on methodological issues as they arise in cognitive neuroscience, particularly around issues of computation, inference from functional brain imaging, and cross-species comparisons of functional architectures.

Miles MacLeod completed his PhD in Philosophy at the University of Vienna in 2010. Since 2015 he has been an Assistant Professor for philosophy of science in practice at the University of Twente. His research interests include scientific cognition in general, cognitive processes of model-building in particular, and mathematical and statistical modeling in scientific contexts.

John Michael completed his PhD in Philosophy at the University of Vienna in 2010. Since 2016 he has been Assistant Professor of Philosophy at the University of Warwick and Affiliated Researcher the Department of Cognitive Science of the Central European University in Budapest. His research interests include the sense of commitment, self-control, joint action, perspective-taking, and other issues at the intersection between philosophy and cognitive science. He currently holds an ERC starting grant investigating the sense of commitment in joint action.

Marcin Miłkowski is Associate Professor in the Institute of Philosophy and Sociology, Polish Academy of Sciences (Warsaw, Poland). For his *Explaining the Computational Mind* (MIT Press, 2013), he received the Tadeusz Kotarbiski Prize from the Polish Academy of Sciences and the National Science Center Award. He is a recipient of the Herbert A. Simon Award for significant contributions in the foundations of computational neuroscience.

Erik Myin is Professor of Philosophy at the University of Antwerp and Director of the Centre for Philosophical Psychology. He has published papers on topics relating to mind and perception in philosophical, interdisciplinary and scientific journals. Two books, *Radicalizing Enactivism: Basic Minds without Content*, and *Evolving Enactivism: Basic Minds Meet Content*, written by Dan Hutto and Erik Myin, were published by MIT Press in 2013 and 2017.

Nico Orlandi is Associate Professor of Philosophy at the University of California at Santa Cruz. Before coming to California, Nico was Assistant Professor at Rice University and a visiting fellow at the Stanford Humanities Center. Nico is the author of a 2014 monograph published by Oxford University Press, and of over fifteen articles on the topics of perception, concepts, mental representation, and inference.

Anco Peeters is a PhD Candidate in Philosophy of Mind and Cognition at the University of Wollongong.

Gualtiero Piccinini (PhD, University of Pittsburgh, 2003) is Professor of Philosophy and Associate Director of the Center for Neurodynamics at the University of Missouri – St. Louis. His book, *Physical Computation: A Mechanistic Account*, was published by Oxford University Press in 2015.

Diane Proudfoot is Professor of Philosophy at the University of Canterbury, New Zealand. She is also Co-Director of the Turing Centre at the Swiss Federal Institute of Technology in Zurich. She was educated at the University of Edinburgh, the University of California at Berkeley (as a Fulbright-Hays scholar), and the University of Cambridge (as an Andrew Carnegie scholar). In 2016 Diane was a Fellow of the Israel Institute for Advanced Studies and in 2017–2018 John Findlay Visiting Professor at Boston University. She and Copeland founded and direct the award-winning online Turing Archive for the History of Computing. Diane has published in the *Journal of Philosophy*, *Artificial Intelligence*, *Scientific American*, and numerous other philosophy and science journals.

William Ramsey is Professor of Philosophy at the University of Nevada Las Vegas. He is the author of *Representation Reconsidered* (Cambridge University Press, 2007) and the co-editor (with Keith Frankish) of the *Cambridge Handbook of Cognitive Science* (Cambridge University Press, 2012) and the *Cambridge Handbook of Artificial Intelligence* (Cambridge University Press, 2014). He has written numerous articles on the nature of mental representation, computational theories of the mind, common sense psychology, and other issues in the philosophy of cognitive science.

Michael Rescorla is a Professor of Philosophy at the University of California, Los Angeles. His research concerns the philosophies of mind, language, and logic.

J. Brendan Ritchie is an FWO [PEGASUS]2 Marie Skłodowska-Curie Fellow in the Laboratory of Biological Psychology, Brain and Cognition Unit, at KU Leuven, Belgium. His philosophical research focuses on the notions of representation and computation utilized in the cognitive and neural sciences. As a scientist his experimental work focuses on the neural basis of visual object categorization, and combines neuroimaging (fMRI, MEG) with modeling of behavior.

Jenelle Salisbury is a PhD student at the University of Connecticut studying philosophy of mind and cognitive science. Her dissertation is on the unity of consciousness and the first-person perspective. She aims to use anomalous cases (such as the split-brain case and the craniopagus case) to inform our conceptions of unity and their neural bases.

Richard Samuels is a Professor of Philosophy and member of the Center for Cognitive and Brain Sciences at Ohio State. He previously held appointments at King's College London and the University of Pennsylvania. He publishes widely on topics in the philosophy of mind, philosophy of psychology, and foundations of cognitive science.

Ruben Sanchez-Romero is a PhD student in Logic, Computation, and Methodology at Carnegie Mellon University. His research is focused on applying statistical causal inference algorithms to brain functional imaging data in order to uncover properties of brain networks at different temporal and spatial scales. He is also member of the Center for Causal Discovery (CCD), a joint effort between Carnegie Mellon University and the University of Pittsburgh.

Susan Schneider is a Distinguished Scholar at the US Library of Congress, a Professor of Philosophy and Cognitive Science at the University of Connecticut, and a faculty member in the Ethics and Technology Group at the Yale University. Within the fields of metaphysics and philosophy of mind, much of her work explores the nature of thought, especially in light of discoveries in cognitive science and work in contemporary metaphysics. She is the author or editor of *Science Fiction and Philosophy*, *The Language of Thought: A New Philosophical Direction*, and *The Blackwell Companion to Consciousness* (with Max Velmans).

Oron Shagrir is Schulman Chair in Philosophy and Cognitive Science and Vice President for International Affairs at the Hebrew University of Jerusalem. He has been a Visiting Research Fellow at a number of institutions, including the Israel Institute of Advanced Studies, the Center for Philosophy of Science at the University of Pittsburgh and the University of Canterbury in New Zealand. Oron received his BSc in Mathematics and Computer Science from the Hebrew University of Jerusalem and gained a PhD in Philosophy and Cognitive Science from the University of California, San Diego. He has published extensively in the philosophy of computing and cognitive science, including papers in *Mind, Philosophy and Phenomenological Research, Philosophical Studies, The Monist, Philosophy of Science, The British Journal for the Philosophy of Science, Synthese, Current Opinion in Neurobiology, Topics in Cognitive Science, Theoretical Computer Science, Communications of ACM*, and *Minds and Machines*, as well as chapters in books published by Oxford University Press, Cambridge University Press, and MIT Press.

Murray Shanahan is Professor of Cognitive Robotics in the Department of Computing at Imperial College London, and a senior research scientist at DeepMind. Educated at Imperial College and Cambridge University (King's College), he became a full professor at Imperial in 2006, and joined DeepMind in 2017. His publications span artificial intelligence, robotics, machine learning, logic, dynamical systems, computational neuroscience, and philosophy of mind. He has written several books, including *Embodiment and the Inner Life* (2010) and *The Technological Singularity* (2015). His main current research interests are neurodynamics, deep reinforcement learning, and the future of AI.

Mark Sprevak is a Senior Lecturer in Philosophy at the University of Edinburgh. His primary research interests are in philosophy of mind, philosophy of science, and metaphysics, with particular focus on the cognitive sciences. He has published articles in, among other places, *The Journal of Philosophy, The British Journal for the Philosophy of Science, Synthese, Philosophy, Psychiatry & Psychology*, and *Studies in History and Philosophy of Science*. His book *The Computational Mind* is forthcoming from Routledge.

Catherine Stinson has graduate training in machine learning from the University of Toronto, and a PhD in History and Philosophy of Science from the University of Pittsburgh. Her research concerns computational methods in cognitive science, integration across fields and levels in the brain sciences, classification in psychopathology, and disorders of body perception. Following a postdoc at the Rotman Institute of Philosophy at the University of Western Ontario, she is working at the intersection of machine learning and healthcare.

Jakub Szymanik is an Associate Professor in the Institute for Logic, Language and Computation at the University of Amsterdam. He is also affiliated with the Department of Linguistics and the Research Priority Area Brain and Cognition both at the University of Amsterdam. He is leading a group studying logic, language, and cognition whose approach can be characterized as a mixture of formal (logic, computational modeling, simulations) and empirical (neurobehavioral experiments, corpus linguistics) methods. He specializes in natural language semantics, especially generalized quantifiers and reasoning.

Rineke Verbrugge is Full Professor at the University of Groningen's Institute of Artificial Intelligence. Since 2002, she has been the leader of the Multi-Agent Systems research group. Her work focuses on logics, multi-agent systems, and social cognition. She received a MSc (cum laude) and a PhD in Mathematics from the University of Amsterdam. Subsequently, she was a post-doc in Prague and Gothenburg, and Assistant Professor at MIT and the Vrije Universiteit Amsterdam. Rineke Verbrugge is chair of the Netherlands Organization for Logic and has chaired events such as the Twentieth European Summer School in Logic, Language and Information (Hamburg, 2008). She has written the book *Teamwork in Multi-Agent Systems: A Formal Approach* with Barbara Dunin-Keplicz (Wiley, 2010). Together with Jan van Eijck, she has been awarded four grants for their large international NIAS-project Games, Action and Social Software (2006–2007). From June 2009 to November 2014, Rineke Verbrugge has led the NWO Vici project "Cognitive Systems in Interaction: Logical and Computational Models of Higher-order Social Cognition", leading to more than 125 articles in international journals and conferences. She is associate editor of the *Journal of Logic, Language and Information*. In 2016, she has been elected member of the Royal Holland Society of Sciences and Humanities.

Daniel A. Weiskopf is an Associate Professor of Philosophy and an associate member of the Neuroscience Institute at Georgia State University. He writes on topics in the philosophy of psychology and philosophy of science, including concepts and cognitive architecture, embodied cognition, interfield modeling, mechanistic explanation, and scientific kinds. He has published numerous articles and is the author, with Fred Adams, of *An Introduction to the Philosophy of Psychology* (Cambridge University Press, 2015).

Farid Zahnoun works at the Centre for Philosophical Psychology at the University of Antwerp. His current central philosophical interest lies in analyzing notions of internal representation, as well as in E-approaches to forms of offline cognition. He was Visiting Researcher at the University of Wollongong (UOW), where he collaborated with Daniel Hutto (September 2016–March 2017).

Carlos Zednik is Assistant Professor at the Otto-von-Guericke University in Magdeburg, Germany. His work centers on scientific explanation in various areas of cognitive science, including psychology and neuroscience, with a particular focus on the explanatory contributions of different mathematical and computational models. In recent work, he has also explored philosophical issues in artificial intelligence.

ACKNOWLEDGMENTS

We would like to thank a number of individuals for helping to make this volume possible: Fahad Al-Dahimi and Jonathan Hoare for copy-editing and helping to prepare the volume for final submission; Adam Johnson for guiding us through the process and providing much needed support and encouragement; and, most important of all, the authors for providing thoughtful, bold, and valuable contributions, for their constructive responses to our comments, and for their patience throughout the production process.

Matteo gratefully acknowledges financial support from the Deutsche Forschungsgemeinschaft (DFG) within the priority program "New Frameworks of Rationality" ([SPP 1516]), and from the Alexander von Humboldt Foundation.

INTRODUCTION

Mark Sprevak and Matteo Colombo

Computational approaches to explain how the mind works have bloomed in the last three decades. The idea that computing can explain thinking emerged in the early modern period, but its impact on the philosophy and sciences of the mind and brain owes much to the groundbreaking work of Alan Turing on the foundations of both mathematical computation theory and artificial intelligence (e.g. Turing, 1936; 1950). Turing's work set the stage for the *computational theory of mind* (CTM), which, classically understood, claims that thinking is a computational process defined over linguistically structured representations.

Championed by Hilary Putnam (1967), Jerry Fodor (1975), Allen Newell and Herbert Simon (1976), and Zenon Pylyshyn (1984) among others, CTM played a major role in cognitive science from the 1960s to the 1990s. In the 1980s and 1990s, connectionism (Rumelhart, McClelland, and the PDP Research Group, 1986) and dynamical systems theory (Thelen and Smith, 1994) began putting pressure on the classical formulation of CTM. Since then, a growing number of cognitive scientists and philosophers have appealed to these alternative paradigms to challenge the idea that the computations relevant to cognition are defined over linguistically structured representations.

Meantime, fueled by increasingly sophisticated machine learning techniques and growing computer power, computers and computational modeling have become ever more important to cognitive science. At the turn of the century, engineering successes in machine learning and computer science inspired novel approaches, like deep learning, reinforcement learning, Bayesian modeling, and other probabilistic frameworks, which straddle dichotomies that previously defined the debate about CTM (e.g. representationalism vs anti-representationalism, logicism vs probability, and nativism vs empiricism). Recently, some researchers have argued that all these theories can be unified by thinking of the mind as an embodied, culturally situated, computational engine for prediction (Clark, 2015).

The Routledge Handbook of the Computational Mind reflects these historical dynamics, engages with recent developments, and highlights future vistas. It provides readers with a comprehensive, state-of-the-art treatment of the history, foundations, challenges, applications, and prospects of computational ideas for understanding mind, brain, and behavior.

The thirty-five chapters of the Handbook are organized into four sections: "History and future directions", "Types of computing", "Foundations and challenges", and "Applications". Although each of the thirty-five chapters in the volume stands alone and provides readers with understanding of a specific aspect of the computational mind, there are several common threads that contribute to the narrative coherence of the Handbook. Some of these threads indicate a departure from past directions; others maintain aspects of the heritage of classical ideas about computation and the mind. We survey these briefly below.

An important thread that is continuous with the origin of CTM is that theorists engage with the details of actual scientific practice. In the Preface of *The Language of Thought*, Jerry Fodor explains that he had two reasons to address the question of how the mind works: first, "the question of how the mind works is profoundly interesting, and the best psychology we have is *ipso facto* the best answer that is currently available. Second, the best psychology we have is still research in progress, and I am interested in the advancement of that research" (1975, p. viii). These two considerations also animate the contributors to this Handbook. Authors rely on the best theories and evidence from the computational sciences to address questions about how the mind works. They also aim to advance research in these sciences, by clarifying foundational concepts, illuminating links between apparently different ideas, and suggesting novel experiments. Authors sometimes disagree about which scientific theories and evidence count as "the best", but their supporting discussion clarifies these disagreements and provides readers with an understanding of differences concerning computational approaches within scientific practice.

Another point of continuity with previous approaches is that many important foundational questions about the computational mind remain largely unresolved. Researchers with different backgrounds and interests continue to wrestle with "classical" questions. Several contributors to the Handbook engage with the problem of computational implementation: What does it mean for a physical system to implement a computation? Other contributors engage with explanatory questions about the relationship between different levels of analysis, such as, for example, the relationship between David Marr's computational, algorithmic, and implementational levels (Marr and Poggio, 1976). An important question here is whether one level of analysis is somehow epistemically privileged when it comes to explain how the mind works. A further set of issues centers on the notion of representation: What kinds of representation occur in the mind and how do they fit with computational models? Several contributors to the Handbook explore the relationship between computation, representation, thought, and action, and how we should understand representation in the context of an embodied and acting agent. Others take up questions about the role of representation in computational explanation, including the format used by representations in the computational sciences.

A final point of continuity with previous treatments concerns the challenge of scalability: How can one go from explaining a few aspects of the mind under limited circumstances to explaining the full range of mental capacities across many demanding, ecologically realistic settings? One aspect of this challenge is associated with the so-called "frame problem". The frame problem was originally formulated as the problem of specifying in a logical language what changes and what does not change in a situation when an event occurs (McCarthy and Hayes, 1969). This relatively specialized problem has been taken as suggestive of a more general difficulty: accounting for the ability of computing systems to make timely decisions on the basis of what is relevant within an ongoing situation. Concerns about computational complexity and tractability compound the frame problem, creating a scalability challenge. At least since Herbert Simon's (1957) work on bounded rationality, a major question faced by computational approaches has been: How can computing systems with limited time, memory, attention, and computing power solve complex, ambiguous, and pressing problems in the real world? Taking the lead from Simon and other pioneers of artificial intelligence (AI), researchers in the computational sciences, including those in this Handbook, develop strategies to cut through the complexity of computational problems and allow computing systems with limited resources to solve complex, real-world problems.

Despite these points of continuity, the contributions in the Handbook also present salient points of departure from previous work on the computational mind. One point of departure is the plurality of approaches we currently observe in the computational sciences. Instead of there being "only one game in town" (Fodor, 1975), there are now many computational approaches to explain how the mind works, each of which illuminates a different aspect of mental phenomena.

The plurality of approaches within the computational sciences has helped to motivate several epistemological and methodological views going under the general banner of 'pluralism'. According to these views, the plurality of computational approaches we observe in the sciences is an essential feature of scientific inquiry into the mind. The explanatory and practical aims of studying the mind are best pursued with the aid of many theories, models, concepts, methods, and sources of evidence from different fields, including philosophy, computer science, AI, psychology, and neuroscience. As several of the contributors to this Handbook suggest, these fields are converging on a pluralistic conception of the computational foundations of the mind that promotes fruitful exchanges on questions, methods, and results.

Pluralist views about the computational mind are reflected in the progressive erosion of dichotomies that have traditionally defined the field. The contributions in this Handbook show that the historical roots of CTM are broad: even at its origins, CTM did not necessitate or reflect a monistic approach to the mind. Today, an increasing number of researchers realize that they do not need to pick between Turing machines, logic, neural networks, probability calculus, and differential equations as "the" approach to the mind. Nor do they need to claim that any one of these approaches is "the" computational theory of the mind. Instead, they are able to choose between diverse questions, problems, and approaches that fall within the computational sciences. These approaches have the power to illuminate different aspects of mental or neural phenomena. None has the monopoly on computation. This has led some researchers to reconceive of apparently competing approaches – such as connectionism or dynamical systems theory – as different aspects of the computational framework rather than as non-computational alternatives.

Work in this area reflects broader trends in the philosophy of science. Many contributors use ideas developed in the context of other sciences to illuminate the practice of the computational sciences. Examples include appealing to work on explanation and the relationship between models and mechanisms; the role of idealization in modeling and perspectivalism about models in general; and the influence of values and social structures on scientific practice. With respect to explanation, philosophers of science have articulated various accounts emphasizing different constraints on what constitutes an explanation. One recent trend salient in this Handbook is to think of scientific explanation in terms of mechanisms and models rather than in terms of laws, general principles, and encompassing theories. A turn to mechanisms and models has informed computational modeling, and raises questions about the conditions under which a computational model has explanatory value. Work on idealization and perspectivalism in the philosophy of science emphasizes that the growth of scientific knowledge is always a situated process carried out by interest-driven human beings interacting in social institutions and seeking to find their way in a complex world. This helps us to understand why there might not be a unique, universally true, computational account of the mind: different inquirers may need different models to answer different questions. Such work also serves to distance current computational approaches from some traditional issues about the metaphysics of mind.

Early computational treatments of mind were closely tied to metaphysical questions like those of the mind–body problem (What is the relationship between mental states and physical states?) and semantic externalism (Does the semantic content of our mental states supervene on brains and bodies or also on the environment?). In this Handbook, these metaphysical debates often take a back seat to questions about the explanatory role of computational models in scientific practice.

One last point of departure from previous treatments arises from the increase in power of computing machinery over recent years. Technological change has contributed to dramatic advances in machine learning and brain simulation. The success of machine learning models is felt in the chapters. Machine learning techniques have inspired models of the mind based around predictive processing, statistical inference, deep learning, reinforcement learning, and related probabilistic notions. Machine learning extracts statistical information by searching large datasets. It uses that information to recognize patterns, make inferences, and learn new tasks like playing video games, board games, or driving a car. A question that occupies many contributors in this Handbook is whether, and to what extent, these techniques also describe the workings of the human mind. While current AI excels at narrowly defined tasks, the problem of how to re-create human general intelligence remains largely unsolved. General intelligence describes the ability to solve many diverse tasks and change goals flexibly and rationally in response to contextual cues. We do not know how humans do this. Reconstructing the process that underlies general intelligence poses a challenge to both current machine learning and computational models of the mind.

As editors, we see *The Routledge Handbook of the Computational Mind* as fulfilling three main goals. First, we see the Handbook as a "time capsule" of current trends, marking points of departure and continuity with respect to classical computational treatments. Since the Handbook crystallizes many of the important ideas we can identify today, it will be a helpful resource for those researchers who will look back at the historical trajectory of the field in a couple of decades or so. Second, we see the Handbook as a volume informing present-day scholars and practitioners of the accomplishments and challenges of computational approaches to the mind. Third, we see the Handbook as a pedagogical resource, appropriate for graduate and advanced undergraduate courses in disciplines ranging from the philosophy of mind and cognitive science, to computational cognitive neuroscience, AI, and computer science.

References

Clark, A. (2015) *Surfing Uncertainty: Prediction, Action, and the Embodied Mind*. Oxford: Oxford University Press.

Fodor, J.A. (1975) *The Language of Thought*. Cambridge, MA: Harvard University Press.

Marr, D. and Poggio, T. (1976) *From Understanding Computation to Understanding Neural Circuitry*. Artificial Intelligence Laboratory. A.I. Memo. AIM-357. Massachusetts Institute of Technology.

McCarthy, J. and Hayes, P.J. (1969) 'Some Philosophical Problems from the Standpoint of Artificial Intelligence', in Michie, D. and Meltzer, B. (eds.) *Machine Intelligence 4*. Edinburgh: Edinburgh University Press, pp. 463–502.

Newell, A. and Simon, H. (1976) 'Computer Science as Empirical Inquiry: Symbols and Search', *Communications of the ACM*, 19, pp. 113–126.

Putnam, H. (1967) 'Psychological Predicates', in Capitan, W.H. and Merrill, D.D. (eds.) *Art, Mind, and Religion*. Pittsburgh, PA: University of Pittsburgh Press, pp. 37–48.

Pylyshyn, Z.W. (1984) *Computation and Cognition*. Cambridge, MA: MIT Press.

Rumelhart, D., McClelland, J., and the PDP Research Group (1986) *Parallel Distributed Processing*, vol. 1. Cambridge, MA: MIT Press.

Simon, H.A. (1957) *Models of Man, Social and Rational: Mathematical Essays on Rational Human Behavior in a Social Setting*. New York, NY: John Wiley and Sons.

Thelen, E. and Smith, L. (1994) *A Dynamical Systems Approach to the Development of Cognition and Action*. Cambridge, MA: MIT Press.

Turing, A. (1936) 'On Computable Numbers, with an Application to the Entscheidungsproblem', *Proceedings of the London Mathematical Society*, 42, pp. 230–265.

Turing, A. (1950) 'Computing Machinery and Intelligence', *Mind*, 49, pp. 433–460.

PART I

History and future directions

1

COMPUTATIONAL THOUGHT FROM DESCARTES TO LOVELACE

Alistair M. C. Isaac

Modern computationalism unites two distinct ideas: the first that reasoning, more generally mental activity, may be decomposed into simple, formal steps; the second that these simple steps may be functionally realized by a physical system. These two ideas follow separate trajectories in the pre-history of the computational mind. Descartes, for instance, developed a detailed account of how paradigmatic psychological processes, such as perception, memory, and emotion, might be realized in a mechanical system, yet he maintained that thought *per se* occupied a separate ontological realm. Leibniz also held that thought could not be reduced to material interactions, yet he endorsed the idea that thought could be decomposed into a sequence of simple formal steps. Overlapping Descartes and Leibniz, both temporally and ideologically, Hobbes combined a mechanistic theory of psychological processes and a computational theory of thought to articulate a precursor to reductive computationalism.

Descartes and Leibniz were both inspired in part by the mechanical and calculational devices of their day. Descartes, for instance, repeatedly draws analogies between psychological processes and automata or clockwork, while Leibniz himself designed the first mechanical calculator that could multiply and divide as well as add and subtract. Nevertheless, a nuanced assessment of the possibility for the mechanical production of complex behavior did not appear until after the technological innovation of the Jacquard Loom in the early nineteenth century. Jacquard introduced the use of punch cards to store complex fabric designs, establishing the possibility that elaborate effects might be the result of simple operations on arbitrarily complex stored instructions. Jacquard's success inspired Babbage's design for the Analytical Engine, which in turn prompted Ada Lovelace's influential 1843 discussion of the precise capacities and limitations of a machine instantiating simple formal operations.

This chapter surveys these issues in turn: the mechanization of psychological phenomena, the conceptualization of thought as computation, and the circumscription of the powers of computation after the introduction of punch card memory.

Automata and the brain

Descartes is often demonized in contemporary philosophy of mind for his dualism, which draws a sharp ontological distinction between body and "soul", or mind. However, Descartes also analyzed many complex phenomena typically treated as "psychological" today in purely mechanistic terms. While our contemporary concept and discipline of psychology did not exist in Descartes' time, and thus his theories can only be categorized as such anachronistically, we can nevertheless retrospectively examine the types of explanation Descartes offered for phenomena now studied by psychologists, such as memory, perception, action, and emotion. In explaining these capacities mechanistically, Descartes drew on his experience with automata and the mechanized novelties of his day, such as the hydraulic amusement parks of Isaac and Salomon de Caus,[1] establishing a research program to explain complex biological behavior by analogy with mechanical artifice.

Descartes' posthumously published[2] *Treatise on Man* begins by asking the reader to consider a man with a body, but not a soul: "nothing but a statue or machine". Just as "clocks, artificial fountains, [and] mills ... have the power to move of their own accord", so also our hypothetical soulless man may engage in complex autonomous motion (Descartes, 1985, p. 99). His nervous system is composed of tiny tubules, through which flows a special fluid, the "animal spirits". The differential flow of the animal spirits through this system of tubes may produce arbitrarily complex behavior, just as the flow of water through hidden pipes in the grottos of the royal garden "is sufficient to move various machines, and even to make them play certain instruments or utter certain words depending on the various arrangements of the pipes through which the water is conducted" (ibid., p. 100).

There is a role for the "rational soul" in this analogy, as "fountain keeper" who may "produce, or prevent, or change" behavior in the system. Nevertheless, the intervention of a soul is not required for many typical, yet complex responses by the soulless man to external stimuli, which Descartes compares to elaborate interactive displays in the royal gardens. Sensory input incites a response from the body just as

> visitors who enter the grottos of these fountains ... unwittingly cause the movements which take place before their eyes. For they cannot enter without stepping on certain tiles which are so arranged that if, for example, they approach a Diana who is bathing they will cause her to hide in the reeds, and if they move forward to pursue her they will cause a Neptune to advance and threaten them with his trident; or if they go in another direction they will cause a sea-monster to emerge and spew water onto their faces.
>
> *(ibid., p. 101)*

Descartes goes on to explain how mechanical cause and effect interaction between a sensory stimulus such as a nearby fire and the soulless man might produce a suitable response, for instance movement away from the fire and a loud exclamation.

Descartes' model for the mechanical operation of brain and nervous system is elaborated further in his *Optics* (1637), *Principles of Philosophy* (1644), and *The Passions of the Soul* (1649). The basic idea is that external stimuli cause vibrations or motions in sensory nerve fibers, and these motions are transmitted to the brain, where they dilate or constrict tubules. The differential flow of animal spirits through these tubules may then inflate or deflate muscles, which in turn pull or push the moving parts of the body to induce action. The soul is needed for sensation proper to occur: "it is the soul which sees, and not the eye" (Descartes, 1985, p. 172); nevertheless, the nature of the sensory input is determined by the type of motion that reaches the brain via the nerves, and the character of the body's response is likewise determined by the resulting pattern of flow of animal spirits through nerve tubules.

Thus every movement we make without any contribution from our will – as often happens when we breathe, walk, eat and, indeed, when we perform any action which is common to us and the beasts – depends solely on the arrangement of our limbs and on the route which the spirits, produced by the heat of the heart, follow naturally in the brain, nerves and muscles. This occurs in the same way as the movement of a watch is produced merely by the strength of its spring and the configuration of its wheels.

(ibid., p. 335)

Even the "passions", emotional or affective states, are determined by mechanical processes within the body. For Descartes, the passions are a form of perception, which we attribute to the soul, but which nevertheless depends for its character on the internal state of the body. Fear, for example, corresponds to a flow of spirits to the heart, causing it to beat more quickly and constrict, as well as a flow to those portions of the brain and body associated with flight, the muscles of the leg and those that turn the back (ibid., p. 342). Likewise, passions such as love and hatred, while serving the natural function of directing our desires toward or away from something external to us, correspond also to physiological changes. In the case of love, the beat of the heart becomes stronger and more regular, digestion more efficient; while in the case of hate, the pulse becomes weak and irregular and digestion is disrupted (ibid., p. 363). These differences depend on the differential manner in which the blood is directed to the internal organs when these passions occur (ibid., p. 364).

These explanations are "mechanistic" in the sense of the seventeenth-century *mechanical philosophy*, namely they appeal solely to extended bodies, interacting through direct contact (Boas, 1952).[3] Despite allowing that a broad array of "psychological" phenomena may be so explained, Descartes maintains that the soul, or mind, has a distinguished functional role, one which cannot be reduced to motion or direct physical contact. In *The Passions* and *The Meditations*, Descartes emphasizes the role of the soul as the seat of will or volition. In *Discourse on the Method* (1637) he suggests two behavioral signs that indicate the presence of a soul (Descartes, 1985, pp. 139–141). The first is the ability to participate in conversation, or otherwise manipulate meaningful symbols:

For we can certainly conceive of a machine so constructed that it utters words, and even utters words which correspond to bodily actions causing a change of its organs (e.g. if you touch it in one spot it asks what you want of it, if you touch it in another it cries out that you are hurting it, and so on). But it is not conceivable that such a machine should produce different arrangements of words so as to give an appropriately meaningful answer to whatever is said in its presence, as the dullest of men can do.

(ibid., p. 140)

The second sign of a soul is the ability to produce truly novel behavior. Those with minds may act in any situation as "reason is a universal instrument", yet mere machines (including, for Descartes, animals) have a limited regime of potential actions, as

… these organs need some particular disposition for each particular action; hence it is for all practical purposes impossible for a machine to have enough different organs to make it act in all the contingencies of life in the way in which our reason makes us act.

(ibid., p. 140)

It is remarkable how Descartes' reflections on the mark of the mental, and the limitations of the mechanical, prefigure those that will recur throughout the history of computationalism. In particular, the idea that novelty, including especially that novelty demonstrated in even the most mundane human conversations, is a sign of intelligent thought finds one instantiation in the Turing test (Turing, 1950). Turing himself takes the worry that artificial devices will never produce novel behavior to be intuitively powerful and historically important, attributing it to Ada Lovelace. For both Lovelace and Turing, and many who have followed in the computational tradition, a key consideration for the question of whether novel behavior may be generated purely through processes decomposable into simple mechanical (physical) interactions is complexity. Is it the case, as Descartes worries, that principled limits on mechanical complexity prevent machines from generating novel behavior, or, as Turing conjectures, that the complexity of machines may outstrip human abilities to predict their actions, producing the appearance of genuine novelty?

Mechanistic theories of brain function have a chequered history after Descartes. Some philosophers adopted a bold reductionism, insisting that Descartes' notion of soul was explanatorily otiose, and that all the complexities of human psychology could be explained in mechanical terms. Such views were characterized by vague, suggestive models of brain mechanism, however, rather than the detailed explanations offered by Descartes.

For instance, Hobbes begins *Leviathan* (1651) with a brief discussion of sensation, imagination, thought, speech, reason, and ultimately volition, all in materialist terms. Nevertheless, Hobbes does not suggest specific brain mechanisms for these psychological phenomena, but makes general comments about how they are in principle nothing but motions. For instance, "All fancies are motions within us, relics of those made in the sense" (ibid., I.iii.2), and sequences of thoughts are merely sequences of these relics, moving in an order determined by past sensory experience and the internal state of the brain. Crucially for Hobbes, volition is not the stumbling block to materialism that it was for Descartes; rather, Hobbes explains will in terms of the beginnings of motion, or "endeavor" (Latin, *conatus*). The passions are persistent states of resistance or endeavor, competing to induce full-fledged motions, and thus actions, within the body. Will is just an *ex post facto* reconstruction, "the last appetite or aversion immediately adhering to the action, or to the omission thereof" (ibid., I.vi.53). As a coherent notion of *conatus* is necessary for physics and mathematics, volition *per se* is no more mysterious than other fundamental aspects of the physical world.

Hobbes' materialism was veiled behind his complex theology and his deference to political authority. Nevertheless, materialism was a dangerous position to maintain in the seventeenth and eighteenth centuries, and those who advocated it explicitly continued to be subject to persecution. Perhaps the most extreme of these was Julien de La Mettrie (1709–1751), whose *Natural History of the Soul* (1745) argued that the natural culmination of Descartes' mechanical philosophy was to incorporate thought and feeling into the material world, attributing them just as much to animals as to humans. This work was burned in effigy at the stake, and La Mettrie was forced to flee to Holland, where he wrote *Man, a Machine* (1748), the reception of which in Leiden forced him to flee again to Prussia, and the protective patronage of Frederick the Great.

Man, a Machine extends Descartes' human-machine analogy to a full-blown materialistic, atheistic monism. It describes the human body as "a self-winding machine, a living representation of perpetual motion", fueled by food and drink (La Mettrie, 1748, p. 32). La Mettrie presents Johann Amman's (1669–1730) work teaching the born deaf to lip-read and communicate by sign language as demystifying language. He conjectures that apes may be taught to sign as well, perhaps even to speak (ibid., p. 40), "because of the great analogy between ape and man" (ibid., p. 39), thereby moving Descartes' first mark of the mental into the animal kingdom, and thus material world. But with language, comes also the power for education and intelligent behavior, and so for La Mettrie, the possibility of ape speech implies complete continuity between animal and human. Even the most cherished of Descartes' powers of the mind, the ability to reason mathematically, is separated from the tricks of a performing animal by degree, not by kind:

> The transition from animals to man is not abrupt. ... A geometer learned the most difficult proofs and calculations the way an ape learns to put on and take off his little hat and to mount his trained dog.
>
> *(ibid., p. 41)*

Yet La Mettrie's only specific addition to Descartes' mechanistic psychology is the conjecture that linguistic thought may be reduced to patterns of vibration: "Just as a violin string or harpsichord key vibrates and produces sounds, so also the strings of the brain echo or repeat the spoken words that produce the sound waves that strike them". In combination with the power of sight to "engrave" images on the brain, these vibrations may instantiate symbolic thought (ibid., p. 42).

Much like Descartes, La Mettrie was inspired to these conclusions in part by his experience with automata, especially those of Jacques Vaucanson (1709–1782), which included a mechanical flute player and an eating and excreting "Digesting Duck" (ibid., p. 69). As before, La Mettrie takes the difference between these achievements to be merely one of degree, and thus conjectures that some "new Prometheus", more skilled than Vaucanson, could construct a conversationally adept automaton: "a *talker*, which can no longer be regarded as impossible" (ibid., p. 69). Nevertheless, the goal of La Mettrie is inspiration rather than demonstration: *Man, a Machine* is more manifesto than scientific treatise, directed at defending atheism and materialism conceptually (and ridiculing arguments against them) rather than systematically developing an empirical theory of mind.

La Mettrie and Hobbes represent exceptions in the post-Cartesian study of mind – serious theories of the brain as a functionally organized mechanism do not reappear until the late nineteenth century. One reason is simply the lack of empirical evidence concerning brain structure: to primitive microscopy, brain tissue looks largely homogeneous and unstructured. Furthermore, a major setback for the scientific project to functionally decompose the operations of the brain occurred with the discrediting of phrenology in the early nineteenth century. It would take the discovery by Broca and others of correlations between specific cognitive deficits and localized brain lesions before functional analysis finally became scientifically respectable again in the 1860s. Then, in the late nineteenth and early twentieth centuries, Ramón y Cajal's new techniques for histological sample preparation allowed him to observe brain structure at a fine enough grain to posit that nerve cells facilitate a directed flow of "nervous current" (Llinás, 2003). Once this microscopic physiological differentiation could finally be observed, theories of neural mechanism graduated from mere "how possibly" explanations to empirically testable hypotheses.

Thought as computation

Hobbes explicitly articulates the thesis that thought is a form of computation in his *De Corpore* (1655). This idea then goes on to inspire Leibniz's attempts to develop a universal language for reasoning. Although much of the subsequent development of logic targeted the norms of good reasoning rather than a description of actual thought, the notion that thought may be *described* as a system of formal operations appears again in Boole's *Investigation of the Laws of Thought* (1854). A puzzle for all these theories is how to reconcile the claim that thought instantiates computational rules with the observed fact of human errors in reasoning.

Hobbes identifies thought with computation, and computation with basic arithmetical operations:

> By RATIOCINATION, I mean *computation*. Now to compute, is either to collect the sum of many things that are added together, or to know what remains when one thing is taken out of another. *Ratiocination*, therefore, is the same with *addition* and *substraction*.
>
> *(Hobbes, 1655, 1.2)*

Hobbes is a nominalist, and thus denies the existence of *universals*, entities that exist simultaneously at multiple locations; so, for instance, there is no further thing *dog* located where all dogs are located, but only the particular dogs themselves. The process of reasoning about general categories, then, is merely the manipulation of *names*, adding or subtracting them from combinations. For instance, we may reason about *man* in general by combining arithmetically the names of his distinctive features, e.g. *body*, *animated*, and *rational*. These combinatorial operations are also characteristic of non-linguistic thought, for instance the perception of a distant person, which proceeds by first triggering the *idea* of *body*, next of *animated*, and finally, as she approaches, of *rational*.

> The idea [the perceiver] has now is compounded of his former ideas, which are put together in the mind in the same order in which these three single names, *body*, *animated, rational*, are in speech compounded into this one name, *body-animated-rational*, or *man*.
>
> *(ibid., 1.3)*

If the person then walks away, as she dwindles from sight, the ideas associated with *rational*, then *animated* are subtracted away, and finally *body* once she disappears from view.

The formal operations of addition and subtraction are inherently normative; they may be performed correctly or incorrectly. If human thought implements these operations, what determines whether reasoning proceeds correctly? Hobbes' extreme nominalism allows him to deny any substantive role for external norms in constraining correct thought. Rather, names are assigned to groupings of particulars arbitrarily, the correct linking between names is merely a matter of definition, and consequently truth itself is "constituted arbitrarily by the inventors of speech" (ibid., 3.9). The correctness or incorrectness of reasoning is thus determined not by some human-independent, objective standard for assessment, but rather our mutual agreement to respect convention, i.e. public arbitration.

> And as in arithmetic, unpractised men must, and professors themselves may, often err and cast up false, so also in any other subject of reasoning, the ablest, most attentive, and most practised men may deceive themselves and infer false conclusions; not but that reason itself is always right reason, as well as arithmetic is a certain and infallible art, but no one man's reason, nor the reason of any one number of men, makes the certainty, no more than an account is therefore well cast up, because a great many men have unanimously approved it. And therefore, as when there is a controversy in

an account, the parties must by their own accord set up for right reason the reason of some arbitrator or judge to whose sentence they will both stand, or their controversy must either come to blows or be undecided, for want of a right reason constituted by nature, so is it also in all debates of what kind soever.

(Hobbes, 1651, I.v.3)

Conversely, the assertion that one has access to some "right reason constituted by nature", or equivalently, the demand to play the role of the arbitrator, is the mark of one who simply wishes to impose their will on others: they "[betray] their want of right reason by the claim they lay to it" (ibid).[4]

Leibniz was also a nominalist of sorts (Di Bella, 2017), but he harshly criticized Hobbes' apparent truth-relativism in passages such as these, and claims to refute it in a number of places (Bolton, 1977). Although rejecting his relativism, the early Leibniz explicitly endorsed Hobbes' central claim about the nature of thought, asserting he "rightly stated that everything done by our mind is a *computation*, by which is to be understood either the addition of a sum or the subtraction of a difference" (Leibniz, 1666, p. 3). The insight that thought is a form of computation guided Leibniz's project to develop a "universal characteristic", or symbolic language for general reasoning; a project he hoped would culminate in the construction of a machine to aid in discovering true theories and resolving disputes (Couturat, 1901). Leibniz made some small progress on the engineering side of this project himself with his *machina arithmetica*, the first mechanical calculator to directly implement multiplication and division, initially described in a paper of 1685.

How does Leibniz resolve the tension between the descriptive assertion that thought is computation and the inherent normativity of computational rules? One crucial point to notice here is that Leibniz conceives of his project to develop a universal computational language as encompassing two distinct types of formal system, a logic of judgment, and a logic of discovery or invention. The logic of judgment concerns correct argument structure, for instance syllogisms. The logic of discovery concerns the determination of possible combinations of ideas; it thus may be used to discover or "invent" new true propositions.

A proposition is composed of subject and predicate; all propositions, therefore, are com2nations. It is, then, the business of inventive logic (as far as it concerns propositions) to solve this problem: 1. given a subject, to find its predicates. 2. Given a predicate, to find its subjects.

(Leibniz, 1666, p. 3)

Thought is computation in the sense that it adds and subtracts ideas. These operations instantiate steps of logical discovery, yet they do not fulfil the norm of a logic of discovery proper, namely to find *all* the permitted combinations between given simple ideas. For this comprehensive combinatorial task, the assistance of a formal language, and its instantiation in a machine, as Leibniz seems to have intended, would serve as a supplement and extension of the limited capacities of human thought.

While the early Leibniz embraces Hobbes' commitment to mechanistic explanations, he denies that the mental may be reduced entirely to materially instantiated motions. Crucially, *conatus*, the infinitesimal beginnings of motion, which Hobbes takes to explain volition and memory, is deemed inadequate to that task by Leibniz. Since material bodies exhibit only the motion resulting from the (potentially) contrary forces (i.e. *conatus*) that impress them, and do not retain any record of such contrary *conatus*, something non-material, suitable for retaining and instantiating this tension as memory, is needed. For the early Leibniz, the solution is to geometrize mind, instantiating it as a single point, within a body and not separate from it, contra Descartes, but nevertheless mathematical rather than material, contra Hobbes.[5]

These considerations also resolve a further puzzle: how the early Leibniz might accept both that thought comprises computation and that material mechanisms may perform computations, and thus aid thought, yet nevertheless hold that material mechanisms themselves are inadequate for mind. For while a material calculating device may implement the mechanics of computation through a series of motions, it lacks any memory of the *conatus* that impelled these motions; yet this memory is required to instantiate sensation, and thus thought proper. One wonders if Leibniz's experience with his own calculating machine may have reinforced this conviction. Leibniz's calculator carried digits during multiplication and long division by changing the relative positions of cogwheels and "stepped drums", cylinders with ridges of different lengths arrayed around their circumference; the relative positions of the cogwheel and drum would ensure the wheel was turned the requisite number of times (corresponding to the number of ridges that engaged it during rotation) to advance the value of the corresponding digit correctly. While this design worked in principle, the actual realizations of it were unreliable due to problems in the machining of their delicate parts. Consequently, slippage between drums and gears meant the ending state of a calculation did not necessarily correspond to the correct combination of the numbers input to the machine by its operator. Just as the mere motions of brain bear no trace of the complex *conatus* that impelled them on their way, the end state of Leibniz's calculator did not bear a determinate mark of the mathematical operation it was set in motion to compute.

These remarks are mere speculation; nevertheless, something like the idea that thought is computation, and yet may be in error due to extrinsic factors affecting its progress, appears explicitly in Boole (1854). Boole's full title illuminates his attitude toward the relationship between thought itself and normative theories of correct reasoning: *An Investigation of the Laws of Thought on Which Are Founded the Mathematical Theories of Logic and Probabilities.* He states at the beginning that his plan is "to investigate the fundamental laws of those operations of the mind by which reasoning is performed" and represent these laws in a formal calculus, but with an ultimate aim of suggesting "some probable intimations concerning the nature and constitution of the human mind" (Boole, 1854, p. 1).

For Boole, the standards for correct reasoning are "not derived from without, but deeply founded in the constitution of the human faculties" (ibid., p. 2). Thus the origin of the normative theories of logic and probability is in a descriptive "science of the mind", a science that is possible because "the operations of the mind are … subject to laws" (ibid., p. 3). Although this endeavor is empirical, it does not itself rest on inductive inference, as do other sciences, since fundamental laws of thought such as those encapsulated in an Aristotelian syllogism may be derived from "the clear apprehension of a single instance" (ibid., p. 4). While Boole does not emphasize the term "computation" as Leibniz did, he nevertheless also represents thought as successions of symbols in a formal language, governed by rules of combination (ibid., ch. 2). However, for Boole, the formal character of the laws of thought does not depend on any "metaphysical speculations" about the mind or underlying causes, but is simply derived empirically from observation, much as the laws of planetary motion do not depend for their validity on knowledge of the cause of gravitation (ibid., pp. 40–41).

If the laws of correct reasoning are laws of the mind analogous to the natural laws we find in physics and astronomy, what explains the observed fact of human error in reasoning? Boole argues that the mere fact they may be violated undermines neither the "existence" nor the "necessity" of the laws of valid reasoning (ibid., p. 408). Rather, the laws of valid reasoning ... form but a *part* of the system of laws by which the actual processes of reasoning, whether right or wrong are governed ... if that system were known to us in its completeness, we should perceive that the whole intellectual procedure was *necessary*, even as the movements of the inorganic world are necessary. ... the phænomena of incorrect reasoning or error ... are due to the interference of other laws with those laws of which *right* reasoning is the product.

(ibid., p. 409)

The interesting puzzle for Boole is thus not so much why humans err in reasoning (this is due to the interference of other causal factors), but rather why one particular subset of the laws that govern thought, namely those he has identified, has a distinguished status (as the laws of correct reasoning).

Boole's system is an algebra, or formal system for operating on values, distinguished by the restriction of variable values to *true* or *false*, or equivalently 1 or 0. It turns out that this restriction suggests the appropriate theoretical foundation for the construction of digital computers, a point first explicitly defended by Claude Shannon (1938, which summarizes results from his 1937 MIT Master's thesis). Nevertheless, the implementation of these ideas in a prototype digital computer appears to date to Atanasoff's 1939 design for the "Atanasoff-Berry Computer", which rediscovered the basics of binary-valued algebra as a means to discretize the fundamentally continuous physics of electrical circuits.[6] So, the computers that in the twentieth century inspired the computational theory of mind were themselves grounded directly in principles inspired in the first instance by the empirical investigation of human reasoning.

Memory, complexity, and novelty

The machines that inspired Descartes and La Mettrie were largely task-specific, with internal mechanisms designed to perform only a single specialized function. In the late eighteenth and early nineteenth centuries, however, a series of technological developments in the textile industry demonstrated the power of stored instructions to produce complex behavior from a simple, but general mechanism. When this possibility was theoretically implemented in the first design for a general-purpose computer, Charles Babbage's Analytical Engine, it inspired Ada Lovelace to sharpen and rearticulate the worry that computational machines are not capable of the genuinely novel behavior that is the mark of human thought.

The basic idea that instructions governing a sequence of operations might be stored in a medium separate from a machine, allowing the machine to produce different effects depending on which instructions are fed to it, appears to date to the eighteenth-century textile industry. Weaving requires passing a weft thread back and forth between arrayed warp threads; by changing which of differently colored warp threads are in front or behind the weft on each pass, the weaver can create patterns in the fabric. The time and labor intensity required to produce complex patterns motivated a sequence of technological developments to aid in this process. In 1725, Basile Bouchon introduced a system for coding the sequence of warp positions defining a pattern with holes punched in a piece of paper – whether a needle connected to each thread of warp was opposite a perforation or solid paper determined whether its respective thread was brought forward or backward for that pass of the weft. While the original implementation of this idea was impractical, a sequence of improvements throughout the eighteenth century culminated eventually in a design suitable for mass production and application, due to Joseph Marie Jacquard (1752–1834).

The Jacquard Loom combined innovations due to Bouchon, the inventor Vaucanson, and others into a single device. Bouchon's paper was replaced with stiff perforated cards, strung in sequence, and mounted above the loom. The process of stepping through the cards was completely mechanized, allowing a single weaver to swiftly produce arbitrarily complex textile patterns coded on the cards. Since the cards could easily be exchanged, a single threading of warp through the loom could be used to produce many different textile patterns. The first Jacquard Loom was completed by 1804, and it soon gained enormous popularity, with the basic mechanism still in use today in some fully automated looms.[7]

Retrospectively, the Jacquard Loom has been interpreted in popular culture as the first programmable device. This assessment is perhaps overly generous, but the Jacquard Loom did constitute a genuine step toward true programmability insofar as it influenced the design of early computers, directly suggesting the use of punch cards for storing instructions. The conceptual importance of the Jacquard mechanism for the history of the computational mind is that it demonstrated how very simple mechanical procedures could produce complex results, so long as they are guided by sufficiently complex instructions. This may at first seem a solution to Descartes' combinatorial worry that, since parts of a mechanism require "particular disposition[s] for each particular action", it would be practically impossible for a machine to produce seemingly complex or novel behavior: the mechanism of the loom's warp has very limited and particular dispositions, but the patterns it produces may be sufficiently elaborate to appear novel. Nevertheless, the origins of that novelty reside entirely in the instructions, and thus Descartes' worry still applies, not now to the powers of the mechanism itself, but to the instructions that drive it. This is essentially the position articulated by Ada Lovelace when considering the limitations of Babbage's Analytical Engine.

Charles Babbage (1791–1871) may rightfully be considered the first to design a general-purpose computational device. His Analytical Engine was conceived to calculate any mathematical function reducible to the primitive operations of addition, subtraction, multiplication, and division. In his exposition of the principles of the Analytical Engine, Maurice Wilkes (1913–2010), himself sometimes credited with constructing "the first practical stored program computer", the EDSAC (Randell 1982, p. 380), argues that "Babbage was moving in a world of logical design and system architecture, and was familiar with and had solutions for problems that were not to be discussed in the literature for another 100 years" (Wilkes, 1977, p. 418). Babbage conceived the Analytical Engine sometime in the 1830s and continued to perfect its design throughout his life. Despite his foresight and ingenuity, the Analytical Engine was never built, due in part to the limitations of nineteenth-century precision machining, and in part to the gross discrepancy between projected cost and practical utility perceived by federal and other potential funding bodies.

Babbage was extremely impressed with the Jacquard Loom, and possessed a finely detailed portrait of Jacquard woven on one of his looms under instructions from 24,000 punch cards. Early in the design of the Analytical Engine he opted to use Jacquard's mechanism for instructing the machine, although he generalized it such that the string of cards could move forward or backward, allowing recursive "loops" in the procedures executed by the Engine. In general, Babbage's design differs from that of all previous calculators (including his own Difference Engine) in the way it functionally differentiates between computational processes and memory. The basic operations of addition, etc. are performed by a centralized "mill" that reads and writes to a "store" of variable values, serving as short-term memory. Two separate sets of Jacquard-style punch cards instruct the machine on the operations to perform, and the locations in the store, respectively, for each calculation.

The Analytical Engine thus embodies a functional architecture that distinguishes between the mechanism that performs computational operations, that which temporarily stores values of short-term relevance to these operations, and that which stores permanent, read-only instructions for guiding computation in the long term. This functional differentiation was rediscovered in the design of modern computers, and codified in the von Neumann architecture, with the added innovation that program instructions themselves could be stored in read-write memory and modified as data (Bromley, 1982, p. 216), before going on to influence information-processing theories of cognitive architecture. In contrast, the mechanistic brains of Descartes, Hume, and La Mettrie implemented memory and calculation within a single mechanism. For instance, on Descartes' model, the flow of spirits through a neural tubule will over time widen it, ensuring that in future spirits are more likely to take that path than others. The width of the tube thus serves as a kind of memory, but its role as memory is not functionally distinct from its role as a conduit for cause and effect relations between sensation and action within the body. This basic model also re-emerges in the twentieth century, with connectionist architectures inspired by low-level models of neural plasticity, such as Hebbian learning.

The most significant exposition of the Analytical Engine published in Babbage's lifetime was an article by the Italian engineer Menabrea (who had attended lectures on the Engine by Babbage), translated and extensively annotated by Ada Lovelace (1815–1852), daughter of the poet Lord Byron. Lovelace was a gifted mathematician and a friend and confidant of Babbage, who employed her own intimate knowledge of the Analytical Engine to flesh out Menabrea's discussion with several detailed algorithms illustrating how the engine might be instructed to calculate complex functions (Menabrea, 1843).

Menabrea himself from the start distinguishes between two aspects of mathematics, "the mechanical ... capable of being expressed by means of the operations of matter", and that which "demands the intervention of reasoning" and "belongs ... to the domain of the understanding" (ibid., p. 669). In summarizing the capacities of the Engine, he emphasizes the importance of the external engineer who interprets and instructs its action, since

> the interpretation of formulæ and results is beyond its province, unless indeed this very interpretation be itself susceptible of expression by means of the symbols the machine employs. Thus, although it is not itself the being that reflects, it may yet be considered as the being which executes the conceptions of intelligence. The cards receive the impress of these conceptions and transmit to the various trains of mechanism composing the engine the orders necessary for their action.
>
> *(ibid., p. 689)*

It is to these remarks that Lovelace's most influential comments for the history of computationalism are appended. She emphasizes the dangers of both "overrating" the capacities of the new device and of "undervaluing" them. On the former, she emphatically denies the power of the Engine to produce any truly novel behavior.

> The Analytical Engine has no pretensions whatever to *originate* any thing. It can do whatever we *know how to order it* to perform. It can *follow* analysis; but it has no power of *anticipating* any analytical relations or truths. Its province is to assist us in making *available* what we are already acquainted with.
>
> *(ibid., p. 722)*

These are the comments that over a hundred years later Turing would call "Lady Lovelace's Objection".

Descartes' argument that mere mechanisms cannot generate novel behavior was founded in his intuitive understanding of the limits of material interaction. In contrast, Lovelace's argument is founded in her own intimate experience writing "programs" for the first general-purpose computer. While she recognized the power of the well-instructed computer, she also keenly felt the importance of human creativity and understanding in the writing of these instructions – it is on this ineliminable human intervention that the powers of the Engine rest. Like Leibniz, she anticipates great benefit from the Engine as an "extension of human power", yet adamantly rejects the possibility that it might replace that power, and thus that the Engine itself could ever arrogate intelligent thought. Likewise, Wilkes finds evidence in Babbage's notes that he was frequently confronted with speculations that the Analytical Engine might genuinely think, and bemoans "the strange fascination exerted over so many minds by the idea of a machine that can think, and the exasperating irrelevance of this to the designer of a calculating machine" (ibid., p. 428).

Conclusion

Several features of the contemporary computational theory of mind have long historical precedent. Two ideas in particular, that psychological phenomena may be explained mechanistically, and that thought is a form of computation, had independent trajectories in the early modern period. These precursors to computationalism were also haunted throughout by the worry that computation, insofar as it is purely mechanical, can never be the source of the true novelty we seem to observe in human thought.

Just as contemporary computationalism has been inspired by the accomplishments and architecture of the digital computer, so also were its precursors inspired by the mechanical achievements of their day. Yet with each innovation, from the mechanized royal grotto that inspired Descartes, through Vaucanson's automata, the Jacquard Loom, and the hypothetical achievements of the Analytical Engine, with an increased understanding of the potential for the mechanized production of complex behavior came also a more focused conception of its limitations.

Acknowledgments

These ideas have benefited from conversations over the years with Justin Leiber, Patrick Suppes, Gary Hatfield, Michael Johnson, and Pauline Phemister. In addition to sources cited in the text, I have also been influenced by the general perspective of Haugeland (1985) and Pratt (1987).

Notes

1 Although there is no direct evidence Descartes witnessed the constructions of the de Caus brothers, the fountain-driven amusements described below closely match other descriptions of their work. Descartes could have viewed their water park in Heidelberg, at the gardens of the Elector of Palatine, sometime in 1619–1620 (Rodis-Lewis, 1998, p. 34; Morris, 1969, p. 453). By some accounts, Descartes even constructed, or considered constructing, automata himself during these formative years (Price, 1964, p. 23; Rodis-Lewis, 1998, p. 68).

2 First published 1664, yet written 1629–1633; Descartes decided against publication upon learning of the condemnation of Galileo by the Inquisition (1985, p. 79).

3 The recent "new mechanism" movement takes a mechanistic explanation to comprise a set of entities and activities, arranged so as to produce the target phenomenon (a representative survey is Bechtel and

Abrahamsen, 2005). As such, it constitutes a generalization of seventeenth-century mechanism, which restricted attention to only a distinguished type of entity, extended bodies, and a distinguished type of interaction, or activity, namely direct contact.

4 For a more thorough elaboration of Hobbes' nominalism and assessment of its apparent skeptical implications, see Krook (1956), Bolton (1977), or Duncan (2017).

5 This interpretation is due to Garber (2009, ch. 1); cf. Phemister (2011); Beeley (2011).

6 Atanasoff (1940); however, the exact origins of the key concepts for digital computing are a matter of much dispute, see for instance Randell (1982); Burks (2003).

7 See for instance Usher (1954, pp. 289–295), for a detailed historical discussion.

References

Atanasoff, J.V. (1940) 'Computing Machine for the Solution of Large Systems of Linear Algebraic Equations', in Randell, B. (1982) *The Origins of Digital Computers: Selected Papers*, 3rd ed. New York, NY: Springer Verlag, pp. 315–335.

Bechtel, W. and Abrahamsen, A. (2005) 'Explanation: A Mechanistic Alternative', *Studies in History and Philosophy of Biological and Biomedical Sciences*, 36, pp. 421–441.

Beeley, P. (2011) 'Leibniz and Hobbes', in Look, B.C. (ed.) *The Bloomsbury Companion to Leibniz*. London: Bloomsbury, pp. 32–50.

Boas, M. (1952) 'The Establishment of the Mechanical Philosophy', *Osiris*, 10, pp. 412–541.

Bolton, M.B. (1977) 'Leibniz and Hobbes on Arbitrary Truth', *Philosophy Research Archives*, 3, pp. 242–273.

Boole, G. (1854) *An Investigation of the Laws of Thought*. New York, NY: Dover.

Bromley, A.G. (1982) 'Charles Babbage's Analytical Engine, 1838', *Annals of the History of Computing*, 4, pp. 196–217.

Burks, A.R. (2003) *Who Invented the Computer?* New York, NY: Prometheus Books.

Couturat, L. (1901) *La Logique de Leibniz*. Translated by D. Rutherford. Available at: philosophyfaculty.ucsd.edu/faculty/rutherford/Leibniz/couturatcontents.php (Accessed: February 23, 2018).

Descartes, R. (1985) *The Philosophical Writings of Descartes*, vol. 1. Translated by J. Cottingham, R. Stoothoff, and D. Murdoch. Cambridge, UK: Cambridge University Press.

Di Bella, S. (2017) 'Some Perspective on Leibniz's Nominalism and Its Sources', in Di Bella, S. and Schmaltz, T.M. (eds.) *The Problem of Universals in Early Modern Philosophy*. Oxford: Oxford University Press.

Duncan, S. (2017) 'Hobbes, Universal Names, and Nominalism', in Di Bella, S. and Schmaltz, T.M. (eds.) *The Problem of Universals in Early Modern Philosophy*. Oxford: Oxford University Press.

Garber, D. (2009) *Leibniz: Body, Substance, Monad*. Oxford: Oxford University Press.

Haugeland, J. (1985) *Artificial Intelligence: The Very Idea*. Cambridge, MA: MIT Press.

Hobbes, T. (1651) *Leviathan*, ed. Curley, E. (1994). Indianapolis, IN: Hackett Publishing.

Hobbes, T. (1655) *De Corpore* (translated as 'Concerning Body'), in Molesworth, W. (ed.) (1839) *The English Works of Thomas Hobbes of Malmesbury*, vol. 1, London: John Bohn.

Krook, D. (1956) 'Thomas Hobbes's Doctrine of Meaning and Truth', *Philosophy*, 31, pp. 3–22.

La Mettrie, J.O. (1748) *Man, A Machine*, ed. Leiber J. (1994) Translated by R.A. Watson and M. Rybalka. Indianapolis, IN: Hackett Publishing.

Leibniz, G.W. (1666) 'Of the Art of Combination', in Parkinson, G.H.R. (ed.) (1966) *Leibniz Logical Papers*. Translated by G.H.R. Parkinson, Oxford: Clarendon Press.

Llinás, R.R. (2003) 'The Contribution of Santiago Ramón y Cajal to Functional Neuroscience', *Nature Reviews Neuroscience*, 4, pp. 77–80.

Menabrea, L.F. (1843) 'Sketch of the Analytical Engine Invented by Charles Babbage', in Taylor, R. (ed.) (1966) *Scientific Memoirs*. Translated by A.A. Lovelace. New York, NY: Johnson Reprint Corporation, pp. 666–731.

Morris, J. (1969) 'Pattern Recognition in Descartes' Automata', *Isis*, 60, pp. 451–460.

Phemister, P. (2011) 'Descartes and Leibniz', in Look, B.C. (ed.) *The Bloomsbury Companion to Leibniz*. London: Bloomsbury, pp. 16–31.

Pratt, V. (1987) *Thinking Machines*. Oxford: Basil Blackwell.

Price, D.J.S. (1964) 'Automata and the Origins of Mechanism and the Mechanistic Philosophy', *Technology and Culture*, 5, pp. 9–23.

Randell, B. (1982) *The Origins of Digital Computers: Selected Papers*, 3rd ed. New York, NY: Springer Verlag.

Rodis-Lewis, G. (1998) *Descartes: His Life and Thought.* Translated by J.M. Todd. Ithaca, NY: Cornell University Press.

Shannon, C.E. (1938) 'Symbolic Analysis of Relay and Switching Circuits', *Transactions American Institute of Electrical Engineers*, 57, pp. 713–723.

Turing, A.M. (1950) 'Computing Machinery and Intelligence', *Mind*, 59, pp. 433–460.

Usher, A.P. (1954) *A History of Mechanical Inventions*, revised ed. Cambridge, MA: Harvard University Press.

Wilkes, M.V. (1977) 'Babbage as a Computer Pioneer', *Historia Mathematica*, 4, pp. 415–440.

2

TURING AND THE FIRST ELECTRONIC BRAINS

What the papers said

Diane Proudfoot and Jack Copeland

This chapter tells the story of the origins of computing – from roomfuls of human computers, through the electromechanical (i.e. relay-based) and electronic computers of the pre-modern era, to the first modern electronic stored-program universal computers in the postwar years. We outline the early computational theories of mind that grew up around these pioneering machines, as well as the first attempts at artificial intelligence (called "machine intelligence" in those days).

As our subtitle indicates, the chapter also describes how news of the computer broke in the media of the time. The late 1940s saw the beginning of an energetic debate on the possibility of machine intelligence: on one side were those who believed electronic computers to be merely jumped-up adding machines, and on the other Alan Turing and a few like-minded thinkers, arguing for machine intelligence and the importance of computation to mind. There are fascinating parallels with modern disputes, for example over the claim that machine intelligence will be the beginning of the end for the human race (see Proudfoot, 2015, for additional parallels).

Newspaper reports are a valuable resource for historians of the computer. (Although past reports are no less prone to inaccuracy than today's stories; naturally we will not be quoting news material that contains factual errors about the history of computing.) Often, newspaper accounts from the dawn of computing are of interest because of the information they supply about how the new technology was perceived at the time: in 1952, the *Illustrated London News* reported Turing as saying that "the daily papers are normally twenty years or so ahead of him and regularly open even *his* eyes in wonderment" (Wood, 1952)!

1 1936 – the universal computing machine

In 1938, the *Manchester Guardian* reported the words of a government statistician, asked to perform a large calculation: he could do it, he said, "if he were given three months free from all other work and an extra staff of twenty computers".[1] In those days, computers were human beings. As late as 1946 the newspapers carried job ads for computers, promising "excellent prospects" and a "[s]alary according to qualifications and experience".[2] A computer was a human clerk who calculated by rote, doing some of the sorts of work done now by electronic computers. The beginning of the end of this era was heralded in 1936 by the publication of Turing's famous "On Computable Numbers, with an Application to the *Entscheidungsproblem*", the paper now widely regarded as laying the foundations of modern computer science. There Turing set out the fundamental logical principles of the modern computer, describing the concept of a *universal computing machine* that operates by means of a program of instructions *stored in the machine's memory*, in the same form as data. By 1952, the press was describing Turing as "possibly England's leading expert on electronic calculators" (Wood, 1952).

Turing's universal computing machine of 1936 was a mathematical model of a human computer. Later, explicating the concept of the electronic digital computer, he said: "The idea behind digital computers may be explained by saying that these machines are intended to carry out any operations which could be done by a human computer" (Turing, 1950, p. 444). The universal computing machine was a major component of Turing's attack on an abstract problem in mathematical logic, David Hilbert's *Entscheidungsproblem*, the decision problem for first-order predicate calculus. (This asks: can a human computer "decide" this calculus – which is to say, can a human computer in principle determine, of each formula of the calculus, whether or not the formula is a theorem of the calculus?) Notwithstanding the highly abstract origin of his computing machine concept, Turing was interested right from the start in the possibility of actually building a universal machine. It was while he was working as a codebreaker at Bletchley Park during the Second World War that he learned of a technology for doing so – pulse electronics.

2 Bletchley Park: The Bombes and Colossi

In September 1939, on the first full day of war with Germany, Turing took up residence at Bletchley Park, a Victorian mansion in the process of becoming Britain's wartime headquarters for military codebreaking. At that time the chief problem facing the codebreakers was Enigma, the machine-generated cipher used by all major branches of the German military. Turing quickly set out to design a machine that would break intercepted Enigma messages. Engineers installed his prototype "Bombe" in the spring of 1940. The Bombe was a programmable parallel computer, designed to solve a specific (non-numerical) problem, and so was very different from the universal or all-purpose computers that we use today. Early models of the Bombe employed relay technology but later models were electronic. Turing's machines (with Gordon Welchman's "diagonal board" giving the Bombes extra power) turned Bletchley Park into an Enigma-breaking factory. The Bombe was, moreover, the first milestone on the road to modern artificial intelligence: it used mechanical search to carry out a task – codebreaking – that required intelligence when done by human beings (Copeland, 2004a).

Soon the codebreakers turned their attention to a new German cipher; this was also machine-generated, but was based on binary code and departed radically from the (by then) well-understood principles of Enigma. Hitler and the German Army top brass used this high-level cipher, which the British codenamed "Tunny". Thomas H. Flowers – who had spent the prewar years pioneering large-scale digital electronics – designed and built a much-needed Tunny-breaking machine, Colossus. His prototype, containing 1,600 vacuum tubes, was installed at Bletchley Park in January 1944. The Colossi (there were nine of them by the end of the war, running 24/7) were the world's first large-scale electronic digital computers. Designed for a narrow range of codebreaking tasks, Colossus was far from being an implementation of Turing's universal machine, and was programmed by routing cables and setting switches – a primitive forerunner of today's keyboard-based programming. But as soon as Turing set eyes on Flowers' racks of high-speed electronic equipment, he knew that digital electronics was the way to build his universal stored-program computer.

In 1945, once the war was over, Turing was hired by London's National Physical Laboratory (NPL) to design an electronic stored-program computer. This was called the Automatic Computing Engine, or ACE, a name chosen in homage to Charles Babbage's Analytical Engine. Turing's plan was that Flowers would construct the ACE at the British Post Office research laboratory in Dollis Hill (the birthplace of Colossus), but unfortunately Flowers' department was loaded up with other key postwar engineering work and he could only spare two engineers to work on the ACE. Progress was slow.

John Womersley, who coined the name "Automatic Computing Engine" and recruited Turing to the NPL – and was described in the press as the "man who inspired the Ace" – explained in a 1950 news interview that his interest in automatic computing machinery was "first aroused in 1936 when the conception of such computers was described by Dr. A. M. Turing".[3] Sir Charles Darwin, Director of the NPL, also emphasized in the media that the ACE sprang ultimately from Turing's "On Computable Numbers", saying in a November 1946 radio talk about the ACE that Turing's aim in his 1936 paper was to discover the "ultimate limitations" of "a machine which would imitate the processes of thought".[4] Darwin said that wartime "developments" involving "electronic valves" were enabling Turing to show "how to make his idea come true" at the NPL.[5] Darwin's letters of the time show that he knew (probably from Turing) that the ACE would use "principles developed … during the war for a certain Foreign Office project", a project involving "Mr. Flowers who has had much experience in … the electronic side of it" (Darwin, 1946a). This is of course a reference to Colossus (although Darwin probably had no detailed knowledge). The route from Turing's 1936 abstract computing machine to the electronic ACE was via the ultra-secret Colossus.

3 Developments in Germany and the United States

Meanwhile, in Germany, Konrad Zuse already had a relay-based general-purpose computer in operation (Copeland and Sommaruga, 2016). Relay-based computers could carry out in minutes or hours calculations that would take human computers weeks or months. Zuse's wartime S1 relay computers (there were three) were used in the Henschel weapons factory, to assist with the manufacture of rocket-propelled missiles. Like Colossus and the Bombe, the S1 was a special-purpose computer, but Zuse's Z3 relay computer was the first working programmable general-purpose digital computer, completed in 1941. Zuse had anticipated elements of the stored-program concept during 1936–1938, but he did not implement stored programming in any of his relay computers (Copeland and Sommaruga, 2016, pp. 89–95). Allied bombs destroyed the Z3 in 1943, but Zuse's Z4 relay computer, completed as the war ended, became the first commercially available general-purpose computer. The Swiss *Eidgenössische Technische Hochschule* (ETH) in Zurich rented the Z4 from Zuse's company; it ran at ETH from 1950 to 1955, and was the core of mainland Europe's first commercial computing center. The pilot model of Turing's ACE, which came to life in 1950, was soon the core of Europe's first commercial *electronic* computing center, in London.

Several early computing projects blossomed in the US (Copeland and Sommaruga, 2016). Howard Aiken's relay-based Harvard Mark 1, in operation by 1943, had much in common with the earlier Z3; built by IBM in New York, the Mark 1 was also known as the IBM Automatic Sequence Controlled Calculator. Earlier, in Iowa, during 1937–1942, John Atanasoff had experimented with a small-scale, special-purpose electronic computer containing approximately 300 vacuum tubes, but overall his machine never functioned satisfactorily. In 1943, Presper Eckert and John Mauchly began work on a large-scale electronic computer named

ENIAC. This first ran in December 1945; the *Chicago Tribune* reported on its front page that the computer – nicknamed the "mechanical Einstein" – "possibly opened the mathematical way to better living for every man".[6]

These machines all belonged to the era preceding stored-programming. ENIAC, like Colossus before it, was programmed by routing cables and setting switches, a process that could take as long as three weeks. Imagine having to do that with your laptop when you wish to switch from word-processing to browsing the web! In 1946 – as Turing worked on the design of the ACE, and as Eckert, Mauchly, and John von Neumann worked on the design of ENIAC's successor, EDVAC – the fundamental problem in computing was how to realize Turing's 1936 concept of a universal stored-program machine in electronic hardware.

4 A revolution of the mind

As this engineering work went on, the idea of computer intelligence – as far as is known, first broached by Turing during the war, at Bletchley Park – began to emerge into the light of day. At the beginning of November 1946, the media reported an address given to the British Institution of Radio Engineers on October 31 by Admiral the Viscount Mountbatten of Burma. Before the war, Mountbatten was the Mediterranean Fleet's Wireless Officer; during the war he was Chief of Combined Operations and then Supreme Allied Commander South-East Asia. Two decades after his 1946 address, Mountbatten said of this speech that he had "had the privilege to disclose for the first time some of the development work which had been undertaken during the war on the electronic computer" (Mountbatten, 1964, p. 14).

In his address, Mountbatten had said: "It is now considered possible to evolve an electronic brain which will perform functions analogous to those at present undertaken by the semi-automatic portion of the human brain". A machine can be built, he said, that "will provide an intelligent – I repeat, intelligent – link" between the information it receives about the "machinery under its control" and the "action necessary to keep the machinery" working as desired (Mountbatten, 1946, pp. 223–224). He continued:

> [M]achines now actually in use can exercise a degree of memory; and some are now being designed to exercise those hitherto human prerogatives of choice and judgement. One of them could even be made to play a rather mediocre game of chess!
>
> *(Mountbatten, 1946, p. 224)*

Mountbatten also predicted a "memory machine", "the size of a large desk", that will store "the whole contents of a colossal reference library of millions of volumes"; with "electronic selection" of its contents, it would be able "to accomplish achievements far beyond the scope of present human attainment". His reference to machines "now actually in use" which display "a degree of memory" may well have included Colossus and other secret memory machines at Bletchley Park. Mountbatten concluded strikingly that "we are really facing a new revolution … a revolution of the mind" (Mountbatten, 1946, p. 224).

In his 1945 design proposal for the ACE (titled "Proposed Electronic Calculator"), Turing had said that his computer "could fairly easily be made to play a rather bad game" of chess (Turing, 1945, p. 389). Probably Mountbatten had Turing's claim in mind, although throughout his speech he referred explicitly to only one computer, the ENIAC. His description of the "electronic brain", though, sounds much more like the ACE: a fast universal machine under stored-program control (as the ACE would be, once constructed) was necessary for the functionality that Mountbatten described. Why, then, did Mountbatten not mention the ACE explicitly? In a letter to the *Times* on November 13, Darwin explained that Mountbatten had been "fully informed" about the ACE, but at the NPL's request "did not mention it explicitly because it had not yet been made public" (Darwin, 1946b). Nevertheless, Mountbatten described the ACE's capacities "correctly in every respect", Darwin said (Darwin, 1946b).

Mountbatten's speech was widely reported in international, national, regional, and even local newspapers, making the front page of several. The newspapers seized on the term "electronic brain". According to one paper, the "whole world of science has been stirred by one revelation … the electronic brain".[7] The public were alleged to be "rather bewildered",[8] fearing that they would be reduced to "moronic button-pushers, lever-pullers, and dial-watchers", in order to "facilitate the Olympian cogitations of an aristocracy of super-minds".[9] The risk was that "the controlled monster" would become "the monster in control", reducing human beings to "degenerate serfs".[10] It was thought that humans might perish entirely, the "victims of their own brain products".[11]

Soon fear spread of job loss through automation. In 1947, the engineer (and member of the NPL executive committee) Sir Clifford Paterson said that "the 'Electronic Brain' was turning the wheels in British factories" and had "already helped to speed output and save labour" (although the following year the cyberneticist William Grey Walter pointed out that the new machines were "very expensive compared with human labour"[12]).[13] The *Press and Journal* asked "What is likely to happen if machines can be made to think?":

> What, then, will be the repercussions on all forms of human labour …? The answer seems fairly clear: they will replace men and women and do their work for them. They will make many people now essential redundant.
>
> *(Godwin, 1949)*

Once a pilot model of Turing's ACE was actually operating, it was said to be "pretty nearly as frightening as the atom bomb".[14] Sixty-plus years later inventor Elon Musk went further, tweeting that artificial intelligence is potentially "more dangerous than nukes".[15] Stephen Hawking and several prominent scientists wrote an article for the US and UK media, expressing similar anxieties. "Success in creating AI would be the biggest event in human history", they said; "Unfortunately, it might also be the last, unless we learn how to avoid the risks". They continued: "One can imagine such technology outsmarting financial markets, out-inventing human researchers, out-manipulating human leaders, and developing weapons we cannot even understand" (Hawking et al., 2014). In 1946, though, news of an "electronic brain" sometimes met with a complacency that is less evident today. As the "product of the human brain", the "new" brain "can never take over completely", according to the *Motherwell Times*;[16] and the *Manchester Guardian* said that, "[h]owever willing and intelligent the mechanical apparatus may be, it is still old Adam who must press the button".[17]

5 Building an electronic brain at the National Physical Laboratory

Turing's views were probably the inspiration for much of Mountbatten's address. When Turing joined the NPL, he announced that he was going to build "a brain".[18] A little later, he said in a letter to the cyberneticist William Ross Ashby (Turing, c. 1946): "In working on the ACE I am more interested in the possibility of producing models of the action of the brain than in the practical applications to computing" (a typically self-dismissive statement from one of the greatest pioneers of scientific computing). Turing's design document "Proposed Electronic

Calculator" also highlighted his interest in computational cognition: "There are indications ... that it is possible to make the machine display intelligence at the risk of its making occasional serious mistakes", he said (Turing, 1945, p. 389).

On November 7, 1946, the *Daily Telegraph* reported the official announcement of the ACE by the British government.[19] The jingoistic British press delighted in the machine's superiority over the ENIAC, which was "just a plain dunce", the *Daily Mirror* said.[20] The ACE, it was explained, could easily be "told" a problem and "remember" what it had been told, whereas the ENIAC required "a laborious process of plugging and switching".[21] "'Ace' will always be trumps", declared the *Daily Mail*.[22]

The *Daily Mail* also said that the ACE would wipe out "a blot on the honour of British science" (Langdon-Davies, 1946) – the blot being that Babbage's Analytical Engine had not been funded. Some British newspapers regarded Babbage's machines as the *fons et origo* of computing machinery: for example, the *Times* said that the Analytical Engine was "certainly the mechanical prototype of the 'electronic brain' of to-day" (Gould, 1946). Mathematician and computing pioneer Douglas Hartree described the Harvard Mark I as "essentially a realisation of Babbage's dream of over a hundred years ago" (Hartree, 1946b); and Womersley (Turing's boss at the NPL) emphasized that "all the basic ideas and the possible things we could do with it [the ACE] had been foreseen by Charles Babbage ... 120 years ago".[23] Since Babbage's day, Britain had "fallen behind other countries in this important form of invention, but it looks as if we are once more taking the lead", said John Langdon-Davies, science editor of the *Daily Mail* (Langdon-Davies, 1946).

It is ironic that Langdon-Davies thought Britain had fallen behind – but he was in no position to know anything about the still ultra-secret Bombes and Colossi. In contrast, W.J. Bentley wrote that "Britain can take full marks for the electronic brain, the amazing mechanical thinker whose existence was recently disclosed by Lord Mountbatten". This was, Bentley said, "entirely a British development", beginning in 1938 when the Radio Department at the Post Office's Dollis Hill research laboratory "were asked to work on an electric machine [the 'Calc'] which would store, memorise and sort out information" (Bentley, 1946).

The day after the ACE was announced, the *Times* published a letter by Hartree. He wrote to "deprecate" Mountbatten's use of the term "electronic brain" – since "it ascribes to the machine capabilities that it does not possess" – and to deny Mountbatten's claim that machines then being designed were capable of "choice" and "judgement". In Hartree's view, these machines can "only do precisely what they are instructed to do by the operators who set them up". They can exercise "a certain amount" of judgment, but only insofar as this has been "fully thought out and anticipated in setting up the machine" and as such (he added in a later letter) is due to the human operator's "judgement and thought" (Hartree, 1946a; 1946b). Hartree hoped, therefore, that use of the term "electronic brain" would "be avoided in future" (Hartree, 1946a). Darwin supported this stance, saying in the *Times* "I wish to associate myself with his [Hartree's] protest"; in Darwin's view, the new computing machines "aspire to imitate" only the part of the brain that is an "unconscious automatic machine producing precise and sometimes very complicated reactions to stimuli", and not the "higher realms of the intellect" (Darwin, 1946b).

Hartree's and Darwin's comments were welcomed in the newspapers. "Far from being a rival of the human mind", it was said, the "new Frankenstein"[24] was merely "the big brother of the sliderule and the adding machine. ... there is nothing more 'mental' about it" (Langdon-Davies, 1946). The "human brain remains unique", and humans will still have to use "wit and judgment".[25] The ACE "knows nothing" about ethics, art or music.[26] "Grey matter (if available) still counts".[27]

In his letter to the *Times,* Darwin said that it was a "loose interpretation" of Mountbatten's words that led to "the present confusion" over the nature of the electronic brain (Darwin, 1946b). But in fact there was a fundamental disagreement about machine intelligence, and this was beginning to be played out in the newspapers. On November 8, 1946, the *Daily Telegraph* reported Turing as saying "that he foresaw the time, possibly in 30 years, when it would be as easy to ask the machine a question as to ask a man"; while Hartree denied "any notion that Ace could ever be a complete substitute for the human brain" – saying "The fashion which has sprung up in the last 20 years to decry human reason is a path which leads straight to Nazism".[28]

Undaunted, in a lecture given four months later on February 20, 1947, Turing offered a breathtaking glimpse of the future of computing, suggesting that the computer will be able to "learn from experience" and that "the machine must be allowed to have contact with human beings in order that it may adapt itself to their standards" (Turing, 1947, pp. 393–394). Machine intelligence experiments would begin, he said, "[a]s soon as one can provide a reasonably large memory capacity" (Turing, 1947, p. 393).

6 Getting the computer revolution underway

It was in June 1948 that the first electronic universal computing machine ran its first program – not, alas, at the NPL, but in Max Newman's Computing Machine Laboratory at Manchester University. It was Newman's 1935 Cambridge lectures that had introduced Turing to Hilbert's *Entscheidungsproblem*, and Newman who had directed the use of the Colossi at Bletchley Park. He shared the dream of using electronics to build Turing's 1936 machine, and it was in his Manchester laboratory that engineers Freddie Williams and Tom Kilburn became the first to achieve this, designing and building a small stored-program computer called simply "Baby". Baby is the distant ancestor of our laptops, mainframes, phones, and tablets.

It was not until 1950 that a pilot model of Turing's ACE came to life. Newspaper reports about "the world's most advanced electronic 'brain'" (which coded problems into pulses traveling "at the speed of light"[29]) said that the pilot model "could provide the correct answer in one minute to a problem that would occupy a mathematician for months",[30] and could in "one-500th of a second … perform calculations which would take a clever mathematician eight minutes".[31] For "practical purposes there is no limit to what Ace can do", the papers said[32] – and all for "about £1 a minute".[33]

The ACE pilot model was preceded in 1949 by Maurice Wilkes' EDSAC at Cambridge University. Wilkes had adapted the American EDVAC design and his British knock-off was running programs some three years before the EDVAC itself. In October 1947 the EDSAC, then in the early stages of construction, was described in the news as a "two-ton 'memory' of steel tubes and mercury". This "new brain" would "have 25 times more 'knowledge' than the American Eniac". Wilkes said that the EDSAC could solve mathematical problems "so complicated that man has never attempted to solve them", delivering the answers "in a matter of seconds".[34] Wilkes also predicted that the machine might make "sensational discoveries in engineering, astronomy, and atomic physics", and even solve "philosophical problems too complicated for the human mind".[35] In January 1950, the EDSAC's inventors were reported to "marvel at the machine they have created". When a problem becomes increasingly difficult, "EDSAC behaves just like a human being. It does not scratch its head – but it hesitates a little. You can almost see it 'thinking'" (Bedford, 1950).

Things were also moving forward rapidly in America (Copeland and Sommaruga, 2016; Copeland et al., 2017). In 1948, the ENIAC was modified to run stored programs, although (unlike Baby and the EDSAC) the programs were read-only. The following year, two full-fledged stored-program computers began working in the US. These were the Eckert-Mauchly BINAC and MIT's Whirlwind (Whirlwind had only a dummy memory at first, and it was two years before its intended high-speed memory was functional). The year 1949 also saw the Australian CSIR Mark I run its first test program.

The year 1948 saw a dazzling array of computing firsts at Manchester, including the first computer-generated digital graphics, the first moving digital images, and early ideas about making the computer generate musical notes (Copeland et al., 2017; Copeland and Long, 2017). In 1949, the press reported that Turing was "trying to teach the machine to play chess", quoting him as saying "Once it has mastered the rules it will think out its own moves".[36] On November 15, 1951, the *Manchester Guardian* announced that the Manchester computer had been "quietly solving a chess problem", using a program written by Dietrich Prinz.[37] This was the Big Bang of computer chess and Prinz was the first person to successfully implement a chess program (Copeland and Prinz, 2017).

Another striking development in 1948 was Turing's anticipation of modern "connectionism", which uses networks of artificial neurons to compute (Copeland and Proudfoot, 1996). This was in his NPL report "Intelligent Machinery", which was in effect the first detailed manifesto of artificial intelligence (Turing, 1948). "Intelligent Machinery" contains the first known suggestion that computing machines can be built out of simple, neuron-like elements connected together into networks. Turing proposed that networks could be "trained" (his term) to perform specific tasks, and he foresaw the need to develop training algorithms, now an important field; he also conceived of the now-standard practice of programming the training algorithm into a computer simulation of the network. However, Turing himself seems never to have programmed a simulation of a neural network (this first occurred in 1954 at MIT[38]).

Another of the firsts in "Intelligent Machinery" was Turing's mention of what is now known as a genetic algorithm, in a brief passage concerning what he called "genetical or evolutionary search" (Turing, 1948, p. 431). Even this early, the gathering computer revolution was beginning to form bonds with biology and brain science.

7 The mind of mechanical man

The mind-machine debate continued in the press. The papers reported Geoffrey Jefferson's lecture "The mind of mechanical man", delivered to the Royal College of Surgeons on June 9, 1949. The next day, the *Times* proclaimed "No mind for mechanical man".[39] Jefferson, the first professor of neurosurgery in the UK, said that those he called "electro-physicists" (computer scientists) greatly underestimated "the extreme variety, flexibility, and complexity" of the nervous system (Jefferson, 1949, p. 1110). In his view, people were being "pushed, gently not roughly pushed" to accept a "great likeness" between electronic circuits and processes of the nervous system, when in fact something "quite different, as yet undiscovered, may happen in those final processes of brain activity that results in what we call, for convenience, mind" (ibid., p. 1108). "All that one is entitled to say", Jefferson argued, is that the mind *might* be like a computer, but "the electrical machine offers no proof that it is so" (ibid., pp. 1108–1109).

According to Jefferson, the human brain has "a fringe left over ... in which free will may act ... a fringe that becomes larger and larger the more complex the nervous system" (ibid., p. 1107). He claimed that "[n]ot until a machine can write a sonnet or compose a concerto because of thoughts and emotions felt, and not by the chance fall of symbols, could we agree that machine equals brain" (ibid., p. 1110). *Punch* poked fun, suggesting that the computer might say "petulantly" that it was "far too busy composing a sonnet" to bother with mathematics (Young, 1949). Turing's response to Jefferson, reported in the *Times*, was tongue-in-cheek but also serious:

> I do not see why [the machine] should not enter any one of the fields normally covered by the human intellect, and eventually compete on equal terms. … I do not think you can even draw the line about sonnets, though the comparison is perhaps a little unfair because a sonnet written by a machine will be better appreciated by another machine.[40]

Overall, opinion in the papers came down on Jefferson's side. Electronic brains, it was said, "may become synthetic men. But they won't have souls" (Godwin, 1949). In a letter to the *Times* on June 14, 1949, the Catholic priest and theologian Illtyd Trethowan said that "responsible scientists will be quick to dissociate themselves from [Turing's] programme". Those who believe that human beings are "free" persons – which "is unintelligible if we have no unextended mind or soul, but only a brain" – "must ask ourselves how far Mr. Turing's opinions are shared, or may come to be shared, by the rulers of our country", Trethowan said grimly (Trethowan, 1949). On June 15, radar pioneer Sir Robert Watson-Watt joined the debate: Trethowan's letter seemed to him "a return to the period of conflict between religion and science", and he was horrified by "any tendency to limit the sphere of truly scientific investigation". Watson-Watt's sympathies were, he said, with those who wished to see "how far the electronic brain will go towards thinking", although he had "not the slightest fear of its coming into competition with the human brain".[41] If "the machine takes charge of the man", Watson-Watt reportedly claimed, "it is because the man is not man-size".[42]

The editorial in the issue of the *British Medical Journal* (BMJ) containing the text of Jefferson's lecture also sided with Jefferson. It allowed that the electronic brain must have "something in common" with the nervous system, since otherwise it could not calculate; but this required only that the machine "reproduce" the "logical processes of numeration" – concluding from this that future machines might "fall in love, write sonnets, or rule their makers" was "bad logic". Poetry, the editorial said, is the expression of "feelings", and what evidence is there that "feelings can be identified, not merely correlated, with electrical rhythms which could be induced in a machine?" In addition, the editors gave a hyperbolic account of the dangers of a "world of machines", foreseeing "tyranny, the concentration camp, the gas chamber, and the cremation oven".[43]

Max Newman (writing in the same issue of the BMJ) conceded the danger that "extravagant powers" will be credited to the new machines, and "conclusions drawn too rapidly about biological analogues". Nevertheless, he said, "caution" was necessary before deciding that machines could *not* think "on the basis of our knowledge of the behaviour of a small pilot model of this very new kind of machine" – Baby – which has been "in rather halting action for a few months". In Newman's view, the question to be asked was not "Can all *kinds* of thought, logical, poetical, reflective, be imitated by machines?" but instead "Can *anything* that can be called 'thought' be so imitated and, if so, how much?" (Newman, 1949, p. 1133).

A few weeks later, the neurophysiologist John Bates weighed in. Bates was the founder of the Ratio Club, a small informal dining club of distinguished physiologists, mathematicians, and engineers who met to discuss cybernetics. (In September 1949 Bates invited Turing to join, saying that the members had "a common interest in the working out of recent advances in communication and computing theory" and were "unanimous in wishing that you would join the company" (Bates, 1949b).) Bates was optimistic about the new science of computing. Biologists, he said, should not "react as if some unwanted electrical gadget was being sold to them" by this new science; in fact, "the progress that is now being made in the science of the classification of mechanisms may ultimately have a liberating influence in biology akin to that brought about by Darwin" (Bates, 1949a).

Bates emphasized two striking ideas that are also found in Turing's work. First, he denied that the question whether the electronic brain was really a *brain* could be settled by appeal to definition. Bates said disparagingly that discussions of whether electronic brains can have "feelings" simply "reduce to verbal definitions", and that Newman's question ("Can *anything* that can be called 'thought' be … imitated and, if so, how much?") likewise seemed "too much bound up with verbal definitions to be satisfactory". (See Section 9 for Turing on defining "thinking".) Second, Bates claimed that it was "absurd" to imagine that the brain functions without calling on the biological principles of "growth and organization – to which there are no mechanical or electrical analogues" (Bates, 1949a). At Manchester, Turing pioneered the study of what he called "morphogenesis", using the computer to simulate biological growth (Turing, 1952). He said, "[N]eurons might be made to grow so as to form a particular circuit, rather than to reach a particular place" (Turing, 1951b). Turing was the first pioneer of what we now call Artificial Life.

8 A new world

In 1951, some of the new computers appeared before the public. Ferranti's Nim-playing machine, "Nimrod" – which interested "everyone from the punter to the pundit", the *Manchester Guardian* said[44] – was on show at the Festival of Britain Science Exhibition in May, and in the same month the ACE pilot model was exhibited for six days at the NPL.[45] On July 7, 1951, the *Manchester Guardian* reported the official opening of the fully-engineered Manchester computer. The computer was provisionally named "Madam" – an acronym for "Manchester Automatic Digital Machine" but also, Freddie Williams said, "because of certain unpredictable tendencies".[46]

Despite public excitement about the new machines, several journalists were unimpressed. The *Daily Mirror* questioned whether the computers were "worth the time and money", or were they "just toys for the boys in the back room?" (Bedford, 1950). The *Economist* asked "No More Clerks?", and pointedly suggested that in "this new world where clerks would be comparatively few … there would have to be a host of highly skilled machine instructors and technicians". Although the question about job losses was a good one, the periodical made a gigantic error when it said that "at the present price of about £55,000 for the latest model, the electronic computing age hardly seems to be just around the corner".[47]

In the same year, Turing gave a lecture titled "Can Digital Computers Think?" on the BBC's Third Programme, a radio channel for talks, music, and drama (Turing, 1951a). Martin Armstrong, the *Listener*'s Spoken Word critic, said of the broadcast that he "was moved every few minutes to hold up my schoolboy hand with a 'Please, Sir … One moment, Sir … Will you explain what you mean, Sir, by …'". In Armstrong's view, saying that a machine thinks is "to define thought as a mechanical process, which is an entirely arbitrary definition". He accused Turing of anthropomorphism: claiming that a machine thinks because it produces mathematical results is, Armstrong said, like "the little girl who tells me that her doll … goes to sleep every night, because, sure enough, it closes its eyes when it is laid in a horizontal position" (Armstrong, 1951).

Turing was well aware that his view was radical. He gave another talk in 1951, titled "Intelligent Machinery: A Heretical Theory" (to "The Fifty One Society" in Manchester), saying:

> "You cannot make a machine to think for you". This is a commonplace that is usually accepted without question. It will be the purpose of this paper to question it.
>
> *(Turing, c. 1951, p. 472)*

In fact the public's attitude to the idea of machine intelligence was already changing. In July 1951, the *Economist* said that the question of machine intelligence was "now far from academic", with the result that the exceptional status of human beings was threatened: "How far is it possible to go in constructing mechanical analogues of human behaviour without stripping man of everything that has been thought to be peculiarly his?", the periodical asked.[48] In the same month the *Manchester Guardian* said that in fact "nobody knows what the Manchester machine will be able to do" – adding that "whatever 'Madam' can do she will do it for Mr Turing".[49]

9 The sinister machine

In 1952, the Manchester computer was described in the papers as a "sinister" machine that "lives and works" at Manchester University.[50] The computer was visibly acquiring new capabilities. In January that year, Newman announced to professional musicians that it could "compose 'very bad tunes'" (according to the *Manchester Guardian*, the next step was a machine that could compose good tunes, but "so far no method of bridging the gap had been devised"). Newman added that human musicians need not worry about "competition from machines"; the machine's activity was "far" from "genuine composition".[51] The press suggested that the computer ought not to be described as capable of composition until it could "turn out a march which is as workmanlike as anything by Sousa" – commenting, though, that human musicians would "be only too pleased to avail themselves of any gadget which enables them to use even less ingenuity than at present".[52]

Williams aired another of the computer's new abilities in the *Manchester Guardian* in February 1952: it could "examine itself for defects when it suspected that it was making errors".[53] An "electronic brain is helping scientists develop a new electronic brain", the press reported;[54] the machine could "diagnose trouble within its own interior" and the next step would be a machine that would "complete the diagnosis by carrying out a surgical operation upon itself".[55] In November 1952, Williams was reported as claiming that the computer "would always win" when playing draughts or chess. "It could make mistakes", he explained, "both purely arithmetical and by misinterpreting its instructions, but both types were rare". Like Hartree, though, Williams held that the machine was no brain: it was "extremely dim and brainless" and "capable only of completely slavish obedience to the wishes and commands of a supervisor, who must do all the thinking".[56] (Williams added drily that the computer "needed 30 well-trained mathematicians to keep it going and three engineers to keep it serviceable".[57])

Turing's second broadcast on the Third Programme, titled "Can Automatic Calculating Machines Be Said to Think?" (Turing et al., 1952), took the form of a symposium in January 1952 with Newman, Jefferson, and the philosopher Richard Braithwaite (like Turing, a Fellow of King's College). The *Listener*'s Martin Armstrong was again provoked, saying "I find it difficult to banish from my mind a conviction of the absurdity of this question":

> It was evident ... at the outset of this discussion that no headway could be made until some sort of shape was imposed on the word *think*. ... Only when we have done so shall we be able to settle the hash of the automatic calculating machine. Meanwhile, is not the question proposed by this programme a meaningless one?

Not until the word "think" has been "accurately defined", can we ever "prove whether or not this machine thinks", Armstrong argued. He continued, "though – between ourselves – I know perfectly well, and so do you, that it doesn't" (Armstrong, 1952). This critique was no doubt prompted by Turing's statement in the broadcast that he didn't "want to give a definition of thinking"; if forced, he said, he "should probably be unable to say anything more about it than that it was a sort of buzzing that went on inside my head" (Turing et al., 1952, p. 494).

The claim that we know that machines do *not* think appeared regularly in the pages of national newspapers. In the *Observer*, essayist E.F.W. Tomlin said that a machine can neither "know" that it is calculating nor "realise when it has failed". A machine does not "choose", Tomlin said, since choosing "must always be a conscious act" (Tomlin, 1952). But others were thinking similarly to Turing. Jacob Bronowski, the mathematician and cultural scholar, claimed that Tomlin's view begged the question: we have no evidence, he said, that "human choice" is in fact any different from a machine's selecting one behavior over another, and the "fact that human beings are conscious of what they are doing in the act of choice does not provide such evidence" (Bronowski, 1952). Machines, Bronowski also said, "can take unpredictable courses, as human beings do".

In 1951 Turing had said, "The whole thinking process is still rather mysterious to us, but I believe that the attempt to make a thinking machine will help us greatly in finding out how we think ourselves" (Turing, 1951a, p. 486). By 1952, what we call computer science, artificial intelligence, and cognitive science had established themselves. Fundamental philosophical problems in these areas were being debated in the newspapers and elsewhere. Also, concerns about job losses due to automation, and about the potential extinction of the human race by artificial super-intelligences, were being publicly discussed – more than half a century before today's anxieties. The "revolution of the mind" had begun.

Notes

1 'Professor Clay Suggests a Biennial Census of Production', *The Manchester Guardian*, November 17, 1938, p. 15.
2 Situations vacant, *The Times* [London, England], April 5, 1946.
3 'Month's Work in a Minute', *The Sheffield Telegraph*, November 30, 1950, p. 4.
4 Darwin as reported in 'Did You Hear That: An Arithmetical Robot', *The Listener*, November 14, 1946, p. 663.
5 Darwin as reported in 'Did You Hear That: An Arithmetical Robot'.
6 'Robot Calculator Knocks out Figures Like Chain Lightning', *Chicago Tribune*, February 15, 1946, p. 1.
7 *The Mercury*, January 3, 1947, p. 5.
8 'Not an "Ace" Brain', *The Courier and Advertiser*, November 11, 1946, p. 2.
9 'The Brain Machine', *The Evening Telegraph and Post*, November 2, 1946, p. 4.
10 'Man and Superman', *The Irish Times*, November 2, 1946, p. 7.
11 'Wellsian Brain', *The Motherwell Times*, November 8, 1946, p. 11.
12 'Did You Hear That? Robot World', *The Listener*, March 11, 1948, p. 413.
13 'Oliphant: Give Science Top Priority', *Daily Mail*, September 26, 1947, p. 3.
14 'London Letter: Ace', *The Irish Times*, December 3, 1950, p. 5.
15 @elonmusk, August 2, 2014.
16 'Wellsian Brain'.

17 'The Unknown Quantity', *The Manchester Guardian*, November 2, 1946, p. 6.
18 Don Bayley in interview with Copeland, 1997.
19 'Britain to Make a Radio Brain', *The Daily Telegraph*, November 7, 1946.
20 'The Adding Machine', *The Daily Mirror*, November 11, 1946, p. 4.
21 'A New Electronic "Brain": Britain Goes One Better', *The Manchester Guardian*, November 7, 1946, p. 8.
22 '"Ace" Will Always Be Trumps', *Daily Mail*, November 7, 1946, p. 3.
23 'Month's Work in a Minute', *The Sheffield Telegraph*, November 30, 1950, p. 4.
24 'Not an "Ace" Brain', *The Courier and Advertiser*, November 11, 1946, p. 2.
25 'Star Question', *The Nottingham Evening Post*, April 13, 1950, p. 4; 'Not an "Ace" Brain'.
26 'Miscellany: Not So Brainy', *The Manchester Guardian*, November 8, 1946, p. 3.
27 'Miscellany: Not So Brainy'.
28 '"ACE" Will Speed Jet Flying', *The Daily Telegraph*, November 8, 1946.
29 'Month's Work in a Minute'.
30 'Month's Work in a Minute: Ace Calculator', *The Times* [London, England], November 30, 1950, p. 3.
31 '£40,000 Electric Brain', *The Evening Telegraph*, November 29, 1950, p. 7.
32 'Month's Work in a Minute: Ace Calculator'.
33 'A New Electronic Calculator: Month's Work in Minute', *The Manchester Guardian*, November 30, 1950, p. 3.
34 Wilkes as quoted in Photo Standalone 1 (no title), *Times Pictorial*, *The Irish Times*, October 25, 1947, p. 3.
35 'A Don Builds a Memory: 4ft Tubes in His Brain', *Daily Mail*, October 2, 1947, p. 3.
36 'Mechanical Brain Is Learning to Play Chess', *The Irish Times*, June 13, 1949, p. 7.
37 '"Brain" Can Solve Chess Problems: But Not Able to Play', *The Manchester Guardian*, November 15, 1951, p. 5.
38 See Farley and Clark 1954 and Clark and Farley 1955.
39 'No Mind for Mechanical Man: An Insoluble Problem', *The Times* [London, England] June 10, 1949, p. 2.
40 'The Mechanical Brain: Answer Found to 300-Year-Old Sum', *The Times* [London, England], June 11, 1949, p. 4.
41 Watson–Watt quoted in 'The Mechanical Brain: Sir R. Watson-Watt on Its Uses', *The Times* [London, England], June 16, 1949, p. 2.
42 'A Man-Sized Man Need Have No Fears', *Daily Mirror*, June 16, 1949, p. 7.
43 'Mind, Machine, and Man', *British Medical Journal* 1 (4616): 1129–1130.
44 'Our London Correspondence', *The Manchester Guardian*, June 21, 1951, p. 6.
45 'Scientific AIDS to Industry', *The Times* [London, England], May 24, 1951, p. 6.
46 'Half a Day for a Lifetime's Calculations: "Madam" with Unpredictable Tendencies', *The Manchester Guardian*, July 7, 1951, p. 3.
47 'No More Clerks?', *The Economist*, July 28, 1951, pp. 206–207.
48 'Fruits of the Mechanical Brain', *The Economist*, July 14, 1951, p. 84.
49 'Half a Day for a Lifetime's Calculations: "Madam" with Unpredictable Tendencies'.
50 'The Last Wonder', *The Irish Times*, March 7, 1952, p. 5.
51 'Very Bad Tunes: But Electronic Machine Can Compose Music', *The Manchester Guardian*, January 4, 1952, p. 2.
52 'Automatic Arias', *The Irish Times*, January 16, 1952, p. 5.
53 'The Electronic "Brain": How Digits Are Stored', *The Manchester Guardian*, February 9, 1952, p. 2.
54 Article 2 (no title), *The Irish Times*, February 9, 1952, p. 15.
55 'Electronic Brain Can Sing Now', *The Courier and Advertiser*, February 28, 1952, p. 3.
56 'This Machine Has Most of the Answers', *The Yorkshire Post*, November 11, 1952, p. 1.
57 'This Machine Has Most of the Answers'.

References

Armstrong, M. (1951) 'It Makes You Think', *The Listener*, London, May 24, p. 851.
Armstrong, M. (1952) 'I *Don't* Think', *The Listener*, London, January 24, p. 157.
Bates, J.A.V. (1949a) 'Mind, Machine, and Man', *British Medical Journal*, 2 (4619), p. 177.
Bates, J.A.V. (1949b) Letter to Turing, September 22. The Wellcome Library, GC/179/B.2.
Bedford, R. (1950) 'A Machine Can Work Out This Problem ... But What Are the Scientists Trying to Get At?', *The Daily Mirror*, London, January 18, p. 2.

Bentley, W.J. (1946) 'A Yorkshireman Is Leading the Team Now Developing the New Electronic Brain: Machine May Link with Body and Think for Us', *Daily Mail*, Hull, November 15, p. 4.

Bronowski, J. (1952) 'Thinking Machines', *The Observer*, London, December 7, p. 2.

Clark, W.A. and Farley, B.G. (1955) 'Generalisation of Pattern Recognition in a Self-Organising System', *Proceedings of the Western Joint Computer Conference*. Los Angeles, March 1–3. New York, NY: ACM.

Copeland, B.J. (2004a) 'Artificial Intelligence', in Copeland, B.J. (ed.) *The Essential Turing*. Oxford: Clarendon Press.

Copeland, B.J. (ed.) (2004b) *The Essential Turing: Seminal Writings in Computing, Logic, Philosophy, Artificial Intelligence, and Artificial Life plus The Secrets of Enigma*. Oxford: Clarendon Press.

Copeland, B.J. and Long, J. (2017) 'Turing and the History of Computer Music', in Floyd, J. and Bokulich, A. (eds.) *Philosophical Explorations of the Legacy of Alan Turing*. Cham: Springer, pp. 189–218.

Copeland, B.J. and Prinz, D. (2017) 'Computer Chess – The First Moments', in Copeland, B.J. et al. *The Turing Guide*. Oxford: Oxford University Press, pp. 327–346.

Copeland, B.J. and Proudfoot, D. (1996) 'On Alan Turing's Anticipation of Connectionism', *Synthese*, 108, pp. 361–377.

Copeland, B.J. and Sommaruga, G. (2016) 'The Stored-Program Universal Computer: Did Zuse Anticipate Turing and von Neumann?', in Sommaruga, G. and Strahm, T. (eds.) *Turing's Revolution*. Basel: Springer, pp. 43–101.

Copeland, B.J. et al. (2017) 'Screen History: The Haeff Memory and Graphics Tube', *IEEE Annals of the History of Computing*, 39, pp. 9–28.

Darwin, C.G. (1946a) Letter to Stanley Angwin, February 22. The Turing Archive for the History of Computing. Available at: www.alanturing.net/turing_archive/archive/p/p02/p02.php.

Darwin, C.G. (1946b) 'The "Electronic Brain"', *Times*, London, November 13, p. 7.

Farley, B.G. and Clark, W.A. (1954) 'Simulation of Self-Organising Systems by Digital Computer', *Institute of Radio Engineers Transactions on Information Theory*, 4, pp. 76–84.

Godwin, G. (1949) 'What Is Likely to Happen If Machines Can Be Made to Think?', *The Press and Journal*, Aberdeen, June 23, p. 2.

Gould, R.T. (1946) 'The "Electronic Brain"', *Times*, London, November 29, p. 5.

Hartree, D.R. (1946a) 'The "Electronic Brain"', *Times*, London, November 7, p. 5.

Hartree, D.R. (1946b) 'The "Electronic Brain"', *Times*, London, November 22, p. 5.

Hawking, S. et al. (2014) 'Transcending Complacency on Superintelligent Machines', *Huffington Post*, April 29.

Jefferson, G. (1949) 'The Mind of Mechanical Man', *British Medical Journal*, 1 (4616), pp. 1105–1110.

Langdon-Davies, J. (1946) 'Electronic Brains Can't Reason', *Daily Mail*, London, November 19, p. 2.

Mountbatten, L. (1946) 'The Presidential Address', *Journal of the British Institution of Radio Engineers*, 6 (6), pp. 221–225.

Mountbatten, L. (1964). 'Address by the Charter President – Admiral of the Fleet, the Earl Mountbatten of Burma, K.G.', *Proceedings of the Indian Division of the Institution of Electronic and Radio Engineers*, 2 (1), pp. 9–14.

Newman, M.H.A. (1949) 'A Note on Electric Computing Machines', *British Medical Journal*, 1 (4616), p. 1133.

Proudfoot, D. (2015) 'Mocking AI Panic', *Spectrum*, 52 (7), pp. 46–47.

Tomlin, E.W.F. (1952) 'Thinking Machines', *The Observer*, London, December 7, p. 2.

Trethowan, I. (1949) 'The Mechanical Brain', *Times*, London, June 14, p. 5.

Turing, A.M. (1945) 'Proposed Electronic Calculator', in Copeland, B.J. et al. (2012) *Alan Turing's Electronic Brain: The Struggle to Build the ACE, the World's Fastest Computer*. Oxford: Oxford University Press (a revised and retitled paperback edition of the 2005 hardback *Alan Turing's Automatic Computing Engine*), ch. 20.

Turing, A.M. (c. 1946) Letter to W. Ross Ashby, The Turing Archive for the History of Computing. Available at: www.alanturing.net.

Turing, A.M. (1947) 'Lecture on the Automatic Computing Engine', in Copeland, B.J. (ed.) *The Essential Turing*. Oxford: Clarendon Press, pp. 362–394.

Turing, A.M. (1948) 'Intelligent Machinery', in Copeland, B.J. (ed.) *The Essential Turing*. Oxford: Clarendon Press, pp. 395–432.

Turing, A.M. (1950) 'Computing Machinery and Intelligence', in Copeland, B.J. (ed.) *The Essential Turing*. Oxford: Clarendon Press, pp. 433–464.

Turing, A.M. (1951a) 'Can Digital Computers Think?' in Copeland, B.J. (ed.) *The Essential Turing*. Oxford: Clarendon Press, pp. 476–486.

Turing, A.M. (c. 1951) 'Intelligent Machinery: A Heretical Theory' in Copeland, B.J. (ed.) *The Essential Turing*. Oxford: Clarendon Press, pp. 465–475.

Turing, A.M. (1951b) Letter to J.Z. Young, February 8. The Modern Archive Centre, King's College Cambridge, K 78.

Turing, A.M. (1952) 'The Chemical Basis of Morphogenesis', in Copeland, B.J. (ed.) *The Essential Turing*. Oxford: Clarendon Press, pp. 519–561.

Turing, A.M. et al. (1952), 'Can Automatic Calculating Machines Be Said To Think?', in Copeland, B.J. (ed.) *The Essential Turing*. Oxford: Clarendon Press, pp. 487–506.

Wood, B.H. (1952) 'Chess Notes', *Illustrated London News*, London, July 19, p. 114.

Young, B.A. (1949) 'Cool and Calculating', *Punch Historical Archive*, London, August 24, p. 208.

3

BRITISH CYBERNETICS

Joe Dewhurst

Introduction

This chapter will explore the role of embodiment in British cybernetics, specifically in the works of Grey Walter and Ross Ashby, both of whom have had a distinctive influence on later research in embodied cognition. The chapter will also consider the relationship between Alan Turing and the British cyberneticists, and contrast Turing's work on computation with the contributions of Walter and Ashby. Contemporary 'embodied' approaches to cognitive science are often contrasted with computational approaches, with the latter being seen as emphasizing abstract, 'disembodied' theories of mind. At their most extreme, proponents of embodied cognition have rejected computational explanations entirely, as is the case with the enactivist tradition. This chapter will conclude by suggesting that the work of the British cyberneticists, which combined computational principles with embodied models, offers a potential route to resolving some of these tensions between embodied and computational approaches to the mind.

Section 1 will give a brief overview of the cybernetics movement, highlighting the relationship between American and British cybernetics. Section 2 will explore Turing's engagement with the Ratio Club (a hub of British cybernetics), and consider themes of embodiment in Turing's own work on computation and artificial intelligence. Section 3 will turn to Walter's experiments in designing autonomous robots, and the similarities between these designs and later work on embodied robotics. Section 4 will discuss the centrality of homeostasis in Ashby's work on cybernetics, and the subsequent influence that it has had on second-order cybernetics and enactivism. Finally, Section 5 will draw all of these themes together and suggest that paying attention to the role of embodiment in cybernetics might offer some insight into how to resolve contemporary disputes concerning the proper place of computation in our theories of mind and cognition.

1 The cybernetics movement in the US and the UK

The cybernetics[1] movement emerged in the post-Second World War US, building on interdisciplinary connections established during the war. The movement was centered around a series of ten interdisciplinary conferences sponsored by the Josiah Macy, Jr. Foundation, held from 1946 to 1953 and focusing primarily on the themes of circular causality and feedback mechanisms.

Key figures associated with the movement in the US included Norbert Wiener (who worked in information theory and control engineering, and further developed the concept of a feedback loop, first introduced in the early twentieth century), John von Neumann (who was instrumental in developing some of the earliest electronic computers), and Warren McCulloch (who along with his collaborator Walter Pitts developed the idea of treating neurons as basic logic gates, and inspired later computational theories of mind).[2] McCulloch's contributions are described elsewhere in this volume (Abrahams, this volume; see also Abrahams, 2016), and the history of cybernetics in the US is relatively well documented (see e.g. Heims, 1993; Edwards, 1996; Dupuy, 2000/2009). Less frequently discussed are the contributions of the British cyberneticists (Pickering, 2010, being a notable exception) which will form the focus of this chapter.

The cybernetics community in the UK was centered around the Ratio Club, an informal dining/discussion group that met intermittently from 1949 to 1958 (see Husbands and Holland, 2008). The club initially met monthly at the National Hospital for Nervous Diseases in Queen Square, London, with the aim of bringing together "those who had Wiener's idea before Wiener's book appeared" (Bates, 1949) to discuss questions and topics relating to cybernetics.[3] After a year the club began to meet less frequently (although still regularly), and in different locations, with several meetings scheduled to take place outside London (Husbands and Holland, 2008, pp. 113–122). After 1953, the frequency of meetings declined further, and by the end of 1955 the club was essentially disbanded, with only one final reunion meeting held in 1958 (ibid., pp. 125–129). Topics for discussion at the club ranged from topics familiar to contemporary cognitive science, such as 'pattern recognition' and 'memory', to topics more specific to the cybernetic milieu, such as 'adaptive behavior', 'servo control of muscular movements', and even 'telepathy' (ibid., p. 116). The club's membership included not only psychologists, psychiatrists, and neurophysiologists, but also physicists, mathematicians, and engineers, reflecting the diverse interests and backgrounds of the cybernetics movement.

Several of the key British cyberneticists also attended one or more of the Macy conferences, and there was significant overlap between the two groups (US and UK), including a 1949 visit by Warren McCulloch to give the opening talk at the inaugural meeting of the Ratio Club (Husbands and Holland, 2012). In this chapter, I will focus primarily on three figures associated with the British cybernetics movement, chosen to highlight the role that embodiment played in British cybernetics. The first of these, Alan Turing, is not normally considered to be a 'cyberneticist', but was a member of the Ratio Club and was highly relevant to the development of cybernetics (and subsequently, artificial intelligence and cognitive science). The other two, Grey Walter and Ross Ashby, are probably the most famous of the British cyberneticists, and have been influential in the development of what has come to be known as 'embodied cognition' (see e.g. Shapiro, 2014; Miłkowski, this volume). By embodied cognition, I have in mind the strong claim that the specific details of a cognitive system's body or environment are essential to our understanding of cognition, and play a constitutive role in cognitive processing, rather than the weak claim that a computational theory of mind must be physically implemented in some form or other (typically assumed to be the brain and/or central nervous system, although some theories are happy to remain neutral about the precise details of the implementation). This chapter will explore the contributions of Turing, Walter, and Ashby to embodied cognition, and consider how the UK cybernetics movement might offer a model for contemporary computational theories of mind that take seriously the role of embodiment in explanations of cognition.

Alan Turing (1912–1954) was born in the UK (in Maida Vale, London), where he lived and worked almost all of his life. He completed his undergraduate degree in mathematics at Cambridge, before being elected a fellow at King's College Cambridge on the strength of his undergraduate dissertation. He subsequently completed a PhD at Princeton with Alonzo

Church, returned to the UK and then spent the Second World War as a cryptanalyst, designing mechanical and computational systems with which to break German ciphers. After the war, he worked on various projects designing early stored-program computers, first at the National Physical Laboratory in London, and then in the mathematics department at the University of Manchester. Towards the end of his life he also became interested in chemical morphogenesis, on which he published an influential paper in 1952.

William Grey Walter (1910–1976) was born in the US to an English father and an Italian-American mother, but moved to the UK in 1915 and remained there for the rest of his life. He was educated in Cambridge as a physiologist, and subsequently made some important early contributions to the development of electroencephalography (EEG). From 1939 until his retirement in 1975 he was based at the Burden Neurological Institute just outside Bristol, where he continued to conduct EEG research, alongside which he developed a personal interest in cybernetics and the general study of brain and behavior. He was a founding member of the Ratio Club, attended the final Macy conference in 1953, and helped organize the first Namur conference ('The First International Congress on Cybernetics') in 1956.

William Ross Ashby (1903–1972) was born in the UK and lived there for most of his life, although from 1961 to 1970 he was based at Heinz von Foerster's Biological Computing Laboratory in Illinois.[4] Ashby's first degree was in zoology, and he also had experience in clinical psychiatry. His contributions to cybernetics included two major books, *Design for a Brain* (1952, republished as a revised edition in 1960) and *An Introduction to Cybernetics* (1956), alongside many other journal articles and research papers. He was also a founding member of the Ratio Club, and an invited speaker at the 1952 Macy conference.

As Pickering (2010, p. 5) notes, it is probably significant that many of the British cyberneticists, unlike most of their American counterparts,[5] had a background in neurobiology and psychiatry, making the question of physical implementation especially salient. Walter's undergraduate degree was in physiology, and he went on to conduct early studies with the then-emerging technique of electroencephalography (EEG), now a staple of neuroscientific research. Ashby initially trained as a zoologist, but went on to work as a clinical psychiatrist and research pathologist. Some of both Walter's and Ashby's contributions to cybernetics were conducted in their spare time, alongside their other responsibilities, lending them what Pickering describes as an "almost hobbyist character" (2010, p. 10). Turing, in contrast, was a mathematician and engineer whose contributions to cybernetics and cognitive science were made during his working life.

In the next section, I will describe how Turing's work relates to cybernetics and embodied cognition, before moving on in Sections 3 and 4 to look at the respective contributions of Walter and Ashby. In each case I will focus on presenting their contributions to cybernetics in terms of the physical models they designed to illustrate these concepts: Walter's early experiments in embodied robotics and Ashby's illustration of ultrastability with his homeostat. Finally, in Section 5 I will suggest that the British cyberneticists offer a model for a potential reconciliation between contemporary computational and anti-computational theories of mind.

2 Turing and the Ratio Club

The focus of this section will be on drawing out the (sometimes overlooked) themes of embodiment that can be found in Turing's work. I will first describe his relationship with the British cyberneticists, before considering how both of his most famous ideas, the eponymous 'Turing machine' and 'Turing test', relate to themes of embodiment.[6] The behavior of the Turing machine, I will suggest, can be understood in terms of cybernetic feedback loops, whilst the role of embodiment in human communication reveals some of the limitations of the original Turing test.

It was agreed unanimously after the first meeting of the Ratio Club that Turing should be invited to join, and he was apparently glad to accept the invitation (Husbands and Holland, 2008, p. 115). He gave two talks at the club, one on 'Educating a Digital Computer' and the other on 'The Chemical Origin of Biological Form' (Boden, 2006, p. 222; Husbands and Holland, 2008, p. 101). He was also in regular communication with at least some members of the club,[7] and would have been familiar with the general principles of cybernetics, which were at the time fairly widespread. It is therefore interesting to consider his views on computation and embodiment in relation to those of the other British cyberneticists.

The Turing machine, original described by Turing in a 1936 paper, is usually characterized as a mechanism consisting of a one-dimensional tape of unbounded length and an automaton that moves along the tape, reading and writing symbols according to a set of simple instructions (see e.g. Barker-Plummer, 2016, sec. 1). Described in this way, it makes sense to think of the tape itself as something like the memory of the system, and therefore as a component of the machine as a whole. Characterizing the machine in this way contributes to an internalistic reading of Turing's account of computation, where every aspect of the computational process is carried out within the system.

However, as Wells (1998) points out, this characterization leaves out an interesting distinction made by Turing in his original description of the machine, which was introduced by analogy with a human 'computer' performing mathematical calculations with a pencil and paper. Here the automaton corresponds to the human computer, whilst the tape corresponds to the paper that they are writing upon, forming what Wells describes as the "environment" of the Turing machine (ibid., 272). Viewed in this way, Turing's account of computation is no longer so obviously internalistic. Whilst the tape could obviously be placed inside the machine (as is typically the case with the memory components of modern electronic computers), it could also remain outside, providing something like an external or distributed memory for the system (cf. Clark and Chalmers, 1998).

Wells argues that this distinction helps to overcome various issues that he identifies with the 'classical' (internalistic) view of computation (ibid., 276–279), and more recently Villalobos and Dewhurst (2017a, sec. 4) have adopted Wells' analysis in order to demonstrate a potential compatibility between computational and enactivist accounts of cognition. Villalobos and Dewhurst argue that the Turing machine, understood in this way, exhibits what is known in the autopoietic/enactivist tradition as 'functional closure', i.e. a form of functional organization where the system's output loops back through its environment (in this case, the tape) in order to form a part of its input (ibid., sec. 5). This notion of functional closure is closely related to the cybernetic notion of a feedback loop; essentially, the claim here is that a Turing machine operates according to a feedback loop that is generated when the symbols written on the tape are in turn read by the machine, meaning that its output at one time-step has become its input at a later time-step. The implementation of a Turing machine (a paradigmatic computational system) can thus be understood with a concept drawn from enactivism (a paradigmatically anti-computational tradition), and which ultimately originated in cybernetics.

In "Computing Machinery and Intelligence", Turing (1950) describes a simple test (now known as the Turing test) for determining whether a machine could pass for a human in a text-based conversation. This test is intended to replace the question 'could a machine think?', which Turing dismisses as "too meaningless to deserve discussion" (ibid., p. 442). It involves a human interrogator having to distinguish between two subjects, one human and the other artificial, with whom they can only communicate through the medium of written messages. The test is 'disembodied' in the sense that no physical details of the machine's implementation are considered relevant to the question of whether or not it is intelligent. It does not need to directly interact with the interrogator, and as such there is no need to program into it an awareness of body language, or tone of voice, or any other aspects of face-to-face communication. It also does not require the ability to regulate its *own* body language or tone of voice, or any other of the myriad complex abilities necessary for synchronous face-to-face communication. This is not to criticize the test as such, but rather to indicate its limitations: it might well serve as an adequate *minimal* test of intelligence, but passing the Turing test in its original form would not guarantee the ability to pass as a human in more general day-to-day interactions.

In responding to what he calls "Lady Lovelace's objection" (Turing, 1950, p. 450), the idea that computers are deterministic and thus incapable of originality, Turing considers the role that learning might play in intelligence, and especially in the generation of novel or surprising behaviors. Later on in the paper he dedicates a whole section to the consideration of building a machine that could learn, and suggests that it might be easier to create a machine simulating the mind of a child, which he considers to be much simpler than an adult's brain. He goes on to propose that by subjecting this 'artificial child' to "an appropriate course of education one would obtain the adult brain" (ibid., p. 456; cf. Sterrett, 2012). It is fair to say that Turing probably underestimated the complexity of a child's brain, but his suggestions in this section do provide an interesting precursor to contemporary approaches to artificial intelligence which focus on developing systems that are able to learn (see Colombo, this volume, for further discussion of learning algorithms). These systems are now commonly designed using a connectionist or neural network approach, which takes inspiration from the structural organization of the biological brain (see Stinson, this volume). In a 1948 report (unpublished until 1968), Turing even provides the outlines of what we might now consider an example of this approach to learning and machine intelligence (Boden, 2006, p. 180; cf. Copeland and Proudfoot, 1996).

By discussing the role of learning in intelligence, and considering an analogy with how a (human) child might learn, Turing pre-empted topics that have now re-emerged in contemporary cognitive science, and that have been of especial interest to those coming from an embodied cognition perspective (see e.g. Flusberg et al., 2010). However, despite acknowledging the role that learning might play in the creation of an intelligent machine, Turing remains fairly dismissive about the idea of embodiment. He does not think that it would be important to give the machine "artificial flesh", or even legs or eyes (1950, p. 434). His conception of intelligence is still very much based around the idea of abstract computational processes, perhaps due to his earlier work on the Turing machine. A universal Turing machine is capable of running any (Turing-computable) program, and thus presumably he was convinced that such a machine, if programmed correctly (whether by its designer or by experience) would be able to produce any answer required by the test. This conception of intelligence is in stark contrast with the work of both Walter and Ashby, for whom (as we shall see) embodiment seems to have played a crucial role in intelligence.

3 Walter and embodied robotics

Whilst Turing's work on machine intelligence was (for the most part) purely theoretical, Walter and Ashby were both more interested in trying to put their theories into practice. In this section, I will consider Walter's early experiments in what we might now call 'embodied robotics', and how these relate to contemporary work in robotics and artificial intelligence. In foreshadowing this contemporary work, Walter's robots provide a connection between the cybernetic notion of embodiment and what has now come to be known as 'embodied cognition', spanning the gulf of several intervening decades of relatively 'disembodied' cognitive science. The focus of this section is on Walter's most memorable contribution to cybernetics, the creation of several artificial 'creatures' (or robots), whose behavior was intended to model the behavior of living organisms and the human brain.

Walter's creations were not entirely original, forming part of an emerging tradition of robotics described by Cordeschi (2002, ch. 3) and Boden (2006, p. 221). During the 1920s and 1930s several researchers had been developing robotic systems based on essentially behaviorist principles, implementing a form of conditioned learning in simple electronic circuits (Cordeschi, 2002, pp. 82–111). For example, one such system consisted of a series of switches connecting a charged battery to several uncharged batteries. If the switch connecting the charged battery was pressed, a light would come on, representing an unconditioned stimulus. When the switch connecting the charged battery was pressed simultaneously with a switch connecting one of the uncharged batteries, the latter would itself become charged, representing a conditioned stimulus (Krueger and Hull, 1931; cf. Cordeschi, 2002, pp. 86–87). These systems were seen as implementing or demonstrating basic aspects of behaviorist theories of learning, and could be taught to navigate their way around simple mazes, in the same manner as the behaviorists' animal subjects. Subsequently, maze-running robots (known as 'rats') were designed independently by Shannon (1951), Wallace (1952), and Howard (1953), each of which operated by systematically exploring a maze until they found their way through it, after which they could 'remember' the route that they had taken and replicate it in future attempts.

Walter's own robots, in contrast to these 'rats' and other similar creations, were not designed for any particular task (such as running a maze), and Walter considered them to be models of how the brain itself might function (Walter, 1953, p. 118; cf. Holland, 2003a, pp. 2096–2097). Walter's 'tortoises', as he called them, were "small electromechanical robots" (Pickering 2010, p. 43), consisting of a chassis with one front wheel and two back wheels, two battery-powered electric motors (one to 'drive' the front wheel and the other to rotate or 'steer' it), and a light-sensitive cell attached to the vertical axis of the front wheel (Walter, 1950a; 1950b; 1951; see also Holland, 2003b). Inside the chassis was a set of basic electronic circuitry connecting the components.[8] When no light was detected, both motors would activate, causing the tortoise to move in a cycloidal path whilst scanning its environment, but as soon as a bright enough light was detected, the steering motor would deactivate, making the tortoise appear to gradually seek out the light. When the light got too bright, however, the steering motor would reactivate, and so the tortoise would tend to wander around in the area it considered to be 'comfortably' illuminated. A switch would also be triggered if its shell was displaced by hitting an obstacle, alternately activating the drive motor and steering motor to allow the tortoise to move away from the obstacle. Later versions of the tortoises would become less sensitive to light as their batteries ran down, allowing them to return to their 'hutches' (which were lit by a bright light) to recharge. Each also had an external light that would switch on when the steering motor was active, appearing 'attractive' to other tortoises, but which would switch off again when its own steering was locked. This caused them to engage in a playful dance, never quite making contact but also never straying too far away – or as Walter put it, "the machines cannot escape from one another, but nor can they ever consummate their 'desire'" (Walter, 1953, pp. 128–129).

Furthermore, with the addition of a behaviorist learning module ('CORA'), and by adjusting various parameters and settings, Walter aimed to use his tortoises to model brain *malfunctions*, or mental illnesses (Walter, 1950a, p. 45; 1951, p. 63; cf. Pickering, 2010, pp. 67–68). In one such arrangement the system could learn to associate a sound (it was equipped with a microphone) with the signals received from detecting a light (which it would usually move towards) and hitting an obstacle (which it would usually move away from). Over time it came to no longer be attracted to the light, and thus was unable to seek out the "nourishment" of its recharging hutch (Walter, 1950a, p. 63). For Walter, then, these robots offered the possibility of an entire theory of human neural activity and the behavior generated by it, although within his own lifetime they remained relatively simplistic and, to a contemporary eye, perhaps not especially impressive.

Although extremely simple in design, the tortoises exhibited complex and apparently purposeful behavior, thus embodying a core cybernetic principle of the emergence of (apparent) teleology from mere mechanism. Crucial here is the role of feedback, first described in the (pre-)cybernetic context by Rosenblueth, Wiener, and Bigelow (1943).[9] Rosenbleuth et al. defined teleological behavior as "behaviour controlled by negative feedback" (ibid., p. 19), and claimed that this definition provided a naturalized account of all teleological (or purposeful) behavior. A system controlled by negative feedback will correct itself when diverted from its 'goal', and so appears to be purposefully aiming for this goal. Walter's robots were also purposeful in this sense, as their reaction to differing levels of illumination served as a form of negative feedback (gradually approaching a distant light, before gradually retreating once it became too bright). Whether, and to what extent, such behavior is 'genuinely' purposeful, or even if it makes sense to ask this question, is beyond the scope of this chapter.

Walter's robotic tortoises foreshadowed the modern development of embodied robotics, emphasizing the emergence of complex behaviors from extremely simple systems. Examples of this approach include Valentino Braitenberg's (1984) book of Walter-style robotic thought experiments,[10] Rodney Brooks' 'subsumption architecture' (1986, see also his 1999), Randall Beer's evolutionary robotics (see e.g. Beer and Gallagher, 1992), Barbara Webb's insect-inspired robots (see e.g. Webb, 1995), and Michael Arbib's work on social robotics (see e.g. Arbib and Fellous, 2004). Brooks' robots in particular bear a resemblance to Walter's tortoises, consisting of deceptively simple computational architectures that interact with their environments to produce relatively complex behaviors. One of the robots built in Brooks' lab, affectionately named 'Herb' (after Herbert Simon), was able to navigate around the laboratory, identifying and collecting up drinks cans and disposing of them appropriately (see Connell, 1989). Walter's approach to robotics was ahead of its time, and in conceiving of his creations as simple models of the human nervous system he foresaw a future tradition of using artificial creations and computer simulations as a means to learn about 'natural' human cognition.

4 Ashby and homeostasis

In contrast with Walter's somewhat sensationalist and media-savvy presentation of his tortoises, Ashby's homeostat was both "less sexy [and] less media-friendly" (Boden, 2006, p. 228). Nonetheless, it provides an interesting model of how the biological concept of homeostasis might be applied to explanations of cognition. His work influenced the development of the enactivist theory of cognition, via Humberto Maturana's autopoietic theory, which extended his analysis of homeostasis to develop the concept of 'autopoiesis'. In this section I will focus primarily on his work on homeostasis, the application of this work in the creation of his 'homeostat', and the influence of his ideas on later developments in embodied cognition.

The concept of homeostasis was originally developed by Walter Cannon (see e.g. his 1929 paper), who used it to describe the mechanisms responsible for maintaining certain vital parameters in living organisms. Norbert Wiener's co-author Arturo Rosenblueth worked at Cannon's laboratory (Dupuy 2000/2009, p. 45), and the general idea of homeostasis was highly influential on the development of cybernetics. Ashby expanded the concept of homeostasis to give a general definition of adaptive systems, including not only biological organisms but any system (whether artificial or natural) that displays homeostatic behavior (1952, ch. 5). His account introduces several additional concepts, such as 'adaptation' (the behavior a system performs to retain stability), 'viability' (the limits within which a system can remain stable), and 'essential variables' (the bounds within which a system remains stable, and beyond which it will collapse into a new configuration). For example, the essential variables of the human body include maintaining a core temperature between (approximately) 36.5 °C and 37.5 °C, beyond which it ceases to be viable and begins to collapse. The account is intended to explain how an adaptive system is able to keep the values of its essential variables within the limits of viability, and how, if it is pushed beyond these limits, it will collapse into a new configuration that may or may not be adaptive. If the core temperature of a human body falls below 36.5 °C, it will either move to seek out a warmer environment, or begin generating and maintaining heat via various mechanisms (including shivering and blood flow constriction), or else become hypothermic and eventually die.

The mechanisms that allow a system to remain stable are essentially versions of the homeostatic mechanisms described by Cannon, but Ashby extended the account to include another set of mechanisms, those of an 'ultrastable' system, which is a system with the ability to adapt its own external environment and/or internal structure to preserve its overall homeostasis (1952, ch. 7). A system of this kind appears to seek out a new viable format, avoiding the threat of a greater and potentially more catastrophic collapse (a cold human seeking out a warmer environment is an example of this). An ultrastable system, Ashby argued, could be considered genuinely intelligent, as it would deploy complex behaviors allowing it to retain structural integrity (1952, ch. 9). Ashby thus developed a general theory of intelligent behavior (i.e. cognition), based around the central idea of biological homeostasis.[11]

In order to illustrate these principles Ashby designed and constructed a model system, the 'homeostat', which exhibited a form of ultrastability (Figure 3.1). The homeostat consisted of a set of four boxes, each containing an induction coil and a pivoting magnetic needle, the latter attached to a wire hanging down into a trough of water. Electrodes placed at the end of each

Figure 3.1 The homeostat, with hanging wires visible at the top of each box. Reproduced with permission of the Estate of W. Ross Ashby (www. rossashby.info)

trough generated a potential gradient in the water, which, via the hanging wire, affected the movement of the needle. The system was set up such that the movement of the needle also modified the current generated by the coil, which in turn influenced the gradient in the water, resulting in a feedback loop between water, needle, and coil (Ashby, 1948, pp. 380 ff.; adapted from Boden, 2006, p. 230).

Each box by itself was not especially interesting, displaying a simple form of feedback, but when connected together the four boxes were able to maintain a stable (homeostatic) equilibrium, with each needle eventually turning to point towards the center of the device. This was achieved by the current generated by each box exerting an influence on each magnet, which in turn adjusts the current, and so on (Ashby, 1952, p. 96). Furthermore, when the maximum value of any one of the four currents exceeded a certain level (its 'essential variables'), a switch would be flipped that "changed the quantities defining the relevant feedback link" (Boden, 2006, p. 231), creating a new configuration and preventing the system entering an uncontrollable feedback loop. By this 'second-order' mechanism the system was able to achieve ultrastability, as it could avoid exceeding its viable limits by adopting a new form of organization.

To Ashby this system presented a simplified model of the basic homeostatic principles and dynamics that he thought were necessary (and perhaps sufficient) for both life and cognition (which for him were continuous with one another). He presented the homeostat at the ninth Macy conference, where it proved to be somewhat controversial. His claim that the system exhibited a form of intelligence was met with incredulity by many of the attendees (Boden, 2006, p. 232), and several of them pointed out that its supposedly 'adaptive' behavior relied essentially on a random search (Boden, 2006, p. 235; Dupuy, 2000/2009, p. 150). Ashby was in fact willing to accept the latter charge, replying "I don't know of any other way that [a] mechanism can do it [i.e. exhibit intelligent behavior]" (ibid.). In a sense he was just taking the cybernetic vision of 'mind as machine' to its logical conclusion, fully automating (and thus 'demystifying') apparently purposeful behavior. Although his reduction of intelligent behavior to random search was extreme, it has in common with other cybernetic approaches the idea that apparently complex behaviors can be explained in terms of simple (and automatable) procedures. Turing's theory of computation also shares this approach, as it explains how to carry out complex mathematical operations in terms of a few basic procedures.

Although its immediate influence was somewhat limited, Ashby's work on homeostasis has gone on to inspire many subsequent theorists in cognitive science. Humberto Maturana's autopoietic theory of cognition draws on Ashby's work (Maturana, 1970; Maturana and Varela, 1980),[12] and this theory subsequently provided the foundation for the contemporary enactivist tradition (Varela, Thompson, and Rosch 1991/2017; see Ward, Silverman, and Villalobos, 2017 for an overview; see also Hutto and Myin, this volume). Enactivism emerged out of what became known as 'second-order' cybernetics (see Froese, 2010; 2011), which aimed to recursively apply cybernetic insights to the analysis of the discipline itself, by acknowledging the role of the observer in scientific experimentation. The movement included Maturana, along with others, such as Heinz von Foerster, who continued applying cybernetic principles after the original movement collapsed.

5 (Dis-)Embodiment in cybernetics and cognitive science

The original cybernetics movement, and British cybernetics in particular, emphasized the role of the body and environment in explanations of cognition. Walter's tortoises were early experiments in embodied robotics, simple systems that exhibited complex behaviors due to their interactions with their environments. Ashby's homeostat applied biological principles in an attempt to model cognitive processes, which he considered to be essentially continuous with one another. Even Turing's work on computational intelligence contained hints of embodiment, insofar as his Turing machine can be interpreted as interacting with an environment, and in the suggestive comments he makes about the relationship between learning and intelligence. Each of these approaches has since been rediscovered by researchers working in the broad tradition of embodied cognition, namely in embodied robotics, enactivism, and connectionism. The British cybernetics tradition also exemplifies how to combine embodied and computational approaches to the study of mind and cognition, and thus how we might be able to reconcile these approaches in the modern day.

Walter and Ashby were not the only British cyberneticists of note, although they were probably the most influential and well-known during the era of the original cybernetics (1946–1953). Other British cyberneticists[13] included Gregory Bateson (1904–1980), an anthropologist who developed the application of systems theory to social groups, and who attended many of the Macy conferences; R.D. Laing (1927–1989), a psychiatrist most well-known for his association with the anti-psychiatry movement; Stafford Beer (1926–2002), who founded the field of 'management cybernetics' and was involved in an attempt to cyberneticize the Chilean economy (see Medina, 2011); and Gordon Pask (1928–1996), an early adopter of cybernetics who contributed to many different areas of research over the years, including educational psychology, systems theory, and human–computer interaction.[14] The last two continued their work after cybernetics had ceased to be popular, and thus provide a continuity of sorts between the classical era and the modern rediscovery of cybernetic principles.

Towards the end of the 1950s the cybernetics movement began to splinter, divided roughly between those who focused more on developing abstract computational models of how cognitive tasks might be solved, and those who focused more on physical implementations of cognitive systems, taking their lead from specific details of the biological brain. Boden (2006, p. 234) calls the latter group the 'cyberneticists', although both groups had their origins in the cybernetics movement. These two groups split not so much due to any deep-seated ideological or theoretical disagreements, but rather as a result of the inherent instability of the cybernetics movement, which cut across (too) many disciplinary boundaries and thus struggled to find a permanent home within any one institution or department.

The computationalist tradition that subsequently became dominant, and remained so for the next few decades, played down the importance of body and world, focusing primarily on abstract models of cognition (Aizawa, this volume; cf. Boden, 2006, p. 236). Insofar as this approach was able to describe general computational principles that might govern cognition it was relatively successful, but since the late 1980s embodied approaches have been making a resurgence, most significantly in embodied robotics and the various versions of enactivism. Both draw on the cybernetic principles and ideals found in the works of Walter and Ashby, emphasizing in particular the importance of the interaction between a system and its environment, and the emergence of cognition out of basic biological processes such as homeostasis.

As Miłkowski (this volume) argues, embodied explanations of cognition need not be at odds with computational ones, as computational principles can be applied to the design of embodied systems. Here it is important to distinguish between the trivial sense in which every computational system must be implemented in some physical medium, and the more interesting sense in which 'embodied' approaches think that specific details of physical implementation might play a role in our explanations of cognition. The classical view of computation accepts embodiment in the trivial sense, but denies that the specific details of physical implementation are essential to our explanations of cognition. Nonetheless, there is scope here for a hybrid approach, where computational theories of mind are implemented in ways that take advantage of the specific details of their embodiment, without necessarily conceding that these details are *essential* for cognition. It might be that certain kinds of implementation allow for aspects of a task to be offloaded onto the body or environment, enabling an efficient solution to a problem, even if there exists a distinct, more computationally intensive solution that could in principle remain implementation-neutral. Given economic and pragmatic constraints, we should prefer the former solution, but this is not to say that the specific details of embodiment are strictly necessary for cognition.

The cybernetics movement in general, and the British cybernetics tradition in particular, offers a useful model for how to integrate computational and embodied approaches. On the one hand, Turing's classical formulation of computation allows for the environment to play a role, whilst on the other hand Walter and Ashby's embodied models of living systems can be implemented computationally, as contemporary work in embodied robotics, dynamical systems research, and connectionism demonstrates. Furthermore, even avowedly anti-computationalist theories such as enactivism can be traced back to the same cybernetic roots as computationalism itself, suggesting that there need not be any fundamental incompatibility between these now apparently divergent approaches (see Villalobos and Dewhurst, 2017b). The enactivist rejection of computationalism relies on the premise that computation requires (semantic) representation, and whilst this has historically been a popular position, it has recently been challenged by a variety of 'mechanistic' accounts of computation (see e.g. Piccinini, 2015). Such accounts may offer a route to reconciliation between enactivism and computationalism, perhaps based around a revival of cybernetic principles.

Conclusion

In this chapter I have presented themes of embodiment in British cybernetics, focusing on the work of two central British cyberneticists, Grey Walter and Ross Ashby. Walter's tortoises represent an early exploration of ideas now described as 'embodied robotics', and Ashby's work on homeostasis inspired the enactivist tradition in embodied cognition. I have also considered themes of embodiment in Turing's work, as despite not typically being considered part of the cybernetic movement, Turing was a contemporary of the British cyberneticists, and attended and presented at their main venue for discussion, the Ratio Club. I suggested that the Turing machine could be considered to interact with an environment of sorts, and that Turing's work on machine learning predicted certain ideas that have now become relatively commonplace. The milieu of British cybernetics therefore presents a model for future work on embodiment and computation, offering the possibility of reconciling two sometimes oppositional traditions.

Acknowledgments

I am grateful to Mark Sprevak, Matteo Colombo, and Owen Holland for providing extensive feedback on earlier drafts of this chapter, and to Mario Villalobos for originally introducing me to cybernetics and autopoietic theory.

Notes

1 The term 'cybernetics' was coined by Norbert Wiener in his 1948 book, and formed part of the title of the later Macy conferences (from the seventh conference onwards).

2 See Wiener (1948), von Neumann (1945; 1952/2000), and McCulloch and Pitts (1943); Rav (2002) provides an overview of the contributions of all three, and describes some of their influences on later scientific developments; Heims (1980) presents a comparative biography of Wiener and von Neumann.

3 In a journal entry dated September 20, 1949, Ashby refers to the formation of a "cybernetics group", and the club seems to have been comfortable using this terminology to refer to themselves.

4 Von Foerster was present at several of the Macy conferences, and edited the proceedings of the latter five conferences. He went on to become highly influential in 'second-order' cybernetics.

5 McCulloch is a notable exception, but neither Wiener nor von Neumann had any background in neurophysiology. Wiener had initially wanted to train as a biologist, but was unable to do so due to his poor eyesight.

6 Turing's later work on 'morphogenesis', which I do not have space to discuss here, also raises themes of embodiment, and marks an early exploration of what we would now call 'artificial life' (Turing, 1952; Proudfoot and Copeland, this volume).

7 In 1949 Turing wrote a letter to Ashby, suggesting that rather than building a physical model of the nervous system, he could instead simulate one on the ACE machine (an early stored-program computer) that Turing was then working on at the National Physics Laboratory (Turing, 1949).

8 Like much of the electronic equipment used by the cyberneticists, this circuitry was analog, meaning that unlike most contemporary (digital) computers it was sensitive to continuous rather than discrete signals.

9 The term 'cybernetic' was not actually coined by Wiener until 1948, but this earlier paper is typically considered part of the cybernetic canon.

10 Braitenberg never mentions Walter by name, but was clearly influenced by his work.

11 Walter's tortoise, 'seeking' to maintain its position at a certain distance from a source of illumination, could also be seen as embodying a kind of homeostatic mechanism.

12 For further discussion of the relationship between Ashby's work and Maturana's autopoietic theory, see Froese and Stewart (2010).

13 Although he died before the movement could really get started, Kenneth Craik (1914–1945) is often associated with the British cybernetics movement. Craik was a psychologist and philosopher whose work pre-empted many of the themes in what would become cybernetics. The Ratio Club was almost named in his honor (Boden, 2006, p. 222), and Walter said of the American cyberneticists that "These people are thinking on very much the same lines as Kenneth Craik did, but with much less sparkle and humour" (Holland, 2003a, p. 2094).

14 Each is discussed in more detail by Pickering (2010).

References

Abrahams, T. (2016) *Rebel Genius: Warren S. McCulloch's Transdisciplinary Life in Science*. Cambridge, MA: MIT Press.

Arbib, M. and Fellous, J.-M. (2004) 'Emotions: From Brain to Robot', *TRENDS in Cognitive Sciences*, 8 (12), pp. 554–561.

Ashby, W.R. (1948) 'Design for a Brain', *Electronic Engineering*, 20, pp. 379–383.

Ashby, W.R. (1949) *Ashby's Journal*, 1928–1972, p. 2624. The W. Ross Ashby Digital Archive. Available at: www.rossashby.info/journal.

Ashby, W.R. (1952/1960) *Design for a Brain*. New York, NY: John Wiley & Sons.

Ashby, W.R. (1956) *An Introduction to Cybernetics*. New York, NY: J. Wiley.

Barker-Plummer, D. (2016) 'Turing Machines', *The Stanford Encyclopedia of Philosophy*, December 21, Zalta, E.N. (ed.), Available at: https://plato.stanford.edu/archives/win2016/entries/turing-machine/ (Accessed: February 14, 2018).

Bates, J. (1949) Letter to Grey Walter, July 27. Unpublished Papers and Records for the Ratio Club. J.A.V. Bates Archive, The Wellcome Library for the History and Understanding of Medicine, London.

Beer, R. and Gallagher, J. (1992), 'Evolving Dynamical Neural Networks for Adaptive Behavior', *Adaptive Behavior*, 1 (1), pp. 91–122.

Boden, M. (2006) *Mind as Machine*. Oxford: Oxford University Press.

Braitenberg, V. (1984) *Vehicles: Experiments in Synthetic Psychology*. Cambridge, MA: MIT Press.

Brooks, R. (1986) 'A Robust Layered Control System for a Mobile Robot', *IEEE Journal on Robotics and Automation*, 2 (1), pp. 14–23.

Brooks, R. (1999) *Cambrian Intelligence*. Cambridge, MA: MIT Press.

Cannon, W. (1929) 'Organization for Physiological Homeostasis', *Physiological Reviews*, 9 (3), pp. 399–431.

Clark, A. and Chalmers, D. (1998) 'The Extended Mind', *Analysis*, 58 (1), pp. 7–19.

Connell, J. (1989) *A Colony Architecture for an Artificial Creature*. MIT Artificial Intelligence Laboratory Technical Report 1151.

Copeland, J. and Proudfoot, D. (1996) 'On Alan Turing's Anticipation of Connectionism', *Synthese*, 108, pp. 361–377.

Cordeschi, R. (2002) *The Discovery of the Artificial*. Dordrecht, Boston, MA, and London: Kluwer Academic Publishers.

Dupuy, J.-P. (2000/2009) *On the Origins of Cognitive Science*. Translated by M.B. DeBevoise. Cambridge, MA: MIT Press.

Edwards, P. (1996) *The Closed World*. Cambridge, MA: MIT Press.

Flusberg, S. et al. (2010) 'A Connectionist Approach to Embodied Conceptual Metaphor', *Frontiers in Psychology*, 1, p. 197.

Froese, T. (2010) 'From Cybernetics to Second-Order Cybernetics', *Constructivist Foundations*, 5 (2), pp. 75–85.

Froese, T. (2011) 'From Second-Order Cybernetics to Enactive Cognitive Science', *Systems Research and Behavioural Science*, 28 (6), pp. 631–645.

Froese, T. and Stewart, J. (2010) 'Life after Ashby: Ultrastability and the Autopoietic Foundations of Biological Autonomy', *Cybernetics and Human Knowing*, 17 (4), pp. 7–50.

Heims, S.J. (1980) *John von Neumann and Norbert Wiener: From Mathematics to the Technologies of Life and Death*. Cambridge, MA: MIT Press.

Heims, S.J. (1993) *The Cybernetics Group 1946–1953: Constructing a Social Science for Postwar America*. Cambridge, MA: MIT Press.

Holland, O. (2003a) 'Exploration and High Adventure: The Legacy of Grey Walter', *Philosophical Transactions of the Royal Society A*, 361, pp. 2085–2121.

Holland, O. (2003b) 'The First Biologically Inspired Robots', *Robotica*, 21, pp. 351–363.

Howard, I.P. (1953) 'A Note on the Design of an Electro-mechanical Maze Runner', *Durham Research Review*, 4, pp. 54–61.

Husbands, P. and Holland, O. (2008) 'The Ratio Club: A Hub of British Cybernetics', in Husbands, P., Holland, O., and Wheeler, M. (eds.) *The Mechanical Mind in History*. Cambridge, MA: MIT Press, pp. 91–148.

Husbands, P. and Holland, O. (2012) 'Warren McCulloch and the British Cyberneticians', *Interdisciplinary Science Reviews*, 37 (3), pp. 237–253.

Krueger, R.G. and Hull, C.L. (1931) 'An Electro-chemical Parallel to the Conditioned Reflex', *Journal of General Psychology*, 5, pp. 262–269.

Maturana, H. (1970) *Biology of Cognition*. Urbana, IL: University of Illinois Press.

Maturana, H. and Varela, F. (1980) *Autopoiesis and Cognition: The Realisation of the Living*. Dordrecht: D. Reidel Publishing Company.

McCulloch, W. and Pitts, W. (1943) 'A Logical Calculus of the Ideas Immanent in Nervous Activity', *Bulletin of Mathematical Biophysics*, 5, pp. 115–133.

Medina, E. (2011) *Cybernetic Revolutionaries*. Harvard, MA: MIT Press.

Piccinini, G. (2015) *Physical Computation: A Mechanistic Account*. Oxford: Oxford University Press.

Pickering, A. (2010) *The Cybernetic Brain*. Chicago, IL: University of Chicago Press.

Rav, Y. (2002) 'Perspectives on the History of the Cybernetics Movement', *Cybernetics and Systems*, 33 (8), pp. 779–804.

Rosenblueth, A., Wiener, N., and Bigelow, J. (1943) 'Behavior, Purpose and Teleology', *Philosophy of Science*, 10 (1), pp. 18–24.

Shannon, C. (1951) 'Presentation of a Maze Solving Machine', in von Foerster, H. (ed.) *Cybernetics: Transactions of the Eighth Conference*, pp. 173–180.

Shapiro, L. (2014) *The Routledge Handbook of Embodied Cognition*. London: Routledge.

Sterrett, S.G. (2012) 'Bringing up Turing's "Child-Machine"', in Cooper, S., Dawa, A., and Lowe, B. (eds.) *How the World Computes*. Dordrecht: Springer, pp. 703–713.

Turing, A. (1936) 'On Computable Numbers, with an Application to the Entscheidungsproblem', *Proceedings of the London Mathematical Society*, 2 (42), pp. 230–265.

Turing, A. (1948) 'Intelligent Machinery', in Copeland, B.J. (ed.) *The Essential Turing: Seminal Writings in Computing, Logic, Philosophy, Artificial Intelligence, and Artificial Life plus The Secrets of Enigma.* Oxford: Clarendon Press, pp. 395–432.

Turing, A. (1949) Letter to W. Ross Ashby, November 19. The W. Ross Ashby Digital Archive. Available at: www.rossashby.info/letters/turing.html.

Turing, A. (1950) 'Computing Machinery and Intelligence', *Mind*, 49, pp. 433–460.

Turing, A. (1952) 'The Chemical Basis of Morphogenesis', *Philosophical Transactions of the Royal Society B*, 237 (641), pp. 37–72.

Varela, F., Thompson, E., and Rosch, E. (1991/2017) *The Embodied Mind.* Cambridge, MA: MIT Press.

Villalobos, M. and Dewhurst, J. (2017a) 'Enactive Autonomy in Computational Systems', *Synthese*. Available at: https://doi-org.ezproxy.is.ed.ac.uk/10.1007/s11229-017-1386-z.

Villalobos, M. and Dewhurst, J. (2017b) 'Why Post-cognitivism Does Not (Necessarily) Entail Anti-computationalism', *Adaptive Behavior*, 25 (3), pp. 117–128.

von Neumann, J. (1945) 'First Draft Report on the EDVAC', report prepared for the U.S. Army Ordnance Department under contract W-670-ORD-4926, in Stern, N. (1981) *From ENIAC to UNIVAC.* Bedford, MA: Digital Press, pp. 177–246.

von Neumann, J. (1952/2000) *The Computer and the Brain.* New Haven, CT and London: Yale University Press.

Wallace, R.A. (1952) 'The Maze-Solving Computer', *Proceedings of the ACM*, pp. 119–125.

Walter, W.G. (1950a) 'An Imitation of Life', *Scientific American*, 182, pp. 42–45.

Walter, W.G. (1950b) 'An Electromechanical Animal', *Dialectica*, 4 (3), pp. 206–213.

Walter, W.G. (1951) 'A Machine that Learns', *Scientific American*, 185, pp. 60–63.

Walter, W.G. (1953) *The Living Brain.* London: Duckworth.

Ward, D., Silverman, D., and Villalobos, M. (2017) 'Introduction: The Varieties of Enactivism', *Topoi*, 36 (3), pp. 365–375.

Webb, B. (1995) 'Using Robots to Model Animals: A Cricket Test', *Robotics and Autonomous Systems*, 16 (2–4), pp. 117–134.

Wells, A.J. (1998) 'Turing's Analysis of Computation and Theories of Cognitive Architecture', *Cognitive Science*, 22 (3), pp. 269–294.

Wiener, N. (1948) *Cybernetics: Or Control and Communication in the Animal and the Machine.* Cambridge, MA: MIT Press.

4

CYBERNETICS

Tara H. Abraham

Introduction

It is quite common in historical and philosophical discussions of computational theories of mind to give foundational status to a groundbreaking paper that appeared in 1943, authored by neuropsychiatrist Warren S. McCulloch and mathematical prodigy Walter Pitts.[1] The paper, entitled "A Logical Calculus of the Ideas Immanent in Nervous Activity", also became foundational in the cybernetics movement. A complex and multivalent field, cybernetics emerged historically in the context of the Second World War and the research of Norbert Wiener on anti-aircraft systems (Wiener, 1948). Out of this grew a central analogy between organisms and machines in terms of purposeful behavior, based on the concept of negative feedback.[2] Over the course of the 1940s, 1950s, and 1960s, cybernetics – as a practice, discipline, and research field – encompassed and influenced work in fields such as information theory, mathematics, psychology, control theory, neurophysiology, psychiatry, and sociology (Kline, 2009); and developed uniquely in the United States, Britain, France, Chile, and the Soviet Union.[3]

Inherent in the McCulloch-Pitts paper, standard accounts hold, were two key ideas: the notion that a Turing machine (an idea which informed their paper, according to McCulloch) is a valuable and potent model of the mind, and that neural networks of varying degrees of abstraction can provide very fruitful models of cognitive processes such as learning and perception.[4] Historically, both ideas fed into various practices in the emerging cognitive sciences of the 1950s, 1960s, and beyond: cognitive psychology, artificial intelligence, philosophy of mind, and computational neuroscience. Ultimately, on the heels of these scientific and philosophical developments – all arguably associated with the emergence and widespread influence of computers and computational systems – the notion that the mind is a computational system gained currency in the cognitive sciences.[5] Other chapters in this volume examine this history more closely.[6]

Yet as this volume also shows, the computational theory of mind (CTM) is not a homogenous entity, and philosophers have devoted much effort to unravelling the different sorts of assumptions about the varied and numerous understandings of what computation actually means in the CTM.[7] Indeed, it is not useful or accurate to speak of *the* computational theory of mind but rather better to speak of many. One point of debate is whether or not it is more appropriate to develop a CTM without reference to the nervous system (e.g. Newell and Simon,

1976), or whether a more fruitful CTM would acknowledge computation as a medium-specific representational process – particularly specific to the central nervous system.

I want to join this effort, yet here I approach this question as a historian, in particular a historian of cybernetics. I wish to problematize the straightforward historical line that is often drawn between the 1943 McCulloch-Pitts paper and current computational theories of mind, in two specific ways. First, the 1943 McCulloch-Pitts paper, while arguably influential for cyberneticians and beyond, did not go unquestioned during this period. To be sure, the McCulloch-Pitts paper quickly became a key component of John von Neumann's design of the digital computer in 1945, and the analogy between the brain and computer became a central metaphor in the cybernetics movement. However, at the famous Macy Foundation-sponsored meetings on cybernetics, held in New York between 1946 and 1953, the McCulloch-Pitts paper almost immediately became the focal point of a long and heated discussion about the value of digital computational processes in modeling the brain and mind.[8] In important ways, the paper sparked a significant amount of disunity amongst members of the cybernetics movement.

Second, the framework of the 1943 paper did not continue to define McCulloch's approach to the mind and brain in a straightforward way. He went on to tackle problems that went beyond abstract logical thought, such as perception and the reliability and stability of the central nervous system in spite of changes in thresholds. Like others in the cybernetics movement, as he engaged with more complex problems in cognition, McCulloch came to admit that neurons are not exclusively digital entities. Further, by focusing on McCulloch's own scientific practices – both theoretical and rhetorical – we can see that the computer metaphor was not a static entity for McCulloch: he had various motivations for employing the computer analogy in his scientific work beyond 1943. It became a point of reference for some of McCulloch's more transgressive scientific practices, for example, in his work as a public figure promoting the cybernetic creed, and in his participation in the unity of science movement.

Examining this trajectory while paying close attention to the various motivations for and obstacles to modeling, we can get a better sense of the complex historical relations between cybernetics and computational theories of mind. While modeling as a scientific practice is at the core of both practices, ends are important here. McCulloch, Pitts, and the other cyberneticians had specific motivations for modeling: McCulloch's goal was consistently to understand the brain and its functioning. By implication, he wanted to provide a rigorous theory of the mind, grounded in neurophysiology. In the end, McCulloch presented his models as guides to experimental work on the brain. In contrast, later practitioners in classical, symbol-based artificial intelligence and cognitive sciences were not concerned about neurophysiological details. If we place the legacy of the 1943 paper in a richer context, and not presume the existence of CTM and read the paper through this lens, we can see that the relationship between cybernetics for CTM is more complex than is often argued.

McCulloch-Pitts, von Neumann, and the computer-brain analogy

In December 1943, a paper appeared in the *Bulletin of Mathematical Biophysics* that expressed the functional relations between arrangements of idealized neurons in terms of Boolean logic (McCulloch and Pitts, 1943). Authored by philosophically minded neuropsychiatrist Warren S. McCulloch and mathematical prodigy Walter Pitts (who was twenty years McCulloch's junior), the paper argued that by modeling neurons as all-or-none entities, one could achieve a workable model of the mind that would provide a foundation for the study of brains and minds – both healthy and diseased. They based this assertion, in part, on the Nobel Prize-winning work of English electrophysiologist Edgar D. Adrian. Adrian (1914) provided experimental verification of the all-or-none nature of the relation between stimulus and response in single nerve fibers: given a threshold of excitation, they either fire and transmit an impulse, or they do not.

In retrospect, McCulloch recalled that Turing's work on computable numbers had also been part of the inspiration for their paper. As they concluded in the 1943 paper:

> It is easily shown: first, that every net, if furnished with a tape, scanners connected to afferents, and suitable efferents to perform the necessary motor-operations, can compute only such numbers as can a Turing machine; second, that each of the latter numbers can be computed by such a net; and that nets with circles can be computed by such a net … This is of interest as affording a psychological justification of the Turing definition of computability and its equivalents … If any number can be computed by an organism, it is computable by these definitions, and conversely.
>
> (McCulloch and Pitts, 1943, p. 129)

While McCulloch and Pitts famously concluded that their theory demonstrated that the mind "no longer goes as ghostly as a ghost" – in essence presenting a theory of the mind – the model also was grounded in assumptions about the functioning of the central nervous system.

Mathematician John von Neumann had learned of the McCulloch-Pitts work from Norbert Wiener, who had worked with Pitts in 1943 at MIT. In August 1944, through the help of Herman Goldstine, von Neumann visited the University of Pennsylvania's Moore School of Electrical Engineering, where, since June 1943, engineers had been working on an electronic calculator known as the ENIAC (Electronic Numerical Integrator and Computer) (Aspray, 1990, p. 34). Problems were quickly seen with the design of the ENIAC, and discussions began on a new computing machine, in which von Neumann participated. Along with Goldstine, John Mauchly, and J. Presper Eckert, von Neumann developed an improved machine, the EDVAC (Electronic Discrete Variable Arithmetic Computer). This was, arguably, one of the first machines to make use of the stored program concept (von Neumann, 1945, pp. 177–246).[9]

Von Neumann had focused on the development of digital systems. In addition to the practical development of high-speed computers, he had an abiding interest in more theoretical matters, a fact that likely drew him to the cybernetics group, an interdisciplinary collection of scientists from across the divides between mathematics, engineering, as well as the medical, human, and social sciences (see Table 4.1). Despite their varied backgrounds, all of the core members – figures like Wiener and McCulloch – as well as more peripheral participants, expressed a shared interest in understanding goal-directed behavior in the content of their various fields in terms of negative feedback mechanisms, as well as employing methods common in mathematics and engineering.

When called upon by the Moore School to draft a report on the EDVAC, von Neumann did not describe the device in the usual "engineering" terms for computing machines: mechanical switches, relays, or vacuum tubes. Instead, the switching elements were the "idealized neurons" of McCulloch and Pitts. As William Aspray (1990, p. 173) aptly noted, this allowed von Neumann to focus on both the logical design of the computer as well as the parallels between the stored-program computer and the human nervous system. Von Neumann devoted an entire section of the report to the neuron analogy, noting that every digital computing device contains relay-like elements having two or more distinct states. Often there are two states, one that exists when there is no outside stimulus, the other when there does exist some outside stimulus. Relay action takes place "in the emission of stimuli by the element whenever it has itself received a stimulus of the type indicated above" (von Neumann, 1945, p. 187). Von Neumann emphasized

Table 4.1 The core members of the original cybernetics group

Disciplinary Background	Members
Mathematics/Engineering	Norbert Wiener
	Walter Pitts
	Claude Shannon
	Julian H. Bigelow
	Leonard Savage
	John von Neumann
Social Sciences/Sociology	Gregory Bateson
	Lawrence K. Frank
	Paul Lazarsfeld
Psychology	Molly Harrower
	Kurt Lewin
	Heinrich Klüver
Neurophysiology/Physiology	Arturo Rosenblueth
	Rafael Lorente de Nó
	Ralph W. Gerard
Psychiatry/Neuropsychiatry	Warren S. McCulloch
	Lawrence S. Kubie
Philosophy	Filmer S.C. Northrop
Ecology	George E. Hutchinson
Anthropology	Margaret Mead
Neuroanatomy	Gerhardt von Bonin
Medicine	Frank Fremont Smith

Source: Adapted from Heims (1993, p. 285)

the analogy of this situation with the neurons of the human nervous system: they are both binary elements and are describable, as McCulloch and Pitts had noted, in a Boolean logic.

Von Neumann's work, in concert with that of McCulloch and Pitts, had a galvanizing effect on the cybernetics movement. In these first few years, the cyberneticians' central analogy was between computing machines and the central nervous system: they explored the potential of computers and their functional architecture for understanding the brain. Following an early meeting, in January 1945, Wiener wrote excitedly to Mexican physiologist Arturo Rosenblueth:

> von Neumann spoke on computing machines and I spoke on communication engin-
> eering. The second day [Rafael] Lorente de Nó and McCulloch joined forces for a
> very convincing presentation of the present status of the problem of the organization
> of the brain. In the end we were all convinced that the subject embracing both the
> engineering and neurology aspects is essentially one, and we should go ahead with
> plans to embody these ideas in a permanent program of research.
>
> *(Wiener, 1945)*

By 1946, McCulloch had persuaded Frank Fremont Smith of the Macy Foundation to sponsor a series of transdisciplinary meetings, which brought together diverse minds to discuss the potential of drawing analogies broadly between organisms and machines and applying math-ematical and modeling practices to the biological, human, and social sciences.[10] The proceedings from the first Macy Meeting on Cybernetics were not published, but Steve J. Heims, in his classic account of the activities of the cybernetics group, reports that the first meeting focused on the brain–computer analogy, as the participants discussed:

> the greater precision of digital machines as compared to the older analog computers, the use of binary rather than decimal representation of numbers, the stored program concept, various methods available for storing and accessing information … Some methods could not be discussed because they were still classified as military secrets. Von Neumann made semi-quantitative comparisons between vacuum tubes and neurons, the overall size of brains and computers, their speed of operation, and other characteristics.
>
> *(Heims, 1993, pp. 19–20)*

Yet, while consensus and enthusiasm defined the meetings at the outset, the metaphor of the brain as a computer – as well as the abstractions and idealizations involved in the modeling practices of McCulloch, Pitts, and von Neumann – began to spark disunity amongst the members of the cybernetics group; mainly along the disciplinary divide between the mathematicians and engineers on the one hand, and the biologists on the other. Often this disunity turned on the perceived potential of the analogy: was it to understand brains better, and direct experiment, or could it help us determine the logical principles that constrict the design of complex, goal-directed systems? The key claim was not that the brain was actually a computer – although McCulloch would employ such dramatic claims in his later rhetorical practices – but rather that if we model the brain in the same sorts of functional terms that defined computing devices, we could simplify the complex problem of how the brain functions. Mathematicians pondered the formal, logical requirements of the analogy – for example, von Neumann argued that using even 10^{10} neurons as "simple relays" would not be enough to account for human abilities (McCulloch, 1949b, p. 31). Neurophysiologists challenged the analogy based on the number of empirical details left out, and pointed out that the functioning of the nervous system overall is more analogical than digital in character.[11] Modeling was not wrong-headed as a scientific practice, but such analogies, to be useful, must be able to fruitfully direct neurophysiological experiment and be empirically consistent and accurate.

Many of the debates turned on whether neurons themselves are actually analog or digital devices. McCulloch, Pitts, and von Neumann used axiomatic methods and deliberately avoided details: the McCulloch-Pitts neurons were idealized, and had little detail about how they functioned, which could actually be shown to be more continuous than discrete.[12] They had ignored physiological, empirical details about how neurons function – in particular, the chemical aspect of transmission based on neurotransmitters, in which continuous variables (e.g. chemical concentrations and electrical fields) play a vital role.[13] Von Neumann similarly treated neurons and his computational units as "black boxes" – that is, he ignored their internal functioning (thresholds, temporal summation, delays). The McCulloch-Pitts neuron was impoverished: it was assumed for the purposes of modeling to be an on–off device.[14] Yet this formal modeling method held the potential, especially for McCulloch, of making sense of the brain's functional organization and phenomena such as memory, perception, and communication.

At the Macy conferences, central to the debates about the McCulloch-Pitts work was not simply the question of the mind as a computer, but of whether the metaphor of the digital computer was in fact an accurate and useful way of understanding the *brain*. As Piccinini and Scarantino (2010) note, the McCulloch-Pitts 1943 paper was about *digital* computation. It was precisely this point that stirred the Macy participants into debate. Discussions began as early as the sixth Macy Meeting in 1949 about the nature of the digital computer itself – at that point not nearly as ubiquitous a scientific object as it became during the 1960s and 1970s (McCulloch, 1949b, p. 30). A large portion of discussion at this meeting stemmed from a pessimistic statement of von Neumann's in 1948, which proposed limitations on the McCulloch-Pitts model and complicated the analogy between organisms and computers:

> First, if a certain mode of behavior can be effected by a finite neural network, the question still remains whether that network can be realized within a practical size, specifically, whether it will fit into the physical limitations of the organism in question. Second, the question arises whether every existing mode of behavior can really be put completely and unambiguously into words … All of this does not alter my belief that a new, essentially logical, theory is called for in order to understand high-complication automata and, in particular, the central nervous system. It may be, however, that in this process logic will have to undergo a pseudomorphosis to neurology to a much greater extent than the reverse.
>
> *(von Neumann, 1951, pp. 310–311)*

In a sense the issue was one of complexity: how many neurons are necessary to account for human abilities and all the functions the human brain performs (McCulloch, 1949b, p. 31)? How are memories stored and how much information can be stored in the human brain? Is this dependent on a minimum number of neurons (Pitts, 1949, p. 60; Gerard, 1949, p. 155)? Discussions also centered on the brain: does the brain really work that way? Are neurons really digital devices (Bateson, 1949, p. 83; Gerard, 1949, p. 155)? In essence, the cyberneticians were debating about how far they could push the brain–computer analogy in order to understand how the central nervous system works. Their discussions often involved empirical details about the brain – neurons, physiology, brain, muscle, and networks. Layered on to this discussion were questions and criticisms about the speculative nature of cybernetic practices – Gerard famously chastised the group for its "as-if" attitude towards understanding the central nervous system and repeatedly urged that the group get "some orthodox neurophysiology into the picture" (Gerard, 1951, p. 171; Savage in Pitts, 1949, pp. 38–39). He went on to critique the brain–computer analogy itself:

> To take what is learned from working with calculating machines and communication systems, and to explore the use of these insights in interpreting the action of the brain, is admirable; but to say, as the public press says, that therefore these machines are brains, and that our brains are nothing but calculating machines, is presumptuous. One might as well say that the telescope is an eye, or that a bulldozer is a muscle.
>
> *(Gerard, 1951, p. 172)*

Even von Neumann, who had been initially responsible for elaborating the brain–computer analogy, by this time found the simplification of neural activity problematic:

> There has been a strong temptation to view the neuron as an elementary unit, in the sense in which computing elements, such as electromechanical relays or vacuum tubes, are being used within a computing machine. The entire behaviour of a neuron can then be described by a few simple rules regulating the relationship between a moderate number of input and output stimuli. The available evidence, however, is not in favour of this. The individual neuron is probably already a rather complicated subunit,

and a complete characterization of its response to stimuli, or, more precisely, to systems of stimuli, is a quite involved affair.

(von Neumann in Gerard, 1951, p. 180)

Von Neumann did not believe that this excluded the possibility of digital mechanisms in the central nervous system. Yet he was pragmatic: after citing several examples of systems which exhibit both analogical and digital characteristics, such as the differential analyzer, he concluded:

> one must say that in almost all parts of physics the underlying reality is analogical, that is, the true physical variables are in almost all cases continuous, or equivalent to continuous descriptions. The digital procedure is usually a human artifact *for the sake of description* [my emphasis].
>
> *(ibid., pp. 181–182)*

Von Neumann knew that physiological evidence had shown continuous variables in neural function, such as chemical transmitters. In the end, core members of the group agreed that the action of the nervous system is not purely digital.

This admission highlights an important feature of the epistemological goals of the cyberneticians, insofar as we can claim a unified position on this point. Theoretical modeling had, from the start, been a key feature of cybernetic practice. Wiener and Rosenblueth had expressed the value of models early on – in their view, there are systems so complex that modeling is the only way to gain a proper understanding of such systems.[15] However, for most cyberneticians, including Warren McCulloch, models served to guide experiment. As the editors of the Macy proceedings concluded at the end of the eighth meeting in 1951 (in part an effort to achieve consensus):

> We all know that we ought to study the organism, and not the computers, if we wish to understand the organism. Differences in levels of organization may be more than quantitative. But the computing robot provides us with analogues that are helpful as far as they seem to hold, and no less helpful whenever they break down. To find out in what ways a nervous system … differs from our man-made analogues requires experiment. These experiments would not have been considered if the analogue had not been proposed, and new observations on biological and social systems result from an empirical demonstration of the shortcomings of our models.
>
> *(von Foerster, Mead, and Teuber in Gerard, 1951, pp. 345–346)*

While the Macy participants were tackling the processes of memory, perception, and communication in terms digital computation, they were continually constrained by the analogy of the computer with the brain, and obligated to account for empirical details in working out a model. This reflects their object of inquiry: while much fluidity existed within the epistemological aims of the brain–computer analogy, ultimately, and especially for McCulloch, the object of investigation was the brain and its functional organization.

McCulloch's modeling practices after 1943

What did the computational brain mean for McCulloch? If we look solely at his 1943 work with Pitts, because of the centrality of the all-or-none principle of neural activity, we could conclude that computation for McCulloch was digital in nature (Piccinini and

Bahar, 2013). Yet this was a bold, audacious abstraction. As discussed above, he, and the other cyberneticians, ultimately knew that the situation was much more complex than that (Lettvin, 1988, p. vi).[16] Overall, McCulloch pushed the brain–computer analogy in several directions that went beyond the Turing-machine focus of the 1943 paper. He used models of neural networks to account for memory (in brains, reverberating chains of neurons) and the perception of universals (universal forms that remain invariant in our perception regardless of scale), he explored the statistical requirements of the number of neurons needed for the brain to function reliably, and he proposed regenerative loops that lead to "errors" in the brain and ultimately mental illness and neurological conditions. In all cases, the computer analogy with the brain was his aid to understanding the mind, but only through the physiology of the brain.

The metaphor of the computer as brain was also powerful in its ability, for McCulloch, to direct experimental investigation. For example, in 1947, to an audience of neurophysiologists, McCulloch praised the brain-computer metaphor as superior to other metaphors to account for the brain's functional organization (McCulloch, 1947, pp. 448–452). In the nineteenth century, McCulloch noted, British neurologist John Hughlings Jackson had conceptualized the motor cortex as a "bass of a piano-accordion whose every button sounds a chord". Another British neurologist, Francis Walshe, had described cortical efferent neurons as akin to "the push-buttons of some monstrous 'juke-box'". Understanding the brain's functioning in terms of input, output, and information processing was superior, McCulloch argued, because it "cleaves to fact, prescribes experiment, predicts outcome, invites refutation" (McCulloch, 1947, p. 448). Other metaphors, such as Jackson's and Walshe's, fail as frameworks for modeling the brain so fruitfully.

McCulloch presented his 1947 work with Pitts on the perception of universals in a similar way: this was a theory of information processing, modeling the recognition of auditory and visual forms using mathematical translations to relate input to output (Pitts and McCulloch, 1947). Their epistemological goal was to generate "hypothetical mechanisms" to guide histological and physiological experiment, and they provided detailed images of the histology of the cerebral cortex. This model formed the basis of McCulloch's famous talk (1951a) at the Hixon Symposium at Caltech in 1948, entitled "Why the Mind Is in the Head". Here, McCulloch called the nervous system "par excellence a logical [i.e. digital] machine" (McCulloch, 1951b, p. 73). Yet he was already concerned with reliability and corruption of information – a limit to the brain–computer analogy:

> no computing machine is as likely to go right under conditions as various as those we undergo … Accordingly to increase certainty every hypothesis should be of minimum logical, or a priori probability so that, if it be confirmed by experiment, then it shall be because the world is so constructed.
>
> *(McCulloch, 1951b, p. 76)*

Participants at the Hixon meeting, most of whom were psychologists, attacked McCulloch on various points, in particular his loose polysemous language surrounding terms like 'goal' and 'purpose', and his various theoretical assumptions concerning neuron structure, behavior, and the cerebral cortex which, neuropsychologist Karl Lashley argued, were not justified by the facts (Lashley, cited in McCulloch, 1951b, p. 100). Responding to some of his critics, McCulloch argued that what he had presented were hypotheses, comprising a "perfectly general theory" that incorporated the principles of design common, he surmised, to both brains and computers. Experiment, in his view, would provide confirmation or refutation:

The hypotheses that I made relating to the nervous system are of the kind that will help me put electrodes in one place to see what is going on in that place and to know what I am looking for, and I expect to hit a snag there very soon. I always have hit snags so far.

(McCulloch, 1951b, p. 132)

In addition to this epistemological role for models, McCulloch had other, more rhetorical purposes in promoting the brain–computer analogy. In a 1949 paper, McCulloch's rhetoric is embedded in the language of engineering: he describes brains as a sub-class of computing machines – the human brain being the "most complicated computing machine there is" (McCulloch, 1949a). That same year, in a paper entitled "Of Digital Computers Called Brains", McCulloch aligned his cybernetic project with the efforts of the American unity of science movement:

It has been said that since the days of Helmholtz no man can understand all science. If by this is meant knowledge of all descriptive details, it is increasingly true. But there are many signs that at the level of theory the most remote of disciplines have developed central ideas that are pulling them together. The wildest speculative analogies of a generation ago turn out to be similar problems in dissimilar materials.

(McCulloch and Pfeiffer, 1949, p. 368)

Indeed, the cyberneticians had been involved in the American unity of science movement since the early 1940s. And philosophers of science of this ilk took notice: for example, Paul Oppenheim and Hilary Putnam cited the work of McCulloch, Pitts, and von Neumann as typifying the sort of micro-reduction of scientific phenomena necessary for attaining scientific unity (Oppenheim and Putnam, 1958).

McCulloch was a modeler. In this practice he had much in common with figures in the nascent field of artificial intelligence during the 1950s and 1960s – indeed he acted as mentor for many of them, such as Marvin Minsky. But McCulloch always sought, with his models, to help us better understand the brain. As we have seen, empirical accuracy was certainly always a sticking point for observers of McCulloch's project and for the cyberneticians themselves.

Conclusions

In terms of scientific practice, cybernetics presents a very specific legacy for current computational theories of mind. Common elements in both pursuits – a concern with the process of computation, and an interest in the mind – are grounded by a fundamental mode of scientific reasoning: modeling. As Mary S. Morgan has noted (see Morgan, 2012), as a style of reasoning in the taxonomy of Alistair Crombie (1994), hypothetical modeling had its historical roots in analogy.[17] In Morgan's own grouping, I would argue, McCulloch and the cyberneticians, like theoreticians in physics, were idealizers – "picking out the relations of interest, and isolating them from the frictions and disturbances which interfere with their workings in the real world to give form to simpler, and 'ideal' world models" (Morgan, 2012, p. 22). Modern computationalists also engage in forms of idealization.

Yet a vitally important aspect of what models are, and how to make sense of modeling as a scientific practice, is how models function in scientific investigation. According to Morgan and Morrison, models can function as autonomous agents and instruments of investigation.[18] Scientific models function as investigative instruments because they involve some form of representation: models typically represent either some aspect of the world, or some aspect of our theories about the world, or both at once. Hence the model's representative power allows it to function not just instrumentally, but to teach us something about the thing it represents.

(Morrison and Morgan, 1999, p. 11)

Certainly, both McCulloch's brand of cybernetics and the work of later computationalists, such as Allen Newell and Herbert Simon, were concerned with foundations,[19] and placed modeling as central to scientific practice. Yet their pursuits differed in important ways.

First, despite their empirical inaccuracies, McCulloch's models aimed to represent and in turn investigate the functioning and functional organization of the human brain. This is apparent as early as McCulloch's 1943 work with Pitts, as well as in the fallout of this paper in discussions amongst the cybernetics group. Their central object of inquiry was not the mind *per se*, but the human brain and central nervous system. Although cybernetics was indeed disunified, and while perception, memory, and learning were all key processes to be explained via models, the main analogy was between the brain and the computer. The cyberneticians spent much time debating and discussing the value and accuracy of the brain as a computing device. Often these discussions expanded into exchanges about the value of theoretical modeling in science – or at least the somewhat exaggerated form of idealization that some core members practiced.

Second, McCulloch had very specific epistemological goals for his models. He was very much interested in the mind, but always via the brain and its physiology: his models, despite being full of abstractions, were always constrained by empirical details about the brain – its properties, its organization. Unlike later investigators probing the potential of understanding the mind via computational processes, McCulloch's models were not ends unto themselves. They were presented as guides for experiment, and he openly admitted he was not always successful in this goal. Furthermore, there was much more to McCulloch's views on the use-fulness of the notion of computation to understanding brains and minds than was contained in his 1943 paper with Pitts. He differed in important ways from the inheritors of the so-called computational project. Unlike later computationalists, McCulloch wanted his models to feed back into the study of the brain in both its healthy and diseased states. McCulloch's models functioned to guide experiment and to provide a foundational element for neurophysiology and psychiatry, as well as for the burgeoning field of cybernetics. McCulloch was after a com-putational theory of the mind via the *brain*, and because of this, his models were held up to a different set of standards. He was speaking to neurophysiologists and neuropsychiatrists, until when at MIT he had acquired a new audience and a new set of inter- and multidisciplinary followers.

Models are ubiquitous in the modern cognitive sciences. While McCulloch acted as mentor to, and influence on, several prominent contributors to the AI project during the 1950s and 1960s, such as Marvin Minsky, the McCulloch-Pitts paper and cybernetics too did not feed directly nor unproblematically into later practices that seem foundational to CTM, in particular artificial intelligence. McCulloch's legacy – and we can tie to this the legacy of cybernetics – lies most strongly in computational neuroscience or even computational cognitive neuroscience – work in these fields strives for more empirically accurate models, and their models incorp-orate knowledge about the brain and neurophysiological data (Rescorla, 2015, p. 27).[20] What emerges from this re-examination of the McCulloch-Pitts work in the context of cybernetics and scientific practice are the very complex and nuanced relations in terms of discipline and culture between cybernetics and the cognitive sciences. Brains, cognition, intelligence, percep-tion, memory, all exist in specific relationships within and across each of these fields. The most important legacy of McCulloch's brand of cybernetics is his attitude that it is easier to build computational models of nervous systems than to study them directly. In a sense, McCulloch and the cyberneticians occupied a transitional space between the AI modelers and the traditional empirical neurophysiologists and neuropsychologists. He was undaunted in the face of criticisms from this latter group: as Lettvin recalled, McCulloch and Pitts "would rather have been clearly wrong than maunderingly vague, as was the accepted style" (Lettvin, 1988, p. ix).

Notes

1 McCulloch and Pitts (1943); examples can be found in Edwards (1996), Piccinini (2004), and Rescorla (2015). For more on their collaboration, see Abraham (2002; 2016, ch. 4).
2 For more on the broad history of the cybernetics movement, see Galison (1994), Heims (1993), Pickering (1995), Edwards (1996), Pickering (2010), Medina (2011), and Kline (2015). Along with the McCulloch-Pitts paper, the other so-called foundational document for cybernetics was a paper by physiologist Arturo Rosenblueth, engineer Julian Bigelow, and mathematician Norbert Wiener (1943), which accounted for purposeful behavior – in both natural and artificial systems – in terms of negative feedback mechanisms.
3 For more on the international context, see Mindell, Segal, and Gerovitch (2003). For more on the Soviet case, see Babintseva (2017).
4 For overviews of these ideas, see Piccinini (2004), Boden (2008), Dupuy (2000).
5 This literature is too vast to cite here; for an overview see Boden (2008) and Rescorla (2015).
6 See e.g. Aizawa (this volume); Garson and Bruckner (this volume); Jaekel and Zednik (this volume).
7 See e.g. Piccinini and Scarantino (2010), Rescorla (2015). For a similar analysis that challenges the notion of psychological categories as natural kinds, see Smith (2005).
8 For more on the Macy meetings, see Edwards (1996, ch. 6) and Heims (1993).
9 See also John von Neumann, *The Computer and the Brain* (2000).
10 For more on the disciplinary dynamics of these conferences and McCulloch's role in them, see Abraham (2016, Chapter 6) and Kline (2015, Chapter 2).
11 See, for example, Gerard (1951).
12 For more on this practice, see Abraham (2003).
13 Henry H. Dale, Otto Loewi, and Walter Cannon had shared the Nobel Prize in Physiology or Medicine in 1936 for their work on chemical transmission in the nervous system.
14 For more on McCulloch's and Pitts' practices of abstraction in their models, see Abraham (2003).
15 For a crisp statement of this perspective, see Rosenblueth and Wiener (1945).
16 The key refutation of McCulloch's digital framework came from Donald MacKay, who was working with McCulloch at the Illinois Neuropsychiatric Institute in Chicago during the early 1950s (MacKay and McCulloch, 1952).
17 See Morgan (2012, p. 15).
18 For explorations of the various uses of models and modeling in scientific practice, see Morrison and Morgan (1999).
19 See Edwards (1996, ch. 6).
20 See Jakel and Zednik (this volume).

References

Abraham, T.H. (2002) '(Physio)logical Circuits: The Intellectual Origins of the McCulloch-Pitts Neural Networks', *Journal of the History of the Behavioral Sciences*, 38 (1), pp. 3–25.
Abraham, T.H. (2003) 'From Theory to Data: Representing Neurons in the 1940s', *Biology and Philosophy*, 18 (3), pp. 415–426.
Abraham, T.H. (2016) *Rebel Genius: Warren S. McCulloch's Transdisciplinary Life in Science*. Cambridge, MA: MIT Press.
Adrian, E.D. (1914) 'The All-or-None Principle in Nerve', *Journal of Physiology*, 47, pp. 460–474.
Aspray, W. (1990) *John von Neumann and the Origins of Modern Computing*. Cambridge, MA: MIT Press.
Babintseva, E. (2017) 'The Cybernetic Effect: The Origins of a New Soviet Psychology of Thinking', *History of Science Society Annual Meeting*, Ontario.

Bateson, G. (1949) 'The Neurotic Potential and Human Adaptation', *Cybernetics: Circular Causal, and Feedback Mechanisms in Biological and Social Systems: Transactions of the Sixth Conference*, in Pias, C. (ed.) (2003) *Cybernetics – Kybernetik: The Macy Conferences 1946–1953*. Zürich and Berlin: Diaphanes, pp. 66–97.

Boden, M. (2008) *Mind as Machine: A History of Cognitive Science* (2 vols.). Oxford: Oxford University Press.

Crombie, A.C. (1994) *Styles of Scientific Thinking in the European Tradition: The History of Argument and Explanation Especially in the Mathematical and Biomedical Sciences and Arts*. London: Duckworth.

Dupuy, J.-P. (2000) *The Mechanization of the Mind: On the Origins of Cognitive Science*. Translated by M.B. DeBevoise. Princeton, NJ: Princeton University Press. (Original work published 1994).

Edwards, P.N. (1996) *The Closed World: Computers and the Politics of Discourse in Cold War America*. Cambridge, MA: MIT Press.

Galison, P. (1994) 'The Ontology of the Enemy: Norbert and the Cybernetic Vision', *Critical Inquiry*, 21 (1), pp. 228–266.

Gerard, R.W. (1949) 'Possible Mechanisms of Recall and Recognition', *Cybernetics: Circular Causal, and Feedback Mechanisms in Biological and Social Systems: Transactions of the Sixth Conference*, in Pias, C. (ed.) (2003) Cybernetics – Kybernetik: The Macy Conferences 1946–1953. Zürich and Berlin: Diaphanes, p. 155.

Gerard, R.W. (1951) 'Some of the Problems Concerning Digital Notions in the Central Nervous System', *Cybernetics: Circular Causal, and Feedback Mechanisms in Biological and Social Systems: Transactions of the Eighth Conference*, in Pias, C. (ed.) (2003) *Cybernetics – Kybernetik: The Macy Conferences 1946–1953*. Zürich and Berlin: Diaphanes, pp. 171–202.

Heims, S. (1993) *Constructing a Social Science for Postwar America: The Cybernetics Group*. Cambridge, MA: MIT Press.

Kline, R. (2009) 'Where Are the Cyborgs in Cybernetics?', *Social Studies of Science*, 39 (3), pp. 331–362.

Kline, R. (2015) *The Cybernetics Moment: Or Why We Call Our Age the Information Age*. Baltimore, MD: Johns Hopkins University Press.

Lettvin, J.Y. (1988) 'Foreword', in McCulloch, W.S. *Embodiments of Mind*. Cambridge, MA: MIT Press, pp. vi–xi.

MacKay, D. and McCulloch, W.S. (1952) 'The limiting informational capacity of a neuronal link', *Bulletin of Mathematical Biophysics*, 14, pp. 127–135.

McCulloch, W.S. (1947) 'Modes of Functional Organization in the Cerebral Cortex', *Federation Proceedings*, 6, pp. 448–452.

McCulloch, W.S. (1949a) 'The Brain as a Computing Machine', *Electrical Engineering*, 68 (6), pp. 492–497.

McCulloch, W.S. (1949b) 'Introductory Discussions', *Cybernetics: Circular Causal, and Feedback Mechanisms in Biological and Social Systems: Transactions of the Sixth Conference*, in Pias, C. (ed.) (2003) *Cybernetics – Kybernetik: The Macy Conferences 1946–1953*. Zürich and Berlin: Diaphanes, pp. 29–40.

McCulloch, W.S. (1951a) 'Why the Mind Is in the Head', in Jeffress, L.A. (ed.) *Cerebral Mechanisms in Behavior: The Hixon Symposium*. New York, NY: John Wiley, pp. 42–111.

McCulloch, W.S. (1951b) *Embodiments of Mind*. Cambridge, MA: MIT Press.

McCulloch, W.S. and Pfeiffer, J. (1949) 'Of Digital Computers Called Brains', *Scientific Monthly*, 69 (6), pp. 369–376.

McCulloch, W.S. and Pitts, W. (1943) 'A Logical Calculus of the Ideas Immanent in Nervous Activity', *Bulletin of Mathematical Biophysics*, 5, pp. 115–133.

Medina, E. (2011) *Cybernetic Revolutionaries: Technology and Politics in Allende's Chile*. Cambridge, MA: MIT Press.

Mindell, D., Segal, J., and Gerovitch, S. (2003) 'From Communications Engineering to Communications Science: Cybernetics and Information Theory in the United States, France, and the Soviet Union', in Walker, M. (ed.) *Science and Ideology: A Comparative History*. London and New York, NY: Routledge, pp. 66–96.

Morgan, M.S. (2012) *The World in the Model: How Economists Work and Think*. Cambridge, UK: Cambridge University Press.

Morrison, M. and Morgan, M.S. (1999) 'Models as Mediating Instruments', in Morgan, M.S. and Morrison, M. (eds.) *Models as Mediators: Perspectives on Natural and Social Science*. Cambridge, UK: Cambridge University Press, pp. 10–37.

Newell, A. and Simon, H.A. (1976) 'Computer Science as Empirical Inquiry: Symbols and Search', *Communications of the ACM*, 19 (3), pp. 113–126.

Oppenheim, P. and Putnam, H. (1958) 'The Unity of Science as a Working Hypothesis', in Feigl, H., Scriven, M., and Maxwell. G. (eds.) *Concepts, Theories, and the Mind-Body Problem*. Minnesota Studies in the Philosophy of Science, Vol. 2. Minneapolis, MN: University of Minnesota Press, pp. 3–36.

Pias, C. (ed.) (2003) *Cybernetics – Kybernetik: The Macy Conferences 1946–1953*. Zürich and Berlin: Diaphanes.

Piccinini, G. (2004) 'The First Computational Theory of Mind and Brain: A Close Look at McCulloch and Pitts's "Logical Calculus of Ideas Immanent in Nervous Activity"', *Synthese*, 141, pp. 175–215.

Piccinini, G. and Bahar, S. (2013) 'Neural Computation and the Computational Theory of Cognition', *Cognitive Science*, 37 (3), pp. 453–488.

Piccinini, G. and Scarantino, A. (2010) 'Computational vs. Information Processing: Why Their Difference Matters to Cognitive Science', *Studies in the History and Philosophy of Science*, 41 (3), pp. 237–246.

Pickering, A. (1995) 'Cyborg History and the World War II Regime', *Perspectives on Science*, 3, pp. 1–48.

Pickering, A. (2010) *The Cybernetic Brain: Sketches of Another Future*. Chicago, IL: University of Chicago Press.

Pitts, W. (1949) in discussion with John Stroud, 'The Psychological Moment in Perception', *Cybernetics: Circular Causal, and Feedback Mechanisms in Biological and Social Systems: Transactions of the Sixth Conference*, in Pias, C. (ed.) (2003) *Cybernetics – Kybernetik: The Macy Conferences 1946–1953*. Zürich and Berlin: Diaphanes, p. 60.

Pitts, W. and McCulloch, W.S. (1947) 'How We Know Universals: The Perception of Auditory and Visual Forms', *Bulletin of Mathematical Biophysics*, 9 (3), pp. 127–147.

Rescorla, M. (2015) 'The Computational Theory of Mind', *The Stanford Encyclopedia of Philosophy*, March 21, Zalta, E.N. (ed.), Available at: http://plato.stanford.edu/archives/win2015/entries/computational-mind (Accessed: September 9, 2016).

Rosenblueth, A., Bigelow, J., and Wiener, N. (1943) 'Behavior, Purpose, and Teleology', *Philosophy of Science*, 10, pp. 18–24.

Rosenblueth, A. and Wiener, N. (1945) 'The Role of Models in Science', *Philosophy of Science*, 12 (4), pp. 316–321.

Smith, R. (2005) 'The History of Psychological Categories', *Studies in History and Philosophy of Biological and Biomedical Sciences*, 36 (1), pp. 55–94.

Von Neumann, J. (1945) 'First Draft Report on the EDVAC', report prepared for the US Army Ordnance Department under contract W-670-ORD-4926, in Stern, N. (1981) *From ENIAC to UNIVAC*. Bedford, MA: Digital Press, pp. 177–246.

Von Neumann, J. (1951) 'The General and Logical Theory of Automata', in Jeffress, L.A. (ed.) *Cerebral Mechanisms in Behavior: The Hixon Symposium*. New York, NY: John Wiley, pp. 1–41.

Von Neumann, J. (2000) *The Computer and the Brain*. New Haven, CT and London: Yale University Press.

Wiener, N. (1945) Letter to Arturo Rosenblueth, January 24. MIT Archives and Special Collections, Box 4, Folder 67, Norbert Wiener Papers.

Wiener, N. (1948) *Cybernetics: Or Control and Communication in the Animal and Machine*. Cambridge, MA: MIT Press.

5

TURING-EQUIVALENT COMPUTATION AT THE "CONCEPTION" OF COGNITIVE SCIENCE

Kenneth Aizawa

Many philosophical accounts of the computational theory of mind focus on Turing machines or Turing-equivalent computational formalisms.[1] Such devices have finite sets of instructions (programs) operating on finitely many symbols with unbounded memory resources that enable them to compute a specific class of functions, the partial recursive functions.[2] The recurrent allusions to Turing machines and Turing-equivalent computing devices suggest that the history of the computational theory of mind is the history of the birth of Turing machines and their subsequent influence.

Such allusions, however, are at times misleading. For one thing, there are important episodes in the history of "the computational theory of mind" where Turing-equivalent computational formalisms had no role.[3] There are cases where the application of the formalism of Turing-equivalent computation to one or another scientific or philosophical issues was not the goal.[4] As a case in point, this chapter will review of some of the papers that are sometimes taken to have been among the founding documents of cognitive science, namely, three of the papers presented at the Symposium on Information Theory at the Massachusetts Institute of Technology in September 1956.[5] These papers are George Miller's "Human Memory and the Storage of Information", Noam Chomsky's "Three Models for the Description of Language", and Allen Newell and Herbert Simon's "The Logic Theory Machine: A Complex Information Processing System". Each of these works reveals a thinker, or thinkers, working on relatively narrow projects which, only in subsequent years, became incorporated into "the computational theory of mind".

To make a few orienting comments about these papers, Miller's "magic number seven" and his hypothesis of "chunking" proposed that, internal to the organism, there are mechanisms that chunk, code, decode, organize, package, process, recode, reorganize, summarize, translate, or transmit information. Miller chose the term "information processing" as a blanket term to cover all of these. Turing-equivalent computation was not discussed. Chomsky was concerned with the structure of linguistic theory and its methods. Central to the 1956 paper were three different types of grammar. Chomsky's interests at this time are often obscured by their subsequent integration into automata theory, computation theory, and the so-called "Chomsky hierarchy".[6]

Finally, Newell and Simon proposed that there are internal, step-by-step procedures by which humans might solve logic problems. Such procedures could provide novel proofs of theorems in Whitehead and Russell's *Principia Mathematica*. While Newell and Simon used computers to simulate their Logic Theorist and they often wrote of the Logic Theorist program, they did not explicitly embrace, at the time, the idea that cognition is a form of Turing-equivalent computation.

Miller

Miller's contribution to the symposium was, to a significant degree, a selection of work that appeared in his better-known and extremely influential paper, "The Magical Number Seven, Plus or Minus Two: Some Limits on Our Capacity for Processing Information", which was itself a reworking of material that he had previously presented at the Eastern Psychological Association meetings held in Philadelphia on April 14–15, 1955. Both of Miller's papers discussed limitations on what Miller called the "span of absolute judgments of unidimensional stimuli" and the "span of immediate memory". Both were meant to challenge a presumed role for Claude Shannon's concept of information in psychological theorizing (Shannon, 1948).

Miller (1956a) introduces the concept of information informally noting that one bit of information enables us to decide between two options, say, more than six feet or less than six feet, whereas two bits enable us to decide between four, three bits between eight, and so on. In experiments in which participants were required to categorize unidimensional stimuli, such as the loudness or frequency of a tone, subjects could only make accurate discriminations among about five to fifteen different tones. In other words, participants found it extremely difficult to judge the frequency category of a tone when the frequency was one among fifteen possible frequencies or more. This means, Miller supposed, that the human discriminatory capacity in such tasks was in the surprisingly limited range of two to four bits per judgment. Miller interpreted this to be a limit on internal mechanisms of judgment, rather than a limit on the receptoral organs, since humans are dramatically better at making comparisons between simultaneously presented stimuli than between sequentially presented stimuli. To illustrate, imagine being in a paint store. One readily sees the difference between two sample colors on adjacent, simultaneously presented swatches of a sample palette, but if the same two samples are presented with a significant time delay, they might both be labeled "cream". Such observations were meant to challenge the behaviorist notion of there being nothing of scientific interest going on behind the scenes of behavior.

Far better known are Miller's results on the span of immediate memory, or what we now might call "short term memory". In a simple protocol, a participant might be read a sequence of symbols, then, after the sequence has been presented, repeat them. The protocol might begin with shorter sequences and progress to longer ones for which the subject is not able to answer correctly. In such experiments, there are two hypotheses concerning the limiting variable on performance. The first, suggested by information theoretic approaches, is that the task will become harder in proportion to the amount of information contained in the sequence. The second is that the task will become harder in proportion to the number of items in the sequence. Thus, according to the first theory, one should be able to remember longer sequences of digits than sequences of letters of the alphabet, since each digit involves less information (one out of ten possibilities) than does a letter of the alphabet (one out of twenty-six possibilities). What one finds, of course, is that both digits and letters have a limit of about seven items.

As with the result on the span of absolute judgments, Miller implicitly supposed that the memory tasks challenged dominant behaviorist conceptions. Miller supposed that our relatively fixed immediate memory capacity forces us to reorganize or recode what is presented to the senses. We must learn how to "chunk" information. As an analogy, he proposes that computer engineers might take the eighteen-digit sequence 010111001001000110, which exceeds immediate memory and group it as 010-111-001-001-000-110. This grouping might then be recoded as 271016, which falls within the span of immediate memory. He further proposes that such chunking is involved in learning to transmit Morse code. Initially, one traffics in dots and dashes, but in time one learns to group them into letters, then words, then phrases.

In interpreting these results, one might suppose that Miller embraces Turing-equivalent computation when he comes to an analogy with computers. He writes,

> Suppose we take literally the assumption that our memory is capable of dealing with only seven items at a time. It is as if we were dealing with a computing machine that has a small, fixed number of storage registers. Each register can accept any of a tremendous variety of different symbols, so the total amount of information that can be stored is quite large.
>
> *(Miller, 1956b, p. 133)*

Notice that Miller does not commit to saying that humans are computing machines, much less that humans are Turing-equivalent computing machines. Instead, the allusion to computers is more like a helpful analogy. For example, in the preceding paragraphs he describes the idea in terms of a "standing room only" hypothesis:

> "Standing room only" hypotheses hold that there are only so many seats available in the mental amphitheater; that there is not time to organize the material properly into supraordinate units in order to fit it into the available number of slots.
>
> *(ibid.)*

It is, perhaps, a less farfetched analogy than one he used earlier:

> Since it is as easy to remember a lot of information (when the items are information-ally rich) as it is to remember a little information (when the items are informationally impoverished), it is economical to organize the material into rich chunks. To draw a rather farfetched analogy, it is as if we had to carry all our money in a purse that could contain only seven coins. It doesn't matter to the purse, however, whether these coins are pennies or dollars. The process of organizing and reorganizing is a pervasive human trait, and it is motivated, at least in part, by an attempt to make the best possible use of our mnemonic capacity.
>
> *(ibid., p. 131)*

Miller does not explicitly discuss Turing-equivalent computation, or any other of the associated concepts, such as effective procedures, recursively computable functions, or any other of the formal apparatus of effective procedures. So, while he was aware of computers and computations, they were not, at this point in time, a driving force in his theorizing. Instead, Miller was nudging the discipline away from reliance on the behaviorist approach and on the use of Shannon information as a tool for understanding certain aspects of human performance. It was only later that Miller's work was linked to Turing-equivalent computation and integrated into "the computational theory of mind".

Chomsky

Chomsky's paper begins, not with a discussion of Turing machines and their kin, but with an introduction to a picture of the structure of linguistic theory.[7] Descriptive linguistics should discover the grammars of individual languages based on a finite set of observations, but then predict indefinitely many other observations. Moreover, it should explain how a language learner could correctly identify the grammar of her language based only on a finite sample of sentences. In addition, Chomsky proposes various methods by which the linguist might develop a linguistic theory. To appreciate this, we may review some of the principal arguments and proposals in the paper.

The first, and simplest, of Chomsky's three models of grammar is the "finite-state grammar". Such a device has a finite number of states S_0, ..., S_q and as it moves from one state to another, it produces a letter from an alphabet A. To produce a sentence (i.e. a sequence of letters), the system begins in S_0 and works its way through a sequence of states, producing multiple letters as it goes, until it halts. The set of all the different sentences the device can produce is the language L of the device.

To show a limitation on finite-state grammars, Chomsky introduces the notion of a dependency. The idea is that a sentence S contains a dependency between the i-th and j-th symbols, if simply replacing the i-th letter of S to produce S_1 leads to an S_1 that is not grammatical, whereas further replacing the j-th letter of S_1 to produce S_2 leads to an S_2 that is grammatical. So, in English, there is an "if-then" dependency in the sentence "If John loves Mary, then Mary loves John". One feature of finite-state grammars, however, is that for any such grammar there is a maximal span of dependence. More formally, there is an integer m such that no sentence S has a dependence spanning more than m letters. English, however, has no such maximal span. "If" and "then" can be separated by an arbitrarily large antecedent in the conditional. So, English cannot have this kind of grammar. Here Chomsky invokes a linguistic methodological principle to the effect that a grammar should generate all and only the set of sentences of the target language.

Chomsky's second model of grammar postulates that sentences have structure over and above the sequence of words. So-called "phrase structure grammars" propose that sentences have categories, such as noun phrase (NP) and verb phrase (VP), into which words ultimately fit (see Figure 5.1). (The fact that such categories are not manifest in the word stream of a sentence constitutes an implicit *prima facie* challenge to behaviorist analyses of verbal behavior.) A phrase structure grammar postulates a vocabulary V, a set of initial strings Σ, and a set of rules F of the form X → Y, meaning rewrite X as Y, where X, Y ∈ V. As a simple example of such a grammar, we have the following:

Σ: sentence
F: sentence → NP VP

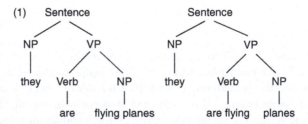

Figure 5.1 Two phrase structures for the string "They are flying planes"

VP → Verb NP
NP → they, plans
Verb → are flying, are

The comma in the third and fourth rules separate different options for replacing the left-hand elements. The application of these rules to Σ in one sequence allows for the construction on the left-hand side of (1), but in another sequence the construction on the right.

The foregoing simple grammar reveals a further limitation on finite state grammars. Notice that the English sentence "they are flying planes" is ambiguous. It can be understood as saying something like "those specks on the horizon are flying planes" or as something like "those pilots are flying planes". The word sequence alone cannot explain this ambiguity, but the differences in the derivations postulated by the phrase structure grammar can. This is a case of what Chomsky calls "constructional homonymy". Here again, Chomsky illustrates a methodological principle by which one can decide among possible grammars: grammars should illuminate the use and understanding of a language.

Within this second model of grammar, Chomsky distinguished context free grammars and context sensitive grammars. The difference is that in a context free grammar the rewrite rules of F allow only a single letter on the left of the "→", whereas in a context sensitive grammar one is allowed rules of the form ZXW → ZYW, meaning that X can be replaced by Y, when these occurrences are flanked by Z and W.

Chomsky's third model of language, transformational grammar, postulates three-part derivations of the sentences of a language. Setting aside all the details, the first part is a phrase structure grammar that generates a "kernel" of sentences of the language. Next, there are more complex transformational rules that transform the tree structures of sentences in the kernel. Because of this, they do something not permitted in the phrase structure component, namely, operate on the derivational history from the phrase structure grammar. Finally, there is a set of morphophonemic rules of the form X → Y, as found in the phrase structure component. These last rules give words (technically, morphemes) their phonemic form.

With the first two models, Chomsky was primarily concerned to find a generative structure that is sufficiently rich as to be able to produce all and only the strings in a given target language, such as English. With the transformational grammar, however, Chomsky focused on an apparatus that he believed would provide some insight into why a set of sentences in a language has the patterns it does. He wanted a grammatical structure with explanatory power. As an example, Chomsky considers three phrases, which we will label as Chomsky did.

(49)   the shooting of the hunters
(50)   the growling of the lions
(51)   the raising of the flowers

While superficially the same in structure, further reflection shows deeper differences. (49) is ambiguous. On one reading, the hunters are the subject of the phrase; they are doing the shooting. On the other reading, the hunters are the object of the phrase; they are the ones being shot. Neither (50) nor (51), however, is ambiguous. (50) only allows the lions to be the subject of the phrase; they are the ones doing the growling. By contrast, (51) only allows the flowers to be the object of the phrase. They are the things being raised. So, this gives us a linguistic phenomenon for which Chomsky sought an explanation. Why are there these patterns among these phrases?

Chomsky proposes that the phrase structure component of English generates two phrases, one of which has the hunters as the subject, e.g. "hunters shoot", and the other of which has the hunters as object, e.g. "they shoot the hunters". He then postulates that there is a transformation T_1 that takes the subject phrase into "the shooting of the hunters" and a second transformation T_2 that takes the object phrase into "the shooting of the hunters". The source of the ambiguity in (49) is, thus, traced back to the phrase structure grammar kernel. The phrase "lions growl" can be modified by T_1 to yield the growling of the lions, as in (50), but one cannot get the "object reading" of (50), because the kernel does not contain "they growled the lions", which could be acted on by T_2. Similarly, the phrase "they raised the flowers" to yield the raising of the flowers, as in (51), but one cannot get the "subject reading" because the kernel does not contain "flowers raised", which could be acted upon by T_1. Thus, Chomsky has resources with which to explain a pattern of sentences in English.

From the foregoing, we can see that Chomsky was concerned to provide some guidance regarding what a theory of grammar must be like, along with various methodological considerations that might be used to decide among candidate grammars for a language. As has been claimed, Chomsky was not, at the time, focused on automata theory or computation theory. Two additional observations might support the foregoing.

First, the three models of grammar to which Chomsky refers in the title of his paper (finite state grammars, phrase structure grammars, and transformational grammars) do not map onto the "models" to be found in the so-called "Chomsky hierarchy" of automata theory and computation theory.[8] While Chomsky (1956), played a seminal role in the development of this hierarchy, we should view this as something of a byproduct of Chomsky's principal interests. The Chomsky hierarchy contains finite state grammars, context free grammars, context sensitive grammars, and recursively enumerable grammars. Each of the grammars that appears later in the list generates a proper superset of the languages generated by grammars earlier in the list. Moreover, it was only later that the equivalences between grammars and automata/computing devices was proven. So, for example, it was the later Chomsky and Schützenberger (1963), paper that showed that context-free grammars could be linked to push-down automata. Landweber (1963) and Kuroda (1964) are sometimes credited with linking context sensitive grammars to linearly bounded automata. The link between recursively enumerable grammars and Turing machines was yet another result.

A second observation concerning Chomsky's interest in linguistics and relative lack of interest in Turing-equivalent computation may be found in comments in a slightly later paper. In 1959, he wrote,

> The weakest condition that can significantly be placed on grammars is that F be included in the class of general, unrestricted Turing machines. The strongest, most limiting condition that has been suggested is that each grammar be a finite Markovian source (finite automaton).
>
> The latter condition is known to be too strong; if F is limited in this way it will not contain a grammar for English (Chomsky, 1956). The former condition, on the other hand, has no interest. We learn nothing about a natural language from the fact that its sentences can be effectively displayed, i.e., that they constitute a recursively enumerable set.
>
> *(Chomsky, 1959, p. 138)*

What this does is reinforce the idea that Chomsky's 1956 project was, in the very first instance, directed to problems of grammar and that it was only later linked to Turing-equivalent computation and integrated into "the computational theory of mind".

Newell and Simon

Newell and Simon's contribution was something of a progress report. In the fall of 1955, Newell and Simon began work on a system that might prove theorems in logic, having a version of the program by December. By June 1956, they had written up their work in a RAND Corporation report, *The Logic Theory Machine: A Complex Information Processing System*.[9] By August, they had run the program on the RAND Corporation's JOHNNIAC computer.[10] Newell and Simon's contribution, thus, made direct use of Turing-equivalent computation by way of programmed digital computers. In their dense presentation, there was not much about their more theoretical views on the nature of reasoning in the mind. Instead, there were extensive discussions of the nuts and bolts concerning the formal aspects of their project. So, for example, Section I described the language, LL, in which the proofs would be written, Section II, the structure of the Logic Theorist program, and Section III simply presented the complete program for the Logic Theorist.[11]

McCulloch and Pitts (1943) had hinted cryptically at the possibility of Turing-equivalent computation constituting cognition. In the space of two sentences, they claimed that it is easily proved that some suitably configured neural networks of McCulloch-Pitts neurons could compute just the numbers that Turing machines could compute. They did not, however, spell out what a Turing machine is, what it is for a Turing machine to compute a number, or how the proof might go.[12] Turing (1950) defended the idea that such computing machines might perform like humans engaged in thought, leaving open, in theory, the idea that computing machines might actually think as do humans.[13]

Newell and Simon's Logic Theorist, however, went beyond the proposals of McCulloch, Pitts, and Turing in a number of concrete ways. First, the Logic Theorist was able to prove thirty-eight of the first fifty-two theorems of Chapter 2 of *Principia Mathematica*, thus showing that computers were more than mere "number factories".[14] Second, the Logic Theorist performed a task that was widely assumed to require thought or intelligence, namely, proving mathematical theorems. Third, the Logic Theorist developed one proof that was more elegant than the one produced by Whitehead and Russell, thereby making the case that a computer could display creativity. The thought here was that the program itself must have come up with the proof, since no one before, including Whitehead and Russell and Newell and Simon, had thought of the proof. The program could, in this sense, produce behavior that went above and beyond what went into it. Fourth, the Logic Theorist provided an account of the kinds of information-bearing structures and information processing that underlie behavior and that would make computers, or humans, intelligent. More specifically, the Logic Theorist embodied the idea that reasoning is a matter of heuristic search.

This last point bears some elaboration as this account of heuristic search embodied much of their theory of reasoning and proved to be extremely influential in subsequent work on artificial intelligence.[15] First, there is the idea of search. Simplifying somewhat, the Logic Theorist is given a theorem of sentential logic, such as $(P \rightarrow -P) \rightarrow P$. The thing sought – a proof – is a sequence of sentences that ends with the theorem. Each sentence in the sequence must be either (a) the standard definition of the material conditional ("$P \rightarrow Q$" as "$-P \vee Q$", where P and Q are schematic letters), (b) one of five axiom schemata, or (c) a sentence derived from one or more preceding sentences by the application of one of four inference rules. Figuring out how to prove a theorem is, thus, a matter of searching for a sequence of sentences that satisfy these conditions.

Next, there is a distinction between algorithms and heuristics. An algorithmic search for a proof would be one that works systematically through all possible sequences of sentences starting with the definition and axiom schemata and ending when finding a sequence of sentences that constitutes a correct proof. It might first check whether the theorem is an instance of the definition schema for the material conditional or one of the five axioms. Next it might check whether the theorem can be obtained by application of one of the inference rules to one or more of the definitions or axiom schemata or earlier theorems. The immediate problem with such an algorithmic solution is that the space of options grows exponentially. Finding a proof this way is practically impossible. In contrast, heuristic search is a matter of using problem-specific information that enables one to pare down the number of options one considers. It is a matter of, say, knowing something about logic, over and above the specification of the proof system. Heuristic search, one might say, is a matter of knowing where to look among the many options. It is this "knowing where to look" that becomes the essence of intelligence and reasoning.

Consider how Turing-equivalent computation figures in Newell and Simon's project. As noted above, in passing, Newell and Simon used an electronic digital computer, JOHNNIAC, to run their Logic Theorist system. Surely, one might think, this shows that they were committed to the idea that cognition is a kind of Turing-equivalent computation. Yet, that is not, apparently, how they thought of the matter. In their subsequent, more theoretical, discussion of the Logic Theorist, Newell, Shaw, and Simon wrote,

> Our position is that the appropriate way to describe a piece of problem-solving behavior is in terms of a program: a specification of what the organism will do under varying environmental circumstances in terms of certain elementary information processes it is capable of performing. This assertion has nothing to do – directly – with computers. Such programs could be written (now that we have discovered how to do it) if computers had never existed. A program is no more, and no less, an analogy to the behavior of an organism than is a differential equation to the behavior of the electrical circuit it describes. Digital computers come into the picture only because they can, by appropriate programming, be induced to execute the same sequences of information processes that humans execute when they are solving problems.
>
> *(Newell, Shaw, and Simon, 1958, p. 153)*

For Newell, Shaw, and Simon, the electronic digital computer is not a model for the mind; they do not – at this point in time – take the mind to be a computer. Instead, they used electronic digital computers as tools for rapidly and precisely churning out the results of their theory of cognition; they are tools for simulating the mind, rather than instantiating the mind. Its role in their work on human psychology is, in this regard, much like the use it might have in a theory of the weather.[16] In a related vein, Newell, Shaw, and Simon did not, at this time, take the mathematical apparatus of Turing-equivalent computational processes to be a mathematics that, even under idealizations such as infinite memory, describes cognitive processes. As with Miller and Chomsky, Newell and Simon were focused on a relatively narrow concern that was only later linked to Turing-equivalent computation and "the computational theory of mind".

Conclusion

Without a doubt the development of the Turing machine and its computational equivalents was an intellectual achievement of the first order, so it is not at all surprising that there have been many cognitive scientists who have put the theory to good use as the basis for a theory of cognition. The hypothesis that cognitive processes are computational processes run on a Turing-equivalent computing machine has certainly received, and certainly deserves, considerable empirical and theoretical attention.

Nevertheless, we should be careful to avoid a simplistic reading of history. Many Turing-equivalent formalisms first appeared in close succession during the mid-1930s, McCulloch and Pitts alluded to them briefly in their seminal and widely-referenced "Logical Calculus" of 1943, and Turing himself was inspired by them in his famous "Computing Machinery and Intelligence" of 1950. So, it is natural to suppose that by the mid-1950s, the theory of Turing-equivalence formalisms was among the founding conceptions of the cognitive revolution. As natural as this may be, however, there are developments in the cognitive revolution – indeed widely respected, seminal developments – where Turing-equivalent computation played at most a secondary role.

This paper has reviewed a few illustrations of the point. Miller's "magic number seven" had little use for Turing-equivalent computation. For Miller, a primary goal was to break away from the tools of formal information theory as a tool for understanding psychological processes. For Chomsky, a primary goal was to understand the structure of grammars of natural language. For Newell and Simon, the primary goal was to advance a theory of reasoning as a matter of heuristic search. For them, computers were merely a tool for quickly showing the consequences of their theory of reasoning. Given their interests, it is not surprising that Miller, Newell, and Simon were not immediately interested in Turing-equivalent computation.

Notes

1 See, e.g., Pylyshyn (1989), Rescorla (2015), and Sprevak (2017). As an exception to the rule, there is Horst (2003). The use of the phrase "Turing-equivalent computation" is meant to sidestep a number of issues. This includes questions about what computation "really" is and what to say about other notions of computation, such as analog computation or hypercomputation. (See, e.g., Copeland, 2002; Pour-El, 1974). It is also meant to be more descriptively informative than is Piccinini's "modern computational theory" (cf. Piccinini, 2004), Piccinini and Scarantino's "digital computation" (cf. Piccinini and Scarantino, 2010), or Rescorla's "Classical Computational Theory of Mind" (cf. Rescorla, 2015).
2 For discussion of these sorts of features, see Rogers (1967), or Rescorla (2015).
3 Another misleading aspect of the references to Turing machines and Turing-equivalent computation is that computation in cognitive science is all about Turing-equivalent computation. See Aizawa (2010).
4 Of course, one famous instance in which Turing machines did play this role was Putnam (1960).
5 Each of these was published in volume 3, issue 2 of the *IRE Transactions on Information Theory*. For some assessment of the significance of these works, see Miller (2003), Bechtel, Abrahamsen, and Graham (2001), Thagard (1996).
6 For a contemporary presentation of this body of theory, see Hopcroft, Motwani, and Ullman (2006), or Sipser (2006).
7 The scope of this project becomes apparent in the light of Chomsky (1955; 1957; 1959).
8 For more on the hierarchy, see Hopcroft, Motwani, and Ullman (2006).
9 See Newell and Simon (1956a).
10 For additional details, see Gugerty (2006); Simon (1996).
11 One elaboration on the ideas implicit in this work may be found in Newell, Shaw, and Simon (1958).
12 For more extensive discussion, see Aizawa (2010).
13 This is not a novel point. It is made in Sprevak (2017), for example.
14 See Feigenbaum and Feldman (1963) for comments on this concern.
15 As an early indicator of this influence, see Feigenbaum and Feldman (1963).
16 Miller seems to support this analysis when he claims "Alan Newell and Herb Simon were using computers to simulate cognitive processes" (Miller, 2003, p. 142).

References

Aizawa, K. (2010) 'Computation in Cognitive Science: It Is Not All about Turing-Equivalent Computation', *Studies in History and Philosophy of Science Part A*, 41 (3), pp. 227–236.

Bechtel, W., Abrahamsen, A., and Graham, G. (2001) 'Cognitive Science, History', *International Encyclopedia of the Social and Behavioral Sciences*. Oxford: Elsevier Science, pp. 2154–2158.

Chomsky, N. (1955) 'The Logical Structure of Linguistic Theory (mimeograph)', *The Logical Structure of Linguistic Theory*. New York, NY: Springer.

Chomsky, N. (1956) 'Three Models for the Description of Language', *IRE Transactions on Information Theory*, 2 (3), pp. 113–124.

Chomsky, N. (1957) *Syntactic Structures*. Berlin: Walter de Gruyter.

Chomsky, N. (1959) 'On Certain Formal Properties of Grammars', *Information and Control*, 2 (2), pp. 137–167.

Chomsky, N. and Schützenberger, M.P. (1963) 'The Algebraic Theory of Context-Free Languages', *Studies in Logic and the Foundations of Mathematics*, 35, pp. 118–161.

Copeland, B.J. (2002) 'Hypercomputation', *Minds and Machines*, 12 (4), pp. 461–502.

Feigenbaum, E.A. and Feldman, J. (1963) *Computers and Thought*. New York, NY: McGraw-Hill.

Gugerty, L. (2006) 'Newell and Simon's Logic Theorist: Historical Background and Impact on Cognitive Modeling', *Proceedings of the Human Factors and Ergonomics Society Annual Meeting*, 50 (9), pp. 880–884.

Hopcroft, J.E., Motwani, R., and Ullman, J.D. (2006) *Introduction to Automata Theory, Languages, and Computation*, 3rd ed. River, NJ: Pearson Education.

Horst, S. (2003) 'The Computational Theory of Mind', *The Stanford Encyclopedia of Philosophy*, December 10, Zalta, E.N. (ed.), Available at: http://plato.stanford.edu/archives/sum2015/entries/computational-mind (Accessed: November 27, 2015).

Kuroda, S-Y. (1964) 'Classes of Languages and Linear-bounded Automata', *Information and Control*, 7 (2), pp. 207–223.

Landweber, P.S. (1963) 'Three Theorems on Phrase Structure Grammars of Type 1', *Information and Control*, 6 (2), pp. 131–136.

McCulloch, W.S. and Pitts, W. (1943) 'A Logical Calculus of the Ideas Immanent in Nervous Activity', *Bulletin of Mathematical Biology*, 5 (4), pp. 115–133.

Miller, G.A. (1956a) 'The Magical Number Seven, Plus or Minus Two: Some Limits on Our Capacity for Processing Information', *Psychological Review*, 63 (2), p. 81.

Miller, G.A. (1956b) 'Human Memory and the Storage of Information', *IRE Transactions on Information Theory*, 2 (3), pp. 129–137.

Miller, G.A. (2003) 'The Cognitive Revolution: A Historical Perspective', *Trends in Cognitive Sciences*, 7 (3), pp. 141–144.

Newell, A., Shaw, J.C., and Simon, H.A. (1958) 'Elements of a Theory of Human Problem Solving', *Psychological Review*, 65 (3), pp. 151–166.

Newell, A. and Simon, H. (1956a) *The Logic Theory Machine: A Complex Information Processing System*. A RAND Corporation report, June 15.

Piccinini, G. (2004) 'The First Computational Theory of Mind and Brain: A Close Look at McCulloch and Pitts' "Logical Calculus of Ideas Immanent in Nervous Activity"', *Synthese*, 141 (2), pp. 175–215.

Piccinini, G. and Scarantino, A. (2010) 'Computation vs. Information Processing: Why Their Difference Matters to Cognitive Science', *Studies in History and Philosophy of Science Part A*, 41 (3), pp. 237–246.

Pour-El, M.B. (1974) 'Abstract Computability and Its Relation to the General Purpose Analog Computer (Some Connections between Logic, Differential Equations and Analog Computers)', *Transactions of the American Mathematical Society*, 199, pp. 1–28.

Putnam, H. (1960) 'Minds and Machines', in Hook, S. (ed.) *Dimensions of Mind*. New York, NY: New York University Press, pp. 57–80.

Pylyshyn, Z.W. (1989) 'Computation in Cognitive Science', in Posner, M.I. (ed.) *Foundations of Cognitive Science*. Cambridge, MA: MIT Press, pp. 51–91.

Rescorla, M. (2015) 'The Computational Theory of Mind', *The Stanford Encyclopedia of Philosophy*, October 16, Zalta, E.N. (ed.), Available at: http://plato.stanford.edu/archives/win2015/entries/computational-mind (Accessed: October 27, 2017).

Rogers, H. (1967) *Theory of Recursive Functions and Effective Computability*. New York, NY: McGraw-Hill.

Shannon, C.E. (1948) 'A Mathematical Theory of Communication', *Bell System Technical Journal*, 27 (3), pp. 379–423.

Simon, H.A. (1996) *Models of My Life*. Cambridge, MA: MIT Press.

Sipser, M. (2006) *Introduction to the Theory of Computation*, 2nd ed. Boston, MA: Thomson Course Technology.

Sprevak, M. (2017) 'Turing's Model of the Mind', in Copeland, J., Bowen, J., Sprevak, M., and Wilson, R. (eds.) *The Turing Guide*. Oxford: Oxford University Press, pp. 277–285.

Thagard, P. (1996) 'Cognitive Science', *The Stanford Encyclopedia of Philosophy*, September 23, Zalta, E.N. (ed.), Available at: https://plato.stanford.edu/archives/fall2014/entries/cognitive-science (Accessed: November 23, 2016).

Turing, A.M. (1950) 'Computing Machinery and Intelligence', *Mind*, 59 (236), pp. 433–460.

Whitehead, A. and Russell, B. (1910) *Principia Mathematica*. Cambridge, UK: Cambridge University Press.

6

CONNECTIONISM AND POST-CONNECTIONIST MODELS

Cameron Buckner and James Garson

This entry covers the past and present development of connectionism in three sections: "Roots", "Revolution", and "Radiation". Roots summarizes the first efforts to assemble neuron-like elements into network models of cognitive function. It includes McCulloch and Pitts' demonstration that their nets can compute any logical function, Rosenblatt's perceptrons, and Hebb's learning rule. The section ends with Minsky and Papert's famous complaint that perceptrons and other simple architectures cannot calculate certain Boolean functions. This sets the stage for a discussion of implementational vs radical interpretations of connectionist modeling. The second section describes the innovations that led to the PDP revolution of the 1980s, including sigmoidal and other activation functions, backpropagation, multi-level nets, and the introduction of simple recurrence. The section explains the new enthusiasm for these models, especially for the power of distributed representations that they employ, and ends with problems that influenced further developments, including the biological implausibility of backpropagation and scaling problems like catastrophic interference. The third section, "Radiation", examines a variety of more recent advances since the PDP heyday. These include multi-network architectures, biologically inspired alternatives to backpropagation, simulations of the effects of neuromodulators, deep convolutional networks, and comparisons between deep learning and Bayesian approaches.

Roots

The early history of connectionism was guided by growing knowledge about the neurological structure of the brain. Once it was clear the brain tissue was composed of cells (neurons) with projecting fibers (axons) connected to input fibers (dendrites) of neighboring neurons, it was natural to try to model the brain and its cognitive abilities with neural networks, collections of neurons with their accompanying connections (synapses). The fundamental questions to solve were:

1 What does a neuron do?
2 How do the synapses affect neural activity?
3 How can neural networks manage to perform useful cognitive tasks?
4 How can neural networks evolve and learn?

The idea that cognitive abilities are the result of connections or associations between components has a long history going from Aristotle through the British Empiricists. It has been an inspiration for the psychological theories of Spencer (1855), James (1890), Lashley (1929), and Thorndike (1932). As more detailed knowledge about neural structure and function developed into the twentieth century, hopes were raised that useful theories about exactly how neural networks could be capable of thought would be in the offing.

The work of McCulloch and Pitts (1949) made a crucial contribution. Their simple binary threshold model of neuron functioning was the first of a series of detailed answers to questions (1) and (2). More importantly, they were able to offer a proof that such nets have computation powers appropriate for cognition, which is an answer in principle to question (3). In the previous decade, Alan Turing (1936) proposed a mathematical characterization of the class of tasks that can be carried out by any rule-governed symbolic process, what we now call the Turing computable functions. McCulloch and Pitts (M&P) showed that their networks are capable of computing basic logical operations, and this yielded a proof that neural nets can perform any task that is Turing-computable. Presuming that thought involves such a process, an explanation of how the brain could think was forthcoming: the neurons of the brain implement a computer that is intrinsically capable of carrying out any rule-governed activity.

But basing a theory of brain function on the model of a computer performing symbolic computation has its downsides. For example, even if a M&P net exists in principle that performs a given complex cognitive function, the architecture needed to carry that out would take immense time and ingenuity for a human to design, construct, test, and refine. How did such intricate and delicate structures come to reside in the brain? In short, there was no clear idea about how to answer question (4).

One strategy for answering this question, which was followed by those who came to be called connectionists, was to look at the computational abilities of simple generic neural layouts, or architectures, and to see how structure might be generated in them via a process that simulates learning. An important inspiration for this strategy was Hebb's proposal (1949) that learning results from strengthening connections between units that act in concert.

Rosenblatt (1958) refined Hebb's suggestions by formulating them in full mathematical detail. He focused on simple two-layer network models, which he called *perceptrons*. Synaptic connections between the two layers (inputs and outputs) were modeled with negative and positive values called *weights*. The weight between input neuron n_i and output neuron n_o was multiplied by the activity of n_i to represent the degree to which n_i's firing contributed to the firing or failure to fire of its target neuron n_o. Two-level networks are essentially limited in their computational abilities. Minsky and Papert famously proved that they cannot even compute the exclusive or truth function (Minsky and Papert, 1969). However, Rosenblatt proposed a learning method for perceptrons and proved that it had the ability to learn any task that perceptrons are capable of performing. Some of his systems also incorporated "trial and error" learning. Here the difference between the actual and desired behavior of the net is calculated (the *error*), and weights are increased or decreased in directions that would minimize that error. Such supervised learning contrasts with Hebb's unsupervised method where associations develop autonomously without feedback on how well the learning process is proceeding.

McCulloch and Pitts' seminal work on how to compute logical functions with networks had a second and very different impact. It was part of the inspiration for the invention of digital computers. As those computers became available and their computational powers increased, it was possible for connectionists, who had previously evaluated their proposals with paper and pencil, to use computers to empirically test the capabilities of their neural network models.

While this provided important new tools, it also generated competition from what we now call the classical or symbolic processing paradigm in artificial intelligence (AI) research. AI researchers developed programs that could mimic human cognitive achievements such as playing checkers (Samuel, 1967), solving word problems in algebra (Bobrow, 1967), or problem-solving in general (Newell and Simon, 1963). Here there was little concern for how these tasks might be performed by the neural assemblies of the brain. The idea was that understanding human intellectual achievements can be carried out at the symbolic processing level, and that while interesting, the problem of how these abilities are actually implemented in the brain is irrelevant to the explanation of cognition.

The canonical story about the history of connectionism in the 1960s is to describe a battle between advocates of the classical paradigm on one hand, and connectionists like Rosenblatt on the other. Classicists supposedly won thanks to Minsky and Papert's (1969) proof that Rosenblatt's perceptrons could not compute the exclusive or function. Rosenblatt was well aware that his two-layer nets had limited capabilities (Rosenblatt, 1958 p. 404), but he held out hope that more could be done with more complex systems. Minsky and Papert conceded that nets with additional layers could overcome the limitations in principle, but lacking a way to extend Rosenblatt's training methods to multi-layered nets, they wrote: "there is no reason to suppose that any of [the perceptron's] virtues carry over to the many-layered versions ... [but it is] an important research problem to elucidate ... our intuitive judgment that the extension is sterile" (1969, p. 232). Minsky and Papert's book was supposed to have demolished support for connectionist research in favor of the classical paradigm. While the effect surely was negative, connectionist research went on, notably in the work of Anderson (1972), Kohonen (1972), and Grossberg (1976), all of which was important for the revolution to come.

Revolution

The 1980s were the Golden Age of Connectionism. Two factors led to its resurgence. The first was widespread unhappiness in the progress of research within the classical paradigm. The early successes in the 1960s led to unrealistic expectations that computers would be programmed to match the intelligence of humans in a decade or two. For example, Herbert Simon predicted "machines will be capable, within twenty years, of doing any work a man can do" (Simon, 1965, p. 96). Not only were those goals not met, the consensus at the end of the 1970s was that the failure to deliver on those promises provided no new lessons that would offer hope for the future. Time was ripe for something new.

The second factor supporting the connectionist resurgence was the culmination of refinements in neural network modeling carried out in the 1970s. Several innovations led to this success, but the most important was the deployment of the backpropagation algorithm for training multi-layered nets, which was first described in Paul Werbos' doctoral dissertation (eventually published in 1994). Experimentation with backpropagation showed that Minsky and Papert's reservations were misguided – there was indeed a way to successfully train multi-layered nets.

Backpropagation works by first calculating the error at the output layer O, which is simply the difference between an output neuron's actual activity and the activity desired. Then neurons in the "hidden" layer H that project to neurons in O are examined, and an error for each is determined by the degree to which its activation would cause (or correct) errors at the output units. Weights between the output and hidden layers are then adjusted slightly in the direction that would minimize error at the output. The same algorithm is applied again to the next layer of neurons that project to those in layer H, and so on all the way back to the input layer. If we imagine a landscape in a space with a dimension for each weight and where the height of the terrain is the error for a given set of weight values, then backpropagation can be seen as a method for traversing the space in the direction that will find the lowest point (lowest error). A secret to the success of backpropagation was the use of graded values for both the activity of neurons and the weights, which smoothed the error landscape so that a search for a minimum was more likely to succeed.

Sejnowski and Rosenberg's (1987) NETtalk, a system that could learn to pronounce English text, was an influential demonstration of the power of backpropagation learning. The data used to train NETtalk contained a large corpus of English words paired with their corresponding phonetic renderings written in a code suitable for controlling a speech synthesizer. Not only did NETtalk learn to accurately associate the text on which it was trained with the correct pronunciation starting from randomly assigned weights, it did a good job of generalizing what it had learned to words that were not in the training set. It was especially impressive that a neural net could learn a task that had posed a genuine challenge to programmers in the classical paradigm. Being able to actually hear the improvement in performance as training proceeded also provided an engaging display.

Rumelhart and McClelland (1986) used backpropagation to train nets to predict the past tense of English verbs. The task is interesting because although most verbs in English form the past tense by adding the suffix '-ed', many of the most frequently used verbs are irregular. After carefully designed training, the network did a good job in learning the past tense of verbs in the training set, and it generalized fairly well to novel verbs, including some irregulars. Rumelhart and McClelland pointed out that partially trained nets displayed overgeneralization errors – such as conjugating 'break' to 'broked' – that are common among children learning English. While this was touted as a sign of the faithfulness of their models, a major controversy ensued concerning just how well their models did match data on actual learning. For example, Pinker and Prince (1988) complained that the system does a poor job with some novel regular verbs, and they used this to argue that neural nets have fundamental limitations in learning general rules. This raised an important issue for connectionist modelers – to demonstrate that nets can learn to generalize properly to approximate rule-based processing that is straightforward from the classical point of view.

The Golden Age reached its apogee with the publication of *Parallel Distributed Processing* (McClelland, Rumelhart et al., 1986), what some considered the "connectionist's bible". This two-volume work both reflected and shaped the burst of new activity that started in the 1980s. Backpropagation held center stage, but the book collected together a wide range of other innovations. It also included a well-organized and sometimes passionate argument for the connectionist paradigm. This clear summary of evidence in favor of connectionism (and a frank admission of some of its failings) set the stage for controversy about the merits of the two paradigms.

Of course one argument was bound to be that neural nets were more faithful to what we know about the physiology of the brain. But there were arguments at the cognitive level as well. For example, neural nets showed a much more robust and realistic response to damage and to noisy input. The loss or random modification of units in a classical computer typically causes catastrophic failure (or none at all, as in the loss of an unused memory location). However, when units of a connectionist model trained with backpropagation are removed, or their connections randomly modified, the network usually continues to function appropriately, albeit less accurately. This "graceful degradation" of function is arguably an essential feature of the brain, which routinely suffers damage and/or random fluctuations in the input.

Another argument in their favor is that neural nets are essentially parallel computers and so especially well adapted to solving problems that require the satisfaction of multiple constraints – such as object recognition, planning, and motor coordination. Although classical computers can be designed with multiple parallel processors, it was argued that the parallel processing solutions offered by neural nets are more natural and efficient. An important consideration in the argument came to be called the 100-step constraint (Feldman and Ballard, 1982). When neurons fire, they require a few milliseconds before they can be active again. Since many complex cognitive abilities (such as recognizing a human face) are accomplished in the 100 millisecond range, it follows that these tasks would have to be carried out in no more than 100 steps on a standard serial computer. But programs actually written to perform such tasks on serial machines require many thousands or even millions of steps. The massively parallel architecture offered by connectionist models promised to explain how the brain manages to perform in a timely way.

A third advantage for connectionism touted by Rumelhart et al. stems from the powerful forms of representation found in neural nets. Networks trained with backpropagation and other learning techniques develop and store information needed to solve a given problem in ways that are unforeseen in the classical paradigm. For example, analysis of NETtalk showed that it learned to represent consonants and vowels not by creating one unit which was active when a vowel was presented, and another for a consonant, but instead by representing the two cases with two different patterns of activity across all the units. This distributed representation of acquired knowledge has the advantage that it will be gracefully degraded if the net is damaged.

These novel representational methods offer other intriguing advantages. Philosophers have generally abandoned the project of defining concepts (say: tiger) through hard and fast rules. Proposed definitions (large striped feline) seem unavoidably prone to exceptions (baby albino tigers). A more attractive option is to think of concepts along the lines of family resemblance (Wittgenstein, 1953, sec. 67) or similarity to a prototype (Rosch, 1975). Here clusters of features help define the degree to which a person shares familial features, although there are no necessary or sufficient conditions for family membership. Representations in connectionist models seem especially well suited to capturing this kind of graded information that lies beyond what can be captured in hard and fast rules (Horgan and Tienson, 1989).

Although evidence for connectionism was persuasive to many in its heyday, a number of worries emerged that have persisted ever since. The first is that the proposed models, especially models of learning processes like backpropagation, may not be so faithful after all, given what we know about the physiology of the brain. First, neural conduction proceeds in a single direction from input (dendrites) to output (axons), but backpropagation requires that an error signal be sent in the reverse direction during training. Some believe in the existence of reverse mechanisms devoted to sending error information (Fitzsimonds, Song, and Poo, 1997), but anatomical information supporting that view has not been persuasive enough to sway all critics (Crick, 1989). More recent work has revealed new mechanisms that might implement backpropagation more faithfully, some of which are mentioned in "Radiation" below. (See Rogers and McClelland, 2014, sec. 5.1 for a recent summary.)

A second matter of deep concern is the massive number of repetitions that are required to train a net to solve even simple problems. Somehow the brain manages to learn using many orders of magnitude fewer repetitions. In fact, there are clear cases where humans master a task from a single case. Such "one-shot" learning is a profound challenge for connectionism. Not only that, but training a net properly can be something of a "black art", involving everything from careful management of how data is presented, to choosing the right parameters concerning the rate of change of the connection values during learning, to selecting the right numbers of units and levels in the architecture, to say nothing of luck.

A third worry may be even more significant: the problem of scale. Research in the classical paradigm was bedeviled by the concern that solutions for toy problems (such as analyzing the grammatical structure of short sentences constructed from a score of English words) fail to work when "scaled up" to tasks found in the real world (analyzing sentences of English in general). Connectionists face a similar problem, namely that training methods used for toy problems fail to generalize to other tasks and more realistic training situations. The clearest and most significant form of this problem has been called "catastrophic interference" or "catastrophic forgetting", the tendency of networks to lose previously learned solutions to classification problems when exposed to new training data (McCloskey and Cohen, 1989). The problem is that connection weight changes required to solve new problems can interfere with the connections required to solve old problems, often overwriting them entirely. This made it very difficult to train the same network over time to solve multiple categorization tasks, something that humans and animals can easily do.

A final objection to connectionism has generated a large literature, especially among philosophers. The focus of the attack was Fodor and Pylyshyn's (1988) claim that connectionists are unable to explain the systematicity of cognition, unless they concede to classicists by adopting classical architecture. Since systematicity is crucial for higher-level cognitive achievements such as language and reasoning, connectionist models are in trouble. By the systematicity of cognition, Fodor and Pylyshyn (F&P) mean that the ability to process one sentence is intrinsically related to the ability to process others with similar structure. For example, anyone who is able to understand 'John loves Mary' also understands 'Mary loves John'. Classicists explain systematicity by assuming that English speakers compute the meaning of 'John loves Mary' by knowing the meanings of the words 'John', 'loves', and 'Mary', and a rule that allows one to determine the meaning of a sentence from the meanings of its constituents. If that is correct, the ability to understand 'Mary loves John' comes for free. F&P grant that connectionists may be able to train nets that recognize both 'John loves Mary' and 'Mary loves John'. The complaint, however, is that nothing about connectionist architecture guarantees that success on one of these tasks entails success on the other. Since purely connectionist networks do not explain systematicity, they are inadequate models of language and reasoning.

The responses to F&P by connectionists and their allies have generated a substantial literature that continues to the present day. Many have pointed out (Aizawa, 1997; Matthews, 1997; Hadley, 1997) that classical architectures do no better at explaining systematicity because there are also classical models that recognize 'John loves Mary' without being able to recognize 'Mary loves John'. In both architectures, further assumptions about the nature of the processing must be made to ensure that 'Mary loves John' and 'John loves Mary' are treated alike. A useful product of the controversy has been a much more careful analysis of the concept of systematicity, in the form of a series of benchmarks (Hadley, 1994) for determining whether the challenge had been met. This led to more focused experimentation on the issue. Whether connectionists have met the most stringent of the systematicity requirements is still controversial. (For a review see Calvo and Symons, 2014.)

The majority of research in the Golden Age used feed-forward nets where information flows in only one direction, from a set of input units (perceptual neurons), through one or more levels of hidden units, to a set of output units (akin to motor neurons). Loops in the flow of information were outlawed, mainly because of difficulties they caused for training. However, the restriction to feed-forward nets is costly, because such a net has no memory of the sequence of steps that occurred during a computation, and that memory is crucial to cognitive tasks such as language processing and even motor control. Elman (1991) deployed a partial solution to the problem with nets that copied activation from the hidden layer back to the input level. He was able to display good results with nets designed to master such relatively difficult problems as subject–verb agreement across intervening relative clauses. This has inspired a school working on connectionist language processing. (For summaries see Christiansen and Chater, 1994; and Rhode and Plaut, 2004.) However, complaints that those nets do not display true mastery of rules persist (Marcus, 1998; 2001).

Work on training nets to manage linguistic tasks has drawn attention to novel forms of representation. The classical view emphasizes the idea that a representation (say 'John loves Mary') requires symbolic constituents ('John', 'loves' and 'Mary') that indicate objects or properties of the world. Constituency is presumed to be essential to efficient coding of information. In connectionist nets, information is captured in the patterns of activation through time of all the neurons. While these patterns may have components, such as the activities of individual neurons, those components are "subsymbolic", in the sense that there is no obvious way to assign them any representational content. The distributed activation that occurs for a complex expression like 'John loves Mary' need not contain any explicit representation of its parts. Although the information about the constituents 'John', 'loves' and 'Mary' can be uncovered through statistical study of net activation patterns, there is no sign that the net needs to explicitly extract this information itself in order to perform language processing tasks (Chalmers, 1990).

Analysis of the linguistic processing performed by Elman's nets illustrates a related idea. The net needed to distinguish grammatical from ungrammatical "sentences" containing relative clauses. The challenge for the sentence below is that 'man' (singular) selects 'runs' despite the intervening plural nouns 'dogs' and 'cats', which select 'run'.

Any **man** that chases dogs that chase cats runs.

When successfully trained to perform such tasks, a statistical analysis of the net's trajectory through the space of all possible activation patterns showed that there was a region of the space containing similar activations that was visited during the processing of Noun Phrases, with subregions for a singular or plural head nouns. During processing of each relative clause following 'man', the trajectory cycled around in that part of the space for a singular head noun, and this explained how the net "knew" to prefer 'runs' despite the distractions posed by the presence of 'dogs' and 'cats'. This illustrates the power of distributed representations to capture complex multidimensional information that helps regulate linguistic processing.

Although activation trajectory coding in a similarity space of activations is an intriguing way to look at the storage and deployment of information about language and the world, Fodor and Lepore (1999) complain that it is simply not up to the task of explaining linguistic meaning. The computation of meaning, they argue, is compositional, that is, the meaning of a complex expression is determined by repeated application of rules that operate on the meaning of its constituents. But similarity alone, they claim, cannot account for compositionality. Since it does not tell the whole story, classical representations with genuine constituency will be needed to fill in the gaps. Churchland (1998) shows that at least some of Fodor and Lepore's objections can be met, although Calvo Garzon (2003) raises new worries. Calvo Garzon's main objection is that if you and I mean the same thing by 'grandmother', then your brain activation pattern for this word and mine must be quite similar. But you and I have massively different collateral information about our grandmothers, so those activation patterns will end up being very different. The problem of collateral information is a challenging one, for it is a non-trivial matter for a theory of representation to disentangle the concepts we share from differences in information we have about them. In any case, further research on neural nets and the brain will be needed to assess the importance of non-classical forms of representation.

One might consider Elman's work to be something of a concession to classicists. The use of simple recurrent nets concedes that some provision for short-term memory is needed and processing memory is a central feature of classical architectures. However, research in the Golden Age was often unconcerned about preserving connectionist "purity" in all conceivable respects. For example, Smolensky (1991) is famous for inventing so-called tensor product methods that allow nets to store information on sentence constituents and to simulate the process of variable binding, both of which are considered classical features.

Evaluation of the debate between classicists and connectionists is complicated by the invention of hybrid architectures containing some classical features (Wermter and Sun, 2000). Miikkulainen (1993) championed an architecture containing different modules that share data coded in activation patterns. The system resembled a classical processor with separate mechanisms for storing and operating on digital "words". This irenic use of hybrid architectures illustrates that many connectionists do not perceive of the classical/connectionist divide as a battlefield (Berkeley, 1997). If hybrid models turn out to be the best accounts of the brain, then the controversy will be moot, for whether classical architecture is required to explain cognition may end up being a matter of degree.

Radiation

The third period that we review – which takes place from roughly 1995 to the present – is marked by a less unified spreading of connectionist research in new directions. Its ambitions tempered and limitations better understood, connectionism ceased to occupy its position as the "next big paradigm", with dynamical systems theory and (later) predictive coding having captured the hearts of revolutionaries (Chemero and Faries, this volume; Hohwy, this volume). Alternatively, Mayor et al. (2014) argue that this loss of the spotlight reflects not the failure of connectionism, but rather its maturation, together with the integration of its central ideas – parallelism, distributed representation, gradual learning, and the importance of reproducing subjects' errors as well as correct performance – into mainstream cognitive science. Either way, connectionist and post-connectionist approaches remain a popular default choice for modelers today, and new advances have continued to push the method's boundaries beyond previous expectations. Gradually, more and more ambitious tweaks have accumulated, made more feasible by further advances in hardware, especially the availability of inexpensive and powerful graphics processing units that can be optimized for training neural networks. In hindsight, one can trace an evolution from standard three-layer connectionist networks to some of the most powerful post-connectionist models today, such as deep convolutional networks, which are characterized by many layers of processing, more efficient forms of backpropagation, fewer non-local connections between layers, and the interpolation of layers with different dedicated functions like convolution and pooling.

Many of the most promising advances arose directly from attempts to address the limitations discussed in the previous section. For example, consider the problem of catastrophic interference, which made it difficult for networks to scale up beyond limited toy classification problems. In practice, avoiding interference often involved carefully interlacing training exemplars for different categorization tasks in the network's training set, so that the connections representing solutions to previous problems were constantly renewed by "refresher" examples. This solution involved rendering training sets yet more biologically implausible, however, as the networks could no longer learn from randomized training data or learn new problems sequentially over time, as humans and animals often do.

Taking inspiration from the larger-scale neuroanatomy of the brain, McClelland, McNaughton, and O'Reilly (1995) proposed that this problem was also faced by biological brains, but was solved through the cooperation of different neural networks with different architectures interacting with one another over time. One network – corresponding to the medial temporal lobes – was regarded as a short-term memory buffer with a rapid learning rate, and another – corresponding to the neocortex – was treated as a long-term memory storage system with a much slower learning rate. The trick was to allow catastrophic interference in the short-term MTL network, which could learn to solve many different problems quickly, and then gradually transfer newly-learned MTL-network representations to the neocortical network over longer periods of time, using interspersed training sessions – which were argued to correspond to patterns of memory consolidation during REM sleep and daydreaming in mammalian brains. Such complementary multi-network architectures are especially popular in cognitive neuroscience, as brain lesions can be simulated by disabling connections between different networks and comparing the resultant performance to the behavior of real lesion patients. Multi-network architectures have been used to model a variety of other phenomena, including not only associative learning and memory (e.g. Gluck and Myers, 1993; 2001) but also interactions between basal ganglia and frontal cortex in working memory (Frank, Loughry, and O'Reilly, 2001) consciousness (Maia and Cleeremans, 2005), and multimodal integration (Bergman et al., 2013).

Another major source of innovation in connectionist theory concerns research on more biologically plausible alternatives to the backpropagation learning rule, with many different alternatives explored. One popular method that can achieve backpropogation-like performance involves activation "recirculation", either using bidirectional activation connections or recurrent connections to transmit error signals around the network without a separate mechanism for backpropagation (Hinton and McClelland, 1988; O'Reilly, 1996). Another family of techniques returns to biological reinforcement learning for inspiration, adjusting weights up a gradient towards reward expectation (rather than error minimization) using a global reward signal (Williams, 1992). So-called "neural gas" networks can learn optimal data representations through a simple Hebb-like rule to gradually adjust activation vectors so that they spread apart and cover a problem's feature space like an expanding gas (Martinetz, Berkovich, and Schulten, 1993; Fritzke, 1995). Other attempts to make connectionist learning more biologically plausible have emphasized the role of neurotransmitters and neuromodulators (such as dopamine and acetylcholine), modeling their effects by bringing about global changes in model parameters such as learning rates or activation functions. Such networks are additionally useful in modeling psychopathologies, which often involve atypical levels of such chemicals (Cohen and Servan-Schreiber, 1992; Siegle and Hasselmo, 2002). Even more recently, however, new findings have rekindled connectionists' romance with backpropagation, such as the finding that random weights work nearly as well for backwards error transmission as weights matching forward activation (thus removing the biologically implausible need for bi-directional synapses – Lillicrap et al., 2016) and evidence that backpropagation-like learning might be implemented by other, independently supported neuroanatomical phenomena, such as spike-timing dependent plasticity (Scellier and Bengio, 2017; Bengio et al., 2017).

One of the most productive modifications to the basic Golden Age, three-layer network has been the addition of more and more hidden processing layers, which can allow networks to represent ever more abstract and hierarchically organized environmental structure. The power of more hidden layers was recognized early on, with connectionists taking inspiration from work on the purportedly hierarchical cascade of visual processing in the mammalian neocortex (Hubel and Wiesel, 1962; Goodale and Milner, 1992). Many hidden layers were deployed especially in autoencoder networks, which can be used to discover optimal compressions of input representations (Plaut and Hinton, 1987). The trick of such networks – which can be visualized to have the shape of an hourglass – is to hook the input and output layers to the same input stream, and pass processing through many internal layers of iterative bottleneck, where each successive layer has fewer nodes than the previous layer until reaching the central bottleneck with very few nodes; processing then continues through larger and larger layers to the output nodes, "reconstructing" the input representation from its sparsest encoding. The bottleneck at the center forces such networks to perform iterative "dimensionality reduction" on the input, allowing them to discover optimally predictive invariances across many input vectors (and often outperforming statistical methods of performing similar feats, such as Principle Components Analysis).

To understand modern deep networks – roughly, those with more than five or ten layers – we must jump backwards in time to a particular landmark, Fukushima's Neocognitron (1980), developed before the Golden Age but then somewhat forgotten until the present. Inspired by Hubel and Wiesel's discovery of two different types of cells in cat visual cortex – dubbed "simple" and "complex", as they had different response profiles – Neocognitron was perhaps the first network to exhibit another core feature common in today's most powerful deep networks, the use of "convolutional" processing that interleaves two different kinds of layers, linear filters and non-linear poolers. Within a convolutional layer, the receptive fields of filter units pass across an array of input values corresponding to the network's input (i.e. spatially across the pixels of a digitized image, or temporally across the auditory data in a sound file); these nodes function roughly like "AND" gates, each trained to detect a linear pattern in the inputs below. Activation from nearby filter units is then aggregated by pooling units in the layer immediately above; the most popular function is now max-pooling, which only passes along activation from the most activated filter unit below (implementing a nonlinear function more like an "OR" gate). Networks interpolating these two kinds of processing are often called "convnets".

Neocognitron was already capable of advanced pattern detection; its insights were neglected for a time only because nobody knew how to successfully train such deeply layered networks with backpropagation, the darling of the Golden Age. Fukushima trained Neocognitron using a complex combination of manual pre-wiring and unsupervised learning; when backpropagation was applied to such deep networks, it tended to settle into poor local minima or fail to stabilize at all (DeMers and Cottrell, 1993). Modelers came to describe the problem as that of "vanishing or exploding gradients", as error signals would either shrink rapidly or grow out of bounds as they were backpropagated through successive layers (Hochreiter, 1991). Reflecting a general pragmatic disposition towards "everything and the kitchen sink", modelers began to experiment with a variety of ad hoc tweaks before, during, and after training to improve the performance of deep networks. For example, Hinton and Salakhutdinov (2006) found that a simple pretraining algorithm to initialize connection weights to plausible default values could greatly improve the performance of backpropagation in deep autoencoders.

Around this time, deep networks began to routinely win machine learning competitions in computer science, leading to an explosion of performance-driven innovation that was little concerned with biological plausibility (Schmidhuber, 2015). Such networks – which are now deployed in a variety of software applications such as Google Image Search – have already achieved superhuman performance in visual recognition. On the benchmark ImageNet recognition task, for example, Microsoft's ResNet overtook human's 5–10 percent error rate with a staggeringly low score of 3.6 percent in 2015 (He et al., 2015), and rates have continued dropping every year since. Winning networks now combine a motley agglomeration of many different techniques, often involving thirty or more layers, ad hoc methods for node addition and removal to avoid over- and under-fitting the input during training, and complex combinations of supervised, unsupervised, and recurrent learning procedures. The diversity of such networks cannot be fully explored here; but suffice it to say that most of these immensely powerful networks can only aspire to biological plausibility in terms of their abstract mathematical properties. Notably, however, some researchers have started dialing back some of this extravagance in order to compare the performance of more biologically plausible convnets with mammalian cortical processing using methods such as array electrophysiology, producing some highly promising early results and ideas for future innovation (Hassabis et al., 2017; Yamins and DiCarlo, 2016).

Interesting open questions regarding modern deep convnets concern (1) their representational properties; (2) *why* they work as well as they do (the so-called "interpretation problem" of deep learning); and (3) mathematical similarities between such networks and other popular modeling techniques, such as Bayesian predictive processing. Concerning the representational properties of such networks, we might wonder what counts as the representational vehicles of such networks – activation in individual hidden layers, entire multi-layer activation vectors, or something more complex yet? The former option could lead to some highly counter-intuitive results for representational contents, as revealed (in a stroke of marketing genius) by Google's "inceptionism" tools, which allow users to explore the processing of a deep convnet by tweaking input images and videos so as to maximize activation in particular hidden layer nodes (Mordvintsev, Olah, and Tyka, 2015). This method revealed that many mid-level nodes in a trained image classifier responded strongly to chimerical input patterns that the team dubbed "pig-snails", "admiral-dogs", and "dog-fish". Do these networks *represent* such non-sense features? And how might attunement to such features facilitate the processing of the network?

Furthermore, we might wonder why such networks work as well as they do – and whether their processing is related in some deeper way to other currently successful methods in AI, such as Bayesian approaches (McClelland, 1998). For example, Patel, Nguyen, and Baraniuk (2015) have argued that deep convnets belong to a family of hierarchical probabilistic classifiers whose strength lies in their ability to model and overcome "nuisance variation" in input, where nuisance variables are sources of variance that are widely present in input but generally not predictive of classification outcome – such as size, position, scale, and orientation in visual tasks, or pitch, tone, and speed in speech recognition. The hierarchical, paired-layer structure of deep convnets allows them to iteratively transform input vectors into intermediary representations that are stable across nuisance variation; the overlapping receptive fields and local connections of convolutional units make them especially good at efficiently detecting complex features in a particular presentation, and the pooling layers make the detection of those features increasingly tolerant to nuisance transformations (see also Hong et al., 2016). Furthermore, when treated in the mathematical abstract, top-down Bayesian classifiers can be obtained by running such transformations in reverse, using them to "render" images by predicting low-level sensory information from high-level classifications. In practice, augmenting "inverted" deep networks with low-level priors or additional generative layers can produce realistic images of novel exemplars in canonical poses (Nguyen et al., 2016), rendering the results of the activity maximization techniques discussed in the previous paragraph more intelligible to human viewers (as well as possibly grounding connectionist models of imagination and episodic planning – Hassabis et al., 2017).

Given this abstract mathematical similarity with hierarchical Bayesian methods – which are also on the ascendancy in cognitive science, vying for position as the most successful method in machine learning – it is natural to contrast the strengths these two approaches, as we once did with classical computationalism. Should hierarchical classification be performed in a "bottom-up" manner, training networks from the attempt to reduce error in high-level classifications using low-level input, or in a "top-down" manner, beginning with a high-level conception of the representational primitives in a problem domain, and revising probabilistic relationships between these primitives to better anticipate low-level input using Bayesian methods? Connectionists tout the greater mechanistic plausibility of their models, and claim that the ability of their networks to discover representational primitives "on their own" allows a much wider exploration of the possible hypothesis space, which may not fit our pretheoretic intuitions (McClelland et al., 2010). On the other side, Bayesians worry that not enough is yet known about neural mechanisms to determine the biological plausibility of specific connectionist proposals and that deep networks usually cannot succeed on more modest, human-like input; they argue instead that beginning with high-level priors is more efficient and produces more intelligible results (Griffiths et al., 2010; Lake et al., 2016). Both approaches support extremely powerful all-purpose machine learning, and only time will tell whether one or the other – or some future hybrid or replacement – will ultimately emerge as the most powerful and biologically plausible approach.

References

Aizawa, K. (1997) 'Explaining Systematicity', *Mind and Language*, 12, pp. 115–136.

Anderson, J. (1972) 'A Simple Neural Network Generating an Interactive Memory', *Mathematical Biosciences*, 14, pp. 197–220.

Bengio, Y. et al. (2017) 'STDP-Compatible Approximation of Backpropagation in an Energy-Based Model', *Neural Computation*, 29 (3), pp. 555–577.

Bergmann, C. et al. (2013) 'A Computational Model to Investigate Assumptions in the Headturn Preference Procedure', *Frontiers in Psychology*, 4 (676), pp. 106–120.

Berkeley, I. (1997) 'A Revisionist History of Connectionism', The University of Louisiana at Lafayette, August 27. Available at: www.ucs.louisiana.edu/~isb9112/dept/phil341/histconn.html (Accessed: February 28, 2018).

Bobrow, D. (1967) 'Natural Language Input for a Computer Problem Solving System', in Minsky, M. (ed.) *Semantic Information Processing*. Cambridge, MA: MIT Press, pp. 133–215.

Calvo, P. and Symons, J. (eds.) (2014) *The Architecture of Cognition: Rethinking Fodor and Pylyshyn's Systematicity Challenge*. Cambridge, MA: MIT Press.

Calvo Garzon, F. (2003) 'Connectionist Semantics and the Collateral Information Challenge', *Mind and Language*, 18, pp. 77–94.

Chalmers, D. (1990) 'Syntactic Transformations on Distributed Representations', *Connection Science*, 2, pp. 53–62.

Christiansen, M. and Chater, N. (1994) 'Generalization and Connectionist Language Learning', *Mind and Language*, 9, pp. 273–287.

Churchland, P. (1998) 'Conceptual Similarity across Sensory and Neural Diversity: The Fodor/Lepore Challenge Answered', *Journal of Philosophy*, 95, pp. 5–32.

Cohen, J.D. and Servan-Schreiber, D. (1992) 'Context, Cortex, and Dopamine: A Connectionist Approach to Behavior and Biology in Schizophrenia', *Psychological Review*, 99 (1), p. 45.

Crick, F. (1989) 'The Recent Excitement about Neural Networks', *Nature*, 337, pp. 129–132.

DeMers, D. and Cottrell, G.W. (1993) 'N-linear Dimensionality Reduction', *Advances in Neural Information Processing Systems*, 5, pp. 580–587.

Elman, J. (1991) 'Distributed Representations, Simple Recurrent Networks, and Grammatical Structure', in Touretzky, D. (ed.) *Connectionist Approaches to Language Learning*. Dordrecht: Kluwer, pp. 91–122.

Feldman, J.A. and Ballard, D.H. (1982) 'Connectionist Models and Their Properties', *Cognitive Science*, 6, pp. 205–254.

Fitzsimonds, R.M., Song, H.J., and Poo, M.M. (1997) 'Propagation of Activity-Dependent Synaptic Depression in Simple Neural Networks', *Nature*, 388 (6641), pp. 439–448.

Fodor, J. and Lepore, E. (1999) 'All at Sea in Semantic Space: Churchland on Meaning Similarity', *Journal of Philosophy*, 96, pp. 381–403.

Fodor, J. and Pylyshyn, Z. (1988) 'Connectionism and Cognitive Architecture: A Critical Analysis', *Cognition*, 28, pp. 3–71.

Frank, M.J., Loughry, B., and O'Reilly, R.C. (2001) 'Interactions between Frontal Cortex and Basal Ganglia in Working Memory: A Computational Model', *Cognitive, Affective, and Behavioral Neuroscience*, 1 (2), pp. 137–160.

Fritzke, B. (1995) 'A Growing Neural Gas Network Learns Topologies', *Advances in Neural Information Processing Systems*, 7, pp. 625–632.

Fukushima, K. (1980) 'Neocognitron: "A Self-Organizing Neural Network Model for a Mechanism of Pattern Recognition Unaffected by Shift in Position"', *Biological Cybernetics*, 36 (4), pp. 193–202.

Gluck, M.A. and Myers, C.E. (1993) 'Hippocampal Mediation of Stimulus Representation: A Computational Theory', *Hippocampus*, 3 (4), pp. 491–516.

Gluck, M.A. and Myers, C.E. (2001) *Gateway to Memory: An Introduction to Neural Network Modeling of the Hippocampus and Learning*. Cambridge, MA: MIT Press.

Goodale, M.A. and Milner, A.D. (1992) 'Separate Visual Pathways for Perception and Action', *Trends in Neurosciences*, 15 (1), pp. 20–25.

Griffiths, T.L. et al. (2010) 'Probabilistic Models of Cognition: Exploring Representations and Inductive Biases', *Trends in Cognitive Sciences*, 14 (8), pp. 357–364.

Grossberg, S. (1976) 'Adaptive Pattern Classification and Universal Recoding: I. Parallel Development and Coding in Neural Feature Detectors', *Biological Cybernetics*, 23, pp. 121–134.

Hadley, R. (1994) 'Systematicity Revisited', *Mind and Language*, 9, pp. 431–444.

Hadley, R. (1997) 'Cognition, Systematicity and Nomic Necessity', *Mind and Language*, 12, pp. 137–153.

Hassabis, D. et al. (2017) 'Neuroscience-Inspired Artificial Intelligence', *Neuron*, 95 (2), pp. 245–258.

He, K. et al. (2015) 'Delving Deep into Rectifiers: Surpassing Human-Level Performance on Imagenet Classification', *Proceedings of the IEEE International Conference on Computer Vision*, pp. 1026–1034.

Hebb, D. (1949) *The Organization of Behavior*. New York, NY: Wiley & Sons.

Hinton, G.E. and McClelland, J.L. (1988) 'Learning Representations by Recirculation', in Anderson, D.Z. (ed.) *Neural Information Processing Systems*. New York, NY: American Institute of Physics, pp. 358–366.

Hinton, G.E. and Salakhutdinov, R.R. (2006) 'Reducing the Dimensionality of Data with Neural Networks', *Science*, 313 (5786), pp. 504–507.

Hochreiter, S. (1991) *Untersuchungen zu Dynamischen Neuronalen Netzen*. Diploma Thesis. Technische Universität München, Institut für Informatik.

Hong, H. et al. (2016) 'Explicit Information for Category-Orthogonal Object Properties Increases along the Ventral Stream', *Nature Neuroscience*, 19 (4), pp. 613–622.

Horgan, T. and Tienson, J. (1989) 'Representations without Rules', *Philosophical Topics*, 17, pp. 147–174.

Hubel, D.H. and Wiesel, T.N. (1962) 'Receptive Fields, Binocular Interaction and Functional Architecture in the Cat's Visual Cortex', *The Journal of Physiology*, 160 (1), pp. 106–154.

James, W. (1890) *The Principles of Psychology*. New York, NY: Dover.

Kohonen, T. (1972) 'Correlation Matrix Memories', *IEEE Transactions on Computers*, C-21, pp. 353–359.

Lake, B.M. et al. (2016) 'Building Machines That Learn and Think Like People', *Behavioral and Brain Sciences*, 40, pp. 1–101.

Lashley, K. (1929) *Brain Mechanisms and Intelligence: A Quantitative Study of Injuries to the Brain*. New York, NY: Dover.

Lillicrap, T.P. et al. (2016) 'Random Synaptic Feedback Weights Support Error Backpropagation for Deep Learning', *Nature Communications*, 7, p. 13276. Available at: http://doi.org/10.1038/ncomms13276.

Maia, T.V. and Cleeremans, A. (2005) 'Consciousness: Converging Insights from Connectionist Modeling and Neuroscience', *Trends in Cognitive Sciences*, 9 (8), pp. 397–404.

Marcus, G. (1998) 'Rethinking Eliminative Connectionism', *Cognitive Psychology*, 37, pp. 243–282.

Marcus, G. (2001) *The Algebraic Mind*. Cambridge, MA: MIT Press.

Martinetz, T.M., Berkovich, S.G., and Schulten, K.J. (1993) '"Neural-gas" Network for Vector Quantization and Its Application to Time-Series Prediction', *IEEE Transactions on Neural Networks*, 4 (4), pp. 558–569.

Matthews, R. (1997) 'Can Connectionists Explain Systematicity?', *Mind and Language*, 12, pp. 154–177.

Mayor, J. et al. (2014) 'Connectionism Coming of Age: Legacy and Future Challenges', *Frontiers in Psychology*, 5 (187), pp. 1–3.

McClelland, J.L. (1998) 'Connectionist Models and Bayesian Inference', in Oaksford, M. and Chater, N. (eds.) *Rational Models of Cognition*. Oxford: Oxford University Press, pp. 21–53.

McClelland, J.L., Botvinick, M.M. et al. (2010) 'Letting Structure Emerge: Connectionist and Dynamical Systems Approaches to Cognition', *Trends in Cognitive Sciences*, 14 (8), pp. 348–356.

McClelland, J.L., McNaughton, B.L., and O'Reilly, R.C. (1995) 'Why There Are Complementary Learning Systems in the Hippocampus and Neocortex: Insights from the Successes and Failures of Connectionist Models of Learning and Memory', *Psychological Review*, 102 (3), p. 419.

McClelland, J., Rumelhart, D. et al. (1986) *Parallel Distributed Processing*. Cambridge, MA: MIT Press.

McCloskey, M. and Cohen, N.J. (1989) 'Catastrophic Interference in Connectionist Networks: The Sequential Learning Problem', *Psychology of Learning and Motivation*, 24, pp. 109–165.

McCulloch, W. and Pitts, W. (1949) 'A Logical Calculus of Ideas Immanent in Nervous Activity', *Bulletin of Mathematical Biophysics*, 5, pp. 115–133. Reprinted in McCulloch, W., Embodiments of Mind. Cambridge, MA: MIT Press.

Miikkulainen, R. (1993) *Subsymbolic Natural Language Processing: An Integrated Model of Scripts, Lexicon and Memory*. Cambridge, MA: MIT Press.

Minsky, M. and Papert, S. (1969) *Perceptrons: An Introduction to Computational Geometry*. Cambridge, MA: MIT Press.

Mordvintsev, A., Olah, C., and Tyka, M. (2015) 'Inceptionism: Going Deeper into Neural Networks', *Google Research Blog*, June 17. Available at: http://googleresearch.blogspot.com/2015/06/inceptionism-going-deeper-into-neural.html (Accessed: June 20, 2015).

Newell, A. and Simon, H. (1963) 'GPS: A Program That Simulates Human Thought', in Feigenbaum, E. and Feldman, J. (eds.) *Computers and Thought*. New York, NY: McGraw-Hill, pp. 279–293.

Nguyen, A. et al. (2016) 'Synthesizing the Preferred Inputs for Neurons in Neural Networks via Deep Generator Networks', *Advances in Neural Information Processing Systems*, 29th Conference on Neural Information Processing Systems, pp. 3387–3395.

O'Reilly, R.C. (1996) 'Biologically Plausible Error-Driven Learning Using Local Activation Differences: The Generalized Recirculation Algorithm', *Neural Computation*, 8 (5), pp. 895–938.

Patel, A.B., Nguyen, T., and Baraniuk, R.G. (2015) 'A Probabilistic Theory of Deep Learning', arXiv preprint, arXiv:1504.00641.

Pinker, S. and Prince, A. (1988) 'On Language and Connectionism: Analysis of a Parallel Distributed Processing Model of Language Acquisition', *Cognition*, 23, pp. 73–193.

Plaut, D.C. and Hinton, G.E. (1987) 'Learning Sets of Filters Using Back-Propagation', *Computer Speech and Language*, 2 (1), pp. 35–61.

Rhode, D. and Plaut, D. (2004) 'Connectionist Models of Language Processing', *Cognitive Studies* (Japan), 120 (1), pp. 10–28.

Rogers, T. and McClelland, J. (2014) 'Parallel Distributed Processing at 25: Further Explorations in the Microstructure of Cognition', *Cognitive Science*, 38, pp. 1024–1077.

Rosch, E. (1975) 'Cognitive Representations of Semantic Categories', *Journal of Experimental Psychology: General*, 104 (3), pp. 192–233.

Rosenblatt, F. (1958) 'The Perceptron: A Probabilistic Model for Information Storage and Organization in the Brain', *Psychological Review*, 65, pp. 386–408.

Rumelhart, D. and McClelland, J. (1986) 'On Learning the Past Tenses of English Verbs', in McClelland, J., Rumelhart, D. et al. (eds.) *Parallel Distributed Processing: Explorations in the Microstructure of Cognition*, vol. 2. Cambridge, MA: MIT Press, pp. 216–271.

Samuel, A. (1967) 'Some Studies in Machine Learning Using the Game of Checkers', *IBM Journal of Research and Development*, 3 (3), pp. 601–617.

Scellier, B. and Bengio, Y. (2017) 'Equilibrium Propagation: Bridging the Gap between Energy-Based Models and Backpropagation', *Frontiers in Computational Neuroscience*, 11 (24). Available at: http://doi.org/10.3389/fncom.2017.00024.

Schmidhuber, J. (2015) 'Deep Learning in Neural Networks: An Overview', *Neural Networks*, 61, pp. 85–117.

Sejnowski, T. and Rosenberg, C. (1987) 'Parallel Networks That Learn to Pronounce English Text', *Complex Systems*, 1, pp. 145–168.

Siegle, G.J. and Hasselmo, M.E. (2002) 'Using Connectionist Models to Guide Assessment of Psycological Disorder', *Psychological Assessment*, 14 (3), p. 263.

Simon, H.A. (1965) *The Shape of Automation for Men and Management*. New York, NY: Harper & Row.

Smolensky, P. (1991) 'Tensor Product Variable Binding and the Representation of Symbolic Structures in Connectionist Systems', in Hinton, G. (ed.) *Connectionist Symbol Processing*. Cambridge, MA: MIT Press, pp. 159–216.

Spencer, H. (1855) *The Principles of Psychology*. New York, NY: D. Appleton and Company.

Thorndike, E. (1932) *The Fundamentals of Learning*. New York, NY: Teachers College, Columbia University.

Turing, A. (1936) 'On Computable Numbers, with an Application to the Entscheidungsproblem', *Proceedings of the London Mathematical Society* (Series 2), 42, pp. 230–265.

Werbos, P. (1994) *The Roots of Backpropagation*. New York, NY: Wiley.

Wermter, S. and Sun, R. (eds.) (2000) *Hybrid Neural Symbolic Integration*. Berlin: Springer-Verlag.

Williams, R.J. (1992) 'Simple Statistical Gradient-Following Algorithms for Connectionist Reinforcement Learning', *Machine Learning*, 8 (3–4), pp. 229–256.

Wittgenstein, L. (1953) *Philosophical Investigations*, ed. Anscombe, G.E.M. and Rhees R. Translated by G.E.M. Anscombe. Oxford: Blackwell.

Yamins, D.L. and DiCarlo, J.J. (2016) 'Using Goal-Driven Deep Learning Models to Understand Sensory Cortex', *Nature Neuroscience*, 19 (3), p. 356.

7

ARTIFICIAL INTELLIGENCE

Murray Shanahan

The long-term aim of the field of artificial intelligence (AI) is to endow computers and robots with intelligence, where *intelligence* might be defined as the ability to perform tasks and attain goals in a wide variety of environments (Legg and Hutter, 2007). In attempting to do this, the field has developed a number of enabling technologies, such as automated reasoning, computer vision, and machine learning, which can be applied to specialist tasks in an industrial or commercial setting. But our concern here is the yet-to-be-realized prospect of *human-level* artificial intelligence, that is to say AI that can match a typical human's capacity to perform tasks and attain goals in a wide variety of environments. A key feature of human-level intelligence is its *generality* (McCarthy, 1987). It can adapt to an enormous variety of environments, tasks, and goals. Achieving this level of generality in AI has proven very difficult. But let us suppose it is possible. What, then, are the philosophical implications? This is the question to be addressed here, after a brief historical account of the field followed by a short sketch of the challenges facing developers of human-level AI.

A very short history

Although lifelike mechanical creatures have appeared in stories since ancient times (Truitt, 2015), discussion of artificial intelligence proper coincided with the advent of general purpose computation, as first characterized mathematically by Alan Turing in the 1930s (Turing, 1936). Ada Lovelace, who speculated on the potential of symbolic computation for composing music, may have glimpsed the possibilities in the nineteenth century. But Turing's 1950 paper, *Computing Machinery and Intelligence*, which introduced what we now call the Turing test, marks the beginning of serious scholarly discussion on the topic (Turing, 1950). Just a few years later, the 1956 Dartmouth Conference took place. Organized by Marvin Minsky and John McCarthy (who coined the term "artificial intelligence"), this event is often considered as inaugurating AI as an academic discipline. Several of the papers presented there, by such pioneers as Newell, Simon, and Selfridge, as well as Minsky and McCarthy, seeded entire research areas.

Throughout the 1960s, '70s, and '80s, artificial intelligence research burgeoned, albeit against a backdrop of periodic hype and disappointment (the so-called AI winters of the mid 1970s and early 1990s). Two ostensibly competing paradigms dominated thinking in this period: symbolic (or classical) artificial intelligence, and connectionism (neural networks). According to the symbolic paradigm, the right architecture for AI is one that manipulates language-like propositional representations according to formal rules. The symbolic paradigm emphasizes high-level cognitive processes, abstracting away from low-level implementation details. The connectionist paradigm, in contrast, draws inspiration from the low-level workings of the biological brain. For connectionist researchers, the right architecture for AI is one that builds on massively parallel, richly interconnected networks of simple neuron-like elements. Representations, according to this way of thinking, are not explicit symbolic entities, but implicit, distributed, and emergent.

While AI researchers are primarily motivated by the engineering challenge of building intelligence into computers and robots, philosophers are more interested in the question of the character of mind. Nevertheless, the division between these two schools of AI is reflected in the philosophy of mind. The symbolic school has an obvious affinity with computational theories of mind of the sort championed by Fodor and others, while the connectionist school is allied to the neuroscience-oriented program of the Churchlands and like-minded thinkers whose primary influence is neuroscience.

By the late 1980s, with little evidence of progress towards human-level artificial intelligence, disillusion with the grand ambitions of the field's founders was commonplace. While many researchers focused on narrow applications of AI technology, roboticist Rodney Brooks attempted to diagnose the problem (Brooks, 1991). His critique disavowed the top-down, disembodied approach of classical, symbolic AI in favor of a bottom-up methodology that prioritized the issue of embodiment. So rather than focusing on reasoning, representation, search, and language, Brooks' program concentrated on robotics, motor control, and sensory feedback, harking back to the early work of cyberneticists such as William Grey Walter (1950). Brooks effectively demonstrated the extent to which intelligent-seeming behavior could be achieved through simple reactive (stimulus–response) rules, without recourse to symbolic representation and reasoning, and thereby inaugurated a new paradigm of cognitive science that put embodiment center stage.

In 1997, IBM's Deep Blue defeated the reigning world chess champion, Garry Kasparov. Nevertheless, at the turn of the millennium, the vision of general purpose, human-level AI seemed as far off as ever. Neither the symbolic nor the connectionist paradigm had got much further than where they were in the 1980s, and Brooks' bottom-up approach was still stuck at the level of sensorimotor foundations, having made little headway with cognitive processes such as planning, inference, or language. The contrast with progress in computer hardware could hardly have been more stark. Keeping pace with Moore's Law, the memory and processing power of the average AI researcher's desktop computer was continuing to increase exponentially, notably in the form of graphics processing units (GPUs), which can be repurposed for general computation enabling their inherent parallelism to be exploited. By the end of the 2000s, this change in hardware was having a significant impact in the field of machine learning.

One technique that particularly benefited from the advent of powerful GPUs was *deep learning*, which uses artificial neural networks organized into multiple layers, where successive layers encode increasingly abstract features of the data (LeCun, Bengio, and Hinton, 2015). Learning in these networks is achieved by slowly modifying the weights of the connections between the artificial neurons. The backpropagation algorithm typically used to do this dates back to the 1970s. But its practical success was limited until the 2000s, when, thanks to the combination of deep networks, big data, and increased computational power, it began to significantly outperform rival machine learning techniques on basic perceptual tasks such as speech recognition and image labelling. The computational power of a GPU is a consequence of its parallelism, and applications that are themselves inherently parallel are best placed to exploit this. Artificial neural networks fit the bill perfectly. GPUs made it possible to train bigger networks with more layers on larger data sets than had previously been feasible.

Towards artificial general intelligence

The recent success of machine learning has precipitated substantial investment from the tech industry, who foresee enormous economic impact for specialist AI technologies in the short- to medium-term. There is also a renewed sense of optimism about the prospects for human-level artificial general intelligence. Indeed, there is now interest in pursuing this goal within industry as well as academia. For example, in 2014, Google purchased London-based start-up DeepMind, whose aim is to "solve intelligence", albeit on a decades-long timescale. In 2016, DeepMind achieved another milestone. Their AlphaGo program defeated one of the world's leading Go players, Lee Sedol, using a combination of deep learning, reinforcement learning, and tree search (Silver et al., 2016). In contrast to the highly specialized technology used in 1997 to conquer chess, these techniques have a general applicability far beyond the game of Go. Nevertheless, even from an optimistic standpoint, a formidable set of obstacles stands in the way of human-level AI. Although we cannot know today what all those obstacles are, or how difficult they are to overcome, it is possible to list some of the most fundamental challenges.

First, there is the challenge of *abstract concepts*. The nature of concepts is, of course, much debated in philosophy. But what I mean here is the ability to see that a set of objects, events, or situations are similar in some important respects and therefore should be treated similarly. Chairs come in many shapes. But we know that they all afford rest, and we know what to bring if someone asks us to find a chair. In the symbolic paradigm, abstract concepts are often taken for granted. For example, the constant symbol "Chair" and the predicate symbol "AffordsRest" might be deployed in a representation without pinning down their meanings. This sort of move allows researchers to investigate the mathematical or computational properties of a representational formalism. But the result has no basis in perception and action, and cannot provide a foundation for recognizing chairs as chairs and treating them as such. In humans, by contrast, everyday concepts like that of a chair are *grounded* in interaction with the physical world. Using machine learning techniques, representations can be similarly grounded in perception. For example, a neural network can be trained using the backpropagation algorithm to compute a mapping from low-level, high-dimensional data to a high-level, more compressed representation. However, today's machine learning methods have very limited powers of abstraction compared to humans.

Second, there is the challenge of *common sense* (Mueller, 2014). Humans are adept at anticipating the physical and social consequences of everyday actions and events. Suppose I am carrying out a particularly odious administrative task which causes me to entertain the possibility of throwing a chair out of the office window. I can easily imagine and describe the physical consequences. The chair will likely be broken into pieces on the road. It may hit and damage a car, or worse, it may injure a person. I can also imagine and describe the social consequences. It is likely someone would call the police. I might end up being prosecuted, and losing my job. So I resist the temptation and get back to the spreadsheet. I don't need to know the exact shapes, dimensions, or orientations of the objects in this scenario to make these predictions. Moreover, it is not an action I have ever witnessed, or even contemplated before. Nevertheless my common sense understanding of the everyday world – of objects, shapes, space, motion, parts and wholes, other minds, beliefs, desires, intentions, and emotions – equips me with this capability. We don't yet know how to endow computers and robots with this sort of generic capacity.

Third, there is the challenge of *creativity* (Boden, 2003). Creativity, in the intended sense, is the tendency to eschew the tried-and-tested and to experiment, sometimes fruitfully. The sort of creativity in question is by no means the province solely of great thinkers, artists, and so on. It is no less the tendency every child has to try things out – crazy things, silly things, but sometimes brilliant things – enabling them to acquire the skills they need to flourish in human society. This would be easy to implement on a computer if it were simply a matter of trying out random actions and ideas. But the combinatorics of everyday life – the sheer number of possible ways to combine and recombine the elements of thought and behavior – renders this infeasible. The difficulty is to confine exploration to combinations of elements that are relevant to an agent's goals, so that a novel yet fruitful combination might be found in a reasonable time. This challenge is related to the *frame problem*, in the wide sense of the term used by philosophers, which is the difficulty of explaining how high-level cognitive processes such as analogical reasoning manage to select the items of information they need from the vast store of potentially relevant information available to them without incurring an impossible computational burden (Shanahan, 2016).

This is surely not a definitive list of the obstacles to achieving human-level artificial general intelligence. Such a list will only be possible with hindsight. From today's standpoint, we can only say that there is an unknown set of conceptual barriers standing in the way. We cannot say for sure what they are or when they will be overcome. But let us suppose these barriers can be overcome. A number of important philosophical questions about the likely nature of the resulting systems then arise. Would they have intentionality? Would they be autonomous? Would they possess selfhood? Would they be conscious? These are the questions we'll be looking at next. But first a few words are in order about the possible forms that a human-level artificial general intelligence might take, as this has a bearing on the answers to those questions.

One axis along which putative future AI systems can be arranged is *biological fidelity* (and to neuroscience in particular). At one extreme, we have whole brain emulation, wherein an exact, digitally simulated copy of an individual's brain is made and run on a computer. At the other extreme, we can imagine (without imagining the details) a human-level AI that is engineered from scratch, according to an architectural blueprint that bears no resemblance to that of the biological brain. In the middle, we have forms of artificial intelligence that take some inspiration from the way the brain functions, but without slavishly copying the brain of any particular species, or indeed adhering to biologically realistic neurons as the underlying computational substrate. From where we stand today, human-level AI seems possible anywhere along this spectrum, and it is impossible to say which is most likely to arrive first.

An orthogonal property of a potential future AI system with general intelligence is the character of its embodiment. A system is *embodied* if its fundamental mode of operation is to control a body situated in a spatial environment, where its input derives from senses mounted on that body and its output is delivered to that body's motor apparatus. An animal is embodied, in this sense, and so is a robot. It is easiest to imagine human-level AI embodied in humanoid form, or perhaps in some other animal-like form. But it's also possible to envisage human-level AI that is disembodied. Although the disembodied personal assistants in today's smartphones and home devices are limited, we can imagine (along with many science fiction writers) a future generation of far more sophisticated, human-level conversational agents. Obviously the intelligence of such a system could not be directly demonstrated on any physical task. Indeed, some authors would claim that human-level intelligence is not feasible without a grounding in interaction with the physical world, although a subset of those authors would countenance the possibility of human-level AI that is virtually embodied in a simulated world.

Consideration of the two axes of biological fidelity and embodiment is only one way to explore what Sloman terms the *space of possible minds* (Sloman, 1984). This space encompasses not only biological intelligence as it has arisen on the Earth, but also every scientifically plausible form of extraterrestrial intelligence, as well as every conceivable form of artificial intelligence, whether implemented by humans or by other occupants of the space of possible minds. To map out this space rigorously is a deep and demanding philosophical task, one that perhaps hasn't received the attention it deserves. For the present article, it's enough to note that human-level artificial intelligence is not necessarily human-like. Indeed, human-like artificial general intelligence is likely to occupy just a tiny portion of the space of possibilities.

Artificial intelligence and intentionality

We often adopt towards computer applications, robots, and other complex artifacts what Dennett terms the *intentional stance* (Dennett, 1987). We speak of them as if they had beliefs, desires, goals, and thoughts – states that are directed at the world and the objects it contains – because this helps us to explain their behavior, to describe it to each other, and to predict it. For example, I might note that my car's navigation system "wants me to turn left because it thinks we're going home", causing my wife to remark that "it will try to make us go over the bridge". Typically we are ignorant of the underlying mechanisms of such systems, and even if we knew how they worked it would be cumbersome to talk about them in those terms. Nevertheless we all know that, when it comes to car navigation systems and the like, the intentional stance is just a useful fiction. My car cannot describe the bridge, or imagine what would happen if it collapsed, or think of another way a person might cross the river. It has never encountered a real bridge or anything resembling one. Indeed it has no idea that there is a world of spatiotemporally located objects out here. So it makes no sense to say that it has beliefs or thoughts that are about anything.

A properly embodied system, such as a robot vacuum cleaner, has a more direct causal connection to the physical world. Its behavior is sensitive to its own location, and to the presence of objects in its immediate environment. Suppose it stops at the edge of the stairs and, adopting the intentional stance, I remark that "it won't move forwards now because it knows there is a drop just in front of it". In this case the drop at issue plays a direct role in the perception–action loop of the robot's controller. The controller will enter into a distinctive state when the robot's sensors detect that there is no floor just in front of it. Because this state relates in a clear and systematic way to a particular state of affairs in the external world, it looks like the robot has, at least, a kind of proto-intentionality. But we are brought up short when the robot does something "foolish", such as repeatedly bumping against a chair leg, backing away then bumping into it again from a slightly different angle. "Well", I might say, "it doesn't *really* know that there is a chair leg there. Otherwise it would realize that it can just go around it". In short, for us to consider the robot as entering a state that is properly speaking *directed at* an object, it must display behavior that is sensitive to the properties of that object that we consider essential.

However, artificial intelligence is becoming increasingly sophisticated. The shortcomings of today's systems will gradually become fewer, and the sorts of mistakes that expose the intentional stance as just a convenient fiction will no longer occur. Eventually, the inclination to remark that a system "doesn't *really* know what a bridge is" or "doesn't *really* know what a chair leg is" will disappear. The question, when that happens, is whether these more sophisticated systems would "really" possess intentionality or not. Would such a system "truly" have mental states that are directed at the world and its objects, or would it merely give the appearance of having such states? A pragmatic way to respond to these questions is to sidestep them. If there are no behavioral ramifications to "really" possessing intentionality, as opposed to merely seeming to possess it, then the distinction plays no useful role in our language, and we may as well do away with it. However, this maneuver, with its overtones of verificationism, is not going to satisfy philosophers who incline to realism with respect to mental states.

Artificial intelligence and autonomy

According to one definition, a system is autonomous to the extent that it can operate without human intervention. By this definition, many existing computer-controlled devices have a degree of autonomy. A robot vacuum cleaner can exit its dock while its owner is away, clean the floor effectively, and return to its dock to recharge. But this is an impoverished notion of autonomy, philosophically speaking. Although such a robot exhibits purposeful behavior, since it has a set of clearly discernible goals towards which all of its actions are oriented, it cannot really be said to act *of its own accord*. It does not weigh up options and deliberately choose between them. Rather, its goals are implicit and fixed, bequeathed to it by its designers.

Now, it could be argued that there is a sense in which no human chooses their own goals, since evolution has given us a set of innate drives, including self-preservation, reproduction, and so on. To which it might be countered that many people seem able to transcend these natural drives, sacrificing their lives for others or rejecting the sexual urge. But there is no need to take sides in this debate to see that what matters when we ascribe autonomy to humans is not so much the primal drives, but rather the apparent sophistication of the process whereby we weigh our options and select our actions. Similar considerations apply to any system based on artificial intelligence. Today's AI systems largely lack sophistication in this respect, so we are not inclined to credit them with making decisions "for themselves" or acting "of their own accord".

On the other hand, we see glimpses of such sophistication. In one of the matches played by AlphaGo, for example, the machine played a move that took both its programmers and the watching Go masters by surprise, a highly unusual move that ultimately led to victory. A "creative" act such as this move suggests that the program has transcended the direct influence of its programmers. In no sense did its programmers select that particular move. We cannot help saying that the machine chose the move for itself. In an important sense, it was doing more than simply what it was told to do, even though on another level it was still (of course) following a series of strict, preordained instructions. The more complex and capable AI systems become, the less jarring it will seem to describe their behavior in terms suggestive of this kind of autonomy.

Artificial intelligence and selfhood

So AI systems of the near future might be said to act of their own accord. But could they ever be said to act *on their own behalf*? To warrant description in such terms, the system's behavior would have to display a degree of sensitivity to its own identity, to the distinction between itself and the rest of the world. The question of embodiment plays a crucial role here. When we speak of an animal looking after itself or protecting itself, we have in mind the attitude it takes towards its own body. Whether or not an animal is capable of recognizing itself in a mirror, every animal understands the boundary of its own body to the extent that it is sensitive to pain or discomfort in its body's parts, and seeks to avoid these sensations. Moreover, every animal understands the energy needs of its own body insofar as many of its actions pertain to the acquisition of food and water. Finally, whether or not an animal properly understands the idea of its own death, it will typically behave in such a way as to preserve its life when threatened.

In short, we find in every animal an inter-related repertoire of behaviors oriented towards its integrity, wellbeing, and continuity, where each of those notions is rooted in the animal's embodiment. Nothing of the sort can be said of any contemporary AI system, even if that system is embodied, meaning that its function is to control a robot. With this precondition for selfhood lacking, we aren't tempted to think of today's AI systems as acting on their own behalf. On the other hand, perhaps there is a faint intimation of nascent selfhood in the robot vacuum cleaner when it senses that its batteries are low and makes its way to the charging dock. Moreover, as robots are built with richer tactile and other senses throughout their bodies, they will become capable of increasingly nuanced responses to potential damage. Perhaps we will gradually become inclined to speak of them as beings in their own right, like humans and other animals.

But when we think of the ways humans act on their own behalf, we have in mind more than attention to bodily needs. Human selfhood is tied up with beliefs, aspirations, memories, personality, and so on, and presupposes a certain continuity in these things. Clearly these considerations are also relevant to the ascription of selfhood to an artificial entity. Indeed, were we to decide that psychological attributes like these, rather than bodily awareness, are the proper grounds for selfhood – for full-blown selfhood of the sort we find in humans – we would be well on the way to granting selfhood to disembodied (future) forms of artificial intelligence. For many philosophers this might feel like a backwards step, a return to a discredited form of Cartesian dualism wherein the mind can be divorced from the body.

Today, no AI system exists, whether embodied or not, that merits the ascription of selfhood. But it isn't hard to imagine an AI system of the near future whose most convenient description is in terms of an ongoing set of beliefs, aspirations, memories, and so on. A system wouldn't necessarily even require human-level intelligence to fit the bill. If we came to treat such systems as if they had selves, as if they acted on their own behalf, perhaps philosophical discussion of whether they "really" have selves, whether they "really" act on their own behalf, would become moot. On the other hand, we can also imagine a future system endowed with human-level artificial general intelligence that seemingly lacked the prerequisites for selfhood. This could be a system whose episodic memory lasted only as long as the immediate task at hand and whose goals were similarly ephemeral. Or it could be a system comprising an amorphous set of functional components assembled on the fly to suit a particular problem in such a way that it had no enduring identity from one brief instantiation to the next.

Artificial intelligence and consciousness

Would a system that possessed human-level artificial general intelligence necessarily be conscious? Of course, the answer to this question depends on what we mean by "consciousness". We associate consciousness with a number of psychological attributes, such as awareness of the world, awareness of inner states, the ability to integrate information, and the capacity for emotion, for suffering and joy (Chalmers, 1996). In humans, these attributes come as a package. But for an artificial entity, we can imagine them occurring separately, or not at all (Shanahan, 2015, ch. 5). So the question of the necessity or otherwise of consciousness for general intelligence has to be broken down into a set of subsidiary questions. Would an AI with general intelligence necessarily have some awareness of the world? Would it need to be aware of its inner states? Would it require the ability to fully integrate perception, memory, and reason? Would it necessarily be capable of suffering?

Let's begin with awareness of the world. Hopefully a picture is by now emerging of the diversity of potential artificial intelligence systems of the future, and as with previous questions of this sort, the answer depends on the particular form the imagined AI will take. A disembodied personal assistant whose job is to answer questions and offer advice might present a convincingly high level of intelligence, yet lack any means of directly sensing the world, or indeed of directly acting on it. Such a system would obviously lack any awareness of the world, so this fundamental aspect of consciousness would be missing. But we might also balk at crediting it with truly general intelligence. Without the ability to interact with complex spatiotemporally extended objects, would we even credit the system with the understanding that there is a world distinct from and external to itself? (The issue harks back to the earlier discussion of intentionality.) And without such an understanding, could we ever say that the system had general intelligence?

There is a good case for answering no to both questions. If the ability to interact with a world of spatially extended objects is a prerequisite for general intelligence then it follows that "awareness" of such a world is a prerequisite. Whether or not awareness of the world in the minimal, behavioral sense alluded to here entails awareness in the full-blown, "phenomenological" sense we associate with consciousness is another matter. However nuanced a robot's responses are to its ongoing situation, it will always be possible to voice the skeptical thought that there is no accompanying phenomenology, that it is not "like anything" for the robot to sense and act within the world. But perhaps, with sufficient exposure to the behavior of a sufficiently sophisticated embodied AI, such philosophical misgivings will simply fall away. After all, the same skeptical thought can always be expressed with respect to another human being.

The possibility of virtual embodiment adds an extra dimension to the debate. Much contemporary AI research involves the development of agents that inhabit simulated 3D environments with more-or-less realistic physics. From a computer science standpoint, such agents are separate entities from the simulated environments they sense and act in, although both are implemented within the same computational substrate. Can such agents be said to be aware of the world they inhabit? There is every reason to suppose that the same behavioral markers we use to attribute awareness of the world to physically embodied creatures could be manifest by a virtually embodied agent in respect of a simulated world. Whether observing its interactions with the simulated environment from the outside, or immersed in that environment ourselves by means of virtual reality, we would no doubt use the same language to describe such an agent as we use in relation to humans and other animals. However, the virtually embodied AI is even more vulnerable to the skeptical voice than the physically embodied agent. Surely (the thought goes) when such an AI reacts to the virtual presence of a virtual object there can be no accompanying phenomenology.

What about awareness of inner states? Is this capability a requirement for having human-level general intelligence? Humans are aware (with more or less acuity) of a variety of inner states, including their own thinking processes and their own emotional state. A person's ability to modulate their behavior and their thinking based on this self-awareness is certainly beneficial. Recognizing mistakes in my past reasoning processes allows me to correct them in the future. And recognizing that my actions resulted from anger rather than judgment will encourage me to keep a cooler head next time. The first of these reflective capabilities would certainly be expected in a human-level AI. But what of the second, self-awareness of emotional states? Are emotional states needed at all for human-level artificial general intelligence? We'll return to this question shortly.

Beforehand, let's consider the question of integration. When we encounter a fellow conscious creature we see in them a certain kind of unity. We expect their behavior to draw on the totality, or the near-totality, of what they know and believe, what they perceive, what they remember, what they want, and so on. When these things do not contribute in a cognitively integrated way to action, it is because something is wrong. The creature (or person) in question is not paying attention, or is "on autopilot", or is suffering from some illness or disorder. Although today's laptop and desktop computers run collections of largely independent applications, it is difficult to envisage a future AI system with human-level general intelligence that displayed a lack of cognitive integration in this sense. Although it might make computational sense to invoke a small set of well-drilled routines in some situations, a system that cannot pool its cognitive resources will often make poorer decisions than one that can. So cognitive integration, a hall-mark of the conscious condition in humans, must also count as a necessary condition for human-level general intelligence in machines.

But let's get back to emotion, which is an altogether different story. There is ample evidence that emotion plays a vital functional role in human decision making (Damasio, 1994). A brain-like human-level artificial general intelligence whose architecture conformed to the biological template would be subject to the same constraints, so we would expect such a system to incorporate emotions in a similar functional role. However, some philosophers will always question whether a system realized in silicon rather than living cells could truly experience emotions as we do – that is to say accompanied by phenomenology – whatever the system's functional organization and outward behavior. Moreover, if an artificial general intelligence were engineered from scratch, with a functional organization very different from that of the biological brain, there would be no reason to assume that it would have even a functional requirement for emotion.

In short, while it is hard to imagine human-level artificial general intelligence without some of the functional attributes we associate with consciousness in humans, such as awareness of the world or cognitive integration, we can imagine a non-human-like artificial general intelligence lacking emotions altogether, both functionally and phenomenologically speaking, and therefore without the capacity for suffering or joy. On the other hand, many philosophers would agree that emotion, though perhaps not necessary, is at least possible in human-level AI, both in a functional role and with accompanying phenomenology, especially if the AI conforms to the blueprint of the biological brain. In the future, the side of this divide that a given AI system falls will clearly have significant moral implications.

The technological singularity

If one day we do succeed in building human-level AI, the implications for humanity are likely to be considerable, not least because the advent of human-level AI is likely to be rapidly followed by AI with superhuman intelligence. Some authors have argued that this will be the result of an *intelligence explosion* (Bostrom, 2014). A human-level AI will be able to create a successor whose intelligence is greater than its own, or to modify itself so as to increase its own intelligence. The resulting system will be capable of engendering an even more intelligent AI, and so the process will go on, potentially at an exponential rate. But even without appealing to self-improvement, it would be possible to effect the transition from human-level AI to superintelligence by more conservative means, such as hardware speed-up. (Attaining human-level AI in the first place appears today the greater challenge.)

Although different authors use the term differently, let us define the *technological singularity* as a putative time in the future when (a) human-level AI has been achieved, (b) superintelligence has rapidly followed, and (c) the resulting impact on humanity is without historical precedent (Shanahan, 2015). The technological singularity may be decades away, or centuries, or it may never occur at all. Nevertheless, the mere possibility raises many philosophically interesting questions. Among the largest of these is the question of whether the outcome would be good for humanity or bad, whether the technological singularity will result in a utopia for humans (Kurzweil, 2005) or a dystopia (business as usual being ruled out by assumption).

At the extreme dystopian end of the spectrum, Bostrom (2014) has argued that superhuman-level AI constitutes an existential risk. His concern is not that the AI of the future will come into conflict with humanity to further its own agenda. Rather, the concern is that we will be unable to specify the goals we want the AI to pursue precisely enough to rule out disastrous unintended consequences. However, as we have seen, there are a wide variety of forms that artificial intelligence might take in the future. At present, we cannot say much about what human- or superhuman-level artificial general intelligence will be like (assuming it arrives at all). Hopefully, if and when this powerful technology becomes a real prospect, we will begin to discern the form, or forms, it will take in time to ensure that its impact on humanity is positive.

To conclude, let us imagine a future in which all goes well in this regard. Suppose that artificial superintelligence is developed, and that it is safely harnessed for the benefit of all humanity. Then some of the oldest questions in philosophy would re-emerge in a new guise, and with an urgency no philosopher in history has had to contend with. What constitutes a good life? How should society be organized and governed? What (if anything) is the ultimate destiny of humankind, and how can we reach for it? It is conceivable that artificial intelligence will give us the power actually to implement whatever answers we, as a species, might agree on, if only such agreement could be reached.

References

Boden, M. (2003) *The Creative Mind: Myths and Mechanisms*, 2nd ed. Abingdon, UK: Routledge.

Bostrom, N. (2014) *Superintelligence: Paths, Dangers, Strategies*. Oxford: Oxford University Press.

Brooks, R.A. (1991) 'Intelligence without Representation', *Artificial Intelligence Journal*, 47, pp. 139–159.

Chalmers, D. (1996) *The Conscious Mind: In Search of a Fundamental Theory*. Oxford: Oxford University Press.

Damasio, A. (1994) *Descartes' Error: Emotion, Reason, and the Human Brain*. New York, NY: Putnam Publishing.

Dennett, D. (1987) *The Intentional Stance*. Cambridge, MA: MIT Press.

Grey Walter, W. (1950) 'An Imitation of Life', *Scientific American*, 182, pp. 42–54.

Kurzweil, R. (2005) *The Singularity Is Near*. New York, NY: Viking Books.

LeCun, Y., Bengio, Y., and Hinton, G. (2015) 'Deep Learning', *Nature*, 521, pp. 436–444.

Legg, S. and Hutter, M. (2007) 'Universal Intelligence: A Definition of Machine Intelligence', *Minds and Machines*, 17, pp. 391–444.

McCarthy, J. (1987) 'Generality in Artificial Intelligence', *Communications of the ACM*, 30 (12), pp. 1030–1035.

Mueller, E. (2014) *Commonsense Reasoning: An Event Calculus Based Approach*, 2nd ed. Burlington, MA: Morgan Kaufmann.

Shanahan, M. (2015) *The Technological Singularity*. Cambridge, MA: MIT Press.

Shanahan, M. (2016) 'The Frame Problem', *The Stanford Encyclopedia of Philosophy*, March 21, Zalta, E.N. (ed.). Available at: http://plato.stanford.edu/archives/spr2016/entries/frame-problem/.

Silver, D. et al. (2016) 'Mastering the Game of Go with Deep Neural Networks and Tree Search', *Nature*, 529, pp. 484–489.

Sloman, A. (1984) 'The Structure of the Space of Possible Minds', in Torrance, S. (ed.) *The Mind and the Machine: Philosophical Aspects of Artificial Intelligence*. Hemel Hempstead, UK: Ellis Horwood, pp. 35–42.

Truitt, E.R. (2015) *Medieval Robots: Mechanism, Magic, Nature, and Art*. Philadelphia, PA: University of Pennsylvania Press.

Turing, A.M. (1936) 'On Computable Numbers, with an Application to the *Entscheidungsproblem*', *Proceedings of the London Mathematical Society*, 2 (42), pp. 230–265.

Turing, A.M. (1950) 'Computing Machinery and Intelligence', *Mind*, 59, pp. 433–460.

PART II

Types of computing

8

CLASSICAL COMPUTATIONAL MODELS

Richard Samuels

Introduction

In this chapter I discuss a familiar class of computational models that have played an influential role in artificial intelligence, computational psychology, and cognitive science – what are often called "classical" or "symbolic" models. In Section 1, I characterize such models, and discuss their relationship to some closely associated ideas. In Section 2, I sketch some putative virtues of classical models. In Section 3, I discuss some of the dimensions along which these models vary, and provide brief illustrations. Finally, in Section 4, I mention some of the more prominent criticisms levelled against the classical modeling paradigm.

1 What is a classical computational model?

The expression "classical computation" only became common currency in cognitive science during the 1980s, largely as a means of contrasting the symbolic tradition with the burgeoning field of connectionist cognitive science (Rumelhart, McClelland, and the PDP Research Group, 1986; Fodor and Pylyshyn, 1988). However, the conception of computation it designates had been influential in AI since the 1950s, and has roots tracing back at least as far as Turing's research in the 1930s (Boden, 2006). Because of this complex history, it is important to distinguish the notion of a classical computational model from a range of associated ideas.

1.1 Classical computational models as a species of process model

There are many kinds of models in cognitive science. For example, some seek to characterize the evolution of a given psychological capacity (Barrett, 2014; Henrich and Tennie, 2017); others model statistical or causal dependencies between salient variables (Ratcliff et al., 2016); and still others seek to make precise some psychologically significant relationship, such as similarity (Tversky, 1977). However, the *prototypical* kind of cognitive models – what are often called "process models" – are primarily oriented towards addressing a kind of how–question. Roughly put: How does human performance (in a particular domain of cognition) come about? Further, the manner in which they seek to answer such questions can be characterized in terms of their target phenomena, and the sorts of features they attribute to their targets:

- *Targets*: Such models purport to explain human performance by characterizing the processes involved in the exercise of some cognitive capacity, or the operation of some functionally characterized cognitive system(s).
- *Features*: These targets are characterized in terms of a combination of familiar kinds of psychological construct: representations; cognitive operations that effect transitions between representational states; and cognitively salient resources, such as memory space, attention, and time (Weiskopf, 2017).

As with all scientific models, cognitive models can be formulated with the aid of quite different representational resources. That is, the modeling *vehicles* can be of different sorts. For example, there are verbal models formulated in a natural language, no doubt supplemented by various pieces of jargon. There are mathematical models, which paradigmatically take the form of an equation or inequality in some mathematical formalism. There are diagrammatic models; and most importantly for our purposes, there are *computational models* where the target aspects of cognition are modeled by a computational system that permits dynamic simulation of the target phenomena. *Classical* computational models (CCMs), in the sense most relevant to the present chapter, are a species of computational, process model.[1]

1.2 Core characteristics of classical models

CCMs are best construed as a broad family of process models that share a core set of characteristics. Perhaps the most obvious is that, *qua* modeling *vehicles*, CCMs are computational systems – paradigmatically, suites of programs run on an ordinary, commercial, digital computer. Yet this is not, of course, a distinctive feature of CCMs, since all computational models take this form. What is distinctive of CCMs is that they characterize their *targets* as computational systems of a particular sort. Slightly more precisely, CCMs represent cognitive processes and systems as involving a kind of *algorithmically* specifiable *symbol manipulation*. What follows is a fairly typical way of spelling out the core aspects of this sort of computation.

Symbolic. If cognition is to be characterized in terms of symbol *manipulation*, one needs *symbols*. Symbols are representations in that they have semantic properties – e.g. they denote or refer. In addition, however, they are much like natural language expressions in that they possess formal or syntactic properties, and belong to a *system* of representations, akin to a language. Such symbol systems invariably contain both primitive symbols, which have no other symbols as parts, and complex symbols built up from primitive ones. Further, these symbol systems are characterized by sets of rules – typically recursive in form – that specify which combinations of symbols are well-formed or grammatical, and also assign meanings to both primitive and well-formed combinations of symbols. In short, symbolic representational systems of the sort relevant to classical computation possess a combinatorial syntax and semantics in much the same way as logical systems, and natural languages, do (Fodor and Pylyshyn, 1988). For this reason, classical models are sometimes called *language of thought* models (Fodor, 1975).

Algorithmic. In addition to syntactic and semantic rules, which define a symbol system, classical computation also presupposes a set of rules, or instructions, which specify *algorithms* for how these symbols are to be manipulated. An algorithm is a precise, stepwise procedure for doing something – of performing a mapping from a class of inputs (the domain) to a class of outputs (the range).[2] That is, it's a way of *computing* a function. Thus, CCMs seek to characterize cognitive processes as algorithmically specifiable processes for computing functions.

Formal. A third assumption embodied in CCMs is that the relevant class of algorithms are *formal* in that the operations specified by the algorithm are defined with respect to the syntactic, as opposed to semantic, properties of symbols. In this regard, they are akin to familiar grade-school algorithms for multiplication and long division, which are formulated in terms of operations on formally characterized items – Arabic *numerals* – and not the things they represent – i.e. numbers. One consequence of this is that the task of classically modeling a cognitive process is entwined with the task of specifying the formal properties of the representations involved. Change the symbol system – e.g. from Arabic to Roman numerals – and one must typically change the algorithm as well.

Interpretable. A final core feature of CCMs is that they characterize cognitive processes as *semantically interpretable.* Although cognitive processes are modeled by formal procedures, the symbols involved have semantic properties as well. As a consequence, it is possible to make sense of – to interpret – the process, not merely as the manipulation of formal tokens, but as mappings from meaningful states to other meaningful states. To return to the example of grade-school arithmetic, although the algorithm for multiplication is specified in term of operations on Arabic numerals, the symbol transitions that occur can be systematically interpreted in terms of the numbers represented – i.e. as finding the product of two or more *numbers.*

1.3 Classical models and "Turing computation"

In addition to the above four features, CCMs are sometimes attributed other characteristics that are incorrectly presumed to be essential. Some of these false presumptions are, I suspect, a consequence of misunderstanding the idea that classicists seek to model "the mind as a Turing machine", or that they "attempt to fit the facts of human cognition to the classical, Turing account of computation" (Fodor, 2001, p. 5).

Turing's research is, of course, extraordinarily influential, in part because it provides a theoretically perspicuous model of (classical) computation. However, CCMs need not – and should not – attribute all the properties of Turing machines to cognitive systems. First, CCMs invariably make different assumptions about the nature of memory. The memory in a Turing machine – the tape – is infinite and unaddressable. In contrast, and for obvious reasons, CCMs do not characterize human memory as infinite; and they almost invariably assume – though often only tacitly – that cognition relies on addressable memory systems (Gallistel and King, 2010).

Second, Turing machines are serial processors, but CCMs need not characterize their targets in this way.[3] Admittedly some highly influential classical cognitive scientists have viewed seriality as an important property of human cognition (e.g. Simon, 1962). Nevertheless, many acknowledge that classical computations can have parallel implementations (Fodor and Pylyshyn, 1988; Gallistel and King, 2010). So, for example, more recent versions of Newell and Laird's SOAR implements symbolic processes, such as production rule activation, in parallel (Ritter, 2005).

Finally, a Turing machine is deterministic in the sense that at any point in a procedure, there is at most one unique next operation it can perform. In contrast, CCMs need not characterize cognition as deterministic. For example, they may posit stochastic processes that involve random number generation, or concurrent operations – both of which suffice for a process being nondeterministic in the relevant sense.

1.4 Classical models and Marr's levels

There is a longstanding tradition in cognitive science of characterizing models or explanations with reference to some hierarchy of levels. The best-known is David Marr's tri-level hierarchy, which I discuss here because it is often construed as a framework for classical modeling (Marr, 1982).

Suppose we seek to characterize some cognitive process or system. Then, each of Marr's level can be characterized by proprietary research questions that require the provision of distinct sorts of descriptions:

* *C-Level*: Computational level descriptions seek to characterize *what* function, or mapping, the system computes, and *why*.
* *A-Level*: Algorithmic level descriptions seek to characterize *how* the computation is performed by specifying (a) the class of symbols that are inputs to and outputs from the system; and (b) the algorithm(s) by which this transformation is accomplished.
* *I-Level*: Implementation level descriptions seek to characterize the physical organization which enables the cognitive process or system to be implemented.

Whether Marr's hierarchy is exhaustive is a matter of some theoretical debate (Peebles and Cooper, 2015). However, the tri-level hierarchy provides a useful way of bringing out certain typical characteristics of classical models.

First, of the three levels, CCMs are clearly best construed as A-level descriptions since they aim to characterize cognitive systems in terms of the algorithmic manipulation of symbols. Second, and relatedly, this observation allows us to see that classical and non-classical cognitive models need not always be incompatible with each other. For example, it may be that some connectionist models are best construed as I-level descriptions, which purport to explain how classical processes might be implemented in the brain (Pinker and Prince, 1988).

Third, since Marr's time, it has become widely accepted by modelers that C-level analyses are critically important to the development of process models – especially CCMs. Among other things, this is because, as Marr stressed, the appropriateness of any given algorithm depends crucially on the nature of the computational problem to be solved (e.g. Griffiths, Lieder, and Goodman, 2015; Bringsjord, 2008b). This was not, however, always a dominant view amongst classicists. Indeed, Marr's motivation for introducing the tri-level hypothesis was to correct what he saw as a major deficiency in the research of his day: a tendency to produce process models without any serious effort at developing rigorous C-level analyses.

Finally, it is worth noting that, as a matter of fact, classical modelers have given far less attention to I-level considerations than to C-level ones. In some cases, this is due to a paucity of relevant I-level information. In other cases, it is a consequence of adopting formalisms that do not readily map onto extant neuroscience (Bringsjord, 2008b).

1.5 Classical models and the computational theory of mind

Historically, a central motivation for classical modeling is the endorsement of the *classical computational theory of mind* (Samuels, 2010; Rescorla, 2015). Though formulated in different ways, the rough idea is this:

CCTM: The mind is literally a classical computational system – an interpretable, formal, symbol manipulator – of some sort; and cognitive processes, such as reasoning and visual perception, just are classical computational processes of some sort.

So construed, CCTM is a kind of empirically motivated, *metaphysical* doctrine, in that it provides a general characterization of what it is to be a mind, or cognitive process (Fodor, 1975; though see Piccinini, 2010, for an alternative construal of CCTM). Moreover, it is a view that has had some highly influential advocates – e.g. Fodor, Pylyshyn, and Gallistel explicitly endorse the view, and Newell and Simon's physical symbol systems hypothesis is a close cousin (Newell and Simon, 1976).

The relationship between CCTM and the classical modeling strategy is a complex one. Clearly, they dovetail with each other. Historically, adherence to CCTM has been a major motivation for developing classical models. Moreover, various kinds of predictive and explanatory success in developing classical models may, in turn, provide support for the doctrine itself.

Nevertheless, it is important to see that classical modelers need not incur a commitment to CCTM – they need not be doctrinal in this way. CCTM is a general thesis regarding the nature of mind and cognition, and CCMs might be scientifically useful even if this general thesis is false. First, it might be that our minds are *hybrid* systems, as some dual process theorists have claimed, where only some cognitive systems are as classicists suppose (Sloman, 1996; see also Anderson, 2007). Alternatively, even if CCTM is entirely inadequate as a metaphysics of mind, CCMs might still be (causal) explanatory at some appropriate level of granularity. (Compare: electrical circuit theory is explanatory in cellular neuroscience, even though no one maintains that neurons *just are* electrical circuits.) Finally, even if CCMs fail to explain human cognition, they might still be useful for other purposes, such as addressing "how-possibly" questions of various sorts.

To summarize: Though the success of the classical modeling enterprise obviously fits well with CCTM, modelers need not be committed to this doctrine since the provision CCMs might be scientifically valuable even if CCTM is false. In Section 3, I will suggest that more recent classical modeling is sometimes of this non-doctrinal variety.

2 Virtues of classical models

Why suppose the goals of cognitive science are fruitfully pursued by developing CCMs? For heuristic purposes, I divide the reasons into two sorts: (a) general methodological virtues, and (b) respects in which CCMs appear peculiarly suited to characterizing aspects of cognition. Whether any of these putative virtues are *unique* to CCMs is an issue of longstanding and ongoing disagreement, which I won't take up here.

2.1 General methodological virtues

Over the past sixty years or so, researchers have claimed that computational models in general, and CCMs in particular, can play a significant role in addressing various methodological concerns in the cognitive and behavioral sciences, including the following:

Prediction and testability. Computational models in general, and CCMs in particular, are useful in that they can generate testable predictions. In particular, they allow for the generation of predictions under different input conditions that can be tested against behavior data.

Avoiding under-specification. Computational modeling requires that researchers be explicit about the assumptions they make. This is especially important in the context of psychological science where, as behaviorists were fond of stressing, much of what passes for theory can be woefully underspecified. Of particular concern is the risk of "explanations" that posit undischarged "homunculi" – sub-processes or sub-systems – that do not so much explain as presuppose the target phenomenon. CCMs help ameliorate this concern because they require the specification and implementation of an algorithmic process. In doing so, they leave nowhere for homunculi to hide.

Avoiding vacuity. Another common behaviorist concern is that intentional psychological explanations may sometimes appear empty because they are too easily generated. Whatever the behavior we seek to understand, it's effortless to retrofit the unobserved mental causes to "explain" it. As Pylyshyn and others note, however, if one demands that psychological explanations take the form of precisely articulated procedures – implementable in the form of programs – this complaint no longer seems plausible. Indeed, far from being too easy, the problem is often that it is too *hard* to develop such models (Pylyshyn, 1984).

Addressing "how"-questions. Many of the most pressing issues in the cognitive and behavioral sciences concern the explanation of *capacities* with which we are already intimately familiar. Put a neurotypical subject in front of a tree under normal lighting conditions, and there's a good chance that they will *see* a tree. Ask such a subject what they see, and there's a good chance that they'll be able to tell you. The principle challenge for psychology is not merely to document such regularities, but to explain *how* instances of such regularities reliably occur. Process models quite generally seek to address such questions, by characterizing the state transitions between initial conditions (e.g. sensory inputs) and a given cognitive or behavioral outcome. CCMs are process models that achieve this goal by specifying a precise stepwise procedure for effecting such transitions. To that extent, they are appropriate for addressing the core explanatory challenge of cognitive science.

Addressing "how-possibly"-questions. There's a well-known and philosophically deeper reason for finding CCMs attractive. Contemporary research on human behavior and cognition occurs within the context of some widespread assumptions that are not easily reconciled. On the one hand, it is almost universally assumed amongst behavioral scientists that human beings are complex physical systems. On the other hand, there is widespread consensus that human behavior is at least partially explained by *representational* processes. In view of this, perhaps the deepest motivation for the classical modeling strategy is that it provides a framework within which these commitments can be reconciled (Haugeland, 1989; Pinker, 2000). CCMs provide *existence proofs* of complex, semantically interpretable physical systems, and in doing so suggest answers to longstanding questions regarding how it is possible for physical systems to exhibit the sorts of psychological capacities we possess.

2.2 The peculiar suitability of classical models

In addition to their general methodological virtues, CCMs appear peculiarly suitable for modeling some apparently pervasive psychological phenomena.

Modeling inferential processes. Closely related to the last point in Section 2.1., many psychological processes appear both causal *and* inferential. This is perhaps most obvious in the case of reasoning, where earlier beliefs are not only causally related to later ones, but also *semantically* related in such a way that the former provide premises for the latter. Yet this phenomenon seems not to be restricted to reasoning. For example, much of our best perceptual psychology proceeds on the assumption that vision, audition, and the like involve "unconscious inference" (Helmholtz, 1867; Scholl, 2005; Olshausen, 2014).

Historically, the inferential character of many psychological processes was perceived as posing a serious challenge: a version of the notorious *homunculus regress*. To explain such rational-cum-causal relations, it seems that meanings themselves must be causally efficacious, which in turn appears to require some inner interpreter – an intelligent subsystem, or homunculus – for which thoughts have meanings. But then the same problem of coordinating semantic and causal relations recurs for the homunculus, resulting in a regress of interpreters. Classical modelers address this problem by rejecting the assumption that rational causation is explicable only if meanings are causally efficacious. Instead they invoke an idea familiar to logicians, that inferences can be characterized in terms of formal rules. (*Modus ponens* is a simple example.) When applied to the task of understanding cognition, the idea is that mental processes are inferential not because of any unexplained sensitivity to meanings, but because they depend on formal rules which, though defined over the syntax of representations, are like logical rules in that they preserve semantic relations. Moreover, since CCMs characterize cognitive processes algorithmically, they are ultimately decomposable into combinations of operations the execution of which requires no intelligence at all. We are thus able to explain the inferential character of cognitive processes without succumbing to regress.

Productivity and systematicity. CCMs are often regarded as suited to modeling aspects of cognition that are productive or systematic (Fodor and Pylyshyn, 1988). This plausibly includes language comprehension and production, planning, deductive reasoning, and perhaps perceptual capacities, such as vision. Roughly put, such cognitive capacities are *productive* at least in the sense that they permit the production of a great many distinct thoughts, many of which are novel. Further, such regions of cognition seem *systematic*, in roughly the sense that the salient representational capacities come in coherent packages. In particular, the ability to be in some cognitive states appears to reliably covary with the ability to be in other semantically related states. To use a well-worn example: so far as we know, there is no-one who can understand the sentence "Mary loves John" and yet lacks the ability to understand the sentence "John loves Mary". The capacity to understand the one, reliably covaries with the capacity to understand the other. *Mutatis mutandis* for a great many cognitive states. Or so it would appear.

Classical modelers have a general approach to modeling systematicity and productivity. In brief, part of the solution is that CCMs are specified relative to a recursively defined combinatorial system of syntactically structured representations. Further, the algorithmic processes defined over this system invariably involve combinatorial operations, sensitive only to the syntax of these representations. In view of this, it is relatively easy to accommodate productive processes because, under minimal assumptions, the system of representations is potentially infinite, and the model has the resources to generate increasingly more complex symbolic structures via the combination of simpler ones. Systematicity is similarly easy to accommodate. If combinatorial operations are defined over syntactic forms, syntactically similar representations will be treated in similar fashion, even where they differ semantically. To return to the well-worn example of "John" and "Mary": Assuming that "John loves Mary" and "Mary loves John" involve the same symbols and share the same syntax, if one of them is producible by the model, then, (given minimal assumptions) so too will the other. This is because the very same computational resources are required for the production of either.

Variables and quantification. Human beings engage in a wide array of cognitive tasks that are readily modeled in terms of operations on variables, often bound by quantifiers. This is perhaps most obvious in the case of natural language, but it appears to occur in a great many other tasks as well, including deductive reasoning, planning, and mathematical cognition. Further, much inductive learning appears to consist in learning the relationships between variables. For example, we are able to learn what Marcus (2001) called "universally quantified, one-to-one mappings", such as identity. These tasks are naturally modeled within the classical framework because variables and quantifiers are readily accommodated within a symbol system, and much classical computation involves operations over such variable structures.

One-shot learning. Human beings engage in various forms of one-shot learning that can exert a significant influence on both our overt behavior and inferential tendencies. Most obviously, this occurs when we acquire new factual information via natural language. As Griffiths et al.

(2010) note, "to a child who believes that dolphins are fish, hearing a simple message from a knowledgeable adult ('dolphins might look like fish but are actually mammals') might drastically modify the inferences she makes". This sort of phenomenon is readily modeled as relying on explicit representations of the sort assumed by classical models. In contrast, it is far from obvious how to accommodate this phenomenon within other modeling frameworks, such as connectionism.

Cognitive flexibility. Amongst the most striking features of human cognition is its *flexibility*. To a first approximation, we appear capable of performing an indefinite range of qualitatively distinct tasks. Or, as Allen Newell once put it: we exhibit a kind of *unlimited qualitative adaptation* (Newell, 1990). One early and powerful motivation for the classical modeling paradigm is that it suggests an elegant account of this phenomenon. Classical computational systems can exhibit this sort of flexibility in that they can execute different sets of instructions designed for different tasks. Faced with the task of explaining human cognitive flexibility, some researchers suggest that a similar account may hold for human cognition as well – that much of our flexibility results from our possession of cognitive mechanisms that are capable of exploiting different bodies of task-relevant procedural knowledge (Newell, 1990).

3 Varieties of classical computational modeling: some illustrations

So far, we have discussed the characteristics, and general virtues, of CCMs. However, different families of classical models have been developed within research programs that vary considerably in their methodological and empirical commitments. As a consequence, there is considerable variation in the sorts of models – and broader modeling practices – which exist within classical paradigms. In what follows, I briefly discuss some of these approaches.

3.1 Heuristic search: early exemplars of classical modeling

Early research by Newell, Simon, and their collaborators aimed not only to provide workable bits of technology, but also to model how human beings solve various cognitive tasks. In addition to possessing the core features of CCMs, programs such as the Logic Theorist and the General Problem Solver (or GPS) incorporated a pair of additional assumptions that exerted a profound influence on subsequent research in AI and cognitive science (Newell and Simon, 1956; 1961).

The first of these assumptions is that much human cognition involves a kind of mental *search* through a space of options – a search space – in order to find a solution to the task at hand. Moreover, since the search space for interesting tasks is almost invariably too large to permit exhaustive search, Newell and Simon further proposed that search needs to be *heuristically* constrained. That is, the model needs to encode various guidelines or "rules of thumb" which constrain the range of options that need be considered in the course of solving the task at hand. For example, GPS used a kind of search heuristic known as means-end analysis, which aims to produce convergence on the solution to a problem by successively reducing the difference between the current state of the system and the goal state.

Within AI the ideas found in Newell and Simon's early work spurred extensive research on heuristic search (see Russell and Norvig, 2010, chs. 3–5), and was instrumental in the development of planning systems, such as STRIPS, which relied on the notions of means-ends analysis and search (Fikes and Nilsson, 1971). Planning research, though dramatically transformed, remains a highly active region of AI (Ghallab, Nau and Traverso, 2016).

From the vantage of contemporary cognitive science, models such as GPS may appear quaint. Nevertheless, the idea that cognition relies on heuristic methods remains an influential one. For example, the "Ecological Rationality" research program, initiated by Gerd Gigerenzer and Peter Todd, relies heavily on the notion of heuristic processes in order to explain our capacity to make decisions in a computationally efficient manner (Todd, Gigerenzer, and the ABC Research Group, 2012). Moreover, whilst not doctrinally committed to a classical view of cognition, many of their models possess the core characteristics of CCMs. This is true, for example, of Gigerenzer and Goldstein's well-known model of the Take-the-Best heuristic, which (roughly) decides between two options – e.g. which of two cities is larger – by using the most valid available discriminating cue, and ignoring the rest (Gigerenzer and Goldstein, 1999).

3.2 Logicism

A second illustration of classical modeling is the logic-based or *logicist* approach. Though it played a prominent role in the development of AI and continues to spur research in applied logic, its influence in contemporary cognitive science is diminished. (For overviews, see Minker, 2000; Bringsjord, 2008a; and Thomason, 2016.)

Starting in the 1950s with the seminal work of John McCarthy and his collaborators, logicists proposed that many of the cognitive problems we confront are fruitfully construed as problems of logical inference (McCarthy, 1959). In slightly more detail, logicists maintain that propositional attitudes – mental states, such as beliefs, judgments, and intentions – are central to human cognition, and that many cognitive processes consist in inferential transitions between such attitudes. In paradigmatic instances of reasoning, for example, one starts with a set of premise beliefs, and infers a conclusion; and when planning one infers new intentions from prior goals, intentions, and beliefs.

If one thinks of cognition in the above way, then formal logic appears directly relevant. In particular, proof theory promises to provide the relevant resources for formally characterizing cognitive tasks in terms of inferential relations between propositional – or declarative – representations.

In terms of Marr's levels, logicism is naturally characterized by the following division of labor. At the C-level, logical formalization is used in order to provide precise specifications of the inferential problems that we solve – e.g. narrative understanding, or spatial reasoning (Thomason, 2016).[4] In view of the range and complexity of the problems we solve, this has resulted in significant developments in formal logic itself, including nonmonotonic logics (Antonelli, 2012), logics for spatial reasoning (Stock, 1997), and logics for temporal reasoning (Ghallab, Nau, and Traverso, 2016).

At the A-level, the core task for logicists is to provide computationally efficient implementations of the solutions specified at the C-level. Though different kinds of implementation are possible, in practice they typically consist in a kind of mechanized proof theory, where relevant information is represented by formulae in a logical language, and computation proceeds by the operation of a theorem-prover, so that new representations can be derived from existing ones, via the application of proof-theoretic rules (Chater and Oaksford, 1991).

Within contemporary AI, perhaps the most well-known example of a logic-based system is Doug Lenat's monumental CYC system, which aims to codify, in machine-usable form, the millions of items of information that constitute human commonsense (Lenat et al., 1990). Within contemporary cognitive science, logic-based models are less commonplace than they once were. Nevertheless, they are found in various fields of research, such as computational linguistics and the psychology of reasoning. For example, Lance Rips PSYCOP is a well-known logic-based model of human deductive reasoning (Rips, 1994). In addition, production systems, such as SOAR and ACT-R – of which more below – bear close ties to logic-based models (Bringsjord, 2008b).

3.3 Cognitive architectures

A third example of classical research concerns the characterization of *cognitive architecture*. Although such architectural models take the form of working computer systems, they possess a pair of features not typical of CCMs in general.

First, in contrast to many CCMs, which tend to target relatively narrow aspects of cognition, models of cognitive architecture seek to provide a comprehensive, detailed specification of how cognition operates across a wide range of domains and tasks. In Newell's (1990) memorable phrase, they are intended to provide "unified theories of cognition". Further, since such models are typically motivated by the idea that much human behavior is a product of complex interactions between systems, they typically specify a variety of systems – e.g. for different sorts of memory, and for different sorts of cognitive process.

Second, in contrast to many CCMs, architectural models pursue the ambitious project of specifying the core set of *basic* computational operations, structures, and resources on which cognition depends. To put the point metaphorically, they purport to specify the sorts of properties that would be described in a "user's manual" for the cognitive system (Fodor and Pylyshyn, 1988). Such properties are assumed to be basic in at least two senses. First, they are presumed to be relatively invariant over the lifespan of the agent. Second, they are typically assumed to be properties of the mind that are presupposed – but not explained – by one's classical account of cognition. As a consequence, it is typically assumed that the explanation of these properties requires recourse to some "lower"-level science, such as neurobiology or biochemistry. Again, none of this is typical of CCMs more generally.

Of course, not all architectural models are classical. For example, Randy O'Reilly's well-known *Leabra* model specifies a connectionist architecture (O'Reilly, Hazy, and Herd, 2017). Nevertheless, since the 1970s, there have been a number of notable efforts to specify cognitive architectures, which are either uniformly classical, or at least hybrid models with classical subcomponents. The SOAR architecture, developed by Allen Newell and John Laird is a prominent example of the former, and John Anderson's ACT-R is an influential version of the latter (Laird, 2012; Anderson, 2007). Versions of these architectures have been around since the 1980s, and have been used to simulate human performance on a broad array of tasks, including arithmetic, categorization, video game playing, natural language understanding, concept acquisition, verbal reasoning, driving, analogy making, and scientific discovery.

Although SOAR and ACT-R are too complex to describe here, it is interesting to note that both architectures contain *production systems* as a core component. Such systems operate on if-then rules, known as productions, in which the antecedent of the rule specifies a condition (e.g. the knight is on square 8), and the consequent an action to be performed when that condition obtains (e.g. move the knight to square 1). Production systems operate via the coordination of three sub-systems: a long-term memory in which the rules are stored, a working memory, and an inference engine. A production rule can be retrieved from long-term memory (or "fired") only if its antecedent condition is met by an element in working memory. The task of the inference engine is to determine which of the rules have all their conditions met, and then to decide which of these should be fired. Over the years, production systems have had various practical applications – e.g. in expert systems such as Mycin and Dendral. But more importantly for present purposes, they have proven exceedingly useful in modeling complex sequences of behavior, such as those that occur in problem solving.

3.4 Bayesian modeling

My final illustration of classical modeling may strike readers as an odd one in that Bayesian research in cognitive science is not ordinarily construed as a form of classicism. And, indeed, there are important differences between Bayesian approaches and the sorts of "good old fashioned" cognitive science mentioned above. For one thing, Bayesian cognitive scientists in general have no doctrinal commitment to CCTM. For another, in contrast to the classical models of old, it is absolutely central to the Bayesian approach that psychological processes are fruitfully construed in terms of *probabilistic* inference of the sort characterized by Bayesian statistics. For all that, some of the models and modeling strategies used by Bayesians bear a striking resemblance to more traditional classical ones; and for this reason, I suggest that some Bayesian modeling is appropriately construed as a non-doctrinal form of classical modeling.

Although there are currently different forms of Bayesianism in the brain and behavioral sciences, researchers in cognitive science typically adopt a methodology, reminiscent of Marr, which starts with C-level analyses. Thus, Griffiths et al. (2010) contrast their Bayesian approach to that of connectionism, and other "mechanism-first" approaches, by noting: "probabilistic models of cognition pursue a top-down or 'function-first' strategy, beginning with abstract principles that allow agents to solve problems posed by the world – the functions that minds perform (2010, p. 357). In other words, Bayesians typically start by providing a C-level analysis of the cognitive task, where they specify the function computed in terms of principles drawn from probability theory, such as those involved in sampling and model selection.

To take a well-known example, suppose that we seek to understand the problem of learning the extension of new words in the absence of negative evidence. When a child learns the word "dog", for instance, it suffices for a teacher to point to a few positive examples – a Chihuahua, a Shetland Sheepdog, and a Boxer, for example – and call them each "dog", without also pointing to, say, a horse or a sunflower and saying "That's not a dog". Within the Bayesian framework, this is naturally construed as a task in which hypotheses are being prioritized according to some probabilistic criterion. Thus, Xu and Tenenbaum (2007) propose that this task and its solution can be partially characterized by a simple but powerful principle of probabilistic inference – the *size principle* – which says that if you are considering a set of nested hypotheses, you should prefer the smallest hypothesis consistent with the available evidence (Perfors et al., 2011).

Most extant Bayesian research is similar to the above in that it aims to provide C-level analyses that specify ideal solutions to computational problems. Moreover, even where algorithmic issues arise, Bayesians are not generally committed to a classical modeling strategy. Nevertheless, some Bayesian models have a distinctly classical flavor. This is so for a pair of reasons. First, Bayesian C-level analyses frequently suggest a role in cognition for complex representational structures of the sort most readily accommodated by classical models – e.g. hierarchically structured category systems, or tree-structured representations (Griffiths et al., 2010). Second, when seeking to explain how ideal solutions might be efficiently approximated by human cognition, Bayesians have pursued a strategy of borrowing techniques from theoretical computer science – such as Monte Carlo methods – which possess characteristics readily accommodated within a classical computational framework – such as variable binding, and compositionally structured hypothesis spaces (Griffiths, Kemp, and Tenenbaum, 2008).

In view of the above, it is perhaps unsurprising that in recent years, some Bayesian researchers have described their own approach to cognitive modeling as relying on what the arch classicist, Jerry Fodor, called a *language of thought* (LOT). In its Bayesian incarnation, however, the LOT is (of course) probabilistic – a *pLOT*. Thus, Piantadosi and Jacobs conclude a recent paper by articulating a conception of Bayesianism that's continuous with, whilst improving upon, the more traditional symbolic approaches that preceded it:

> The pLOT is not a revolutionary new theory that promises to overthrow existing paradigms; it is a resurgent old theory that promises to integrate many approaches into a unitary framework ... we argue that it provides one of the most promising frameworks for cognition, combining the compositionality of symbolic approaches with the robustness of probabilistic approaches, thereby permitting researchers to formulate and test theories that do not acquiesce to the poles of major debates.
>
> *(Piantadosi and Jacobs, 2016)*

4 Challenges to classical models

The classical paradigm has been subject to a bewildering array of objections; and though there isn't the space to consider them in detail here, I propose to briefly discuss some of the more prominent ones.

4.1 A priori *philosophical objections*

One sort of objection is not so much directed at CCMs as the metaphysics of mind with which they are associated. Specifically, such arguments purport to show on broadly *a priori* grounds that CCTM is false. Perhaps the most well-known of these objections is Searle's Chinese Room argument, which is sometimes taken to show that CCTM is false because performing the right computations is insufficient for such cognitive capacities as understanding. The argument proceeds via a thought experiment:

> A native English speaker who knows no Chinese [is] locked in a room full of boxes of Chinese symbols (a database) together with a book of instructions for manipulating the symbols (the program). Imagine that people outside the room send in other Chinese symbols which, unknown to the person in the room, are questions in Chinese (the input). And imagine that by following the instructions in the program the man in the room is able to pass out Chinese symbols which are correct answers to the questions (the output).
>
> *(Searle, 1999)*

From outside it seems the system understands Chinese. But according to Searle, no matter what program the man executes, he won't know what the symbols *mean*. Thus mastery of syntactic operations – of the program – is insufficient for semantics; and since understanding a sentence requires a grasp of what the sentence *means*, running a program is insufficient for understanding as well. Further, Searle maintains that the conclusion generalizes. What's true of natural language understanding is also true for cognition more generally. Running a program, no matter how good, is insufficient for cognition.

The critical discussion surrounding Searle's argument is too large to consider in detail here. (See Searle, 1980, and responses; and, Preston and Bishop, 2002, for further discussion.)

It should be noted, however, that even if Searle is correct about the inadequacy of CCTM, it is far from clear that this would render classical modeling scientifically moribund. For as we saw earlier, the two are logically independent. In addition, it is not obvious that Searle's argument undermines CCTM. One common response is that, as an objection to CCTM, it misses the mark. Classicists do not claim that executing the right program is, by itself, sufficient for thought. This would require the acceptance of a claim that classicists routinely deny: that computational role – the way the program uses a representation – determines its meaning. Rather, what classicists maintain is that cognitive processes are computational processes operating on semantically evaluable representations, whilst *leaving open* – indeed frequently endorsing – the option that semantic properties are determined by something other than computational role, such as causal relations to the environment (Fodor, 1990). Thus according to this response, the conclusion of Searle's argument is wholly compatible with the truth of CCTM.

4.2 Arguments from mathematics

A second family of objections seeks to draw out implications for the classical paradigm from well-known results in mathematics – most famously Gödel's incompleteness theorems (Gödel, 1934; Lucas, 1961; Penrose, 1989). These arguments take a variety of forms; but the general idea is that the mathematical result implies limitations on computational systems, which the human mind allegedly exceeds. In the case of Gödel's results, the limitation is, roughly, that for any formal system – such as a classical computer – which is both consistent and capable of expressing the truths of arithmetic, there will be truths that are not provable in the system. Further, it is argued that since we are capable of appreciating such truths, human minds are not classical computers.

Again, this sort of argument has generated an extensive literature. (For an overview, see Franzén, 2005.) Once more, I restrict myself to two comments. First, even if sound, it is unclear how severe the consequences for the classical paradigm would be. This is because extant mathematical arguments, even if sound, would only show that some human cognitive capacities exceed those of computers. Yet this is wholly compatible with most of our capacities being amenable to classical modeling.

Second, the extant mathematical arguments invariably depend on empirical assumptions regarding the extent of our cognitive powers. But as many commentators have noted, these assumptions are at best highly idealized (Shapiro, 1998; 2003). Why, for example, suppose that we can always see whether or not a given formalized theory is consistent, or that we are capable of formulating our own Gödel sentence? It is, to put it mildly, unobvious that these are powers we possess.

4.3 Explanatory limitations

A third family of criticisms maintains that the classical paradigm lacks the resources to explain various important psychological phenomena. In some cases, the "objection" consists of little more than drawing attention to an obviously complex psychological phenomenon, and persuasively asserting that no mere computer model could explain, or exhibit, such a capacity. Claims regarding the prospects of modeling creativity often have this flavor (Boden, 2004). In other cases, the focus is on phenomenally conscious states – such as, perceptual experiences or emotions – where there is, in Nagel's memorable phrase, "something that it is like to be" in those states (Nagel, 1974). The claim, in brief, is that classical models cannot provide a satisfactory account of how organisms can have such states because phenomenal properties are not plausibly characterized in terms of computational or functional roles (Haugeland, 1989; Chalmers, 2004).

The above concerns are seldom met with consternation by proponents of the classical paradigm. In the case of creativity, whatever the ultimate prospects for a satisfactory computational explanation, it should be unsurprising that no such account currently exists, since we lack good explanations of the *prosaic* cognitive capacities on which creativity depends. If we currently lack good explanations of *humdrum* cognition, why on earth would we expect to possess good explanations for exceptional cognition?

In the case of conscious experience and emotion, researchers are similarly unperturbed, though for different reasons. For in these cases, many classicists already *accept* the criticism. Though some brave theorists suggest that a computational account of phenomenal consciousness might be in the offing (McDermott, 2001), a more typical response is to construe classicism, not as an approach to all mental phenomena, but only to what we might loosely term the "cognitive mind". On such a view, phenomenal consciousness as such is simply not a plausible target for classical modeling.

In contrast to the above, the final example of a putative explanatory limitation that I discuss here is of genuine concern to classical researchers. This is because it appears to challenge the prospects of modeling some of the core phenomena of cognitive science – reasoning, planning, and learning, for example. The issue in question is often subsumed under the heading of the *frame problem*, and concerns our ability to determine what information is *relevant* to the tasks we perform (Ford and Pylyshyn, 1996). In particular, when making plans or revising our beliefs, we somehow manage to identify what information is relevant to the task at hand and ignore the rest. How is this "relevance sensitivity" to be explained in classical terms? It is implausible that we survey *all* our beliefs since such a strategy would require more time and computational power than we possess. Some more computationally feasible process is required. Yet many doubt such a process can be specified in classical terms. It has been suggested, for example, that relevance is unlikely to be explicable in classical terms because it is a *holistic* property of thought, in roughly the sense that the relevance of a given thought depends on a broad array of "surrounding conditions", such as one's background beliefs and intentions (Fodor, 2001; Haugeland, 1989).

Conclusion

In this chapter, I outlined the core aspects of classical computational models, enumerated their main virtues, and provided brief illustrations, both historical and contemporary. Further, I briefly discussed the relationship between classical modeling, and a range of associated ideas; and I sketched some of the more common objections to the classical approach. Although the cognitive sciences have changed dramatically since the early work of Newell and Simon, classical modeling retains a significant role in contemporary research.

Notes

1 Two terminological points. First, talk of "models" is relatively recent. More typically, early exponents of classical modeling spoke of programs as "theories" or "explanations" as opposed to models. Moreover, in recent years, "classical computation" is most typically used by computer scientists in contradistinction to *quantum* computation (Yu et al., 2002). On this use of "classical", computational systems that would be categorized as non-classical by cognitive scientists – e.g. connectionist models – are classical (i.e. non-quantum) systems.

2 Of course, algorithms satisfy a number of constraints: (a) each step in the procedure is moronic in that it requires no ingenuity or intelligence to carry out; (b) no insight or ingenuity is required to determine what the next step in the procedure is; and (c) if each step is followed exactly, the procedure is guaranteed to produce some determinate outcome in a finite number of steps.

3 Of course, the model, *qua* program, is typically run on a serial computer. However, this is also true of PDP models.
4 Roughly put, the rules of the logical system are used to specify the function in intension that is computed in the course of performing a given inferential task.

References

Anderson, J.R. (2007) *How Can the Human Mind Occur in the Physical Universe?* New York, NY: Oxford University Press.

Antonelli, G.A. (2012) 'Non-Monotonic Logic', *The Stanford Encyclopedia of Philosophy*, December 21, Zalta, E.N. (ed.), Available at: https://plato.stanford.edu/archives/win2016/entries/logic-nonmonotonic/ (Accessed: January 18, 2018).

Barrett, H.C. (2014) *The Shape of Thought: How Mental Adaptations Evolve.* New York, NY: Oxford University Press.

Boden, M.A. (2004) *The Creative Minds: Myths and Mechanisms*, 2nd ed. London: Routledge.

Boden, M.A. (2006) *Mind as Machine: A History of Cognitive Science*, vol. 1. Oxford: Oxford University Press.

Bringsjord, S. (2008a) 'The Logicist Manifesto: At Long Last Let Logic Based Artificial Intelligence Become a Field Unto Itself', *Journal of Applied Logic*, 6 (4), pp. 502–525.

Bringsjord, S. (2008b) 'Declarative/Logic-based Cognitive Models', in Sun, R. (ed.) *Cambridge Handbook of Computational Psychology*. Cambridge, UK: Cambridge University Press.

Chalmers, D. (2004) 'How Can We Construct a Science of Consciousness?', in Gazzaniga, M.S. (ed.) *The Cognitive Neurosciences III*. Cambridge, MA: MIT Press, pp. 1111–1119.

Chater, N. and Oaksford, M. (1991) 'Against Logicist Cognitive Science', *Mind and Language*, 6 (1), pp. 1–38.

Fikes, R. and Nilsson, N. (1971) 'STRIPS: A New Approach to the Application of Theorem Proving to Problem Solving', *Artificial Intelligence*, 2 (3–4), pp. 189–208.

Fodor, J. (1975) *The Language of Thought.* Cambridge, MA: Harvard University Press.

Fodor, J. (1990) *A Theory of Content and Other Essays.* Cambridge, MA: MIT/Bradford Press.

Fodor, J. (2001) *The Mind Doesn't Work That Way.* Cambridge, MA: MIT Press.

Fodor, J. and Pylyshyn, Z. (1988) 'Connectionism and Cognitive Architecture: A Critical Analysis', *Cognition*, 28, pp. 3–71.

Ford, K.M. and Pylyshyn, Z.W. (eds.) (1996) *The Robot's Dilemma Revisited: The Frame Problem in Artificial Intelligence.* New York, NY: Ablex.

Franzén, T. (2005) *Gödel's Theorem: An Incomplete Guide to Its Use and Abuse.* Wellesley, MA: A.K. Peters.

Gallistel, C.R. and King, A. (2010) *Memory and the Computational Brain.* Malden, MA: Wiley-Blackwell.

Ghallab, M., Nau, D., and Traverso, P. (2016) *Automated Planning and Acting.* Cambridge, UK: Cambridge University Press.

Gigerenzer, G. and Goldstein, D.G. (1999) 'Betting on One Good Reason: The Take the Best Heuristic', in Gigerenzer, G., Todd, P.M., and the ABC Research Group. *Simple Heuristics That Make Us Smart.* New York, NY: Oxford University Press, pp. 75–95.

Gödel, K. (1934) 'On Undecidable Propositions of Formal Mathematical Systems', reprinted with corrections in Davis, M. (ed.) (1965) *The Undecidable: Basic Papers on Undecidable Propositions, Unsolvable Problems and Computable Function.* Hewlett, NY: Raven Press, pp. 41–81.

Griffiths, T. et al. (2010) 'Probabilistic Models of Cognition: Exploring Representations and Inductive Biases', *Trends in Cognitive Sciences*, 14 (8), pp. 357–364.

Griffiths, T.L., Kemp, C., and Tenenbaum, J.B. (2008) 'Bayesian Models of Cognition', in Sun, R. (ed.) *The Cambridge Handbook of Computational Cognitive Modeling*. Cambridge, UK: Cambridge University Press.

Griffiths, T., Lieder, F., and Goodman, N. (2015) 'Rational Use of Cognitive Resources: Levels of Analysis between the Computational and the Algorithmic', *Topics in Cognitive Science*, 7 (2), pp. 217–229.

Haugeland, J. (1989) *Artificial Intelligence: The Very Idea.* Cambridge, MA: MIT Press.

Helmholtz, H. (1867) *Handbuch der physiologischen Optik*, 3. Leipzig: Voss.

Henrich, J. and Tennie, C. (2017) 'Cultural Evolution in Chimpanzees and Humans', in Muller, M., Wrangham, R., and Pilbeam, D. (eds.) *Chimpanzees and Human Evolution.* Cambridge, MA: Harvard University Press, pp. 645–702.

Laird, J.E. (2012) *The SOAR Cognitive Architecture.* Cambridge, MA: MIT Press.

Lenat, D. et al. (1990) 'Cyc: Toward Programs with Common Sense', *Communication of the ACM*, 33 (8), pp. 30–49.

Lucas, J.R. (1961) 'Minds, Machines, and Gödel', *Philosophy*, 36 (137), pp. 112–137.

Marcus, G.F. (2001) *The Algebraic Mind: Integrating Connectionism and Cognitive Science*. Cambridge, MA: MIT Press.

Marr, D. (1982) *Vision*. San Francisco, CA: W.H. Freeman.

McCarthy, J. (1959) 'Programs with Common Sense', in *Proceedings of the Teddington Conference on the Mechanization of Thought Processes*. London: Her Majesty's Stationary Office, pp. 75–91.

McDermott, D. (2001) *Mind and Mechanism*. Cambridge, MA: MIT Press.

Minker, J. (ed.) (2000) *Logic-Based Artificial Intelligence*. Dordrecht: Kluwer Academic Publishers.

Nagel, T. (1974) 'What Is It Like to Be a Bat?', *The Philosophical Review*, 83 (4), pp. 435–450.

Newell, A. (1990) *Unified Theories of Cognition*. Cambridge, MA: Harvard University Press.

Newell, A. and Simon, H.A. (1956) 'The Logic Theory Machine: A Complex Information Processing System', *IRE Transactions on Information Theory*, IT-2, pp. 61–79.

Newell, A. and Simon, H.A. (1961) 'Computer Simulation of Human Thinking', *Science*, 134 (3495), pp. 2011–2017.

Newell, A. and Simon, H.A. (1976) 'Computer Science as Empirical Enquiry: Symbols and Search', *Communications of the ACM*, 19 (3), pp. 113–126.

Olshausen, B.A. (2014) 'Perception as an Inference Problem', in Gazzaniga, M. and Mangun, R. (eds.) *The Cognitive Neurosciences*, 5th ed. Cambridge, MA: MIT Press, pp. 295–304.

O'Reilly, R.C., Hazy, T., and Herd, S. (2017) 'The Leabra Cognitive Architecture: How to Play 20 Principles with Nature and Win!', in Chipman, S.E.F. (ed.) *The Oxford Handbook of Cognitive Science*. Oxford: Oxford University Press, pp. 91–116.

Peebles, D. and Cooper, R.P. (eds.) (2015) 'Thirty Years after Marr's Vision: Levels of Analysis in Cognitive Science', *Topics in Cognitive Science* (special issue), 7 (2), pp. 185–381.

Penrose, R. (1989) *The Emperor's New Mind: Concerning Computers, Minds, and the Laws of Physics*. New York, NY: Oxford University Press.

Perfors, A. et al. (2011) 'A Tutorial Introduction to Bayesian Models of Cognitive Development', *Cognition*, 120 (3), pp. 302–321.

Piantadosi, S.T. and Jacobs, R. (2016) 'Four Problems Solved by the Probabilistic Language of Thought', *Current Directions in Psychological Science*, 25, pp. 54–59.

Piccinini, G. (2010) 'The Mind as Neural Software? Understanding Functionalism, Computationalism, and Computational Functionalism', *Philosophy and Phenomenological Research*, 81 (2), pp. 269–311.

Pinker, S. (2000) *How the Mind Works*. New York, NY: Norton.

Pinker, S. and Prince, A. (1988) 'On Language and Connectionism', *Cognition*, 28, pp. 73–193.

Preston, J. and Bishop, M. (eds.) (2002) *Views into the Chinese Room: New Essays on Searle and Artificial Intelligence*. New York, NY: Oxford University Press.

Pylyshyn, Z. (1984) *Computation and Cognition*. Cambridge, MA: MIT Press.

Ratcliff, R. et al. (2016) 'Diffusion Decision Model: Current Issues and History', *Trends in Cognitive Sciences*, 20 (4), pp. 260–281.

Rescorla, M. (2015) 'The Computational Theory of Mind', *The Stanford Encyclopedia of Philosophy*, March 21, Zalta, E.N. (ed.), Available at: http://plato.stanford.edu/archives/win2015/entries/computational-mind (Accessed: January 18, 2018).

Rips, L.J. (1994) *The Psychology of Proof: Deduction in Human Thinking*. Cambridge, MA: MIT Press.

Ritter, F.E. (2005) 'SOAR', in Nadel, L. (ed.) *Encyclopedia of Cognitive Science*. Hoboken, NJ: Wiley. Available at: http://proxy.lib.ohio-state.edu/login?url=https://search.credoreference.com/content/entry/wileycs/soar/0?institutionId=4358 (Accessed: February 2, 2018).

Rumelhart, D., McClelland, J.L., and the PDP Research Group (1986) *Parallel Distributed Processing*, vol. 1. Cambridge, MA: MIT Press.

Russell, S. and Norvig, P. (2010) *Artificial Intelligence: A Modern Approach*, 3rd ed. Upper Saddle River, NJ: Prentice Hall.

Samuels, R. (2010) 'Classical Computationalism and the Many Problems of Cognitive Relevance', *Studies in History and Philosophy of Science*, 41, pp. 280–293.

Scholl, B.J. (2005) 'Innateness and (Bayesian) Visual Perception: Reconciling Nativism and Development', in Carruthers, P., Laurence, S., and Stich, S. (eds.) *The Innate Mind: Structure and Contents*. Oxford: Oxford University Press, pp. 34–52.

Searle, J. (1980) 'Minds, Brains and Programs', *Behavioral and Brain Sciences*, 3, pp. 417–457.

Searle, J. (1999) 'The Chinese Room', in Wilson, R.A. and Keil, F. (eds.) *The MIT Encyclopedia of the Cognitive Sciences*. Cambridge, MA: MIT Press, pp. 115–116.

Shapiro, S. (1998) 'Incompleteness, Mechanism, and Optimism', *Bulletin of Symbolic Logic*, 4, pp. 273–302.

Shapiro, S. (2003) 'Mechanism, Truth and Penrose's New Argument', *Journal of Philosophical Logic*, 32 (1), pp. 19–42.

Simon, H. (1962) 'The Architecture of Complexity', *Proceedings of the American Philosophical Society*, 106 (6), pp. 467–482.

Sloman, S.A. (1996) 'The Empirical Case for Two Systems of Reasoning', *Psychological Bulletin*, 119, pp. 3–22.

Stock, O. (1997) *Spatial and Temporal Reasoning*. Dordrecht: Kluwer Academic Publishers.

Thomason, R. (2016) 'Logic and Artificial Intelligence', *The Stanford Encyclopedia of Philosophy*, December 21, Zalta, E.N. (ed.), Available at: https://plato.stanford.edu/archives/win2016/entries/logic-ai/ (Accessed: January 18, 2018).

Todd, P.M., Gigerenzer, G., and the ABC Research Group (2012) *Ecological Rationality: Intelligence in the World*. New York, NY: Oxford University Press.

Tversky, A. (1977) 'Features of Similarity', *Psychological Review*, 84 (4), pp. 327–352.

Weiskopf, D. (2017) 'The Explanatory Autonomy of Cognitive Models', in Kaplan, D.M. (ed.) *Explanation and Integration in Mind and Brain Science*. Oxford: Oxford University Press, pp. 44–69.

Xu, F. and Tenenbaum, J.B. (2007) 'Sensitivity to Sampling in Bayesian Word Learning', *Developmental Science*, 10 (3), pp. 288–297.

Yu, A. et al. (2002) *Classical and Quantum Computation*. Boston, MA: American Mathematical Society.

9

EXPLANATION AND CONNECTIONIST MODELS

Catherine Stinson

Introduction

Connectionist models are widely used in the cognitive sciences, and well beyond. This is so despite the fact that some critics have charged that we can't learn about cognition using connectionist models (Fodor and Pylyshyn, 1988). Although researchers who use connectionist models have offered a number of defenses of their methods (Smolensky, 1988; McClelland, 1988), and there is growing empirical evidence suggesting that these models have been successful in advancing cognitive science, there is no consensus on how they work. This chapter explores the epistemic roles played by connectionist models of cognition, and offers a formal analysis of how connectionist models explain.

The question of what sorts of explanations connectionist models offer has not received much (positive) attention. Understanding how these explanations work, however, is essential in evaluating their worth, and answering questions such as: How convincing is a given model? What makes a connectionist model successful? What kinds of errors should we look out for?

For the sake of comparison, I begin with a brief look at how other types of computational models explain. Classical AI programs explain using abductive reasoning, or inference to the best explanation; they begin with the phenomena to be explained, and devise rules that can produce the right outcome. Including too much implementation detail is thought to hinder the search for a general solution. Detailed brain simulations explain using deductive reasoning, or some approximation to it; they begin with the raw materials of the system and first principles they obey, and calculate the expected outcome. Here, inaccuracies or omissions of detail can lead to incorrect predictions. Connectionist modeling seems to combine the two methods; modelers take constraints from both the psychological phenomena to be explained, and from the neuroanatomical and neurophysiological systems that give rise to those phenomena. The challenge is to understand how these two very different methods can be combined into a successful strategy, rather than a failure on both counts. I'll focus on the problem of why using neural constraints should be a good strategy, even if those neural constraints aren't correct in their details.

To answer this question I look at several examples of connectionist models of cognition, observing what sorts of constraints are used in their design, and how their results are evaluated. The marks of successful connectionist models include using structures roughly analogous to neural structures, accurately simulating observed behavioral data, breaking down when damaged in patterns analogous to neurological cases, and offering novel, empirically verifiable predictions.

I argue that the point of implementing networks roughly analogous to neural structures is to discover and explore the generic mechanisms at work in the brain, not to deduce the precise activities of specific structures. As we will see, this method depends on the logic of tendencies: drawing inductive inferences from like causes to like effects. This can be combined with neuropsychological evidence, which is evaluated using graph theoretical reasoning.

How computational models explain

Computational models are especially important in cases where experimenting directly on the target system is not practicable, or the system is very complex. Opening a human skull and poking around is very invasive, so this kind of intervention can only be done in exceptional cases like during treatment of Parkinson's disease or epilepsy (Engel et al., 2005). In these rare cases, single cell recordings and electrical stimulation interventions can sometimes be done on awake, behaving patients, providing important validation of models arrived at by other means. These studies are necessarily of short duration, and usually are restricted to particular brain regions, making them quite limited in terms of what can be investigated. Furthermore, these recordings are made from brains affected by pathology, and usually in patients taking medication (Mukamel and Fried, 2012). Care must be taken when drawing inferences from studies of atypical brains to neurotypical populations.

Several non-invasive means for indirect measurement from and intervention on human brains are also available. Technologies like transcranial magnetic stimulation, positron emission tomography, functional magnetic resonance imaging, and electroencephalography all provide valuable information about human brain functioning, but all of these methods face practical limitations like noise and limited spatial or temporal resolution.

Human experiments can be supplemented by experimenting on model species like sea slugs, mice, or macaque monkeys, but these animal models also face limitations. Most animals can't perform complex laboratory tasks, and few if any can give verbal feedback, making it very difficult to investigate higher cognitive processes. In addition, it cannot be taken for granted that the brains of non-human animals process information in the same way that human brains do.

Human brains are also extremely complex, consisting of in the order of 100 billion neurons, each with thousands of synaptic connections on average, not to mention the elaborate structures within each neuron, the chemical soup surrounding them, and all the other cells in the brain whose functions are only beginning to be understood. Computational models have the capacity to quickly analyze how complex systems evolve over time, and/or in a variety of situations, making them invaluable for investigating human brain functioning.

Explanation in classical AI

Other chapters of this volume are dedicated to the history and explanatory uses of classical AI, but for our purposes here, a few brief notes will be helpful. Consider first the birthplace of classical AI: McCarthy et al.'s (1955) Dartmouth Proposal. In this proposal it is conjectured that "every aspect of learning or any other feature of intelligence can in principle be so precisely described that a machine can be made to simulate it" (McCarthy et al., 1955). The authors optimistically suggest that one summer would be sufficient to make significant progress on the problem of machine intelligence. The idea is that we can come to understand intelligence by precisely constructing a machine that reproduces the phenomenon.

More details about how this method is meant to work are found in Newell and Simon's pioneering 1961 paper. Newell and Simon begin by analyzing behavioral phenomena into protocols: transcripts of subjects speaking aloud about their thought processes while they solve a problem. The AI project is then to "construct a theory of the processes causing the subject's behavior as he [*sic*] works on the problem, and to test the theory's explanation by comparing the behavior it predicts with the actual behavior of the subject" (Newell and Simon, 1961, p. 2012).

It is clear from the section of the text titled "Nonnumerical Computer Program as a Theory" that Newell and Simon intend for their programs to be scientific theories that explain the behavioral phenomena. At the time, the "Received View" of scientific theories (see Winther, 2016), supposed that theories are sets of statements cast in predicate logic, and the prevailing deductive-nomological account of scientific explanation (Hempel and Oppenheim, 1948) supposed that empirical observations, such as the subjects' problem-solving behavior, could be explained by logically deducing observation statements from statements of laws and antecedent conditions. For Newell and Simon, the antecedent conditions would correspond to the input problem, the theory would be the sequence of symbolic expressions contained in the program, and the logically deduced outputs of the program would be the observation statements. At the heart of their approach is the postulate later dubbed the "physical symbol system hypothesis" (Newell and Simon, 1976), that the processes going on inside the subject are, like their program, operations on symbols.

Established scientific theories can be used to deduce predictions, but Newell and Simon were still at the theory-building stage. The defense of their physical symbol system hypothesis "lies in its power to explain the behavior" (Newell and Simon, 1961, p. 2012). In other words, Newell and Simon were judging the success of their AI program as a theory of problem solving by comparing its output to human behavior. A program that counts as a good theory should produce output that matches the known behavioral data. The fact that the program gives rise to the same output is a reason for believing that the cognitive process might be the same as the program. This is an abductive inference, or an inference to the best explanation. The inference has the form,

$$\frac{T \to O \qquad O}{T} \qquad (1)$$

where T stands for the theory/program, and O for the observed behavior. If the program produces the right output, it is a candidate explanation of the observed behavior, and in the absence of any other adequate explanation, which was plausibly the case in 1961, that program is by default the best explanation.

Newell and Simon's defense of the physical symbol system hypothesis – the assumption that any explanation of cognition should take the form of symbol manipulations – is that making this assumption led to a string of successful explanations of cognitive tasks. Phenomena that previously could not be explained suddenly became tractable with the help of that one trick. As they say, "The processes of thinking can no longer be regarded as completely mysterious" (Newell and Simon, 1961, p. 2016). One reasonable criterion to use when deciding between candidate explanations is unity; a single assumption that helps to explain many phenomena is preferable to multiple assumptions, all else being equal.

A more contemporary statement of this strategy can be found in Coltheart et al.'s defense of classical AI models of reading. They say, "the adequacy of the theory can be rigorously assessed by simulation. Are all the effects observed in the behavior of people when they are carrying out the cognitive activity in question also seen in the behavior of the program?" and "if there is no other theory in the field that has been demonstrated through computational modeling to be both complete and sufficient, resting on laurels is a reasonable thing to do until the emergence of such a competitor" (Coltheart et al., 2001, 204). This clearly describes inference to the best explanation.

Explanation in realistic brain simulations

"Simulation" has been used in the previous examples in a way that is common in discussions of cognitive models, but notably different than its meaning in other fields. In physics and climate science, what I'll call a true simulation starts from a fundamental theory, usually consisting of differential equations that describe the behavior of elementary entities like particles. A true simulation then churns through calculations based on these equations to generate a description of the state of the system at various time points (Humphreys, 1990). Often the purpose is to predict outcomes like weather forecasts, cosmological events, or the properties of a newly synthesized material. In true simulations, the inference is deductive, and has the form,

$$\frac{T \to O \qquad T}{O} \tag{2}$$

where T stands for the fundamental theory as instantiated in the program, and O for the observed outcome. In practice, true simulations are not perfect deductive tools; the starting point may not correspond exactly to the state of the world of interest, and numerical approximations are generally needed to solve the fundamental equations.

Some approaches to computational modeling in cognitive science aspire to model the brain from the bottom up, starting by modeling brain anatomy and/or physiology in detail, like true simulations. The goal of the Blue Brain project is "to simulate the brains of mammals with a high level of biological accuracy and, ultimately, to study the steps involved in the emergence of biological intelligence" (Markram, 2006). Another large-scale, anatomically detailed simulation by Izhikevich and Edelman incorporates "multiple cortical regions, corticocortical connections, and synaptic plasticity" (Izhikevich and Edelman, 2008, p. 3593). Eliasmith's Spaun focuses on "explaining how complex brain activity generates complex behavior" with a simulation that generates "behaviorally relevant functions" (Eliasmith et al., 2012). In these projects, getting the anatomical and physiological details correct is a high priority.

Explanation in connectionist models

Connectionist models of cognition, in particular the Parallel Distributed Processing (PDP) approach, likewise incorporate details of neural anatomy and physiology. As the introduction to the PDP 'bible' states, "One reason for the appeal of PDP models is their obvious 'physiological' flavor: They seem so much more closely tied to the physiology of the brain than are other kinds of information-processing model" (McClelland and Rumelhart, 1986, p. 10). Although this statement suggests an intention to model the physiology of the brain, the physiological similarities between PDP models and real brains are quite loose, unlike true simulations, which try to get the details exactly right.

Like classical AI, connectionist models have the primary aim of reproducing cognitive phenomena. It is not immediately obvious how classical AI's top-down methods can be combined with brain simulation's bottom-up methods. Of particular concern is how incorporating neural constraints is meant to help when these constraints are taken only very loosely. If we view connectionist modeling through the lens of classical AI and deductive-nomological explanation, it might look like the inference structure is only a slight variation on Inference 2, such that:

$$\frac{T^* \to O \qquad O \qquad t_1,...,t_n \in T^*}{T} \qquad (3)$$

where T^* is a model that loosely approximates T, and $t_1,..., t_n$ are statements from T (describing physiological constraints on brains) that are included in the model T^*.

This assumes that the purpose of adding physiological constraints on brains is to increase the strength of the inference to T. However, if n is small relative to the number of facts in T, the benefit of adding them to the premises would be negligible, which would undermine connectionism's claims about the importance of physiological plausibility. Another problem is that the model T^* only loosely approximates T. In order to make an inference to the best explanation, T would need to be established as a candidate explanation for O, but here it is T^* that implies O. If this were an accurate interpretation of connectionist methodology, these would be serious problems, however, Inference 3 gets connectionist methodology very wrong.

During the period between 1961 and 1986, the "Received View" of scientific theories and the corresponding deductive-nomological account of scientific explanation were largely scrapped (see Woodward, 2017). I don't think connectionists have the aim of constructing theories at all, but rather models (see Morgan and Morrison, 1999; Winsberg, 2001; Bailer-Jones, 2009 for accounts of scientific modeling). With this in mind, we shift from interpreting T as a theory that entails all the facts about the target system, to interpreting T as the target system itself (or in propositional terms, we can think of this as the set of all facts that are true of the target system).

In the next section I analyze several examples of connectionist modeling work. I argue that connectionist models are meant to explore the mechanisms operative in the target system. On this account, explaining cognitive phenomena using connectionist models involves reasoning about mechanisms, which operates using the logic of tendencies. In Stinson (2018) I connect this argument about how connectionist models explain to the philosophical literature on idealization in modeling, and explore examples from other scientific fields where abstract, idealized models likewise offer explanatory advantages over highly detailed models.

Connectionist explanation examples

In this section I look in some detail at examples of connectionist models from several areas of cognitive science research. I begin by looking at the models described in De Pisapia et al.'s (2008) review of connectionist models of attention and cognitive control. By looking closely at how the studies are described, I discern four criteria by which the success of these models is judged. Consideration of models from several other areas of cognition confirm that connectionist models of cognition typically follow this pattern.

First, the models reviewed in De Pisapia et al. (2008) all try to capture known neurophysiological characteristics of the brain. For instance, many of the models implement feature maps corresponding to the representations computed in brain areas V1, PP, and IT. Some of the models also capture more specific details about hypercolumns, patterns of inhibitory connections, neuronal dynamics, etc. This reflects the belief that "models which make strong attempts to incorporate as many core principles of neural information processing and computation as possible are the ones most likely to explain empirical data regarding attentional phenomena across the widest-range of explanatory levels" (De Pisapia et al., 2008, p. 423). But importantly, the neural plausibility is always limited to general or core features, not every detail.

The second criterion is that the models are expected to simulate or replicate known empirical results from psychology. For instance, "Simulations using biased competition model[s] were found to be successful in accounting for a number of empirical results in visual search" (De Pisapia et al., 2008, p. 431). The competing feed-forward models are evaluated in the same terms: "these models have been effective in capturing the known neurobiology of low-level visual processing, while at the same time simulating findings from the empirical visual search and natural scene viewing" (De Pisapia et al., 2008, p. 432).

Third, the models are judged based on their ability to explain clinical phenomena, like the cognitive effects of brain lesions and other neurological conditions. The models need both to

> agree with behavioral results coming from the basic experimental paradigms and with the data from brain-damaged patients suffering from attentional impairments … the true strength of these models lies in their ability to model the qualitative pattern of impairments associated with neuropsychologically-based attentional disorders, such as the spatial neglect syndrome.
>
> *(De Pisapia et al., 2008, p. 432)*

Fourth, many of the models generate predictions about what the result of novel experimental scenarios should be, which can later be verified in the lab. One model "provided novel predictions about how patients with object-based neglect might perceive objects when they are joined with cross-links or brought towards each other" (De Pisapia et al., 2008, p. 431). In another case, "reaction time slopes … obtained by model simulations were successful in predicting subsequent psychophysical investigations" (De Pisapia et al., 2008, p. 431).

These four criteria for successful connectionist modeling of cognition are also apparent in many other studies. For example, O'Reilly et al.'s model of working memory "is biologically plausible. Indeed, the general functions of each of its components were motivated by a large base of literature spanning multiple levels of analysis, including cellular, systems, and psychological data" (O'Reilly and Frank, 2006, p. 312). In addition to simulating "powerful levels of computational learning performance" (O'Reilly and Frank, 2006, p. 284), it also models clinical results by testing "the implications of striatal dopamine dysfunction in producing cognitive deficits in conditions such as Parkinson's disease and ADHD" (O'Reilly and Frank, 2006, p. 313). McClelland et al.'s model of memory likewise tries to be "broadly consistent with the neuropsychological evidence, as well as aspects of the underlying anatomy and physiology (McClelland, McNaughton, and O'Reilly, 1995, p. 419). Suri and Schultz (2001) model the anatomy of the basal ganglia, including only pathways that exist in the brain and through which feedback is thought to actually travel; and Billings et al. (2014) design the units in their "anatomically constrained model" to match properties like the diameters and densities of granule cells and mossy fibers in the cerebellum.

Sejnowski, Koch, and Churchland (1988), focusing on vision, describe connectionist models as "simplifying brain models" which "abstract from the complexity of individual neurons and the patterns of connectivity in exchange for analytical tractability" (Sejnowski, Koch, and Churchland, 1988, p. 1301). One of the advantages they list of connectionist modeling over experimental techniques is that "New phenomena may be discovered by comparing the predictions of simulation to experimental results" and they note that "new experiments can be designed based on these predictions" (Sejnowski, Koch, and Churchland, 1988, p. 1300). The models they describe are not only consistent with previous experimental measures, they also make "interesting predictions for ... responses to visual stimuli" (Sejnowski, Koch, and Churchland, 1988, p. 1303).

Plaut et al. (1996) likewise try to simulate both experimental results, and the patterns of breakdown in clinical cases in their model of reading, as well as generating testable predictions. Some of the empirical results that the model replicates are that high-frequency and consistent words are named faster than low-frequency and inconsistent words, and that these two effects interact (Plaut et al., 1996, pp. 7–8). In addition, "damaging the model by removing units or connections results in a pattern of errors that is somewhat similar to that of brain-injured patients with one form of surface dyslexia" (Plaut et al., 1996, p. 8). Finally, the assumptions of the model can be used "to derive predictions about the relative naming latencies of different types of words. In particular ... why naming latency depends on the frequency of a word" (Plaut et al., 1996, p. 21).

Although this sample of papers has not been entirely systematic, it is representative in that it covers three decades of work, four core areas of cognition (attention, memory, language, and vision), many of the main players in the field and several types of paper (experiment, theoretical paper, and review). Certainly there are connectionist models of cognition that do not meet all four criteria (and perhaps some that meet none of the four). I do not claim that this pattern is universal, merely typical, and as we'll see later, some components can be dropped without greatly affecting the form of the inference. In the next section I offer an analysis of the kind of explanation offered by this sort of model.

How connectionist models explain

Recall that classical AI's explanations of cognition employ inference to the best explanation, which involves finding a candidate explanation, then, as Coltheart put it, resting on one's laurels until a reasonable competitor comes along. Connectionist models of cognition not only provide the competition, but also make plain the methodological fragility of classical AI's dependence on inference to the best explanation. As Sejnowski puts it, "Although a working model can help generate hypotheses, and rule some out, it cannot prove that the brain necessarily solves the problem in the same way" (Sejnowski, Koch, and Churchland, 1988, p. 1304). In other words, simulating the behavior only shows that you have a candidate explanation; it does not show that you have the right explanation, i.e. one that produces the behavior in the "same way".

For connectionists, the "same way" means looking to the anatomy and physiology of the brain, because whatever the right explanation of cognition is, it must be at least possible to implement it with brainy stuff. Connectionists talk about taking constraints from both physiology and psychology, as though they are employing an inferential pincer movement, narrowing the space of possibilities from two flanks at once (although search may not be an apt metaphor for model building, because the domain is infinite, and there are no halting conditions).

A more promising way of understanding connectionist methodology is hinted at in each of the papers cited above. They all talk about the constraints they take from brains in terms of basic, or general principles. Here are some quotes to that effect: "modeling is often crucial if we are to understand the implications of certain kinds of basic principles of processing" (McClelland, 1988, p. 107); "connectionist modeling provides a rich set of general computational principles that can lead to new and useful ways of thinking about human performance" (Plaut et al., 1996, p. 2). "The study of simplifying models of the brain can provide a conceptual framework for isolating the basic computational problems and understanding the computational constraints that govern the design of the nervous system" (Sejnowski, Koch, and Churchland, 1988, p. 1300).

The point is evidently not to model the brain in detail, but rather to model the basic processing principles used by the brain.

McClelland, McNaughton, and O'Reilly (1995) describe this strategy in their paper about why there are two learning systems in hippocampus and neocortex. They focus on the phenomenon of memory consolidation, a gradual process that can take many years. Their goal is a model of learning and memory that goes beyond just reproducing the observed phenomena. They want to make sense of why, from a design perspective, there are two separate memory systems, and to figure out what the functional importance of gradual consolidation is. They ask,

> Is the phenomenon a reflection of an arbitrary property of the nervous system, or does it reflect some crucial aspect of the mechanisms of learning and memory? Is the fact that consolidation can take quite a long time – up to 15 years or more in some cases – just an arbitrary parameter, or does it reflect an important design principle?
>
> *(McClelland, McNaughton, and O'Reilly, 1995, p. 419)*

In cases like this, some details, like the timing of consolidation, take on particular importance for figuring out how a phenomenon is produced. Models recreate select physiological or anatomical details of their target systems, not to strengthen the inference from model to target slightly, as in Inference 3, but in order to test the significance of those details. If that detail is changed, is there a qualitative change in overall performance? An arbitrary property can be altered without a qualitative change in performance, but a crucial aspect of the mechanism cannot. Instead of acting as piecemeal support for the theory, these details are used to probe the design of the mechanism.

Talk of mechanisms, as in the quote from McClelland, McNaughton, and O'Reilly (1995) above, is common in discussions of connectionist methodology, but not so in classical AI, where algorithms are the main concern. For connectionists, producing the behavior in the "same way" means more than just having the right algorithm. While an algorithm provides a schematic specification of processes or activities and their coordination, a mechanism specifies both the algorithm plus the entities or parts involved in these activities, and their organization. (For accounts of mechanism, see Machamer, Darden, and Craver, 2000; Glennan, 2002; Bechtel and Abrahamsen, 2005.) Machamer, Darden, and Craver (2000) stress this dualist nature of mechanisms.

The anatomical facts that are recreated in connectionist models provide a schematic specification of mechanism entities. Entities in mechanisms are not to be confused with implementation details. Rather than being specific details about the hardware or software on which an algorithm is run, mechanism entities are more like the types of structures required by an algorithm. A sorting algorithm might require a memory store and a read/write device, for example. A description of a mechanism makes explicit those entities that an algorithm takes for granted.

This focus on mechanisms rather than algorithms also helps explain why a fair bit of attention is paid to simulating neurological damage in connectionist modeling. One way of testing whether a property is an arbitrary or crucial feature of a mechanism's design is to see what happens when you remove or break it. Cognitive neuropsychology is the study of "what one can learn about the organization of the cognitive system from observing the behavior of neurological patients" (Shallice, 2001, p. 2128). By analyzing the kinds of cognitive deficits represented in neurological case studies, one can construct hypotheses about how cognitive mechanisms are designed. Connectionist modeling incorporates this strategy.

Traditionally neuropsychology depends on the assumption that cognitive functions are localized to specific brain regions, so that injuries affecting discrete brain regions can be correlated with deficits in specific cognitive functions. Historically, the affected brain regions would be assessed postmortem, but contemporary cognitive neuropsychology also makes use of neuroimaging data to localize lesions.

The logic involved in using data from cognitive neuropsychology to develop cognitive theories has been discussed at length elsewhere (Shallice, 1988; Bub, 1994a; 1994b; Glymour, 1994). In this literature brain anatomy and physiology are represented abstractly as directed graphs, where nodes correspond to anatomical locations where particular functions are performed, and edges correspond to connections between these functional units, through which data is communicated. Lesions to different parts of the graph then give rise to distinct functional disturbances. For instance, in one of the field's pioneering papers, Lichtheim (1885) posits that a lesion to the "centre of motor representation of words" would give rise to symptoms like "Loss of (a) volitional speech; (b) repetition of words; (c) reading aloud" (Lichtheim, 1885, p. 320). For each neurological subject, there must be a way of lesioning the graph such that the available paths through the graph correspond to the profile of that patient, i.e. their characteristic set of capacities.

The upshot of these methodological discussions in cognitive neuropsychology is as follows. Consider the possible cognitive theories as a set of possible directed graphs. Given sufficient lesion data, the correct theory should be a minimal graph whose set of path-sets contain all the profiles corresponding to dissociations seen in the neurological data (Bub, 1994a, p. 850). As a shorthand, I'll write this as $T^N =_{min} G^N$, where T^N stands for the cognitive model, and G^N refers to the set of graphs that can account for neurological data N. (As Glymour (1994) points out, T^N may not be unique.)

Connectionist models are more powerful than traditional cognitive neuropsychology, because they are not limited by the availability of neurological subjects with specific injuries, and they need not assume localizability of functions. Localized injuries can be simulated by damaging all the nodes in one region of the network. Other sorts of injuries can be simulated by modifying the network as a whole, such as by adding noise, changing connection weights, or adjusting the learning rule.

Connectionist modeling efforts do not use the formal approach of choosing minimal graphs, but share cognitive neuropsychology's rationale for simulating neurological data. Intuitively, the approach requires that the mechanism be such that there are distinct ways of damaging it that would result in each of the patterns of neurological deficits that have been observed, without being unnecessarily complex. (How to assess the complexity of a mechanism is a good question, but one I'll leave unanswered.) The wrong mechanism would yield a qualitatively different pattern of deficits. In cognitive neuropsychology, brain regions and their connections are treated abstractly as nodes and connections in graphs, but still can tell us a lot about cognitive architecture.

Connectionist models are likewise abstract yet informative about cognitive architecture. They are reusable, multi-purpose tools that can be reconfigured in a variety of contexts. As McClelland et al. say of their model, "These are not detailed neural models; rather, they illustrate, at an abstract level, what we take consolidation to be about" (McClelland, McNaughton, and O'Reilly, 1995, p. 420). That connectionist models are abstract or idealized is sometimes raised as a criticism; if connectionist models were supposed to explain the way true simulations do, their lack of realistic detail would be a serious problem. However, connectionist models aim to discover only the generic properties of the mechanisms they implement, not all the details. The reasoning involved in discovering how generic mechanisms work is nothing new; in fact, it was described by Mill (1843).

According to Mill, in order to analyze causes and effects, we must first decompose each scenario into single facts (which for Mill can be states of affairs, events, or propositions). What counts as a single fact, or how far down we have to go in the decomposition, depends on our purpose (Mill, 1843, III: p. 187). We then observe which facts cause which others by observing which follow from which, as circumstances vary. The advantage of experiments is that

> When we have insulated the phenomenon we're investigating by placing it among known circumstances, we can vary the circumstances in any way we like, choosing the variations that we think have the best chance of bringing the laws of the phenomenon into a clear light.
>
> *(Mill, 1843, III: p. 189)*

When a regularity is discovered, such that one set of facts (such as a particular arrangement of working parts) tends to be followed by another set of facts (such as a particular pattern of behaviors), we have what I'll call a generic mechanism. According to a popular recent account, "Mechanisms are regular in that they work always or for the most part in the same way under the same conditions. The regularity is exhibited in the typical way that the mechanism runs from beginning to end" (Machamer, Darden, and Craver, 2000, p. 3). Mechanisms may operate regularly only within certain ranges of parameter values, and the sameness of their results may be qualitative, or likewise specify a range of values. In general, they are like causes tending to produce like effects. Although they are loosely defined and not perfectly predictable, generic mechanisms are useful in a variety of contexts.

An illustrative example is lateral inhibition, which was first described in retinal ganglion cells (Hartline, 1940a; 1940b), but later discovered to be "ubiquitous to all sensory areas of the brain" (Macknik and Martinez-Conde, 2009). Retinal ganglion cells have inhibitory connections to their immediate neighbors. The strength of the inhibitory signal is proportional to the activation of the cell the signal originates in. This means that when one cell is stimulated, its neighbors are inhibited. For a cell to fire strongly, most of its neighbors can't also be stimulated. Retinal ganglion cells respond to object contours or edges, which are characterized by abrupt changes in illumination. Compared to neurons in the middle of uniform patches of illumination, which are inhibited by all of their neighbors, neurons at edges receive less inhibition, so have higher relative activity. This tends to sharpen responses even further, because this activation and inhibition is ongoing. As a result, even fairly faint edges are sharpened.

The lateral inhibition mechanism has been used to explain several other biological phenomena where contrasts are detected or enhanced. One example is cell type differentiation in embryology. Cells that start to develop earliest, and are on track to specialize for a particular purpose, such as forming a particular organ, send out protein signals that act as chemical inhibitors. These inhibitory proteins prevent surrounding cells from taking on the same job, which means that the neighboring cells specialize for something different. Small initial differences in developmental schedules make for stark contrasts in developmental outcomes.

There are also economic and sociological analogues. If communities decide to focus their limited resources on their most promising students or athletes, and if the amount of investment made is in proportion to their skills, this results in a widening of the gap between the skills of the most promising and the rest. In this sort of scenario, the most promising students or athletes get more resources to the detriment of less promising ones, which makes the best improve more quickly, further widening the skill gap between stars and non-stars.[1] Another example is the convention that ping-pong or pool tables in pubs are kept by the winner of a match. This means that the better players improve more quickly, because they get more practice, at the expense of mediocre players who get less practice in virtue of being kicked off the table after each try.

These examples vary widely in their details, but all share some very general structural properties, and have qualitatively similar effects. This is the sort of general processing principle that connectionist models are designed to discover and explore. First we discover, through a combination of mathematical demonstration and empirical observation, that a certain type of mechanism (e.g. networks with inhibitory connections among neighbors) tends to give rise to a certain type of behavior (e.g. contrast enhancement). We then make use of that knowledge to make sense of how brain structures (e.g. the retina) give rise to cognitive phenomena (e.g. edge detection).

The connection between the target system T and our model T^* is that both instantiate the same general mechanism type. We can infer that the properties of the one apply to the other based on their shared type membership. For instance, the actual retinal ganglion cell network and our connectionist model of it both belong to the general type of lateral inhibition networks. We can explore the properties of the type using the model T^*, then infer that the properties we observe, O^*, also belong to the target system T.

The first part of the strategy is making novel empirical predictions. The gap between T^* and T can be narrowed not only by showing that the model confirms the observations made in the target system, or $T^* \rightarrow O$, but also by showing that predictions work in the opposite direction. Confirming the predictions of the model in the target system does two things: it rules out gerrymandered models that are designed to give the desired output without sharing underlying properties, and it shows that the similarities between theory and model run in both directions. The latter builds confidence that the model and theory belong to the same type. Being the same type of mechanism also involves sharing the entities that are crucial to the design of the mechanism, having qualitatively similar behavior, and having the same pattern of breakdown when damaged.

Because connectionist models are used during many stages of research, there is no single inference type that fits all cases. One important example is inferring that an established model can predict the behavior of a target system, In this case, the form of the inference might look like this:

$$\frac{T^* \rightarrow O^* \quad T, T^* \in M^T}{T \rightarrow O^*} \tag{4}$$

The first premise states that the model produces a set of predicted observations O^*. The second premise states that the model and target system instantiate the same mechanism type M^T. Using the logic of tendencies, we can infer that like causes (T and T^*) should have like effects, so the model's predictions, O^*, should also be true in the target system.

Another example is inferring that the model is adequate, given what is known about the target system. In this case, the form of the inference might look like this:

$$\frac{T \rightarrow O \quad T, T^* \in M^T}{T^* \rightarrow O} \tag{5}$$

As with any inductive inferences, explanations using the logic of tendencies are susceptible to error. First, if the mechanism's operation is not very regular or reliable (for example, a stochastic mechanism), the model may predict different outcomes than the target in some cases, despite both being examples of the same mechanism type. Second, the output of the model is never exactly the same as the target phenomenon, so additional arguments are sometimes needed to establish that they are similar enough. The details left out will sometimes make a difference. Third, the experimental and neurological data on which assumptions about the design of the mechanism are based are of course incomplete, so a model that is adequate at one time can be ruled out by later evidence.

Given this new understanding of how connectionist models work and what the risks of error are, we can rethink the sorts of criticisms of connectionist models that are and aren't viable. For stochastic mechanisms, we should look for results that summarize probability distributions over many randomized trials rather than single runs. Because some details will always differ between model and target, results should be considered tentative until several variations with different details and assumptions all agree. Both of these suggestions are already standard practice in connectionist modeling. A more novel result is that blanket criticisms of connectionist models as either too detailed or not detailed enough are off the mark, as long as the level of detail is appropriate to the research question. Very detailed models are not only less widely applicable, but also more susceptible to being overridden by new discoveries in neurophysiology. We should expect earlier models to be more abstract, and later models to be more detailed about select parts of the mechanism. This pattern is already apparent in connectionist modeling research. Often it is the more general models rather than the more specific that receive the most critical attention, but it should be the reverse.

Despite these caveats, connectionist modeling is a powerful and nuanced set of methods that allow for the possibility of explaining cognition at many scales of generality or specificity. It can also offer explanations of how and why cognitive deficits occur as a result of particular sorts of brain lesions, which promises clinical payoffs.

Conclusion

I began by offering formal accounts of how classical AI and true simulations explain. Classical AI uses inference to the best explanation, as was clear from the methodological claims made in both older and contemporary sources. Simulation tries to deduce predictions from detailed bottom–up models. Connectionist models are puzzling in that they seem to try to do a little of each, which should undermine both modes of explanation.

I arrived at a four–part analysis of the explanatory features of connectionist models. First, details of the neurophysiology of the brain are built into the models. Second, the output of the models reproduce known psychological data. Third, damaging the models reproduces patterns of deficits found in neurological cases. Finally, good models make novel empirical predictions that can be experimentally verified. I noted that connectionist models are intended to explore the generic mechanisms operating in the brain, and illustrated the relevant notion of mechanism with the example of lateral inhibition.

I then constructed a formal analysis of the explanations offered, which interprets connectionist models and the cognitive theories they represent as sharing membership in a type of mechanism. The inferences made from connectionist models to cognitive phenomena can be understood as involving the logic of tendencies. Models and targets that instantiate the same general mechanisms can be expected to have similar output.

One of the motivations for offering an account of how connectionist models explain is that doubts have been raised as to whether they are relevant to cognition at all. Although connectionist models have been contributing to our understanding of the mind for several decades now, there has been little understanding of how they work. I hope that this chapter will shed some light on this question.

Note

1 This was rumored to be the case in a figure skating club near my childhood home, where 1988 Olympic silver medalist Elizabeth Manley trained.

References

Bailer-Jones, D.M. (2009) *Scientific Models in Philosophy of Science*. Pittsburgh, PA: University of Pittsburgh Press.

Bechtel, W. and Abrahamsen, A. (2005) 'Explanation: A Mechanist Alternative', *Studies in the History and Philosophy of Science, Part C*, 36 (2), pp. 421–441.

Billings, G. et al. (2014) 'Network Structure within the Cerebellar Input Layer Enables Lossless Sparse Encoding', *Neuron*, 83 (4), 960–974.

Bub, J. (1994a) 'Is Cognitive Neuropsychology Possible?', *Philosophy of Science*, 1, pp. 417–427.

Bub, J. (1994b) 'Models of Cognition through the Analysis of Brain-Damaged Performance', *The British Journal for the Philosophy of Science*, 45 (3), pp. 837–855.

Coltheart, M. et al. (2001) 'DRC: A Dual Route Cascaded Model of Visual Word Recognition and Reading Aloud', *Psychological Review*, 108 (1), pp. 204–256.

De Pisapia, N., Repovs, G., and Braver, T.S. (2008) 'Computational Models of Attention and Cognitive Control', in Sun, R. (ed.) *Cambridge Handbook of Computational Psychology*. Cambridge, UK: Cambridge University Press, pp. 422–450.

Eliasmith, C. et al. (2012) 'A Large-scale Model of the Functioning Brain', *Science*, 338 (6111), pp. 1202–1205.

Engel, A.K. et al. (2005) 'Invasive Recordings from the Human Brain: Clinical Insights and Beyond', *Nature Reviews Neuroscience*, 6 (January), pp. 35–47.

Fodor, J.A. and Pylyshyn, Z. (1988) 'Connectionism and Cognitive Architecture: A Critical Analysis', *Cognition*, 28, pp. 3–71.

Glennan, S. (2002) 'Rethinking Mechanistic Explanation', *Philosophy of Science*, 69 (S3), pp. 342–353.

Glymour, C. (1994) 'On the Methods of Cognitive Neuropsychology', *The British Journal for the Philosophy of Science*, 45 (3), pp. 815–835.

Hartline, H.K. (1940a) 'The Effects of Spatial Stimulation in the Retina on the Excitation of the Fibers of the Optic Nerve', *American Journal of Physiology*, pp. 700–711.

Hartline, H.K. (1940b) 'The Receptive Fields of Optic Nerve Fibers', *American Journal of Physiology*, pp. 690–699.

Hempel, C. and Oppenheim, P. (1948) 'Studies in the Logic of Explanation', *Philosophy of Science*, 15, pp. 135–175.

Humphreys, P. (1990) 'Computer Simulations', *PSA: Proceedings of the Biennial Meeting of the Philosophy of Science Association*, 1990 (2), pp. 497–506.

Izhikevich, E.M. and Edelman, G.M. (2008) 'Large-scale Model of Mammalian Thalamocortical Systems', *Proceedings of the National Academy of Sciences*, 105 (9), pp. 3593–3598.

Lichtheim, L. (1885) 'On Aphasia', *Brain*, 7, pp. 433–484.

Machamer, P., Darden, L., and Craver, C.F. (2000) 'Thinking about Mechanisms', *Philosophy of Science*, 67 (1), pp. 1–25.

Macknik, S.L. and Martinez-Conde, S. (2009) 'Lateral Inhibition', in Goldstein, E.B. (ed.) *Encyclopedia of Perception*. London: Sage. Available at: http://dx.doi.org.myaccess.library.utoronto.ca/10.4135/9781412972000.n166.

Markram, H. (2006) 'The Blue Brain Project', *Nature Reviews Neuroscience*, 7 (2), pp. 153–160.

McCarthy, J. et al. (1955) 'A Proposal for the Dartmouth Summer Research Project on Artificial Intelligence', August 31. Available at: http://raysolomonoff.com/dartmouth/boxa/dart564props.pdf (Accessed: October 26, 2016).

McClelland, J.L. (1988) 'Connectionist Models and Psychological Evidence', *Journal of Memory and Language*, 27, pp. 107–123.

McClelland, J.L., McNaughton, B.L., and O'Reilly, R.C. (1995) 'Why There Are Complementary Learning Systems in the Hippocampus and Neocortex: Insights from the Successes and Failures of Connectionist Models of Learning and Memory', *Psychological Review*, 102 (3), pp. 419–457.

McClelland, J. and Rumelhart, D.E. (1986) *Parallel Distributed Processing: Explorations in the Microstructure of Cognition*, vol. 2: *Psychological and Biological Models*. Cambridge, MA: MIT Press.

Mill, J.S. (1843) 'A System of Logic: Ratiocinative and Inductive', Available at: www.earlymoderntexts.com (Accessed: October 26, 2016).

Morgan, M.S. and Morrison, M. (1999) *Models as Mediators: Perspectives on Natural and Social Science*. Cambridge, UK: Cambridge University Press.

Mukamel, R. and Fried, I. (2012) 'Human Intracranial Recordings and Cognitive Neuroscience', *Annual Review of Psychology*, 63 (1), pp. 511–537.

Newell, A. and Simon, H.A. (1961) 'Computer Simulation of Human Thinking', *Science*, 134 (3495), pp. 2011–2017.

Newell, A. and Simon, H.A. (1976) 'Computer Science as Empirical Inquiry: Symbols and Search', *Communications of the ACM*, 19 (3), pp. 113–126.

O'Reilly, R.C. and Frank, M.J. (2006) 'Making Working Memory Work: A Computational Model of Learning in the Prefrontal Cortex and Basal Ganglia', *Neural Computation*, 18, pp. 283–328.

Plaut, D.C. et al. (1996) 'Understanding Normal and Impaired Word Reading: Computational Principles in Quasi-regular Domains', *Psychological Review*, 103 (1), pp. 56–115.

Sejnowski, T., Koch, C., and Churchland, P. (1988) 'Computational Neuroscience', *Science*, 241 (4871), pp. 1299–1306.

Shallice, T. (1988) *From Neuropsychology to Mental Structure*. Cambridge, UK: Cambridge University Press.

Shallice, T. (2001) 'Cognitive Neuropsychology, Methodology of', in Wright, J. (ed.) *International Encyclopedia of the Social and Behavioral Sciences*. Amsterdam: Elsevier, pp. 2128–2133.

Smolensky, P. (1988) 'On the Proper Treatment of Connectionism', *Behavioral and Brain Sciences*, 11, pp. 1–74.

Stinson, C. (2018) 'What Artificial Neurons Tell Us about Real Brains', Article under review.

Suri, R.E. and Schultz, W. (2001) 'Temporal Difference Model Reproduces Anticipatory Neural Activity', *Neural Computation*, 13 (4), pp. 841–862.

Winsberg, E. (2001) 'Simulations, Models, and Theories: Complex Physical Systems and Their Representations', *Philosophy of Science*, 68 (3), pp. S442–S454.

Winther, R.G. (2016) 'The Structure of Scientific Theories', *The Stanford Encyclopedia of Philosophy*, March 21, Zalta, E.N. (ed.), Available at: https://plato.stanford.edu/archives/win2016/entries/structure-scientific-theories/ (Accessed: October 26, 2016).

Woodward, J. (2017) 'Scientific Explanation', *The Stanford Encyclopedia of Philosophy*, September 21, Zalta, E.N. (ed.), Available at: https://plato.stanford.edu/archives/fall2017/entries/scientific-explanation/ (Accessed: October 26, 2016).

10

DYNAMIC INFORMATION PROCESSING

Frank Faries and Anthony Chemero

Introduction

Computational and dynamical approaches to the mind are widely assumed to entail incompatible sciences of cognition. So foundational is the divide between the two approaches, it is said, that the latter constitutes a denial of the former. Indeed, the roots of the divide do run deep, and dynamical approaches do pose challenges to the core of the prevailing computational view. However, there is at least one sense in which the approaches can be seen as, at the very least, complementary, such that there may be a common ground for intellectual transactions between the two camps. It is the purpose of the present chapter to stake out that common ground.

This chapter will proceed as follows. The first section will provide an introduction to dynamical systems theory, including its methods, central features, and the ways it is taken to conflict with computational theories. The second section will resolve these conflicts, by showing that at least two points on which these theories are presumed to conflict need not be seen as conflicts. Dynamical and computational approaches to cognition are often taken to be incommensurable because of the issue of mental representation, and the location of the boundaries of cognition. We hope to demonstrate that commitments about these issues do not necessarily commit one to a particular approach to cognition. The third section shows that, because computational and dynamical approaches are, at the very least, complementary, the source of conflict is not the approaches themselves, but the dogmatic '–isms' to which theorists commit themselves. The fourth section introduces a view of dynamical and computational explanations which is sufficiently broad to encompass both kinds of explanation. We call this dynamical information processing (DIP). DIP is broadly compatible with computational explanation, but drawing from insights in embodied cognition, extended cognition, and ecological psychology. DIP enables us to defend a pluralistic view of explanation in cognitive science – one which calls a truce to dogmatic conflict and proposes a framework by which computational and dynamical approaches can be mutually supporting.

Dynamical systems theory

It has become clear in recent decades that the framework of dynamics provides a powerful scheme for revealing the temporal organization of complex biological systems. Because cognition is an activity of a biological system, this suggests that dynamics may be an appropriate framework for explaining the mind. This framework relies on the mathematical tools of dynamical systems theory (hereafter DST) including differential equations, geometric state-space analysis, and other visualization techniques including attractor landscapes and bifurcation diagrams (cf. Strogatz, 2014). These tools provide a useful framework for the modeling, analysis, and visualization of time series data, i.e. data gathered from repeated measurement of a system changing over time. Central to this toolkit is a set of differential equations or difference equations, which contain variables and parameters which capture how different features of the target system change over time. What makes DST powerful as an explanatory tool is that dynamical models can be used to track and predict the mutual influence of multiple system variables or parameters over time. Generally speaking, a dynamical system is a mathematical object which describes the change in state of a system over time. Importantly, the state of the system in the future is dependent, in some principled way, on its current state.

An important feature of many differential equations is that they are, strictly speaking, unsolvable. Despite this feature, DST is able to use computational techniques to simulate solutions to these unsolvable differential equations. These simulated solutions qualitatively model the long-term behavior in terms of trajectories in a geometrically-defined *state space*, or set of all values (or *states*) that the variables of a particular system can take over time. The particular variables of the system's state define the dimensions of the space, such that the total number of dimensions of state space corresponds to the total number of state variables of the system. (These spaces will sometimes have more than three dimensions, so will be difficult to visualize.) The differential equations define a *vector field*, or rules of evolution of the system over time by assignment of magnitudes and directions of change at each point in the state space. A trajectory is a continuous sequence of states through the vector field given an initial state of the system. The state space of any given set of differential equations will thus be composed of the set of trajectories of that system. Very often, dynamical systems will converge on a particular region of the state space. States of these systems will be pushed into certain regions, regardless of the point at which the system starts. These regions are either single points (*fixed points*) or particular trajectories (*limit cycles*). Convergence is due to the system's topology, or the layout of points in the state space which push the system towards fixed points or along certain trajectories. Finally, continuous changes in the *control* or *order parameters* shape the state space over time. Order parameters, also known as collective variables, summarize the behavior of a system's components. Changes in order parameters will thereby amount to changes in the system's components. Continuous quantitative change in control parameters leads to non-continuous qualitative change in the topology of a state space. The change in attractor landscape can be smooth and continuous, but in other cases, abrupt changes in the landscape can occur once values of control parameters cross particular thresholds, as in the case of *bifurcation*.

As a concrete example, consider the simplified neural network model described in Beer (1995). This system consists of two simulated neurons fully interconnected in a network described by the following two equations:

$$\dot{y}_1 = -y_1 + w_{11}\sigma(y_1 - \theta_1) + w_{21}\sigma(y_2 - \theta_2),$$

$$\dot{y}_2 = -y_2 + w_{12}\sigma(y_1 - \theta_1) + w_{22}\sigma(y_2 - \theta_2),$$

where y_i is the state of the ith neuron, σ is a sigmoidal activation function, θ controls the activation threshold, and w_{ij} is the weight of the connection between the ith and jth neuron. Each differential equation describes the behavior of a simulated neuron over time. Because there are two equations necessary to describe the neural network, and because the equation for one neuron refers to the equations for the other neuron, these equations are said to be coupled. What this means is that the behavior of one simulated neuron necessarily depends on the behavior of the other. Starting from some initial state x_0, defined as some set of values for the variables in these equations, the equations will describe the trajectory of the system as it unfolds over time.

As mentioned above, one interesting aspect of the behavior of certain dynamical systems is the stable pattern into which trajectories from a wide variety of initial states will converge. Some systems will diverge to infinity or exhibit seemingly random patterns. However, some systems will eventually converge to limit cycles, or a set of points which, if a dynamical system ever falls into, the system will remain in indefinitely. Some particularly interesting limit sets in dynamical systems are attractors and repellors. Attractors are stable limit sets which draw all trajectories passing through nearby states toward them. The set of states which converge on the attractor is called its basin of attraction. In contrast, unstable limit sets are called repellors, and these sets push trajectories passing through nearby states away from them. Possible plots of typical trajectories through state space, or phase portraits, qualitatively illustrate these limit sets.

The features listed above highlight the utility of dynamical systems theory in cognitive science. One virtue of dynamical systems theory is in allowing theorists to build up a dependency matrix of possible behaviors of a system on external parameters. This provides for better prediction of a system's behavior based on the manipulation of a few variables. That these variables can be coupled affords the ability to describe the interactions which account for a system's behavior. Lastly, because many dynamical systems are nonlinear, theoretical applications employing dynamical systems tools will be well-equipped to model aspects of cognition which exhibit nonlinearity.

Versus computational theory

The mathematical theory of computation is a well-established branch of mathematics. It studies which functions are computable by some algorithm or subset of computational systems. It is characterized in detail in several other chapters in this volume (see Aizawa, this volume; and Samuels, this volume). With regard to the sciences of the mind, computational theories characterize the behavior of cognitive systems by appeal to the computations they perform. At a minimum, this involves some kind of isomorphism or mapping between a "physical" description and a "computational" description of the cognitive system (Putnam, 1960). The plausibility of this mapping is often taken to be a measure of the adequacy of the computational characterization of the target system. If there is such a mapping between a physical description and a computational description, the system can be said to be "computing" the function defined by the computational description's inputs and outputs.

Prior to the rise of the dynamical framework, the computational theory of mind (hereafter CTM), or the hypothesis that cognition is, or can best be described as, a computational process, was the dominant framework in cognitive science. Since that time, advances in mathematical computational theory, as well as growing diversity of theoretical backgrounds among cognitive scientists, has led to increased distinctions among computational theories which might be of relevance to the study of the mind. The classical view of computation held by Fodor (1981) and Pylyshyn (1984), as well as Newell and Simon (1976), is the narrow view that cognition is symbolic (digital) computation, and is committed to the claim that cognitive capacities are underpinned by mental representations (Fodor and Pylyshyn, 1988). Initially the dominant view of computation, this view eventually gave way to competing notions of computation, including broad digital computation (Searle, 1990; Putnam, 1988), generic computation (Piccinini and

Scarantino, 2011), connectionist computation (Rumelhart and McClelland, 1986), and neural computation (Piccinini and Bahar, 2013), and many more besides. While these views may not agree on all points (e.g. is computation symbolic or sub-symbolic? Digital, analog, or *sui generis?*) they are unified in their commitment to the tools of mathematical computational theory in the explanation of the mind.

Because of this, we may say that an important feature which distinguishes dynamical and computational explanations of cognition is the tools they use. Dynamical explanations focus "on the structure of the space of possible trajectories and the internal and external forces that shape the particular trajectory that unfolds over time" (Beer, 2000, p. 96), and are expressed as a set of differential or difference equations that describe how the system's state changes over time. In contrast, computational explanations tend to focus on the structure and content of the representations employed and the nature and efficiency of the algorithms used, and are expressed using the tools of computational theory, which take as input representations of the problem to be solved, which are then manipulated using general knowledge about the problem domain (Beer, 2000). There is an important caveat here: the distinction we are drawing is about the *explanatory practices of cognitive scientists.* Dynamical cognitive scientists do not believe that cognitive systems or their components solve differential equations; rather, they believe that differential equations feature in the best explanations of cognitive systems. For example, we suggested that the activity of the simulated two-neuron dynamical system described above is best explained using the tools of DST, but those neurons are not doing calculus. In contrast, some computational cognitive scientists believe that brain areas are actually computing solutions to differential equations. For example, Mazurek et al. (2003) explain the activity of several cortical areas as computing temporal integrals. This is a computational explanation, even though there is calculus involved. The key distinction here is between a cognitive scientist explaining cognition using calculus and a cognitive scientist explaining cognition as the target system to be explained solving differential equations (i.e. doing calculus).

Though not explicitly stated, there are a few assumptions which seem to underlie the CTM. We shall attempt to extract those assumptions and lay them bare here. Computational explanation assumes that cognition is the manipulation of mental representations, and that this manipulation takes place entirely in the brain.

Representation

An attractive idea for CTM is that, because computation generally involves manipulation of symbols, and these symbols (a) correspond to features of environmental stimuli, and (b) are instantiated by biological processes (typically neural firings), then computation involves a strict mapping between biological processes and features of environmental stimuli. Therefore, particular patterns of neural firings *represent* particular features of the environment. However, contrary to Fodor's exclamation that there can be "no computation without representation", CTM is not necessarily representational. For instance, if the mind is computational in the sense described by the connectionist (Rumelhart and McClelland, 1986), then it is debatable whether the system can be said to truly make use of "mental representations" in any strong sense. Likewise, certain kinds of generic computation are not necessarily representational (Piccinini and Scarantino, 2011; Piccinini and Bahar 2013; Piccinini, 2015).

Nevertheless, the notion that computational explanation makes use of representation is a recalcitrant one. Without any specific claims about representation, this notion still tends to emerge in that computational modeling of various cognitive capacities trades in representational terms. That is, various structures within the model are often identified as contributing logical operations over a set of defined inputs. This simple statement seems representational through and through. What defines the inputs is their correspondence to the things which they represent. The logical operations which the various structures contribute are manipulations of those representations to produce an output. Moreover, the very objects of inquiry in computational modeling are often representational themselves. A computational model of working memory, for instance, seeks to discover, among other things, where and how working memory occurs in the brain. Importantly, if one assumes that memory is representational, this does not commit one to a representationalist theory. But it certainly lends itself to investigation using representational machinery. Thus the notion of cognition as a kind of "mirror to the world" has permeated current methodology in computationalist cognitive science.

Brain-bound systems

If human brains are modeled as computers and human cognitive processes are modeled as computational processes occurring in them, it seems reasonable to expect that cognitive processes are *inside* the individual. Imagine an everyday laptop computer. Every piece of data processed by that computer is processed *inside* that computer. Even if the data is not *stored* on that computer, when it is processed *by* that computer, it is processed *inside* of it.

Because of this, the brain is the physical system of interest in much of computational cognitive science. Often, if anything other than the brain is involved in a computational explanation, it is only by virtue of being an *input* to the brain. Thus, sensory stimuli are mere *transductions* of the source of the stimuli into electrochemical impulses which carry information about that source. Again think of an ordinary laptop. The pattern of movements of fingers over the keyboard is a part of the computing process only insofar as there are patterns of electrical signals being input to the software which carry information about those patterns of movement.

The dynamical approach in cognitive science

On its face, what defines the dynamical approach is a commitment to explaining cognition using the mathematical tools of dynamical systems theory. (As we noted above, this is very different from the claim that cognitive systems themselves solve differential equations.) Among philosophers and cognitive scientists, this commitment to using the mathematical tools of dynamical systems theory is often taken to entail a radical view according to which dynamical models constitute an approach entirely distinct from computationalism. There are commonly two cuts which can be made to divide dynamical approaches from computational ones. We shall explore each of these here.

Versus the computational approach

As sketched in the first section, the dynamical and computational approaches disagree over mental representation and the boundaries of cognition. However, these are false points of contention. We shall attempt to resolve these points of contention here.

Radical embodied cognitive science

As mentioned above, one common assumption about the computational approach is that it is necessarily representational; however, there are computational approaches which violate this assumption (see Piccinini and Scarantino, 2011; Piccinini and Bahar, 2013; Piccinini, 2015).

Often, the dynamical approach is presumed to circumvent the need for mental representation. Radical embodied cognitive science is emblematic of this view (Chemero, 2009). However, there are dynamical approaches which are themselves representational (viz. Clark, 1997; 2015; Izhikevich, 2007). Thus the representationalism/anti-representationalism distinction does not cut cleanly across the computational/dynamical divide. As such, it seems inappropriate to claim it as a central point of contention between the two camps.

Brain-body-environment

As mentioned above, it is commonly held that if cognitive states are computational states, and if cognitive states are just brain states, then computational states are simply brain states. That is, if we accept CTM, then our computational explanations of cognition must be explanations of the brain. However, this belief is not necessary for CTM, or even the computational approach in general. Computational states are identified by their functional role. This function will, of course, place constraints on the kinds of physical structures which can instantiate them. However, nothing about this requires that those physical structures all be in the brain.

Wilson has advanced a view of computation which goes beyond the brain in identifying component structures. This view, known as "wide computationalism" (Wilson, 1994), holds that any element in the brain, in the body, or in the environment can fill the functional role required to carry out a particular computation. This view accords with the "extended mind" tradition (Clark and Chalmers, 1998). An example of a process which is computationally wide in the sense described by Wilson is multiplication of large numbers by hand. If one is asked to multiply 2488659 by 396602, one begins by working from right to left, performing component multiplications, storing the intermediate solutions somewhere (usually on paper), moving one step left, then repeating the process. As Wilson claims, "[t]he problem solving activity itself need not and does not take place solely in one's head ... A crucial part of the process of multiplication, namely, the storage of mathematical symbols, extends beyond the boundaries of the individual" (Wilson, 1994, p. 355–356). Thus, the commitment to internalism, or the view that all mental structures are located squarely in the skull, is unnecessary for a commitment to the computational approach. A computational approach, and even the CTM, leaves room for elements of the computational system to exist in the brain, body, or environment.

Explanation and –isms

In this section, we will make a series of distinctions among kinds of explanation in the cognitive and neural sciences. We will also distinguish between explanations and –isms. None of this is intended to be controversial. The purpose of this will be to argue that if we set monistic –isms aside we can see a heretofore unexplored explanatory possibility, one that casts certain kinds of whole-animal activity of the sort that is typically explained dynamically in information processing terms.

Given the compatibilities sketched above, we claim that the primary feature that distinguishes dynamical and computational explanations of cognition is the toolkit they use. As we noted above, following Beer (2000), computational explanations focus on the structure and content of the representations employed and the nature and efficiency of the algorithms used, and are expressed using the tools of computational theory, which typically take as input representations of the problem to be solved, which are then manipulated using general knowledge about the problem domain. By contrast, a dynamical explanation focuses on the structure of the space of possible interactions of sets of cognition-relevant variables and the forces that shape the actual trajectory that we observe, and are expressed as a set of differential or difference equations that describe how the system's state changes over time.

The source of this contrast should be clear. Because animals and environments exhibit mutuality, and thus bodies and brains co-evolve and are intertwined with their environments, on the dynamical approach an animal's brain, body, and environment are viewed as coupled dynamical systems. Because explanations of cognitive systems will include elements of the brain, body, and environment, an explanatory tool is required that can apply across the borders of brain, body, and environment. Moreover, because one of the fundamental units of perception is the change in stimulus, it is only fitting that the dynamical approach should rely on tools that describe changes in the agent and its environment over time. Dynamical systems theory is well positioned to do both.

To illustrate by way of example, consider the following pair of equations, taken from Beer (1995):

$$\dot{X}_A = A\big(X_A;\ S(X_E)\big)$$

$$\dot{X}_E = E\big(X_E;\ M(X_A)\big)$$

Here, A and E are taken to model the organism and its environment, respectively, as continuous-time dynamical systems. $S(X_E)$ and $M(X_A)$ are functions which couple environmental variables to organismic parameters and from organismic variables to environmental parameters, respectively. The equations do not describe the way various internal and external factors cause changes in the behavior of the organism. Instead, dynamical models like this explain the way the entire system – the relevant features of the organism and environment – unfolds over time.

Natural regions of explanation

Although Beer's well-known description of the nature of dynamical explanations in cognitive science casts them as applying only to animal-environment systems, there is no real reason that they cannot also apply to the activity of brains. Indeed, dynamical explanations have been a part of neuroscience for decades. For example, the Hodgkin-Huxley model of neuronal action potentials (Hodgkin and Huxley, 1952), which is foundational in modern neuroscience, is a set of differential equations. Other pioneering dynamical neuroscientists include Walter Freeman (1995; 2001; Freeman and Kozma, 2000), Herman Haken (2007), and Gyorgi Buzsaki (2006). More recently, Scott Kelso, who was an early adopter of dynamical explanation in animal-environment systems, has turned these tools to the study of the brain (Kelso, 2012). In fact, Kelso and his colleagues generally use the very same equations they used to study animal-environment systems to dynamically model brain activity (Kelso, Dumas, and Tognoli, 2013), implying that the cognitive systems instantiate the same dynamic at multiple scales. Similarly, although computational explanation works most naturally as a mechanistic explanation of activity that occurs in the brain, it can also be applied to broader animal-environment systems. Perhaps the most discussed version of what Rob Wilson has called 'wide computationalism' is Kirsh and Maglio's experiments on Tetris players (Kirsh and Maglio, 1995). The game involves rotating four-squared polyform blocks in seven different configurations to fit into open spaces at the bottom of the screen. They found that players tended to rotate the 'zoids' on the monitor to see whether they would fit into spaces at the bottom of the screen. Kirsh and Maglio suggested that this rotation was a way of making internal computational processes more efficient, by trading easy motor and visual processes (key presses and seeing) for difficult cognitive processes (mental rotation of irregular shapes). Kirsh and Maglio argue that the external rotation is part of the computation that enables Tetris players to play the game.

Explanatory emigration

Dynamical and computational explanations each have natural regions of explanation, types of entities to which they apply most easily – the former, wide agent-environment system; the latter, narrow brain-internal systems – but this in no way conflicts with their application outside their more natural homes. Going further, there is no need for conflict between computation and dynamical explanations, whether narrow or wide. Computational and dynamical explanations just tend to focus on different aspects of cognition: computational explanations tend to focus on ways in which brains or animal-environment systems process information; dynamical explanations tend to focus on real-time change in highly coupled, multi-part systems. What do conflict are computationalism and dynamicism. Computationalism is the view that cognitive systems are computational systems and, therefore, computational explanation is the appropriate explanation of them; dynamicism is the view that cognitive systems are dynamical systems and, therefore, dynamical explanation is the appropriate explanation of them. A computationalist would reject dynamical explanations as unable to account for cognitive systems; a dynamicist would reject computational explanations as unable to account for cognitive systems. We find neither of these views plausible. Human cognition is as complex a subject matter as there is, and it is possible that any one kind of explanation will be insufficient to explain all of it (Dale, 2008; Chemero and Silberstein, 2008; Dale, Dietrich, and Chemero, 2009). In the current context in cognitive science, and probably for the next several decades, we will likely need both computational and dynamical explanations.

Dynamical information processing

For the rest of this chapter, we will assume that both dynamical and computational explanations of both brain-bound and agent-environment phenomena are valuable contributions to cognitive science. This assumption enables us to endorse what we will call 'dynamical information processing' (DIP), a kind of explanation of the ongoing activity of animal-environment systems that is both dynamical and computational. What we are calling DIP here was discussed briefly in Chemero (2009), where it was pointed out, following Rowlands (2006), that sometimes animals process environmental information by moving their bodies. To make sense of DIP, we need to understand the variety of information that exists in the environment, and see some examples of the way that this information can be used, manipulated, and created by bodily movement.

The information that is processed in DIP is the variety that Gibson (1966; 1979) discussed. Given the strong historical connection between the dynamical approach in cognitive science and Gibsonian ecological psychology (see Chemero, 2009; Käufer and Chemero, 2015), it might not be all that surprising that Gibson's theory of environmental information is the key to combining dynamics and computation. Environmental information, according to Gibson, is different from Shannon information; it is neither syntactic, nor quantifiable. Energy arrays in the environment have structure. The light, for example, that is available at any point of observation has reflected off all of the non-occluded surfaces that surround that point of observation. Given the laws of chemistry and optics, the character of light at the point of observation will be lawfully structured by its reflection off those surfaces. Gibson put this by saying that the light available to animals *specifies* the surfaces; the light having the structure it does guarantees that the surfaces are the way they are. It is this relationship between the structured light and the surfaces that allows the light to carry information about the surfaces.

Gibson argued that perception is direct, unmediated contact with the environment. For this to be possible, Gibson argued that information is plentiful in the environment, and is sufficient for animals to make the discriminations they need to make without resorting to internal computational processes. This view is in direct opposition to the claims made by computational cognitive scientists, who think that the information available in the stimulus is impoverished, and that computational processing in the brain is required to transform ambiguous stimuli into awareness of the environment. For example, to determine how far away a person is, perceivers need to use the apparent size of the person in combination with stored assumptions about the typical size of people to compute distance. This might seem true, if the input to, say, visual perception is a pair of distorted, upside-down retinal snapshots. Indeed, it is sometimes impossible to tell whether the objects in photographs are three-dimensional objects or cardboard cutouts. But perception, for Gibson, is not a process that begins at sensory surfaces, but is a state of the agent-environment system. Gibson includes the environment as a crucial element of perception in order to remove the need for an intermediary, and thus maintain that perception is direct. Perception occurs in moving around the environment in such a way as to uncover, transform, and create the information that unambiguously specifies both objects and affordances. Information, in Gibson's sense, is processed during exploration of the environment in the perception–action cycle.

As an example, consider visual information about some feature of the environment, say whether a particular landscape contains a cliff, or whether a vertical rectangle in front of you is an open or shut door. Gibson's view is that we are not comparing instantaneous snapshots of that landscape to make an unconscious inference about whether or not there is a cliff, but rather that changes in visual information caused by our bodily movements specify the layout. Consider an object approaching in your visual field. The instantaneous retinal image is ambiguous with regard to the actual distance of the object given the portion of the visual field it currently takes up. What is not ambiguous, however, is the pattern of change over time. (See Figure 10.1.) The top part of the figure depicts two sticks that cast the same instantaneous retinal image, along

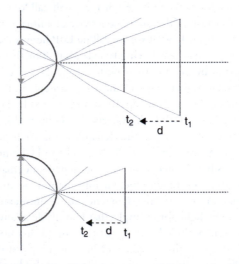

Figure 10.1 An illustration of specificity given motion. Used with permission from Kevin Shockley (personal communication)

with the change in the image size as the longer one moves toward the point of observation. The bottom part of the image depicts only the shorter stick, and change in image size as it moves toward the point of observation. Movement generates the information that specifies which stick is present.

Gibson's approach, therefore, is to look for reliable structure that is lawfully generated by bodily movement. Thus, to tell whether the rectangular contour in front of you is an open or closed door requires that you move, and register changes in the optical flow (i.e. differences in outward flow in ambient optic array inside the rectangular contour relative to change in ambient optic array outside the rectangular contour). The movement generates and transforms optic flow such that information that was not available is made available as to whether the door is open or closed. We call this dynamical information processing. (See Figure 10.2.)

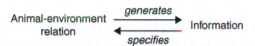

Figure 10.2 The information cycle in perception. Used with permission from Kevin Shockley (personal communication)

One example of this is postural sway. Ordinary body sway consists primarily of small fore–aft motions of the body's center of mass relative to the gravitational and inertial forces in the environment. These motions create a slight displacement of the head and eyes relative to the environment. This displacement produces optic flow. When the ground surface and the illuminated environment are stationary, parameters of the optic flow, such as its direction, amplitude, and frequency, are deterministically related to the corresponding parameters of body sway. For this reason, the optic flow provides information about body sway that can be useful in controlling sway, and help maintain standing balance. One prominent method for studying relations between vision and body sway is the *moving room paradigm* (Lee and Lishman, 1975). This paradigm uses a room constructed so that the walls are not attached to the floor, and can be moved. By moving the room subtly, researchers create optic flow that simulates the optical consequences of body sway; a sudden, relatively large movement of the room toward (or away from) the participant can simulate the optical consequences of falling forward (or backward). When standing persons are exposed to experimentally generated optic flow they tend to respond by coupling body sway to the flow. The implication here is that body sway thus contributes to stability of vision by coupling to the optic flow. That is, body sway generates information available in optic flow that is used to control the sway, and in so doing, enable standing balance.

An experiment conducted by Balasubramaniam and colleagues (2000) examined postural balance in terms of two underlying subsystems of postural sway. Postural balance, on this view, is the result of medio–lateral (ML; side to side) and anterior–posterior (AP; front to back) sway. Earlier studies (Paulus et al., 1989; Riley et al., 1997) showed that postural fluctuations in "quiet stance", or the undirected maintenance of upright posture, serve two essential functions, exploratory (obtaining information about current postural dynamics) and performatory (making corrections and adjustments to those dynamics on the basis of the obtained information), and that ML and AP sway are directly related to distance or size of a fixed target. However, these studies have taken place with participants standing with feet side-by-side, with the only task being to stand still. In these cases, fluctuations in AP and ML sway will be independent (Winter et al., 1993). However, Balasubramaniam et al. predicted that in tasks which require both precision and postural stability, like that of an archer trying to hit a target, the patterns of ML and AP fluctuation will be quite different. Competing demands of precision and stability gave rise to systematic, interrelated variation in ML and AP fluctuation patterns as a function of orientation of the target. In later work, Balasubramaniam and Wing (2002) demonstrated that the fact that AP sway is more prominent than ML sway in humans is functional, i.e. for vision, rather than anatomical, i.e. caused by the direction of feet. To demonstrate this, they had participants engage in a task that required participants to precisely aim at a target to their sides. When they do so, ML sway becomes more prominent than AP sway. That is, participants sway more in the direction their eyes are pointed. The transformations of the light that occur during sway, which (1) are caused by the participant's motion, (2) are lawfully determined by the relationship between the moving participant and the target, and (3) enable the participant to maintain their orientation to the target and their upright posture is what we call dynamical information processing.

Finding similar ways in which animals transform and generate information about their environment via action, i.e. ways in which they dynamically process environmental information has been the most important business of ecological psychology for the last several decades. That work is often technical, and generally uses the mathematical tools of dynamical systems theory (cf. von Holst, 1973; Turvey and Carello, 1996; Van Orden, Holden, and Turvey, 2005). But DIP is visible in much more mundane examples. We heft the bag to see if we can carry it; we lean to the left to see around something; we re-position our head to enhance the temporal disparity of sounds arriving at our ears and hear where the sound is coming from. Each of these is a case of dynamical information processing: we engage in overt action to create and/or transform – to process – the information available to us.

Where is the processing?

So far, this chapter has shown that there is a brand of dynamical explanation which is broadly consistent with computational explanation, drawn from insights in embodied cognition, extended cognition, and ecological psychology. We have called it dynamical information processing. The environment is full of information of the Gibsonian sort. Our skillful, typically non-reflective, exploratory actions systematically transform the information available to us. Dynamical information processing suggests that humans and other animals are indeed computers of a sort, since they are information processors. However, it does not suggest that brains are information processors.

DIP is unlike the computational information processing typical in computational explanations. Brains are elements of the brain-body-environment, but they are not automatically given preferential status in the carrying out of cognitive activity. There may be some behaviors which rely more heavily on the brain, just as there may be behaviors which rely more heavily on the ears, or on features of the environment, or even on other agents. Indeed, dynamical information processing leaves open the possibility that some information processing may not require brains. DIP is consistent with the notion of a computational cognitive system. However it does not imply, in attempting to study it, looking at the brain is the only (or even the best) way to understand cognition.

DIP is not the same as wide computational explanation. Wide computational explanations are committed to what is sometimes called 'information offloading' (Hutchins, 1995; Kirsh and Maglio, 1995). Information offloading occurs when some aspect of a cognitive process that might be done by the brain is offloaded to the environment to simplify processing demands. This need not be restricted to the vehicles which will be transformed in the process of the computation. It is not only that information that is to be processed that is offloaded to the environment, as when, say, you write a number down to save it for future calculation. Any aspect of a cognitive process is a candidate for offloading. This includes not only the information to be processed, but the processing itself. In contrast, with DIP it is not entirely clear that information is being processed in any particular place. The transformations in information occur at the scale of the entire animal-environment system, so it is the entire system that may be said to be processing the information. Importantly, however, the information processing in the sway and standing balance examples discussed above involve no information offloading. There is no information or information processing that could have been in the brain, but was placed in the environment for convenience or efficiency during sway and balance. The information processed in sway is necessarily in the environment.

As noted above, work by Mark Rowlands (2006) is an important precursor to DIP, and what he calls 'deeds' can shed light on the nature of the processing involved. Deeds are bodily movements that animals engage in, purposely and skillfully, but without intentional underpinnings required for them to be classified as full-blown actions. Actions are done intentionally, and are typically composed of many, hierarchically nested skillful movements. These are deeds. To use the example above, a participant in an experiment might intend, because of instructions given by an experimenter, to point a laser pointer at an object on the wall. To do so, the participant will sway, predominantly in the direction of gaze. She will also move her eyes, head, and neck. The sway and other bodily movements are what Rowlands identifies as deeds, and are part of the dynamical information processing that the agent is engaged in. Likewise, in the case of the postural sway, the act of standing still (i.e. upright balancing) is going to require many deeds to complete. That is, in maintaining an upright posture, a human being will engage in both AP and ML swaying. Neither of these individual sway directions will be sufficient for the act of standing still. Likewise, maintaining an upright posture is also required to stand still, but this is not sufficient to stand still. Instead, standing still will require a series of ongoing sub-processes. These sub-processes are deeds.

Deeds, on this conception, perform the same information-transforming processes which a computational view would ascribe to sub-personal, internal computational processes. The exploratory movements an agent implements to uncover invariant features of the optic array, for instance, take the place of computational processes which construct a mental representation based on the retinal image. In this way DIP explanations complement traditional computational explanations. A robust DIP account of cognitive processes will highlight aspects of the agent-environment system which exhibit strong coupling behavior. This, in turn may constrain subsequent computational explanations of cognition by relieving the brain of some of its processing duties. The result is a finer-grained depiction of the role of the brain in cognition, and one which can increase the precision of scientific inquiries of the brain. The main difference lies is the tools being used to discover and analyze these features. In the case of deeds, explanations will be put forth in the language of dynamical systems theory. In contrast, computational explanations will tend not use these tools. The dynamics of postural sway and optic flow, for instance, can be modeled as coupled oscillators (Dijkstra, Schöner, and Gielen, 1994; Giese et al., 1996; Stoffregen et al., 2000).

What the above analysis has shown is that there is a view of dynamical and computational explanations which is sufficiently broad to satisfactorily encompass both kinds of explanation: dynamical information processing. The difference between these two traditions, on this view, does not lie in a commitment to any particular –ism. Instead, a DIP should be seen as player in a pluralistic view of computational and dynamical explanations in the cognitive sciences.

Conclusion

The purpose of this chapter has been to stake out a common ground between computational and dynamical approaches. It has been shown that many of the traditional lines along which the dynamical/computational distinction has been drawn are inappropriate. First, it is typically presumed that commitments to mental representations serve to distinguish computational from dynamical approaches, with computational views lying on the representational side, and dynamical views on the anti-representational side. However, because there are computational views which are non-representational, and dynamical views which are representational, drawing the line along representational lines is inappropriate. Second, computational views are typically presumed to entail internalism with respect to their instantiations. That is, computations performed by cognitive systems are typically taken to be performed by components *internal* to the system. With regard to human cognitive systems, these components are taken to be parts of brains. However, the existence of wide computationalism has shown that such a commitment is unnecessary to the computational approach. Finally, a division has been made between computational and dynamical approaches on the basis of commitments to *mechanistic explanation*. However, since the dynamical approach expresses a methodological preference, and not a claim about explanation, this division in unsatisfactory. That is, one can adopt the dynamical or computational approach without making any specific claims about mechanisms or explanations.

Having cleared the ground for a broadly compatible approach to computational and dynamical approaches, we endorsed a kind of explanation that we call dynamical information processing. It is hoped that DIP can represent an epistemic truce, and engender a commitment to mutually supporting scientific exploration. It is too early to call the battle between frameworks in cognitive science; in fact, it could be that future cognitive science is neither computational nor dynamical. Until a verdict is reached, DIP allows us to still make genuine, non-adversarial progress toward understanding cognition.

Acknowledgment

Anthony Chemero was supported by the Charles Phelps Taft Research Center while working on this chapter.

References

Balasubramaniam, R., Riley, M.A., and Turvey, M.T. (2000) 'Specificity of Postural Sway to the Demands of a Precision Task', *Gait and Posture*, 11 (1), pp. 12–24.

Balasubramaniam, R. and Wing, A.M. (2002) 'The Dynamics of Standing Balance', *Trends in Cognitive Science*, 6 (12), pp. 531–536.

Beer, R. (1995) 'A Dynamical Systems Perspective on Agent-Environment Interaction', *Artificial Intelligence*, 72, pp. 173–215.

Beer, R. (2000) 'Dynamical Approaches to Cognitive Science', *Trends in Cognitive Sciences*, 4, pp. 91–99.

Buzsaki, G. (2006) *Rhythms of the Brain*. New York, NY: Oxford University Press.

Chemero, A. (2009) *Radical Embodied Cognitive Science*. Cambridge, MA: MIT Press.

Chemero, A. and Silberstein, M. (2008) 'After the Philosophy of Mind: Replacing Scholasticism with Science', *Philosophy of Science*, 75 (1), pp. 1–27.

Clark, A. (1997) *Being There: Putting Brain, Body and World Together Again*. Cambridge, MA: MIT Press.

Clark, A. (2015) *Surfing Uncertainty: Prediction, Action, and the Embodied Mind*. New York, NY: Oxford University Press.

Clark, A. and Chalmers, D. (1998) 'The Extended Mind', *Analysis*, 58, pp. 7–19.

Dale, R. (2008) 'The Possibility of a Pluralist Cognitive Science', *Journal of Experimental and Theoretical Artificial Intelligence*, 20, pp. 155–179.

Dale, R., Dietrich, E., and Chemero, A. (2009) 'Explanatory Pluralism in Cognitive Science', *Cognitive Science*, 33, pp. 739–742.

Dijkstra, T.M.H., Schöner, G., and Gielen, C.C.A.M. (1994) 'Temporal Stability of the Action-Perception Cycle for Postural Control in a Moving Visual Environment', *Experimental Brain Research*, 97 (3), pp. 477–486.

Fodor, J. (1981) 'The Mind-Body Problem', *Scientific American*, 244, pp. 114–125.

Fodor, J. and Pylyshyn, Z. (1988) 'Connectionism and Cognitive Architecture: A Critical Analysis', *Cognition*, 28, pp. 3–71.

Freeman, W. (1995) 'The Hebbian Paradigm Reintegrated: Local Reverberations as Internal Representations', *Behavioral and Brain Sciences*, 18 (4), p. 617–626.

Freeman, W. (2001) *How Brains Make up Their Minds*. New York, NY: Columbia University Press.

Freeman, W. and Kozma, R. (2000) 'Local-Global Interactions and the Role of Mesoscopic (Intermediate-range) Elements in Brain Dynamics', *Behavioral and Brain Sciences*, 23 (3), p. 401.

Gibson, J.J. (1966) *The Senses Considered as Perceptual Systems*. Boston, MA: Houghton Mifflin.

Gibson, J.J. (1979) *The Ecological Approach to Visual Perception*. Boston, MA: Houghton Mifflin.

Giese, M.A. et al. (1996) 'Identification of the Nonlinear State-Space Dynamics of the Action-Perception Cycle for Visually Induced Postural Sway', *Biological Cybernetics*, 74 (5), pp. 427–437.

Haken, H. (2007) *Brain Dynamics: An Introduction to Models and Simulations*. New York, NY: Springer-Verlag.

Hodgkin, A.L. and Huxley, A.F. (1952) 'A Quantitative Description of Membrane Current and Its Application to Conduction and Excitation in Nerve', *Journal of Physiology*, 117, pp. 500–544.

Hutchins, E. (1995) *Cognition in the Wild*. Cambridge, MA: MIT Press.

Izhikevich, E. (2007) *Dynamical Systems in Neuroscience: The Geometry of Excitability and Bursting*. Cambridge, MA: MIT Press.

Käufer, S. and Chemero, A. (2015) *Phenomenology: An Introduction*. Cambridge, UK: Polity Press.

Kelso, J.S. (2012) 'Multistability and Metastability: Understanding Dynamic Coordination in the Brain', *Philosophical Transactions of the Royal Society of London B: Biological Sciences*, 367 (1591), pp. 906–918.

Kelso, J.S., Dumas, G., and Tognoli, E. (2013) 'Outline of a General Theory of Behavior and Brain Coordination', *Neural Networks*, 37, pp. 120–131.

Kirsh, D. and Maglio, P. (1995) 'On Distinguishing Epistemic from Pragmatic Action', *Cognitive Science*, 18 (4), pp. 513–549.

Lee, D.N. and Lishman, J.R. (1975) 'Visual Proprioceptive Control of Stance', *Journal of Human Movement Studies*, 1 (2), pp. 87–95.

Mazurek, M.E. et al. (2003) 'A Role for Neural Integrators in Perceptual Decision Making', *Cerebral Cortex*, 13, pp. 1257–1269.

Newell, A. and Simon, H. (1976) 'Computer Science as Empirical Inquiry: Symbols and Search', *Communications of the Association for Computing Machinery*, 19, pp. 113–126.

Paulus, W. et al. (1989) 'Differential Effects of Retinal Target Displacement, Changing Size and Changing Disparity in the Control of Anterior/Posterior and Lateral Body Sway', *Experimental Brain Research*, 78, pp. 243–252.

Piccinini, G. (2015) *Physical Computation: A Mechanistic Account*. Oxford: Oxford University Press.

Piccinini, G. and Bahar, S. (2013) 'Neural Computation and the Computational Theory of Cognition', *Cognitive Science*, 37 (3), pp. 453–488.

Piccinini, G. and Scarantino, A. (2011) 'Information Processing, Computation, and Cognition', *Journal of Biological Physics*, 37 (1), pp. 1–38.

Putnam, H. (1960) 'Minds and Machines', in Hook, S. (ed.) *Dimensions of Mind: A Symposium*. New York, NY: Collier, pp. 138–164.

Putnam, H. (1988) *Representation and Reality*. Cambridge, MA: MIT Press.

Pylyshyn, Z. (1984) *Computation and Cognition*. Cambridge, MA: MIT Press.

Riley, M.A. et al. (1997) 'Influences of Body Lean and Vision on Postural Fluctuations in Stance', *Motor Control*, 1, pp. 229–246.

Rowlands, M. (2006) *Body Language: Representation in Action*. Cambridge, MA: MIT Press.

Rumelhart, D. and McClelland, J. (1986) *Parallel Distributed Processing*, vol. 1. Cambridge, MA: MIT Press.

Searle, J. (1990) 'Is the Brain's Mind a Computer Program?', *Scientific American*, 262, pp. 26–31.

Stoffregen, T.A. et al. (2000) 'Modulating Postural Control to Facilitate Visual Performance', *Human Movement Science*, 19 (2), pp. 203–220.

Strogatz, S.H. (2014) *Nonlinear Dynamics and Chaos: With Application to Physics, Biology, Chemistry, and Engineering*, 2nd ed. Cambridge, MA: Westview Press.

Turvey, M.T. and Carello, C. (1996) 'Dynamics of Bernstein's Level of Synergies', in Latash, M.L. and Turvey, M.T. (eds.) *Dexterity and Its Development.* Mahwah, NJ: Lawrence Erlbaum, pp. 339–376.

Van Orden, G.C., Holden, J.G., and Turvey, M.T. (2005) 'Human Cognition and 1/f Scaling', *Journal of Experimental Psychology: General*, 134 (1), pp. 117–123.

von Holst, E. (1973) *The Collected Papers of Erich von Holst*, vol. l: *The Behavioral Physiology of Animal and Man.* Translated and edited by R. Martin. Coral Gables, FL: University of Miami Press. (Original work published 1939).

Wilson, R. (1994) 'Wide Computationalism', *Mind*, 103 (411), pp. 351–372.

Winter, D.A. et al. (1993) 'An integrated EMG/Biomechanical Model of Upper Body Balance and Posture during Human Gait', *Progress in Brain Research*, 97, pp. 359–367.

11

PROBABILISTIC MODELS

David Danks

A plethora of probabilistic models

The world is a fundamentally noisy and variable place: few events must occur; our measurements are rarely perfectly accurate; and relations are almost never deterministic in nature. Instead, there is uncertainty and error of various types in all our experiences, as shown by just the slightest reflection on everyday life. Sometimes, caffeine helps me to be more alert, but not always. Sometimes, my dog barks at strangers, but not always. Nonetheless, cognitive systems (including people) must be able to learn and reason appropriately despite this ineliminable noise and uncertainty. And in addition to variability in our experiences, human behavior is itself noisy and uncertain; people do not (and often should not) act identically in seemingly identical situations or contexts. Computational models of human cognition must have some way to handle all of the noise, uncertainty, and variability; many do so with probabilities, as the probability calculus is a standard computational framework for capturing and working with noise and uncertainty, whether in the world or the reasoner.[1] As one illustrative example, almost all theories of category judgments (such as "Is this a dog?") are probabilistic in nature: they allow for uncertainty in both the world – the same observation might sometimes be a dog, sometimes a wolf – and in the human categorizer – the same observation can probabilistically yield one of several possible judgments.

Although probabilities might be a standard tool for a computational cognitive model to capture noise and uncertainty, they nonetheless raise significant challenges for explanation and prediction. At a high level, the core underlying issue is that probabilistic models do not provide specific predictions for single cases or particular behaviors; instead, they only provide predictions about (features of) collections of behaviors. Almost any sequence of events is consistent with almost any probability distribution, although it might be highly improbable, and so our explanations and predictions do not operate in the usual ways. Instead, we need to rethink the explanations and predictions that these models provide. In this chapter, we consider these issues, as well as some of the novel benefits and advantages that probabilistic cognitive models can potentially provide beyond possible descriptive adequacy. Because the focus here will be on more conceptual issues, there will be few technical details. There are many useful introductions available elsewhere for readers interested in the precise mathematical formulations of probabilistic models in general (Koller and Friedman, 2009; Ross, 2009), and probabilistic cognitive models in particular (Chater, Tenenbaum, and Yuille, 2006; Perfors et al., 2011). In addition, we will focus on cognitive models, rather than neurocomputational ones. Although many models of neural phenomena are probabilistic in nature (e.g. Doya et al., 2007; Ganguli and Simoncelli, 2014), we will restrict our attention to more cognitive models (though many of the observations apply with minor adjustments to neurocomputational models).[2]

At a high level, probabilities can be incorporated into a computational cognitive model in two different, not mutually exclusive, ways. First, representations in the cognitive system can include or employ probabilities, where we take a very broad view of the notion of "representation". Any cognitive system must encode, whether explicitly or implicitly, key information about its environment, and these encodings will frequently involve probabilities to capture noise and uncertainty about the surrounding environments and contexts. For example, representations of causal structure are often modeled as probabilistic (causal) graphical models (Danks, 2014; Griffiths and Tenenbaum, 2005), which explicitly use a joint probability distribution to represent the noisy causal relations in the world. Or some Bayesian cognitive models represent theoretical knowledge as distinct hypotheses (perhaps probabilistic, perhaps deterministic) with probabilities that encode strength of belief (Griffiths, Kemp, and Tenenbaum, 2008; Perfors et al., 2011). A more implicit use of probabilities can be found in exemplar theories of categorization. These theories represent a category by a set of (definite, non-probabilistic) previously observed instances, and so appear to be non-probabilistic. However, those exemplars (plus a similarity metric) implicitly encode the probability of observing various types of individuals (Ashby and Maddox, 1993); that is, these categories actually correspond to probability distributions, even though they are not typically written in that way. In all of these cases, the cognitive model encodes or represents the world as a fundamentally noisy place; probabilities here are used to capture indeterminism in the environment, at least from our perspective.

Second, probabilities can be used in a computational cognitive model to capture noise and indeterminism in the cognitive agent herself. Experience, observations, and context rarely fully determine people's cognitive activity, at least at the level of our cognitive models. For example, our choices between two similar options will exhibit a degree of noise: given seemingly the same choice, we will sometimes pick option A and other times option B. Similar indeterminacy can be found in many other cognitive processes, and so our models of the agent's cognitive processes often include probabilities (even when the agent's representations are non-probabilistic in nature). In general, we can usefully distinguish between three types of cognitive processes, though no bright lines can necessarily be drawn to separate them: (i) learning; (ii) reasoning or inference; and (iii) acting or decision making. A probabilistic learning process might yield different learned representations, even if identical observations and initial knowledge or prior beliefs are provided as inputs. A probabilistic reasoning process might yield different judgments or beliefs, even given identical representations and context as input. A probabilistic decision-making process might yield different choices, even if given as input identical representations, beliefs, context, and goals. In each case, identical input to the process can yield different outcomes, and probabilities are used to capture this indeterminism.

Of course, probabilities can enter into a computational cognitive model at more than one place. For example, consider models of category acquisition and categorization – how we learn particular concepts, and then employ them for novel cases. In almost all cases, this cognitive process is noisy and indeterministic, and so should presumably involve probabilities. However, those probabilities can occur in representation (e.g. Rehder, 2003), learning (e.g. Love, Medin, and Gureckis, 2004), reasoning (e.g. Nosofsky and Palmeri, 1997), or more than one of the above (e.g. Tenenbaum and Griffiths, 2001). That is, we face an underdetermination problem: we know that probabilities have to appear *somewhere*, but we do not have the necessary data to determine whether they occur in representations, processes, or both. Often, the same behavioral phenomena can be modeled using (a) deterministic representations and probabilistic processes; (b) probabilistic representations and deterministic processes; or (c) both probabilistic representations and processes. Of course, most (complex) cognitive models face underdetermination challenges, but the problem here is even harder, as we do not even know what *type* of components (probabilistic vs deterministic) should be employed in our model.

This introductory section has talked about computational cognitive models as though they apply to particular individuals; that is, cognitive models were discussed in the context of explaining the cognitive processes of particular individuals. In fact, though, many of our cognitive models are fundamentally ambiguous about whether they describe individuals or populations. In many contexts, this ambiguity is innocuous, but probabilistic models are not such a context. Suppose that we observe variability in behavior for a group of people who have all seemingly been exposed to the same information (e.g. experimental stimuli in the lab). This variability could arise from everyone having the same probabilistic cognition, or from people having different deterministic cognition, or a mixture of the two. As a non-cognitive example, suppose that I flip many different coins and find approximately 50 percent heads, 50 percent tails. This "behavior" could arise at the population level because each individual coin is fair and balanced, or because half of the coins are two-headed and half two-tailed, or because we have a mix of these two extremal possibilities. More generally, any population-level probability distribution can be explained by probabilities *within* the individuals, or by probabilities *across* the individuals (or a combination). Perhaps we behave differently from one another because our cognition is fundamentally probabilistic, or perhaps because we have variability in our initial beliefs and subsequent experiences. The challenge for many of our computational cognitive models is that they describe average or population-level behaviors without explicitly stating whether the model is also an individual-level one. Often, it is implied that the models apply to particular individuals (not just the population), but that is frequently not explicitly stated. And in many cases, we lack the evidence to distinguish between the various possibilities, as we need repeated observations of each person in order to establish whether their particular cognition is probabilistic, and such repeated measures can be quite difficult and expensive to obtain. In the remainder of this chapter, we will see several places where this ambiguity – do the probabilities in the cognitive model capture within-individual or across-individual variability? – matters in the use, interpretation, and explanatory power of probabilistic cognitive models.

Explanation and prediction with probabilistic models

We begin by thinking about prediction using probabilistic models, as that is key to thinking about their explanatory power (as well as many other uses of probabilistic models). Importantly, probabilistic cognitive models will generally not predict any specific behavior at all, but rather a range and likelihood of possible behaviors (regardless of where the probabilities are located in the model). These predictions can thus be quite difficult to assess or use, precisely because they are logically consistent with almost anything. Almost any sequence of data will be logically consistent with almost any probabilistic cognitive model, though the data might be quite unlikely. We thus need to rethink the exact content and target of our predictions and explanations.

It is perhaps easiest to see the issues by considering a non-cognitive example. Suppose that I am flipping a fair coin – that is, a coin that has a 0.5 probability of coming up heads. The predicted possibilities for flips of this coin include every possible sequence of heads and tails; some sequences might be exceptionally improbable, of course, but they are nonetheless possible. In the case of probabilistic cognitive models, almost any behavior will be predicted to be possible, though the model might predict that this behavior should be unlikely or rare. One reaction would be to conclude that probabilistic cognitive models are therefore untestable or useless, as they do not constrain the possibility space for behavior. This reaction is too quick, however, as we can instead shift to thinking about whether the observed behavior is likely or expected. Of course, we cannot test the likelihood of a single instance, and so we must also shift our focus from predicting a single behavior to predicting properties of sequences or collections of behaviors. This change raises anew the issue from the end of the previous section: if our focus is on collections of behavior, then we have to be very careful to distinguish between (a) collections formed from multiple behaviors by a single person; and (b) collections formed from behaviors by multiple people. Probabilistic cognitive models for (a) can be used to generate predictions for (b), but not vice versa. Hence, if our only observations are of type (b), then we will likely face additional underdetermination in terms of confirmation and plausibility.

With this understanding of the predictions of probabilistic cognitive models in hand, we can turn to the explanations provided by a well-tested, well-confirmed probabilistic cognitive model. There are multiple explanatory virtues (as we will discuss in the next section), but we can first focus on the role of prediction in explanation. Predictive power is important because all theories of explanation hold that an explanans **S** should, in some sense, show why an explanandum *E* was expected, likely, inevitable, or otherwise followed naturally. Different theories of explanation provide different ways to explicate the idea of "following naturally", but all of those explications are connected in some way with predictive power. As a result, the approach that we employ for prediction in probabilistic cognitive models must also apply to the explanatory power of those models. In particular, probabilistic models cannot provide the same types of explanations, or same explanatory power, as deterministic cognitive models.

Consider some probabilistic cognitive model *M* and any arbitrary, though relevant, behavior *B*. As long as *M* assigns non-zero probability to *B*, then *M* can always give an "explanation" of *B*: the fact that *M* implies *B* is possible means that there is *some* sequence in *M* that results in *B*, and this sequence shows how *B* could have been produced (if *M* were true). But this means that the mere existence of an *M*-explanation is quite uninformative, since we know *a priori* that we will almost certainly be able to provide a story about how *B* could have been produced, regardless of what *B* turns out to be. And if a theory can "explain" any possible data, then it arguably provides no explanation at all. One natural response is to argue that *M* provides an explanation only if it shows that *B* is highly likely or highly probable. The problem, though, is that improbable things sometimes happen, and so this constraint implies that we will sometimes have no explanation for some *B* (i.e. the improbable ones). For example, a sequence of ten heads when flipping a fair coin is highly improbable – it will happen only around 0.1 percent of the time when one does ten coin flips – but if it does happen, then it would be quite strange to say that we have no explanation at all.[3] More generally, many probabilistic cognitive models predict that any particular, specific behavior *B* will be relatively improbable, even though they might well be able to provide a causal or mechanistic account of how *B* was generated.

At this point, there are two natural moves that one can make. First, we can change our understanding of the behavior to be explained. In the coin-flipping case, any particular sequence is improbable, but sequences with certain shared features might be much more probable; for example, a sequence with five heads and five tails, regardless of order, occurs 24.6 percent of the time. Hence, we can perhaps save the requirement that an *M*-explanation should show how *B* is probable (or at least, not too improbable) by focusing on particular features of *B*, rather than *B* exactly. In the case of probabilistic cognitive models, this move typically requires shifting from explanations of a particular behavior *B* to explanations of *collections* of behaviors $B_1, \ldots, B_n$. That is, *M* no longer provides an explanation of how a specific behavior, decision, or judgment resulted, but instead explains how features of a *distribution* of behaviors results, whether within a single person over time, or across a number of different people. These explanations of higher-level behavioral patterns are different than what we might have expected, but can be exactly what we want and need in certain contexts.[4] For example, if I am trying to understand causal reasoning, then I do not necessarily need to know how each particular causal judgment is generated, but only how they are usually generated, or the variability in how they can be generated, or the factors that are causally and/or explanatorily relevant to variation in those judgments. Individual people can be idiosyncratic in many different ways, and it might simply be unreasonable to think that we could give satisfactory explanations for how each specific behavior is generated; human cognition might simply be too complex a system. At the same time, we need to recognize that explanations of group-level phenomena or collections of behaviors (including those of the same person at different points in time) are importantly different from those that explain specific individual behaviors. We have changed our target, and so our explanations are arguably weaker in important ways. For example, they no longer explain any particular cognitive or behavioral event.

A second response is to shift away from asking whether M makes B probable or not, and instead focus on the sequence of events identified by M in its purported explanation of B. That is, we can require our M-explanations to provide an account of what actually happened to result in B. There are many debates about whether cognitive and neuroscientific explanations must be causal, mechanistic, or have some other shared feature (e.g. Craver, 2007; Kaplan and Craver, 2011; Lange, 2013; Ross, 2015). However, we do not need to engage with those debates here, as all of the parties agree that explanations identify a particular sequence of events that led to B. Those debates are about whether there are further constraints on that sequence, such as requiring it to be a causal sequence or mechanism. Regardless of that question, B presumably resulted from a sequence of events, and identification of that sequence provides one kind of explanation. Thus, a probabilistic M can perhaps provide a non-probabilistic explanation of B. Unfortunately, as noted earlier, we know *a priori* that we will almost always be able to postulate *some* sequence of events in M that would lead to B. The key question for explanations of this type is whether the postulated sequence actually occurred, and that determination requires that we observe much more than just B. This second strategy – shift to focusing on actual sequences of events – might be the right one in some cases, but comes at a cost: we only have grounds to believe those M-explanations about how B actually resulted if we have much more information about the particular case. The mere observation of B is clearly not sufficient, since we can almost always generate a "how possibly" M-explanation.

The overall message is that probabilistic cognitive models generally provide explanations of how some behavior resulted only if we (i) weaken our expectations by shifting to features of collections of behavior (by the same or different individuals); or (ii) strengthen our measurement capabilities by observing intermediate states or events that culminated in the behavior. Given this choice, we might instead pursue a completely different response by changing the desired type of explanation to account for *why* the behavior occurred (rather than *how*). In particular, many probabilistic cognitive models have been offered as "rational" or "optimal" models that can tell us why some behavior occurred, even if nothing can be said about how it was generated. For example, a *rational* model of categorization (Anderson, 1991; Goodman et al., 2008; Tenenbaum and Griffiths, 2001) aspires to explain people's category judgments by showing it to be optimally correct behavior. These theories do not specify the processes or structures by which these judgments were produced, but they can nonetheless explain why people act as they do: namely, people are trying to succeed at the task of categorization, and these responses are the right way to do that. The explanation here is analogous to what one might say when asked to explain why a calculator reads '17' when '8+9=' is entered: namely, that's the right answer, and properly functioning calculators are designed to give the right answer. This explanation gives us no information about how the calculator functions, but it nonetheless can explain the calculator's "behavior". Of course, human cognition is not necessarily "designed" like a calculator is, and so we must provide additional information (Danks, 2008). Nonetheless, this different type of explanation – a why-explanation rather than how-explanation – is another response to the difficulty of explaining human behavior.

Why-explanations are not restricted to probabilistic cognitive models, but they are particularly common for those models, partly for reasons that we explore in the next section. For now, we focus on the requirements and explanatory power of these why-explanations. To have a full why-explanation, we need to show not only that the behavior is optimal for human cognizers in these environments, but also that people act in this way *because* the behavior is optimal (Danks, 2008). The second requirement is crucial, as optimality alone does not tell us why the behavior occurred if, in fact, that optimality played no role in leading to the behavior. In the calculator case, the why-explanation depends partly on the calculator being correctly designed; a similar claim is required for why-explanations of human behavior. Of course, we do not need to have a full causal story about the role of past (optimal) performance. For example, it is sufficient to show that there are ontogenetic or phylogenetic pressures that will push people to act more optimally. And given a demonstration of optimality and its cognitive relevance, then not only do we arguably know why some behavior occurred, but we can also predict what would happen if the environment or task shifted (assuming the individual had time to learn and adapt).

This why-explanation is limited in certain important ways. For example, and in contrast with a causal-mechanical how-explanation, we can make only limited predictions about what might happen if the cognitive system is damaged or altered in some way. We can presumably expect that it will be different in *some* way, but we cannot predict how exactly it will change, nor whether it will be able to recover or adapt to this damage. We also do not avoid the problem of predicting single cases: if the optimal behavior is to act probabilistically (as in, for example, certain foraging situations), then we will still have to shift our explanandum to properties of collections of behaviors. Nonetheless, these why-explanations do represent a qualitatively different type of explanation from the usual causal-mechanical-computational ones found in cognitive science.

Explanation beyond prediction

One key feature of explanations is that they show why or how something occurred, but there are plausibly other explanatory virtues or functions. In particular, explanations are often thought to play a unifying role (Kitcher, 1981), though the nature of this unification is not always clear. In the case of probabilistic models, the unification function is often touted as an important aspect that speaks in favor of the models. These arguments all begin with the observation with which this chapter started: the world is a fundamentally noisy and uncertain place (from our perspective). The proponents of probabilistic models then typically argue that the probability calculus, or Bayesian updating, or some other probabilistic model is the normatively correct way to handle noise and uncertainty (e.g. Chater, Tenenbaum, and Yuille, 2006; Chater and Oaksford, 2008; Oaksford and Chater, 2007). Thus, these arguments claim that probabilistic cognitive models provide explanatory unification in virtue of being the (purported) correct way to handle a world like ours. The shared language of probabilities in all of these models of diverse cognitive phenomena provides a further unification: they are all instances of probabilistic inference, reasoning, specification, etc., and so these cognitive processes and behaviors are just different manifestations of the same type of theoretical "machinery" (leaving aside the question of whether they share any neural "machinery").

There is a sense in which the conclusion of these arguments is correct, as our cognition surely must be robust in the face of various types of noise, uncertainty, or indeterminism. It would be bizarre if our cognitive processes had no way of representing and responding (perhaps implicitly) to this variability. And to the extent that we think that different cognitive phenomena do involve similar types of processes or representations, we should favor model-types that are widely successful. So to the extent that probabilistic cognitive models have significant, widespread *descriptive* explanatory success, then we might hope that we can develop an argument that future probabilistic models should be judged as more plausible. However, this unificationist argument makes no reference to rationality or optimality claims, and so we must provide further argument that rationality or optimality considerations provide a further (explanatory) reason to favor probabilistic cognitive models, rather than ones based in other non-deterministic processes.

The standard arguments for why-explanations in probabilistic cognitive models depend on the claim that all rational, optimal, or normative models *must* be probabilistic; in particular, they must satisfy the probability calculus. This claim justifies assertions that probabilistic models are the "correct" or "appropriate" way to handle uncertainty, which thereby privileges those models (when they are approximately descriptively correct). There are many different defenses of this claim in the literature (many collected in Oaksford and Chater, 2007). For example, Dutch book arguments show that failing to conform to the probability calculus can lead to decisions that are individually sensible (from the decision-maker's point of view) but are jointly guaranteed to end badly. Or convergence arguments show that no method of changing one's beliefs can consistently do better than if one changes strengths of belief according to the probability calculus. Many of these arguments are deployed specifically in favor of Bayesian models – that is, models in which belief change or inference occurs through conditionalization as given by Bayes' Rule – but they often are appropriate for probabilistic models more generally. The details also obviously can matter in these arguments for the crucial claim, but the key here is simply that they all aim to establish strong, perhaps even identity, relations between the class of probabilistic models and the class of rational/optimal models.

However, there is an issue with the way that these arguments are used. In every case, the arguments show (at best) that probabilistic models, reasoning, or updating are *one* good way to handle uncertainty, not that they are the *only* or *uniquely* good (or rational, or optimal, or correct) way (Eberhardt and Danks, 2011). More specifically, "probabilistic" and "rational" are theoretically independent notions: one can have probabilistic, non-rational models, and also non-probabilistic, rational models. Although probabilistic models are often rational or optimal, they are not privileged in that way. As just one example, consider the cognitive task of learning from experience. There have been numerous arguments that Bayesian conditionalization is the rational way to learn – that is, given a new piece of evidence, the changes in one's probabilities over various options (i.e. learning from a probabilistic perspective) should change in accordance with Bayes' Rule (Teller, 1973; 1976). The normative force of these arguments arises from Bayesian conditionalization ensuring probabilistic coherence over time, or consistency of plans in light of new information, or convergence to the truth (when it is learnable), or other such desirable features. But in every case, there are alternative methods – sometimes, infinitely many such methods – that also satisfy that desideratum (Douven, 1999; Eberhardt and Danks, 2011). Bayesian conditionalization is normatively defensible, but not uniquely normatively privileged, compared to other methods for shifting belief, or other (often more qualitative) representations of uncertainty.

This story repeats itself for essentially every argument in favor of the rationality of probabilistic models and methods: they are normatively defensible, but not normatively unique. Moreover, explanatory unification (of the sort proposed at the beginning of this section) depends on uniqueness, not simply defensibility. Probabilistic models and methods were argued to provide some extra explanatory power that goes beyond "mere" descriptive adequacy, but the additional explanatory power depends on the number of alternatives. If probabilistic models and methods are only one of many possibilities, then we have only a very weak normative explanation of why the brain/mind employs them (if it does). We cannot claim that these models are inevitable because "a rational agent couldn't have done otherwise", precisely because there are many different things that a rational agent could do instead. That is, the question "Why probabilistic models?" cannot be answered with "Because they are inevitable for rational agents", despite suggestions to the contrary from proponents of those models.

Despite these issues, there is still an important sense in which probabilistic models and methods can provide a type of explanatory unification, though one grounded in their descriptive rather than normative virtues. These theories employ a common template or schema for the specification of the model, methods, and techniques (Danks, 2014, ch. 8). We can thus understand the mind as consisting of many distinct instantiations of the same underlying type of representation or process, such as joint probability distributions or Bayesian updating processes (Colombo and Hartmann, 2017). To the extent that we expect there to be similarities within the mind, the shared schema of a probabilistic method or model implies that the collection of probabilistic models has greater explanatory power than the "sum" of the individual model's explanatory powers. That is, the shared probabilistic schema implies mutually reinforcing support,[5] at least to the extent that we expect that different aspects of the mind/brain should have some degree of similarity. One might worry about this last qualifier, as there are many arguments that the mind/brain should and does exhibit substantial modularity, and we might have no particular reason to think that modules share a model- or method-schema (Carruthers, 2006; Fodor, 1983; Tooby and Cosmides, 1992). However, we also have no reason to think that modules *cannot* have a shared schema, as apparently module-specific phenomena can instead arise because of distinct prior knowledge, experience, or expectations (Samuels, 1998). General arguments for modularity do not speak directly against "schema-based" explanatory unification. We thus find that probabilistic models do arguably have some (potential) additional explanatory power if they are as widespread as proponents claim, but it is based in their descriptive similarity, not a shared normative base.

Conclusion

We live in a noisy, uncertain world, and probabilistic models, methods, and reasoning are a natural way to tackle such environments. We should thus be unsurprised that probabilistic models are ubiquitous in modern cognitive science: they are found in models of essentially every area of the mind/brain, from very early perception (Ganguli and Simoncelli, 2014; Lee and Mumford, 2003), to both simple low-level (Courville, Daw, and Touretzky, 2006; Xu and Tenenbaum,) and complex high-level (Chater, Tenenbaum, and Yuille, 2006; Oaksford and Chater, 2007) cognition, to motor activity (Kording and Wolpert, 2006; Wolpert and Kawato, 1998). They have been employed to understand even phenomena that are sometimes thought to be non-computational, such as emotions (Seth, 2013). At the same time, there are very real challenges in understanding the explanations that such models and methods provide. Almost any behavior is consistent with almost any (plausible) probabilistic cognitive model, and so many of the standard theories of prediction and explanation do not apply. Instead, we must shift how we think about explanation with these models. Instead of explaining a single particular instance, we can: explain features of the collections of phenomena (in individuals or groups); or collect additional measures that ground the particular explanation; or shift to providing why-explanations rather than how-explanations. Each of these strategies has been employed with probabilistic cognitive models, thereby enabling widespread use of these powerful types of models.

Notes

1 Probabilities are not the only way to address this issue – fuzzy sets (Zadeh, 1965) are another representational framework – but we focus on probabilistic models for reasons of space.
2 We will also largely ignore debates about whether probabilities are subjective degrees of belief, physical propensities, limiting relative frequencies, or something else. In context, it is almost always clear how the probabilities are intended in these cognitive models.
3 In fact, *any* specific sequence of heads and tails will happen only 0.1 percent of the time when one flips a coin ten times, so we would actually have to say that we cannot provide an explanation for any particular sequence, though as noted below, we could arguably explain certain properties of the sequence (e.g. proportion of heads being greater than, say, 0.4).
4 As a non-cognitive example, note that this is exactly what we do in most thermodynamic models: we focus on predictions and explanations of properties of the distribution of particle locations, rather than specific particle locations.
5 This interdependence can be made precise in terms of intertheoretic constraints (Danks, 2014).

References

Anderson, J.R. (1991) 'The Adaptive Nature of Human Categorization', *Psychological Review*, 98, pp. 409–429.
Ashby, F.G. and Maddox, W.T. (1993) 'Relations between Prototype, Exemplar, and Decision Bound Models of Categorization', *Journal of Mathematical Psychology*, 37, pp. 372–400.
Carruthers, P. (2006). *The Architecture of the Mind*. Oxford: Oxford University Press.
Chater, N. and Oaksford, M. (eds.) (2008) *The Probabilistic Mind: Prospects for Bayesian Cognitive Science*. Oxford: Oxford University Press.
Chater, N., Tenenbaum, J.B., and Yuille, A. (2006) 'Probabilistic Models of Cognition: Conceptual Foundations', *Trends in Cognitive Sciences*, 10 (7), pp. 287–291.
Colombo, M. and Hartmann, S. (2017) 'Bayesian Cognitive Science, Unification, and Explanation', *British Journal for the Philosophy of Science*, 68 (2), pp. 451–484.
Courville, A.C., Daw, N.D., and Touretzky, D.S. (2006) 'Bayesian Theories of Conditioning in a Changing World', *Trends in Cognitive Sciences*, 10 (7), pp. 294–300.
Craver, C.F. (2007) *Explaining the Brain: Mechanisms and the Mosaic Unity of Neuroscience*. Oxford: Oxford University Press.
Danks, D. (2008) 'Rational Analyses, Instrumentalism, and Implementations', in Chater, N. and Oaksford, M. (eds.) *The Probabilistic Mind: Prospects for Bayesian Cognitive Science*. Oxford: Oxford University Press, pp. 59–75.
Danks, D. (2014) *Unifying the Mind: Cognitive Representations as Graphical Models*. Cambridge, MA: MIT Press.
Douven, I. (1999) 'Inference to the Best Explanation Made Coherent', *Philosophy of Science*, 66, pp. S424–S435.
Doya, K. et al. (eds.) (2007) *Bayesian Brain: Probabilistic Approaches to Neural Coding*. Cambridge, MA: MIT Press.
Eberhardt, F. and Danks, D. (2011) 'Confirmation in the Cognitive Sciences: The Problematic Case of Bayesian Models', *Minds and Machines*, 21 (3), pp. 389–410.
Fodor, J.A. (1983) *The Modularity of Mind*. Cambridge, MA: MIT Press.
Ganguli, D. and Simoncelli, E.P. (2014) 'Efficient Sensory Encoding and Bayesian Inference with Heterogeneous Neural Populations', *Neural Computation*, 26 (10), pp. 2103–2134.
Goodman, N.D. et al. (2008) 'A Rational Analysis of Rule-based Concept Learning', *Cognitive Science*, 32 (1), pp. 108–154.

Griffiths, T.L., Kemp, C., and Tenenbaum, J.B. (2008) 'Bayesian Models of Cognition', in Sun, R. (ed.) *The Cambridge Handbook of Computational Cognitive Modeling*. Cambridge, UK: Cambridge University Press.

Griffiths, T.L. and Tenenbaum, J.B. (2005) 'Structure and Strength in Causal Induction', *Cognitive Psychology*, 51 (4), pp. 334–384.

Kaplan, D.M. and Craver, C.F. (2011) 'The Explanatory Force of Dynamical and Mathematical Models in Neuroscience: A Mechanistic Perspective', *Philosophy of Science*, 78 (4), pp. 601–627.

Kitcher, P. (1981) 'Explanatory Unification', *Philosophy of Science*, 48, pp. 507–531.

Koller, D. and Friedman, N. (2009) *Probabilistic Graphical Models: Principles and Techniques*. Cambridge, MA: MIT Press.

Kording, K.P. and Wolpert, D.M. (2006) 'Bayesian Decision Theory in Sensorimotor Control', *Trends in Cognitive Sciences*, 10 (7), pp. 319–326.

Lange, M. (2013) 'What Makes a Scientific Explanation Distinctively Mathematical?', *British Journal for the Philosophy of Science*, 64, pp. 485–511.

Lee, T.S. and Mumford, D. (2003) 'Hierarchical Bayesian Inference in the Visual Cortex', *Journal of the Optical Society of America A*, 20 (7), pp. 1434–1448.

Love, B.C., Medin, D.L., and Gureckis, T.M. (2004) 'SUSTAIN: A Network Model of Category Learning', *Psychological Review*, 111, pp. 309–332.

Nosofsky, R.M. and Palmeri, T.J. (1997) 'An Exemplar-based Random Walk Model of Speeded Classification', *Psychological Review*, 104, pp. 266–300.

Oaksford, M. and Chater, N. (2007) *Bayesian Rationality: The Probabilistic Approach to Human Reasoning*. Oxford: Oxford University Press.

Perfors, A. et al. (2011) 'A Tutorial Introduction to Bayesian Models of Cognitive Development', *Cognition*, 120 (3), pp. 302–321.

Rehder, B. (2003) 'A Causal-model Theory of Conceptual Representation and Categorization', *Journal of Experimental Psychology: Learning, Memory, and Cognition*, 29, pp. 1141–1159.

Ross, L.N. (2015) 'Dynamical Models and Explanation in Neuroscience', *Philosophy of Science*, 82 (1), pp. 32–54.

Ross, S.M. (2009) *Introduction to Probability Models*, 10th ed. Cambridge, MA: Academic Press.

Samuels, R. (1998) 'Evolutionary Psychology and the Massive Modularity Hypothesis', *The British Journal for the Philosophy of Science*, 49 (4), pp. 575–602.

Seth, A.K. (2013) 'Interoceptive Inference, Emotion, and the Embodied Self', *Trends in Cognitive Sciences*, 17 (11), pp. 565–573.

Teller, P. (1973) 'Conditionalization and Observation', *Synthese*, 26, pp. 218–238.

Teller, P. (1976) 'Conditionalization, Observation, and Change of Preference', in Harper, W.L. and Hooker, C.A. (eds.) *Foundations of Probability Theory, Statistical Inference, and Statistical Theories of Science*. Dordrecht: Reidel, pp. 205–259.

Tenenbaum, J.B. and Griffiths, T.L. (2001) 'Generalization, Similarity, and Bayesian Inference', *Behavioral and Brain Sciences*, 24, pp. 629–641.

Tooby, J. and Cosmides, L. (1992) 'The Psychological Foundations of Culture', in Barkow, J.H., Cosmides, L., and Tooby, J. (eds.) *The Adapted Mind: Evolutionary Psychology and the Generation of Culture*. Oxford: Oxford University Press, pp. 19–136.

Wolpert, D.M. and Kawato, M. (1998) 'Multiple Paired Forward and Inverse Models for Motor Control', *Neural Networks*, 11, pp. 1317–1329.

Xu, F. and Tenenbaum, J.B. (2007) 'Word Learning as Bayesian Inference', *Psychological Review*, 114 (2), pp. 245–272.

Zadeh, L. (1965) 'Fuzzy Sets', *Information and Control*, 8, pp. 338–359.

12

PREDICTION ERROR MINIMIZATION IN THE BRAIN

Jakob Hohwy

1 Introduction

Prediction error minimization (PEM) is becoming increasingly influential as an explanatory framework in computational neuroscience, building on formal developments in machine learning and statistical physics (for recent research, introductions, and philosophical discussion, see Friston, 2010; Hohwy, 2013; Clark, 2016a; Metzinger and Wiese, 2017). This chapter reviews the main motivation for working within the framework, and then explains PEM in more detail, tying it in with fundamental considerations in theoretical neurobiology. I shall argue that PEM provides a unified account of brain processes for mind, cognition, and action.

The chapter is organized as follows. Section 2 begins with the problem of perception, that is, how there can be unsupervised representation of the environmental causes of our sensory input. It then sets out what appears to be the most promising candidate for solving the problem of perception: hierarchical Bayesian inference. Section 3 goes deeper and more abstract than Bayesian inference, and explains the background for PEM, namely the free energy principle (FEP), which is an extremely general description within theoretical neurobiology of what it means to be a biological persisting organism in the changing world. Surprisingly, from that move springs a wealth of explanatory prowess displaying the approach as a comprehensive, unified, computational account of perception, action, and attention. FEP immediately promotes a comprehensively epistemic conceptualization of brain function that is then cast in more heuristically friendly terms with the notion of PEM, and which then connects back to the Bayesian brain, or, rather the brain that approximates the hierarchical Bayesian inference that was introduced in Section 2. Section 4 develops PEM's commitments for brain processes by specifying the general types of processing needed for long-term prediction error minimization that can occur in an unsupervised manner and yet approximate inference and thereby give rise to perception. Section 5 conceives these PEM-processes as mechanism sketches, and looks toward ways of filling out these sketches. Throughout, there is consideration of questions from philosophy of science and mind about the explanatory import of this type of computational theory, working towards the view that PEM, in contrast to many other computational theories, substantially constrains the underlying neuronal mechanisms.

2 An approach to the problem of perception: hierarchical
Bayesian inference

The problem of perception has a long history in philosophy. Versions of it arise in Plato, in Descartes, in early thinkers like Ibn al Haytham, in the debates amongst empiricists and rationalists such as Locke, Hume, Spinoza, and Leibniz, and comes to a head in Kant's work. Kant considered the necessary conditions for the possibility of perception from the starting point of an organism bombarded by the manifold of sensory input. He proposed a set of *a priori* forms of intuition and categories that 'filter' the sensory input and makes perception possible, leaving the external 'thing-in-itself' essentially unknowable. Though Kant continued to be hugely influential in mainstream philosophy, an important development of his work came in Helmholtz' scientific writings, in particular, around his *Optics*. Helmholtz agrees with the Kantian way of setting up the problem of perception but he objects to the implied skepticism and the idea that we passively filter the sensory manifold through the *a priori* categories. Rather, the perceptual system is engaged in active exploration of the sensorium, much like a scientist explores nature. This gives rise to the notion of perception as a type of unconscious inference:

> The 'psychical activities' leading to perception … are in general not conscious, but rather unconscious. In their outcomes they are like inferences insofar as we from the observed effect on our senses arrive at an idea of the cause of this effect. This is so even though we always in fact only have direct access to the events at the nerves, that is, we sense the effects, never the external objects.
>
> *(Helmholtz, 1867, p. 430)*

This idea has proven influential with many variants in psychology and cognitive science following Helmholtz and, more recently, an explosion of research in machine learning and theoretical neurobiology (Hatfield, 2002).

In contemporary terms, Kant's problem is about how a system can develop (statistical) models of the causes of the input to its sensors without being supervised by an external entity that already knows the mapping between external causes and internal effects. Obviously, supervised systems, though by no means technically easy to engineer, are not going to explain how perception arises in the first place. The aim is therefore to answer the question of how unsupervised perception is possible. This constraint on what can be used in the explanation is captured neatly by Helmholtz, namely that we only "sense the effects, never the external objects". We somehow perceive the world just on the basis of our stored belief and current sensory evidence, and without helping ourselves to independent information about the causes. The challenge in much cognitive science and philosophy of mind has been to deliver an answer to this question that does not either 'smuggle in' some conception of external supervision or, instead, leaves the internal processes of the system cut adrift from the world, unable to heed Helmholtz's warning against the skeptical dangers of the full Kantian picture.

The first step is to fully follow Helmholtz and conceive this as a problem of causal inference: what are the causes of the sensory input? This is challenging because no simple scheme can overcome the inherent (and very Humean) problem for causal inference, namely that there are no necessary relations between causes and effects: the same effect (e.g. retinal image) can have many different causes, and vice versa. This is a many–many problem for causal inference, which aims to infer a one–one type solution (e.g. the retinal image of a moving light was caused by an approaching car, not a firefly).

The approach that has the best potential to solve the problem, and which eventually leads to PEM, is in a sense really simple, though it has much underlying, complex mathematics. A solution to the problem of perception can only work with the resources that the system (e.g. the brain) has access to. As Helmholtz points out, this includes the current sensory input. But this is not all that is available, there is also the internal model built up on the basis of prior experience. That gives two things, which could be compared with each other: the model (or predictions generated by the model) and the current sensory input (or evidence).

This simple scheme is then applied to perception. On an input of a flashing orange light, the system can use its prior knowledge to disambiguate between different hypotheses (the indicator of a turning car, or the light of an emergency vehicle?). The best answer is the one that generates the least prediction error. Already here, the story recruits many levels of representation and becomes highly context-dependent. How likely is it that there is a turning car versus an emergency vehicle at this location, what is the time series of sensory input from indicator lights on a car versus the flashing lights on an emergency vehicle, and so on? The suggested idea is that perceptual inference is a process that arrives at revised models of the world, which accurately represent the world.

So far, this is merely a heuristic description, closely aligned with Helmholtz's initial comparison of perception to the scientific process of theory confirmation. The account needs in addition some constraints on the use of prior knowledge to disambiguate and interpret the sensory input in perceptual inference. The question is how much prior knowledge should be trusted (after all, emergency vehicles are not that rare). Similarly, there needs to be some constraints on the use of prediction errors to update the internal model (after all, how clearly were the flashes actually observed?).

With such constraints in place, we could move to solving the problem of perception because there would then be a principled way of arriving at a mapping of causes and input-based representations of causes. Specifically, conditional probability functions would assign different probabilities to different values of the hidden parameter when the sensory input is known to be a particular value.

The constraints call for a principled weighting of priors and the prediction errors conveyed through the sensory evidence. That principle is given by Bayes' theorem, $p(h \mid e) = p(e \mid h)p(h) / p(e)$. The likelihood, $p(e \mid h)$, conveys the fit between the hypothesis and the sensory evidence, which together with the actual sensory evidence allows us to calculate the prediction error, and $p(h)$ gives the probability of the prior hypothesis, before the evidence is observed, which indicates how much it should be trusted. The appeal to Bayes is pivotal because we have then the opportunity to move straight from the problem of perception to what is often considered a paragon of rationality, namely Bayes' rule for updating credence functions over time. Perception, if it were to be Bayesian, would in other words be a rational process, a process naturally captured in terms of inference, hypothesis, evidence, and prediction.

It is convenient to treat these probability distributions (or in the continuous case, probability density functions, though I will suppress this distinction here for simplicity) as normal (or Gaussian) distributions, since such distributions can be represented with their sufficient statistics, their mean and variance. We use the inverse of the variance to get the *precisions* of the distributions; this is mathematically convenient in this treatment because precisions can be summed. The higher the precision the more 'narrow' the distribution is around the mean. Then we turn to a notion of Bayesian *inference*, where the update of the prior to get the posterior (and thus the prior for the next inference step) is governed by the ratio of precisions of the prior and likelihood.

The prior and likelihood thus each have a mean, m and x, and a precision π_p and π_l. Bayes' theorem can then be expressed in terms of the mean of the prior, m (i.e. the prediction), the mean of the likelihood, x, from which m is subtracted to yield the magnitude of the prediction error. A *weight* is attached to the prediction error given by the prior and posterior precisions, where the posterior precision is the sum of the prior and likelihood precisions. The result is that the prediction error is weighted more if the likelihood precision is high – the sensory signal is precise and more should be learned from the current sensory input. Conversely, the weight on the error is less if the prior is precise – if much is already known then it is unlikely that new information should move the prior around. The weight then determines the rate with which the posterior shifts in the light of new information – the learning rate.

In this simple understanding of Bayesian inference, the learning rate given by the weight on the prediction error will decline over time, as more evidence is accumulated for the prior, making it ever more precise. That does not correspond well with the way we tend to learn and unlearn things over the day and during the course of our lives. In other words, the learning rate needs to be variable, depending on the context and how the world around us changes.

A variable learning rate can be accommodated in empirical, *hierarchical* Bayes. Here the simple Bayesian inference rule is iterated at multiple levels of a hierarchy and the weight is made to depend on the expected precisions at each given level and the levels above. This means the learning rate reflects a large number of expectations for the evolution of precisions and means over multiple time scales. For example, the volume of cars turning depends on the time of day, and there are many ambulances and police cars expected in the city on Saturday nights. In such a hierarchy, model revision happens in two parts, for means and for precisions, and there will be prediction errors for both (sometimes called value prediction errors and volatility prediction errors – VAPE and VOPE (see Mathys et al., 2014, for the notion of hierarchical inference and variable learning rates).

The internal model that results from repeated steps of hierarchical Bayesian inference replicates the causal structure of the environment. For example, if a regular relation between two environmental causes (a player shooting a basketball) begins to deliver unexpected results (the ball begins to drift left) because a new cause is interfering (the wind is picking up), then the internal model will have to posit this further, interfering cause in addition to the causes already inferred (the player and the ball). The causal net of the environment and the causal net represented in the internal model will mirror each other. Causal inference therefore becomes model-focused and holistic rather than point-like, where the relevant information, gleaned through prediction errors, is captured in the relations between causes. In this perspective, perception arises from the currently best performing structured hypothesis generated under the internal model. Representation of the world comes about through structural isomorphism with, or recapitulation of, the causal structure of the world (Gładziejewski, 2016; Kiefer and Hohwy, 2017).

Hierarchical Bayesian inference is then what is required for Helmholtz's unconscious perceptual inference. It builds in both learning and inference, as the priors over several spatiotemporal scales in the hierarchy are revised in the light of prediction error. It means that perceptual inference is suited to an organism (or indeed artificial system) operating in a changing, uncertain world. Perception would then be a rational, Bayesian, process that optimally integrates prior knowledge with current evidence in a manner sensitive to the changing context.

There is some reason to believe that the brain actually behaves according to hierarchical Bayesian inference (Iglesias et al., 2013; Vossel et al., 2015), and a large body of research that describes perceptual and cognitive phenomena in a more general Bayesian perspective; though not always with a hierarchical framework (Knill and Richards, 1996; Chater, Tenenbaum and Yuille, 2006; Yuille and Kersten, 2006).

How does this get us nearer an account of what the brain is actually doing, and how it may manage to be Bayesian in any substantial sense rather than a merely descriptive or heuristic sense? We know, for example, that we are pretty bad at consciously performing Bayesian inference (Kahneman, Slovic and Tversky, 1982) so it may be hard to believe that we are good at unconscious Bayesian inference (for wider discussion of Bayesian explanations, see Colombo and Seriès, 2012). Notice also that here we have just described things in terms of Bayesian inference and, whereas we have mentioned predictions and prediction errors, the story has not been about prediction error *minimization*, PEM. To progress the discussion to these topics, I will first go back to the ambitious source of PEM, namely the free energy principle, FEP.

3 From FEP to PEM to the Bayesian brain

FEP is a principle, not a law, meant to describe living organisms (this section is based on the free energy principle literature, which in this guise begins with Friston (2010); an important early version of the energy literature is Hinton and Sejnowski (1983); see Kiefer and Hohwy (in press) for an introduction). FEP begins with a trivial observation, that organisms exist, and proceeds with a platitude, that if an organism exists, then it must be characterizable by a model of the states in which the organism is most likely to be found. This is a platitude because to exist an organism must be occupying some subset of states rather than be dispersed through all states (cf. decomposing, unable to maintain its own boundary). To exist is then to be such – and act such – that one is not found in states that would be surprising given the model that characterizes the organism. In other words, an existing organism must be able to minimize surprise (in this technical sense of that notion, which differs from the psychological notion of being surprised).

The question then is how the organism, or as we shall call it, the agent, manages to minimize surprise. The problem here is that the agent cannot know *a priori* what its true model is. To know that it would have to average over an indefinite number of copies of itself across all possible states to figure out which ones are surprising. More subtly, even if the agent had the knowledge given to it, it is not clear what it would do with that knowledge in and of itself to enable it to maintain itself in its expected states. We could, perhaps, rephrase this problem as 'the problem of life'. Just as with the problem of perception, where there is a prohibition of uninferred knowledge of the distal causes of sensory stimuli, here there is a prohibition of uninferred knowledge of the states that would allow the organism to maintain its organismic boundaries. And as in the problem of perception, the knowledge cannot simply be served up, pre-digested by a benign informant or supervisor. This suggests there may be deep similarities between these problems.

How *does* an agent then know which states would allow it to maintain its organismic boundaries? The free energy principle solves this problem by noting that the organism has access to the (probabilistic notion of) free energy and that free energy bounds surprise such that minimizing free energy implicitly minimizes surprise. This may sound obfuscated, because we have not yet explained the notion of free energy. It is a probabilistic notion (with strong conceptual links back to statistical physics) and for our purposes here we can mainly consider it the long-term average of prediction error. Hence the idea is that the long-term average prediction error bounds the surprise such that an organism that is able to minimize prediction error in the long-term average will thereby minimize surprise.

The notion of free energy bounding surprise is somewhat complex. Here I give one, simplified heuristic route to this notion, which begins with the notion of exact Bayesian inference, as considered in the previous section (I again suppress the distinction between distributions and densities; for a more comprehensive tutorial, see Bogacz, 2017). Recall that the aim is to infer the posterior probability of the hypothesis h given the evidence e, $p(h \mid e)$. Bayes' rule says that $p(h|e) = p(e|h)p(h)/p(e)$ but in the full continuous case computing this directly may require trying to solve intractable complex integrals in the marginal probability function for the denominator. So, instead, we can adopt a *recognition* model, $q(h)$, and try to make that distribution *approximate* the true posterior, $p(h|e)$.

We then need a measure of the approximation of the two probability distributions. This measure is the Kullbach–Leibler divergence, or relative entropy, between $q(h)$ and $p(h|e)$, expressed as $KL(q(h) \| p(h|e))$. The KL divergence is either 0 or positive and measures the difference in average information between two probability distributions. That is, the entropies (average information) are subtracted and parts of the expression are reorganized as a log ratio, such that, schematically, $KL(p \| q) = \Sigma p(i)\log(p(i)/q(i)) = -\Sigma p(i)\log(q(i)/p(i))$.

Using the fact that $p(h|e) = p(e,h)/p(e)$, it can be shown that $KL(q(h) \| p(h|e)) + \Sigma q(h)\log$ $p(e,h)/q(h) = \log p(e)$. Here $\log p(e)$ is the log probability of e, which is the surprise. Since we are considering $p(h|e)$, the evidence e is given and this means that $\log p(e)$ is a fixed negative value (negative because it is the log of a value between 0 and 1) and this in turn constrains what happens on the left side of the equation. Specifically, since e is given, just $q(h)$ can vary and as we do that in the second term, which is always negative, we must be controlling the KL divergence, which is never negative (this relation between the terms is easy to verify with a simple set of numbers). The second term is thus a lower bound on the log probability of the evidence, often written as L, so that the overall expression can be simplified to $KL + L = \log p(e)$. This shows that we can approximate the true posterior just by manipulating $q(h)$ to maximize the function for L, $\Sigma q(h)\log p(e,h)/q(h)$, rather than attempt to engage in exact inference. This type of approximation is central to the whole framework. By simply working on the recognition distribution, $q(h)$, it will get closer and closer to just the exact Bayesian inference, $p(h|e)$.

How can $q(h)$ be used to perform this job? Here we turn to *variational* Bayes, according to which one deals with the parameters of the model, h, one by one, assuming that the other parameters are known even though in fact they are not (Bishop, 2007; Bogacz, 2017). As the parameters are each varied, the recognition density $q(h)$ as it were wobbles around and begins to approximate the true posterior, $p(h|e)$. Since we are both approximating the posterior $p(h|e)$ and improving the lower bound on the (log) probability of the evidence, this means changing parameters so as to maximize the joint probability of the hypothesis h and the evidence e. Minimizing free energy can then be understood as improving the fit, over time, of its hypotheses and the evidence, or making the evidence less surprising, given the model. This is a job the agent can perform, since it just assumes a model (it varies the model parameters) and knows its own sensory input. The beauty is that by doing so it must approximate exact inference and improve the bound on surprise. If the joint probability remains high in the long-term average, then the agent accumulates evidence for its own model, and, since we have tied the model to the agent, this means that it is providing evidence for its own existence.

Consider then what an agent can do to maximize the joint probability of model and evidence. First, it may revise the model in the light of the evidence; this is along the lines discussed above and corresponds to *perception*. Second, it may sample evidence that fits with the hypotheses generated from the model. This goes beyond the quasi-formal description above because now we are actively changing (or generating) the evidence, but it is key to the free energy principle because it corresponds to *action* and thereby it begins to explain what the agent does to maintain its own existence, or stay in its expected states. Since even action leads to approximation to the true posterior, action is called 'active inference'. Third, the agent may *simplify* its model, getting rid of overly complex parameters that are not needed to explain away prediction error in the long run. Fourth, the agent should mobilize all the relevant knowledge at its disposal in order to regulate the learning rate in a context-dependent manner; that is, the agent should *integrate* its beliefs with each other in order to generate good predictions of the ever-changing sensory input. A fifth process cuts across the others (and relates intrinsically to the fourth), namely *precision* optimization, or learnt sensitivity to the strength of priors and input, which is needed to assign weights in the optimal, variable manner.

How should all this then speak to the notions of Bayesian inference in the previous section? Mathematically (and making the Laplace assumption that distributions are normal), by engaging in variational Bayes, exact inference must be approximated. As promised earlier, this can be expressed more heuristically in terms of prediction error. Consider that if one engages in Bayesian inference, then over the long-term average, prediction error will be as small as it can be, given irreducible noise (there will always be some variation around the mean that cannot be eliminated). That is, if the inference converges on the mean as a result of following Bayes' rule, then the accumulated prediction error cannot be any smaller. If inference converges on another value as a result of using some non-Bayesian rule, then there will have to be more prediction error. This is the link from Bayesian inference to prediction error minimization: follow Bayes and error will be low.

Variational Bayes can be conceived heuristically as turning this relation around and saying that if a system cannot do exact inference but is nevertheless able to minimize its long-term average prediction error by whatever tool it has at its disposal, then it will approximate exact Bayesian inference. Of course FEP says that the system should minimize error (or maximize the joint probability of hypothesis and evidence). So, an approximate notion of Bayesian inference in the brain follows from FEP, though interestingly, FEP begins not with the problem of perception but with the problem of life.

The overall picture is intricate. First there is the generative model, which generates 'top-down' predictions on the basis of the internal model. Then there is the recognition model, $q(h)$, which approximates the otherwise intractable posterior of exact inference, $p(h|e)$. The recognition model inverts the generative model: as the KL-divergence moves toward zero, the recognition model becomes the true posterior, that is, $q(h)$ infers the causes given the evidence. All this connects to the hidden external causes in the world through the assumption that exact inference represents the world because it is based on optimal, rational, integration of prior knowledge and current evidence that, skeptical scenarios aside, leads to structural resemblance between world and internal model.

There is thus a promising solution to the problem of perception because accurate internal models can arise on the basis of processing information that the organism has at its disposal and can operate on without supervision, namely the internal model and the sensory evidence. The processing is feasible because, at least, it does not require trying to solve intractable mathematical problems. This answers the question about our ability to engage in Bayesian inference: even though we are poor at conscious, exact Bayesian reasoning we may be good at simply keeping prediction error low. Later, we will discuss whether this is something the brain is actually doing and in what sense.

Notice that at the outset we focused on prediction error minimization – PEM – rather than the Bayesian brain, or the free energy principle. PEM adds the simplifying Laplace assumption, that distributions (density functions) are normal (or 'Gaussian'), to FEP, which allows us to conceive of free energy as the long-term average prediction error. This is useful because then PEM becomes a heuristic expression of FEP, which is easy to understand in particular in its role as solving the problem of perception. In the remainder of the chapter, I will simply talk of PEM in this FEP-infused sense of long-term average prediction error minimization, which approximates hierarchical Bayesian inference.

In the literature, there has been much focus on *predictive coding*. I prefer the notion of PEM over predictive coding because predictive coding is a specific type of 'process theory' for PEM with its own versions and characteristics (see Spratling, 2017). Process theories can be thought of as concrete algorithmic implementations of the overall computational scheme set out by FEP's use of variational Bayes, often given various assumptions. This is a more restrictive focus than what I shall take here. Predictive coding, in particular, has no role for action, whereas PEM incorporates action (for a process theory for active inference, see (Friston, FitzGerald et al., 2016).

The philosophical literature often uses the notion 'predictive processing' as shorthand for the suite of solutions offered by FEP (Clark, 2016a). There is no substantial difference between PEM and predictive processing but I prefer PEM because 'predictive processing' fails to focus on the central aspect that the agent only predicts because it is in the business of *minimizing* error, which makes it inherently epistemic in nature – PEM is in the business of accumulating evidence for the given model.

4 PEM processes

The question then is what the brain is actually supposed to be doing throughout this PEM process. Consider again the five aspects of PEM suggested above: perceptual inference, active inference, simplification, integration, and precision-optimization. Each of these can be supposed to help minimize error. Importantly, their respective contributions to minimize error must be considered in the long-term average. Rampant revision of the internal model to any momentary sensory input would make the model 'accept' any possible state with the consequence that it would cease to exist (recall, to exist is to be found on some and not all possible states). Stubborn insistence on the internal model as the exclusive driver of prediction error minimization through selective sampling is unrealistic since it assumes the world is unchanging. In both the case of excessive perceptual and active inference, we can expect that the prediction error will increase in the long run. Essentially, too much perceptual inference assumes the agent is not relatively persistent through time, and too much active inference assumes the world is more persistent than it really is – both of which are faulty assumptions that will drive prediction error up in the long term. A balance must be struck between perceptual and active inference, to achieve a long-term rate of prediction error minimization consistent with existence of the agent.

Model simplification is driven by the standard statistical modeling idea that overfitting a model to noise will generate more prediction error in the long term even if it can deal somewhat well with current sensory input. An overly complex model will see too many spurious details and miss out on the underlying patterns generating the input in the longer term. Conversely, an overly simple model will also generate excessive prediction error as it abstracts away from real patterns in the environment that generate sensory input that could be explained away. Again, a balance must be struck between complexity and simplicity, to optimize the long-term average of prediction error minimization. Integration of prior beliefs should be considered over multiple time scales, such that long-term causal regularities can help inform current sensory input. Learning must then happen over these time scales.

All of these four processes must be governed by expected precisions of the prediction errors, which leads to relative weighting of them in inference (where weights sum to one). The agent needs to have beliefs about levels of irreducible noise to know how much it should seek to drive down prediction error, and it must have expectations for how much explainable uncertainty can occur and how complex the model should be made to explain away such uncertainty (for an early account of kinds of uncertainty in hierarchical inference, see Mumford, 1992). Similarly, in action the agent must choose between policies to achieve its expected states (that is, sample its expected inputs) based on the expected precisions of those states and policies. Precision optimization is therefore what allows the agent to take a long-term perspective on perception, action, and simplification.

Precision optimization is itself reasonably mapped onto a cognitive process, namely attention (Feldman and Friston, 2010; Hohwy, 2012). Attention is about moving the processing load around depending on the expected precision of the sensory input in perception or as outcomes of action. As just explained, this is what precision optimization does. Notice that precision optimization is a much broader notion than cognitive science normally takes attention to be. Expected precisions are essential for standard cases of Bayes optimal multisensory integration, and precision optimization is what determines the balance between action and perception (Brown et al., 2013; Hohwy, 2016b).

So here is the suite of carefully integrated and balanced processes the brain must be engaged in to minimize the KL-divergence between the generative and recognition models, and thereby perceive the world. Change the representational units of the model when there is prediction error, minimize error relative to predictions of what the sensory input should be, prune and add representational parameters, and continuously update its own expectations of how noisy and uncertain these processes all are and bring these expectations of precision to bear on the processes. Importantly, these are not processes of actual, exact Bayesian inference, rather, as we have seen, they are processes that will tend to minimize long-term prediction error and thus approximate the outcome of such exact inference.

There is a pleasing overlap between these processes and the Helmholtzian analogy to scientific practice. There is also an echo of contemporary debates about *inference to the best explanation* (or abduction) where what makes an explanation best is its ability to generate precise predictions, generate fruitful new experiments, together with its simplicity and level of integration (see Lipton, 2004; Seth, 2015); notice that the overlap with inference to the best explanation is not perfect since the core ingredient of 'explanatoriness' is not part of the PEM picture (cf. Roche and Sober, 2013). The echo of inference to the best explanation is relevant because it is somewhat more plausible that we can engage in such inference than in exact Bayesian inference, which we are notoriously poor at consciously, and seems mathematically intractable.

In the brain, we should then expect to see activity that corresponds to these processes. There should be neural populations capable of encoding sufficient statistics and that can generate top-down predictions and bottom-up prediction errors, which are gain-modulated (also in the pre-stimulus phase) in the light of expected precisions. Prediction error should be attenuated in unchanging environments as evidence is accumulated and an increasingly good fit is established between prior belief and sensory evidence, and priors should decrease over time as the world is expected to change. There is considerable scientific activity exploring these predictions, and a growing body of empirical evidence in its favor (for reviews and examples, see, e.g., Alink et al., 2010; Hesselmann et al., 2010; Sadaghiani et al., 2010; Den Ouden, Kok, and De Lange, 2012; Lieder et al., 2013; Kok, Failing, and De Lange, 2014; Aru et al., 2016; Chennu et al., 2016; Gordon et al., 2017). There is an emerging body of literature developing the process theory for active inference, to sit alongside the predictive coding process theory of perceptual inference (Friston, FitzGerald et al., 2016). There is some evidence casting new light, in favor of active inference (Brown et al., 2013), on familiar phenomena such as sensory attenuation during self-generated action (Van Doorn et al., 2015; Laak et al., 2017). Complexity reduction is thought to characterize some perceptual illusions (Hohwy, 2013), it may be the brain's mode of function when deprived of sensory input, as during sleep (Hobson and Friston, 2012), and has been explored in terms of the evolution of prediction error minimization over the life span that would be expected to have increasingly simple models, accompanied with being more sanguine in the face of prediction error (Moran et al., 2014).

Viewed like this, PEM offers theory unification. Perception, action, and attention are all explained as different aspects of the brain's attempt to minimize long-term average prediction error (for discussion of unification, see, e.g., Danks, 2014; Colombo and Hartmann, 2017). Does PEM offer anything new, or is it just unification by shallow re-packaging of existing theories in probabilistic vernacular? I have been arguing that, from a theoretical, philosophical perspective, it does offer something new and unique, namely a plausible solution to the problem of perception that unifies mental and cognitive phenomena in one framework. But it is true that in some cases, it is re-casting existing theories in new terms. For example, it is a re-description of the elements of biased competition theory of attention (Desimone, 1998; Feldman and Friston, 2010). It does offer something new to our understanding of attention, nevertheless. First, PEM lends the theory support over other theories of attention: even though it may not immediately offer new predictions that the existing theory could not offer (though it might), the fact that PEM is part of a unified theory means that it indirectly integrates the existing theory with explanations of other domains. Second, re-casting the biased competition theory of attention in PEM-terms expands the scope for the theory, since action is itself viewed as the upshot of biased competition between hypotheses for current and future states; in other words, PEM affords a challenging understanding of action as fundamentally an attentional phenomenon. Third, in the probabilistic guise of PEM, biased competition is explained as precision weighted prediction error minimization, where weights sum to one. This means that allocation of attention is understood as more than a manifestation of ways to navigate an information bottleneck and instead as the necessary upshot of hierarchical Gaussian filtering of the sensory input. Fourth, PEM's account of attention provides a principled explanation of the difference between endogenous and exogenous attention in terms of different learnt or innate expectations for precisions (Hohwy, 2013, ch. 9). For further discussion of the explanatory power of PEM, see Hohwy (2013); Clark (2016a).

5 PEM mechanisms in the brain

So far, the overall PEM-picture is that prediction error is minimized by processes akin to those of inference to the best explanation. By invoking those processes, PEM goes considerably beyond the typical, more phenomenological level of explanation for the Bayesian brain that just observes that much perceptual and cognitive function can be described in Bayesian terms. PEM tells us something about what the underlying mechanism is like, which is not offered by a phenomenological account in terms of exact inference. This defines at least a mechanism sketch (Piccinini, 2006; Piccinini and Craver, 2011; for discussion, see also Rusanen and Lappi, 2016), which tells us to look for hierarchical message passing involving processes of prediction, precision optimization, active sampling, complexity reduction, and integration.

The mechanism sketch also suggests that it is the same one, relatively simple mechanism that is replicated throughout the areas and levels of the cortical hierarchy: representation and error units tied together with pathways for passing information about sufficient statistics within the level, with further intrinsic connectivity for regulating gain in the light of prediction error precision, and extrinsic connectivity for receiving prediction errors (both VAPE and VOPE) from levels below and passing predictions down, and receiving predictions from above and passing prediction errors up.

A collection of such neuronal populations will be able to minimize prediction error over the long term because together the predictions combine non-linearly such that the sensory input from the noisy external world with its interacting causes can be well matched, and in turn the representation units will implicitly invert the top–down generative model, as explained earlier. It can also be hypothesized that the basic mechanism will have to encode conditional expectations for hidden *causes* (i.e. the brain's best estimate as to what is driving the changes in the physical world) and conditional expectations of the hidden *states* (i.e. the brain's best estimate about the actual 'physics' of the external world that drives the responses of the sensory organs). That is, there needs to be some translation of how the occurrence of a cause in the world affects the sensory organs such that those effects can be predicted (Friston, 2008; Kanai et al., 2015).

Research is underway for describing this mechanism in neurobiologically realistic terms, in terms of canonical microcircuits (Bastos et al., 2012), and advanced neuroimaging methods are being developed for capturing not just the causal relations (cf. effective connectivity) between levels of the cortical hierarchy (that maps on to the levels of hierarchical inference) but also causal relations within the microcircuits at each level (Friston et al., 2017; Pinotsis et al., 2017), with empirical studies of, for example, pain perception lending support (Fardo et al., 2017).

If indeed PEM message passing describes effective connectivity intrinsic to cortical canonical microcircuits, and extrinsic effective connectivity between hierarchical brain areas, then the brain's actual biological hardware can be said to fill in the mechanism sketch. The brain then literally is an organ for long-term average prediction error minimization – an epistemic or self-evidencing organ (Hohwy, 2016a; see Kiefer, 2017, for further discussion of literal inference in the brain). Neuronal populations predict, explain away sensory input, revise or accumulate evidence for the model, and so on. There will of course be levels of neuroscientific explanation where it becomes harder to retain a clear view of this epistemic mechanism, perhaps as we drill down and observe neurotransmitter function and the function of individual neurons at the molecular level. But it will be difficult to rid the picture of the epistemic framework since the actual causal influences between neuronal populations serve epistemic purposes. For example, there is emerging work connecting interventions on different types of neurotransmitters (dopamine, acetylcholine, noradrenaline) to different aspects of hierarchical Bayesian inference (Marshall et al., 2016), and thereby establishes a link between PEM and neuropharmacology. This has potential for application to mental disorder and would imply that a range of mental disorders are inherently epistemic.

6 Concluding remarks: neuronal epistemics

This chapter took as its point of departure the problem of perception and described how it can be solved by a system that approximates hierarchical Bayesian inference through long-term prediction error minimization. This is more than a computational approach to perception, it is tied to extremely general considerations about life from theoretical neurobiology. This deeper perspective suggests that the computational processes of hierarchical message passing provides a mechanism sketch of what the brain is actually doing – it engages in inherently epistemic, self-evidencing processes. Given its basis in neurobiological theory, and the dearth of alternative theories with much capacity to explain unsupervised perception, it is tempting to conclude that mind and cognition must be explained in terms of the processes that can minimize long-term average prediction error (or free energy). On this view, perception and cognition *are* just long-term average prediction error minimization. Multiple realizations of the processes are possible, of course, since brains can at least in principle be made of different stuff, but at the level of the mechanism sketch, it is tempting to argue for identity (for discussion of levels of computational explanation, see Craver, 2007; Eliasmith and Kolbeck, 2015).

This raises interesting and difficult questions about the scope and range of the PEM approach into the phylogenetic tree of biological organisms (Sims, 2016), among the biological parts within each organism, and beyond and between multiple organism and organisms and objects around them. Should we accept that single-celled organisms like *E.coli* selectively sample the environment and that it is a manifestation of inherently epistemic processes, or, that groups of people can implement perceptual inference? There is considerable philosophical debate about these and other questions about our conceptions of mind, perception, and cognition in nature (Allen and Friston, 2016; Clark, 2016b; Gallagher and Allen, 2016; Hohwy, 2016a; Kirchhoff, 2016; Clark, 2017; Hohwy, 2017; several contributions to Metzinger and Wiese, 2017).

References

Alink, A. et al. (2010) 'Stimulus Predictability Reduces Responses in Primary Visual Cortex', *The Journal of Neuroscience*, 30 (8), pp. 2960–2966.

Allen, M. and Friston, K.J. (2016) 'From Cognitivism to Autopoiesis: Towards a Computational Framework for the Embodied Mind', *Synthese*. Available at: https://doi.org/10.1007/s11229-016-1288-5.

Aru, J. et al. (2016) 'Early Effects of Previous Experience on Conscious Perception', *Neuroscience of Consciousness*, 2016 (1). Available at: https://doi.org/10.1093/nc/niw004.

Bastos, A.M. et al. (2012) 'Canonical Microcircuits for Predictive Coding', *Neuron*, 76 (4), pp. 695–711.

Bishop, C.M. (2007) *Pattern Recognition and Machine Learning*. Dordrecht: Springer.

Bogacz, R. (2017) 'A Tutorial on the Free-Energy Framework for Modelling Perception and Learning', *Journal of Mathematical Psychology*, 76 (Part B), pp. 198–211.

Brown, H. et al. (2013) 'Active Inference, Sensory Attenuation and Illusions', *Cognitive Processing*, 14 (4), pp. 411–427.

Chater, N., Tenenbaum, J.B., and Yuille, A. (2006) 'Probabilistic Models of Cognition: Conceptual Foundations', *Trends in Cognitive Sciences*, 10 (7), p. 287–291.

Chennu, S. et al. (2016) 'Silent Expectations: Dynamic Causal Modeling of Cortical Prediction and Attention to Sounds That Weren't', *The Journal of Neuroscience*, 36 (32), pp. 8305–8316.

Clark, A. (2016a). *Surfing Uncertainty: Prediction, Action, and the Embodied Mind*. New York, NY: Oxford University Press.

Clark, A. (2016b) 'Busting Out: Predictive Brains, Embodied Minds, and the Puzzle of the Evidentiary Veil', *Noûs*, 54 (4), pp. 727–753.

Clark, A. (2017) 'How to Knit Your Own Markov Blanket', in Metzinger, T.K. and Wiese, W. (eds.) *Philosophy and Predictive Processing*. Frankfurt am Main: MIND Group. Available at: DOI: 10.15502/9783958573031.

Colombo, M. and Hartmann, S. (2017) 'Bayesian Cognitive Science, Unification, and Explanation', *The British Journal for the Philosophy of Science*, 68 (2), pp. 451–484.

Colombo, M. and Seriès, P. (2012) 'Bayes in the Brain: On Bayesian Modelling in Neuroscience', *The British Journal for the Philosophy of Science*, 63 (3), pp. 697–723.

Craver, C. (2007) *Explaining the Brain: Mechanisms and the Mosaic Unity of Neuroscience*. New York, NY: Oxford University Press.

Danks, D. (2014) *Unifying the Mind: Cognitive Representations as Graphical Models*. Cambridge, MA: MIT Press.

Den Ouden, H.E., Kok, P., and De Lange, F.P. (2012) 'How Prediction Errors Shape Perception, Attention and Motivation', *Frontiers in Psychology*, 3, art. 548. Available at: https://doi.org/10.3389/fpsyg.2012.00548.

Desimone, R. (1998) 'Visual Attention Mediated by Biased Competition in Extrastriate Visual Cortex', *Philosophical Transactions of the Royal Society of London B*, 353, pp. 1245–1255.

Eliasmith, C. and Kolbeck, C. (2015) 'Marr's Attacks: On Reductionism and Vagueness', *Topics in Cognitive Science*, 7 (2), pp. 323–335.

Fardo, F. et al. (2017) 'Expectation Violation and Attention to Pain Jointly Modulate Neural Gain in Somatosensory Cortex', *NeuroImage*, 153, pp. 109–121.

Feldman, H. and Friston, K. (2010) 'Attention, Uncertainty and Free-Energy', *Frontiers in Human Neuroscience*, 4 (215). Available at: https://doi.org/10.3389/fnhum.2010.00215.

Friston, K. (2008) 'Hierarchical Models in the Brain', *PLoS Computational Biology*, 4 (11), e1000211.

Friston, K. (2010) 'The Free-Energy Principle: A Unified Brain Theory?', *Nature Reviews Neuroscience*, 11 (2), pp. 127–138.

Friston, K., FitzGerald, T. et al. (2016) 'Active Inference: A Process Theory', *Neural Computation*, 29 (1), pp. 1–49.

Friston, K.J., Preller, K.H. et al. (2017) 'Dynamic Causal Modelling Revisited', *NeuroImage*. Available at: https://doi.org/10.1016/j.neuroimage.2017.02.045.

Gallagher, S. and Allen, M. (2016) 'Active Inference, Enactivism and the Hermeneutics of Social Cognition', *Synthese*. Available at: https://doi.org/10.1007/s11229-016-1269-8.

Gładziejewski, P. (2016) 'Predictive Coding and Representationalism', *Synthese*, 193 (2), pp. 559–582.

Gordon, N. et al. (2017) 'Neural Markers of Predictive Coding under Perceptual Uncertainty Revealed with Hierarchical Frequency Tagging', *eLife*, 6, e22749.

Hatfield, G. (2002) 'Perception as Unconscious Inference', in Heyer, D. and Mausfeld, R. (eds.) *Perception and the Physical World*. New York, NY: John Wiley & Sons, pp. 113–143.

Helmholtz, H.V. (1867) *Handbuch der Physiologishen Optik*. Leipzig: Leopold Voss.

Hesselmann, G. et al. (2010) 'Predictive Coding or Evidence Accumulation? False Inference and Neuronal Fluctuations', *PloS One*, 5 (3), e9926.

Hinton, G.E. and Sejnowski, T.J. (1983) 'Optimal Perceptual Inference', *Proceedings of the IEEE Conference on Computer Vision and Pattern Recognition*. Washington, DC, June, pp. 448–453.

Hobson, J.A. and Friston, K.J. (2012) 'Waking and Dreaming Consciousness: Neurobiological and Functional Considerations', *Progress in Neurobiology*, 98 (1), pp. 82–98.

Hohwy, J. (2012) 'Attention and Conscious Perception in the Hypothesis Testing Brain', *Frontiers in Psychology*, 3, art. 96. Available at: https://doi.org/10.3389/fpsyg.2012.00096.

Hohwy, J. (2013) *The Predictive Mind*. Oxford: Oxford University Press.

Hohwy, J. (2016a) 'The Self-Evidencing Brain', *Noûs*, 50 (2), pp. 259–285.

Hohwy, J. (2016b) 'Prediction, Agency, and Body Ownership', in Engel, A., Friston, K., and Kragic, D. (eds.) *The Pragmatic Turn: Toward Action-Oriented Views in Cognitive Science*. Cambridge, MA: MIT Press, pp. 109–210.

Hohwy, J. (2017) 'How to Entrain Your Evil Demon', in Metzinger, T.K. and Wiese, W. (eds.) *Philosophy and Predictive Processing*. Frankfurt am Main: MIND Group. Available at: DOI: 10.15502/9783958573048.

Iglesias, S. et al. (2013) 'Hierarchical Prediction Errors in Midbrain and Basal Forebrain during Sensory Learning', *Neuron*, 80 (2), pp. 519–530.

Kahneman, D., Slovic, P., and Tversky, A. (eds.) (1982) *Judgment under Uncertainty: Heuristics and Biases*. London: Macmillan.

Kanai, R. et al. (2015) Cerebral Hierarchies: Predictive Processing, Precision and the Pulvinar, *Royal Transactions of the Royal Society B*, 370 (1668), pp. 1–13.

Kiefer, A. (2017) 'Literal Perceptual Inference', in Metzinger, T.K. and Wiese, W. (eds.) *Philosophy and Predictive Processing*. Frankfurt am Main: MIND Group. Available at: DOI: 10.15502/9783958573185.

Kiefer, A. and Hohwy, J. (2017) 'Content and Misrepresentation in Hierarchical Generative Models', *Synthese*, pp. 1–29. Available at: DOI 10.1007/s11229-017-1435-7.

Kiefer, A. and Hohwy, J. (in press) 'Representation in the Prediction Error Minimization Framework', in Symons, J., Calvo, P., and Robins, S. (eds.) *Routledge Handbook to the Philosophy of Psychology*. Oxford: Routledge.

Kirchhoff, M.D. (2016) 'Autopoiesis, Free Energy, and the Life–Mind Continuity Thesis', *Synthese*, pp. 1–22. Available at: DOI 10.1007/s11229-016-1100-6.

Knill, D.C. and Richards, W. (eds.) (1996) *Perception as Bayesian Inference*. Cambridge, UK: Cambridge University Press.

Kok, P., Failing, M.F., and de Lange, F.P. (2014) 'Prior Expectations Evoke Stimulus Templates in the Primary Visual Cortex', *Journal of Cognitive Neuroscience*, 26 (7), pp. 1546–1554.

Laak, K.-J. et al. (2017) 'Attention is Withdrawn from the Area of the Visual Field Where the Own Hand Is Currently Moving', *Neuroscience of Consciousness*, 3 (1). Available at: DOI: 10.1093/nc/niw025.

Lieder, F. et al. (2013) 'A Neurocomputational Model of the Mismatch Negativity', *PLoS Computational Biology*, 9 (11), e1003288.

Lipton, P. (2004). *Inference to the Best Explanation*. London: Routledge.

Marshall, L. et al. (2016) 'Pharmacological Fingerprints of Contextual Uncertainty', *PLOS Biology*, 14 (11), e1002575.

Mathys, C.D. et al. (2014) 'Uncertainty in Perception and the Hierarchical Gaussian Filter', *Frontiers in Human Neuroscience*, 8 (825). Available at: DOI: 10.3389/fnhum.2014.00825.

Metzinger, T. and Wiese, W. (eds.) (2017) *Philosophy and Predictive Processing*. Frankfurt am Main: MIND Group.

Moran, R.J. et al. (2014) 'The Brain Ages Optimally to Model Its Environment: Evidence from Sensory Learning over the Adult Lifespan', *PLoS Computational Biology*, 10 (1), e1003422.

Mumford, D. (1992) 'On the Computational Architecture of the Neocortex. II. The Role of Cortico-cortical Loops', *Biological Cybernetics*, 66, pp. 241–251.

Piccinini, G. (2006) 'Computational Explanation in Neuroscience', *Synthese*, 153 (3), pp. 343–353.

Piccinini, G. and Craver, C. (2011) 'Integrating Psychology and Neuroscience: Functional Analyses as Mechanism Sketches', *Synthese*, 183 (3), pp. 283–311.

Pinotsis, D.A. et al. (2017) 'Linking Canonical Microcircuits and Neuronal Activity: Dynamic Causal Modelling of Laminar Recordings', *NeuroImage*, 146, pp. 355–366.

Roche, W. and Sober, E. (2013) 'Explanatoriness Is Evidentially Irrelevant, or Inference to the Best Explanation Meets Bayesian Confirmation Theory', *Analysis*, 73 (4), pp. 659–668.

Rusanen, A-M. and Lappi, O. (2016) 'On Computational Explanations', *Synthese*, 193 (12), pp. 3931–3949.

Sadaghiani, S. et al. (2010) 'The Relation of Ongoing Brain Activity, Evoked Neural Responses, and Cognition', *Frontiers in Systems Neuroscience*, 4 (20), pp. 1–14.

Seth, A.K. (2015) 'The Cybernetic Bayesian Brain: From Interoceptive Inference to Sensorimotor Contingencies', in Metzinger, T.K. and Windt, J.M. (eds.) *Open MIND*. Frankfurt am Main: MIND Group. Available at: DOI: 10.15502/9783958570108.

Sims, A. (2016) 'A Problem of Scope for the Free Energy Principle as a Theory of Cognition', *Philosophical Psychology*, 29 (7), pp. 967–980.

Spratling, M.W. (2017) 'A Review of Predictive Coding Algorithms', *Brain and Cognition*, 112, pp. 92–97.

Van Doorn, G. et al. (2015) 'Attenuated Self-tickle Sensation Even under Trajectory Perturbation', *Consciousness and Cognition*, 36 (November), pp. 147–153.

Vossel, S. et al. (2015) 'Cortical Coupling Reflects Bayesian Belief Updating in the Deployment of Spatial Attention', *The Journal of Neuroscience*, 35 (33), pp. 11532–11542.

Yuille, A. and Kersten, D. (2006) 'Vision as Bayesian Inference: Analysis by Synthesis?', *Trends in Cognitive Sciences*, 10 (7), p. 301.

PART III

Foundations and challenges

13

TRIVIALITY ARGUMENTS ABOUT COMPUTATIONAL IMPLEMENTATION

Mark Sprevak

1 Introduction

Triviality arguments seek to show that computational implementation in physical systems is trivial in some worrisome way. A triviality argument might show that a theory of implementation attributes computations to too many physical systems, or that it attributes too many computations to those physical systems that compute, or both. Triviality arguments threaten to make trouble both for computational functionalism (the metaphysical claim that implementing a certain computation is sufficient for having a certain mental state or process) and for computational explanation in science (the scientific practice of explaining mental and behavioral phenomena in terms of physical computations).

In this chapter, I examine four triviality arguments. These are arguments of Ian Hinckfuss, John Searle, Hilary Putnam, and David Chalmers. Their arguments may appear to give us cause for dismay. However, seen in a more positive light, they help us formulate an improved theory of computational implementation and choose between competing alternatives. If a theory of computational implementation blocks, or otherwise avoids bad consequences of, a triviality argument, that is a desirable property of the theory. Depending on how bad the consequences, it may even be a necessary property of the theory. Triviality arguments mark out red lines that a theory of implementation should not cross.

In Section 2, I describe the aim of a theory of computational implementation. In Section 3, I discuss the structure and target of a triviality argument. In Section 4, I give four triviality arguments about implementation. In Section 5, I explore how far these triviality arguments reach – how trivial is "trivial"? In Section 6, I reply to the objection that we should simply accept the conclusions of the triviality arguments. In Section 7, I describe some popular lines of response to the triviality arguments. In the Conclusion, I argue that we should learn to love the triviality arguments: they shine light on what would otherwise be murky territory for theory builders. I also propose a theory of implementation that aims to minimize the cost of responding to triviality arguments: pluralism about computational implementation.

2 Computational implementation

Roughly speaking, a theory of implementation aims to describe the conditions under which a physical system does and does not implement a computation.[1] More precisely, a theory of implementation aims to tell us, for a physical system, X, and abstract computation, Y, the conditions under which "X implements Y" is true or false. X may be any physical system – an electronic PC, a brain, or the entire universe. Y may be any abstract formal computation – a Turing machine, a cellular automaton, an artificial neural network, or a C++ program.[2] A theory of implementation tells us which conditions the physical system needs to satisfy for it to implement the computation. Such a theory gives us the *truth conditions* of claims about computational implementation. This serves not only as a semantic theory but also to explicate the concept (or concepts) of computational implementation as they appear in the computational sciences. A theory of implementation says what we mean by our talk of computational implementation and explains how it reduces to (hopefully straightforward) conditions regarding abstract computations and physical systems.

A theory of implementation is sometimes also described as a theory of the computational implementation *relation*. The relation is envisioned as a metaphysical bridge between the abstract realm of mathematical entities (Turing machines, finite state automata, …) and the concrete realm of physical systems (electronic PCs, brains, …). The relation either obtains or does not obtain between specific abstract entities and specific physical systems. If it obtains, then the physical system implements the computation; if not, then not. Conceived this way, a theory of implementation has an explicitly metaphysical task: to describe a special metaphysical relation within our ontology. Although fine as an informal gloss, describing the goal of a theory of computational implementation in these terms is a strategic error. It hypostatizes the implementation relation as part of the description of the problem and it lumbers us with the task of explaining how such a relation fits into our wider ontology. These are not problems that we need to take on from the start. The truth of claims about physical systems implementing computations does not require the existence of a special metaphysical relation between mathematical entities and physical objects. Still less does it require the existence of mathematical entities to stand in such a relation. Rendering claims about computational implementation true or false no more requires the existence of a special metaphysical relation than rendering claims that use the expression "the average man" true requires the existence of a special metaphysical object, the average man. A metaphysical relation of computational implementation may exist, but it is not a commitment that a theory of computational implementation need make at outset.

Instead, a theory of implementation should aim to answer two questions about the truth conditions of *talk* about computational implementation:

COMP Under which conditions is it true/false that a physical system implements a computation?
IDENT Under which conditions is it true/false that a physical system implements one computation rather than another?

The first question concerns the computational status of a physical system. The second concerns its computational identity.[3] Neither has an easy or uncontroversial answer.

In seeking to answer COMP and IDENT, a theory of implementation should provide a theory that is extensionally adequate. The computational sciences already (explicitly and implicitly) classify physical systems into those that compute and those that do not. They further classify members of the class of computing systems by their computational identity. Many complex judgments are made here, but a few simple ones can be briefly stated: electronic PCs compute and their plastic cases do not; my electronic PC is running Microsoft Word and not Grand Theft Auto; not every electronic PC in the world is currently running the Tor browser. These judgments would be regarded as "obviously correct" by a scientist or engineer with a working grasp of computational implementation. Such judgments, made with confidence and receiving widespread agreement in the relevant scientific arenas, are important data points for a theory of implementation to capture.

A good theory of implementation need not capture every single data point or find every one of its claims vindicated in existing practice. We might expect some degree of divergence between what the theory of implementation says and current judgments in science. A violation of extensional adequacy may be small or large. At the small end, it may be accommodated by minor adjustments or qualifications to existing scientific practice. At the large end, such accommodation may not be possible. A theory of implementation may say that current scientific practice is massively in error. It may say that all (or nearly all) physical systems implement all (or nearly all) computations. There is no question here of accommodation. Instead, we are put in a bind: reject the scientific practice or reject the theory of implementation. The triviality arguments aim to demonstrate a violation of extensional adequacy of the latter kind.

It is worth noting that extensional adequacy is only one desideratum of a good theory of implementation. Other desiderata include that the theory of implementation be *explanatory*: it should explain computational implementation in terms of notions that are better understood than computational implementation. The theory should be *non-circular*: it should explain computational implementation in terms of notions that are not themselves explained by computational implementation. The theory should be *naturalistic*: it should not make the truth of implementation claims depend on human beliefs, interests, or values.[4] In Section 7, we will see that theories of implementation that avoid the triviality arguments often do so at the cost of giving up one or more of these other desiderata.

3 Triviality arguments

Triviality arguments attack the extensional adequacy of a theory of implementation. They may focus on a violation of extensional adequacy with respect to COMP, IDENT, or both. Triviality may arise because a theory of implementation attributes computations to too many physical systems, attributes too many computations to systems that compute, or both.

The target theory of computational implementation in this chapter is a "mapping" account of computational implementation. A mapping account is a theory of implementation that practitioners in the computational sciences tend to produce when questioned. It is also the starting point for almost every more sophisticated theory of implementation. A mapping account of implementation says that a sufficient condition for computational implementation is the existence of an isomorphism[5] between the physical states and transitions of a physical system and the abstract states and transitions of a computation:[6]

(M) A physical system X implements a formal computation Y if there is a mapping f that maps physical states of X to abstract states of the formal computation Y, such that: for every step-wise evolution $S \rightarrow S'$ of the formalism Y, the following conditional holds: if X is in physical state s where $f(s)=S$ then X will enter physical state s' such that $f(s')=S'$

In Section 7, we will see that more sophisticated theories of implementation treat M as a necessary but not a sufficient condition for computational implementation. Part of the motivation for this comes from recognition that unmodified M is vulnerable to triviality arguments.

M is simple, clear, explanatory, non-circular, and naturalistic. M also explains why computations are multiply realizable. Different physical systems (silicon chips, vacuum tubes, brass cogs and wheels, neurons) can implement the same computation because, despite their physical differences, their various physical activities can be isomorphic to the same abstract structure.

4 The arguments

It is worth noting two points before proceeding.

First, the triviality arguments do not depend on M alone. Additional assumptions, including empirical assumptions about the typical behavior of physical systems, are required. These assumptions may be true, but they are unlikely to be necessary truths. In other possible worlds, M may provide non-trivial implementation conditions.

Second, an unproblematic claim about implementation is sometimes confused with the triviality claims. This claim is that any physical system could, under the right circumstances, implement any given computation. A rock could, if we were to make tally marks on it, compute the addition function. A wall could, if we were to attach electromagnets to control its physical states the right way, run Microsoft Word. That any given physical system *could*, in the right circumstances, implement an arbitrary computation is not at issue in the triviality arguments. What is at issue is whether these systems *do* implement that computation. One might expect there to be a difference between the two. (Compare: all hydrogen atoms could be used as fuel, but not all are.) The triviality arguments aim to show that this expectation is false. (Almost) all physical systems don't merely have the *potential* to implement any given computation, they actually *are* implementing it. The threat of the triviality arguments is thus not a threat about universal *realizability* in some modally qualified sense, but a threat about universal *realization*.

4.1 Hinckfuss' pail

William Lycan describes a thought experiment originally suggested by Ian Hinckfuss:

> Suppose a transparent plastic pail of spring water is sitting in the sun. At the micro level, a vast seething complexity of things are going on: convection currents, frantic breeding of bacteria and other minuscule life forms, and so on. These things in turn require even more frantic activity at the molecular level to sustain them. Now is all this activity not complex enough that, simply by chance, it might realize a human program for a brief period (given suitable correlations between certain micro-events and the requisite input-, output-, and state-symbols of the program)? And if so, must the functionalist not conclude that the water in the pail briefly constitutes the body of a conscious being, and has thoughts and feelings and so on? Indeed, virtually any physical object under any conditions has enough activity going on within it at the molecular level that, if Hinckfuss is right about the pail of water, the functionalist quickly slips into a panpsychism that does seem obviously absurd.
>
> *(Lycan, 1981, p. 39)*

There is no mention of trivial implementation here, but there is a clear violation of extensional adequacy. Physical systems that we do not normally think of as implementing computations (pails of water) are implementing computations and, perhaps more worryingly, their computational identity is shared with that of our brains and bodies. Hinckfuss is assuming some form of computational functionalism. He argues that the pail implements the same computation as the human brain and body, and for this reason it has the same mental properties as us.

Hinckfuss' thought experiment may be unnerving, but it is not obvious that it is fatal to M.

First, it is not obvious that the conclusion is unacceptable. Even if we follow the chain of reasoning to its conclusion, panpsychism is arguably not an untenable position (Chalmers, 1996a; Goff, 2017; Strawson, 2006). There are good reasons, however, to jump off before we reach the conclusion. Computational functionalists rarely claim that every aspect of mental life supervenes on the computation that a physical system performs. Usually, this claim is made only for a subset of mental life: non-conscious aspects of mental life (Block, 1978; Chalmers, 1996a) or aspects of mental life that exclude cognitive processes like central cognition (Fodor, 2000). If one were to remove these aspects of mental life from the thought experiment, it may no longer seem absurd or even objectionable that a pail of water could, over a brief time interval, share the same computations as our brain and body.

Second, it is not clear how the thought experiment is supposed to produce a triviality result. What is imagined is the *possibility* of an unusual implementation. We need a reason to think that such an implementation is actual in order to have a triviality result. There are plenty of strange physical possibilities: spontaneous unmixing of scrambled eggs, movement of all molecules of air in the room into one corner, quantum tunneling of my legs through the floor. Most of the time, science and engineering assumes that these events will not happen. It is safe to do so because, even though the events are physically possible, they are unlikely. Perhaps a pail of water implementing the same computation as a human brain and body is like that. If so, it does not provide a reason to think that computational implementation is trivial.

4.2 Searle's wall

John Searle describes a different thought experiment:

> [I]t is hard to see how to avoid the following results: 1. For any object there is some description of that object such that under that description the object is a digital computer. 2. For any program and for any sufficiently complex object, there is some description of the object under which it is implementing the program. Thus for example the wall behind my back is right now implementing the Wordstar program, because there is some pattern of molecule movements that is isomorphic with the formal structure of Wordstar. But if the wall is implementing Wordstar, then if it is a big enough wall it is implementing any program, including any program implemented in the brain.
>
> *(Searle, 1992, pp. 208–209)*[7]

Consider, according to M, why Searle's electronic PC implements WordStar. Inside his PC are many microscopic physical changes: changes in electrical, thermal, vibrational, and gravitational state of the physical parts of his PC. His PC implements WordStar because among these physical changes is one set of changes – the set of electrical changes – that has a structure that is isomorphic to the formal structure of WordStar. Searle claims that the same is true of his wall. Inside the wall are many microscopic physical changes: there are atoms and molecules undergoing electrical, thermal, vibrational, and gravitational changes. Searle suggests there are *so many* patterns of physical activity inside his wall that there is certain to be at least one pattern with a structure isomorphic to the formal structure of WordStar. Therefore, just like his PC, his wall implements WordStar. The same reasoning applies to other computations and to other physical systems provided they are "sufficiently complex".

Again, there are problems with this argument that should leave one unpersuaded.

First, the restriction to physical systems that are "sufficiently complex" is underspecified. If "sufficiently complex" means *having enough patterns of activity*, this would be a restatement of what needs to be shown for triviality: that the physical system has enough patterns for trivial implementation. We need an independent characterization of the class of physical systems affected by triviality. We need some idea how large this class is, which systems it contains, and whether its members are relevant to scientific practice. If instead one defines "sufficiently complex" in terms of a system's physical size – as Searle seems to suggest – small enough physical systems relevant to scientific practice may be immune to the challenge.

Second, and more worryingly, why should we believe, even of the largest physical systems, that there are always enough patterns of physical activity to make implementation trivial? One might agree with Searle that a wall contains many patterns of activity. But one might not accept that it contains *every* pattern of physical activity – or that it contains a specific pattern, such as one isomorphic to WordStar. How can we be *sure*, as Searle says, that the wall contains this particular pattern? Searle needs to show, not just that there are *many* patterns of physical activity, but that we should be *certain* there is a pattern isomorphic to any abstract computation.

4.3 Putnam's rock

In the Appendix of *Representation and Reality* (1988), Hilary Putnam presents an argument that addresses the preceding concerns. While Searle and Hinckfuss aim to show that a trivializing mapping exists but do not actually show us the mapping, Putnam provides a method for finding the relevant mapping. Given a physical system, X, and formal computation, Y, Putnam demonstrates how to map X's states to Y's states so that X implements Y according to M. Putnam also provides a characterization of the class of physical systems vulnerable to trivial implementation.

Putnam restricts his triviality argument to inputless finite state automata (FSAs).[8] In Section 5, we will see how to extend his argument to other types of computer. Putnam says that the class of physical systems that are vulnerable to his triviality argument is the class of physical systems that are "open". An "open" physical system is one that is not isolated from, and therefore is in causal interaction with, its environment. Nearly all physical systems in which we are interested are open in this sense.[9] To illustrate his argument Putnam chooses a simple inputless FSA that transits between two abstract states, $A \rightarrow B \rightarrow A \rightarrow B$. He argues as follows.

Pick any open physical system (say, a rock) and any time interval, t_0 to t_n. Consider the "phase space" of the rock over this time interval. The phase space is a representation of every one of the rock's physical parameters, including the physical parameters of the rock's constituent atoms, molecules, and other microscopic parts.[10] Over time, the rock will trace a path through its phase space as its physical parameters change. The rock's physical parameters will change due to endogenous physical causes (its atoms changing state, vibrations, atomic decay, etc.), and because of external causal influences (gravitational, electromagnetic, vibrational, etc.). Putnam argues that some external influences are certain to play the role of "clocks" for the rock: due to these influences the rock will not return to precisely the same set of values of its physical parameters in the time interval. Putnam calls this the "Principle of Noncyclical Behavior". Putnam argues that this principle is likely to be true of any open physical system.[11]

Consider the rock's phase-space trajectory from t_0 to t_n. By the Principle of Noncyclical Behavior, this path will not cross itself at any point. Putnam assumes that the path through phase space is also continuous in time: the path passes through a different point in phase space at each moment in time. Putnam calls this the "Principle of Continuity". Provided these two principles hold, each point in the rock's trajectory falls within a unique region of its phase space. Putnam divides the rock's phase space into four regions through which the rock's state travels during the time interval, and he labels these r_1, r_2, r_3, r_4. These regions describe the rock's state during four, equally spaced time intervals between t_0 and t_n. Regions in phase space are groups of possible physical states. A region in phase space therefore defines a possible physical state *type* for the system. Consequently, we can describe the rock's physical state during the time interval in the following way: in the first time interval, the rock is in the physical state type defined by r_1; in the second, it is in the physical state type defined by r_2; in the third, in the physical state type defined by r_3; and in the fourth, in the physical state type defined by r_4.

Using regions of phase space to characterize the rock's physical state type is a powerful tool. It reveals that the rock undergoes multiple changes in its physical state type during the time interval. One set of such changes is this: $r_1 \rightarrow r_2 \rightarrow r_3 \rightarrow r_4$. But, Putnam observes, it is not the only set of changes. The rock also undergoes the following changes: $r_1 \lor r_3 \rightarrow r_2 \lor r_4 \rightarrow r_1 \lor r_3 \rightarrow r_2 \lor r_4$. In other words, as well as traveling through four neighboring regions of its phase space (r_1, r_2, r_3, r_4), the rock oscillates between two disjoined regions of its phase space ($r_1 \lor r_3$ and $r_2 \lor r_4$). It is worth stressing that there is nothing objectionable about identifying a physical state type of a system with a disjunction of regions of that system's phase space. Many physical state types used for legitimate implementation are defined this way: for example, net thermal energy and net electric charge. The physical states that implement the computational states of electronic PCs are often highly disjunctive: they are diverse configurations of electrical signals that could occur in multiple electronic components scattered throughout the machine. Putnam maps $r_1 \lor r_3$ to computational state A and $r_2 \lor r_4$ to computational state B. We now have an isomorphism between the physical states and transitions of the rock and the formal states and transitions of the FSA. According to M, the rock implements the FSA. The same reasoning applies to other physical systems and other inputless FSAs. Every open physical system implements every inputless FSA under M.

There are three common objections to Putnam's argument.

First, Putnam's argument assumes that any disjunction of regions in phase space defines a legitimate physical state type for implementing a computational state. We have already seen there is nothing inherently objectionable about mapping a disjunction of phase-space regions to a single computational state. However, it is less clear whether constructing a mapping from an *arbitrary* disjunction of phase-space regions is permissible. Critics of Putnam suspect that some disjunctions of phase space are "legitimate" candidates to implement a computational state, whereas others are not. The problem is that it is hard to say *which* disjunctions are legitimate and *why*. As we will see in Section 7, answering this question turns out to be the central point on which theories that aim to replace M disagree. Which further conditions – semantic, teleological, causal, natural kind, pragmatic, etc. – should a disjunction of physical states satisfy to count as a "legitimate" implementer of a computational state?

Second, many computations have inputs (and outputs), but Putnam's triviality argument only applies to inputless FSAs. Putnam's response is that although *physically specified* inputs and outputs would partially constrain implementation, the computational states that lie between input and output would still be open to his triviality argument. A separate reply, developed by Godfrey-Smith (2009) and Sprevak (2012), is that the inputs and outputs of computations are rarely specified physically. Inputs and outputs are typically described as abstract states within the abstract computational formalism (e.g. as numerals, characters, strings, or activation values). These abstract states could, in principle, be implemented by any physical state type (electrical signals, vibrations in the air, turns of a brass cog). As abstract states, computational inputs and outputs seem just as vulnerable to Putnam's triviality argument as internal computational states.[12]

Third, a computer should not be destroyed by arbitrarily small physical changes. But there is no guarantee that the mappings described by Putnam would hold under (even slightly) different physical conditions, e.g. if one photon more had hit the rock before t_0. The mapping given by Putnam also only covers FSA states that actually occur during the computation. It does not cover abstract states or transitions that could have occurred but did not. Computers, especially complicated ones, often have states and transitions that are not instantiated on a given run but that could have been under other conditions.[13] On the basis of these two points, one might propose two counterfactual conditions that a genuine implementation of a computation should satisfy. First, the physical transitions identified by the mapping should be "reliable": they should not fail under arbitrarily small physical changes. Second, the mapping should be "exhaustive": it should map every abstract state and transition of the computer to a physical state and transition. Putnam's argument only tells us about what *actually* happens to the physical system, so it cannot guarantee that either of these counterfactual conditions are satisfied.

4.4 Chalmers' clock and dial

The counterfactual objection to Putnam's triviality argument was once believed to be fatal (Block, 1995; Chalmers, 1995; Chrisley, 1995; Maudlin, 1989). Chalmers (1996b) showed that this assumption is wrong. He constructed a more sophisticated triviality argument, based on Putnam's, that satisfies the counterfactual conditions.

Chalmers defines a "clock" as a component of the physical system that reliably transits through a sequence of physical states over the time interval.[14] He defines a "dial" as a physical component of the system with an arbitrary number of physical states such that if it is put into one of those states it stays in that state during the time interval. Chalmers' counterfactually strengthened triviality result is that every physical system with a clock and a dial implements every inputless FSA.

The argument involves a similar construction to Putnam's, but over possible, as well as actual, trajectories in phase space. In one respect the construction is simpler, since the only states that need to be considered are the physical system's clock and dial; the other physical states can be safely ignored. Chalmers' strategy is to identify a mapping between each formal FSA state and a disjunction of physical states $[i,j]$ of the implementing system, where i corresponds to a numbered clock state, and j to a numbered dial state, and show that the relevant physical states stand in the right counterfactual relations to each other.

Suppose the system starts in physical state $[1,j]$. It will reliably transit to $[2,j]$, $[3,j]$, and so on, as the clock progresses. Suppose that the system starts its actual run in dial state 1. The start state of the FSA can then be mapped to $[1,1]$, and the subsequent abstract states of the FSA to $[2,1]$, $[3,1]$, and so on. At the end of this mapping process, if some FSA states have not come up, then choose one of those formal states as the new start state of the FSA and map $[1,2]$ to it. Then pair physical states $[2,2]$, $[3,2]$, and so on with the abstract states that follow in the evolution of the FSA. Continue until all the un-manifested states of the FSA have been considered. Now, for each abstract state of the FSA, we have a non-empty set of associated physical states $\{[i_1, j_1], [i_2, j_2], \ldots, [i_n, j_n]\}$. Map the disjunction of these states to each FSA state. The resulting mapping between physical and formal states satisfies the counterfactually strengthened version of M.

Chalmers argues that almost all open physical systems have a clock and a dial. If for any reason a physical system does not have a clock or a dial, they can be added by attaching a watch to the physical system. If trivial implementation can be achieved simply by adding a watch to a rock, something has clearly gone wrong with the account of implementation.

5 The reach of the arguments

None of the preceding arguments show that every physical system implements every computation. In what sense do they show that implementation is "trivial"? Broadly speaking, we can measure their strength along three dimensions: time and chance, physical systems, and abstract computations.

First, time and chance. One reason why Hinckfuss' argument seems weak is that trivial implementation is only claimed for a brief time period and conditional on some lucky accident. Searle's argument tries to pump our intuitions to raise the chance of trivial implementation happening more often and over a longer time interval, but he gives no proof that this must occur. The arguments of Putnam and Chalmers are unrestricted in their time interval. They also provide a higher degree of certainty (conditional on various empirical assumptions) that trivial implementation occurs in that time interval. The time interval (t_0 to t_n) could, in principle, be as long or short as one likes: one second, one year, or 10^9 years (provided the physical system is still around).

Second, physical systems. Hinckfuss and Searle suggest that only macroscopic systems (like walls or pails of water) are vulnerable to trivial implementation. On Putnam's account, a physical system is vulnerable to trivial implementation provided it satisfies the Principles of Noncyclical Behavior and Continuity. On Chalmers' account, a physical system is vulnerable to trivial implementation provided it has a clock and a dial. There is no reason why the conditions described by Putnam and Chalmers cannot be satisfied by microscopic as well as macroscopic systems. A few atoms, or even a single atom, could vary its state in such a way as to satisfy the conditions. Thus, Putnam's and Chalmers' arguments appear to threaten not just macroscopic systems but also systems that are small or simple in Hinckfuss' and Searle's terms.

Third, abstract computations. Which abstract computations are trivially implemented? Familiar abstract computations include FSAs, Turing machines, register machines, pushdown automata, cellular automata, random access machines, and artificial neural networks. These, however, are just a tiny sample from the vast population of possible computational architectures. Which abstract computers are subject to trivial implementation? We can put an upper bound on the triviality arguments here. Some computers are impossible to implement in a physical system. Plausible examples of such include infinitely accelerating computers (for which each step takes place faster than the previous step), computers that use infinite time or storage, and computers that manipulate real-valued quantities with unlimited precision.[15] These abstract computers are normally regarded as *notional* computers and studied for their formal properties alone (for example, proving which sentences in the arithmetic hierarchy they decide). They cannot be, and they are not intended to be, physically implemented. The triviality arguments thus have a limit. Not every abstract computation is trivially implemented because not every abstract computation is implementable.

Searle claims that all "programs" are trivially implemented. However, it is hard to be sure what he means by this. In computer science, a "program" refers to a piece of data that plays a certain role within a certain kind of computer, a programmable computer. Programmable computers are a relatively small sub-population within the class of abstract computers (most Turing machines are not programmable). A physical system that implements a program must *ipso facto* implement a programmable computer. Searle thinks that his triviality result applies to a wider range of computers than just the programmable ones. Therefore, he does not seem to have the above definition of "program" in mind. It appears that the term has a more generic meaning, roughly synonymous with *algorithm* or *computational method*. But then his argument is unrestricted with regard to formal computations, and we have seen that this is not right.

Chalmers and Putnam restrict their triviality claims to only one type of computer: inputless FSAs. We have seen how to extend their claims to FSAs with inputs and outputs. What about other abstract computers? Below, I argue that their triviality claims generalize, beyond FSAs, to all abstract computers with finite storage. More to the point, their claims generalize to every *physically implementable* computer.

The argument for this generalization relies on three premises:

1. There is an isomorphism between the physical activity of any open physical system, A, (with a clock and dial) and any FSA, B.
2. If there is an isomorphism between A and B, and an isomorphism between B and C, then there is an isomorphism between A and C.
3. There is an isomorphism between any computer with finite storage, C, and an FSA, B.

The first premise is the conclusion of the triviality arguments. The second premise states the formal property of transitivity of the isomorphism relation. The third premise requires justification, which is given below. The argument runs as follows. Pick any open physical system, A, and any abstract computer with finite storage, C. By premise 3, there is an isomorphism between C and some FSA, B. By premise 1, there is an isomorphism between A and FSA B. By premise 2, there is an isomorphism between A and C. Hence, A implements C.

Justifying premise 3 is not hard. The state of any abstract computer with finite storage, C, can be redescribed by a single monolithic "state" variable, X. The state variable, X, enumerates every possible way in which that abstract computer could be. For example, each value of X ($x_1, x_2, \ldots, x_n$) may denote a possible tape and head state combination for a Turing machine, a possible grid pattern for cells of a cellular automaton, and a possible setting of activation levels and weights for an artificial neural network. Since C has finite storage, its monolithic state variable X can only take a finite number of possible values – otherwise, one could use it to gain a computer with infinite storage. The next value of C's monolithic state variable is determined by its current value.[16] For example, the next value (tape and head state combination) of a Turing machine is determined by its current value (tape and head state combination). The behavior of C can then be fully described by a directed graph (perhaps a large one) of C's state variable and possible transitions between its values (and any inputs or outputs where relevant). This directed graph uniquely specifies an FSA, B. Conversely, FSA B, under the scheme for labeling ways C could be with values of a giant state variable, uniquely specifies C. This establishes an isomorphism between B and C, which is what premise 3 requires.

The class of abstract computers with finite storage is a large one. There are good reasons for thinking it contains the class of abstract computers that are physically implementable.[17] Any physical implementation of a computer only has access to finite physical resources to do its work. These resources may be plentiful (e.g. all the energy and time in the system's forward light cone), but they are finite. This means that any physical implementation of a computer will eventually fail on a large enough input. For example, any PC one builds will eventually fail to recognize $\{a^n b^n \mid n \geq 0\}$ for large enough n. A physical system only has finite resources and so it only has finite storage. Consequently, a physical system can only implement an abstract computer with finite storage. The upper limit on storage is likely to be large – large enough that it is often ignored. We often *idealize* electronic PCs by treating them as if they had unlimited storage. But strictly speaking, only implementation of abstract computers with finite storage is possible.

The preceding points indicate that the triviality arguments have a very far reach indeed. There is no space between the abstract computers that *can* be implemented and those that are implemented *trivially*. The triviality arguments are effectively unrestricted in this respect. If an abstract computation is physically implementable, it is trivially implemented.[18]

6 What is so bad about trivial implementation?

One might wonder whether we should just accept that computational implementation is trivial. After all, M has many other virtues: it is simple, clear, explanatory, and makes the truth of claims about computational implementation objective. Perhaps these virtues are worth the cost of accepting that implementation is trivial.

However, M would remain problematic for at least three reasons:

1. M's violation of extensional adequacy needs explanation.
2. Combined with computational functionalism, M entails panpsychism.
3. M drains computational explanations in the sciences of their power.

All of these considerations have some force, but I will argue that the third consideration is the most significant.

The premise of the current response is that violating extensional adequacy is a price worth paying to keep M. Given this, it is not immediately obvious how pointing (again) to violation of extensional adequacy has any further persuasive force. Violating extensional adequacy may be bad, but the defender of M already admits it. The question is whether there are further problems that she needs to address as a consequence. One such problem is to explain *why* M diverges so much from the judgments of experts in the computational sciences and what we should do about this. A hard-nosed revisionist might suggest that we have discovered that the experts in the computational sciences were wrong and they should revise their claims about computational implementation accordingly (e.g. start saying that PC cases do run Grand Theft Auto). A less revisionary response would be to explain away the disagreement between M and existing scientific practice by appeal to pragmatic factors. For example, one might say that computational implementation is, strictly speaking, trivial but this is not displayed in scientific practice – and need not be so displayed – because scientists attend to, and talk about, only the implementations that interest them. Other implementations are objectively there, but they are not of interest and so they are not discussed. Talk of "the" computations that a physical system implements should be interpreted as a pragmatic shorthand to direct our attention to the implementations that interest us and away from those that do not.[19]

The second consideration raises problems for M but only conditional on computational functionalism being true. Computational functionalism claims that if a physical system implements certain computations then it has certain mental states and processes. According to the triviality arguments, nearly every physical system implements nearly every computation. Consequently, nearly every physical system has nearly every mental state and process.

Computational functionalism was popular in the 1970s and 1980s (Block, 1978; Fodor, 1987; Putnam, 1975). But it is not clear how widely the view is endorsed today, even in the qualified versions described in Section 4.1. Current cognitive science appeals to physical computations to explain behavior and mental processes. However, contemporary cognitive science is usually silent about whether those computations are metaphysically sufficient for mental life. Consequently, it is unclear how much weight, if any, to accord consideration 2 as a source of problems for M.

The third consideration should cause more concern. Cognitive science explains, predicts, and describes human behavior and mental processes in terms of computations. Decision making, categorization, inference, and belief revision are explained by the brain implementing distinctive computations. Cognitive science explains particular aspects of behavior and mental processing (behavioral or psychological "effects") by appeal to the brain implementing specific computations. Specific effects occur because the brain implements one computation rather than another. This explanatory methodology is threatened by the triviality results. If implementation is trivial, then no distinctive computations are implemented by the brain. The brain, like almost every other physical system, implements almost every computation. Explaining psychological effects by appeal to distinctive computations cannot work because there are no distinctive physical computations. Granted that computational explanation is important in cognitive science, accepting the triviality results while continuing to pursue cognitive science looks hard.

7 How to respond to triviality arguments

There is widespread agreement that unmodified M makes computational implementation trivial. There is also widespread agreement that trivial implementation is incompatible with the explanatory goals of cognitive science. Unfortunately, there is no agreement about what to do about it. Competing proposals try to modify M in different ways in order to block the triviality arguments. These proposals tend to fall into four broad categories.

Physical/causal structure proposals. These proposals dive deeper into the physical and causal nature of physical systems to find differences that matter for implementation. Chalmers (1996b) claims that physical states that implement distinct abstract states should be "independent" components of the physical system. What "independent" means here is not entirely clear although Chalmers suggests that it means the physical states occupy different spatial regions. Unfortunately, as he acknowledges, this condition is too strong; it rules out legitimate implementations (Sprevak, 2012). As an alternative, Godfrey-Smith (2009) suggests that physical states that implement the same abstract state should be "physically similar" to each other and "physically different" from those that implement different abstract states. Again, the meaning of "physical similarity" is unclear but in any case the condition is too strong. Two physical states within the same computation that implement different abstract states may not just be physically similar, they may be physically identical. This happens in virtualized machines and in an ordinary PC when memory is reorganized during a memory remap (Sprevak, forthcoming).

Semantic proposals. Some physical computers manipulate representations. For example, an electronic PC manipulates electrical signals that represent numbers when it computes an answer to an addition problem. Semantic accounts of implementation suggest that only those physical systems that manipulate representations implement computations. As Fodor said, "[t]here is no computation without representation" (1981, p. 180). The computational identity of a physical system is determined by which representations it manipulates and how it manipulates them (Shagrir, 2010; Sprevak, 2010). Walls and rocks do not implement computations because they do not contain representations, or if they do, they do not manipulate them in the right way. Like the physical/causal proposals, semantic proposals face the worry that they are too strong. Not every physical computation manipulates representations. Some computers, like parsers, appear to be "purely syntactic" and do not manipulate representations at all (Piccinini, 2008).

Teleological proposals. Physical parts of a computer often have teleological functions related to the computation. For example, a memory unit inside a PC has the teleological function of storing data. Teleological accounts of implementation suggest that only physical systems with the right teleological functions implement computations. The computational identity of a physical system is determined by the teleological functions of its parts and how those parts are related (Bontly, 1998; Piccinini, 2015). Walls and rocks do not implement computations because they do not have the teleological functions associated with computing. Like the physical/causal and semantic proposals, teleological proposals face the worry that they are too strong. Teleological functions are relational properties: they depend on the physical system satisfying conditions about how users treat it, the intentions of designers, the system's evolutionary history, or the system's possible successes in particular environments. Yet an intrinsic physical duplicate of a computer – one that lacks these relations – still seems to be a computer. A further wrinkle is that naturalistic accounts of teleological function suggest that naturalized teleological functions are sparsely instantiated and have a large degree of indeterminacy in their identity (Burge, 2010; Shea, 2013). It is unlikely there is a sufficiently rich and determinate set of natural teleological functions to ground the computational claims of cognitive science.

Anti-realist proposals. Physical computers are often physical systems that are useful to us, or salient to us, as computers in light of our human interests, values, and our human cognitive and perceptual machinery. An electronic PC is a convenient means for us to implement a word processing program, in a way that a rock is not. Anti-realist accounts suggest that it is because certain physical systems offer a useful means for us to implement a computation that they implement that computation. The computational identity of a physical system is determined by how the physical properties of the system interact with our human-centered interests and perceptual and cognitive abilities. Computers have physical activity that we can observe, predict, or manipulate in appropriate ways. Walls and rocks do not implement computations, notwithstanding their isomorphism to abstract computations, because we cannot conveniently exploit those isomorphisms to do computational work. The relevant isomorphisms are "there" but worthless to us because we do not know how to control the physical states that map to relevant computational inputs, outputs, or intermediate states. "Usefulness" here is not simply a matter of subjective utility. One person wanting something to implement a computation shouldn't make it so. An anti-realist account of implementation would likely appeal to what is generally useful, explanatory, perspicuous, informative, or practicable in science.

Anti-realism is ultimately the route down which Searle and Putnam wish to push us. Their goal is to show us, not that computational implementation is trivial, but that computational implementation *unconstrained by human interests and values* is trivial. Unlike physical/causal, semantic, and teleological proposals, anti-realism gets the extension of computational implementation more or less correct. It fits closely with the judgments associated with COMP and IDENT in existing computational practice. However, it has a cost. Anti-realism gives up on the *naturalistic* desideratum of a theory of computational implementation. Anti-realism guarantees that computational implementation is not a natural or objective matter of fact.

Indeed, to the extent that implementation is non-trivial, computational implementation is 100 percent a function of our (perhaps a broad "our" referencing a scientific community) interests, values, and perceptual and cognitive abilities. Scientific explanations that appeal to computational implementation would have to acknowledge this. They explain by invoking a mind-dependent, observer-relative notion. Given that computational explanation in cognitive science is valued as a way to understand the mind in objective, non-mind-dependent terms, this should cause worry.

8 Conclusion

Triviality arguments teach us that unmodified M is unacceptable. We have seen little agreement about how to respond to them. Different theorists plump for different options, with different costs, in order to block the triviality arguments. It is unfortunate that there is so little agreement here. But on the positive side, it is good that triviality arguments provide significant, hard-to-meet constraints on theorizing. Without constraints that push back against us, we would be theorizing about implementation in the dark. The triviality results are not an embarrassment. They provide a valuable source of information that can guide us towards improved theories of computational implementation.

What would be a fair price to pay to avoid the triviality arguments? Each option canvassed in Section 7 incurs a cost. Typical costs were that the theory is too strong or that it gives up on the naturalistic desideratum of a theory of implementation. Before closing, I wish to suggest that we can minimize costs by adopting a form of pluralism about computational implementation. Each of the constraints described in Section 7 has some element of truth in it: it describes how implementation is constrained in *some* circumstances. The mistake the accounts make is that they say implementation is constrained in the same way in *every* circumstance. Scientific practice allows for more diversity than that: implementation may be sometimes constrained one way, sometimes in another. The relevant constraints in different circumstances could invoke physical relations, semantic content, teleological functions, or human-centered interests and values. The problem we saw in Section 7 was that appealing to a single constraint does not do the work in all circumstances (or at least not without cost). A pluralist account of computational implementation says that the factor that constraints implementation varies between contexts. Whatever constraint can be claimed present (without cost!) in that context – be it physical, semantic, teleological, or pragmatic – does the work of constraining implementation in that context. Absent such constraints, implementation is of course trivial. But in any context where implementation is not trivial, at least one such constraint kicks in. If more than one constraint is available, then conflicting claims about implementation may arise (e.g. the system both implements a computation and does not implement the computation relative to different standards). This may result in groups of researchers talking past each other, or more commonly, acknowledgment that there is a legitimate sense in which the relevant physical system does and does not perform the computation. A pluralist approach offers answers to COMP and IDENT that reflect the nuances of scientific practice while avoiding the costs of a one-size-fits-all approach to the triviality arguments.

Acknowledgment

I would like to thank Matteo Colombo for helpful comments on a previous version of this chapter.

Notes

1 The discussion in this chapter is phrased in terms of physical implementation. If there are non-physical states – qualia, ectoplasm, etc. – a theory of implementation may aim to cover their computational implementation conditions too.

2 I do not consider here how we should characterize the class of abstract computations. For the purpose of this chapter, I assume that we know (at least roughly) which abstract formal descriptions count as computations.

3 Attribution of multiple computational identities to a physical system is common in the sciences. Sometimes the computations are related: for example, when a physical system satisfies several related formal computational descriptions (e.g. gradient descent, backpropagation, AdaGrad, and some specific machine-learning Python program). Sometimes the computations are not related: for example, when the physical system has a sufficient number of physical properties to support the attribution of multiple unrelated computational models. Anderson (2014) argues that the brain is a computing system of the latter type.

4 See Sprevak (2012) for more on these desiderata. See Piccinini (2015) for discussion of additional desiderata.

5 The mapping relation is sometimes called a "homomorphism". The correct term depends on how one groups physical states into physical state types, which as we will see, is controversial.

6 This condition is adapted from Chalmers (2012).

7 Although Searle's argument is phrased in terms of programs, I will understand it here as covering any abstract computation; for discussion, see Section 5.

8 See Hopcroft and Ullman (1979); Sudkamp (1998) for a description of FSAs.

9 One possible exception is the entire universe (Copeland et al., 2018).

10 Putnam only considers the classical properties of physical systems. It is not clear how quantum mechanical properties would constrain implementation under M.

11 Poincaré's recurrence theorem says that physical systems, if they satisfy certain conditions, return to a total physical state arbitrarily close to that of their initial conditions after a sufficiently long time. However, this theorem only applies to closed systems and the Poincaré recurrence period for an open system is likely to be extremely long – longer than the lifetime of the universe.

12 For more on this point, see discussion of the "transducer layer" in Godfrey-Smith (2009) and "strong" and "weak" input–output constraints in Sprevak (2012).

13 See Maudlin (1989) for an illustration of this point with Turing machines.

14 Chalmers' "clock" is different from the clocks in Putnam's argument. Putnam's clocks are external signals that cause the system's physical state to evolve in a non-cyclical way. Chalmers' clocks are inside the system and they change their physical state in a counterfactually robust way.

15 Blum et al. (1998); Copeland (2002); Piccinini (2011).

16 I focus here only on deterministic computers. It is worth considering how the argument might generalize further to non-deterministic computers. This would require proving a version of the Putnam/Chalmers triviality result for non-deterministic FSAs. One way to do this would be to augment their assumptions to require that the physical system contain some random physical element. One could then partition the random element's physical state into physical types with appropriate probabilities for the FSA's states and map abstract states of the non-deterministic FSA to appropriate disjunctions of triples of states of the clock, dial, and random element. What would remain is to prove a non-deterministic analogue of premise 3. This would require showing that there is an isomorphism between any non-deterministic computer with finite storage, C, and some non-deterministic FSA, B. The argument could follow the line of reasoning given in the main text for premise 3.

17 See Rabin and Scott (1959).

18 Chalmers (2012) aims to block this consequence for his preferred computational architecture, combinatorial state automata, by modifying M to require that computational states be implemented by "independent" components of a physical system; see Section 7 for discussion.

19 A parallel could be drawn with how Lewis (1970) and Mackie (1974) treat causes and background conditions. According to Lewis and Mackie, there is no objective distinction between a cause and a background condition. They defuse disagreement between this and our everyday talk (which does distinguish between causes and background conditions) by appeal to the pragmatics of causal discourse. Talk of causes and background conditions is a pragmatic device to direct our attention to the causes that interest us.

References

Anderson, M.L. (2014) *After Phrenology: Neural Reuse and the Interactive Brain*. Cambridge, MA: MIT Press.

Block, N. (1978) 'Troubles with Functionalism', in Savage, C.W. (ed.) *Perception and Cognition: Issues in the Foundations of Psychology*, Minnesota Studies in the Philosophy of Science, vol. 9. Minneapolis, MN: University of Minnesota Press, pp. 261–325.

Block, N. (1995) 'The Mind as the Software of the Brain', in Smith, E.E. and Osherson, D.N. (eds.) *An Invitation to Cognitive Science*, vol. 3: *Thinking*. Cambridge, MA: MIT Press, pp. 377–425.

Blum, L., Cucker, F., Shub, M., and Smale, S. (1998) *Complexity and Real Computation*. New York, NY: Springer.

Bontly, T. (1998) 'Individualism and the Nature of Syntactic States', *The British Journal for the Philosophy of Science*, 49, pp. 557–574.

Burge, T. (2010) *Origins of Objectivity*. Oxford: Oxford University Press.

Chalmers, D.J. (1995) 'On Implementing a Computation', *Minds and Machines*, 4, pp. 391–402.

Chalmers, D.J. (1996a) *The Conscious Mind*. Oxford: Oxford University Press.

Chalmers, D.J. (1996b) 'Does a Rock Implement Every Finite-state Automaton', *Synthese*, 108, pp. 309–333.

Chalmers, D.J. (2012) 'A Computational Foundation for the Study of Cognition', *Journal of Cognitive Science*, 12, pp. 323–357.

Chrisley, R.L. (1995) 'Why Everything Doesn't Realize Every Computation', *Minds and Machines*, 4, pp. 310–333.

Copeland, B.J. (2002) 'Accelerating Turing Machines', *Minds and Machines*, 12, pp. 281–301.

Copeland, B.J., Shagrir, O., and Sprevak, M. (2018) 'Zuse's Thesis, Gandy's Thesis, and Penrose's Thesis', in Cuffano, M. and Fletcher, S. (eds.) *Computational Perspectives on Physics, Physical Perspectives on Computation*. Cambridge, UK: Cambridge University Press, pp. 39–59.

Fodor, J.A. (1981) 'The Mind–Body Problem', *Scientific American*, 244, pp. 114–125.

Fodor, J.A. (1987) *Psychosemantics*. Cambridge, MA: MIT Press.

Fodor, J.A. (2000) *The Mind Doesn't Work That Way*. Cambridge, MA: MIT Press.

Godfrey-Smith, P. (2009) 'Triviality Arguments against Functionalism', *Philosophical Studies*, 145, pp. 273–295.

Goff, P. (2017) *Consciousness and Fundamental Reality*. Oxford: Oxford University Press.

Hopcroft, J. and Ullman, J. (1979) *Introduction to Automata Theory, Languages, and Computation*, 2nd ed. Reading, MA: Addison-Wesley.

Lewis, D.K. (1970) 'Causation', *The Journal of Philosophy*, 70, pp. 556–567.

Lycan, W.G. (1981) 'Form, Function, and Feel', *The Journal of Philosophy*, 78, pp. 24–50.

Mackie, J.L. (1974) *The Cement of the Universe*. Oxford: Oxford University Press.

Maudlin, T. (1989) 'Computation and Consciousness', *The Journal of Philosophy*, 86, pp. 407–432.

Piccinini, G. (2008) 'Computation without Representation', *Philosophical Studies*, 137, pp. 205–241.

Piccinini, G. (2011) 'The Physical Church–Turing Thesis: Modest or Bold?', *The British Journal for the Philosophy of Science*, 62, pp. 733–769.

Piccinini, G. (2015) *The Nature of Computation*. Oxford: Oxford University Press.

Putnam, H. (1975) 'The Mental Life of Some Machines', in *Mind, Language and Reality: Philosophical Papers*, vol. 2. Cambridge, UK: Cambridge University Press, pp. 408–428.

Putnam, H. (1988) *Representation and Reality*. Cambridge, MA: MIT Press.

Rabin, M.O. and Scott, D. (1959) 'Finite Automata and Their Decision Problems', *IBM Journal of Research and Development*, 3, pp. 114–125.

Searle, J.R. (1992) *The Rediscovery of the Mind*. Cambridge, MA: MIT Press.

Shagrir, O. (2010) 'Brains as Analog-Model Computers', *Studies in History and Philosophy of Science*, 41, pp. 271–279.

Shea, N. (2013) 'Naturalising Representational Content', *Philosophy Compass*, 8, pp. 496–509.

Sprevak, M. (2010) 'Computation, Individuation, and the Received View on Representation', *Studies in History and Philosophy of Science*, 41, pp. 260–270.

Sprevak, M. (2012) 'Three Challenges to Chalmers on Computational Implementation', *Journal of Cognitive Science*, 13, pp. 107–143.

Sprevak, M. (forthcoming) 'Review of Susan Schneider, *The Language of Thought: A New Philosophical Direction*', *Mind*.

Strawson, P.F. (2006) 'Realistic Monism: Why Physicalism Entails Panpsychism', *Journal of Consciousness Studies*, 13, pp. 3–31.

Sudkamp, T.A. (1998) *Languages and Machines*, 2nd ed. Reading, MA: Addison-Wesley.

14

COMPUTATIONAL IMPLEMENTATION

J. Brendan Ritchie and Gualtiero Piccinini

Introduction

Some things compute, others do not. Digital computers do, and perhaps minds, but not rocks. Or so it seems. Determining what conditions a physical system must satisfy in order to compute is the focus of theories of computational implementation, or physical computation. In this chapter we explore some implications of these theories for the computational theory of mind (CTM). After highlighting some general features of implementation, we review the theories on offer and how they address the challenge of pancomputationalism, namely, the thesis that every physical system computes. We argue that satisfying minimal desiderata for theories of implementation – to avoid the most damaging form of pancomputationalism – sharply limits the degree to which psychology is autonomous from neuroscience. In particular, if the mind is computational and physically implemented, then psychology constrains the kinds of structure and organization to be found in the nervous system, and neuroscience constrains the kinds of computation to be posited by psychologists.

The computational mind and implementation

Strong versions of CTM maintain that the nature of mental states is wholly computational. Weak versions of CTM maintain that at least some cognitive phenomena are explained by mental computations, although there may be more to the nature of mental states than computational properties. For example, weak CTM is compatible with the view that mental states have qualitative aspects (qualia) whose nature is not wholly computational. The notion of implementation is important to both strong and weak CTM; any view that considers the mind to be computational, in whole or in part, must give an account of what it takes for a computation to be physically implemented.

Implementation may be defined as a relation between an abstractly defined computation and the concrete physical process that carries it out. Accordingly, there are two ways to think about computation. First, we may investigate computation abstractly, by formally defining systems such as Turing machines. This is the focus of the mathematical theory of computation, an important branch of mathematics. Second, computations are also a kind of concrete physical process, such as the operations of a Turing machine implemented with motorized Lego pieces.

An account of implementation aims to specify the conditions under which a physical system performs a computation defined by a mathematical formalism – it is a theory of physical computation. If our mind is computational, there must be a fact of the matter regarding how it is physically implemented.

The details depend on the kind of computation being implemented. The most familiar is digital computation, which is the notion defined by the classical mathematical theory of computation. Alternatively, mental computations may be analog or of some other kind (Eliasmith, 2003; Piccinini and Bahar, 2013). We propose to focus on computation in a general sense that includes these particular kinds – digital computation, analog computation, and so on – as species. Whatever form of abstract computation is at play, when implemented, the physical operations will qualify as a form of *generic* physical computation (Piccinini and Scarantino, 2011). A generic computation involves the processing of a vehicle (a variable or value of a variable) in accordance with a rule that is defined over the vehicles. The rule specifies a mapping from inputs (and possibly internal states) to outputs. The physical process changes a portion of the vehicle. For example, if a physical system implements a Turing machine, the physical process alters one of the digits on the tape in accordance with the rule that defines the Turing machine.

Crucially, since the rule is only sensitive to variations of the vehicles along a certain dimension, the vehicles can be of any physical medium, so long as they allow for the appropriate degrees of freedom. In this respect, the rules and the vehicles over which they are defined are *medium-independent* (Garson, 2003). For example, it does not matter what physical material is used to implement a Turing machine, so long as the cells in the tape can take two possible values and the active component flips those states in accordance with the rule. In contrast, although baking a cake is also a physical process that follows a rule, the type and quantity of each ingredient matters a great deal to making the cake turn out right. Since baking a cake is not a medium-independent process, it is not a physical computation (*qua* cake baking).

Medium independence is connected to the vexed issue of multiple realizability. Many supporters of CTM have long argued that mental properties are multiply realizable – they can be physically realized in different ways (e.g. Fodor, 1975; 1978). This is important because according to many of these supporters, if mental properties are multiply realizable, psychology is autonomous from neuroscience (more on that shortly). But capturing the precise sense in which mental properties (or any other properties) are multiply realizable has proven controversial. Here we adopt the account of Piccinini and Maley (2014). We assume that realization is a relationship between a property of a whole system and properties and relations of the components of a system at the mechanistic level immediately below, with the realized property consisting of a proper subset of the causal powers of the lower-level properties and relations that realize it. The property is multiply realizable when different kinds of components, different arrangements of the same kinds of components, or different arrangements of different kinds of components, can produce the same property.

As an example, consider a standard zinc-carbon dry cell battery connected to an LED. The battery produces an electrical current of ~1.5 V, which powers the diode so that the circuit as a whole produces light within the visible spectrum. Replacing the battery with one of equivalent voltage does not qualify as multiple realization. For example, a single zinc-copper lemon cell or potato battery from science class produces insufficient current for powering an LED and producing visible light. But a magnesium-copper lemon cell will reliably produce the required voltage (Swartling and Morgan, 1998), as will a zinc-copper potato battery if the tuber is first boiled (Golberg, Rabinowitch, and Rubinsky, 2010). Despite the very different physical composition, these batteries contribute the same causal power to the circuit. Though a single zinc-copper lemon or raw potato cell is insufficient to power the LED, an array of them will produce enough voltage. Since the array introduces variation in both the arrangement and the kinds of components, we have a different realization of the property (producing visible light) than the single battery circuit.[1]

Multiple realizability in this sense is exhibited by classic examples like single-chamber versus compound eyes, which vary both in structure and components across species (Aizawa and Gillett, 2011; Land, 2005; Polger and Shapiro, 2016), as well as computing systems. For example, the same logic circuit can be implemented by different combinations of logic gates, and the same logic gate can be implemented using different technologies. Crucially, medium independence is a stronger condition than multiple realizability in the sense we have defined. Medium independence entails multiple realizability, though not vice versa. Even though different circuit arrangements might power our LED in order to produce visible light, only some media will produce sufficient voltage. In contrast, implementing computations only requires that, whatever the physical medium, it possess the right degrees of freedom and functional organization.[2]

In summary, a commitment to computational psychology presupposes a fact of the matter about implementation, or physical computation. It entails not only multiple realizability, but also medium independence. What, then, *is* implementation?

What is implementation?

A theory of implementation specifies the conditions a physical system must satisfy in order to carry out a computation. There are many desiderata relevant to such a theory:

Metaphysical adequacy: does it entail there is a fact of the matter about whether a physical system computes?

Explanatory adequacy: does it allow that some of a system's capacities may be explained by what it computes?

Extensional adequacy: does it ensure that paradigmatic cases of computing systems do compute, and paradigmatic cases of non-computing systems do not?

These desiderata provide a standard of evaluation for the theories that we review. The more that are satisfied, the better the theory. Crucially, the challenge of pancomputationalism is related to all of these desiderata.[3]

Theories of implementation

For simplicity we will frame our discussion in terms of digital computation and descriptions of state types and transitions. A physical system implements a computation when there is an appropriate mapping between the computational state types and transitions and the physical microstate types and transitions.[4] Theories of implementation specify what this mapping is like as well as any further conditions that must also be satisfied.

As a concrete example, consider a simple finite-state automaton, M, with four internal states (S_0, S_1, S_2, S_3), four inputs (i_1, i_2, i_3, i_4), two outputs (o_1, o_2), and a starting state (S_0). The state-transition function for M consists of the following rules:

If in S_0 with input i_1, then transition to S_1 with output o_1.
If in S_0 with input i_2, then transition to S_2 with output o_1.
If in S_1 with input i_2, then transition to S_3 with output o_2.
If in S_1 with input i_3, then transition to S_0 with output o_1.

If in S_2 with input i_1, then transition to S_3 with output o_2.
If in S_2 with input i_4, then transition to S_0 with output o_1.
If in S_3 with input i_3, then transition to S_2 with output o_1.
If in S_3 with input i_4, then transition to S_1 with output o_1.

In other words, for M to reach S_3 and produce o_2, it must receive inputs i_1 and i_2 in sequence, and first transition to one or the other intermediate state. The other two inputs return M from S_3 to the intermediate states, and then to S_0. The state diagram for M is depicted in Figure 14.1 (cf. Scheutz, 2001, p. 5, Figure 2).[5]

Now consider the simple physical system, P, similar to the circuit described earlier, but with two switches on the wire connecting the battery cathode to the LED (Figure 14.2). Supposing that the initial configuration of P is that both switches are open, it is *prima facie* plausible that P implements M. To illustrate why, we turn to some of the theories of implementation on offer.

According to *weak mapping accounts* there is a mapping between subsets of the physical microstates of a system and the computational states, such that the state transitions between the physical microstates mirror those between the computational states. Such an account captures part of why P might implement M, given the following mapping: S_0 maps onto P when both switches are open, S_1 and S_2 map onto P when (respectively) the first or second switch is closed, and S_3 maps to P when both are closed. Correspondingly i_1 and i_2 map (respectively) to the closing of the first and second switch, i_3 and i_4 map to opening the first and second switch (respectively), o_1 corresponds to the LED being off, and o_2 to it being on.

The problem with weak mapping accounts is that they allow too many mappings. Consider a different mapping between M and P in which the causal history plays a role. Again the initial state of P corresponds to S_0, and when a switch is closed it is in a state corresponding to either S_1 or S_2. The difference is that if the first switch is closed (input i_1, state S_1), and then it is opened again, the re-opening maps to i_2 (not i_3) and P is now described as being in a state corresponding to S_3 (not S_0). While potentially coherent, this may seem like an odd way of mapping M to P, since two equivalent (sets of) physical microstates of P, in which both of P's switches are open, now map to two distinct computational states, S_0 and S_3, based on a difference in causal history.

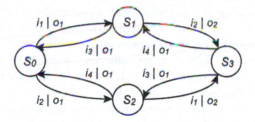

Figure 14.1 The state diagram for finite-state automaton M

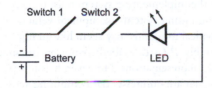

Figure 14.2 The circuit diagram for physical system P

Allowing for such arbitrary computational descriptions seems to make physical computation a feature of how we describe physical systems, rather than what they do.

Robust mapping accounts restrict what sort of mapping is allowable. In particular, a counterfactual account requires that any allowable mapping must be counterfactual-supporting, so that if a physical system had gone into a different microstate, which maps onto a different computational state, then it would have followed the corresponding state-transition rule. In this respect, an implementation mapping must track lawful and reliable microstate transition types, which can be specified independently of the computations a system might implement (Chalmers, 1996; Copeland, 1996). A pure counterfactual account requires nothing other than these dependencies. A causal account requires that the computational state transitions map to causal relations between physical microstates (Chalmers, 1996; Scheutz, 2001). A dispositional account requires that the physical system manifest a disposition to transition from one microstate type into another (Klein, 2008a). One may further require that the microstate types map to distinct components of a physical system (Chalmers, 2011). Causal and dispositional accounts are closely related to counterfactual accounts, since they presuppose the same counterfactuals that are appealed to by a pure counterfactual account, although some have argued that they have additional advantages such as being more extensionally adequate (cf. Klein, 2008a, p. 145). Crucially, all robust mapping accounts block the odd mapping between M and P described above. If I close and then open the first switch, P transitions from one state to another, and back again. If both switches being open corresponds to S_0 and output o_1, then under robust mapping accounts re-opening the first switch after closing it (input i_3 not i_2) returns the system to S_0 and o_1, rather than transitioning it to S_3 and output o_2.

So far we have said that the mapping between M and P is a *prima facie* plausible case of implementation. However, one might reasonably question whether P is computing anything when the switches are closed in sequence. One way to address this query is to introduce additional conditions on implementation. There are two main proposals.

When we ordinarily think of computing, typically we imagine systems that manipulate symbols – states with semantic content. *Semantic accounts* of implementation make this property constitutive of all forms of computation. In a slogan: "no computation without representation" (Fodor, 1981, p. 180; see also Cummins, 1983; Fodor, 1975; 1978, among many others).[6] Semantic accounts are perhaps the dominant view in philosophy of mind, in part because the mind is commonly thought to be representational. They are also closely related to the widespread view that computation is information processing in some sense (Piccinini and Scarantino, 2011). Perhaps unsurprisingly, then, there are many such accounts on offer, which vary with respect to what states qualify as representations, how they are individuated, what kind of content they have, and how they get their content. For example, when it comes to individuating computational states based on their representational content, the main debate is whether the content is *wide* (i.e. individuated by aspects of the world that are external to a system), or *narrow*, reflecting solely intrinsic properties of the system.

Whatever the details, all semantic accounts introduce a further condition on implementation, in so far as the states of the implementing system must be content-bearing representations. Since many paradigmatic computing systems manipulate vehicles that are also symbols (e.g. a computer hard drive in its typical uses), this may seem like an improvement on robust mapping accounts. For example, plausibly P (as described) is not an instance of physical computation because none of its states are representations. However, it is less plausible that M is not computational. Finite-state automata are quintessential computing systems, but their internal states need not be defined as having semantic content, or receive a semantic interpretation. This is true of M, which was characterized solely in terms of a set of internal states, inputs and outputs, and a state-transition function. Under a strict semantic account, M is not computational. This seems to run counter to computability theory, which does not require that computational states be representations. Perhaps more pressing, the very notion of a symbol seems to require a non-representational way of individuating computational states (Piccinini, 2004). For these reasons, semantic accounts may not be the best way to improve on robust mapping accounts.

A different approach is to build on the strengths of robust mapping accounts while adding further non-semantic conditions. This is the direction taken by *mechanistic accounts* of implementation, according to which a physical system implements a computation when it is a certain kind of functional mechanism. A functional mechanism is an organized system of components each with its own functions. When the components are combined in the appropriate way and are operating properly, their joint activities constitute the capacities exhibited by the mechanism. This notion comes from accounts of constitutive explanation according to which we explain phenomena by finding mechanisms – that is, by decomposing a system into its relevant components and showing how the components' activities produce the phenomenon (Bechtel and Richardson, 1993; Glennan, 2002; Machamer, Darden, and Craver, 2000). According to the mechanistic account of implementation, a physical system computes in the generic sense when it is a mechanism that has the teleological function of processing medium-independent vehicles in accordance with a rule defined over the vehicles (Piccinini, 2007; 2015; cf. also Kaplan, 2011; Miłkowski, 2013; Fresco, 2014).

The mechanistic account builds on the strengths of robust mapping accounts, as it requires a decomposition of a physical system into components and the dependencies between them, in line with theories of mechanistic explanation. Like semantic accounts, it adds further conditions, chiefly, that a physical system have the teleological function of carrying out certain processes. Its appeal to teleological functions captures an important feature of many instances of physical computation – typically systems that compute are either designed or selected to do so, and this explains how they acquired their teleological functions. Thus P, as described, does not implement M since it does not have the function of computing, though it is easy to imagine situations where it might acquire it. We can imagine a situation where P is a component of a computing device built of switches and LEDs. The important point is that, under the mechanistic account, determining whether a physical system implements some computation requires taking account of not just the mapping, but also the function of the mechanism.[7]

The challenge of pancomputationalism[8]

According to pancomputationalism, all physical systems compute something. This claim can vary in its severity. According to *unlimited* pancomputationalism, every physical system carries out every computation – or, somewhat more weakly, every physical system with sufficient complexity carries out a large number of distinct computations (Putnam, 1988; Searle, 1992). According to *limited* pancomputationalism, every physical system performs at least one computation (Chalmers, 2011; Scheutz, 2001).[9]

Unlimited pancomputationalism is a radical thesis. When conjoined with a strong version of CTM it entails panpsychism or something close to it, because it entails that whatever computational system constitutes the mind is implemented by every sufficiently complex physical system (Chalmers, 1996, p. 310). By the same token, it renders CTM both trivially true and nearly vacuous, because it entails that any putative computational explanation of cognition is implemented not only by ordinary cognitive systems but also by every other sufficiently complex physical system. Unlimited pancomputationalism also presents a challenge for theories of implementation. If a theory cannot avoid unlimited pancomputationalism, neither can it satisfy our desiderata. Such a theory is metaphysically inadequate, since it entails that physical computation need not be an objective property of the operation of a system, as well as explanatorily inadequate, since the fact that a system computes would not reflect anything distinctive of the system's capacities. Finally, it is extensionally inadequate, since it deems paradigmatic cases of non-computing physical systems such as hurricanes, digestive systems, and rocks computational just like digital computers and Turing machines.

Limited pancomputationalism has less extreme consequences. It does not entail panpsychism, and theories that allow for it may be metaphysically adequate. However, it is controversial whether theories of implementation that are consistent with limited pancomputationalism are also explanatorily and extensionally adequate.

What arguments are there for unlimited pancomputationalism? One approach is to start from the premise that implementation is purely a matter of how an observer interprets a physical system. Given any physical system of sufficient complexity, it can be described as implementing some computation (Searle, 1992). The first rigorous arguments come from Putnam (1988). Consider a finite-state automaton, M^*, that simply transitions between these two states in sequence: S_0, S_1, S_0, S_1, S_0, S_1, S_0. Putnam further considers an arbitrary physical system, P^*, within an arbitrary time interval that goes through different maximal physical states at times t_1, ..., t_7. Given a disjunctive mapping between the computational states and maximal physical microstates (S_0 maps to the microstates that occur at t_1, t_3, t_5, and t_7; S_1 maps to the microstates that occur at t_2, t_4, and t_6), Putnam claims that P^* implements M^*, even if it is an ordinary rock. This argument does not yet challenge CTM directly since M^* does not have inputs or outputs. But Putnam's argument may be strengthened by considering that the different inputs and outputs of an ordinary finite-state automaton can be encoded in the initial and final states of an inputless and outputless finite-state automaton. If this is done, the conclusion of Putnam's argument becomes the following: any physical system (of rather minimal complexity) implements any finite-state automaton.

While even more elaborate arguments for unlimited pancomputationalism can be generated (Chalmers, 1996; Godfrey-Smith, 2009), Putnam's argument illustrates that they rely, either implicitly or explicitly, on a weak mapping account of implementation. In contrast, any robust mapping account has the resources to block such arguments, since it requires, at a minimum, counterfactual restrictions on the (independently specifiable) microstate changes of a physical system.[10] Thus a rock does not implement M^* during an arbitrary time interval because it does not flip back and forth between microstates belonging to two different sets so as to mirror the state transitions of Putnam's finite-state automaton. However, robust mapping accounts do not typically have the resources to avoid limited pancomputationalism, which impugns their extensional adequacy. While our circuit P might not implement the automaton M, it might implement M^* when the switch is simply flipped back and forth in sequence. Similarly, consider a rock in the desert, not during an arbitrary time interval, but rather over the course of a few days. Each day the rock heats and then cools, as the sun rises and falls. The desert rock implements M^* even under some robust mapping accounts.

Some accept that robust mapping accounts either entail (or are consistent with) limited pancomputationalism (Chalmers, 2011; Scheutz, 2001; Sprevak, 2012), and try to assuage concerns about explanatory and extensional adequacy: rather than it being the property of computing *simpliciter* that provides a demarcating criterion for these desiderata, it is computation of the right, non-trivial sort that is important. In contrast, a relative strength of the mechanistic account is that it requires no such hedging of the desiderata, since by adding functional requirements, it provides resources for avoiding even limited pancomputationalism.

In summary, there are several accounts of implementation on offer. An important feature of all plausible accounts is that a robust, counterfactual-supporting mapping is necessary, and likely sufficient, for meeting the challenge of *unlimited* pancomputationalism (though additional constrains are needed to avoid *limited* pancomputationalism). This can be thought of as a constraint on any non-trivializing theory of implementation. As we shall now see, this requirement has important implications for CTM.

Implementation and autonomy

While theories of implementation grew in part out of discussion of CTM, the implications of these theories are underappreciated. To help remedy this, we will highlight some consequences of these theories for the doctrine that psychology, or psychological explanation, is autonomous from neuroscience.

We focus on two forms of autonomy. The first is autonomy as *irreducibility of laws*: psychological laws cannot be reduced to lower-level laws, in the sense that the generalizations of the higher-level science cannot be derived from or replaced by those of a lower-level science (Fodor, 1975; 1978; Kitcher, 1980; Richardson, 2008). The second is autonomy as *lack of direct constraint*. A higher-level explanation puts direct constraints on a lower-level one if and only if the capacities it describes constrain the possible organized components that can exhibit those capacities. The lower-level explanation constrains the higher-level one when the reverse dependency holds and the components, and their organization, constrain what functional properties the system can realize (Cummins, 1983; Piccinini and Craver, 2011).

There is of course one kind of indirect constraint that all agree on, which is that our psychological capacities must be somehow realized, or in the case of computational psychology, implemented (Cummins, 1983; 2000). However, any conditions on implementation robust enough to avoid unlimited pancomputationalism are inconsistent with both of the above forms of autonomy. To see why, we first turn to the classic argument for autonomy, which rests on multiple realizability.

Multiple realizability and arguing for autonomy

The classic argument for autonomy of laws rests on a few assumptions. First, psychological natural kind predicates are projectable, in the sense that if some members of a kind have a property, one is justified in inferring that others have that property (Kim, 1998; Klein, 2008b). Second, projectability is a necessary condition for being a scientific kind. Third, psychological kinds are multiply realizable (we assume in the sense articulated earlier) and the set of lower-level realizing kinds forms an open, disjunctive list. Given these assumptions, the argument goes as follows (Fodor, 1975; 1978; 1997).

Consider again our circuit P, and now imagine a different physical system, P', which consists of a 2-bit hard drive with two nanometer-sized regions of magnetic grains that can be flipped between two magnetizations by a read-write head. Suppose further that P and P' are each part of computing machines, so they implement M. When we consider any of the states of these two systems, there seems to be little that they physically have in common. Such a motley crew of physical implementations, it is claimed, share nothing in common beyond their computational properties, as the microphysical states and organization of the two systems are radically different. For this reason, they lack any lower-level properties that can be specified independently of the higher-level computational description. That is, there is no lower-level projectable natural kind predicate that applies to all the realizers of a computational state.

The same is supposed to be true of the realizers of our mental states. If they share no lower-level property, they cannot form a scientific lower-level kind. Any attempt to group the open disjunction of possible realizers at the lower level will define a putative kind that is "gerrymandered" (Fodor, 1997), or "disjoint and disparate" (Richardson, 2008, p. 530), since the disjunctive members have "nothing in common" beyond the fact that they realize the same psychological kind (Kitcher, 1980, p. 137). And if a putative kind is so gerrymandered and disparate, no lower-level laws apply to it. Therefore, the higher-level laws cannot be derived from or replaced by any lower-level ones. In sum, since psychological kinds are multiply realizable, there are no independently specifiable nomic generalizations in the lower-level science on to which the psychological generalization can be mapped.

One observation about this argument is that it also speaks in favor of autonomy from direct constraints. Since the mapping from the lower- to higher-level kinds is many-to-one, we cannot tell what properties the realizing system has simply from the fact that it manifests the higher-level property or kind (Sober, 1999, p. 545). For if there is a unity at one level and a disunity at the other, such that there are no shared lower-level properties, then it is hard to see how there can be any direct constraints between the two.

An implementation dilemma

Defenders of autonomy for psychological explanation generally do not consider how their view relates to conditions on implementation (though see Fodor, 1978). This is significant, since we will now argue that any theory of implementation that can avoid unlimited pancomputationalism is incompatible with either form of autonomy.

The incompatibility is immediately clear when it comes to autonomy from direct constraints. Any theory of implementation that is at least robust entails that there are direct constraints. On the one hand, the grouping of physical microstates into sets related by counterfactual-supporting state transitions restricts what computations it can carry out. On the other, any medium-independent property puts restrictions on what physical systems can realize it, as the system must have the appropriate degrees of freedom and counterfactual-supporting microstate transitions (Piccinini, 2015, p. 123). The composition and organization of the brain constrains what it can compute, and if some aspect of cognition is explained computationally, then the brain must have the right sort of organization to implement it. So if our brain implements computations in a nontrivial manner, there are direct constraints.

There is also no autonomy of laws if our account of implementation is at least robust. As we pointed out earlier, the physical medium is immaterial to implementing a computation, so long as a medium possesses the appropriate degrees of freedom and organization. Nonetheless, these degrees of freedom reflect the independent dynamics of a physical system, and a system will only implement a computation, in a non-trivial sense, if the microstate transitions support counterfactuals that mirror the computational state transitions. For example, if we encounter systems that implement some computation, we can infer what other physical systems must be like in order to implement the same computation, even if we do not know what components these other systems are made of or their specific physical capacities. We can infer that they must have transitions between microstates that support certain types of counterfactuals, or have a causal organization of an appropriate sort (i.e. one sufficient to establish a robust mapping). In short, possessing the appropriate degrees of freedom and microstate transitions is *itself* a shared property of any system that implements a particular computation.

To illustrate, consider again M and its two implementations P and P'. Even though the two systems have different physical properties, at an appropriate level of abstraction they are equivalent in degrees of freedom and functional organization. And for any other physical system that implements the same computation, we can also project that it consists of vehicles and internal dynamics that exhibit the appropriate degrees of freedom and functional organization – if they did not, then they would not implement the same computation (cf. Klein, 2008b). Of course none of this shows that there are physical scientific kinds that range over all the properties of all the diverse implementations. However, a lack of *any* lower-level projectability is essential to the argument for autonomy going through. The fact that different implementations share some of their properties therefore undermines the argument.

So robust accounts of implementation appear incompatible with the main argument for autonomy. If we endorse a weak mapping account, however, there are no projectable properties across implementations or direct constraints, because there are no restrictions on implementation mappings. This allows that a physical system might have nothing in common organizationally with the computation it implements (cf. Fodor and Pylyshyn, 1988, p. 63). So if we endorse a weak mapping account, autonomy may be preserved. Still this is a Pyrrhic victory, since a weak mapping account lacks the resources to avoid unlimited pancomputationalism. So a cost of saving autonomy is a theory of implementation that is metaphysically, explanatorily, and extensionally inadequate. Defenders of autonomy face what we may call an *Implementation Dilemma*:

Horn 1: Endorse the weak mapping account in order to save autonomy. Since the weak mapping account allows for unlimited pancomputationalism, every (sufficiently complex) physical system implements whatever computations constitute or explain our cognitive capacities. Thus we obtain an undesirable form of panpsychism.

Horn 2: Endorse at least a robust mapping account, avoiding unlimited pancomputationalism, while still maintaining autonomy. But since autonomy is incompatible with physical implementation under a robust mapping account, the only way to consistently endorse both theses is to hold that the computations that constitute or explain our cognitive capacities are not physically implemented. Thus we obtain an undesirable form of dualism concerning psychological properties.

It should go without saying that both horns of the dilemma are dreadful. The first horn leads us to a form of panpsychism that is especially undesirable, because it is grounded in the weakness of the account of implementation rather than any evidence or argument that every physical system has a mind. The second horn leads us to a form of dualism that is also especially undesirable, because it is also grounded in the weakness of the account of implementation. The only viable option, then, is to reject autonomy.

Doing without autonomy

The preceding might be unwelcome news to those who maintain that psychological explanation is autonomous. There are a few avenues of resistance. First, one might challenge the idea that degrees of freedom and counterfactual-supporting state transitions are projectable properties across all physical systems that implement a computation. Second, one might hope for an account of implementation that is less than robust, but nonetheless avoids unlimited pancomputationalism.

Such moves are unlikely to succeed, in part because theories of implementation drive a wedge between multiple realizability and lack of projectability. To illustrate, suppose a causal account of implementation, according to which the computations carried out by a physical system are wholly determined by its causal capacities. If the diverse implementations of a computation share no projectable properties, not even in their degrees of freedom, then any property that one has, another must lack. Thus, there must be an implementation that lacks a causal organization that exhibits the appropriate degrees of freedom. But then the system implements a *different* computation. This sort of argument has been used to reject the idea that there are genuinely multiply realizable kinds (Klein, 2008b) or that there is little or no multiple realizability (Polger and Shapiro, 2016). A better response is to let go of the idea that multiple realizability entails a lack of projectability. It is not multiple realizability that should be called into question, but autonomy.

Furthermore, these rejoinders are unmotivated. Traditionally autonomy was the cost of preserving the legitimacy of psychological explanation and avoiding classic reductionism. However, rather than establishing the reduction of psychology to neuroscience, lack of autonomy is equally compatible with a multi-level integrationist approach to the explanation of cognition, in which computation takes pride of place (Boone and Piccinini, 2016).

Conclusion

Theories of implementation attempt to characterize what conditions a physical system must satisfy in order to compute. Interest in this topic grew out of discussion of whether the mind is computational. As we have shown, there are a diverse number of theories on offer, some more adequate than others. We have also argued that if the mind is computational in an interesting sense, then psychology and neuroscience directly constrain each other.

Acknowledgments

Thanks to our audience at EPSA 2017. Thanks to the editors for helpful feedback. This material is partially based upon work supported by the National Science Foundation under grant no. SES-1654982 to Gualtiero Piccinini. This project has received funding from the FWO and European Union's Horizon 2020 research and innovation program under the Marie Skłodowska-Curie grant agreement No 665501, in the form of an FWO [PEGASUS]² Marie Skłodowska-Curie Fellowship (12T9217N) to J. Brendan Ritchie.

Notes

1 This example raises the difficult question of how to individuate different realizations of a single property (Shapiro, 2000). For example, changing the brand of dry cell battery, or breed of potato, does not seem to produce different realizations. We touch on this issue in note 2.

2 Polger and Shapiro (2016, p. 166) deny the entailment from medium independence to multiple realizability, but it is unclear why. If a property is medium-independent, it is *ipso facto* multiply realizable by any medium with enough degrees of freedom. Perhaps Polger and Shapiro confuse medium independence with realization by mechanisms that differ in irrelevant features. For example, winged corkscrews made of steel versus aluminum are *not* distinct realizations because they remove corks from bottlenecks in the same way. The rigidity of both steel and aluminum is the relevant common property of both corkscrews (Shapiro, 2000). In contrast, consider different technologies that implement the same computing system – such as electronic or electromechanical implementations of the same logic design. They are different realizations that perform the same computations in relevantly different ways. This becomes clear if one attempts to process the medium employed by an electronic computer using an electromechanical one, or vice versa; it will not work. The same is true if one attempts to substitute an electromechanical relay for an electronic circuit within an electronic computer (or vice versa). So this is a case of genuine multiple realizability, but it is also more than that. Whereas in ordinary multiple realizability the property being realized may be defined in terms of specific physical effects (e.g. removing corks from bottlenecks), computational properties are defined more abstractly, in terms of relations between variables with certain degrees of freedom (Piccinini, 2015). This is why computation is not just multiply realizable, but also medium-independent.

3 Piccinini (2015, pp. 11–15) includes being able to explain miscomputation and taxonomizing different kinds of computation as other desiderata to be captured. Here we focus on the three in the main text because they are most relevant to pancomputationalism.

4 Here by "computational states and transition" we mean physical macrostates and transitions between macrostates that are defined in a medium-independent way, which may be implemented by appropriate sets of physical microstates and transitions between microstates.

5 Implicit in our description of M is that it can only receive certain inputs when in certain internal states. For example, if in S_0 it can only receive i_1 or i_2 as inputs. Also, it can never receive the same input in sequence.

6 Importantly, semantic accounts are distinct from the view that computations are sensitive to semantic properties (Rescorla, 2012). One may endorse the former and not the latter (e.g. Fodor, 1980), or vice versa (for discussion, see Piccinini, 2015, pp. 32–33).

7 For example, if the LED turns itself off, this may not be a malfunction if the light being off is a computational state; but it will be a malfunction if the function of the device is to produce visible light.

8 A more detailed treatment of pancomputationalism can be found in Sprevak (this volume).

9 A related form of pancomputationalism, *ontic* pancomputationalism, holds that the nature of the physical universe is entirely computational. Here we set ontic pancomputationalism aside. For discussion see Anderson and Piccinini (2018).

10 A contrary opinion is offered by Scheutz (2012), who argues that even causal accounts (Chalmers, 2011) lead to unlimited pancomputationalism.

References

Aizawa, K. and Gillett, C. (2011) 'The Autonomy of Psychology in the Age of Neuroscience', in Illari, P.M., Russo F., and Williamson, J. (eds.) *Causality in the Sciences*. Oxford: Oxford University Press, pp. 202–223.

Anderson, N.G. and Piccinini, G. (2018) 'Ontic Pancomputationalism', in Cuffaro, M.E. and Fletcher, S.E. (eds.) *Physical Perspectives on Computation, Computational Perspectives on Physics*. Cambridge, UK: Cambridge University Press, pp. 23–38.

Bechtel, W. and Richardson, R.C. (1993) *Discovering Complexity*. Princeton, NJ: Princeton University Press.

Boone, W. and Piccinini, G. (2016) 'The Cognitive Neuroscience Revolution', *Synthese*, 193 (5), pp. 1509–1534.

Chalmers, D.J. (1996) 'Does a Rock Implement Every Finite-state Automaton?', *Synthese*, 108 (3), pp. 309–333.

Chalmers, D.J. (2011) 'A Computational Foundation for the Study of Cognition', *Journal of Cognitive Science*, 12 (4), pp. 323–357.

Copeland, B.J. (1996) 'What Is Computation?', *Synthese*, 108 (3), pp. 335–359.

Cummins, R.C. (1983) *The Nature of Psychological Explanation*. Cambridge, MA: MIT Press.

Cummins, R.C. (2000) '"How Does It Work?" vs. "What Are The Laws?" Two Conceptions of Psychological Explanation', in Keil, F. and Wilson, R. (eds.) *Explanation and Cognition*. Cambridge, UK: Cambridge University Press, pp. 117–144.

Eliasmith, C. (2003) 'Moving beyond Metaphors: Understanding the Mind for What It Is', *The Journal of Philosophy*, 100 (10), pp. 493–520.

Fodor, J.A. (1975) *The Language of Thought*. Cambridge, MA: Harvard University Press.

Fodor, J.A. (1978) 'Computation and Reduction', in Savage, C.W. (ed.) *Perception and Cognition: Issues in the Foundations of Psychology*. Minneapolis, MN: University of Minnesota Press.

Fodor, J.A. (1980) 'Methodological Solipsism Considered as a Research Strategy in Cognitive Psychology', *Behavioral and Brain Sciences*, 3 (1), pp. 63–73.

Fodor, J.A. (1981) 'The Mind–Body Problem', *Scientific American*, 244 (1), pp. 114–123.

Fodor, J.A. (1997) 'Special Sciences: Still Autonomous after All These Years', *Noûs*, 31 (s11), pp. 149–163.

Fodor, J.A. and Pylyshyn, Z.W. (1988) 'Connectionism and Cognitive Architecture: A Critical Analysis', *Cognition*, 28 (1–2), pp. 3–71.

Fresco, N. (2014) *Physical Computation and Cognitive Science*. New York, NY: Springer.

Garson, J. (2003) 'The Introduction of Information into Neurobiology', *Philosophy of Science*, 70 (5), pp. 926–936.

Glennan, S. (2002) 'Rethinking Mechanistic Explanation', *Philosophy of Science*, 69 (S3), pp. S342–S353.

Godfrey-Smith, P. (2009) 'Triviality Arguments against Functionalism', *Philosophical Studies*, 145 (2), pp. 273–295.

Golberg, A., Rabinowitch, H.D., and Rubinsky, B. (2010) 'Zn/Cu-vegetative Batteries, Bioelectrical Characterizations, and Primary Cost Analyses', *Journal of Renewable and Sustainable Energy*, 2 (3), 033103.

Kaplan, D.M. (2011) 'Explanation and Description in Computational Neuroscience', *Synthese*, 183 (3), pp. 339–373.

Kim, J. (1998) *Mind in a Physical World*. Cambridge, MA: MIT Press.

Kitcher, P. (1980) 'How to Reduce a Functional Psychology?', *Philosophy of Science*, 47 (1), pp. 134–140.

Klein, C. (2008a) 'Dispositional Implementation Solves the Superfluous Structure Problem', *Synthese*, 165 (1), pp. 141–153.

Klein, C. (2008b) 'An Ideal Solution to Disputes about Multiply Realized Kinds', *Philosophical Studies*, 140 (2), pp. 161–177.

Land, M.F. (2005) 'The Optical Structure of Animal Eyes', *Current Biology*, 15 (9), pp. R319–R323.

Machamer, P., Darden, L., and Craver, C.F. (2000) 'Thinking about Mechanisms', *Philosophy of Science*, 67 (1), pp. 1–25.

Miłkowski, M. (2013) *Explaining the Computational Mind*. Cambridge, MA: MIT Press.

Piccinini, G. (2004) 'Functionalism, Computationalism, and Mental Contents', *Canadian Journal of Philosophy*, 34 (3), pp. 375–410.

Piccinini, G. (2007) 'Computing Mechanisms', *Philosophy of Science*, 74 (4), pp. 501–526.

Piccinini, G. (2015) *Physical Computation: A Mechanistic Account*. Oxford: Oxford University Press.

Piccinini, G. and Bahar, S. (2013) 'Neural Computation and the Computational Theory of Cognition', *Cognitive Science*, 37 (3), pp. 453–488.

Piccinini, G. and Craver, C. (2011) 'Integrating Psychology and Neuroscience: Functional Analyses as Mechanism Sketches', *Synthese*, 183 (3), pp. 283–311.

Piccinini, G. and Maley, C.J. (2014) 'The Metaphysics of Mind and the Multiple Sources of Multiple Realizability', in Sprevak, M. and Kallestrup, J. (eds.) *New Waves in Philosophy of Mind*. Houndmills, UK: Palgrave Macmillan, pp. 125–152.

Piccinini, G. and Scarantino, A. (2011) 'Information Processing, Computation, and Cognition', *Journal of Biological Physics*, 37 (1), pp. 1–38.

Polger, T.W. and Shapiro, L.A. (2016) *Multiple Realization Book*. Oxford: Oxford University Press.

Putnam, H. (1988) *Representation and Reality*. Cambridge, MA: MIT Press.

Rescorla, M. (2012) 'Are Computational Transitions Sensitive to Semantics?', *Australasian Journal of Philosophy*, 90 (4), pp. 703–721.

Richardson, R.C. (2008) 'Autonomy and Multiple Realization', *Philosophy of Science*, 75 (5), pp. 526–536.

Scheutz, M. (2001) 'Computational versus Causal Complexity', *Minds and Machines*, 11 (4), pp. 543–566.

Scheutz, M. (2012) 'What It Is Not to Implement a Computation: A Critical Analysis of Chalmers' Notion of Implementation', *Journal of Cognitive Science*, 13 (1), pp. 75–106.

Searle, J.R. (1992) *The Rediscovery of the Mind*. Cambridge, MA: MIT Press.

Shapiro, L.A. (2000) 'Multiple Realizations', *The Journal of Philosophy*, 97 (12), pp. 635–654.

Sober, E. (1999) 'The Multiple Realizability Argument against Reductionism', *Philosophy of Science*, 66 (4) pp. 542–564.

Sprevak, M. (2012) 'Three Challenges to Chalmers on Computational Implementation', *Journal of Cognitive Science*, 13 (2), pp. 107–143.

Swartling, D.J. and Morgan, C. (1998) 'Lemon Cells Revisited: The Lemon-powered Calculator', *Journal of Chemical Education*, 75 (2), pp. 181–182.

15

COMPUTATION AND LEVELS IN THE COGNITIVE AND NEURAL SCIENCES

Lotem Elber-Dorozko and Oron Shagrir

Introduction

Many neuroscientists, cognitive scientists and philosophers take it that nervous systems, and even their single cells, perform computations and that these computational operations play a role in producing and explaining cognition. Scientists and philosophers also tend to account for neuro-cognitive phenomena within one or another framework of levels.

How are these two trends – the computational approach and the framework of levels – integrated in the foundations of cognitive science? The answer to this question is by no means simple, and largely depends on what one means by *levels* and by *computation*. Leveled hierarchies have been used to present various, sometimes conflicting, viewpoints. While some have presented such hierarchies to argue for the reduction of all levels to one fundamental level (Oppenheim and Putnam, 1958), others have used them to support the autonomy of different scientific practices (Cummins, 1983), still others presented them as a comprehensive way to explain cognitive phenomena (Marr, 1982). Moreover, *levels* can be understood as levels of description (Pylyshyn, 1984), analysis (Marr, 1982), organization (Churchland and Sejnowski, 1992), mechanisms (Bechtel, 1994; Craver, 2007), and more.[1]

The nature of computation and computational explanation is also a hot topic, with answers spanning semantic (Shagrir, 2006; Sprevak, 2010), syntactic (Stich, 1983), causal (Chalmers, 2011), mechanistic (Miłkowski, 2013; Piccinini, 2015), algorithmic (Copeland, 1996) and other approaches. We will discuss here three approaches to computational explanations and how they fit in a framework of levels. One is David Marr's (1982) three-level analysis in which the top-level consists of computational-level theories. Another is offered by Cummins (1983; 2000; see also Fodor, 1968; Haugeland, 1978), who proposes that computational explanations are a sort of functional analysis, and that they are autonomous to some extent from the lower implementation (e.g. neurological) level. A third, more recent, picture views computational explanations as mechanistic explanations (Piccinini, 2007; 2015; Piccinini and Craver, 2011; Kaplan, 2011; Miłkowski, 2013; Fresco, 2014) that are not autonomous from a lower implementation level.

The chapter does in no way provide an exhaustive survey of all the literature concerning computation and levels; nor does it offer a systematic analysis of the relations between them. Our aim is far more modest: We focus on on-going debates concerning the place of computational explanations within a leveled approach to the study of neuro-cognitive phenomena. As a teaser, we start with a quick mention of three influential pictures of levels that had their influence on the pictures described in more depth along the chapter.

We begin with a picture that deals with scientific practice in general, but greatly influenced frameworks for explanation in cognitive science. Oppenheim and Putnam (1958) discuss levels of scientific discourse, each employing its own predicates and laws (e.g. atoms, molecules, living things). The levels are hierarchically ordered such that "Any thing of any level except the lowest must possess a decomposition into things belonging to the next lower level" (ibid., p. 9). Oppenheim and Putnam use this framework to argue that, based on empirical evidence, it is very likely that there is a "unity of science". This means that each level can be reduced into its next lower level so that any observational data explainable by the former is explainable by the latter. Because reduction is transitive, all levels can be reduced into one united fundamental level. "In this sense, Unity of Science is an alternative to the view that it will eventually be necessary to *bifurcate* the conceptual system of science, by the postulation of new entities or new attributes" (ibid., p. 13).

A second picture, that deals specifically with explanation of cognition, is offered by Zenon Pylyshyn (1980; 1984; 1989), and is consonant with the framework offered by Allen Newell (1980; 1982).[2] Pylyshyn advances a tri-level framework with the aim of providing foundations for the classical view in cognitive science.[3] Assuming that cognition is classical (e.g. digital and programmed) computation, it would be best to account for cognition at different levels, whereas each level describes the same system/process from a different perspective. Pylyshyn enumerates "three autonomous levels of description" (1984, p. 259). The top level is the semantic (or knowledge) level. This level explains why people, or other complex computing systems, do certain things by stating their goals as well as "showing that these are connected in certain meaningful or even rational ways" (Pylyshyn, 1989, p. 57). The symbol (or syntactic, algorithmic, or functional) level demonstrates how the semantic content is encoded by symbolic expressions; it also specifies the structure of these expressions and the regularities by which they are manipulated. The physical (or biological) level specifies how the entire system is realized in physical structures.[4] While each level describes different aspects of a computing system, Pylyshyn argues that the distinctive feature of the computational approach is that it addresses cognition in terms of a formal symbolic, algorithmic level of analysis (1980, p. 111).[5] The computational level is not detached from the semantic and the physical levels; it constrains and is constrained by them. The levels are autonomous in the sense that each addresses different questions and conforms to different principles (1984, p. 259).

A very different picture is offered by Patricia Churchland and Terrence Sejnowski (1992) in *The Computational Brain*. Their starting point is "that there are levels of organization is a matter of fact" (ibid., p. 11). When talking about "levels of organization", Churchland and Sejnowski take it, similarly to Oppenheim and Putnam (1958), that objects belonging to a lower-level are smaller in size, and are also parts of objects that are at the higher level (Figure 15.1). This is in contrast to Pylyshyn who often talks about levels of description in which the entities at a lower level (e.g. symbolic) are very often not part of entities at the higher level (e.g. semantic content).[6] Another difference is that most or all of the levels mentioned by Churchland and Sejnowski (Figure 15.1) fall within Pylyshyn's physical/biological level. Moreover, while Churchland and Sejnowski certainly associate computing with information processing, they do not talk about distinct semantic or functional levels. As they see it, computational studies contribute to the "co-evolution" of research in different levels. This approach, they posit, is key to the understanding of brain and cognitive function. While Pylyshyn's view – levels of description – is reflected in Cummins' and to a lesser extent in Marr's writings (Sections 1 and 2), the mechanistic approach adopts levels with part–whole relations, similarly to the "levels of organization" view (Section 3) and the tension between these different frameworks is the basis for many debates today.

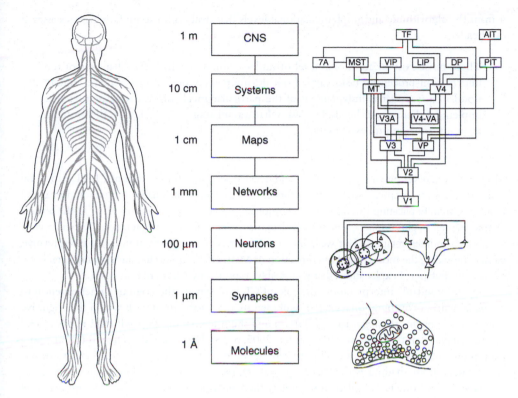

Figure 15.1 Levels of organization in the nervous system
Source: Adapted with permission from Churchland and Sejnowski (1988)

1 Marr's computational-level theories

In *Vision*, Marr famously advances a three-level approach to the study of visual processes and to the study of cognition more generally. The "most abstract" is the computational level (CL), which "is the level of *what* the device does and *why*" (1982, p. 22). The role of the *what* aspect is to specify what is computed. The job of the *why* aspect is to demonstrate the appropriateness and adequacy of what is being computed to the information-processing task (ibid., pp. 24–25). We will discuss the computational level in more detail below. The algorithmic level characterizes the system of representations that is being used, e.g. decimal vs binary, and the algorithm for the transformation from input to output. The implementation level specifies how the representations and algorithm are physically realized. Marr's levels are not levels of organization, where the entities at higher level are composed of entities at the level below it. He refers to his levels as "levels of analysis", whereas each such level provides a further understanding of the visual phenomenon. Marr's levels are similar to Pylyshyn's levels in that each level employs its own methods to analyze the cognitive system, and in that the interaction between the (distinct) levels is essential for a complete account of the explanandum phenomenon, e.g. some visual task. However, some identify Marr's "computational level" with Pylyshyn's semantic level, and Marr's *algorithmic level* with Pylyshyn's *symbolic level*. We challenge this view and will elaborate on it more below.

Marr says that "it is the top level, the level of computational theory, which is critically important from an information-processing point of view" (1982, p. 27), and he distinguishes it from the algorithmic and implementational levels that deal with the underlying processes at our heads:

> There must exist an additional level of understanding at which the character of the information-processing tasks carried out during perception are analyzed and understood in a way that is independent of the particular mechanisms and structures that implement them in our heads. This was what was missing – the analysis of the problem as an information processing task.
>
> *(ibid., p. 19)*

Marr, however, never provided a systematic and detailed account of his notion of CL. He moves on to advance a set of computational theories of specific visual tasks which had a tremendous impact on vision research. Explicating the notion of a computational-level theory and its place in the leveled picture was left to philosophers, who provided, in turn, very different interpretations. We will review some of these interpretations. But we want to emphasize that our motivation is not interpretative, namely providing the most faithful interpretation of Marr. Our aim is to highlight an important feature of computational explanations that is (arguably) captured by Marr's notion of CL.[7]

On the "standard" interpretation, the role of CL is to specify the cognitive phenomenon to be explained: "A computational analysis will identify the information with which the cognitive system has to begin (the *input* to that system) and the information with which it needs to end up (the *output* from that system)" (Bermúdez, 2005, p. 18). Thus edge-detection is the mapping from representations of light intensities to representations of physical edges (e.g. object boundaries). Shape-from-shading is the mapping from representations of shading to representations of shape, and so on. The explanation itself is then provided mainly at the algorithmic level (Ramsey, 2007, pp. 41–42). This interpretation is inspired by Pylyshyn's three-layer picture on which the top-level is some "semantic" level, and it is the middle, symbolic, level, that explains how the system performs cognitive capacities. But it is not completely in accord with Marr who separates the computational and algorithmic levels and assigns to the computational level a unique explanatory role.[8] The standard interpretation is right in saying that Marr's computational level can be seen as delineating the explanandum for the algorithmic and mechanistic levels. What is ignored, however, is the fact that this delineation has itself a major explanatory role in the account of the visual task (Shagrir and Bechtel, 2017).

Lawrence Shapiro (1997) interprets CL as providing a task analysis of the visual task. He writes:

> [A]t the computational level of theory the theorist describes what I shall call *chief* tasks and *service* tasks … the chief task of the visual system is the derivation of 3-D shape representations from information encoded in 2-D images. Service tasks are those tasks the completion of which contribute to the achievement of the chief task.
>
> *(ibid., p. 134)*

In particular, he argues, the information-processing description of the service tasks, in terms of informational content, contributes to the understanding of the chief task. This is in accord with the functional picture of computational explanations – discussed in the next section – according to which the capacity of a system ("chief task") is explained in terms of the capacities of the components ("service tasks") of which it is composed. According to Shapiro, only after this task is completed, we turn to the algorithmic level that specifies "the algorithms and representations that can in fact solve the chief and service tasks" (ibid., p. 136).

There are indeed cases where the information-processing descriptions of service tasks (e.g. stereo disparity) account for the chief task (e.g. stereo vision). But the paradigm cases of computational theories that Marr and his students advance – edge-detection, stereo disparity, and structure-from-motion – do not aim to provide task analyses. For example, the theory of stereo disparity demonstrates that the system computes a matching function that must satisfy the constraints of uniqueness and continuity (these constraints reflect, in turn, certain facts about the visual field). In many cases, the functional strategy proposed by Shapiro better fits with Marr's algorithmic level than with his computational level. Thus, while the computational level aims to explain what the system is computing and why it is computing it, a decomposition of the task will usually explain how the task is achieved and such a description is more in accord with a description of an underlying algorithm.

Gualtiero Piccinini and others (Piccinini and Craver, 2011; Piccinini, 2015; Boone and Piccinini, 2016b; see also Kaplan, 2011, p. 343) describe Marr's computational and algorithmic levels as *sketches* of mechanisms (see Section 3 on mechanisms). A sketch of a mechanism is a description in which some structural aspects of the mechanism are missing. Once these missing aspects are filled in, the description turns into "a full-blown mechanistic explanation"; the sketches themselves can be thus seen as "elliptical or incomplete mechanistic explanations" (Piccinini and Craver, 2011, p. 284). They are, in a way, a guide or a first step towards the structural components that constitute the full-blown mechanistic explanations. Piccinini would probably agree with Shapiro that the computational (and algorithmic) level provides a task analysis, but he argues that a task analysis is a mechanistic sketch (Piccinini and Craver, 2011), and computational explanations are mechanistic explanations (Piccinini, 2015).

Piccinini is right to observe that both the computational and algorithmic levels are abstract, in that they omit certain structural aspects of the mechanism (both levels are also abstract in the sense that they provide mathematical or formal descriptions). We disagree, however, that these levels provide weak or incomplete explanations (see Section 3). What seems even more troublesome is the attempt to lump Marr's computational and algorithmic levels together. If anything, it is the algorithmic and implementational levels that belong together as both look *inside* the computing system to the operations that enable it to compute a function. The algorithmic level (much like the implementation level) is directed to the *inner working* of the system, i.e. to causal relations between sub-components. In contrast, the computational level looks *outside*, to identifying the computed function and to relating it to the environment in which the system operates (Shagrir and Bechtel, 2017).

Frances Egan (1995; 2010; 2017) argues that CL provides a mathematical specification of the input–output mathematical function that the system computes (then the algorithmic level specifies the algorithm by means of which the system computes this function, and the implementation level specifies how this algorithm is implemented in the brain): "The top level should be understood to provide a function-theoretic characterization", and "the theory of computation is a mathematical characterization of the function(s) computed" (Egan, 1995, p. 185). Thus, for example, the computational theory of early vision provides the mathematical formula $\nabla^2 G * I$ as the computational description of what the retina does.[9] This, according to Egan, is an explanatory formal theory.[10] It is not, however, a representational theory:

> *Qua* computational device, it does not matter that input values represent *light intensities* and output values the rate of change of *light intensity*. The computational theory characterizes the visual filter as a member of a well understood class of mathematical devices that have nothing essentially to do with the transduction of light.
>
> *(Egan, 2010, p. 255)*

The cognitive, intentional, characterization is what Egan terms a *gloss* on the mathematical characterization provided by the computational theory; but it is not part of the theory.

Egan nicely captures the way Marr characterizes the *what* aspect of CL. The job of this element is to provide a precise specification of *what* the system does, and the precise specification of what the retina does is provided by the formula $\nabla^2 G * I$. However, Egan downplays the fact that there is another component to CL, namely, the *why* aspect. So it seems that Marr thinks that CL has to cover another aspect, beyond providing mathematical characterizations.

A more recent interpretation emphasizes the role of the environment in Marr's notion of computational analysis (Shagrir, 2010; Bechtel and Shagrir, 2015; Shagrir and Bechtel, 2017). According to this interpretation, the aim of the *what* element is to characterize the computed (typically input–output) function in precise mathematical terms. The aim of the *why* is to demonstrate why the computed function is pertinent to the visual task. Thus to take the theory of edge-detection, the *what* element characterizes the operations of early visual processes as computing the zero-crossings of (Laplacian) second derivative filterization of the retinal images. The aim of the *why* is to say why the visual system computes derivation, and not (say) factorization or exponentiation, for the task of edge-detection. Saying that the computed function leads to representations of edges just reiterates the *why* question. After all, computing derivation in very different environments – where sharp changes in illumination conditions occur very frequently or along the solid faces of surfaces – would not lead to representations of edges. So why is derivation pertinent to edge-detection in our visual environment?

Marr associates the *why* aspect with what he calls *physical constraints*, which are physical facts and features in the physical *environment* of the perceiving individual (1982, pp. 22–23). These are constraints in the sense that they limit the range of functions that the system could compute to perform a given visual task successfully. In the case of edge-detection one relevant constraint is that sharp changes in reflection (e.g. illumination conditions) often occur along physical edges such as object boundaries. Thus by detecting the zero-crossings of the second-derivative operators the visual system captures the sharp changes in light reflection in the visual field (whereas the latter changes can be described in terms of extreme points of first-derivatives or zero-crossings of second derivatives of the reflection function). The claim, more generally, is that a computational analysis appeals to the physical constraints in order to underscore some structural similarities (or morphism) between the visual systems and the visual field, and these, in turn, serve to demonstrate the appropriateness and adequacy of the computed function to the information-processing task.

To sum up, Marr's notion of CL has provoked a variety of interpretations which reflect, to a large extent, the views of the interpreters about the nature of computational explanations and levels in cognitive science. Often, these interpretations assimilate the computational level with the algorithmic (e.g. Ramsey and Shapiro) and even with the implementation (e.g. the mechanistic view) level. We take these views to miss an important aspect of CL, namely, how the computation reflects the environment. Nonetheless, these views have their own merits. In the next two sections we will discuss two of these views (the functional and the mechanistic) in more detail.

2 Computational explanation as functional analysis

An influential position in philosophy of cognitive science, advocated mostly at the end of the twentieth century, is that cognitive capacities are explained by appeal to (simpler) cognitive functions and their interaction (Fodor, 1968; Haugeland, 1978; Cummins, 1983; 2000).

For example, the "capacity to multiply 27 times 32 analyzes into the capacity to multiply 2 times 7, to add 5 and 1, and so on" (Cummins, 2000, p. 126). According to this position there are two levels at which a system can be described: the functional level and the physical level. The functional level, addressed in psychological research, describes properties and activities as having a functional-teleological role; often the states and activities are presumed to have some intentionality, e.g. activities are described as computations, information-processing tasks, and semantic tasks. The physical level, addressed in neuroscience, describes physical structures and properties, without a functional interpretation. On this view, computational explanations, that describe computing functions, are functional analyses that reside at the functional level because they analyze the capacity and not the realizing system. As Cummins writes: "Turing machine capacities analyze into other Turing machine capacities. Since we do this sort of analysis without reference to a realizing system, the analysis is evidently not an analysis of a realizing system but of the capacity itself" (2000, p. 125).

The functional and structural levels are levels of description, where the same system is described from different viewpoints. The functional and structural descriptions are taken to be autonomous and distinct from one another and it is usually stated that both are required for a complete explanation of the phenomenon (Fodor, 1968; Cummins, 1983). This position is radically different from the, then very popular, philosophical view advocated by Oppenheim and Putnam (1958); Oppenheim and Putnam argued that as science advances we expect types and theories in all scientific fields to be reduced to types and theories in physics. Therefore, phenomena that are explained today by theories that are outside the field of physics will someday be explained by a theory in physics. In contrast, proponents of the functional analysis view rely on the unique intentional features of cognition to suggest that science will and should remain divided to (at least) two levels that use different, unique explanations: the functional and structural levels.

In support of the claim that functional analysis is distinct from structural description, it is common to invoke Leibniz's gap. One argues that even if we had all the information about brain processes, specified in neurological terms, we still could not deduce from it which functions are computed at the functional level. Also, when functionally analyzing a capacity, it is explained by decomposing it to simpler functions. To give an example of a computational explanation, choosing the next move in a chess game can be decomposed into simpler computations such as: computing the value of each state of the board, computing the probability of the board being in each state several moves from now, etc. These computations in turn are explained by decomposing them into simpler functions. But no matter how simple, the explaining activities are always also described functionally. In order to explain a function in structural rather than functional terms a different, non-functional, explanation is required (Haugeland, 1978; Cummins, 2000). Thus, although there are part–whole relations in functional analysis, according to this view these parts and wholes remain at the same, functional, level and what differentiates the levels is the type of description (functional vs structural). In this, this view follows Pylyshyn (1984; 1989), who presents a framework where different levels of description differ according to the aspects of the system they describe, and differs from Churchland and Sejnowski (1992), who describe levels of organization where the levels stand in part–whole relations.

In support of the claim that the functional level is autonomous from the structural level, it is common to invoke multiple realization. Several people have argued, against the reductionist view (Oppenheim and Putnam, 1958), that it is extremely improbable that a specific type of mental state could be realized only by a single physical type. It is much more likely that mental properties have multiple possible physical realizations and therefore cannot be reduced to a single physical type (Putnam, 1980; Fodor, 1974). In a similar vein, it is indicated that functions and computations are often actually realized in different physical media. For example, both an eighth-grade student and an electronic calculator can subtract numbers, but the physical systems realizing the computation are different. One might conclude that "functional analysis puts very indirect constraints on componential analysis" (Cummins, 1983, p. 29; 2000, p. 126) and the practice of functional analysis of the mental can continue without paying much attention to the underlying neurology. On this framework science is bifurcated into the investigation of the functional and the investigation of the physical, where each can continue separately.

While this picture is similar to Marr's framework in that the levels are levels of description, with computational descriptions at the top level, this view interprets computational explanations as explanations that decompose functions into other functions and it does not address Marr's emphasis on explaining *what* and *why* at the CL. As stated in Section 1, computational explanations as functional analyses are akin to Marr's algorithmic level. Moreover, Marr presented an integrative framework for explanation, whereas this view emphasizes the autonomy and distinctness of explanations at the functional and structural levels.

This disunity of science has been criticized by Lycan (1987, ch. 4). Lycan argues that functional and structural phenomena are not divided into two levels. According to Lycan, there are multiple levels, so that upper-level types are composed of lower-level types and explained by them. Functional descriptions become more structural as we descend down the levels. He illustrates this by referring to a possible functional analysis of a *face recognizer* (1987, pp. 43–44). According to this example, one sub-function that composes the *face recognizer* is an *analyzer*, which takes the visual picture as input and returns a binary vector computed from the picture. This *analyzer*, in turn, consists of a *projector*, that projects a grid on the picture and a *scanner* that runs through the squares and returns "1" or "0" for each square. One of the sub-functions that compose the *scanner* is a *light meter* that registers the degree of lightness in a square, which in turn is composed of *photosensitive chemicals*, and so forth. Lycan asks:

> Now at what point in this descent through the institutional hierarchy (from *recognizer* to *scanner* to *light meter* to *photosensitive substance* ...) does our characterization stop being teleological, period, and start being purely mechanical, period? I think it is clear there is no such point.
>
> *(1987, p. 44)*

Under this framework, a functional analysis of a capacity takes us one step closer to a structural description.

More recently, Piccinini and Craver (2011) have taken a stance similar to Lycan and argued that functional analyses are elliptical mechanistic explanations. Similar to functional analyses, mechanistic explanations (see also Section 3) explain phenomena by appealing to components and their interaction. Unlike functional analyses, they include details about the structure of the components. Piccinini and Craver argue that functional analyses should include structural information as well because, regardless of whether the functional is multiply realized in the structural, the functional directly constrains the structural and vice versa. As an illustration they write: "stirring (a sub-capacity needed in cooking) is the manifestation of (parts of) the cook's locomotive system coupled with an appropriate stirring tool as they are driven by a specific motor program" (2011, p. 293). The functional, in this case stirring, constrains the structural, in this case an appropriate stirring tool. "If the cook lacks a stirring tool but still manages to combine ingredients thoroughly, we should expect that the mixture has been achieved by other means, such as shaking" (2011, p. 293). Therefore, to know whether a functional analysis is indeed a true explanation of a capacity we must know at least that the postulated functions can take place in the structure of the brain. (This is also pointed out by proponents of functional analysis, see Cummins 2000; Fodor 1968.)

Both Lycan (1987) and Piccinini and Craver (2011) contest the claim that there are two autonomous levels of description and instead suggest a picture where levels are levels of organization (recall Churchland and Sejnowski, 1992) that stand in part–whole relations. On this picture both functional and structural descriptions persist throughout the levels in varying degrees.

The debate about the autonomy of functional analyses is still ongoing. Shapiro (2016) disputes Piccinini and Craver's claims and argues for the autonomy of functional descriptions from structural descriptions. He points out that practically every explanation is constrained to some extent by physical details and that this should not be sufficient to threaten the autonomy of a functional explanation. He argues that while details about implementation are useful in supporting theories, they are not the only kind of evidence used to this effect; behavioral experiments are frequently used. Therefore, explanations in psychology can be shown to describe the actual causal structure without appeal to implementation details (see also Weiskopf, 2011). Moreover, even when implementation details are used to support a theory, their confirmatory role does not make them part of the explanation itself, which may be completely functional.

This being said, scientific practice today clearly favors an integrated approach, as demonstrated in cognitive neuroscience. Today, a wide variety of methods allows scientists to investigate neural activity in various time and space scales; such methods include single-unit and multi-unit electrophysiology, calcium imaging, fMRI, gene-expression profiling, and more. Other methods such as optogenetics and gene trapping allow scientists to intervene on the activity of specific neurons and genes and observe the behavioral results. It is not surprising to see that many publications today relate cognitive phenomena with neural activity, sometimes at the level of gene transcription or spine growth. To name just a few examples, inhibition of dorsal subiculum neurons during recall has been shown to impair long-term memory in certain tasks (Roy et al., 2017); "grid cells" that fire when the animal is in specific locations in a grid-like manner were identified in the entorhinal cortex (Fyhn et al., 2004); and a large family of at least one hundred genes (today estimates are at 1,000) has been found to encode proteins that are odor receptors, responsible for odor recognition (Buck and Axel, 1991).

Furthermore, as knowledge about brain structures expands, it is becoming more and more common to base computational models on known anatomical structures in the brain. One such example is a "covariance based plasticity" learning algorithm, where learning is mediated through plasticity in the synapses of a network model (Loewenstein and Seung, 2006). Another famous example is deep-learning networks, which have been inspired by the hierarchical nature of the visual cortex. Often, activity in simulated neurons in these networks is compared with activity in visual brain areas (Lee, Ekanadham, and Ng, 2007).

Much is still unknown about the complex relation between structure and function in the brain and those who point at possible ways to integrate the structural and functional do so with caution. Nonetheless, it is clear that today the study of the functional is not moving forward independently from the structural. On the contrary, much scientific effort today is dedicated to the investigation of their relation. This calls for a framework that integrates computational-functional properties and structural properties (Boone and Piccinini, 2016b). Such a view will be presented in the next section.

3 The mechanistic approach to computation

The mechanistic approach to explanation in the cognitive and neural sciences has been widely advocated in recent years (Bechtel and Richardson, 1993; Machamer, Darden, and Craver, 2000; Glennan, 2002; Craver, 2007; Kaplan, 2011; Piccinini and Craver, 2011; Miłkowski, 2013; Boone and Piccinini, 2016b). According to this approach, many explanations in neuroscience and cognitive sciences are mechanistic. As a general formulation we can say that "Mechanisms are entities and activities organized such that they are productive of regular changes from start or set-up to finish or termination conditions" (Machamer, Darden, and Craver, 2000, p. 3). Mechanistic models explain phenomena by describing their underlying mechanism. For example, release of neurotransmitter when the axon is depolarized is explained by a detailed description of a process that begins with depolarization of the axon that causes opening of calcium channels, and is terminated when fusing of neurotransmitter vesicles to the cell membrane causes neurotransmitter to be released (see Piccinini and Craver, 2011, for more detail). Mechanistic explanations are hierarchical; each explanatory capacity can itself be explained mechanistically (Figure 15.2). Here, the levels stand in part–whole relations. Computational and structural descriptions can exist in the same level and are both part of the same mechanistic explanation.

The argument that computational explanations are mechanistic is similar to the one presented in Section 2 for functional analyses; a model has not been shown to be an explanation until it has been shown to describe the actual causal structure (Kaplan, 2011; Kaplan and Craver, 2011; Piccinini and Craver, 2011; Miłkowski, 2013; Boone and Piccinini, 2016b).[11] Once a model describes the actual causal structure that underlies a phenomenon it is a *mechanistic model*. Consequently, computational models either do not describe causal relations among components

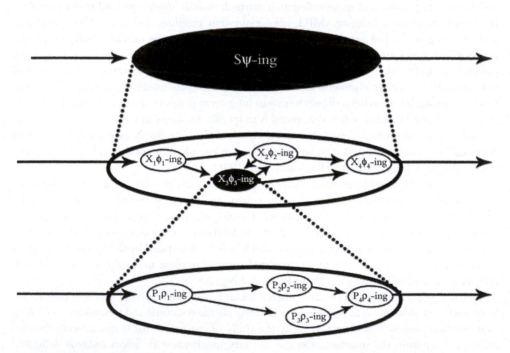

Figure 15.2 An example of a hierarchy of mechanistic explanations. S is the system, Ψ is the explanandum activity, X_i and P_i are the *explanans* components and Φ_i and ρ_i are their respective activities
Source: Adapted from Craver (2007)

and are therefore not explanatory, or they do and are therefore mechanistic. In this regard, structural information about the implementing system is taken to be necessary to confirm that a model is an explanation. Similar arguments are made for the claim that Marr's computational level is an incomplete mechanistic explanation – a mechanistic sketch (Kaplan, 2011; Piccinini and Craver, 2011; Piccinini, 2015; Boone and Piccinini, 2016b).

The mechanistic approach allows us to consider the unity of science independently from questions about multiple realization. There is only one way to explain – by describing causal structures – but higher levels need not be reducible to lower levels in the way envisioned by Oppenheim and Putnam (1958), which implies that all phenomena are explicable at the lowest level. Instead, phenomena at all levels are explained mechanistically and the hierarchy of mechanistic explanations connects phenomena from different levels. Furthermore, because details about implementation are required to turn a computational model into an explanation, computational explanations cannot be taken to be autonomous from implementation, even if they are multiply realized in different implementations. By this, the mechanists answer, in a novel way, some of the challenges to the unity of science posed by the functional analysis view (Craver, 2007, ch.7; but see a criticism of this framework in Levy, 2016).

However, the mechanistic approach received many criticisms which can be divided into two main objections. The first is that computational explanations are not mechanistic and therefore an integrated-leveled framework of mechanistic explanation is incorrect. The second is that it is still unclear from the mechanists' arguments how any framework can integrate computation into mechanisms while still maintaining the explanatory value of computational description.

3.1 Arguments for the non-mechanistic nature of computational explanations

The argument that computational explanations are not mechanistic usually follows one of three lines of objection. One line of objection is that at least part of computational theory in cognitive neuroscience addresses certain why-questions whose answers do not track causal relations in the mechanistic sense. According to the mechanists, mechanistic explanations are causal explanations in that they track the causal structure that is relevant to the explanandum phenomenon. Some argue, however, that computational explanations (models) do not necessarily refer to causal relations in answering these why-questions.

Chirimuuta (2014), for example, argues that some computational models ("interpretative models") address "the question of why nervous systems operate as they do" (Dayan and Abbott, 2001), and involve explanations which typically make reference to efficient coding principles, and not to causes. Her main example is the normalization equation that models the cross-orientation suppression of simple cell response in the primary visual cortex and in other systems. As it turned out, the response of cells in V1 is significantly reduced ("suppressed") if the preferred stimuli are super-imposed by other stimuli with different, non-preferred, orientation. Heeger (1992) accounts for the phenomenon with a normalization model that states that in addition to the excitatory input from LGN, each V1 cell also receives inhibitory inputs from its neighboring V1 cells (that are sensitive to lines in different angles). This normalization equation – which quantitatively describes the cells' responses – is later found to describe other parts of the nervous system (Carandini and Heeger, 2012). This, Chirimuuta says, raises the following question: "Why should so many systems exhibit behavior described by normalization equation?" The answer, she continues, is non-causal, but refers to principles of information theory: "For many instances of neural processing individual neurons are able to transmit more information if their firing rate is suppressed by the population average firing rate" (2014, p. 143).[12]

A second argument that computational explanations are not mechanistic is that they are not necessarily decompositional. There are network (computational) models that do not decompose the explanandum capacities into sub-components and their organization. Rathkopf (2015) argues that mechanistic explanations apply to nearly decomposable systems (Simon, 1962) where nodes in each module have more and perhaps stronger connections with each other than with nodes outside the module. Many network models, however, provide non-decompositional explanations for non-decomposable systems, where part–whole decomposition is not possible. For example, a network model that accounts for patterns of traffic in a road network explains the amount of traffic in each road by appealing to dependence relations that span over the entire network. Thus explaining why a certain road connecting two edges has lighter traffic depends on the structure and organization of the entire network; it cannot be explained by decomposing the network into separate components and their organization. Similar network-dependent properties may be identified in neural networks. Related points are made by Weiskopf (2011), who points out the existence of noncomponential models in cognitive science and by Huneman (2010) who argues that in some cases the explanation does not appeal to causal structure, but to the topological or network properties of the system.[13]

A third argument is related to abstraction. According to the mechanistic framework, explanations must be situated in an actual causal structure so details about how the computational model is implemented in the physical system are required to make it an explanation. This claim is a crucial part in the argument that computational explanations are mechanistic. Levy and Bechtel (2013) argued that there are cases where the relevant explanatory information abstracts away from most structural details. Many mechanists agree with this claim and maintain that abstract explanations are still directly constrained by implementation and hence not autonomous from it (Craver and Darden, 2013; Boone and Piccinini, 2016a; Craver, 2016; Kaplan, 2017). For example, many computational theories posit digital computation, and until it is shown that this is implemented in the structure of the system these theories are not substantiated (Piccinini and Bahar, 2013). As described in Section 2, Shapiro (2016) has pointed out that constraints do not necessarily prevent autonomy.

3.2 The problem of integration of the computational and the mechanistic

Even if one is not convinced by the previous arguments, one might wonder how computational explanations are integrated within the mechanistic hierarchy. One option is viewing computational explanations as sketches of mechanisms, and, as such, they are weak, partial, or elliptical explanations. According to this picture, computational explanations nicely integrate within the mechanistic framework, in that computational properties and implementational properties belong to the same level of mechanism. When adding to the computational sketches the missing structural properties we get a full-blown mechanistic explanation of a given phenomenon.

But as Haimovici (2013) points out, this picture can prove to be problematic for the mechanistic view. Often, computational explanations are taken to be a central part of explanation in cognitive and neural sciences, even by proponents of the mechanistic view (Piccinini and Bahar, 2013). If computational explanations are merely sketches, then they cannot be considered good explanations by themselves. On the other hand, if we combine structural and computational details to get a full-fledged mechanistic explanation, the resulting explanation is no longer medium-independent (i.e. multiply realizable in different media), which is a feature that is commonly required from computation (Piccinini and Bahar, 2013; Piccinini, 2015).

The other option is that computational explanations are medium-independent, yet can be full-blown mechanistic explanations. They are full-blown to the extent that they refer to relevant medium-independent properties (Piccinini, 2015). But this option immediately raises two other issues. One is that computational explanations are distinct (and perhaps autonomous). Granted that computational explanations are full-blown mechanistic ones; they are nevertheless distinct from implementational mechanistic explanations. Computational explanations refer to medium-independent properties, whereas implementational explanations are about medium-dependent, implementational, properties. In other words, we can reformulate the distinctness thesis around the medium-independent/medium-dependent distinction instead of the dismissed functional/structural distinction. One might argue that the medium-independent/medium-dependent distinction suffices to support the thesis that computational explanations are distinct (and arguably autonomous) from the implementational level.

The other issue is that the relation between computational and implementational properties is often not a part–whole relationship. Piccinini proposes that:

> Computing systems, such as calculators and computers, consist of component parts (processors, memory units, input devices, and output devices), their function and organization. Those components also consist of component parts (e.g., registers and circuits), their function, and their organization. Those, in turn, consist of primitive computing components (paradigmatically, logic gates), their functions, and their organization. Primitive computing components can be further analyzed mechanistically but not computationally.
>
> *(Piccinini, 2015, pp. 118–119)*

But, given that under the mechanistic framework explanation is decomposition into parts, one can wonder how "primitive computing components can be further analyzed mechanistically but not computationally". The logic gate is implemented as a whole by some physical, electrical, circuit. Its inputs and outputs are implemented by some physical properties, e.g. voltages. This physical circuit, including the input and output voltages, can be further analyzed mechanistically but not computationally. However, the implementation relation itself is not a part–whole relation, hence not a mechanistic analysis or explanation. For example, the physical voltages that implement the input and output channels of the gates – typically characterized by digits, 1s and 0s – are not parts of the digits. So one can provide a mechanistic explanation of the implementing voltages, but it is not clear what is the mechanistic explanation of the primitive computing components such as the implemented digits.

Furthermore, even if the logic-gate/voltage relation were a mechanistic, part–whole, relation, it is still left unclear how a higher-level computational level is analyzed mechanistically both by underlying computational and implementational levels. Take the computational level that consists of "component parts (e.g. registers and circuits), their function, and their organization". Let us call it C_1. The components of C_1 can be further analyzed, computationally, by the computational components of an underlying computational-level C_0, which "consist of primitive computing components (paradigmatically, logic gates), their functions, and their organization". However, the computational components of C_1 (e.g. registers and circuits) are also realized in some implementational, medium-dependent, physical properties that belong to another mechanistic level, P. But how are P and C_0 related in the mechanistic hierarchy? P and C_0 must be different because the first describes physical implementation details and the latter, medium-independent properties. It is also not possible for one description to be at a lower level than the other. The properties of C_0 are certainly not parts of the properties of P and vice versa. It seems that we have here two different hierarchies, one computational, C_0, C_1, C_2, ..., and one implementational, P_0, P_1, P_2, ... (presumably there are further implementational levels below P_0). But it is left unclear how the two are related to each other.

Furthermore, under the possibility that computations can be multiply realized in different physical structures, the mechanist is faced with a bigger problem – not just one computational hierarchy and one mechanistic hierarchy, but many mechanistic hierarchies. The mechanist has to show how each of these can be fitted within a single computational hierarchy.

The result of the issues raised here is surprisingly similar to the framework presented in Section 2. There are two distinct explanatory hierarchies for the same system: one functional and the other structural; they do not seem to integrate. While mechanists attempt to offer an alternative to this divided view, their work is not yet complete. Those who want to argue that computational explanations are mechanistic explanations will have to address these issues.

4 Summary

This chapter focused on the relation between computation and different frameworks of levels. While the viewpoints presented here are radically different from each other, they can all be seen as positions in a debate about a central philosophical question: are computational and functional explanations distinct from neuroscientific and mechanistic explanations, or do they belong to the same kind of explanation even though they might sometimes occur at different levels? There are those who have rejected the possibility that computational explanations are inherently different from neuroscientific explanations. They favor a framework where cognitive phenomena are described in levels of part–whole relations, specifically of mechanisms, where phenomena at different levels are all explained similarly. This view allows for the same kind of explanation to persist throughout the cognitive system, at the expense of the unique explanatory power of computational explanations. The main criticism of this view is that it has not yet been shown how computational and implementational descriptions can yield a single unified explanation in a way that does not diminish the central role computation has in the explanation of cognitive and neural phenomena.

Those who believe that functional and computational descriptions are distinct from physical descriptions must adopt a view with two levels of description, as proponents of the functional analysis view do. In contrast to the previously described view, these folks emphasize what is different between the computational and physical, and endow computational explanations with irreplaceable explanatory power and autonomy from physical descriptions. This comes at the expense of the unity of explanation in science. Moreover, current experimental practice clearly favors an integrated approach, where physical and computational properties are commonly integrated. Marr adopts a softer stance, according to which computational explanations have a distinct explanatory role, but only when they are integrated with the algorithmic and implementation explanations is the explanation complete. His approach has received many interpretations that are consistent with both the views presented above. According to the interpretation of CL favored by us, Marr's view emphasizes the relation between the cognitive system and the environment in explanation, a relation that is often overlooked.

The questions at the heart of this debate concern fundamental issues in the philosophy of cognitive science about the relation between the computational and the physical. Surely, the ongoing debate on the correct leveled framework for computation will serve as an instructive case for the philosophy of science in general.

Acknowledgments

We thank Jens Harbecke, Arnon Levy, Gualtiero Piccinini, Mark Sprevak, and Matteo Colombo for helpful comments. This research was supported by a grant from the GIF, the German-Israeli Foundation for Scientific Research and Development.

Notes

1   See Craver (2007, ch. 5) for a review.
2   The term knowledge level arrives from Newell (1982) who also terms the second level "symbolic".
3   In the earlier writings, Pylyshyn (1984) talks about cognitive science, but later on, perhaps with the rise of the rival connectionist approach, he confines the proposed tri-level framework to the classical view (1989, p. 57).
4   This tri-level picture bears similarities to Dennett's tri-stance picture (Dennett, 1971), which offers to account for the behavior of complex systems. The semantic level parallels in some respects the intentional stance. The design stance has some affinities with the functional aspects of Pylyshyn's symbolic level, and the physical stance is similar to the physical level.
5   As can also be seen in Section 2, the "computational levels" are often contrasted with the physical levels, where the computational levels are identified with functional and semantic levels (Block, 1995), and sometime exclusively with a syntactic level (Fodor, 1994, pp. 7–16).
6   Some take levels of organization to be levels of nature that describe leveled objects in the world, while levels of description are levels of science that describe the relations between scientific theories or models (Craver, 2007, ch. 5). We do not discuss this distinction in this chapter.
7   See Shagrir and Bechtel (2017) for a detailed discussion of these interpretations.
8   No wonder that these interpreters have commented that "Marr, very confusingly, calls it [the top level] the 'computational' level" (Sterelny, 1990, p. 46). Dennett (1994, p. 681) and Ramsey (2007, p. 41, note 43).
9   The term I stands for a two-dimensional array ("the retinal image") of intensity values detected by the photoreceptors (which is the input). This image is convoluted (here signified by '$\star$') through a filter $\nabla^2 G$, where G is a Gaussian and ∇^2 is a second-derivative (Laplacian) operator. This operation is arguably performed in the retinal ganglion cells.
10   A similar viewpoint is expressed by van Rooij (2008). An important variant of this view associates the computational level with an idealized *competence* and the algorithmic and implementation levels with actual performance (Horgan and Tienson, 1994; Frixione, 2001; Polger, 2004; Rusanen and Lappi, 2007).
11   The commitment to an "actual causal structure" can be interpreted either ontologically or epistemically. Often, proponents of the mechanistic view maintain that explanations make ontic commitments about the causal structures in the world (Craver, 2014). Weiskopf (2011) argued that the distinction between possible models and actual explanations is epistemic and determined by the degree to which the model accommodates available evidence. This line of thought is continued in (Colombo, Hartmann, and Van Iersel, 2015), who suggest an antirealist version of mechanistic explanation, in which coherence with existing scientific theories plays a large role in supporting mechanistic models.
12   This aligns with Bechtel and Shagrir's suggestion that Marr's computational theories aim to answer certain why-questions about the relation of the computed function and the physical world, and that answering these questions does not involve causal structure. See also Rusanen and Lappi (2016) who argue that Marr's computational theories track non-causal, formal, and abstract dependence relations.
13   In response, mechanists have argued that these network models turn out to be explanatory only when they describe causal structures and therefore should still be considered mechanistic (Craver, 2016).

References

Bechtel, W. (1994) 'Levels of Description and Explanation in Cognitive Science', *Minds and Machines*, 4, pp. 1–25.
Bechtel, W. and Richardson, R.C. (1993) *Discovering Complexity: Decomposition and Localization as Strategies in Scientific Research*. Princeton, NJ: Princeton University Press.

Bechtel, W. and Shagrir, O. (2015) 'The Non-Redundant Contributions of Marr's Three Levels of Analysis for Explaining Information-Processing Mechanisms', *Topics in Cognitive Science*, 7, pp. 312–322.

Bermúdez, J.L. (2005) *Philosophy of Psychology: A Contemporary Introduction*. Abingdon, UK: Routledge.

Block, N. (1995) 'The Mind as the Software of the Brain', in Osherson, D.N. et al. (eds.) *An Invitation to Cognitive Science*. Cambridge, MA: MIT Press, pp. 170–185.

Boone, W. and Piccinini, G. (2016a) 'Mechanistic Abstraction', *Philosophy of Science*, 83, pp. 686–697.

Boone, W. and Piccinini, G. (2016b) 'The Cognitive Neuroscience Revolution', *Synthese*, 193, pp. 1509–1534.

Buck, L. and Axel, R. (1991) 'A Novel Multigene Family May Encode Odorant Receptors: A Molecular Basis for Odor Recognition', *Cell*, 65, pp. 175–187.

Carandini, M. and Heeger, D.J. (2012) 'Normalization as a Canonical Neural Computation', *Nature Reviews Neuroscience*, 13, pp. 51–62.

Chalmers, D.J. (2011) 'A Computational Foundation for the Study of Cognition', *Journal of Cognitive Science*, 12, pp. 323–357.

Chirimuuta, M. (2014) 'Minimal Models and Canonical Neural Computations: The Distinctness of Computational Explanation in Neuroscience', *Synthese*, 191, pp. 127–153.

Churchland, P.S. and Sejnowski, T.J. (1988) 'Perspectives on Cognitive Neuroscience', *Science*, 242, pp. 741–745.

Churchland, P.S. and Sejnowski, T.J. (1992) *The Computational Brain*. Cambridge, MA: MIT Press.

Colombo, M., Hartmann, S., and van Iersel, R. (2015) 'Models, Mechanisms, and Coherence', *British Journal for the Philosophy of Science*, 66, pp. 181–212.

Copeland, J. (1996) 'What Is Computation?', *Synthese*, 108, pp. 335–359.

Craver, C.F. (2007) *Explaining the Brain*. Oxford: Oxford University Press.

Craver, C.F. (2014) 'The Ontic Account of Scientific Explanation', in Kaiser, M.I. et al. (eds.) *Explanation in the Special Sciences: The Case of Biology and History*. Berlin: Springer Verlag, pp. 27–52.

Craver, C.F. (2016) 'The Explanatory Power of Network Models', *Philosophy of Science*, 83, pp. 698–709.

Craver, C.F. and Darden, L. (2013) *In Search of Mechanisms: Discoveries across the Life Sciences*. Chicago, IL: University of Chicago Press.

Cummins, R. (1983) *The Nature of Psychological Explanation*. Cambridge, MA: MIT Press.

Cummins, R. (2000) '"How Does It Work?" vs. "What Are the Laws?" Two Conceptions of Psychological Explanation', in Keil, F. and Wilson, R.A. (eds.) *Explanation and Cognition*. Cambridge, MA: MIT Press, pp. 117–145.

Dayan, P. and Abbott, L.F. (2001) *Theoretical Neuroscience: Computational and Mathematical Modeling of Neural Systems*. Cambridge, MA: MIT Press.

Dennett, D.C. (1971) 'Intentional Systems', *Journal of Philosophy*, 68, pp. 87–106.

Dennett, D.C. (1994) 'Cognitive Science as Reverse Engineering: Several Meanings of "Top-Down" and "Bottom-Up"', in Prawitz, D., Skyrms, B., and Westerstahl, D. (eds.) *Logic, Methodology and Philosophy of Science IX*. Amsterdam: Elsevier Science, pp. 679–689.

Egan, F. (1995) 'Computation and Content', *Philosophical Review*, 104, pp. 181–203.

Egan, F. (2010) 'Computational Models: A Modest Role for Content', *Studies in History and Philosophy of Science*, 41, pp. 253–259.

Egan, F. (2017) 'Function-Theoretic Explanation and Neural Mechanisms', in Kaplan, D.M. (ed.) *Explanation and Integration in Mind and Brain Science*. Oxford: Oxford University Press, pp. 145–163.

Fodor, J. (1968) *Psychological Explanation: An Introduction to the Philosophy of Psychology*. New York, NY: Random House.

Fodor, J. (1974) 'Special Sciences (Or: The Disunity of Science as a Working Hypothesis)', *Synthese*, 28, pp. 97–115.

Fodor, J. (1994) *The Elm and the Expert*. Cambridge, MA: MIT Press.

Fresco, N. (2014) *Physical Computation and Cognitive Science*. New York, NY: Springer.

Frixione, M. (2001) 'Tractable Competence', *Minds and Machines*, 11, pp. 379–397.

Fyhn, M. Molden, S., Witter, M.P., Moser, E.I., and Moser, M. (2004) 'Spatial Representation in the Entorhinal Cortex', *Science*, 305, pp. 1258–1264.

Glennan, S. (2002) 'Rethinking Mechanistic Explanation', *Philosophy of Science*, 69, pp. S342–S353.

Haimovici, S. (2013) 'A Problem for the Mechanistic Account of Computation', *Journal of Cognitive Science*, 14, pp. 151–181.

Haugeland, J. (1978) 'The Nature and Plausibility of Cognitivism', *Behavioral and Brain Sciences*, 1, pp. 215–226.

Heeger, D.J. (1992) 'Normalization of Cell Responses in the Cat Striate Cortex', *Visual Neuroscience*, 9, pp. 181–197.

Horgan, T. and Tienson, J. (1994) 'A Nonclassical Framework for Cognitive Science', *Synthese*, 101, pp. 305–345.

Huneman, P. (2010) 'Topological Explanations and Robustness in Biological Sciences', *Synthese*, 177, pp. 213–245.

Kaplan, D.M. (2011) 'Explanation and Description in Computational Neuroscience', *Synthese*, 183, pp. 339–373.

Kaplan, D.M. (2017) 'Neural Computation, Multiple Realizability, and the Prospects for Mechanistic Explanation', in Kaplan, D.M. (ed.) *Explanation and Integration in Mind and Brain Science*. Oxford: Oxford University Press, pp. 164–189.

Kaplan, D.M. and Craver, C.F. (2011) 'The Explanatory Force of Dynamical and Mathematical Models in Neuroscience : A Mechanistic Perspective', *Philosophy of Science*, 78, pp. 601–627.

Lee, H., Ekanadham, C., and Ng, A.Y. (2007) 'Sparse Deep Belief Net Model for Visual Area V2', *Advances in Neural Information Processing Systems*, 20, pp. 873–880.

Levy, A. (2016) 'The Unity of Neuroscience: A Flat View', *Synthese*, 193, pp. 3843–3863.

Levy, A. and Bechtel, W. (2013) 'Abstraction and the Organization of Mechanisms', *Philosophy of Science*, 80, pp. 241–261.

Loewenstein, Y. and Seung, H.S. (2006) 'Operant Matching Is a Generic Outcome of Synaptic Plasticity Based on the Covariance between Reward and Neural Activity', *PNAS*, 103, pp. 15224–15229.

Lycan, W. (1987) *Consciousness*. Cambridge, MA: MIT Press.

Machamer, P., Darden, L., and Craver, C.F. (2000) 'Thinking about Mechanisms', *Philosophy of Science*, 67, pp. 1–25.

Marr, D. (1982) *Vision: A Computational Investigation into the Human Representation and Processing of Visual Information*. Cambridge, MA: MIT Press.

Miłkowski, M. (2013) *Explaining the Computational Mind*. Cambridge, MA: MIT Press.

Newell, A. (1980) 'Physical Symbol Systems', *Cognitive Science*, 4, pp. 135–183.

Newell, A. (1982) 'The Knowledge Level', *Artificial Intelligence*, 18, pp. 87–127.

Oppenheim, P. and Putnam, H. (1958) 'Unity of Science as a Working Hypothesis', in Feigl, H., Scriven, M., and Maxwell, G. (eds.) *Minnesota Studies in the Philosophy of Science*, vol. 2. Minneapolis, MN: Minnesota University Press.

Piccinini, G. (2007) 'Computing Mechanisms', *Philosophy of Science*, 74, pp. 501–526.

Piccinini, G. (2015) *Physical Computation: A Mechanistic Account*. Oxford: Oxford University Press.

Piccinini, G. and Bahar, S. (2013) 'Neural Computation and the Computational Theory of Cognition', *Cognitive Science*, 34, pp. 453–488.

Piccinini, G. and Craver, C.F. (2011) 'Integrating Psychology and Neuroscience: Functional Analyses as Mechanism Sketches', *Synthese*, 183, pp. 283–311.

Polger, T. (2004) *Natural Minds*. Cambridge, MA: MIT Press.

Putnam, H. (1980) 'The Nature of Mental States', in Block, N. (ed.) *Readings in Philosophy of Psychology*, 1, pp. 223–231.

Pylyshyn, Z.W. (1980) 'Computation and Cognition: Issues in the Foundation of Cognitive Science', *Behavioral and Brain Sciences*, 3, pp. 111–132.

Pylyshyn, Z.W. (1984) *Computation and Cognition*. Cambridge, MA: MIT Press.

Pylyshyn, Z.W. (1989) 'Computing in Cognitive Science', in Posner, M.I. (ed.) *Foundations of Cognitive Science*. Cambridge, MA: MIT Press, pp. 49–92.

Ramsey, W. (2007) *Representation Reconsidered*. Cambridge, UK: Cambridge University Press.

Rathkopf, C. (2015) 'Network Representation and Complex Systems', *Synthese*, 195, pp. 1–24.

Roy, D.S. et al. (2017) 'Distinct Neural Circuits for the Formation and Retrieval of Episodic Memories', *Cell*, 170, pp. 1000–1012.

Rusanen, A. and Lappi, O. (2007) 'The Limits of Mechanistic Explanation in Neurocognitive Sciences', *Proceedings of the European Cognitive Science Conference*. London: Francis and Taylor.

Rusanen, A. and Lappi, O. (2016) 'On Computational Explanations', *Synthese*, 193, pp. 3931–3949.

Shagrir, O. (2006) 'Why We View the Brain as a Computer', *Synthese*, 153, pp. 393–416.

Shagrir, O. (2010) 'Marr on Computational-Level Theories', *Philosophy of Science*, 77, pp. 477–500.

Shagrir, O. and Bechtel, W. (2017) 'Marr's Computational Level and Delineating Phenomena', in Kaplan, D.M. (ed.) *Explanation and Integration in Mind and Brain Science*. Oxford: Oxford University Press, pp. 190–214.

Shapiro, L.A. (1997) 'A Clearer Vision', *Philosophy of Science*, 64, pp. 131–153.

Shapiro, L.A. (2016) 'Mechanism or Bust ? Explanation in Psychology', *British Journal for the Philosophy of Science*, 68, pp. 1037–1059.

Simon, H.A. (1962) 'The Architecture of Complexity', *Proceedings of the American Philosophical Society*, 106, pp. 467–482.

Sprevak, M. (2010) 'Computation, Individuation, and the Received View on Representation', *Studies in History and Philosophy of Science Part A*, 41, pp. 260–270.

Sterelny, K. (1990) *The Representational Theory of Mind*. Oxford: Blackwell.

Stich, S.P. (1983) *From Folk Psychology to Cognitive Science: The Case against Belief*. Cambridge, MA: MIT Press.

van Rooij, I. (2008) 'The Tractable Cognition Thesis', *Cognitive Science*, 32, pp. 939–984.

Weiskopf, D.A. (2011) 'Models and Mechanisms in Psychological Explanation', *Synthese*, 183, pp. 313–338.

16

REDUCTIVE EXPLANATION BETWEEN PSYCHOLOGY AND NEUROSCIENCE

Daniel A. Weiskopf

Introduction

Reductionism is one of the most divisive concepts in the popular and philosophical lexicon. Over the past century it has been championed, declared dead, resurrected, and reformed many times over. Its protean character reflects the circumstances of its birth in the polarizing mid-twentieth-century debates over the unity of science. While the totalizing ideal of unified science has lost its luster, localized reductionist projects continue to flourish. In this chapter I sketch the goals and methods of one prominent form of reductionism within the mind-brain sciences and consider the prospects for non-reductionist alternatives.

Defining reductive explanation

First, we can distinguish *ontological* and *methodological* reductionism.[1] *Ontological reductionism* centers on the question of whether the kinds appealed to in psychology are ultimately anything "over and above" those appealed to in neuroscience. Reductionists hold that taxonomic distinctions among psychological kinds will align with those made among neuroscientific kinds, so that the way that psychology carves up its domain simply falls out of the way that neuroscience does. Ontological antireductionism maintains that psychological kinds are not necessarily visible using only the classificatory apparatus of neuroscience.

Methodological reductionism claims that the explanatory constructs of psychology are ultimately dispensable in favor of those drawn from neuroscience. Psychological explanations are only epistemic stopgaps that will, in the end, turn out to be replaceable by neuroscientific explanations. Methodological antireductionists, by contrast, champion the autonomy of psychological explanation. They hold that psychological explanations either cannot be fully dispensed with in favor of neuroscientific ones, or at least that they *need* not be.

Reductive explanation is an interfield project. A *field* centers on a set of problems, relevant facts, and phenomena that bear on their solutions, explanatory goals and norms, and distinctive experimental techniques, materials, and methods (Darden and Maull, 1977). The question is how the problems, phenomena, and explanations generated within one field can be related to those in the other, given that they may have strikingly different ontologies and explanatory frameworks (Poeppel and Embick, 2005). Answering this question requires developing specially tailored interfield theories.

Within the classic Nagelian framework, reduction was an intertheoretic relation: a theory T_1, identified with a systematic body of laws, reduces to another theory T_2 when T_1 can be logically derived from T_2, under certain background conditions. When theories are drawn from different fields or domains that each employ their own specialized vocabulary, a set of connecting ("bridge") principles linking these terms is required to allow the deduction to go through. The condition of *connectability* ensures that the ontology of the two theories can be aligned appropriately, while the condition of *derivability* shows why the laws of the reduced theory *must* hold, given the lower-level laws and these connections.

Nagel's model illustrates the constraints that have traditionally governed philosophical accounts of reduction.[2] An adequate interfield reduction should have two characteristics. First, it should preserve the ontology of the reduced field. Ontological conservatism is what separates reduction from straightforward elimination. This means that something like Nagel's connectability principle must be part of any non-eliminative reduction. Second, it should preserve (and possibly extend) the reduced field's explanatory insights. Moving to the reducing field should not involve a major loss of explanatory power or generality. Both of these are matters of degree, since pruning, revision, and parameterization of the phenomena and generalizations of both fields is standard in interfield mapping.

An interfield theory aims to show how and why the elements of the participating fields relate systematically to each other. To offer a *reductive* explanation, an interfield theory should show how the ontology and explanatory constructs of the reduced field systematically *depend* on those of the reducing field. That is, it should give a theoretically illuminating account of how the kinds posited in psychology are *realized* or *implemented* by their physical substrate. The dependence condition is crucial because interfield theories exist in many non-reductive contexts of inquiry. We can attempt to integrate two fields or two models, such as general relativity and quantum field theory, by subsuming them in a single framework without assuming that one must be reduced to the other.

What distinguishes reductionist interfield theorizing is that it is both *conservative* and *directional*: the ontology and explanatory content of one field depends on that of another, such that the existence of the higher categories, as well as the explanations that they are part of, can be accounted for solely by the existence and activities of entities within the lower field.

Finally, reductionism is associated with a set of distinctive heuristics and research strategies (Wimsatt, 2006). While these do not strictly define a reductionist project they are strongly indicative of one. They include attempting to articulate a system's microcomponents that serve as the sole causal basis for generating and explaining its macrolevel properties and behavior (a maneuver Rob Wilson (2004) dubs "smallism"), positing identities between entities and processes in the target and the reducing field (McCauley and Bechtel, 2001), and localizing higher-level functions within discrete microcomponents. Reductionist strategies tend to represent the direction of ontological priority, control, and explanation within a system as being internal and bottom-up. The more it is necessary to draw on external, higher-level, and contextually variable factors in explaining the properties of a system, the less traction these heuristics will get.

The ontology and methodology of cognitive modeling

Cognitive modeling is one of the main tools used in psychology to describe and understand the mental and behavioral capacities of humans and other organisms. A *cognitive model* includes:

1 a characterization of the *target cognitive capacity* itself: its input–output profile, the experimentally derived phenomena associated with it, its distinctive patterns of effects, its normal and abnormal developmental trajectory, and its relationships to other cognitive capacities;
2 an *ontological inventory*: a set of representational vehicles along with their distinctive properties such as format and informational content, processes that create, combine, store, retrieve, and otherwise transform and operate over them, and resources that can be used in this processing such as memory registers and attentional allocation and processing cycles;
3 an *organization* or *structure*: a specification of the way that these ontological elements are grouped into stable cognitive systems, the regularities and laws that they obey, the rules and paths of influence by which they can interact and influence one another, the control structures that dictate what operations will happen when, and the basic properties of the cognitive architecture in which they are embedded.

Often the role of cognitive modeling is not merely to inferentially bridge the gap between behavior and brain structures (Love, 2016), but to do so by describing real psychological structures. *Realism* is a causal thesis: a realistic model should describe causally active elements and operations of the cognitive system, such that the dynamics of these elements is capable of producing the input–output profile and patterns of phenomena associated with the target capacity. The posited elements should not simply be instrumental fictions, useful in generating predictions but not themselves influencing the system's behavior.[3]

Causally interpreted cognitive models make several commitments with respect to their elements. First, these elements should be the sorts of things that can be manipulated and intervened on to produce specific effects. A model can be regarded as describing part of the total cognitive state that the system can be in. The set of possible states corresponds to possible assignments of values to variables regarding the system's representations, processes, and resources. The model should accurately capture the patterns of manipulation of these state variables that are possible and the range of effects that varying each element produces. Cognitive models are maps of salient *intervention points* in a psychological system.

Second, these elements should be *robust* (Wimsatt, 1994): there should be a set of independent but converging operations (measurement procedures, experimental protocols, and the like) that can detect and track the state of the system's components. The greater the number of distinct epistemic pathways that exist to detect a component the more confidence we can have that it exists apart from our schemes of modeling and measurement.

Third, the model should successfully generate *predictions* about how the cognitive system will behave under various conditions that conform to the observed phenomena, and also generalize in a natural (non-ad hoc) way to new results. This is a basic criterion of empirical adequacy. Numerous model-fitting techniques can be applied to see whether the model is capable of capturing a dataset.

Cognitive models themselves are neutral with respect to physical or neurobiological structures.[4] The aim of integrating cognitive and neural models is twofold. With respect to a single cognitive model, showing that it can be successfully neurally integrated is thought to provide extra evidence in its favor. With respect to two or more cognitive models that are equivalent in terms of their predictive value, the ability to better integrate one model rather than the others provides some evidential advantage for it. In both scenarios, appeal to the *neural plausibility* of cognitive models provides a field-external constraint on psychological theorizing (Butler, 1994).

Mack, Preston, and Love (2013) offer a nice example of the latter use of neural data in model adjudication. Both prototype and exemplar models of categorization can capture the same range of behavioral data, which has led to a stalemate between the two views. However, latent parameters of the two models corresponding to the degree of match between a stimulus and a stored representation can be correlated with global and local patterns of fMRI-measured brain activity in participants who are performing categorization tasks. These correlations suggest that many participants are using exemplar strategies, though a substantial minority use prototype or mixed approaches. These patterns can also be used to isolate regions to be investigated in future studies, meaning that not only can cognitive models be discriminated, hypotheses about their implementations may also be framed. We turn now to one specific proposal about the form these hypotheses might take.

Mechanistic integration as a reductive interfield strategy

Many scientific fields center on discovering and elucidating mechanisms (Andersen, 2014a; 2014b; Bechtel, 2008; 2009; Bechtel and Abrahamsen, 2005; Craver, 2007; Craver and Darden, 2013; Darden, 2001; Glennan, 2002; Zednik, 2015). The explanatory target of mechanistic analysis is an entity's or a system's function – its capacity to carry out a certain sort of activity or to fill a causal role. Humans have the capacity to store and retrieve a limited number of items from memory; the liver has the function of removing toxins from the bloodstream; pyramidal cells have the function of generating action potentials. The question of how each function is carried out is answered by specifying a mechanism.

Mechanisms are organized sets of entities plus their associated activities and processes. Mechanistic analysis is a species of componential causal analysis: it requires decomposing the target system into its component parts, placing them within the overall organization of the system, locating them relative to one another, and understanding their activities and operations: what they do and how they contribute to the performance of the system's overall function. Wimsatt (2007) explicitly links this form of mechanistic analysis with reduction: "a reductive explanation of a behavior or a property of a system is one that shows it to be mechanistically explicable in terms of the properties of and interactions among the parts of a system" (2007, pp. 670–671).

Mechanistic discovery is often intrafield, as in the case of applying cellular and molecular techniques to understand how the action potential is generated or the process by which neurotransmitters are transported and released into synaptic gaps. When applied as an interfield strategy, mechanistic analysis involves correlating the elements of our cognitive ontology with those of neuroscience, or in Kaplan and Craver's (2011) terms, discovering a *model-to-mechanism mapping*. In practice this implies a strong preference for localizing elements and operations of the cognitive system in discrete, spatially contiguous, "natural"-seeming components of the neural system (Coltheart, 2013). An integration is successful to the extent that this sort of localized mapping of cognitive onto neural structures preserves the explanatory power of the original cognitive model to capture its distinctive phenomena and effects.

When applied to computational models, interfield mapping requires showing how computational states and processes are implemented in neural hardware. Many competing theories of computational implementation exist (Chalmers, 1994; 1996; 2011; Copeland, 1996; Gallistel and King, 2010; Miłkowski, 2011; Rescorla, 2014; Shagrir, 2012). These typically involve imposing some form of structural constraints (normally spelled out in physical or causal terms) on the underlying hardware. One that explicitly draws on mechanistic insights is due to Gualtiero Piccinini (2015). On Piccinini's account, a *computing system* is identified with a kind of mechanism that has the function of carrying out generic computations: "the processing of vehicles by a functional mechanism according to rules that are sensitive solely to differences between different portions (i.e., spatiotemporal parts) of the vehicles" (2015, p. 121), where these rules conform to a mathematical function from inputs and current states to outputs. The vehicles of computation consist of "spatiotemporal parts or portions", often a concatenated sequence of digits that can take on finitely many discrete states.[5]

Piccinini emphasizes that while computation is "medium independent" (ibid., p. 122) in that it only attends to some of the physical properties of the implementing medium and not others, nevertheless implementing a computation places tight structural constraints on the nature of computational realizers. These must be met for it to be true that a system is computing a certain function:

> In real systems, structural components lie between the input and the output, and they are organized to exhibit that capacity. Whether the components satisfy the given task analysis depends on whether the components include structures that complete each of the tasks. If no such structures can be identified in the system, then the task analysis must be incorrect.
>
> *(ibid., p. 90)*

Such comments reveal a commitment to *componential realism*: in order for a cognitive model to offer a good causal explanation, there needs to be real structural components of a neurobiological mechanism that correspond to the elements of that model and that carry out the operations of those elements. Elements of cognitive models, in short, must map onto mechanistic structural components of the brain. In the absence of such a mapping, the explanations that the model offers are simply false, and accepting them would be "to give up on the idea that there is a uniquely correct explanation" (ibid., p. 91) of the system's behavior. The idea that distinct computational elements must map onto independent physical components (however those are identified) also plays a key role in Chalmers' (1996) theory of implementation, and it embodies a similar componential realist thought.

A similar structural condition is proposed by Bechtel and Hamilton (2007) in discussing the role of localization heuristics in mechanistic analysis: "Discovery of an operation that cannot be linked to a part of the structure poses the question of whether that operation is indeed being performed and if so, by what component". The ability to localize functions in identifiable parts of structures underwrites mappings between entities in different fields. Operations that can't be tied to working parts of mechanisms are suspect.

A successful mechanistic reduction will map elements of a model onto mechanistic parts in such a way that the workings of those parts causally explains the phenomena that the model does. Insofar as it offers such direct constraints, the componential realism condition offers an advance over previous criteria of neural plausibility, which were grounded in an often impressionistic sense of similarity between cognitive models and the brain. The element-to-part aspect of the mapping guarantees ontological conservatism. It further satisfies the directional explanatory condition on reduction: the causal operations of neural components explain how they carry out the functions ascribed by the model.

Limits of mechanistic reduction

The success of mechanistic reduction turns on the existence of a smooth mapping from cognitive models onto neural mechanisms. However, it is at present an open question how well-aligned these mappings will be. Several writers have raised doubts about this possibility, proposing instead that cognitive and neural models may *cross-classify* the causal structure of the brain (Shapiro, 2015; Stinson, 2016; Weiskopf, 2011a; 2016), meaning that elements of the former often cannot be correlated with elements of the latter. While few have argued that *no* cognitive elements map onto neural mechanisms, that there might be such failures as a matter of course has been explored seriously.

Stinson, for example, notes that research in the psychology of attention and memory has generated models that do not in any obvious way map onto underlying neural systems. Attentional models use diagrams of information flow through a sequence of layers consisting of perceptual processors, memory stores of varying durations, filters, selectors, and channels. Other elements, such as sequences of encoders for generating representations of particular types of properties, and controllers where higher-level intentional processing can direct the flow of information, are also present. In practice these models are assessed autonomously: while they can be *used* as templates for neural localization, the fact that these elements may not correspond with distinct parts of neural mechanisms has not led to their abandonment within psychology.

Consider a case of interfield taxonomic mismatch. Psychologists distinguish semantic, episodic, and autobiographical forms of declarative memory, and the distinctions among these types has traditionally been made on the basis of behavioral and lesion studies (Tulving, 1983). It was initially suggested that each cognitive system could be localized in a distinct neural region. However, Burianova and colleagues (Burianova and Grady, 2007; Burianova, McIntosh, and Grady, 2010) showed that coordinated activity in a common network of areas including the left lingual gyrus, left hippocampus, and right caudate nucleus is implicated in all three forms of retrieval. The three forms share a substantial, albeit distributed, anatomical basis. If mechanisms are spatially and structurally delimited, this seems *prima facie* reason to conclude that these are not in fact separate cognitive kinds, since they share a common realizer (Greenberg and Verfaellie, 2010).

Recent work in systems neuroscience suggests there are principled reasons that such mismatches, in which cognitive kinds are split, fused, and intermingled at the level of neural implementation, may be common. The *massive redeployment* (or *neural recycling*) *hypothesis* proposes that the brain consists of a set of interconnected and highly multifunctional processing units that are reused in tasks across many different domains (Anderson, 2010; 2014; 2015; Dehaene, 2011; Dehaene and Cohen, 2007). Successful task performance, particularly in higher cognition, involves coordinating processing across a distributed suite of regions whose activities can be dynamically reconfigured to execute many distinct cognitive functions (Sporns, 2011).

This hypothesis has several consequences. The first is that much of our cognitive activity is neurally *distributed* or *holistic*: particular cognitive operations and entities are spread out across a broad network of brain regions. The second is that neural components are highly *multifunctional*: these regions each participate in and contribute towards the execution of many distinct cognitive functions. The third is that neural activation is *context-sensitive* and *non-local*: the contribution that each component region makes towards carrying out these functions is determined in part by the ongoing behavior of the other components that have been recruited and the overall task being executed (Bechtel, 2012; Bressler and Kelso, 2016; Meehan and Bressler, 2012; Nathan and Del Pinal, 2015).

Points one and two imply a striking consequence, namely that the neural basis for many distinct cognitive functions may be intractably *entangled*. Entanglement occurs when it is difficult or impossible to pull the spatial realization of one function apart from that of another. There are several ways in which spatially overlapping realizers may make distinct functional contributions. There might be rapid physical reconfiguration of the neural wiring within a region, or different properties of a fixed wiring configuration might allow it to execute multiple functions when put in various activation contexts. In these cases the same region might contain several overlapping physical parts from the standpoint of cognitive realization. The declarative retrieval network mentioned above may be an example. Another possibility is that a single physical structure is inherently multifunctional, so that several cognitive elements genuinely correspond to only a single neural component. In less radical cases, there will still be significant overlap between the network regions implicated in many different functions (Crossley et al., 2013).

To insist that functional differences *must* force us to type physical structures differently is to illegitimately impose a classification scheme that makes the 3M constraint true by fiat. The phenomenon of entangled realizers poses a challenge to reduction because it is often assumed that wholly distinct cognitive elements must be mapped onto wholly distinct neural mechanisms (or parts of mechanisms). This is not strictly implied by componential realism, but it is closely allied with it: what *makes* a cognitive element real is its distinctive mechanistic realization, and to the extent that such failures of fit arise, they are evidence against the posited cognitive ontology (Poldrack, 2010).

The third point poses an additional challenge to many approaches to mechanism. As Woodward (2013) has argued, mechanisms are the class of componential causal explanations in which the behavior of the components obeys principles of stability, modularity, and fine-tuning. In many types of dynamical systems, including neural networks and genetic regulatory networks, however, these constraints may not apply.[6] In particular, the processing contribution of each region seems to depend non-locally on the contributions of other regions and on the overall cognitive function that is being carried out: what a part is doing in a context depends on what many other parts are also doing, and changing the cognitive context can also change the contribution made by that particular part (Sporns, 2014).

Since explaining the behavior of the parts may require referring not only to causal factors outside of the parts themselves (looking outwards) but also to factors individuated at the cognitive level (looking upwards), a reductionist explanatory strategy that attempts to capture the cognitive properties of the system purely in terms of bottom-up interactions among stable components may not be appropriate. The more it is necessary to look outwards and upwards in describing the contextual parameters that govern the system's behavior – and even the behavior of the parts themselves – the less reductionist the integration becomes.

Some mechanists respond to these worries by claiming that mechanisms need not obey constraints of spatiotemporal contiguity and unity, so that their parts may potentially be widely scattered and intermingled (Piccinini and Craver, 2011). But it is important to resist liberalizing the notion of a mechanistic part or component to include *anything* that an element of a cognitive model can be mapped onto. "Parts" must have greater integrity than this, and such a move trivializes the mechanistic thesis by declaring anything that realizes a cognitive structure to be, *de facto*, a mechanism.

The mechanist program initially took enormous care to explicate the constraints on mechanisms, and to separate mechanistic explanation from other approaches to complex systems (Bechtel and Richardson, 2010, p. 147).[7] Accordingly, we ought to preserve conceptual space for the possibility of non-mechanistic realization of complex functions. By collapsing the notion of a mechanism into the notion of a realizer, the thesis loses its force as an empirical hypothesis about the best research strategies for understanding systems like the mind/brain.

Towards a realistic antireductionism

The challenges just canvassed can be summed up as follows. First, the network structure of the brain might not resemble the paradigm examples of mechanisms. Second, even if these dynamical brain networks are best understood as mechanisms, it might not be possible to understand how they function in a reductive, bottom-up fashion. Third, even if a bottom-up mechanistic analysis is possible, this analysis might not include spatially circumscribed working parts that correspond neatly to the elements in our best-confirmed cognitive models.

These nested possibilities represent three different failure modes for the program of mechanistic reductive analysis: in one case, there are no mechanisms to map cognitive operations onto, and in the other two cases the mapping fails to be reductive either because the bottom-up directionality assumption fails, or because the mapping is not ontologically conservative. The antireductionist challenge, then, runs as follows. Reductive explanation requires mapping cognitive elements onto structures (working parts) within neural mechanisms. Further, cognitive elements are only real when (or to the extent that) they map onto these structures, as the componential realism claim requires. Failures of model-to-mechanism mapping along any of these lines would not only constitute a failure of reductive explanation, but would pose a daunting challenge to the cognitive ontology that psychological models are committed to. In the remainder of this discussion I will sketch a possible defense of realism from within this antireductionist framework.[8]

Recall that realism is a causal thesis: for a model element to exist requires that it have some sort of causal significance. One proposal for how to understand causal claims is in terms of *interventions* or *manipulations* (Campbell, 2006; 2008; 2010; Woodward, 2003; 2008). On an interventionist conception, X causes Y just in case, relative to certain background conditions, if there were a single intervention on X (and only on X), then the value of Y would change. X and Y here are state variables that can take on several possible values, and interventions or manipulations consist in events of making these variables have one such value rather than another. The relationships between variables imply that counterfactuals hold systematically and contrastively between all pairs of values, such that if X were manipulated to have the value x_a, then Y would have the value y_a, and so on. In the circumstances where the system's state changes obey such counterfactuals, it is true to say that changes in the value of X cause changes in the value of Y.

Interventionism as an account of causal explanation is closely linked with experimental procedures that are designed specifically to vary certain conditions and determine what effect, if any, these changes will have on a creature's cognition and behavior. It is therefore tailor made for understanding the cognitive models that psychology generates, since these are developed in response to precisely such interventions (Rescorla, 2017). Within Baddeley's model of working memory, for example, the phonological loop is assumed to be insensitive to semantic relations, so manipulations of these properties should not affect maintenance of information, whereas phonological similarity should increase the confusability of items in memory. The fact that these representational manipulations produce the predicted outcomes is evidence in favor of a component system with the hypothesized properties (Baddeley, 2012).

Similarly, systems analyses of cognitive capacities (boxologies) can generally be interpreted in interventionist terms, since they are visual representations of abstract structures characterized in terms of clusters of intervention points. In models of attention, for instance, there is a distinction between passive and dynamically tunable filters: the former only allow certain "preset" representations into working memory, while the latter can be adjusted by the current contents of working memory. In practice this comes down to whether intervening on the content of working memory will change the types of information that are allowed in on future trials, particularly whether information on task-irrelevant dimensions will make a difference (Pratt and Hommel, 2003). These diagrams, in short, can be regarded as guides to thinking about patterns of interventions rather than as proto-hypotheses about physical or mechanistic structures.

Interventionism, then, suggests an alternative conception of realism according to which in order for a model element to be causally real, it needs to correspond to system state variables that can be manipulated to alter outcomes in specific ways. This ties model elements fairly directly to experimental procedures in psychology. However, these variables do not need to correspond to structural components of the system's physical realization base, or more specifically to parts of mechanisms. They may instead be entities (akin to collective variables) that can't be mapped onto anything that would constitute a neuroanatomically or physiologically recognizable constituent of the brain. This opens up the desired conceptual space by showing how causal realism about psychological kinds can co-exist with their holistic, entangled realization.

Objections and replies

The first objection to the antireductionist picture sketched here targets its permissiveness *vis-à-vis* holistic realization. This objection has been pressed by Peter Godfrey–Smith (2008), who notes that contemporary functionalism is committed to functionally characterized components that are "level-bound": they are both causally real and capable of supporting explanations of the system's behavior, but also only visible from the ontological perspective of a particular level (2008, p. 66). Against this possibility, he argues that entities at the cognitive level must ultimately be discharged in terms of "*bona fide* parts, or states of *bona fide* parts" (ibid., p. 68), which alone can underwrite a "literally correct causal description" (ibid., p. 70) of the system.

More formally, citing Chalmers' (1996) account of computational implementation, Godfrey-Smith posits a

> requirement that each CSA [combinatorial state automaton] substate be mapped onto a *distinct spatial region* of the implementing system … a theory of implementation must exclude a mapping in which each CSA substate is mapped holistically to a partial specification of the physical state of the entire system.
>
> *(2008, p. 68)*

When doing computational psychology, we must, in short, move from merely conjectured entities in models to more seriously grounded components of mechanisms.

As we have seen, however, the interventionist conception differs with the componential realist on the conditions for saying that a model element is causally real. It is sufficient that it be the locus of a cluster of interventionist counterfactuals, rather than having any direct mapping onto mechanistic parts. Realization requires that the system be organized in some such way that these counterfactuals are true of it, not that it be organized in a specifically mechanistic way.

A second objection centers on the role of dissociation studies in (dis)confirming cognitive models. Neural interventions can sometimes dissociate cognitive functions that are modeled as being part of the same system, and this is often regarded as evidence against cognitive theories that lump them together. If realizers are routinely widely entangled, it will often be possible to influence several functions at once by selective neural interventions on their common basis regions, and this might suggest that our current cognitive ontologies are mistaken in regarding these functions as separate.

However, cognitive models themselves do not imply any counterfactuals about what would happen if various types of neural interventions were performed. The illusion that they do stems from reading them as componential realists tend to, namely as preliminary sketches or hypotheses about neural structure. From an interventionist standpoint, though, they merely describe relations among manipulable cognitive entities. The fact that a specific neural intervention may disrupt the pattern of counterfactuals that are true of these cognitive entities does not undermine the fact that they nevertheless hold in the routine circumstances when they are assessed against the background of the normal, intact neural system. Putting the point differently, the fact that manipulating X normally results in changes to Y doesn't say anything about whether there is some third thing such that manipulating it might affect them both.

A related objection is that the case for entanglement has been overstated. It might turn out that all psychological constructs *can* be discriminated neurally from one another, even though some can only be discriminated *weakly* (Lenartowicz et al., 2010). (Weak discrimination here means that the brain regions of interest involved in each tasks tapping each construct overlap largely but not entirely.) Therefore, there are no true cases of constructs that are indiscriminably entangled, and no distinct-realizer violations. However, this overlooks an important point: if such small differences are allowed to count against entanglement then they cannot *also* be used as evidence to motivate elimination of constructs from our cognitive ontology. The two claims stand and fall together. A construct might be only weakly neurally discriminable but still be robustly detectable and manipulable using psychological methods.

Finally, the interventionist's criterion of realism may be thought to be overly liberal. Without pinning down cognitive elements to well-behaved mechanistic components, we may be unable to distinguish between models that capture real causal structure and those that are merely phenomenological, hence not explanatory. It will, in short, be too easy to declare that a psychological model is realized – the view does not make enough discriminations to allow us to separate real from fictional constructs.

This criticism might be fair if interventionism failed to make any principled distinction between phenomenological and explanatory computational models. But it clearly does this. An example of a widely applied and highly predictive model is Latent Semantic Analysis (Landauer and Dumais, 1997). LSA is, in effect, a data-mining technique for analyzing a large corpus of text and generating a high-dimensional representation of the associations among the words and phrases contained therein. These representations can be used to simulate performance on vocabulary tests and the Test of English as a Foreign Language (used as a measure of English proficiency for non-native speakers), and have also been harnessed for automated grading of student essays. However, there are few studies showing that they can be intervened on and manipulated in a way that systematically affects human lexical processing. Since the association matrices that LSA outputs are not plausible targets of intervention, the model's predictive facility is no evidence of their psychological reality – a conclusion that would hold even if LSA were a far more "neurally realistic" model.

Conclusion

As the limited success of reductionist interfield strategies indicates, a theory of how computational and other representational elements in psychological models are implemented remains in many ways elusive. The possibility I have sketched and defended here is one on which psychological kinds are neurally realized, but the realization relation might be a hopelessly entangled one. At least some of the empirical evidence currently leans in this direction. If this situation turns out to be intractable and persistent the mind–body relationship might turn out to be considerably more epistemically opaque than reductionist heuristics have traditionally assumed it to be. In forging a path forward, integrative modeling in the mind/brain sciences may at last be shedding the habits of thought and practice that characterized its reductionist past.

Notes

1 This distinction is explicated in Schaffner (1993). For discussion of other types of reduction and their relationships, see Bickle (2006), Theurer and Bickle (2013), Horst (2007), Kaiser (2015), Kim (2005; 2008), Sarkar (1992), Theurer (2013), and Wimsatt (1974; 2006).

2 Kenneth Schaffner's Generalized Reduction/Replacement model (1993) is the most extensive attempt to preserve the basic insights of Nagelian reduction.

3 A caveat: some cognitive modelers aim only for empirical adequacy, and even mechanistic models can have non-realist interpretations (Colombo, Hartmann, and Van Iersel, 2015). Causal interpretation is often partial, meaning that only some elements are treated in a realistic way, while others are fictions or simplifications that facilitate ends such as computational simulation. Little guidance is provided by a model itself as to which of its components should be interpreted causally, hence it is not always straightforward to determine the degree of a model's realistic commitments. The thesis of realism is not the same as Kaplan and Craver's (2011) "3M constraint", since that requires that model elements map onto components of mechanisms, while realism only requires that there be a mapping to causally significant components, without assuming that these must be mechanistically organized. The relevance of this will become clear in later sections.

4 In this sense they are functional kinds, like many others that occur in the special sciences. For discussion and critique of the notion of a functional kind, see Reydon (2009), Weiskopf (2011b), and Buckner (2014).

5 Symbols are strings of digits that are potentially semantically interpreted. Though Piccinini doesn't hold that semantics is essential to computational description, models in computational psychology typically treat them as vehicles of thought, i.e. as having content that is relevant to the cognitive task the system is carrying out.

6 The objection from failures of modularity is also pressed by Fagan (2012), who offers a revised mechanistic account in response to it. See Glymour (2007) for a metaphysical picture similar to the one sketched here.

7 For related worries about the cogency of the reductionist's notion of a mechanistic part, see Franklin-Hall (2016), Nicholson (2012), and Teller (2010).

8 Another argument to this conclusion, though one that takes a different route, appears in Egan (2018).

References

Andersen, H. (2014a) 'A Field Guide to Mechanisms: Part I', *Philosophy Compass*, 9 (4), pp. 274–283.

Andersen, H. (2014b) 'A Field Guide to Mechanisms: Part II', *Philosophy Compass*, 9 (4), pp. 284–293.

Anderson, M.L. (2010) 'Neural Reuse: A Fundamental Organizational Principle of the Brain', *The Behavioral and Brain Sciences*, 33 (4), pp. 245–266.

Anderson, M.L. (2014) *After Phrenology*. Cambridge, MA: MIT Press.

Anderson, M.L. (2015) 'Précis of *After Phrenology*: Neural Reuse and the Interactive Brain', *Behavioral and Brain Sciences*, 39, pp. 1–22.

Baddeley, A.D. (2012) 'Working Memory: Theories, Models, and Controversies', *Annual Review of Psychology*, 63, pp. 1–29.

Bechtel, W. (2008) *Mental Mechanisms: Philosophical Perspectives on Cognitive Neuroscience*. New York, NY: Routledge.

Bechtel, W. (2009) 'Looking Down, Around, and Up: Mechanistic Explanation in Psychology', *Philosophical Psychology*, 22 (5), pp. 543–564.

Bechtel, W. (2012) 'Referring to Localized Cognitive Operations in Parts of Dynamically Active Brains', in Raftopoulos, A. and Machamer, P. (eds.) *Perception, Realism, and the Problem of Reference*. Cambridge, UK: Cambridge University Press, pp. 262–284.

Bechtel, W. and Abrahamsen, A. (2005) 'Explanation: A Mechanist Alternative', *Studies in History and Philosophy of Biological and Biomedical Sciences*, 36 (2), pp. 421–441.

Bechtel, W. and Hamilton, A. (2007) 'Reduction, Integration, and the Unity of Science: Natural, Behavioral, and Social Sciences and the Humanities', in Kuipers, T. (ed.) *General Philosophy of Science: Focal Issues*, vol. 1. Amsterdam: North Holland, pp. 377–430.

Bechtel, W. and Richardson, R.C. (2010) *Discovering Complexity*. Cambridge, MA: MIT Press.

Bickle, J. (2006) 'Reducing Mind to Molecular Pathways: Explicating the Reductionism Implicit in Current Cellular and Molecular Neuroscience', *Synthese*, 151 (3), pp. 411–434.

Bressler, S.L. and Kelso, S. (2016) 'Coordination Dynamics in Cognitive Neuroscience', *Frontiers in Systems Neuroscience*, 10 (September), pp. 1–7.

Buckner, C. (2014) 'Functional Kinds: A Skeptical Look', *Synthese*, 192, pp. 3915–3942.

Burianova, H. and Grady, C.L. (2007) 'Common and Unique Neural Activations in Autobiographical, Episodic, and Semantic Retrieval', *Journal of Cognitive Neuroscience*, 19 (9), pp. 1520–1534.

Burianova, H., McIntosh, A.R., and Grady, C.L. (2010) 'A Common Functional Brain Network for Autobiographical, Episodic, and Semantic Memory Retrieval', *NeuroImage*, 49 (1), pp. 865–874.

Butler, K. (1994) 'Neural Constraints in Cognitive Science', *Minds and Machines*, 4 (2), pp. 129–162.

Campbell, J. (2006) 'An Interventionist Approach to Causation in Psychology', in Gopnik, A. and Schulz, L.E. (eds.) *Causal Learning: Psychology, Philosophy, and Computation*. Oxford: Oxford University Press, pp. 58–66.

Campbell, J. (2008) 'Interventionism, Control Variables and Causation in the Qualitative World', *Philosophical Issues*, 18 (1), pp. 426–445.

Campbell, J. (2010) 'Control Variables and Mental Causation', *Proceedings of the Aristotelian Society*, 110, pp. 15–30.

Chalmers, D.J. (1994) 'On Implementing a Computation', *Minds and Machines*, 4 (4), pp. 391–402.

Chalmers, D.J. (1996) 'Does a Rock Implement Every Finite-State Automaton?', *Synthese*, 108 (3), pp. 309–333.

Chalmers, D.J. (2011) 'A Computational Foundation for the Study of Cognition', *Journal of Cognitive Science*, 12, pp. 323–357.

Colombo, M., Hartmann, S., and Van Iersel, R. (2015) 'Models, Mechanisms, and Coherence', *British Journal for the Philosophy of Science*, 66 (1), pp. 181–212.

Coltheart, M. (2013) 'How Can Functional Neuroimaging Inform Cognitive Theories?', *Perspectives on Psychological Science*, 8 (1), pp. 98–103.

Copeland, B.J. (1996) 'What Is Computation?', *Synthese*, 108 (3), pp. 335–359.

Craver, C.F. (2007) *Explaining the Brain*. Oxford: Oxford University Press.

Craver, C.F. and Darden, L. (2013) *In Search of Mechanisms*. Chicago, IL: University of Chicago Press.

Crossley, N.A. et al. (2013) 'Cognitive Relevance of the Community Structure of the Human Brain Functional Coactivation Network', *Proceedings of the National Academy of Sciences*, 110 (28), pp. 11583–11588.

Darden, L. (2001) 'Discovering Mechanisms: A Computational Philosophy of Science Perspective', in Jantke, K.P. and Shinohara, A. (eds.) *Discovery Science*. Berlin: Springer, pp. 3–15.

Darden, L. and Maull, N. (1977) 'Interfield Theories', *Philosophy of Science*, 44 (1), pp. 43–64.

Dehaene, S. (2011) *The Number Sense*. Oxford: Oxford University Press.

Dehaene, S. and Cohen, L. (2007) 'Cultural Recycling of Cortical Maps', *Neuron*, 56 (2), pp. 384–398.

Egan, F. (2018) 'Function-Theoretic Explanation and the Search for Neural Mechanisms', in Kaplan, D.M. (ed.) *Explanation and Integration in Mind and Brain Science*. Oxford: Oxford University Press, pp. 145–163.

Fagan, M.B. (2012) 'The Joint Account of Mechanistic Explanation', *Philosophy of Science*, 79 (4), pp. 448–472.

Franklin-Hall, L.R. (2016) 'New Mechanistic Explanation and the Need for Explanatory Constraints', in Aizawa, K. and Gillett, C. (eds.) *Scientific Composition and Metaphysical Ground*. London: Palgrave, pp. 41–74.

Gallistel, C.R. and King, A.P. (2010) *Memory and the Computational Brain*. Malden, MA: Wiley-Blackwell.

Glennan, S. (2002) 'Rethinking Mechanistic Explanation', *Philosophy of Science*, 69 (September), pp. 342–354.

Glymour, C. (2007) 'When Is a Brain Like the Planet?', *Philosophy of Science*, 74 (3), pp. 330–347.

Godfrey-Smith, P. (2008) 'Reduction in Real Life', in Hohwy, J. and Kallestrup, J. (eds.) *Being Reduced*. Oxford: Oxford University Press, pp. 52–74.

Greenberg, D.L. and Verfaellie, M. (2010) 'Interdependence of Episodic and Semantic Memory: Evidence from Neuropsychology', *Journal of the International Neuropsychological Society: JINS*, 16 (5), pp. 748–753.

Horst, S. (2007) *Beyond Reduction*. Oxford: Oxford University Press.

Kaiser, M.I. (2015) *Reductive Explanation in the Biological Sciences*. Dordrecht: Springer.

Kaplan, D.M. and Craver, C.F. (2011) 'The Explanatory Force of Dynamical and Mathematical Models in Neuroscience: A Mechanistic Perspective', *Philosophy of Science*, 78 (October), pp. 601–627.

Kim, J. (2005) *Physicalism, or Something Near Enough*. Princeton, NJ: Princeton University Press.

Kim, J. (2008) 'Reduction and Reductive Explanation: Is One Possible without the Other?', in Hohwy, J. and Kallestrup, J. (eds.) *Being Reduced*. Oxford: Oxford University Press, pp. 93–114.

Landauer, T. and Dumais, S. (1997) 'A Solution to Plato's Problem: The Latent Semantic Analysis Theory of Acquisition, Induction, and Representation of Knowledge', *Psychological Review*, 104 (2), pp. 211–240.

Lenartowicz, A. et al. (2010) 'Towards an Ontology of Cognitive Control', *Topics in Cognitive Science*, 2 (4), pp. 678–692.

Love, B.C. (2016) 'Cognitive Models as Bridge between Brain and Behavior', *Trends in Cognitive Sciences*, 20 (4), pp. 247–248.

Mack, M.L., Preston, A.R., and Love, B.C. (2013) 'Decoding the Brain's Algorithm for Categorization from Its Neural Implementation', *Current Biology*, 23 (20), pp. 2023–2027.

McCauley, R.N. and Bechtel, W. (2001) 'Explanatory Pluralism and Heuristic Identity Theory', *Theory and Psychology*, 11 (6), pp. 736–760.

Meehan, T.P. and Bressler, S.L. (2012) 'Neurocognitive Networks: Findings, Models, and Theory', *Neuroscience and Biobehavioral Reviews*, 36 (10), pp. 2232–2247.

Miłkowski, M. (2011) 'Beyond Formal Structure: A Mechanistic Perspective on Computation and Implementation', *Journal of Cognitive Science*, 12 (4), pp. 359–379.

Nathan, M.J. and Del Pinal, G. (2015) 'Mapping the Mind: Bridge Laws and the Psycho-neural Interface', *Synthese*, 193 (2), pp. 637–647.

Nicholson, D.J. (2012) 'The Concept of Mechanism in Biology', *Studies in History and Philosophy of Science Part C*, 43 (1), pp. 152–163.

Piccinini, G. (2015) *Physical Computation*. Oxford: Oxford University Press.

Piccinini, G. and Craver, C.F. (2011) 'Integrating Psychology and Neuroscience: Functional Analyses as Mechanism Sketches', *Synthese*, 183 (3), pp. 283–311.

Poeppel, D. and Embick, D. (2005) 'Defining the Relation between Linguistics and Neuroscience', in Cutler, A. (ed.) *Twenty-First Century Psycholinguistics: Four Cornerstones*. Hove, UK: Taylor and Francis, pp. 103–120.

Poldrack, R.A. (2010) 'Mapping Mental Function to Brain Structure: How Can Cognitive Neuroimaging Succeed?', *Perspectives on Psychological Science*, 5 (6), pp. 753–761.

Pratt, J. and Hommel, B. (2003) 'Symbolic Control of Visual Attention: The Role of Working Memory and Attentional Control Settings', *Journal of Experimental Psychology, Human Perception and Performance*, 29 (5), pp. 835–845.

Rescorla, M. (2014) 'A Theory of Computational Implementation', *Synthese*, 191 (6), pp. 1277–1307.

Rescorla, M. (2017) 'An Interventionist Approach to Psychological Explanation', *Synthese*, pp. 1–32. Available at: https://doi.org/10.1007/s11229-017-1553-2.

Reydon, T.A.C. (2009) 'How to Fix Kind Membership: A Problem for HPC Theory and a Solution', *Philosophy of Science*, 76 (5), pp. 724–736.

Sarkar, S. (1992) 'Models of Reduction and Categories of Reductionism', *Synthese*, 91 (3), pp. 167–194.

Schaffner, K.F. (1993) *Discovery and Explanation in Biology and Medicine*. Chicago, IL: University of Chicago Press.

Shagrir, O. (2012) 'Computation, Implementation, Cognition', *Minds and Machines*, 22 (2), pp. 137–148.

Shapiro, L.A. (2015) 'Mechanism or Bust? Explanation in Psychology', *The British Journal for the Philosophy of Science*, 68 (4), pp. 1037–1059.

Sporns, O. (2011) *Networks of the Brain*. Cambridge, MA: MIT Press.

Sporns, O. (2014) 'Contributions and Challenges for Network Models in Cognitive Neuroscience', *Nature Neuroscience*, 17 (5), pp. 652–660.

Stinson, C. (2016) 'Mechanisms in Psychology: Ripping Nature at Its Seams', *Synthese*, 193 (5), pp. 1585–1614.

Teller, P. (2010) 'Mechanism, Reduction, and Emergence in Two Stories of the Human Epistemic Enterprise', *Erkenntnis*, 73 (3), pp. 413–425.

Theurer, K.L. (2013) 'Seventeenth-Century Mechanism: An Alternative Framework for Reductionism', *Philosophy of Science*, 80 (5), pp. 907–918.

Theurer, K.L. and Bickle, J. (2013) 'What's Old Is New Again: Kemeny-Oppenheim Reduction at Work in Current Molecular Neuroscience', 17 (2), pp. 89–113.

Tulving, E. (1983) *Elements of Episodic Memory*. Oxford: Oxford University Press.

Weiskopf, D.A. (2011a) 'Models and Mechanisms in Psychological Explanation', *Synthese*, 183, pp. 313–338.

Weiskopf, D.A. (2011b) 'The Functional Unity of Special Science Kinds', *British Journal for the Philosophy of Science*, 62 (2), pp. 233–258.

Weiskopf, D.A. (2016) 'Integrative Modeling and the Role of Neural Constraints', *Philosophy of Science*, 83 (5), pp. 674–685.

Wilson, R.A. (2004) *Boundaries of the Mind: The Individual in the Fragile Sciences – Cognition*. Cambridge, UK: Cambridge University Press.

Wimsatt, W.C. (1974) 'Reductive Explanation: A Functional Account', *Philosophy of Science*, pp. 671–710.

Wimsatt, W.C. (1994) 'The Ontology of Complex Systems: Levels Of Organization, Perspectives, and Causal Thickets', *Canadian Journal of Philosophy*, 20, pp. 207–274.

Wimsatt, W.C. (2006) 'Reductionism and Its Heuristics: Making Methodological Reductionism Honest', *Synthese*, 151 (3), pp. 445–475.

Wimsatt, W.C. (2007) 'Aggregate, Composed, and Evolved Systems: Reductionistic Heuristics as Means to More Holistic Theories', *Biology and Philosophy*, 21 (5), pp. 667–702.

Woodward, J. (2003) *Making Things Happen*. Oxford: Oxford University Press.

Woodward, J. (2008) 'Mental Causation and Neural Mechanisms', in Hohwy, J. and Kallestrup, J (eds.) *Being Reduced*. Oxford: Oxford University Press, pp. 218–262.

Woodward, J. (2013) 'Mechanistic Explanation: Its Scope and Limits', *Aristotelian Society*, Supplementary Volume, 87 (1), pp. 39–65.

Zednik, C. (2015) 'Heuristics, Descriptions, and the Scope of Mechanistic Explanation', in Braillard, P.-A. and Malaterre, C. (eds.) *Explanation in Biology*. Dordrecht: Springer, pp. 295–318.

17

HELMHOLTZ'S VISION
Underdetermination, behavior and the brain

Clark Glymour and Ruben Sanchez-Romero

Underdetermination is a misfit between theoretical ambitions, data, and methods of inference, where the ambition is to find kinds of truth about some system of interest, whether the cosmos or the brain or whatever is beneath or between. Underdetermination comes in different forms. Given a goal, say to identify the causal relations among a set **S** of variables in a system or class of similar systems, measurements of a set **V** of variables may be insufficient to distinguish any of the members of the possible collections of causal relations among the **S** variables no matter how large the sample sizes for values of variables in **V**. For brevity, we will call that "structural" underdetermination. Alternatively, the variables in **V** may suffice for correct estimation of **S** but only with samples that are larger than feasible. We will call that "sample" underdetermination. Again, aspects of the structure may be unidentifiable because of sheer computational complexity – we could not, for example, search exhaustively among the roughly $4^{10,000,000,000}$ possible causal structures for the more than 100,000 or so time-series variables measured by contemporary functional magnetic resonance scans of the brain. We call this "computational" underdetermination. And, of course, depending on the estimation method used, the estimates of causal relations or other parameters may carry with them uncertainties expressed as probabilities. The difficulties are not mutually exclusive.

Underdetermination is relational, not all or none. It might, for example, be possible to identify quantities that are in a certain range but not outside that range, or causal relations that are sufficiently strong but not weaker. The solutions to underdetermination are to find better data, use better statistical methods, or to abandon the ambition, perhaps to substitute one that is more feasible. Underdetermination has haunted psychology, and does so still, although the scope and details and kinds of uncertainty have changed. In what follows, we offer a brief historical survey of attempts to fathom the physical mechanisms of mind as computational systems, followed by a consideration of some of the concrete versions of underdetermination in contemporary neuropsychology.

In the conception of Hermann Helmholtz and his associates, Ernst Brücke and Emil du Bois Reymond and their students, mental phenomena were ultimately a piece of physiology, like breathing, and the ambition of psychology should be to unravel their physical mechanisms, as with any other physiological process (von Helmholtz, 1847). The work of Ramón y Cajal (1988) invited the view (to which Ramón y Cajal subscribed) of the functioning brain as a kind of signaling system, what we would, but they did not, call a computational information processing system (Glymour, 1991). Their views still form the background to cognitive psychology, especially cognitive neuropsychology. But from the beginning, the connections between behavior and whatever computational machinery is at work in the brain were radically underdetermined, structurally underdetermined.

Twentieth-century psychology began with two paradigms relating the mental and the physical, both inherited from the previous century. They can as well be thought of in retrospect as different models of computation. On the one hand, mental processes and their behavioral manifestations are the product of activities in local regions of the brain, and of physical but meaningful signaling relations – information transfer – between those regions. The activities themselves are of some unknown kind, electrical or chemical or something, but allowing of psychological descriptions. The signaling relations pass some quantity to and through nerve cells. What is passed between nerve cells was equally underdetermined; electrical charge was a candidate, but so were unknown chemicals; recognizing the uncertainty, Freud called it "Q" for "Qualitat". The brain is a "semantic computer" in which clusters of connected neurons represent external objects and their relations – Freud's example is the infant's representation of a mother's breast – the activation of that cluster of neurons is sent to motor neurons that move the baby's head and mouth. The modular conception, for example of the view of aphasia advocated by one of Brücke's colleagues, who was also Freud's teacher, Theodor Meynert, Professor of Psychiatry at Vienna, held that word inputs were interpreted in one region, Wernicke's, the interpretation was passed to another region, Broca's, where a response was formulated, and finally sent to a motor region (Meynert, 1884). This picture was buttressed both by nineteenth-century experiments on dogs that localized regions for motor responses, and especially by nineteenth-century discoveries through autopsy of quasi-localization of brain damage in people with marked behavioral abnormalities of speech and vision – aphasias and agnosias. On the other hand, mental phenomena are the result of collective activities and joint signaling within a network of connected neurons distributed throughout the entire brain or some large piece of it, e.g. the cortex. The influence of one neuron or collection of neurons on another *means* nothing. On this view, there are no brain locales admitting psychological descriptions. This was, for example, Freud's 1891 account of aphasias. In both views, the brain is what we would describe as a computational device with a lot of unspecified structure – issues such as analog versus digital had not arisen in the nineteenth-century neuropsychology. In the first view, it is a device that passes information in a more or less rich semantical sense – the signals passed *mean* something, and in each unit something is done to the physical representations of those meanings. In the second view, meanings, if there are such things, are aspects of different collective physical activities and transmissions.

The divide was not just about localization versus globalization in the nervous system, about modularity versus connectionism. It was about whether a traditional *psychological* science whose mental entities and processes are realized by distinct physical mechanisms is possible. On the first view, normal and abnormal behaviors are in correspondence with physical processes having parts that can break and linkages that can be severed; on the second view, not so much if at all. The second line is one theoretical source of behaviorism, evidenced explicitly in the work of Edwin Thorndike (1905): roughly there can be no psychological mechanisms because there are no physical parts that correspond to our psychological attributions. All one can learn is regularities between sensory input to the brain and motor output, because really that's all there is. Mental phenomena really are, as Gilbert Ryle put it, the ghost in the machine, the whole, black-box, undecomposable, mysterious machine.

Sigmund Freud, who, lest we forget, was trained at Vienna, the center of late nineteenth-century neuroscience, and who studied with Brücke and at one time planned to study with Helmholtz, embraced aspects of each of the two views, the second notably in his book on aphasia. Eventually, in the last chapter of *The Interpretation of Dreams*, he quasi-articulated a merger of the two paradigms, reverting to the language of neurophysiology in an attempt to explain the neural mechanism of repression. While behaviorists explicitly abandoned the ambition to establish the mechanisms of mind, others in the first half of the twentieth century, Donald Hebb and Clark Hull for example, abandoned the obligation to establish their theoretical conjectures. Hebb, who essentially followed the second paradigm, described physical realizations of mental states as distributed "ensembles" of neural activity, and more famously proposed what psychology textbooks now call the "Hebb synapse" as a mechanism for learning: signals to a neuron from a source somehow make the neuron more susceptible to receiving subsequent signals from the same source. Freud had fully articulated what is now called the Hebb synapse forty years before Hebb wrote, and it is probably in other places in the literature of late nineteenth-century neuropsychology. Hull, and a generation of learning theorists, modeled psychology on a sort of axiomatic quasi-biological pseudo physics, whose fundamental entities are "drives". Neither Hebb nor Hull could make a convincing empirical argument for their conceptions from the evidence available to them. Hebb's "ensemble" account endures as one model in neuropsychology; Hull's is only history.

Everything changed in the middle of the twentieth century with the availability of digital computers and programming languages. The impact of the digital computer for statistics, and through that, for investigations of how the brain produces behavior, were enormous. Statistics was born from computational challenges at the end of the eighteenth century, and the challenges continued in the first half of the twentieth. Before the digital computer, Bayesian statistics was a mere toy: posterior probabilities could only be computed in simple cases, and there were no means of estimating causal relations among large numbers of variables. The digital computer prompted the development of computationally demanding algorithms for these kinds of statistical estimates. We will later describe some of the ways these developments have proved valuable for investigating cognitive mechanisms.

The first effect of the digital computer on cognitive psychology was to produce a cornucopia of theorizing and enable computational illustrations, without, however, much empirical validation. Essentially, psychologists could now program descriptions of a hypothetical mental machine, a series of sequential states of computational structures – usually with some psychological functional story attached – in between digital representations of input and output. The programs were tuned *post facto* to reproduce experimental behavioral data, or aspects of it. Prominent examples include the SOAR programs initiated by Allen Newell and his collaborators and students, and John Anderson's ACT-R programs. There are thousands of papers applying these or related frameworks. Much of this work reads like computational psychoanalytic theory, with different theoretical entities and better behavioral data; indeed, the mixed local and connectionist framework of Anderson's early work has strong analogies with Freud's *Project for a Scientific Psychology*, and in recent years, Anderson, like Freud, has essayed neural analogues of his computational data structures. The SOAR project even had sociological anticipations. Like the Viennese Psychoanalytic Society, SOAR became a bit of a cult whose meetings were closed to doubters. In contrast, workers such as Anderson and Herbert Simon were entirely open.

The problem with these efforts was that digitally encoded finite pieces of behavior can be simulated by an infinity of programs. Some of this reached to absurdity. When the introduction to a volume of simulation theories for developmental psychology (Klahr and Langley, 1987) claimed that the SOAR programming language is the "language of thought", an editor of the volume was asked (by one of us), which study in his volume could not be simulated in BASIC. (None, he admitted.) Response time data, and the known speed of neural transmission, limited the algorithmic possibilities, but not enough (Luce, 1986). Some of these psychological efforts were paralleled by similar work in artificial intelligence – what John Haugeland called GOFAI, good, old-fashioned artificial intelligence – and some, like the ACT-R architecture, did double duty, and in the latter role have proved quite valuable, notably in automated instruction (Austin and Anderson, 2008).

A counter-movement purported to describe the brain as a "dynamical system", which is as informative as announcing that the brain is carbon based. Shorn of computational considerations, most, but not all, of this work was little more than hand waving about "basins of attraction", "attractors", "multiple causality", and such, or *post facto* simulations of simple psychological experiments. The work of Linda Smith and Esther Thelen provides any number of examples including children's reaching in a version of the classic Piaget experiment in which a child learns to reach for an object that she has seen hidden (Smith and Thelen, 2003). The negative inspiration seems to have been a thorough dislike of computational conceptions of cognitive processes – which have a pedigree from Thomas Hobbes to Herbert Simon and points in between. The positive inspiration seems to be (or have been) a kind of natur-philosophical holism in which the internal and external are inseparable, philosophy filtered more through Heidegger than Goethe. Despite the scientific paraphernalia, it remains that there are no empirical means available for identifying distinguishing features of non-linear dynamical systems from external physical measurements of a brain doing cognitive tasks, let alone for identifying the kinds of mechanisms that Helmholtz's project envisioned.

Like it or not, admit it or not, psychologists in the middle of the last century, and for some time after, were stuck with a hard epistemological fact. The great aim of cognitive science as Helmholtz envisioned it is to figure out how humans develop so as to be able to do all of the things we call "cognitive". It aims to describe the internal mechanics – biological mechanics – and relations with the rest of the world that make possible the common features of normal human cognition, and to describe how these mechanisms and relations develop through infancy and childhood, and how their normal functioning produces the varieties of normal cognition and how damage to them produces cognitive anomalies.

Mechanics is computation. Most generally, a computer is any system that can output the value of a function from values of variables to which the machine is set. In that conception, a computer is so only with respect to an identification of variables, something it is up to humans, as investigators in whatever science, to provide. So conceived, most computers are analog and compute but a handful of functions; the digital conception of computation from Alan Turing's work, and John von Neumann's idea of a stored program, generated the specialized notion of "computation" that is now the common usage. Current biology commits cognitive psychology to the general computational framework: the neuron is an input–output "device" that transmits signals from neurons to neurons; whether the computational code of neural spiking is analog or digital or some of each is still debated (Mochizuk and Shinomoto, 2014).

Meanwhile, psychology aimed to make a science of mind using the traditional sorts of evidence available to psychologists: behavior under experimentally controlled conditions, errors, self-reports of mental processes, and response times. The most obvious and most ignored fact was that on almost every dimension Helmholtz's ambition, even specialized pieces of it, was radically, structurally underdetermined by this sort of evidence. For every way of describing the body of phenomena psychologists could establish, there are a multitude of possible computational processes in between that could accommodate them, and implementations of the theories, such as SOAR and ACT-R, were essentially limited programming systems for which alternative programming systems could provide the same input–output relations, as with the SOAR and BASIC programs for developmental psychology noted above. The biological, computational mechanisms of mind remained hidden within the black box of the brain.

What was needed to reduce structural underdetermination and allow the kind of theory of mind Helmholtz envisioned was a way to see inside the box, to acquire data that would bring theories of cognition closer to physiology and to the neural mechanisms of computation. Some psychologists, such as Zenon Pylyshyn, adamantly opposed the very idea (Pylyshyn, 1986) on the grounds that psychology ought to be an "autonomous" science. The opposition was a tacit admission that the variables in then-current cognitive psychological models of behavior had little or no established connection with biology. Even connectionist computational models had no biological basis for their learning algorithms, which required information to be "backpropagated" from output variables in the network. Then, in the 1970s, and most dramatically in 1990, physical techniques emerged that could see aspects of the processes at work inside the brain box – without opening it. They included electroencephalography, proton emission tomography, and magnetic resonance imaging. The last, in the form of "functional" magnetic resonance emerged as the workhorse of contemporary cognitive neuropsychology, and we will focus on it. Psychology quickly changed towards the vision of Helmholtz and Ramón y Cajal. By the mid 1990s mathematical psychologists such as Gregory Ashby were suddenly working with brain images.

Magnetic resonance is an interaction between the magnetism of the nuclei of atoms and electromagnetic radiation having the frequencies of radio waves. Ignoring a lot of details involving Nobel prizes, protons have a magnetic moment and in an external magnetic field that moment precesses, in analogy to the precession of the Earth's rotation about its axis. The chemical environment of a proton produces an external magnetic field, and others can be experimentally imposed. The frequency of precession determines the Larmor frequency – the "resonance" frequency of electromagnetic radiation that can be absorbed and re-radiated. A scheme of external magnetizations and radio frequency pulses allows identification of the spatial locations of variations in magnetic fields in living tissue, and it was established that different tissues in the human body can be thus distinguished. Hemoglobin, the substance in the blood that carries oxygen hither and thither in the body, exists in two states, oxygenated and deoxygenated, with different magnetic properties, and that difference influences the magnetic fields around such molecules. In 1990, Ogawa and his collaborators discovered that variations in the concentrations of the two states of hemoglobin can be distinguished by nuclear magnetic resonance, the Blood Oxygenation Level Dependent (BOLD) signal, and fMRI was born. The idea is that neural cell metabolism, including spiking, requires oxygen, and so differences in neural activity will be correlated with differences in ratios of deoxygenated and oxygenated hemoglobin in the environment of the neuron. The details of how this creates a detectible magnetic resonance signal are uncertain. One prominent theory is that neuron spiking in a region creates an excess of deoxygenated hemoglobin in the neighborhood, which causes a rush of oxygenated hemoglobin into the area, which briefly produces an excess of the normal concentration, and whose magnetic effects are detectible. In any case, the BOLD signal is well correlated with other measures of oxygenation and neural physiology, and so it is taken as an indirect measure of the physiological activity of collections of nerve cells.

The BOLD signal is a series over time of measurements, typically about one measurement every two seconds or so, much slower than the (apparently quite variable) time for a potential difference to propagate down an axon and release chemicals received by synapses. BOLD signals register collective effects of hundreds of thousands of neurons in small regions, or "voxels", typically more than 2 cubic millimeters in volume but more recently about 1 cubic millimeter, containing perhaps 50,000 nerve cells. For the whole brain, fMRI measurement yields a time series of each of these voxels. Inside an fMRI machine is not a comfortable place to be, so a measurement session is unlikely to last more than an hour, often less. A half hour scanning session would yield a few hundred momentary recordings of the signal from each voxel.

The typical fMRI study is concerned with what Patrick Suppes disparaged as "real estate": identifying which regions of the brain are especially active or inactive when a subject is given a stimulus or asked to perform a simple task during scanning. More recently, there have been a burst of studies of what is called the "resting state" where no stimulus is given and no response is required. Research demonstrates that features of the stimulus can be predicted from patterns of BOLD signals over the brain. (Amazing as that is, we are a long way from "mind-reading" – we cannot put a subject in a machine with the instruction "think hard about one thing" and determine from the BOLD signals what she is thinking.) But all of this is well short of addressing the underdetermination of the computational cognitive physiology envisioned in the nineteenth century and after. If the brain works by passing signals around (ultimately, rather simple signals: *discharge an action potential!*), what is the computational wiring, and which crescendos of signals are intermediate between stimulus and output, and how specific are the causal traces to particulars of input and output, to stimulus and context? None of this is addressed by using holistic patterns of brain activity to infer aspects of a stimulus, and identifying the "regions of interest" that are especially active or inactive in response to a stimulus is rather like identifying some of the objects in an electronic circuit that heat up when a current is applied, but without knowing the circuitry or what the objects do to the current and voltage, or which pieces of circuitry are involved in which input–output relations. Some neural circuitry might serve as an amplifier, increasing an aggregate signal. Some circuitry might serve as a damper or governor, reducing or modulating a signal. Some processes might be feed-forward, from source to sink, while some processes may involve feedback from source to sink to source, through intermediate steps. These are the kinds of questions about computational mechanisms in the brain that we imagine Helmholtz would have wanted answered. (It is notable, if coincidental, that Helmholtz devised a coil that generates a uniform magnetic field.)

Fitting the methodology to the goals is critical to avoid unnecessary underdetermination, or worse perhaps, mis-determination. For the purposes of Helmholtz's vision, fMRI methodology has largely been a misfit. Empirical attempts to infer computational circuitry from BOLD signals have for the most part been of two forms. One is to directly connect any "regions of interest" – i.e. clusters of voxels known to be especially active or inactive under some stimulus – if and only if their time series are correlated. These results are almost always described as "functional connectivity", but in view of the usual usage of "function", that is a wild misnomer. The correlation of BOLD time series can be produced by a variety of mechanisms, only two of which are that the signals from one region are caused by neural activities in another. (Consider, for example, that two variables will be correlated if they have no influence on one another but do have a common cause.) Describing correlations as "circuitry", as is often done, is obfuscation, covering underdetermination with misdescription.

Another, more sophisticated method is to estimate causal relations from regression methods. Regression is the oldest causal search procedure there is, with sources in the nineteenth century. The basic idea is to estimate the correlation of two variables *conditional on all* other measured variables – that is, the linear effect that variation in one variable would have on variation in another if the first were the cause and the second the effect, and no other variables changed their values. In estimating computational circuitry in an fMRI experiment, we do not initially know which time series are causes of which others – except that the stimulus is not caused by the neurons of the experimental subject. So, when the regression procedure estimates the connection between two variables, X and Y, it may very well be conditioning on one or more variables that are joint effects of X and Y. But easy algebra shows that if X and Y are uncorrelated, and Z is influenced by both X and Y, then X and Y will be correlated conditional on Z. The procedure, in other words, is liable to false positives. That aside, no directions of influence can be determined by this method: regression presupposes that the potential causes (the regressors) have already been distinguished from their effects (the outcomes).

Because fMRI measurements are time series for each voxel, and causes precede effects, which measured events cannot be causes of others is determined by the data. This allowed the application of time series methods for causal inference introduced into economics by Clive Granger in the 1960s. "Granger causation" is essentially regression of measurements at later time steps on measures at some fixed numbers of time steps earlier. It has been widely applied in fMRI studies, but careful simulation studies (Smith et al., 2011) show that for fMRI it is badly inaccurate, producing both false causal connections and missing connections correctly found by other less popular methods.

There are several other analytical methods that can use fMRI to identify both causal connections and their directions and whose accuracies are vindicated to some degree either by animal experiments or by simulations with causally simple models of the BOLD generating process, or both. Here is where the statistical power of the digital computer bears on Helmholtz's vision. The methods include LiNGAM, which uses independent components analysis (ICA) to find the independent sources of a signal (Shimuzu et al., 2006). Because all models of the BOLD signal assume there are independent noises or disturbances affecting each variable, ICA methods can decompose each voxel time series into the noise terms that affect it directly or indirectly. If A causes B, the noise directly affecting A will indirectly affect B, but not vice versa, and the ICA decomposition therefore determines a causal order among the time series. LiNGAM unfortunately suffers from sample underdetermination – unrealistically long time series are required for accurate results. Another method, GIMME (Gates and Molenaar, 2012) uses a method embedded in the LISREL programs widely used in psychometrics. Using the time series, the method systematically searches for direct influences of one time series variable on another, trying to optimize a fit between empirical correlations and the best estimate of the correlations obtained from a model at any stage of the search. GIMME has performed quite well in simulation tests, but is limited to a few dozen variables. It suffers from computational underdetermination. Modifications of two of the oldest search methods for graphical causal models, so-called "Bayes net methods" – the PC algorithm modified to PC-Max and the quasi-Bayesian Greedy Equivalence Search (GES), modified to Fast Greedy Equivalence Search (FGES) – are both reasonably accurate and through parallelization can be applied to tens of thousands of variables. FGES has even recovered a sparse causal graph with a million variables, and has been applied to over 50,000 voxels of fMRI scans (Ramsey et al., 2017). These methods can take advantage of the time series ordering of measurements, or ignore it, but they work somewhat better when the time ordering is not used. Finally, but not least, there are a number of "non-Gaussian" and non-linear procedures that, given that a pair of variables have a causal connection, can estimate the direction of influence (Zhang and Hyvärinen, 2008). While it is a truism that correlation underdetermines causal direction, correlation is only the second term, or "moment", in a power series expansion of a probability distribution. Higher-order terms, for example representing the skew of a distribution, *can* distinguish directions. So far, the most accurate search procedures available for voxel to voxel connections combine these non-Gaussian methods with PC-Max or FGES searches.

There have been both silly and less silly criticisms of efforts in cognitive neuropsychology to identify the mechanisms of thought, the mind's causal arrows. It was boldly announced that a

BOLD signal could be obtained from a dead fish, which, since any variations in magnetic field strengths in the body will create a signal, is no surprise. The argument is roughly analogous to pointing a microscope at a superficially smooth surface on Earth and proclaiming any irregularities seen are comparable in size to the "mountains" on the moon seen through Galileo's telescope. A more interesting criticism has been offered by Jonas and Kording (2017), who simulated, down to the transistor level a microprocessor controller for three video games, and made simulated time-series measurements of activities of elements of the simulated microprocessor. They applied "currently popular" data analysis methods to the data to try to reconstruct the causal relations between microprocessor units or aggregations of those units. One of their procedures was to separately disable each individual transistor – and infer that the transistors for which a game failed to boot are the "unique" causes of that game. "We might thus conclude they are uniquely responsible for the game – perhaps there is a Donkey Kong transistor or a Space Invaders transistor". Another of their experiments applied Granger causal inference to time series of measurements from areas of their simulator, finding correct connections, false connections and missing true connections. Jonas and Kording may be right about what is "currently popular" but their study would have been more to the point if they had instead used the "best available" methods. What features of the causal structure of a system can be identified from damages to internal circuitry using changes in input/output behavior has been studied using formal learning theory (Glymour, 2001), but that was not considered. What inferences to neural causal roles can be made from variations in fMRI signals concomitant with changes in behavior has been studied and debated as "reverse inference" in neuropsychology (Machery, 2014; Glymour and Hanson, 2016), but that was not considered. Granger causal methods are, as noted, sub-optimal for learning fMRI time series, and all of the statistical methods discussed above depend for accuracy on non-deterministic relations among the measurable variables; the microprocessor simulator was deterministic. There are simulators that more accurately capture the BOLD signal and the processes generating it – why simulate a microprocessor? Jonas and Kording (2015) prefer Bayes models which they have applied to identify neuronal cell types. Why not use exact Bayesian methods to identify causal relations between voxels? Because identifying causal structures, even feed-forward causal structures by strictly Bayesian methods is a *very* hard computational problem. It can be done for about twenty variables.

While available methods can identify structures that amplify (as in Figure 17.1) or regulate feed-forward influences and feedback cycles, and can be applied at the voxel level of resolution, there remains an enormous structural, computational and sampling underdetermination

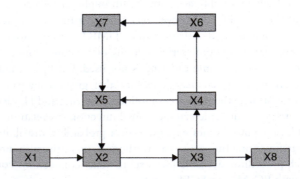

Figure 17.1 Depending on the signs of the connections, this circuit can serve as an amplifier or governor of the X3 → X8 connection

of neural influences from imaging data. The "classical" cognitive psychologists had difficulty linking their variables to biological variables; mechanistic neuropsychology has troubles in the other direction: finding which specific combinations of local neural activities organized in causal crescendos produce which specific measurable behaviors. Perhaps, as the Churchlands so often warned and Thorndike believed, there is no match, any more than our folk classifications of trees and fishes match their biological classifications. But beyond reflex and involuntary movements, matching neural processes to behavioral features may be too much to ask, just as we would not expect a physicist to be able to define "billiard ball" in purely physical terms or predict every detail of the motion of billiard balls when struck by a cue (pool table surfaces differ, billiard ball surfaces and composition differ, strikes by cues differ, etc.). There is trouble in the middle as well, between neuron and behavior: there is no sure guide to which arrays of neurons act coherently, as a unit, when cognitive tasks are done. The spatial resolution of instruments, whether magnetic resonance or EEG or whatever, need not be nature's spatial resolution in creating a thought or a motion. Further, computational and statistical underdetermination combine to limit how informative various methods can be. When the relations among variables are very dense, as they are with neurons and even with neurons aggregated to voxels, no known methods can accurately retrieve more than a fraction of the connections, and of those, only the strongest.

The brain is no longer a black box, rather more a semi-opaque box whose complexity and ethical inviolability leave underdetermined much of the detail of how it does what it does, even when measured and estimated by our best available methods. We have a long way to go before, if ever, Helmholtz's vision of psychology is realized and underdetermination becomes a matter of Kuhnian puzzle solving or billiard ball calculation, but the underdetermination we face is not, as it was for Thorndike, grounds for abandoning Helmholtz's vision. Striving and falling short, we learn more.

Acknowledgments

We thank Joseph Ramsey, Biwei Huang, Kun Zhang, and Madelyn Glymour of the CABAL group at Carnegie Mellon for discussions and for some of the work referenced here. Research reported in this publication was supported by grant U54HG008540 awarded by the National Human Genome Research Institute through funds provided by the trans-NIH Big Data to Knowledge (BD2K) initiative. The content is solely the responsibility of the authors and does not necessarily represent the official views of the National Institutes of Health.

References

Austin, R. and Anderson, J. (2008) *E-Schooling: Notes from a Small Island*. Abingdon, UK: Routledge.

Gates, K. and Molenaar, P (2012) 'Group Search Algorithm Recovers Effective Connectivity Maps for Individuals in Homogeneous and Heterogeneous Samples', *Neuroimage*, 63 (1), pp. 310–319.

Glymour, C.N. (1991) 'Freud's Androids', in Neu, J. (ed.) *The Cambridge Companion to Freud*. Cambridge, UK: Cambridge University Press, pp. 44–85.

Glymour, C.N. (2001) *The Mind's Arrows: Bayes Nets and Graphical Causal Models in Psychology*. Cambridge, MA: MIT Press.

Glymour, C.N. and Hanson, C. (2016) 'Reverse Inference in Neuropsychology', *The British Journal for the Philosophy of Science*, 67 (4), pp. 1139–1153.

Jonas, E. and Kording, K.P. (2015) 'Automatic Discovery of Cell Types and Microcircuitry from Neural Connectomics', *ELife*, 2015 (4), e04250, pp. 1–21.

Jonas, E. and Kording, K.P. (2017) 'Could a Neuroscientist Understand a Microprocessor?', *PLOS Computational Biology*, 13 (1), pp. 1–23.

Klahr, D. and Langley, P. (1987) *Production System Models of Learning and Development*. Cambridge, MA: MIT Press.

Luce, R.D. (1986) *Response Times: Their Role in Inferring Elementary Mental Organization*. Oxford: Oxford University Press.

Machery, E. (2014) 'In Defense of Reverse Inference', *The British Journal for the Philosophy of Science*, 65 (2), pp. 251–267.

Meynert, T. (1884) *Psychiatrie. Klinik der Erkrankungen des Vorderhirns, begründet auf dessen Bau, Leistungen und Ernährung*. Vienna: W. Braumüller.

Mochizuk, Y. and Shinomoto, S. (2014) 'Analog and Digital Codes in the Brain', *Physical Review E*, 89 (2), pp. 1–8.

Pylyshyn, Z.W. (1986) *Computation and Cognition: Toward a Foundation for Cognitive Science*. Cambridge, MA: MIT Press.

Ramón y Cajal, S. (1988) *Cajal on the Cerebral Cortex: An Annotated Translation of the Complete Writings*. Translated and edited by J. DeFelipe and E.G. Jones. Oxford: Oxford University Press.

Ramsey, J.D. et al. (2017) 'A Million Variables and More: The Fast Greedy Equivalence Search Algorithm for Learning High-dimensional Graphical Causal Models, with an Application to Functional Magnetic Resonance Images', *International Journal of Data Science and Analytics*, 3 (2), pp. 121–129.

Shimizu, S. et al. (2006) 'A Linear Non-Gaussian Acyclic Model for Causal Discovery', *Journal of Machine Learning Research*, 7, pp. 2003–2030.

Smith, L. and Thelen, E. (2003) 'Development as a Dynamical System', *Trends in Cognitive Science*, 7, pp. 343–348.

Smith, S. et al. (2011) 'Network Modelling Methods for fMRI', *NeuroImage*, 54, pp. 875–891.

Thorndike, E.L. (1905) *Elements of Psychology*. New York, NY: A.G. Seiler.

von Helmholtz, H. (1847) *Uber die Erhaltung die Kraft*. Berlin: G. Reimer.

Zhang, K. and Hyvärinen, A. (2008) 'Distinguishing Causes from Effects Using Nonlinear Acyclic Causal Models', *Journal of Machine Learning Research, Workshop and Conference Proceedings (NIPS 2008 Causality Workshop)*, 6, pp. 157–164.

18

THE NATURE AND FUNCTION OF CONTENT IN COMPUTATIONAL MODELS

Frances Egan

Introduction

Much of computational cognitive science construes human cognitive capacities as representational capacities, or as involving representation in some way. Computational theories of vision, for example, typically posit structures that represent edges in the distal scene. Neurons are often said to represent elements of their receptive fields. Despite the ubiquity of representational talk in computational theorizing there is surprisingly little consensus about how such claims are to be understood. The point of this chapter is to sketch an account of the nature and function of representation in computational cognitive models.

A commitment to representation presupposes a distinction between representational *vehicle* and representational *content*. The vehicle is a physically realized state or structure that carries or bears content. Insofar as a representation is causally involved in a cognitive process, it is in virtue of the representational vehicle. A state or structure has content just in case it represents things to be a certain way; it has a 'satisfaction condition' – the condition under which it represents accurately.

The representational vehicles in so-called 'classical' computational systems are *symbols*, physical structures characterized by a combinatorial syntax, over which computational processes are defined. Symbols are tailor-made for semantic interpretation, for 'hanging' contents on, so to speak. But not all computational systems are symbol-manipulating systems. For example, connectionist models explain cognitive phenomena as the propagation of activation among units in highly connected networks; dynamical models characterize cognitive processes by a set of differential equations describing the behavior of the system over time. The systems so described do not operate on symbols in any obvious sense. There is a good deal of controversy about whether these systems are genuinely representational. For the most part, the dispute concerns whether such systems have representational vehicles, that is, states or structures causally involved in cognitive processes that are plausibly construed as candidates for semantic interpretation. In this chapter we will put this issue aside, abstracting away from questions about the bearers of content, and focus on the nature and function of representational content itself.

Adequacy conditions on an account of content for computational systems

We can identify several widely accepted constraints on an account of content for computational neuroscience:

1 The account should provide the basis for the attribution of *determinate* contents to computational states or structures.
2 The account should allow for the possibility that the posited states can *mis*represent.

The idea is that genuinely representational states represent *robustly*, in the way that paradigmatic mental states such as beliefs represent; and they should allow for the possibility of *getting it wrong*.

There is a constitutive connection between constraints (1) and (2). If the theory cannot underwrite the attribution of determinate satisfaction conditions to a mental state (type), then it cannot support the claim that some possible tokenings of the state occur when the conditions are not satisfied, and hence would misrepresent. For example, suppose that we want to capture the idea that a frog's tongue snapping at a BB in the laboratory constitutes a misrepresentation. This requires excluding BB-caused tokenings from the content-determining conditions of the internal state. Partitioning possible tokenings of the state into veridical instances on the one hand and misrepresentations on the other requires an antecedent specification of the state's content.

3 The account should be *naturalistic*.

Typically, this constraint is construed as requiring a specification, in non-semantic and non-intentional terms, of (at least) a sufficient condition for a state or structure to have a particular content. Such a specification would guarantee that the theory makes no illicit appeal to the very phenomenon – meaning – that it is supposed to explain. This idea motivates so-called *tracking* theories, discussed below. But we will see that this is not the only way to interpret the naturalistic constraint. More generally, the constraint is motivated by the conviction that intentionality is not *fundamental*:[1]

> It's hard to see … how one can be a realist about intentionality without also being, to some extent or other, a reductionist. If the semantic and the intentional are real properties of things, it must be in virtue of their identity with (or maybe supervenience on) properties that are themselves *neither* intentional *nor* semantic. If aboutness is real, it must be something else.
>
> *(Fodor, 1987, p. 97)*

> There are no "ultimately semantic" facts or properties, i.e. no semantic facts or properties over and above the facts and properties of physics, chemistry, biology, neurophysiology, and those parts of psychology, sociology, and anthropology that can be expressed independently of semantic concepts.
>
> *(Field, 1975, p. 386)*

Philosophers of mind of a materialistic bent have traditionally been interested in computationalism in part because it seeks to characterize mental processes as *mechanical* processes – processes guaranteed to be physically realizable, whose specification invokes no mysterious mental substance, properties, or events. Its success would pave the way for a naturalistic reduction of the mind, and so of intentionality. Or so it has been hoped.

Finally,

4   The account should conform to actual practice in computational cognitive science.

Proposals for computational content

Let us turn now to the central question: how do states/structures posited in computational models get their meaning? I will discuss some popular proposals and indicate outstanding problems with each before sketching what I take to be the correct view. My discussion of the popular candidates will necessarily be very brief.

Tracking theories

Most theories of content explicate intentionality in terms of a privileged relation between the tokening of an internal state and what the state represents. Thus the state is said to 'track' (in some specified sense) the external condition that serves as its satisfaction condition. Tracking theories are explicitly naturalistic – both the relation and the relata should be specified in non-intentional and non-semantic terms – but they differ in their accounts of the representation relation.

Information-theoretic theories

Very roughly, according to information-theoretic accounts, an internal state S means *cat* if S is caused by the presence of a cat, and certain further conditions obtain.[2] Further conditions are required to allow for the possibility of misrepresentation, that is, for the possibility of some S-tokenings *not* caused by cats but, say, by large rats on a dark night. A notable problem for information-theoretic theories is the consequence that everything in the causal chain from the presence of a cat in the distal environment to the internal tokening of S, including cat-like patterns in the retinal image, may appear to satisfy the condition, and so falls into S's extension. Thus, information-theoretic theories typically founder on constraint (1), failing to underwrite determinate contents for mental states. The outstanding problem for such theories is to provide for determinacy without illicit appeal to intentional or semantic notions. Yet further conditions may sufficiently constrain content but if the proposed meaning-determining relation becomes too baroque it will fail to be explanatory, leaving us wondering *why* it determines content.

Teleological theories

According to teleological theories, internal state S means *cat* if S has the natural function of indicating cats. The view was first developed and defended in Millikan (1984), and there are now many interesting variations on the central idea.[3] Teleosemanticists have been notoriously unable to agree on the natural function of states of even the simplest organisms.[4] Let's focus on a widely discussed case. Does the inner state responsible for engaging a frog's tongue-lashing behavior have the function of indicating (and hence representing) *fly*, *frog food*, or *small dark moving thing*? Teleosemanticists, at various times, have proposed all three. Suppose we settle on *fly*. Wouldn't a *fly stage* detector or an *undetached fly part* detector serve the purpose of getting nutrients into the frog's stomach equally well?[5] The problem is that indeterminate functions cannot ground determinate contents. Each of various function-candidates specifies a different satisfaction condition; unless a compelling case can be made for one function-candidate over the others, teleosemantics runs afoul of constraint (1). Moreover, the argument should not appeal to intentional or normative considerations (such as what makes for a good explanation), on pain of violating the naturalistic constraint.

Structural similarity theories

A third type of tracking theory appeals to the type of relation that holds between a map and the domain it represents, that is, structural similarity or isomorphism. Cummins (1989), (Ramsey 2007), and Shagrir (2012) have proposed variations on this idea. Of course, since similarity is a symmetric relation but the representation relation is not, any account that attempts to ground representational content in similarity will need supplementation by appeal to something like *use*. Moreover, as the saying goes, "isomorphisms are cheap". A given set of internal states or structures is likely to be structurally similar to any number of external conditions. The question is whether structural similarity can be sufficiently constrained to underwrite determinate contents while still respecting the naturalistic constraint.

The upshot of this short discussion is that tracking theories face formidable problems, but it would certainly be premature to write them off. One might simply conclude that more work needs to be done. It is worth noting, however, that despite the fact that there is no widely accepted naturalistic foundation for representational content, computational theorists persist in employing representational language in articulating their models. For example, vision theorists talk of structures posited in the course of visual processing *representing* edges in the scene. Neuroscientists talk of cells in the hippocampus ('place cells') *representing* locations in the local environment. The apparent mismatch between the theories of content developed by philosophers pursuing the naturalistic project and the actual practice of computational theorists in ascribing content cries out for explanation; it motivates a different sort of account. Before sketching an account that better fits the practice I shall consider very briefly a couple of other proposals.

Phenomenal intentionality

It has recently been suggested by proponents of the *phenomenal intentionality research program* (PIRP)[6] that rather than looking to external relations between states of the subject and distal objects or properties to ground determinate content, as tracking theorists propose, we should look inside to the subject's phenomenal experience. Indeed, Horgan and Graham (2012) claim that phenomenally based intentionality is the source of all determinacy of thought content, even for the deeply unconscious, sub-personal states posited by computational theories of cognition. Intriguing though the suggestion is, it has a number of problems. PIRP theorists reject the naturalistic constraint, as it is normally understood, but there are more serious worries. In the first place, the view finds no support in the actual practice of computational theorists, who typically look to an organism's behavior and to the environment in which the behavior is normally deployed when they assign representational content to computational states. They look to characteristic patterns of error. On a smaller scale, neuroscientists look to features of a neuron's receptive field. They do not look to the way things seem to the subject; though, of course, their theories often have implications for the subject's phenomenal experience. So the suggestion fails to comply with constraint (4), the requirement that an account of representational content should conform to actual practice in computational cognitive science. Second, and more importantly, whatever the current state of practice, the proposal is at odds with a fundamental commitment of computationalism, viz. the idea that thought is, at bottom, a *mechanical* process. This commitment underwrites the promise of artificial intelligence. Maybe a mechanical account of phenomenal consciousness will eventually be forthcoming, explaining not only our own phenomenal experience but also paving the way for the creation of machine consciousness. But if so, the phenomenal intentionality program gets the grounding relation backwards. It will be computation that fixes the determinate content of phenomenal experience, not the other way around.

Content eliminativism

A natural reaction to the problem of grounding content might be to reject content altogether, as Noam Chomsky does.[7] According to Chomsky, characterizing an internal structure as 'representing an edge' or 'representing a noun phrase' is just loose talk, at best a convenient way of sorting structures into kinds determined by their role in processing. As Chomsky puts it, "the theory itself has no place for the [intentional] concepts that enter into the informal presentation, intended for general motivation" (1995, p. 55). In a later work he goes on to say:

> I do not know of any notion of "representational content" that is clear enough to be invoked in accounts of how internal computational systems enter into the life of the organism. And to the extent to which I can grasp what is intended, it seems to me very questionable that it points to a profitable path to pursue.
>
> *(Chomsky, 2003, p. 274)*

Chomsky is on to something important here. Structures posited by computational theories *are* sorted into kinds by their role in processing. And though they are often characterized by their contents, to take representational talk too seriously *is* to conflate the theory with its informal presentation. But content eliminativism doesn't follow, because Chomsky is wrong to conclude that content plays no explanatory role in computational cognitive models. These claims will be defended in the next section.

A deflationary account of content

The most popular accounts of content for computational theorizing – tracking theories – share two central commitments:

1 Mental representations have their contents *essentially*: if a particular internal structure had a different content it would be a different (type of) representation. In other words, computational theories individuate the states and structures they posit partly in terms of their content.
2 Content is determined by a privileged naturalistic relation holding between a state/structure and the object or property it is about.

In this section I will sketch an alternative picture of the nature and function of representational content in computational theorizing[8] – what I call a *deflationary* account of content – characterized by the rejection of the above two claims.

I begin by calling attention to two central features of computational theorizing:

1 Computational theories of cognitive capacities provide what I call a *function-theoretic* characterization of the capacity.
2 A computational theory (including the function-theoretic characterization, and the specification of algorithms, structures and processes) is accompanied by what I call an *intentional gloss*.

These two features, to be spelled out below, determine two kinds of content that play distinctive roles in computational theorizing.

Mathematical content

Marr's (1982) theory of early vision purports to explain edge detection, in part, by positing the computation of the Laplacean of a Gaussian of the retinal array. The mechanism takes as input intensity values at points in the image and calculates the rate of intensity change over the image. In other words, it computes a particular smoothing function. Marr's theory is typical of perceptual theories in this respect: perceptual systems compute smoothing functions to eliminate noise. Shadmehr and Wise's (2005) computational account of motor control explains how a subject is able to grasp an object in view by computing the displacement of the hand from its current location to the target location, i.e. by computing vector subtraction. Seung et al. (1996; 1998; 2000) hypothesize that the brain keeps track of eye movements across saccades by deploying an internal integrator. These examples illustrate an explanatory strategy that is pervasive in computational cognitive science. I call the strategy *function-theoretic explanation* and the mathematical characterization that is central to it *function-theoretic characterization* (hereafter FT).[9] Theories employing the strategy explain a cognitive capacity by appeal to an independently well-understood mathematical function under which the physical system is subsumed. In other words, what gets computed, according to these computational models, is the value of a mathematical function (e.g. addition, vector subtraction, the Laplacean of a Gaussian, a fast Fourier transform) for certain arguments for which the function is defined. For present purposes we can take functions to be mappings from sets (the arguments of the function) to sets (its values). Inputs to the component of the Shadmehr/Wise mechanism that computes vector subtraction represent vectors and outputs represent their difference. More generally, the inputs of a computationally characterized mechanism represent the arguments and the outputs the values of the mathematical function that canonically specifies the task executed by the mechanism. Hence, the FT characterization specifies a kind of content – *mathematical* content – and this content is essential to the computational characterization of the mechanism. If the mechanism computed a different mathematical function, and hence was assigned different mathematical contents, it would be a different computational mechanism.

The mathematical functions deployed in computational models are typically well understood independently of their use in such models. Laplacean of Gaussian filters, vector subtraction, fast Fourier transforms, and so on, are standard items in the applied mathematician's toolbox. An FT description provides an abstract, domain-general, environment-neutral characterization of a mechanism. It prescinds not only from the cognitive capacity that is the explanatory target of the theory (vision, motor control, etc.) but also from the environment in which the capacity is normally exercised.

What I will call the *computational theory proper* comprises a specification of (i) the mathematical function(s) computed by the device (the FT characterization), (ii) the specific algorithms involved in the computation of the function(s), (iii) the representational structures that the algorithms maintain, and (iv) the computational processes defined over these structures. I shall call elements (i)–(iv) the *computational component* of the theory proper. These core elements provide an environment-independent characterization of the device. They have considerable counterfactual power: they provide the basis for predicting and explaining the behavior of the device in any environment, including environments where the device would fail to exercise any cognitive capacity at all. Of course, the theorist must explain how computing the value of the mathematical function, in the subject's normal environment, contributes to the exercise of the cognitive capacity that is the explanatory target of the theory. Only in *some* environments would computing the Laplacean of a Gaussian help an organism to see. In our environment this computation produces a smoothed output that facilitates the detection of sharp intensity gradients across the retina, which, when they occur at different scales, typically correspond to physically significant boundaries – changes in depth, surface orientation, illumination, or reflectance – in the scene. Thus the 'theory proper' will also include (v) such environment-specific facts as that a co-incidence of sharp intensity gradients at different scales is likely to be physically significant, corresponding to object boundaries in the world. I shall call element (v) the *ecological component* of the computational theory proper. Together these five elements of the theory proper suffice to explain the subject's manifest cognitive capacity.

Cognitive contents

So far nothing has been said about domain-specific representational content. In general, the inputs and outputs of computational mechanisms are characterized not only in abstract terms, as the arguments and values of the specified mathematical function; they are typically also characterized as representing properties or objects relevant to the cognitive capacity to be explained. I call such contents *cognitive contents*. In ascribing cognitive contents the theorist may look for a distal causal antecedent of an internal structure's tokening, or a homomorphism between distal and internal elements, but the search is constrained primarily by the cognitive capacity that the theory is developed to explain. Vision theorists will look to properties that can structure the light in appropriate ways; thus they construe the states and structures they posit as representing light intensity values, changes in light intensity, and further downstream, changes in depth and surface orientation. Theorists of motor control construe the structures they posit as representing positions of objects in nearby space and changes in body joint angles. And the assignment of task-specific cognitive contents will be justified only if the theorist can explain how the posited structures are used by the system in ways that facilitate the cognitive capacity in question.

Cognitive contents, I will argue, are not part of the essential characterization of the device and are not fruitfully regarded as part of the computational theory proper. They are ascribed to facilitate the explanation of the relevant cognitive capacity, though, as noted above, the five elements of the theory proper are strictly speaking sufficient to explain the system's success (and occasional failure). Cognitive contents are best construed as an *intentional gloss* on a computational theory. The primary function of an intentional gloss is to illustrate, in a perspicuous and concise way, how the computational/mathematical theory addresses the intentionally characterized phenomena with which we began and which it is the job of the theory to explain. Cognitive content is the 'connective tissue' linking the sub-personal mathematical capacities posited in the theory and the manifest personal-level capacity that is the theory's explanatory target.

Let me spell out how this works in practice by focusing more closely on the early vision example, although the strategy is general. The computation of the Laplacean of a Gaussian is, of course, presumed to be physically realized in the brain; accordingly, Marr's theory specifies a structure – EDGE[10] – that is the output of this processing. Why would a vision theorist call the structure "EDGE"? Since the structure is individuated by its role in processing, the theorist could have highlighted aspects of its shape, as Marr did for BLOB and BAR, or assigned it an arbitrary name, such as "INTERNAL STRUCTURE #17". Calling the structure "EDGE" highlights its role in the complex process whereby the subject ultimately comes to recover the three-dimensional layout of the scene. So the structure, the output of the processes that compute the Laplacean of a Gaussian, is glossed in commonsense terms as *EDGE*. To say that the structure *represents* edges is 'shorthand' for the facts that constitute the ecological component of the theory, typically facts about robust covariations between tokenings of the structure and distal property instantiations under normal environmental conditions. These facts explain the organism's visual capacity, and they say nothing about representation.

Recall Chomsky's claim that characterizing an internal structure as 'representing an edge' or 'representing a noun phrase' is simply a convenient way of sorting structures into kinds determined by their role in processing. Chomsky is right that the posited structures are individuated by their computational roles, but wrong to conclude that content serves no legitimate function. The intentional gloss, in assigning contents appropriate to the relevant cognitive domain, shows that the theory addresses its explanatory target, a capacity which is often characterized, pretheoretically by commonsense, in intentional terms (for example, *seeing what is where*).

In addition to the explanatory context – the cognitive capacity to be explained – various pragmatic considerations play a role in determining an appropriate intentional gloss. Given their role in explanation, candidates for cognitive content must be salient or tractable. The structure EDGE represents a change in depth, surface orientation, illumination, or reflectance, but if the distal causes of a structure's tokening are too disjunctive the theorist may decide to assign a proximal content to the structure,[11] motivated in part by a desire to help us (that is, theorists and students of vision) keep track of what the mechanism is doing at a given point in the process.

We can see the extent to which pragmatic considerations figure in the ascription of content by revisiting some of the problems encountered by tracking theories in their attempt to specify a naturalistic content-determining relation. Far from adhering to the strict program imposed by the naturalistic constraint, as understood by tracking theorists, the computational theorist, in assigning content to posited internal structures, *selects* from all the information in the signal what is relevant for the cognitive capacity to be explained and specifies it in a way that is salient for explanatory purposes. Typically, pragmatic considerations will privilege a distal cause (the cat) over a proximal cause (cat-like patterns in the retinal image). Recall the dispute among teleosemanticists about whether the frog's internal state represents *fly* or *frog food* or *small dark moving thing*. The dispute is unlikely to be settled without reference to specific explanatory concerns. If the goal of the theoretical project is to explain the frog's role in its environmental niche, then *fly* content might be privileged. Alternatively, if the goal is to explain how the frog's visual mechanisms work, then *small dark moving thing* might be preferable. In other words, explanatory focus resolves indeterminacy. Turning to Quinean indeterminacy, the ontology implicit in public language privileges *fly* over *fly stage*. But none of these content choices are naturalistically motivated – the naturalistic constraint prohibits appeal to specific explanatory interests or to public meaning.

So we see, then, a *second* function of representational content: to characterize posited internal structures in a way that makes perspicuous their causal role in a process that typically extends into the environment. The content ascription *selects* what is salient in a complex causal process, given specific explanatory concerns. The upshot is quite a different take on the widely accepted view that the content of an internal state or structure *causally explains* the role that the state plays in cognitive processing.[12] This view puts the explanatory cart before the horse. A content ascription captures a salient part of the causal nexus in which the state is embedded. So, for example, construing the frog's internal state as representing *fly* emphasizes the causes of its tokening in the frog's normal ecological niche (its production); construing it as representing *frog food* emphasizes downstream nutritional effects of its tokening (its consumption). Thus it is no surprise that content *looks* to be causally explanatory – one of its jobs is to characterize internal structures/ states in a way that makes perspicuous their causal role in a cognitive process, again, given specific explanatory concerns. But content itself doesn't causally explain anything.

It is time to take stock. The view of content sketched here rejects the two central commitments of tracking theories: (1) Mental representations have their contents *essentially*; and (2) Content is determined by a privileged naturalistic relation holding between the state/structure and the object or property that it is about.

It is typically cognitive (domain-specific) contents that tracking theories take to be both essential to explanations of cognitive capacities and determined by a privileged naturalistic relation. I have argued that the structures posited by computational theories do not have their cognitive contents essentially. If the mechanism characterized in mathematical terms by the theory were embedded differently in the organism, perhaps allowing it to sub-serve a different cognitive capacity, then the posited structures would be assigned different cognitive contents. If the subject's environment were different, so that the use of these structures by the device did not facilitate the execution of the specified cognitive task, then the structures might be assigned no cognitive contents at all. And the various pragmatic considerations cited above might motivate the assignment of different cognitive contents to the structures. Moreover, since pragmatic considerations typically *do* play a role in determining cognitive contents, these contents are not determined by a naturalistic relation.

Turning to mathematical contents: whatever the ontological status of mathematical objects, it is unlikely that any naturalistic relation holds between the structures posited in the theory and (just) the mathematical objects specified by the FT characterization. Nonetheless, mathematical content *is* essential. The various scenarios discussed above would not affect the attribution of mathematical content, because the FT characterization is a canonical specification of what the device does. To characterize the device as computing a mathematical function *just is* to interpret its inputs and outputs as representing the arguments and values of the function respectively; if the FT characterization is essential, as I have argued, then so is the mathematical content that it determines.

Revisiting the adequacy conditions

I shall conclude by considering this deflationary account of content in light of the adequacy conditions for a theory of content for computational neuroscience.

Condition (1) requires that the account provide the basis for the attribution of *determinate* contents to computational states or structures. The deflationary theory does better in this respect than tracking theories, all of which have trouble grounding determinate content in a naturalistic relation. Once the role of specific explanatory interests and other pragmatic factors in content attribution is fully appreciated, determinacy is to be expected.

Condition (2) requires that the account allow for the possibility of *mis*representation. There is no mystery about how misrepresentation arises in the deflationary account. Cognitive contents are ascribed to internal structures on the basis of the cognitive capacity to be explained, what is happening in the subject's normal environment when the structures are tokened, and various pragmatic considerations discussed above. Normally, the structure is tokened when and only when the specified external condition obtains. But occasionally something goes wrong. In low light, a shadow may be mistaken for an edge. In an Ames room at Disney World, where the light is systematically distorted, the subject will misjudge the character of the local space. In such circumstances, the structure whose cognitive content is *edge* is tokened in response to a shadow or some other distal feature, and the mechanism misrepresents a shadow as an edge. The mechanism computes the same mathematical function it always computes, but in an abnormal situation (low light, distorted light, etc.) computing this mathematical function may not be sufficient for executing the cognitive capacity. Lest one think that a tracking theorist could avail herself of a similar story about misrepresentation, keep in mind that the structures have their (determinate) cognitive contents only in the gloss, where various pragmatic considerations provide the additional constraints necessary to support an attribution of misrepresentation. Misrepresentation, like veridical representation, is confined to the intentional gloss.[13]

Condition (3) requires that the account be naturalistic. At first blush, it may seem that the appeal to explanatory and other pragmatic considerations in the determination of cognitive content compromises the deflationary account's naturalistic credentials. That isn't so, because the pragmatic elements and the contents they determine are 'quarantined' in the intentional gloss, to use Mark Sprevak's (2013) apt expression. The theory proper of a cognitive capacity ((i)–(v) above) does not traffic in ordinary (i.e. cognitive domain-specific) representational contents. The theory proper provides a full description of the capacity sufficient to explain the organism's success at the cognitive task; the intentional gloss serves the various heuristic purposes described above.

Recall that the primary motivation for the naturalistic constraint is the conviction that intentionality is not fundamental, and the hope among materialistically minded theorists of cognition that computationalism will contribute to a naturalistic reduction. Specifying non-intentional and non-semantic sufficient conditions for an internal state's having its determinate content – the project that tracking theorists have set for themselves – is only one way that a reduction might be accomplished, and not a particularly promising way if, as I have argued, content attribution in computational practice is rife with pragmatic elements. But insofar as the deflationary account sketched here is an accurate representation of that practice, computational neuroscience is making some progress toward a naturalistic reduction of intentionality. I don't want to overstate the point: computational theories appeal to unreduced mathematical content. But a well-confirmed computational theory of a cognitive capacity that included an account of how the mechanism is realized in neural structures would be a significant step toward a reductive explanation of intentionality in that cognitive domain. States and structures that are characterized in the theory in terms of their computational role have meaning and truth conditions only in the intentional gloss, where they are used to show that the theory addresses the phenomenon for which we sought an explanation.

One of Chomsky's motivations for eliminating representational content is the desire to purge the cognitive sciences of normative and intentional notions – such talk as 'solving a problem', 'making a mistake', 'misrepresenting' – which he thinks reflect our parochial interests, and hence have no place in legitimate science. But such austerity is neither necessary nor appropriate. The project, after all, is to understand our own mentality. The intentional gloss characterizes computational processes in ways congruent with our commonsense understanding of ourselves, ways that the theory itself eschews. It fills a kind of explanatory gap between the scientific and the manifest image, to put the point in Wilfrid Sellars' (1963) terms.

Finally, condition (4) requires that the account conform to actual practice in computational cognitive science. The deflationary account improves on its competitors in two significant respects: (1) it recognizes the role played in computational models by a mathematical characterization of a mechanism, and hence the attribution of mathematical content, and (2) it explicitly acknowledges the role of pragmatic considerations in the ascription of ordinary representational content.

Notes

1 The recent resurgence of panpsychism notwithstanding.
2 See Dretske (1981) and Fodor (1990) for the most developed information-theoretic accounts. Further conditions include the requirement that during a privileged learning period only cats cause S-tokenings (Dretske, 1981) or that non-cat caused S-tokenings depend asymmetrically on cat-caused S-tokenings (Fodor, 1990).
3 See Matthen (1988), Papineau (1993), Dretske (1995), Ryder (2004), Neander (2006; 2017), and Shea (2007) for other versions of teleosemantics.
4 See the discussion of the magnetosome in Dretske (1986) and Millikan (1989).
5 See Quine (1960).
6 The expression is from Kriegel (2013).
7 See Chomsky (1995; 2000). For another eliminativist view see Stich (1983).
8 See Egan (2013) for elaboration of the account sketched here.
9 See Egan (2017) for elaboration of FT explanation.
10 I will use upper case to denote structures whose individuation conditions are given by their roles in processing, i.e. non-semantically.
11 For example, zero-crossings in Marr's theory represent discontinuities in the image.
12 For a sample of the literature promoting this idea see Dretske (1988), Segal and Sober (1991), and Rescorla (2014).
13 The structures characterized abstractly in the theory by the FT specification can also misrepresent. If the mechanism overheats or is exposed to a harmful substance it may fail to compute its normal mathematical function, for example, miscomputing, and hence misrepresenting, the sum of a vector addition as some other value.

References

Chomsky, N. (1995) 'Language and Nature', *Mind*, 104, pp. 1–61.
Chomsky, N. (2000) 'Internalist Explorations', in *New Horizons in the Study of Language and Mind*. Cambridge, UK: Cambridge University Press, pp. 164–194.
Chomsky, N. (2003) 'Reply to Egan', in Antony, L. and Hornstein, N. (eds.) *Chomsky and His Critics*. Oxford: Blackwell, pp. 268–274.
Cummins, R. (1989) *Meaning and Mental Representation*. Cambridge, MA: MIT Press.
Dretske, F. (1981) *Knowledge and the Flow of Information*. Cambridge, MA: MIT Press.
Dretske, F. (1986) 'Misrepresentation', in Bogdan, R. (ed.) *Belief: Form, Content, and Function*. Oxford: Oxford University Press, pp. 17–36.
Dretske, F. (1988) *Explaining Behavior*. Cambridge, MA: MIT Press.
Dretske, F. (1995) *Naturalizing the Mind*. Cambridge, MA: MIT Press.
Egan, F. (2013) 'How to Think about Mental Content', *Philosophical Studies*, 170, pp. 115–135.
Egan, F. (2017) 'Function-Theoretic Explanation and the Search for Neural Mechanisms', in Kaplan, D.M. (ed.) *Explanation and Integration in Mind and Brain Science*. Oxford: Oxford University Press, pp. 145–163.
Field, H. (1975) 'Conventionalism and Instrumentalism in Semantics', *Nous*, 9, pp. 375–405.
Fodor, J.A. (1987) *Psychosemantics*. Cambridge, MA: MIT Press.
Fodor, J.A. (1990) 'A Theory of Content II: The Theory', in *A Theory of Content and Other Essays*. Cambridge, MA: MIT Press, pp. 89–136.
Horgan, T. and Graham, G. (2012) 'Phenomenal Intentionality and Content Determinacy', in Schantz, R. (ed.) *Prospects for Meaning*. Boston, MA: De Gruyter, pp. 321–344.
Kriegel, U. (2013) 'The Phenomenal Intentionality Research Program', in Kriegel, U. (ed.) *Phenomenal Intentionality*. New York, NY: Oxford University Press, pp. 1–26.
Marr, D. (1982) *Vision*. New York, NY: Freeman.
Matthen, M. (1988) 'Biological Functions and Perceptual Content', *Journal of Philosophy*, 85, pp. 5–27.
Millikan, R. (1984) *Language, Thought, and Other Biological Categories*. Cambridge, MA: MIT Press.
Millikan, R. (1989) 'Biosemantics', *Journal of Philosophy*, 86, pp. 281–297.
Neander, K. (2006) 'Content for Cognitive Science', in Papineau, D. and McDonald, G. (eds.) *Teleosemantics*. Oxford: Oxford University Press, pp. 140–159.
Neander, K. (2017) *A Mark of the Mental: In Defense of Informational Teleosemantics*. Cambridge, MA: MIT Press.

Papineau, D. (1993) *Philosophical Naturalism*. Oxford: Blackwell.

Quine, W.V. (1960) *Word and Object*. Cambridge, MA: MIT Press.

Ramsey, W. (2007) *Representation Reconsidered*. Cambridge, UK: Cambridge University Press.

Rescorla, M. (2014) 'The Causal Relevance of Content to Computation', *Philosophy and Phenomenological Research*, 88, pp. 140–159.

Ryder, D. (2004) 'SINBAD Neurosemantics: A Theory of Mental Representation', *Mind and Language*, 19, pp. 211–240.

Segal, G. and Sober, E. (1991) 'The Causal Relevance of Content', *Philosophical Studies*, 63, pp. 1–30.

Sellars, W. (1963) 'Philosophy and the Scientific Image of Man', in *Science, Perception, and Reality*. New York, NY: Humanities Press.

Seung, S.H. (1996) 'How the Brain Keeps the Eyes Still', *Proceedings of the National Academy of Science USA*, 93, pp. 13339–13344.

Seung, S.H. (1998) 'Continuous Attractors and Oculomotor Control', *Neural Networks*, 11, pp. 1253–1258.

Seung, S.H. et al. (2000) 'Stability of the Memory of Eye Position in a Recurrent Network of Conductance-based Model Neurons', *Neuron*, 26, pp. 259–271.

Shadmehr, R. and Wise, S. (2005) *The Computational Neurobiology of Reaching and Pointing: A Foundation for Motor Learning*. Cambridge, MA: MIT Press.

Shagrir, O. (2012) 'Structural Representations and the Brain', *British Journal for the Philosophy of Science*, 63, pp. 519–545.

Shea, N. (2007) 'Consumers Need Information: Supplementing Teleosemantics with an Input Condition', *Philosophy and Phenomenological Research*, 75, pp. 404–435.

Sprevak, M. (2013) 'Fictionalism about Neural Representations', *The Monist*, 96, pp. 539–560.

Stich, S. (1983) *From Folk Psychology to Cognitive Science: The Case against Belief*. Cambridge, MA: MIT Press.

19

MAPS, MODELS AND COMPUTATIONAL SIMULATIONS IN THE MIND

William Ramsey

1 Introduction

Computational accounts of the mind are often framed as accounts that treat the mind as an "information processer"; yet, as many writers recognize, it is not always clear just what this means. One way of understanding information processing is rooted in the idea that cognitive activity involves the manipulation and exploitation of inner representational states and structures. Yet again, although there is considerable agreement among cognitive scientists and philosophers of mind about the explanatory need for internal representations in theories of cognitive processes,[1] there has been less clarity and agreement about the nature of the representations. In fact, there have been disagreements about their form, disagreements about the way in which representations acquire their content, disagreements about their explanatory role, and, perhaps most importantly, disagreements about the manner in which they function as representations. The perspective I want to illuminate in this chapter involves a particular *type* of representation that has a long history in computational accounts and that is increasingly viewed as a promising way to make sense of representation in the brain. Commonly referred to as "S-representation" (see below for more on this label), this type of representation is based upon some form of structural similarity between a representational system on the one hand, and the item, process, condition, or relations represented on the other hand. In large measure, the notion is motivated by our use of models, maps, and simulations in our own problem-solving activities. Just as we use external models and maps to acquire information, make predictions, and navigate through the world, so too, investigators claim that the computational brain uses its own neural models and maps to perform various cognitive tasks.

To shed light on this picture of mental representation and its role in computational accounts of the mind, this chapter will have the following organization. In Section 2, I'll present a general explanation of this notion of representation and discuss some of its central aspects. I'll also say a bit about how it differs from another prominent notion of representation in cognitive science. In Section 3, I'll provide a few illustrations of how this notion of representation has appeared in computational accounts of the mind. Section 4 will address some common criticism of this way of thinking of representation in the brain, and Section 5 presents a brief conclusion.

2 S-representation(s)

Our understanding of mental representation has often been inspired by our understanding of representation outside of the brain (Godfrey-Smith, 2006). One such common sort of non-mental representational device exploits the existence of some sort of structural similarity or homomorphism between the representational system on the one hand, and the thing represented (the intentional object) on the other. Maps, models, various diagrams and most types of simulations represent by virtue of mirroring or matching various properties and relations of the intentional object. These types of devices invoke a particular style of representation, sometimes called "S-representation" (following Cummins, 1989); the 'S' can be interpreted as standing for "structural" or "simulation" or "surrogative", since all of these terms designate key dimensions of this notion. Often, the intentional object of S-representation is referred to as the representational "target".

Consider how we use a map to get around. The map serves as a useful guide because it carries information about some terrain or cityscape. It carries this information not by linguistically describing the terrain, nor by possessing elements that are triggered by environmental stimuli. Instead the map carries and transmits information by replicating the proportional spatial relations of significant features of the terrain in a two-dimensional format (though not exactly). A map presents to us a type of replica of the region that we can then use to form beliefs about distances, possible routes, current locations, and so on. The lines and marks on the map represent features of the landscape (roads, paths, buildings, streams, etc.) by standing *in* for those elements in a structurally similar facsimile of that terrain. The representation relation is grounded in a shared lay-out that preserves spatial arrangement and thus allows the representational elements of the map to function as proxies for elements of the real world.

The same thing happens when we build a model of something and use its behavior to simulate and thus inform us of the target's behavior. When used properly, a structurally accurate model of an airplane or a well-designed computer simulation of a storm will act in ways that, although not exactly like their targets, are similar enough in important respects to the ways that real planes and storms behave to be highly informative. Thus, we can use these models to make predictions, explain anomalies, identify causally relevant factors, and so on. As with a map, the constituent elements of a model or simulation represent by standing in as surrogates for whatever real world elements with which they share the same structural "position"; for example, a tail flap on a model plane stands in for the tail flap of the real airplane and thereby represents it.

Models, maps, and simulations almost never replicate all of the different items, properties, and relations of the target domain. For example, a map typically leaves out factors that are not essential to the informative role it is designed to play. The map replicates the relative distances, locations, and perhaps names of various buildings, but it typically does not bother to present impertinent information about the buildings' colors or structural composition. Thus, although S-representation is based upon some sort of similarity between the representation and target, this should not be interpreted too literally or formally.[2] Even the pertinent features, like the relative positions, are not normally replicated with 100 percent accuracy. A map of Chicago is still an extremely useful guide for getting to the Sears Tower, even if the position of the Sears Tower on the map is very slightly further from the Lakeshore, proportionally, than it is in real life.

Most writers insist that genuine representation is impossible unless there exists the potential for misrepresentation or falsehood. S-representation provides a natural way of understanding how misrepresentation is possible. Misrepresentation can occur when there is sufficiently large *dis*-similarity between the representational system and the thing represented – where the pertinent similarity relations break down. For example, while a map of Chicago can be very slightly off regarding the position of the Sears Tower, it cannot be presented as north of the Lincoln Park. Any such map would falsely represent (misrepresent) the position of the Sears Tower. If a computer simulation of a storm depicts wind speeds in excess of 70 mph, whereas the real storm has winds that never exceed 50 mph, then this would be a clear case of misrepresentation. Just as broken mirrors can create distorted images in various ways, so too there are a variety of ways in which S-representations can distort (and thereby misrepresent) the "image" it presents of reality. Just how much dissimilarity is tolerable for what can be described as accurate representation, as opposed to how much dissimilarity (and what sort of dissimilarity) entails misrepresentation is a notoriously thorny issue; the matter typically depends upon the specific details of how a particular map or model is used.

In various discussions of S-representation, there is sometimes ambiguity regarding exactly what counts as the actual representational vehicles. On the one hand, authors sometimes treat the representational vehicle as the model or map itself, however it happens to be instantiated. On this interpretation, S-representations share a structural similarity with their intentional objects. On the other hand, we can also think of the representational vehicles as the constituent elements of a model or map. On this interpretation, S-representations typically do *not* share any sort of structural similarity with their intentional objects. An X on a map is a representation of buried treasure not because the buried treasure is X-shaped, but instead because the X is at the location on the map that is shared by the corresponding location of the terrain the map replicates. Sometimes writers appear to vacillate between these different interpretations – sometimes calling both the map/model and their constituent elements "the representations" (Swoyer, 1991). Here, we do not need to decide which usage is best, or even if there is anything wrong with treating both sorts of things as different types of S-representations. However, we should note that these two sorts of things cannot function as representations in exactly the same way. A map can be used as a representation because *it* is structurally similar to its intentional objects, whereas the X on a map plays a representational function because it *participates* (as a surrogate) in the broader representational system that is structurally similar.

As we've seen, S-representations represent by virtue of some sort of structural similarity between the representational system and the target. But the exact nature of this structural similarity varies with regard to complexity. In some cases, the matter is relatively straightforward. A good model of an airplane is (typically) just a miniature version of the airplane, and thus has the same spatial/physical structure. Its parts are physically related in a manner that is proportionally similar to the relations of the parts of the target; the only real difference is size. But not every model replicates the relevant structural relations in this way. Consider a typical organizational chart representing the hierarchy of some large corporation or university. It depicts mid-level bosses and managers as being spatially above their subordinates, and the boss's bosses as above them, and so on. But, of course, the different managers and their subordinates are seldom *spatially* related in this way. Instead, the spatial relations of the model serve as analogs for the command and control relations in the organization. Because the spatial relations on the chart track the authority relations in a systematic way (e.g. the metaphorically "higher" the position in the organization, the literally higher the spatial position on the chart), spatial relations can serve as a substitute for authority relations.

Models thereby often replace not just entities and their parts with proxies, but also relations, properties, values, and a host of other dimensions of the target domain. Mathematical models replace nearly every aspect of the target domain with mathematical entities and relations; computational simulations do the same with computational entities and processes. But if certain types of relations and properties of the target can be replaced in the model with other kinds of relations and properties, then it can be asked: in what sense are the model and its target really "structurally similar"? In the case of the corporation's organizational chart, it seems clear that representing relations must share certain abstract properties (like transitivity) with their represented, real-world counterparts. But how much of this is required, and which sort of abstract properties must be shared can vary between models and types of models.

One analysis that addresses some of these issues is an elaborate yet helpful paper by Chris Swoyer (1991). In this paper, Swoyer also identifies the type of problem-solving typically involved in the use of S-representations as "surrogative reasoning". The basic idea is easy to grasp. Because various structural and relational features of the S-representational system correspond to a variety of features of the represented system, then known or learnable facts about the representational system can generate new knowledge about the represented system. We might start with questions about the target system that, for whatever reason, cannot be answered by direct examination. So we instead directly examine (explore, investigate, etc.) the pertinent aspects of the representational system – the aspects that mirror the target system in a way that pertains to our question. This examination yields a pseudo-answer with regard to our original question – "pseudo" only because it applies to the representational system instead of the target. However, this pseudo-answer can be converted into a real answer when we transfer this understanding onto the target domain, a projection that is warranted by the structural similarity between the two systems. As Swoyer puts it:

> Structural representation enables us to reason directly about a representation in order to draw conclusions about the things that it represents. By examining the behavior of a scale model of an aircraft in a wind tunnel, we can draw conclusions about a newly designed wing's response to wind shear, rather than trying it out on a Boeing 747 over Denver. By using numbers to represent the lengths of physical objects, we can represent facts about the objects numerically, perform calculations of various sorts, then translate the results back into a conclusion about the original objects. In such cases we use one sort of thing as a surrogate in our thinking about another, and so I shall call this *surrogative reasoning*.
>
> *(1991, p. 449)*

If you think about how we navigate with a map, or how we use a model to make predictions, we often engage in exactly this sort of surrogative reasoning, albeit so quickly and effortlessly that we hardly notice. Indeed, it is easy to imagine developing a system that mechanizes this process – that examines an inner model of some target domain and then uses this information for solving various problems associated with that domain. Computational systems are exactly this sort of mechanism; thus, in computational theorizing about the mind, S-representation and surrogative reasoning have become commonplace, as we'll see in Section 3.

Although our focus here is on an approach to representation that is based on structural similarity, it should be noted that this is not the only approach to understanding representation in computational models of cognition. A popular alternative approach combines *two* common notions of non-mental representation. With regard to the *form* or *structure* of the representation, public language representations provide the inspiration. Representations in the brain are treated as words and sentences in a language of thought. Just as with public language, the syntactic arrangement of such "Mentalese" sentences, however they are realized in the brain, serves as a determinant of content, giving rise to a "combinatorial semantics" (Fodor, 1975). But this fails to explain the content or semantics of the *basic* representational units – the "words" of Mentalese.[3] Here, inspiration commonly comes from representational devices like thermometers or smoke detectors – things that represent by virtue of being caused by the presence of the represented entity or by the represented condition. Thus, basic representational units in the brain are alleged to represent by virtue of being reliably activated by (and, for the most part, *only* by) the things that they represent. A cognitive state is a representation of John if and only if it carries information about John by virtue of being properly caused by (or nomically dependent upon, an "indicator" of, etc.) the presence of John (Fodor, 1987; Dretske, 1988). This account of representation is inspired by, among other things, certain neurological theories that treat the responsiveness of neurons to certain stimuli as revealing the representational role of those neurons (Lettvin et al., 1959; Hubel and Weisel, 1968).[4]

Consequently, the causal or "indicator" notion of representation is typically treated as a competitor to the S-representation account we have been discussing. The two accounts appear to exploit different sorts of relations in the manner by which they provide information – structural similarity vs causal dependency. Yet it is also possible to view the two accounts as explaining different *dimensions* or *aspects* of a single representational theory. In addressing the question of how something can *function as* a representation in the brain, the S-representation story provides a plausible answer. Neural states function as representations by serving as stand-ins for elements of the target domain in some larger computational system whose structure is sufficiently similar to the target to be exploited for surrogative reasoning. In addressing the question of how something functioning as a representation in this way comes to have the specific content it does, causal links to elements in the target domain help provide an intuitive answer. A neural map is a map of terrain X (and not some other, similar terrain) because it was terrain X that caused the internal map to come about and acquire the exploitable structure it possesses. Alternatively, perhaps elements of a neural map are reliably activated when the corresponding location is nearby. The key point here is that it is at least possible that both the structural story and the causal/dependency story will have an important role to play in our final mature account of representation in computational cognition (Ramsey, 2016).

3 S-representation and the computational mind

In the last section, we saw how a type of representation that is based upon some sort of structural mirroring between the representation and the represented is generally understood and how it allows for a specific type of problem-solving and calculation. Here we will look how this notion of representation is invoked as an explanatory posit in computational accounts of cognition. In truth, virtually every area of cognitive modeling has involved theories that appeal to representations of this sort. This includes various accounts of reasoning, knowledge representation, memory, learning, navigation, perception, language comprehension, motor control, and several other cognitive competencies. In this section I'll provide three examples involving logical reasoning, knowledge representation, and animal navigation. Yet before jumping in, it will help to first clear away some potential confusion about how the term "model" arises in computational cognitive science. There are, in fact, two distinct notions that are easily conflated.

The first of these applies to our scientific theorizing in all domains about any given phenomenon and, moreover, our attempts to simulate that phenomenon (system or process) on a computer. To test various theories and to generate predictions about the system or process in question, we often construct computer programs that simulate the relevant phenomenon or system as proposed by the theory. So, for example, to test and deploy a theory of hurricane behavior, meteorologists use computer models to simulate storm activity under a variety of different sets of conditions. We employ this strategy in cognitive science just like the other sciences. We build theoretical and computational models of what researchers believe happens in the brain (at some level of analysis) when we engage in different cognitive activities. The second and very different notion of a model is that of an explanatory posit in certain (though not all) theories of cognition. With this notion, the claim is that the brain itself uses models or simulations when it engages in certain cognitive activities. To explain how the brain performs some cognitive task, it is claimed that it exploits an inner structure that is functioning as some sort of model or map that is structurally similar to a target which is relevant to the cognitive task in question. Putting these two notions of "model" together, we can say that some (though not all) models of cognition claim that the brain itself uses inner models for performing certain cognitive tasks. So some, but not all, scientific modeling pertains to cognition, and some, but not all, cognitive modeling invokes neurological models as an explanatory posit.

In accounting for human reasoning, one of the most important and dominant theories is due to the work of Philip Johnson-Laird (1983; 2006; 2013). Inspired by the work of Kenneth Craik (1943), Johnson-Laird argues that we perform a variety of cognitive tasks using representational structures that he describes as mental models with a structure "corresponding to the structure of what it represents ... its parts are interrelated in the same way that the parts of the entities that it represents are interrelated" (2013, pp. 651–652). Affirming his commitment to computationalism, Johnson-Laird insists "the construction of mental models, the communication of their contents, and reasoning on the basis of such representations, are nothing more than computational processes" (1983, p. 12).

Johnson-Laird invokes these mental models to explain a variety of cognitive abilities, including language comprehension, imaging and a host of other things. But his account is perhaps most fully developed, especially from a computational perspective, with regard to inference and logical reasoning. In particular, the account is committed to explaining the striking range of abilities humans display in understanding and processing different forms of basic arguments. To take a toy example, we can ask why it is that we do so much better completing valid arguments of the syntactic form,

(1)   All As are Bs
(2)   All Bs are Cs
(3)   Therefore ...

as opposed to arguments of the form,

(1')   All As are Bs
(2')   No Cs are As
(3')   Therefore ...

Johnson-Laird explains this difference by insisting that the premises are psychologically represented, not by syntactically structured, quasi-linguistic representations as presented above (with syntactic structures that share the same complexity), but instead by set models of each premise. A model for premise (1), "All As are Bs", might involve an imagined set of As, all of which are Bs, with some Bs that are not As:

A = B
A = B
A = B
...
B

The model for premise (2) is similar:

B = C
B = C
...
C

The union of the models (premises (1) and (2)) yields a complex schema like this:

A = B = C
A = B = C
A = B = C
...
B = C
B = C
...
C

Here the appropriate conclusion, "All As are Cs", can be ascertained in the conjoined models with relative ease. But what about the second argument? It involves a different second premise: "No Cs are As". The model for this premise would look something like this:

C
C
C
A
A
A

The argument combines this premise with the model for premise (1), yielding a schema like this:

C
C
C
_____

A = B
A = B
B

Here, the conjoined models fail to make obvious the proper conclusion; hence, more psycho-logical effort and more model testing is required to yield the proposition that some Bs are not Cs (and not something fallacious like "No B is C"). This proposal thereby explains an important fact about our reasoning capacity, and although this is a toy example (inspired by Johnson-Laird's more sophisticated treatment), it illustrates how the mental model approach is different from other accounts of computational representations, such as quasi-linguistic approaches involving explicitly represented inference rules. Various major research programs on the nature of reasoning and inference are now grounded in the mental models outlook (see, for example, Oakhill and Garnham, 1996; Schaeken et al., 2007)

Another important area of cognitive research pertains to the way we store information, a field of research commonly known as *knowledge representation*. A great deal of this work is carried out by investigators in artificial intelligence, although it also overlaps with psychological research on the nature and structure of conceptual knowledge. According to many theories in this domain, knowledge is stored by structures that are best described as small-scale models of the target domain. For example, one popular account of how we represent conceptual knowledge invokes structures called hierarchical semantic networks (Collins and Quillian, 1969). Semantic networks consist of interconnected nodes, whereby the individual nodes and connections correspond to the elements, properties, relations (especially super- and subordinate relations) of the represented subject. One such hierarchical semantic network is shown in Figure 19.1. Here, a small portion or our conceptual memory involving dogs and birds is captured by a graphic representation. Much like the corporate hierarchy chart we discussed in Section 2, proposed semantic networks of this sort possess a structure that tracks the non-spatial ontological structure of whatever bit of reality they represent. In this way, they are representational models that encode information in a structure-sensitive way.

To some degree, semantic networks like these helped inspire the interactive activation models of memory retrieval that later helped serve as the foundation for the connectionist revolution in cognitive modeling (see Rumelhart and McClelland, 1986). Indeed, while many accounts of knowledge representation are based upon classical computational architectures, it should be noted that the newer connectionist tradition also presents accounts of information storage and retrieval that are often thought to rely upon representations that, to some degree, mirror the structure of the target domain.[5]

A third area of cognitive research where the model/map notion of representation has found a home is cognitive ethology, and in particularly research on animal navigation and the use of cognitive maps. The notion of cognitive maps used for navigation was first introduced by Tolman

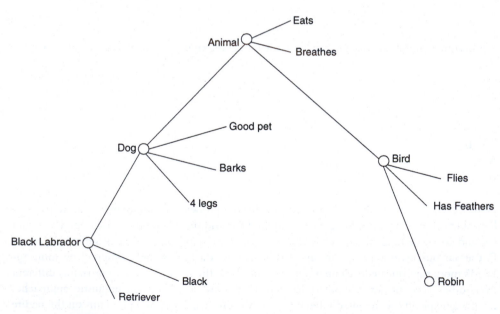

Figure 19.1 Sample hierarchical semantic network
Source: Inspired by Collins and Quillian (1969)

(1948).[6] It has since gained steady support, particularly with the work of John O'Keefe and Lynn Nadel and various others (O'Keefe and Nadel, 1978; Gallistel, 1998; Burgess and O'Keefe, 2002). These researchers claim that certain hippocampal structures of several animals serve as maps of the organism's environment. For example, Burgess and O'Keefe have argued that arrays of neural networks in the hippocampus of rats form something akin to a Cartesian coordinate system that is used both to store coordinate positions and to perform vector calculations which in turn navigate the rat through different terrains (Burgess and O'Keefe, 2002). It is natural to treat these neural transformations as implementing something like a working map, with elements functioning as S-representations of the target domain. Moreover, a critical element of this research involved the discovery of "place cells" – neurons that become highly activated when the rat gets close to specific locations in the environment. Consequently, to some degree, these neural maps appear to implement both elements of representation discussed toward the end of Section 2 – map-like structures with elements that function as S-representations and causal/dependency relations that tie the content of such representations to specific elements in the world (Ramsey, 2016).[7]

4 Challenges to S-representation in cognitive modeling

The claim that the brain uses internal neuronal structures that function as representations by somehow modeling various things in the world has been criticized in a variety of ways. While some of these difficulties have yet to be fully resolved, there are a number of promising strategies for handling them that provide some reason for optimism.

Some criticisms of S-representation are grounded in much broader concerns that aren't unique to the explanatory role they play computational accounts of cognition. For example, it is sometimes argued that structural similarity (or resemblance) cannot be the basis for a representation relation because similarity relations are symmetrical whereas representation is asymmetrical (Goodman, 1968). Concerns such as these can be handled by supplementing our understanding of representational systems with further details about the way such systems actually function in the real world. For instance, we can cheerfully agree that structural similarity goes both ways, and thus admit that, in principle, either item could be used as a structural representation of the other (e.g. we *could* use the lay-out of the actual city to learn facts about a map of the city). But it is far from clear why this should be a problem. Representations are functional entities that earn their status in part by virtue of how they are used. The fact that we could use a city to learn about a map in no way undermines the much more mundane representational status of a map that serves to provide information about a city.

Other criticisms are more serious and are directed at the specific claim that the brain uses any sort of structural representations. One of these concerns a problem of content indeterminacy. As many have noted, structural similarities are cheap, and any given system can be said to be structurally similar to many different things. How do we pick among these to designate the real content of the representation? In the case of artifacts like maps, we can appeal to the intentions of the map's creators to determine the actual target. But no one creates the inner representations in our brains with the intention of providing them with a specific content. So, if a neural array is, in some sense, and to varying degrees, homomorphic with many different things, which of these is the thing it is supposed to represent?

While we cannot appeal to the intentions of a map maker to fix the target of representational systems in the brain, there are other factors that *can* serve to fix content. For instance, as was mentioned in Section 2, neural systems that function as models or maps form in response to various causal interactions between the agent and its environment. So, intuitively, if an organism successfully uses some sort of internal map for guidance, then the map represents the specific terrain that contributed to the map's formation. The terrain contributes to the map's formation *vis-à-vis* some type of learning process during the organism's meanderings. The fact that there may be other terrains in the world that are structurally similar to the internal map has no bearing on the determinacy of the map's content. That's because the content is determined not solely by the similarity relation, but also by the relevant causal relations that helped to bring the representational system into existence. This is just one of many possible ways in which a theory of S-representations can be supplemented in a manner to avoid the primary problem of content indeterminacy.

A different worry concerns the neural plausibility of inner maps and models. No one committed to cognitive maps seriously thinks that the neurons in our brains somehow physically line up in a way that is spatially similar to their representational targets, as with paper maps. And, of course, even if there were such neuronal maps and models, there would be no one inside our skulls to exploit them in the same way we exploit external maps and models. Consequently, proponents of S-representation need to say something about the neurological implementation of structures that are supposed to be structurally similar to things in the world, and just how this is exploited by the system.

To some degree, the neural plausibility worry is a difficulty that plagues nearly all accounts of representational vehicles in the brain, including those more dependent upon conventional, quasi-linguistic symbolic structures. Consequently (and fortunately), a standard response to this worry is open to those who invoke mental maps and models. The response is that in computational models of cognition, there are levels of analysis and description that are more abstract than the physical, implementation details. It is at a more abstract, algorithmic level of analysis where models and maps reside. To adopt an old observation, if you look inside the physical structure of a conventional computer, at the wires and circuits, you won't see anything that resembles any of the things that conventional computers are used to model or simulate. Even in a computational system that is currently running a storm simulation, there will be nothing at the physical operations of the computer that resembles blowing wind or falling rain. Yet we know that there is a higher level of analysis involving more abstract computational structures and operations that simulate exactly those meteorological events. The same point applies to computational accounts of neurological activities exploiting surrogative reasoning. In fact, as we briefly saw in Section 3, there have been various accounts of how neuronal computing may actually be using something like a Cartesian coordinate system to encode spatial and location information.

In Section 2 we saw that the notion of structural similarity that is at the heart of S-representation comes with a cluster of difficult questions that are not easily answered, especially when the representational system substitutes new kinds of relations and properties for the relations and properties of the elements of the target domain, as typically happens in computational systems. Critical questions include: How can a computational process be characterized as "structurally similar" to various non-computational processes and entities? Is the relevant homomorphism objectively real, or is it observer-dependent and thus a function of our explanatory interests? How unnatural or forced can interpretations be that connect a model to a target, and still have the model qualify *as* a model of the target (Cummins, 1989)? Also, how is it that the brain exploits the structural similarity between the representation and whatever is represented? Finding the correct answers to these and related questions is a primary goal of a growing number of philosophical and scientific programs working on representation (see, for example, O'Brien and Opie, 2004; Rescorla, 2009; Shagrir, 2012; Shea, 2013; 2014; Morgan, 2014).

While space does not allow us to give these questions the attention they deserve, I would like to recommend a sort of pragmatic outlook to them, at least in certain explanatory contexts. We should remember that when a computational, neurological, or some other type of theory attempts to explain some cognitive ability by invoking some posit, there is a fairly overt promise of an explanatory pay-off by adopting this perspective. But such a pay-off requires that the perspective not be too arduous to adopt. In the case of S-representation, treating the relevant neural/computational structure as a model of some target must be sufficiently simple to produce the alleged enhancement in our understanding. Presumably, the amount of work needed for such a perspective will depend to some degree upon who is adopting the perspective and upon how "natural" he or she finds it to view the structure *as* a map or model. We also need to understand how the relevant structural similarity is, as such, exploited by the system (Shea, 2014). If the computational mechanism or process in question shares various structural or organizational similarities with its target, and if it is relatively easy to see how these similarities are taken advantage of by the system, then there should be no real problem in regarding the structure as playing the role of a model/map/simulation. But if the alleged similarities are very hard to discern, or if it is extremely difficult to make sense of how the system is employing the structure *as* a representational mechanism, then even if such an analysis is in principle possible, it may not be worth the effort. We might be better off adopting a strictly causal/mechanical perspective that abandons the representational outlook altogether. Consequently, as this research moves forward we should do our best to avoid treating neural/computational processes as the modeling of something else when the *only* reason for doing so is the temptation to think that the brain solves various problems the surrogative way that we often do.

5 Conclusion

Despite the worries discussed in the last section, I believe there is growing support for the idea that if we are going to understand cognition as a process that is both computational and representational in nature, then an essential part of that picture will involve an appeal to S-representations. That is, we will need to treat at least certain neural structures as implementing computational states and operations that are functioning not as linguistic structures or as indicators, but as models, maps and simulations of various aspects of the world. Fortunately, this picture of representation in the brain is both attractive and robust, holding considerable promise as an explanatory posit that will substantially improve our understanding of a wide array of different cognitive capacities.

Of course, that doesn't mean there is no more work to be done in making sense of this notion of cognitive representation. Quite the contrary, we are really only getting started. Still, as I've suggested here, there is little reason to think the obstacles are insurmountable or to deny that a strong shift toward S-representation (and perhaps away from a quasi-linguistic understanding of computational representation) is a move in the right direction.

Acknowledgments

I would like to thank the volume editors, Mark Sprevak and Matteo Colombo, for their extremely helpful comments and suggestions on an earlier draft of this chapter.

Notes

1 There have also been dissenting voices. For those who reject the need to invoke representations in theories of cognition, see, for example, Thelan and Smith (1994); Beer (1995); Hutto and Myin (2012); Ramsey (2017).
2 Some writers, including myself (Ramsey, 2007), have used the term "isomorphism" to describe the relevant relation, but this notion (as it is understood formally) is perhaps too strong. 'Homomorphism' might get closer to the sort of structural similarity intended; still, there might be those worried about the way these terms are used in mathematics who will complain. Since I am not doing mathematics, my use of 'homomorphism' is based simply on the Greek roots, meaning, roughly, 'same form'. For those who oppose this looser meaning, please feel free to substitute whatever term you think best captures the kind of similarity that exists between a map or model, and its target.
3 These are treated by many, like Fodor (1975), as concepts.
4 Further research in this area explores the different ways in which information is encoded (and decoded) in neurons. See, for example, Rolls and Treves (2011).
5 See, for example, Sejnowski and Rosenberg (1987).
6 It should be noted that at least some regard Tolman's rejection of behaviorism as less clear, and treat his discussion of cognitive maps as a shorthand for capturing behavioral dispositions.
7 For further discussion of cognitive maps, see Rescorla (2009).

References

Beer, R.D. (1995) 'A Dynamic Systems Perspective on Agent–Environment Interaction', *Artificial Intelligence*, 72, pp. 173–215.

Burgess, N. and O'Keefe, J. (2002) 'Spatial Models of the Hippocampus', in Arbib, M.A. (ed.) *The Handbook of Brain Theory and Neural Networks*, 2nd ed. Cambridge, MA: MIT Press.

Collins, A.M. and Quillian, M.R. (1969) 'Retrieval Time from Semantic Memory', *Journal of Verbal Learning and Verbal Behavior*, 8 (2), pp. 240–247.

Craik, K. (1943) *The Nature of Explanation*. Cambridge, UK: Cambridge University Press.

Cummins, R. (1989) *Meaning and Mental Representation*. Cambridge, MA: MIT Press.

Dretske, F. (1988) *Explaining Behavior*. Cambridge, MA: MIT Press.

Fodor, J.A. (1975) *The Language of Thought*. Cambridge, MA: Harvard University Press.

Fodor, J.A. (1987) *Psychosemantics*. Cambridge, MA: MIT Press.

Gallistel, C.R. (1998) 'Symbolic Processes in the Brain: The Case of Insect Navigation', in Scarorough, D. and Sternberg, S. (eds.) *An Invitation to Cognitive Science*, vol. 4: *Methods, Models and Conceptual Issues*, 2nd ed. Cambridge, MA: MIT Press, pp. 1–51.

Godfrey-Smith, P. (2006) 'Mental Representation, Naturalism, and Teleosemantics', in MacDonald, G. and Papineau, D. (eds.) *Teleosemantics*. Oxford: Oxford University Press, pp. 42–68.

Goodman, N. (1968) *Languages of Art: An Approach to a Theory of Symbols*. Indianapolis, IN: Bobbs-Merrill Company.

Hubel, D. and Weisel, T. (1968) 'Receptive Fields and Functional Architecture of Monkey Striate Cortex', *Journal of Physiology*, 195, pp. 215–243.

Hutto, D. and Myin, E. (2012) *Radicalizing Enactivism: Basic Minds without Content*. Cambridge, MA: MIT Press.

Johnson-Laird, P. (1983) *Mental Models: Towards a Cognitive Science of Language, Inference and Consciousness*. Cambridge, MA: Harvard University Press.

Johnson-Laird, P. (2006) *How We Reason*. Oxford: Oxford University Press.

Johnson-Laird, P. (2013) 'The Mental Models Perspective', in Reisberg, D. (ed.) *The Oxford Handbook of Cognitive Psychology*. Oxford: Oxford University Press, pp. 650–667.

Lettvin, J. et al. (1959) 'What the Frog's Eye Tells the Frog's Brain', *Proceedings of the Institute of Radio Engineers*, 47, pp. 1940–1951.

Morgan, A. (2014) 'Representations Gone Mental', *Synthese*, 191 (2), pp. 213–244.

Oakhill, J. and Garnham, A. (1996) *Mental Models in Cognitive Science: Essays in Honor of Phil Johnson-Laird*. East Sussex, UK: Psychology Press.

O'Brien, G. and Opie, J. (2004) 'Notes Towards a Structuralist Theory of Mental Representation', in Clapin, H., Staines, P., and Slezak, P. (eds.) *Representation in Mind: New Approaches to Mental Representation*. Amsterdam: Elsevier, pp. 1–20.

O'Keefe, J. and Nadel, L. (1978) *The Hippocampus as a Cognitive Map*. Oxford: Oxford University Press.

Ramsey, W. (2007) *Representation Reconsidered*. Cambridge, UK: Cambridge University Press.

Ramsey, W. (2016) 'Untangling Two Questions about Mental Representation', *New Ideas in Psychology*, 40, pp. 3–12.

Ramsey, W. (2017) 'Must Cognition Be Representational?', *Synthese*, 194 (11), pp. 4197–4214.

Rescorla, M. (2009) 'Cognitive Maps and the Language of Thought', *The British Journal for the Philosophy of Science*, 60 (2), pp. 377–407.

Rolls, E. and Treves, A. (2011) 'The Neural Encoding of Information in the Brain', *Progress in Neurobiology*, 95 (3), pp. 448–490.

Rumelhart, D. and McClelland, J. (1986) *Parallel Distributed Processing*, vols. 1 and 2. Cambridge, MA: MIT Press.

Schaeken, W. et al. (eds.) (2007) *The Mental Models Theory of Reasoning: Refinements and Extensions*. Mahwah, NJ: Lawrence Erlbaum Associates.

Sejnowski, T.J. and Rosenberg, C.R. (1987) 'Parallel Networks That Learn to Pronounce English Text', *Complex Systems*, 1, pp. 145–168.

Shagrir, O. (2012) 'Structural Representations and the Brain', *British Journal for the Philosophy of Science*, 63, pp. 519–545.

Shea, N. (2013) 'Millikan's Isomorphism Requirement', in Ryder, D., Kingsbury, J., and Williford, K. (eds.) *Millikan and Her Critics*. Oxford and Malden, MA: Wiley-Blackwell, pp. 63–80.

Shea, N. (2014) 'Exploitable Isomorphism and Structural Representation', *Proceedings of the Aristotelian Society*, 64 (2), pp. 123–144.

Swoyer, C. (1991) 'Structural Representation and Surrogative Reasoning', *Synthese*, 87, pp. 449–508.

Thelan, E. and Smith, L. (1994) *A Dynamic Systems Approach to the Development of Cognition and Action*. Cambridge, MA: MIT Press.

Tolman, E. (1948) 'Cognitive Maps in Rats and Men', *Psychological Review*, 55, pp. 189–208.

20

THE COGNITIVE BASIS OF COMPUTATION

Putting computation in its place

Daniel D. Hutto, Erik Myin, Anco Peeters and Farid Zahnoun

> Computing is normally done by writing certain symbols on paper.
> *(Alan Turing, 1936, p. 249)*

Use of computational models and talk of computation is rife in explanations of cognition. In philosophical hands, this anodyne observation about explanation is transformed when it is augmented by the claims that computational processes are metaphysically real processes that are either necessary or sufficient for cognition. Whether advanced in its weaker, necessity, or stronger, sufficiency guise, the underlying idea is that computation is *a*, if not *the*, explanatory basis for cognition. Call this underlying idea the Computational Basis of Cognition thesis, or CBC.[1]

The CBC maintains that if biological minds or artificial systems are capable of cognition then they must, in one way or another, compute. The CBC motto is: no cognition without computation. With respect to the special case of putative brain-based, neural computations, advocates of CBC hold that such computations form the basis of, and explain, a wide range of cognitive operations. These not only include perception, attention, language-processing, and reasoning but also canonical acts of overt computation – like adding fractions, solving equations, generating proofs – that feature in specialized symbol-manipulating, rule-based practices. Notably in the latter cases, the direction of explanation runs from the covert to the overt in that overt computational processes are taken to be explained by covert computational processes and not the other way around.

The CBC can be supported in various ways, employing different theories of computation. In Section 1, we introduce representationalist theories of computation that might be used to ground the CBC, identify what motivates them, and raise concerns about such theories. Sections 2 and 3 focus on the prospect of grounding the CBC in non-representational theories of computation. Ultimately, we question the ability of such theories to deliver a metaphysically robust, naturalistic account of computation of the sort needed to support the CBC.[2] In the final section, we articulate the alternative possibility to the CBC – namely, that computation may depend on semantically-laden cognition and not the other way around. We put forward a reversed rival of the CBC – one that, we argue, avoids the problems encountered by both representational and non-representational causal-mechanistic theories of computation and which is consistent with the known facts about how minds and brains work.

1 The computational basis of cognition: representationalist theories

Some defenders of the CBC embrace representational theories of computation. Representational theories of computation propose that computations are always and everywhere operations over symbols and that symbols have both representational and syntactic properties essentially (Salisbury and Schneider, this volume). In promoting this style of theory, Fodor, perhaps the staunchest of its advocates, maintains that "all symbol tokens have intentional contents and … syntactic structure – constituent structure in particular – that's appropriate to the content they have" (Fodor, 1987, pp. 135–137; see also Fodor 1990, p. 167; 1975, p. 198).

There are two interlocking assumptions at the heart of representational theories of computation. The first assumption is that symbols are taken to be individuated partly by their syntactic structure. It is their syntactic structure that links them inferentially to other symbols. Symbols are assumed to have a kind of 'shape', analogous to the shapes of the syntactical forms of natural language sentence tokens, where such shapes have structural properties that cannot be understood solely in terms of their physical properties. Nevertheless, it is the fact that the syntactic properties of symbols can be implemented concretely in physical systems that makes computational processes mechanically possible.

The second assumption is that symbols are also taken to be partly individuated by what they are about – namely, what they denote or refer to. Crucially, according to the 'received view', as Sprevak (2010) dubs it, a symbol's representational properties determine which computations, if any, are taking place. For theorists attracted to this view, the fact that symbols have the representational properties that they do solves the otherwise intractable problem of computational individuation; namely, determining whether a given process is a computational process by specifying which function or rule is being carried out.

To borrow an example from Sprevak (2010), consider an electrical system which receives either 0V or 5V at its two input nodes. The system will output 5V only if its two input nodes receive 5V, as specified in Table 20.1. At first sight, the system may be thought to implement a classic AND-gate. However, this assumes that the 5V output has a '1' or 'true' value. But 5V could have a '0' or 'false' value, in which case the system would be implementing an OR-gate.

Apparently, the non-semantic properties of the input–output patterns alone are insufficient to determine which of the two values are in play and hence which computational function is being implemented. Yet the problem is overcome if, as Sprevak (2010) claims, "Appeal to representation allows us to decide between these two options … [and that] the difference between an implementation of an AND gate and an OR gate is a difference in representational content" (Sprevak 2010, p. 269).

This observation motivates the idea that representational contents are needed to specify which computational functions are being carried out. Generalizing, the lesson to be drawn from this case is that representational contents are needed to do the heavy lifting in fixing

Table 20.1 A specification of an electrical system

IN1	IN2	OUT
0V	0V	0V
0V	5V	0V
5V	0V	0V
5V	5V	5V

computational identities and that "the functions a system computes are always characterized in semantic terms" (Shagrir, 2001, p. 382).

In sum, the problem of computational individuation can apparently be dealt with if it is assumed that "representational content plays an essential role in the individuation of states and processes into computational types" (Shagrir, 2006, p. 393). Realistically construed, as O'Brien and Opie (2009) put it, computation is, at least partly, dependent upon and "governed by the contents of the representations it implicates" (p. 53). The cost of accepting that computational states and input–output-functions are essentially, if only partially, individuated semantically is to accept that: "there is no computation without representation" (Fodor, 1981, p. 180).

Ultimately, the price of the representationalist solution to the problem of computational individuation may be too high for defenders of the CBC who also advocate explanatory naturalism. For to make a representational theory of computation work we need a theory that tells us "what counts as representation" and "what gives representations their content" (Piccinini, 2015, p. 29; see also Chalmers, 2011; 2012).[3]

Naturalists who subscribe to a representational theory of computation and hope to use it to mount a credible defense of the CBC are, in the end, obliged to supply a grounding theory of content. In line with the CBC such a theory would need to explain how computational vehicles gain their contents without making appeal to the norms and rules supplied by sociocultural practices. The reasoning is straightforward: if, as the CBC assumes, computation is required for cognition, and if cognition is required for sociocultural practices, then, by implication, computation is required for sociocultural practices. This places an important constraint on the CBC: if there can be no computation without representation then the representations in question must be accounted for independently of and prior to the emergence of socialcultural practices.

Yet despite many dedicated efforts, we currently lack a tenable naturalized theory of content – given in causal, informational, or biological terms or some combination thereof – that satisfies the demands of the CBC. Without such a theory as a principled means of allocating contents to vehicles, representational theories of computation remain, at best, programmatic and promissory. Certainly, for anyone attracted to explanatory naturalism, such theories do not supply a secure foundation for the CBC here and now.[4]

In what other ways might the CBC be defended, assuming that these concerns constitute reasons to steer clear of representationalist theories of computation?

Several philosophers have proposed that a tenable non-representational notion of computation is already well within our reach. There are various theories on the market that attempt to define computations solely in formal, structural, or mechanical terms (e.g. Chalmers, 2011; Miłkowski, 2013; Piccinini, 2015). As their collective name indicates, all of the theories in this family seek to demonstrate how "computation can be fully individuated without appeal to semantic content" and how "there is computation without representation" (Piccinini, 2015, p. 33).[5] As such, should any of these theories prove workable it would supply an account of computation that avoids the need to naturalize semantic content.

Ultimately, with respect to the CBC, more is required. As far as securing the CBC goes, the crucial test of any tenable non-semantic theory of computation is whether it articulates a notion of computation that will prove foundational in the sciences of the mind. Thus, the pivotal question is: are there any tenable non-semantic theories of computation and, if so, can they play such a role?

In the end, there are reasons to doubt that non-semantic theories can provide an account of computation needed to do the sort of explanatory work required for securing the CBC. A full survey of such theories and their potential to secure the CBC is beyond the scope of this chapter. Still, it is possible to highlight the main sort of challenges this class of theories faces by focusing on two representative samples.

2 The computational basis of cognition: a non-semantic, functional theory

Drawing on a long tradition inspired by the properties of Turing machines, Chalmers (2011; 2012) offers a functionalist account of computation – one that is meant to capture the core understanding of computation as it figures in the formal theories of computer scientists. The central assumption of this functionalist theory is that a computation is a formalism that specifies a system's causal topology – namely, its fine-grained organizational structure – by specifying the system's inputs, outputs, internal states and their transitions.[6]

To this account of what computations are, Chalmers adds a general theory of what it takes for a physical system to implement a computation. On a rough-and-ready rendering, such implementation occurs when the causal structure of some concrete physical system formally mirrors the structure of the computation. It follows from this theory of computational implementation that computations abound in nature since any appropriately organized physical system will implement at least one computation.

With respect to the CBC, Chalmers (2011; 2012) makes an important claim about cognition – one that goes beyond his general theories of computation and computational implementation. He holds that, perhaps with some exceptions, cognitive properties and processes are maximally indifferent to the material substrates of the systems in which they are implemented: they are distinguished in being organizationally invariant.[7] A property or process is organizationally invariant if it can be implemented concretely in some physical system merely by implementing its causal topology.

Chalmers denies that every physical process has this feature. Digestion, he contends, does not. This is because he assumes that digestion requires particular physio-chemical properties. Changing the material substrates in certain respects, but retaining the causal topology, does not guarantee digestion. For cognitive processes on the other hand, merely retaining its causal topology and implementing it by any material means secures that the implementation is a *bona fide* instance of cognition.

There are two problems in attempting to secure the CBC by appeal to the supposed organizational invariance of cognition. First, and this is the principal concern, even if it turns out that cognition has the property of being organizationally invariant, the fact that cognition is computational in Chalmers' general sense would not explain why cognition has this special feature. Chalmers simply highlights that, on his account, cognition is special because it can be implemented in any system that preserves the relevant causal topology. Yet his appeal to cognition's alleged computational nature would not explain this special status, even if it turns out to be analytically true.

Second, it is contentious whether cognition actually differs in kind from other processes, like digestion, in being maximally indifferent to its material substrates. As far as anyone knows cognition may depend to a much greater extent on its material substrates than Chalmers imagines. After all, it is no accident that sensory systems have the particular material properties that they have. This is because having such properties appears to be required if they are to fulfil their cognitive functions. As Dennett (1997) observes, "in order to detect light … you need something photosensitive" (p. 97). This is the case not just for natural but also for artificial eyes. Even though there is still some degree of flexibility in how visual perception might be achieved, this fact places significant limits on what materials might be used for visual systems to get their cognitive work done.

The story is not importantly different when it comes to the cognitive contributions of brains:

> The recent history of neuroscience can be seen as a series of triumphs for the lovers of detail ... the specific geometry of the connectivity matters ... the location of specific neurotransmitters and their effects matters ... the architecture matters ... the fine temporal rhythms of spiking patterns matter, and so on.
>
> (Dennett, 2005, p. 19)[8]

It may be that for some cognitive operations only certain physical properties matter, such as the timing of neuronal spiking patterns. Still, it would not follow that such properties are abstract and substrate-indifferent as opposed to being concrete and substrate-sensitive. As Polger and Shapiro (2016) emphasize in resisting the former interpretation, "the frequency of the spike train of a neuron or neural assembly ... is a property of neurons as neurons, not just as implementers of some supraneural process" (p. 164).

In short, it would be hard to deny that cognitive processes depend on particular materials despite exhibiting varying degrees of substrate-neutrality.[9] What is not established is that cognitive processes are maximally substrate-neutral such that it is possible to re-create all their relevant causal patterns in alternative media. Thus, on the question of whether cognition exhibits organizational invariance the jury is still out.

What if the claim that cognition is organizationally invariant fails to garner empirical support? Is there still enough strength in an unvarnished Chalmers-style functionalist theory of computation to establish the CBC? In one sense, it might appear so. After all, the cornerstone assumption of Chalmers' theory is that anything with a causal structure that can be specified by means of a computational formalism implements a computation.

Towl (2011) complains that this feature of a Chalmers-style theory of computation makes it overly permissive: namely, it threatens to trivialize the notion of computation. He asks us to consider a game at a pool table. It is easy enough to characterize the physical events of the game – such as the movement of the balls – as implementing a form of vector addition in terms of direction and velocity. But what explanatory advantage is conferred by treating the activity of the balls as implementing computations? What is explained by supposing the balls and the pool table are in fact computing vector sums? As Towl stresses, the situation would be entirely different if we used the movements of the balls to compute sums or if we connected the movement of the balls to a specialized device that was dedicated to the purpose of computing sums.

This type of complaint does not trouble Chalmers' general theory. He admits that his account of computation may fail to capture useful distinctions required for certain explanatory purposes. That is fine so long as it serves other needs. He is attracted to a pluralism that allows him to isolate the value of his general theory of computation to picking out and demarcating the formal subject matter that is of special interest to the computational sciences (Chalmers, 2012).[10]

Yet even if the pluralist reply holds up, Chalmers' general theory of computation would at most answer a classifactory need: it would not have the explanatory punch needed to defend the CBC. After all, even if we suppose that brains, just like pool tables, implement computations in the way that Chalmers' general theory assumes, we would need a story about how and why any such computations make a difference to and explain cognition.

In the end, if our understanding of the computational theory of cognition is based solely in a Chalmers-style general theory of computation then it loses "much of its explanatory force" (Piccinini, 2015, p. 55). Thus, the price of guaranteeing the CBC by appeal to Chalmers' theory of computation is that the CBC is rendered trivially true but explanatorily hollow with respect to the needs of the sciences of the mind (O'Brien, 2011; Ritchie, 2011; Rescorla, 2012).

3 The computational basis of cognition: a non-semantic, mechanistic theory

Piccinini (2015) advances a mechanistic account of computation which is designed to overcome the sorts of problems faced by more liberal functionalist theories of computation. It operates with a generic definition of computation that restricts the class of physical computing systems to a sub-class of functional mechanisms. The central plank of this theory is that to qualify as a computing system a mechanism must have the function to manipulate medium-independent vehicles according to rules as one of its teleo-functions.

The key assumptions of this theory are as follows: A vehicle is understood as a variable – a state that can take different values and change over time – or a specific instance of such a variable (Piccinini, 2015, p. 121). Vehicles are manipulated "according to rules that are sensitive solely to differences between different portions (i.e., spatiotemporal parts) of the vehicles" (ibid., p. 121; see also Piccinini and Bahar, 2013, p. 458). Rules are here understood broadly and in non-representational terms: rules are simply input to output maps. Finally, and crucially, all concrete computations and their vehicles are deemed medium-independent because they can be described and defined "independently of the physical media that implement them" (Piccinini, 2015, p. 122).[11]

In operating with a much more restrictive theory of what counts as a physical computation than its purely functionalist rival, Piccinini's mechanistic theory demarcates computing systems from other sorts of functional devices in a way that avoids pan-computationalism. Consequently, by its lights, digestive systems and pool tables lack the special features just mentioned needed to qualify as computing systems. Moreover, with respect to the CBC, this theory looks, *prima facie*, far better placed than its functionalist rival to deliver the required explanatory goods.

There is one apparent obstacle to defending the CBC by appeal to a mechanistic theory of computation of this sort. It is that there are clear dissimilarities between what happens in brains and what happens in artifactual computers. Indeed, looking solely at the character of neural activity it has been observed that brains are not executing computations of any familiar kind – brains are not performing digital or analog computations. Summarizing an analysis of a wide range of findings, Piccinini and Bahar (2013) openly acknowledge this fact, reporting that, "in a nutshell, current evidence indicates that typical neural signals, such as spike trains … are neither continuous signals nor strings of digits" (p. 477).

Can we infer from these observations that brains are not performing any kind of computation? No. Piccinini and Bahar (2013) conclude that brains are performing computations of a special variety, maintaining that neural computation happens in its own special way – namely that "neural computation is sui generis" (p. 477; see also Piccinini, 2015, p. 223). Of course, this inference is not obligatory. If the above evidence were all we had to go on then we would be equally justified in concluding that brains do not compute.

Why then suppose, in light of such findings and the constraints of a mechanistic theory of computation, that the neural processes that contribute to explaining cognition are computational? Piccinini and Bahar (2013) supply an argument based on the following assumptions: cognition involves information processing of a kind that requires the manipulation of "vehicles based on the information they carry rather than their specific physical properties" (p. 463). Therefore, cognition requires the manipulation of medium independent vehicles. Hence, the neural processes that contribute to cognition must involve the manipulation of medium-independent vehicles.[12]

Voltage changes in dendrites, neuronal spikes, neurotransmitters, and hormones are offered as prime examples of neurocomputational vehicles. Piccinini and Bahar (2013) hold that such neural events and entities qualify as medium-independent vehicles because the properties which are relevant for their cognitive work – such as firing rates and patterns – can be defined in abstract terms. Thus, these authors claim, this makes such vehicles unlike the other, putatively more concrete properties of the neural systems that implement them.

It is questionable, however, that the neural events and processes that underpin cognition actually have the feature of being medium-independent. There is reason to doubt that neural events could contribute to cognitive work if that work really requires the concrete manipulation of medium-independent vehicles. The trouble is that if medium-independent vehicles are defined by their abstract properties then it is unclear how such vehicles could be concretely manipulated. Understanding how neural processes can be sensitive to concrete, medium-dependent properties presents no conceptual difficulty. By contrast, we have no conception of how concrete neural processes could causally manipulate abstract, medium-independent vehicles. Certainly, the defenders of the mechanistic theory of computation offer no account of how such manipulations might be achieved.

Again, there is no barrier to understanding how neural events can be sensitive to only specific aspects of a concrete structure. Nor is there a barrier to understanding how an analogue of that neural process could be sensitive to the same aspect of an analog structure in a materially different system. But that does not make either the imagined neural process or its analogue sensitive to a medium-independent property. Neither process is sensitive to what the other process is sensitive to. Rather, they are both sensitive to some aspect of physical structures that can be given a medium-independent description.

Polger and Shapiro (2016) diagnose the source of confusion that gives rise to belief in abstract medium independent vehicles, as one of conflating the abstractness which is a feature of computational models with features of "the processes being modelled" (p. 166). Elaborating, they observe that "the apparent medium independence of computational explanations owes to the fact that they model or describe their phenomena in topic-neutral or abstract ways rather than to the abstractness or multiple realizability of their objects" (ibid., p. 155).

In the end, it turns out that medium independence is not a property of physical token processes, but rather is a relational or comparative property of several processes. As a result, one can have medium-independent descriptions of processes – descriptions which abstract from certain substrate-related properties and mention properties which can be found in different substrates – but one cannot have concrete vehicles that are medium-independent.

Happily, the dimensions of variation in physical systems to which neural events are sensitive need not be construed as medium-independent vehicles. They may simply be dimensions of variation in the concrete properties of certain structures. Nor need the lawful changes involved in being sensitive to certain properties of such structures be thought of in terms of the rule-bound manipulation of medium-independent vehicles. They might simply be systematic changes that conform to specific patterns.

In sum, these considerations cast serious doubt on the possibility of employing a non-semantic mechanistic theory of computation to support the CBC.

4 The cognitive basis of computation: a sociocultural theory

As the preceding analysis reveals, there are serious problems with the most promising existing proposals for securing the CBC. As things stand, there is no compelling evidence or theoretical argument for supposing that computation is the, or even an, explanatory basis of cognition.

Where in the world, then, do we find computations and how do they relate to minds? There is another possibility to consider – one left hanging at the end of the first section: namely, that computation may depend on cognitive activity and not the other way around. The kind of cognition in question, we propose, is that which only arises within and is integrally bound up with specific sociocultural normative practices.

In locating computations in nature, we seek to revive the original model of a computational system (see, Copeland and Proudfoot, this volume; Isaac, this volume) which was that of "a person – a mathematician or logician manipulating symbols with hands and eyes, and pen and paper (The word 'computer' originally meant 'one who computes')" (Thompson, 2007, p. 7). Accordingly, in the originary case computing first arises along with the emergence of "a sophisticated form of human activity" (ibid., p. 7).

Computation originally consists of symbol manipulating operations carried out by people. Sociocultural practices make it the case that certain operations with symbols are properly identifiable and individuated as computations: the reason is because it is only within such practices that computational operations and manipulations have a home. Such computations are semantically laden, in the sense that statements which express particular computational operations, such as the result of calculating a derivative function, are true or false. The surrounding context and practices of such manipulations determines whether a given manipulation of symbols is an instance of computing or not. This is because both the current use and the larger history of a person or system determines whether the manipulation forms part of, say, a particular computational operation, some other computational operation, or none at all. Borrowing an example from Michael Rescorla, it is the surrounding history and practices that determine whether a child in a contemporary context, while performing an arithmetic operation over numerals, is computing in the decimal system and not in some other system like base-13 (Rescorla, 2013).

Sociocultural practices for structurally manipulating tokens in specific ways that accord with an established practice is plausibly not only the basis for how human beings compute, it is likewise the basis for artificial forms of computation. We often rely on artifacts and artificial systems to compute with and for us. We can compute by writing with chalk on blackboard; by moving the beads of an abacus; or by pressing the keys of a calculator. In such circumstances, we compute with chalk and board, with the abacus, or with the calculator. Yet, focusing on the last case, we not only compute with calculators, we also say that calculators compute. The only relevant difference is that computing with an abacus requires moving the beads around, while computing with a calculator requires pressing some keys and then letting the mechanics of the machine take care of the rest.

Importantly, when we construct artificial computing devices we do so by relying on, and re-arranging concrete physical materials, so that they acquire a structure that suits our goals. There is no reason to assume that, before these materials or processes are put to computational use by us, they already compute. In other words, constructing computers consists in transforming material devices and processes that do not compute into devices and processes that we can compute with. The computational properties of these devices depend on the surrounding sociocultural activities of which they become part. Accordingly, we can think of Turing machines that manipulate meaningless strings as simply not computing until those strings are put to use for specific purposes.

Perhaps some of the processes occurring in brains are, at some level of abstraction, similar to the kinds of processes found in our computational artifacts. But that does not imply that the brain computes, only that we can draw analogies between these two kinds of processes. Neither does the fact that people can compute 'in their heads', without engaging in overt manipulation of symbols, show that in such cases the brain computes. Even in these cases, it is the person that computes. The fact that computing relies on, and would not be possible without the occurrence of specific brain processes does not entail that those brain processes themselves are computations.

If brains are not computing when contributing to cognition then what are they doing? Neural activity is sensitive to relations of covariance, and such sensitivity drives cascades of neural activity that influence and constrain organismic responsiveness. But such coordinated activity need not be thought of as processing information or, thereby, as a kind of computation. That assumption is not necessary to explain the work that brains do in enabling organisms to "get a grip on the patterns that matter for the interactions that matter" (Clark, 2016, p. 294). Well-calibrated neural activity can systematically influence and constrain organismic responding, and even maintain connections with specific worldly features without the brain engaging in any computations. In other words, neurodynamics can be, and apparently should be, conceived of in terms of coordinated cascades rather than in terms of information processing computations (Hutto and Myin, 2017, epilogue).

Why take this sociocultural proposal about the basis of computation seriously? As we have seen there are inherent difficulties in supposing that computation arises in nature independently of and prior to socioculturally based practices of someone or something computing for a purpose.

How, on our account, does our sociocultural account of computation relate to cognition? If the analysis and arguments of this chapter hold up then we have reason to try to invert the explanatory order proposed by the Computational Basis of Cognition thesis. We must reverse the polarity of standard thinking on this topic, and ask how it is possible that computation, natural and artificial, might be based in cognition and not the other way around.

If specific sociocultural practices are a necessary and sufficient explanatory basis of computation, and those practices are themselves cognitively based, then it follows that computation is also cognitively based. Of course, the cognitive basis need not itself be representational (see Hutto and Myin, 2013; 2017; Hutto and Satne, 2015); and if we are correct, on pain of circularity, it cannot be computational either.

Acknowledgments

Daniel Hutto thanks the Australian Research Council, Discovery Project DP170102987 'Mind in Skilled Performance', and Erik Myin and Farid Zahnoun thank the Research Foundation Flanders (FWO), projects G048714N 'Offline Cognition' and G0C7315N 'Getting Real about Words and Numbers', for funding that enabled the completion of the primary research informing this chapter. We are also grateful to Mark Sprevak and Matteo Colombo for their invitation to contribute, and for their excellent and helpful feedback.

Notes

1 Notably the CBC, in either its necessity or sufficiency variant, is a much stronger thesis than the thesis "that concept of computation lies at the very foundation of cognitive science" (O'Brien, 2011, p. 381). Thus a prominent neurocentric version of the CBC espouses that: "brains perform computations and neural computations explain cognition" (Piccinini, 2015, p. 207). Piccinini and Bahar (2013) trace an industrial strength, neural variant of the CBC – that neural activity simply *is* computation – back to McCulloch and Pitts (1943). Whether articulated in stronger or weaker form, the CBC has more or less enjoyed the status of the received view in the sciences of the mind ever since the advent of the cognitive revolution: see Piccinini (2015, p. 207) for a long list of those who have defended this idea in some shape or form since the 1970s forward. Indeed, support for the neural variant of the CBC runs so deep that, as Piccinini and Bahar (2013) report, many cognitive scientists even "consider it common-sensical to say that neural activity is computation and that computation explains cognition" (p. 454).

2 For reasons of space we do not discuss other, less widely endorsed theories of computation. See Piccinini (2015, chs. 2–4) for a more systematic review of other positions and the problems they face.

3 Representational theories of computation are accused of having feet of clay. Those at the vanguard of these debates have observed that, "the notion of semantic content is so ill-understood that it desperately needs a foundation itself" (Chalmers, 2011, p. 334).

4 As long as semantic or representational content is understood in terms of having satisfaction conditions of some kind – for example, truth or accuracy conditions – then there are reasons to think that no naturalistic theory of content is anywhere in sight. To supply such a theory would require overcoming the Hard Problem of Content (Hutto and Myin, 2013; 2017). Until that problem is dealt with, there is no gain in appealing to semantic or contentful properties that allegedly permeate and individuate computational processes.

5 Importantly, non-semantic accounts of computation can allow that computations can involve the manipulation of vehicles bearing representational contents. This can be the case, according to such theories, just so long as representational contents are not taken to be essential to the existence of computational processes (Chalmers, 2011; Miłkowski, 2013; Piccinini, 2015).

6 According to Chalmers (2011) a causal topology is "the abstract causal organization of the system: that is, the pattern of interaction among parts of the system, abstracted away from the make-up of individual parts and from the way the causal connections are implemented" (p. 337).

7 Chalmers (2011) observes that not all aspects of cognition will be organizationally invariant: any aspect of cognition that partly depends on the actual make-up of the environment will not. He gives knowledge and belief as examples, on the assumption that their contents are fixed by external factors. Famously, if content externalism holds, whether one has a belief about water or not depends on the actual physio-chemical make-up of the relevant substances in the world one occupies.

8 Importantly, on this score Chalmers (2012) acknowledges that "locations, velocities, relative distances and angles are certainly not organizational invariants: systems with same causal topology might involve quite different locations, velocities and so on" (p. 216).

9 Even Chalmers allows that digestion can survive some changes to its physio-chemical substrate so long as the relevant causal patterns are preserved (2011, p. 338). Thus digestion may be at one end of the substrate–neutrality spectrum and certain cognitive processes at the other.

10 It is far from obvious that Chalmers is right on this score – viz., that his general theory adequately captures such scientific commitments. There is a great deal of disagreement in the field about which notion of computation is in fact deployed in computability theory and computer science (Piccinini, 2008, p. 6; Rescorla, 2017, p. 8).

11 Piccinini cites Garson as the inspiration for his strong construal of medium independence (see Garson, 2003). An earlier formulation of medium independence can be found in Haugeland (1989) when he speaks of formal systems being realized in "any number of different media" (p. 58).

12 See Hutto and Myin (2013; 2017) for reflections about the nature of information that support the idea that cognition involves medium-dependent information sensitivity as opposed to medium-independent information processing.

References

Chalmers, D. (2011) 'A Computational Foundation for the Study of Cognition', *Journal of Cognitive Science*, 12 (4), pp. 323–357.

Chalmers, D. (2012) 'The Varieties of Computation: A Reply', *Journal of Cognitive Science*, 13 (3), pp. 211–224.

Clark, A. (2016) *Surfing Uncertainty: Prediction, Action and the Embodied Mind*. Oxford: Oxford University Press.

Dennett, D.C. (1997) *Kinds of Minds: Towards an Understanding of Consciousness*. London: Phoenix.

Dennett, D.C. (2005). *Sweet Dreams: Philosophical Obstacles to a Science of Consciousness*. Cambridge, MA: MIT Press.

Fodor, J.A. (1975) *The Language of Thought*. Cambridge, MA: Harvard University Press.

Fodor, J.A. (1981) *Representations: Philosophical Essays on the Foundations of Cognitive Science*. Cambridge, MA: MIT Press.

Fodor, J.A. (1987) *Psychosemantics: The Problem of Meaning in the Philosophy of Mind*. Cambridge, MA: MIT Press.

Fodor, J.A. (1990) *A Theory of Content and Other Essays*. Cambridge, MA: MIT Press.

Garson, J. (2003) 'The Introduction of Information into Neurobiology', *Philosophy of Science*, 70 (5), pp. 926–936.

Haugeland, J. (1989) *Artificial Intelligence: The Very Idea*. Cambridge, MA: MIT Press.

Hutto, D.D. and Myin, E. (2013) *Radicalizing Enactivism: Basic Minds without Content.* Cambridge, MA: MIT Press.

Hutto, D.D. and Myin, E. (2017) *Evolving Enactivism: Basic Minds Meet Content.* Cambridge, MA: MIT Press.

Hutto, D.D. and Satne, G. (2015) 'The Natural Origins of Content', *Philosophia*, 43 (3), pp. 521–536.

McCulloch, W.S. and Pitts, W. (1943) 'A Logical Calculus of the Ideas Immanent in Nervous Activity', *The Bulletin of Mathematical Biophysics*, 5 (4), 115–133.

Miłkowski, M. (2013) *Explaining the Computational Mind.* Cambridge, MA: MIT Press.

O'Brien, G. (2011) 'Defending the Semantic Conception of Computation in Cognitive Science', *Journal of Cognitive Science*, 12 (4), pp. 381–399.

O'Brien, G and Opie, J. (2009) 'The Role of Representation in Computation', *Cognitive Processing*, 10 (1), pp. 53–62.

Piccinini, G. (2008) 'Computation without Representation', *Philosophical Studies*, 137 (2), pp. 205–241.

Piccinini, G. (2015) *Physical Computation: A Mechanistic Account.* Oxford: Oxford University Press.

Piccinini, G. and Bahar, S. (2013) 'Neural Computation and the Computational Theory of Cognition', *Cognitive Science*, 37 (3), pp. 453–488.

Polger, T.W. and Shapiro, L.A. (2016) *The Multiple Realization Book.* Oxford: Oxford University Press.

Rescorla, M. (2012) 'How to Integrate Representation into Computational Modelling, and Why We Should', *Journal of Cognitive Science*, 13 (1), pp. 1–38.

Rescorla, M. (2013) 'Against Structuralist Theories of Computational Implementation', *The British Journal for the Philosophy of Science*, 64 (4), pp. 681–707.

Rescorla, M. (2017) 'Levels of Computational Explanation', in Powers, T.M. (ed.) *Philosophy and Computing*, vol. 128. Cham: Springer, pp. 5–28.

Ritchie, J.B. (2011) 'Chalmers on Implementation and Computational Sufficiency', *Journal of Cognitive Science*, 12 (4), pp. 401–417.

Shagrir, O. (2001) 'Content, Computation and Externalism', *Mind*, 110 (438), pp. 369–400.

Shagrir, O. (2006) 'Why We View the Brain as a Computer', *Synthese*, 153, pp. 393–416.

Sprevak, M. (2010) 'Computation, Individuation, and the Received View on Representation', *Studies in History and Philosophy of Science*, 41, pp. 260–270.

Thompson, E. (2007) *Mind in Life: Biology, Phenomenology, and the Sciences of Mind.* Cambridge, MA: Harvard University Press.

Towl, B.N. (2011) 'Home, Pause, or Break: A Critique of Chalmers on Implementation', *Journal of Cognitive Science*, 12 (4), pp. 419–433.

Turing, A.M. (1936) 'On Computable Numbers, with an Application to the *Entscheidungsproblem*', *Proceedings of the London Mathematical Society*, 2nd series, 42 (1), pp. 230–265.

21

COMPUTATIONAL EXPLANATIONS AND NEURAL CODING

Rosa Cao

Introduction

The notion of *computation* is ubiquitous in discussions of the aims and advances of cognitive science and neuroscience. This is partly a practical matter, since computational models are used in the analysis of everything from behavioral performance in cognitive tasks to massive brain imaging data sets to fine-scaled neural activities. But beyond the practical utility of computational tools, the computational approach – *computationalism* – represents a commitment to a theoretically and philosophically motivated conception of the nature of the brain *as* a computational system, and the nature of cognition as a computational process.

Computation is often closely associated with semantic notions, and talk of "representation" is everywhere in neuroscience. Despite appearances, however, semantic notions are rarely doing significant work in neuroscientific explanations; rather, computational descriptions are motivated primarily by other considerations. By contrast, representation often plays an ineliminable role in talk of computation in psychology. Consequently, talk of computation in neuroscience has little bearing on substantive psychological or philosophical theses about the role of computation in cognition, when those are committed to representationalism about computation. I'll discuss how putative representational contents are assigned in neuroscientific practice, and provide examples of how computation talk arises independently of representational ascriptions.

Computation in neuroscience

Let's turn to neuroscientific practice. The first thing to note is that computation is commonly used in a very permissive way, and neuroscientists rarely concern themselves explicitly with a theory of implementation that specifies the mapping from physical states or processes to abstract computational ones. Quite often it might simply seem appropriate to describe as computational anything the brain does, given the background *presumption* that the brain is an information-processing system, and that this is essentially equivalent to saying that it is a computational system.

But even within an information processing system, not all the relevant causal processes need be informational. Just as one might flex one's fingers before getting down to some serious typing, so neural activity may be important for physical *conditioning* or otherwise preparing the brain for *other* important processes to happen, such as opening up the window for plasticity, creating synchronized activity, and so on. My typing is aimed at setting down information, but the flexing of the fingers beforehand only facilitates the later muscle motions; it is not itself an information-bearing action relative to the goal of setting down whatever the content of the page will be. Similarly, action potentials could be involved in maintaining channel conditions for more effective transmission of information, or be part of the causal mechanism for driving a motor response, rather than being directly involved in the transmission of information.

A number of papers from the Shenoy group characterize the primary role of activity in motor cortex as *mechanistic* rather than representational.[1] They argue that their data is best explained if "preparatory [neural] activity provides the initial state of a dynamical system whose evolution produces movement activity. Our results thus suggest that preparatory activity may not represent specific factors, and may instead play a more mechanistic role" (Churchland et al., 2010). Interestingly, this causal-mechanistic role is *still* characterized by the authors as *computational*, "Neurons in many cortical areas ... systematically modulate their activity during the delay. Thus, these motor related areas appear to be engaged in computation prior to the movement" (Shenoy, Sahani, and Churchland, 2013) – suggesting that in fact all that they meant by "computational" is the minimal sense of playing some functional role in the system.

This kind of computation-talk is explicitly cheap. It could be eliminated with no loss in explanatory power or scientific insight. But in other cases, something more ambiguous is happening. Computations have a particular algorithmic structure involving mathematical operations, and we claim that these operations are somehow implemented in the physical processes taking place in the brain. Such a role for computation is best characterized in terms of a *structural* notion of computation, where there exists some mapping between physical states (and the causal transitions between them) and computational states (and the transitions between them specified by the algorithm), but no semantic notions are directly implicated.

Sometimes, there is a further idea that computation is not just being carried out in neural processes, but also that it is being performed over neural representations. This would seem to imply that a semantic notion of computation is being employed, but we should be careful. In order to understand what this involves, we need to understand what representation talk in neuroscience actually comes to.

Neural representation and the neural code

Notions of representation

The dominant paradigm in much of neuroscience remains representational. It is focused on finding *tuning curves*, that capture the selective response properties of neurons to some stimuli and not others. It looks for correlations between states of the world (either stimuli or motor outputs) and the patterns of neural activity evoked by or evoking them. But what notion of representation can be derived from these causal and correlational facts?

A robust notion of representation requires that any content we find in the system is playing a genuine representational role in the system, independent of any interpretation that we as observers may be projecting onto the system. In addition to not being observer-dependent, robust content should support misrepresentation, and it should be sufficiently determinate and non-disjunctive to support practical predictions about the system's behavior.

In this section I'll describe how the contents of neural representations are determined in practice, before turning to whether the principles implicit in these assignments really license attribution of robust semantic content.

Because "representation" is also used in a number of different ways in neuroscience, I'll start with a brief catalog. Sometimes we talk about particular cells or groups of cells as representing features *with* the activation patterns that are elicited by those features. Here, activation patterns (e.g. spike trains in one or more cells) will be the vehicles of representation. Other times, people pick out particular brain areas or groups of cells *themselves* as representations, e.g. "the hand representation" in the sensory homunculus. In this sense, the representation is the bit of the brain where activity occurs that is relevant to dealing with information about the hand. While these distinctions are useful, none of them are crucial to my point here; whether we take neural representations to be the physical parts of the brain themselves, the processes taking place in them, content gets assigned in the same sorts of ways.

There is also a third notion imported from computer science via Marr, which uses "representation" to mean something more like a *scheme* of representation, the way Arabic numerals are our number representation – a scheme or system by which we represent items (numbers) in a particular domain. This third notion is more like a coding scheme. When people talk about a system *learning* a representation in this sense, it means that the system is establishing a scheme to keep track of relevant states of the world, likely by mapping them to distinct internal states. Learning a representation of (say) a set of images, then, is what allows a system to categorize them. I should also note that there is some evidence that codes are dynamic – that the response properties of cells change depending on recent history and context. This introduces an extra degree of freedom, but I will ignore this complication in what follows.

In practice, representational contents are assigned to neural vehicles (usually spike trains from single neurons, or activation maps of larger brain regions) on the basis of a few heuristic principles. Taken together, these heuristic principles constitute a mix of some intuitive functional commitments about what the brain, perceptual systems, and neural activity is *for*, a basic causal theory of content, and some optimality assumptions stemming from a kind of methodological adaptationism. I should note that these principles are *descriptive* of neuroscientific practice, but they do not constitute any kind of prescriptive standard. Since their initial articulation in the early days of neurophysiology,[2] they have become so internalized that the content assignments they underlie tend to come first, and any explicit justification of the practice comes later, if at all.

The correlation principle

The most fundamental of these is the *correlation principle*, that is, that particular kinds of contents are associated with particular input channels. At the coarsest level, this gives us contents specific to particular sensory modalities.[3] Thus we find visual information in visual cortex, and auditory information in auditory cortex and so forth – *because* visual cortex receives a huge amount of input from the eyes, which are optimized for sensitivity to lighting conditions and photons bouncing off things in the environment, and not optimized to respond to sound waves. The specificity is guaranteed by how different groups of cells are hooked up to particular physical inputs.

We also know that the anatomical connectivity of the first few stages in sensory processing roughly preserves spatial organization, so that (for example) adjacent cells in the retina (which in turn are positioned to likely receive information about nearby visual stimuli) project to adjacent cells in early visual areas. By determining a cell's receptive field, we can narrow down which parts of the environment (in egocentric, or more precisely, sensor-centric space) it is causally sensitive to.

We also find *feature* selectivity, where some cells or groups of cells appear to be selectively responsive to particular features. The best known examples are again in vision: cells in primary visual cortex are sensitive to oriented edges, for example – they exhibit their strongest firing response when edges of the right orientation are present in their receptive fields (Hubel and Wiesel, 1959); the FFA brain region exhibits its strongest response when presented with *faces*, or visual stimuli that share the most prominent visual features of faces, with two eyes and a mouth arranged in the normal way (Kanwisher, McDermott, and Chun, 1997).

The proportionality principle

Another heuristic might be called the *principle of proportionality*. Barlow argued that the strength of a neural signal should scale with the strength of the stimulus. There is substantial evidence for this in many sensory domains (louder, brighter, harder stimuli evoke more spikes, higher contrast stimuli evoke more reliable responses, etc.). It's not always obvious what "stronger" means: we have to figure out what the relevant dimension is along which to measure magnitude or intensity. But all else being equal, the *importance* of what is being conveyed by the signal is thought to be well-correlated with the number of spikes evoked.[4]

For a given encoding unit, we infer that more spikes (or better synchronized spike patterns) mean a stronger, or more salient, or more certain stimulus. The background presumption here is that a stronger stimulus is more important (perhaps one more relevant to the creature's interests), and thus should have a stronger effect on the system, mediated by a physically effective neural signal (see Panzeri et al., 2017).

This is actually a relatively strong assumption, for it presumes that the dimensions that an outside observer takes to be relevant are also the ones coded for by the system, and on the same scale. Followed slavishly, it rules out codings that map *decreases* or *pauses* in firing to *increases* in environmental variables of interest.

There are other methodological issues: if we look only for cells that march in lockstep to environmental variables that we have presupposed to be relevant, then we may miss cells that have more complex response patterns but which are nonetheless involved in the capacity we are investigating (e.g. "mixed selectivity cells").[5] The situation is even worse if we have failed to guess the right environmental variables (and we might expect this happens quite often, as perhaps the classic puzzle of "complex cells" in visual cortex demonstrates).

One way to address these issues is to look downstream – what role do the signals play with respect to the rest of the system? How are they used?

The decodability principle

The *decodability principle* says that the content of a representation depends on what the recipient of the signal can make of it. While the specifics of neural decoding have been given much less attention than the specifics of neural encoding – in part because they are much less practically accessible – the principle itself is intuitive: whenever we have encoding, we must also have decoding, in which the information in the signal is extracted and put to use in the brain's cognitive economy, whether in driving behavior or other cognitive functions, especially if we take seriously the idea that neurons are using signals to *communicate* with each other.

However, most often *decoding* is used to refer to something that *scientists* do in trying to interpret brain activity. But only if the scientist is plausibly in the same position as the brain itself with respect to the signal can we equate the two. So for example, although we can "decode" something about stimulus information in sensory areas by looking at changes in blood oxygenation level in different parts of the brain, it is unlikely that the brain itself employs blood oxygenation levels as a way to encode stimulus features, and thus we do not ascribe content to these oxygenation 'signals'.

The prominence of feature-coding for many years led to neural codes being expressed in terms of what neural firings a scientist might expect to observe, given the presentation of a particular experimental stimulus. But this is relative to the scientists' background beliefs and ways of carving up the world, whereas what matters for neuroscience is explaining the role of the signal in the cognitive processes of the organism, i.e. how the organism can make effective use of the signal.[6] Thus, as Rieke et al. (1999) have argued, we ought to invert the dependence relation; the relevant quantity is not what can be inferred by an outsider about the signal from the stimulus, or P(signal|stimulus), but rather what can be inferred ("inferred") by the brain itself about the stimulus from an incoming neural signal, or P(stimulus|signal). This last quantity – the probability of some stimulus occurring, given the spike train in question – should be taken to be the content of that spike train. Again, the relevant reference class for these stimuli will have to be fixed by "common sense", and thus informed by the correlation principle, but whatever it is, it should be one that it is reasonable to expect the system itself to have.

Attending to what a signal is used *for* in the system brings us closer to a notion of content that goes beyond mere correlational-information-carrying. It appeals at least implicitly to the function of the signal in the system. It also allows the correlation principle to be generalized to more cognitive domains. For example, researchers have identified non-sensory areas as being responsible for "representing" everything from rules for behavior to the expected *values* associated with a particular stimulus.[7]

Ideally, the above three principles taken together would provide relatively stable content assignments. What we actually get is consensus in a few canonical cases, but much less agreement as we move to less well-studied areas, especially away from the sensory periphery.[8]

Neural content, function, and the problems of misrepresentation and indeterminacy

Without providing a full metasemantic theory of robust representational content, we can't say definitively that the contents ascribed to neural vehicles don't meet the criteria. But at least *prima facie*, the principles governing neuroscientific practice in assigning content are too weak to support the requirements laid out earlier: observer-independence, misrepresentation, and sufficient determinacy to support practical predictions.

The correlational principle is ultimately based on causal facts about the system – it says that signals encode information about their causes, and that their contents depend on their downstream effects. At least for sensory signals, all that is required is a pattern of selective responsiveness to particular stimuli or stimulus features for a neuron to be pegged as representing that feature, and its firing activity to be identified as the vehicle of that representation.

More precisely, assignments of content to neural vehicles exhibit two problematic features. First, our principles fail to provide a way to distinguish between very different stimuli that a cell may be equally responsive to. That means that we also cannot distinguish contents that are quite different from the point of view of psychology. In the language of feature coding, features fall into large and perhaps disjunctive equivalence classes as far as the neural activity they evoke is concerned.

Imagine a single neuron in V1, selective for edges of a particular orientation in its receptive field. It achieves its maximum firing rate for a vertically oriented edge. It also exhibits a higher firing rate for high-contrast "strong" stimuli than lower contrast ones (thus obeying Barlow's principle of proportionality). In the case where that neuron is firing at 80 percent of maximum, it could be indicating either a vertical stimulus at (say) 80 percent contrast, or an edge oriented at approximately 72 degrees (rather than its maximally preferred 90 degrees) but at 100 percent contrast, and any number of combinations of these. What are we to say about its representational content? If it is "really" representing one of these, it seems unclear *which*.

Or suppose we observe the activity of an inhibitory fast-spiking cell in somatosensory cortex of a rat, and we observe that it fires more in response to the deflection of one particular whisker than otherwise. What is the function of that activity? We could say that it serves to indicate that that whisker was deflected, or that it serves to sharpen the response of nearby excitatory cells, which in turn serve to indicate that that whisker was deflected, or that it serves to normalize the response of the circuit as a whole, in order to subserve somatosensation ... and so on. Any and all of these seem plausible; moreover, they do not seem to be hypotheses that could really be tested by collecting more data about how the whisker now responds in various situations.

Second, we do not seem to have the resources to identify cases of *misrepresentation*. Neural firing always has *some* causal antecedent or another – if we simply identify the content of that firing with the causal antecedent, then there can never be misrepresentation. What we need is some way of saying what the neuron is *supposed* to be firing in response to – what it has the *function* to indicate to the system. Then, when it fires in response to something *else* (say because of noise in the system), we get to say that it is *mis*representing. So if we have a way to assign functions to neural activity, then we might be able to solve both the problem of misrepresentation or error and the problem of indeterminacy.[9]

Where can we find scientifically respectable normative functions? One way of getting teleonomy is by looking for the evolutionary or selective function of a trait. As Wright has it, *X has the function to Y iff it is the case that X exists as a consequence of its doing Y*.[10] But even leaving aside the epistemic difficulties with ascertaining such functions for neurons given the inaccessibility of evolutionary and even developmental history, I doubt that this is the notion that neuroscientists actually rely on in practice.

Strangely enough, however, neuroscientists seem almost completely unconcerned with the possibility of disjunctive or indeterminate contents. I submit that this is because in practice, functions are often defined by *tasks*. That is, they are imposed by the experimenter: we set the experimental subject some task – perhaps to produce some motor response in response to some stimulus feature over a number of trials. And then, we presume that whatever processes are differentially activated by that task (as opposed to those active in some control condition which does not involve the cognitive capacity of interest but is otherwise as similar as possible) have the function to do whatever it is they are doing to make successful completion of the task possible.

So in one sense, function ascriptions are impossible to get "right", and worse, there might be no objective, natural, fact of the matter about them (though nothing I've said here establishes this for any particular case). And in another sense, they are experimentally accessible and relatively clear-cut – but somewhat *ad hoc* and dependent on the interpretation of the particular experiment. Once we *accept* the determinate function attribution stipulated by the particular task of interest, we can have as much determinacy and error as a robust notion of representation requires. But this is at the cost of making the representational ascriptions interest-relative and perspectival, although still instrumentally useful in context. In that way, our content assignments remain permissive in a sense that makes it difficult to make sense of computationalism as an objective fact about cognitive systems (unless computationalism is not committed to representationalism).

Representation as taxonomy; computation as modeling

One plausible alternative understanding of talk of representational states or computational processes in neuroscience is as *shorthand* for physical states and physical processes (particular patterns of activity that we observe in certain characteristic situations) that do not otherwise have a convenient taxonomy.[11] Function (and thus content) ascriptions then serve the purpose of *summarizing* whatever existing set of response properties have been characterized. So for example, we might talk about the representation (or engram) of a particular location in order to pick out just that collection of cells that respond to location-dependent features that were active while an animal was in that location (and no others).[12]

The use of computational or representational language as merely a naming convention may also explain the explicit commitment in some quarters to the kind of pan-computationalism that says that every physical system computes *something* – namely whatever mathematical operations might be used in the model that accurately describes its behavior.

Once the specifications of the particular naming convention have been established, we can translate back and forth between the empirically accessible physical facts and the computational model. In this way, a computational model can also make testable claims about the causal relations between vehicles and thus some claims about the "bits of matter" moving around in the system, and how *they* interact. It tells us something about the causal structure of what is happening during the computation, and the mechanism carrying it out.

These mappings won't be unique, however. Single cells may be said to compute normalizations, or summations of their inputs; there can be as many computational ascriptions in the brain as there are plausible physical quantities to measure, at all scales of size and abstraction. Is this a problem?

Suppose that different mathematical functions (and thus different computational hypotheses) are assigned to the same physical process by different scientific observers. There may then be disagreements about whether, say, a particular circuit is merely summing its inputs, averaging them, or multiplying them – disagreements that cannot be resolved by additional observations about the physical behavior of the circuit, no matter how numerous or detailed. For example, if earlier states are supposed to represent "two" and "three", nothing constrains us to say that the later state represents "five" rather than "six" – structurally they would be the same. (The operations of addition and multiplication over positive numbers are isomorphic.)[13]

However, *once* the parties to the debate also agree on a specific mapping from numerical values to measurable neural firing rates (or some other physical quantity), the disagreement becomes empirical, and can be resolved. As long as we do not imbue the particular computational model with too much significance (recognizing instead that it is partly determined by a stipulative and pragmatically motivated mapping convention), there is no harm done.

The canonical neural computation

Now let's look at an example of modeling explanation of this kind in more detail. Carandini and Heeger (2012) argue for the existence of a canonical neural circuit – a processing motif that is repeated over and over again in different parts of the brain, subserving quite different abilities. They characterize this circuit as performing the computational operation of "divisive normalization". They compare this to other computations that they take to be well-established that the brain (or a particular neuron/neural circuit) performs: exponentiation (thresholding) and linear filtering (summation of receptive fields).

The CNC is defined by a transformation from input (either to a cell or to a circuit) to output (usually measured from a single cell). The authors are impressed at the effectiveness of the normalization equation that they posit in *accurately describing* observed responses from a wide variety of systems, each with different underlying physical architectures. That is, the normalization equation predicts the spiking rate of a cell (or group of cells) *j*, in response to different input profiles, which might themselves be spiking rates of cells that synapse onto *j*, or environmental stimulus features (say gratings of different contrasts) further upstream.

$$R_j = \gamma \frac{D_j^n}{\sigma^n + \sum_k D_k^n}$$

Carandini and Heeger argue that that normalization brings "functional benefits to computations", that it is involved in processes from object recognition (perceptual) to value encoding (cognitive), and that it is a way of *connecting* behavior to cellular mechanisms (2012, pp. 60–61). That is, they talk as though this kind of neural computation helps us to connect neural activity to higher-level function (i.e. characterized cognitively or psychologically in representational terms), just as the computationalist program promises.

I think this is misleading. Rather, the CNC exemplifies the mode of computational explanation in which we construct *models* of neural processes, models which neither depend on nor license any assignment of semantic content (although they may certainly be *compatible* with such assignments were we to find ourselves needing or wanting them on *independent* grounds). Moreover, when we look at the specific examples they give, the phenomena explained are themselves (merely) neural-level phenomena, rather than cognitive ones. Among them are early sensory responses in the retina, early cortical responses in V1, some effects in visual-spatial attention, and only somewhat more tenuously, some responses in non-perceptual brain areas such as value-sensitive neurons in LIP. So for example, "normalization explains why responses of V1 neurons saturate with increasing stimulus contrast, irrespective of stimulus orientation, and therefore irrespective of firing rate" (Carandini and Heeger, 2012, p. 54).

Certainly normalization *describes* the saturating responses of V1 neurons. That is, with the right parameters *n*, γ, and σ, it accurately predicts their firing rate as we increase stimulus contrast. Furthermore, it describes the input–output relationship of stimulus to firing *compactly*. And finally, it posits a *function* – signal processing – for the activities observed.

Thus we posit gain control as a function of a circuit whose activities satisfy the normalization equation, because gain control allows for an increased range of sensitivity, which we know that the system exhibits (behaviorally), and which we think is furthermore appropriate given the function of the system as a whole (to allow the organism to see and respond effectively in a range of background conditions). Normalization is a *way* of achieving gain control, and thus normalization partly explains the system's success (of being sensitive across different background conditions).

I've said that the function of the circuits performing the CNC is essentially *signal processing* – whether in the form of gain control (e.g. optimizing the dynamic range of the system to sensory inputs across different background conditions), or efficient coding (e.g. minimizing informational redundancy in the inputs to visual cortex). Other potentially desirable outcomes of signal processing might include increased fidelity, robustness, strength (amplitude), etc. This processing makes the signal more useful to downstream processes, whatever *those* may be.

There are two features of signal processing that are relevant here. First, it is *insensitive* to content. As Shannon (1948) pointed out on the first page of his classic paper, signals *may* have meaning (i.e. there is *some* mapping from particular patterns of signals to particular contents), but any semantic details are "irrelevant to the engineering problem".[14] And second, notice that the point of *communication* is to *reproduce* a message, *not* to transform it, or change it in any way. So although a communications system may only approximate a message in its output, the normative goal or *function* is faithful *reproduction* rather than *transformation* or change.[15]

But no (non-trivial) cognitive process[16] is explained by mere transmission; what matters is that the content *changes* over the course of the process that is called "computation". For any interesting computationalist process, features are highlighted, others are discarded, messages are combined, massaged, *transformed*. And so the existence of non-transformative signal processing in many neural circuits does not seem to furnish additional support for computationalism, despite being representative of much talk about neural computation.

Instead, what the CNC and other forms of neural computation are doing is better described as a kind of signal *packaging*. That is, without changing the information content of the signal, they optimize its non-semantic features, for example by providing amplification, reducing noise, or improving resolution across a wide range of conditions.

There is a fascinating discussion by Webb (2006) that suggests that there is a principled reason for all this. What we want robust representation for is some kind of standing-in-for (*à la* Haugeland, 1993) in *mental* or *psychological* representation – or even if Haugeland's is not quite the right characterization, representations ought to play *some* kind of distinctive functional role in the system beyond serving as a mere causal intermediary (also see Ramsey, 2007; 2016) between the system and the environment. Perhaps they allow for the evaluation of hypotheticals or planning.[17] Webb implies that the very *idea* of encoding/decoding rules this out – encoding is all about *preserving* information while packaging it for transmission (see also Bergstrom and Rosvall (2009) for a statement of this). Encoding and decoding *qua* signal processing or mere transduction steps are thus computationally sterile with respect to content, and so any neuroscientific notion of "representation" that derives entirely from encoding must be also.

Isn't semantic computation supported by inference to the best explanation?

To the extent that neuroscientists talk about representation of non-perceptual cognitive entities as options or values or confidences, they will assign the contents according to more or less the same procedure as described earlier for perceptual features – that is, by picking out patterns of brain activity whose occurrence is *correlated* with when they think these representations will be tokened, and that in turn is given by a coarse-grained psychological model which may be understood as computational in a semantic sense. We then look for matches to that coarse-grained model in the patterns of neural activity. Does finding these correlates lend support to the computational model, or ground it in neuroscientific data? There is an overwhelming presumption in the field that it does, but is it justified?

I outline a kind of bootstrapping inference to the best explanation below, where if all the pieces fall into place, it seems we ought to accept that the activity of neural circuits is best understood as performing a computation in the sense of transforming robust representational contents.

We start by assuming that the system under investigation *is* computing, and take a best guess at what the relevant vehicles of computation are. By default, patterns of neural spiking are the candidates, being well-situated to be differentially responsive to whatever inputs the computations need to be sensitive to, and drive whatever outputs the computation is supposed to produce control over.

We then construct a computational or mathematical model that accurately describes and predicts the transformation of those vehicles. Once the model has been validated on new (or reserved) data, we look to see what relationship between contents and vehicles (if any) would make those computational transformations adaptive or useful given what we know about the function of the system as a whole.

If it turns out that there are natural assignments of contents to neural vehicles that allow for these satisfying interpretations of neural activity as performing a useful computation, then we say that those vehicles really do have those contents. And then we see how well those content ascriptions support further inferences that may be tested in turn. Only when this edifice stands the test of time and investigation may we consider the initial assumption (that the system was performing semantic computation) as well as the intermediate inferences (that the vehicles really do have the robust representational contents that a satisfying gloss on the computational model assigns them) validated.

This is a best case scenario. And each of these steps presents some epistemic hazard – where in practice the line between theft and honest toil is faded and scuffed. It is crucial that when we look for natural interpretations of quantities or variables in our computational models in terms of representational content, that it is done in a non-question-begging way – in which the models could turn out to be wrong.

For example, it would not be fair to *stipulate* the content of observed neural activity to match a particular computational hypothesis *before* having undertaken model validation and followed out some of the later inferences. Nor would it do to tailor the mapping from contents to physical signals to accommodate whatever patterns of activity we in fact observe to a computational model to which we had some prior commitment.

Evaluating computationalist hypotheses about neural activity must be a *holistic* enterprise – requiring simultaneous commitment to a package of hypotheses about content, conventional mappings for computation, and explanatory depth. Two interesting consequences follow.

First, computational hypotheses can't be fully tested *locally* – part of the validation involves looking at new task contexts involving the same putative neural vehicles and contents, but requiring different computations in order to achieve distinct goals. (In practice, for many models this may not happen as much as it ought to ... or even at all.) And second, it is not only a bonus virtue of computational explanations that they connect neural phenomena with cognitive phenomena, but also a *requirement* – any semantic computational explanation that does *not* make contact with higher-level functions of the system will be difficult to justify as part of this strategy of inference to the best explanation.

It is doubtful that the best case scenario obtains often, if at all, in computational neuroscience concerned with the activities of neurons. Perhaps the strongest case can be made for the model of a reward prediction error system in the VTA apparently coding for variables required to implement the temporal difference (TD) learning algorithm.[18] In that work, it was clear that the VTA was involved in learning expectations about certain patterns of stimuli (cues and impending rewards). These are components of the same kinds of tasks that the pre-existing TD algorithm had been developed to address.[19] Researchers were struck by the similarity between response patterns of the dopamine neurons and the values of the error variable in the learning algorithm, and found that, at least qualitatively, the algorithm predicted the response patterns.

But even in this the most touted success of computational neuroscience, the validation and the model development happened together (not independently, as we would like). Moreover, it's not clear how much further the results take us. How faithfully do neural responses in other populations match the variables in the model? What new predictions can we make about the actual architecture of the brain? Can it accommodate new data? (See Redgrave and Gurney, 2006, for some critiques.)

In any case, success in this bootstrapping mode where semantic content seems to be playing a genuine explanatory role is the exception, not the rule.

Upshots

I have tried to argue that the notion of computation most common in neuroscience has explanatory virtues that might be more aptly described as those of *computational modeling*. Neural computation and neural representation are, in practice, thinner, more liberal, and more observer-relative notions than the types of computation and representation often assumed in theoretical psychology or computational cognitive science. Thus the success of computational modeling provides no support for the more ambitious computationalist project of connecting neural computation (as construed by neuroscientists) to a computational theory of mind or cognition.

To take the language in papers such as Carandini and Heeger's at face value is to accept a notion of computation that is almost universally applicable. The computations involved are transformations of physical inputs and outputs, and might be less contentiously characterized as computational *models* of those physical transformations. Since no particularly robust notion of representation is involved in these computations, it would be a mistake to think that characterizing the computations performed by neurons is equivalent to characterizing cognition – or that duplicating those computations under a convenient (but arbitrary) implementation convention in, say, artificial neural networks, will be sufficient to reproduce cognitive processes.

Since neuroscientists are unlikely to stop using the term *computation* any time soon, honest advocates of computationalism should be clear on the difference between neural computation and the computations required for the unifying computationalist thesis. None of this is to say that the computationalist program is hopeless, only that neural computation is not the right place to look for its justification.

Notes

1 See Churchland et al. (2010); and Shenoy, Sahani, and Churchland (2013).
2 Especially in Barlow (1961; 1972).
3 As Mueller hypothesized in 1838 in his doctrine of "specific nerve energies". While the actual "energies" in the specific nerves are the same, it seems to be the particular pathways and areas that determine the content. And while it's true that *once the system is set up*, it doesn't matter what kind of stimulus is used to excite a particular input pathway, the *initial* assignment of modality to a brain area does seem to be determined by the causal source of the input. So, *given* a normal adult brain, stimulating the auditory nerve electrically will produce effects consistent with some sort of auditory experience, *as if* some sound had been played. But the *reason* for this is that, under normal conditions, *only* auditory stimuli will excite neurons in an auditory area (that area itself being defined as encompassing only those cells that immediately respond to auditory stimuli under normal conditions). The specification of "normal conditions" is usually left to common sense, with all the attending practical advantages and theoretical disadvantages.
4 That importance might result from internal factors such as attention, certainty, or differences in expected reward as well as external features of the stimulus itself (Ikeda and Hikosaka, 2003; Ma and Jazayeri, 2014; Stachenfeld, Botvinick, and Gershman, 2017).
5 Hardcastle et al. (2017) argue that any reliable statistical relationship should count as encoding, and explore a few relatively simple non-linear ones. This allows for much more flexibility in potential codes.
6 Traditional feature coding advocates might respond that any information available in the signal is likely to be exploited by the system. If we assume that the brain is *optimally* adapted to process information, then whatever code used for the transmission of information from area to area must also be maximally efficient, carrying as much relevant information through the channel as allowed by the information-theoretic limits. Even if not always true, the assumption will be a useful heuristic in the manner of methodological adaptationism, in that it helps us not to *miss* features that *have* been selected for. Adopting this optimality assumption allows us to assume that if the information is visible to the experimenter, then it

is also available to the system itself. While somewhat contentious within the neuroscience community (given the tension with any non-trivial decodability constraint), it is often assumed in practice. (Much of William Bialek's work (Bialek, de Ruyter van Steveninck, and Tishby, 2007) exemplifies strong adaptationism; see Carandini et al. (2005) for arguments on the other side.)

7 Examples include reward prediction error representations in the midbrain dopaminergic system (Schultz, Dayan, and Montague, 1997), rule representations in the prefrontal cortex (Wallis, Anderson, and Miller, 2001), and negative reward value in the lateral habenula (Hikosaka, 2010).

8 This is so despite the fact that some of the most well-known examples of neural "representation" are found further from the periphery, for example, in the hippocampus and nearby medial temporal lobe areas. More contentious examples include representations of "rules" in prefrontal areas, representations of threat or value in subcortical structures, and representations of planned action sequences in motor and premotor areas. And of course, perhaps *the* best confirmed computational model of a cognitive system is that of the subcortical dopaminergic reward system.

9 Many believers in robust representation at the psychological level (e.g. Burge, 2010, chs. 8–9) have *not* found naturalistic accounts of content that appeal to information plus function to be particularly convincing, at least in part because of the difficulty in identifying functions properly.

10 Wright (1973).

11 See Sprevak's (2013) 'Fictionalism about neural representations" for a similar view.

12 Here's a typical usage, from Liu, Ramirez, and Tonegawa (2014): "distinct populations of cells in the DG represent contexts A and C (figure 4a–e), enabling the manipulation of context-specific memories at the level of defined neural populations". Another example: "the NCM contains (part of) the neural representation of the tutor song, while the song system nucleus HVC may be a locus for a neural representation of the bird's own song" (Bolhuis et al., 2012). Here it is clear that "part of" is meant *physically*, and the neural representation of the tutor song is just the set of cells involved in the storage of a song (i.e. activated during the process in which the song is "encoded" in memory).

13 Also see Shea (2013) for an illustration of this point with a block-counting process.

14 More acutely: signals don't need to be semantic at all. They are simply whatever we want the channel to *preserve*. Signal processing can be done on signals with content (such as cell phone transmissions), but it can also be done on signals that don't *stand for* anything at all (e.g. astronomical measurements from a radio telescope).

15 This is not really a perfectly clear distinction; really it is more like the distinction between signal and noise. Once you know what the signal is supposed to be, everything else is noise. So there is a sense in which whatever processing it takes to get specific responses for faces in FFA can be cast as "merely filtering out the non-face noise" from the full visual input signal. That would seem to be missing the point. Similarly, if the goal is to transmit only the most important or task-relevant information, then getting rid of everything else can be called signal processing. But perhaps this is unfair (although less unfair than the face case), since the signal might be quite deeply buried, and it is only post hoc that we can say, oh *this* was the signal all along. I think that most of Carandini and Heeger's cases it is fair to call genuine (mere) signal processing, but perhaps the receptive field remapping behind attentional modulation (as described in Wu, 2014) falls closer to what ought to qualify as content processing.

16 Perhaps the one exception here is memory storage and retrieval (and even there, we have good evidence that there is transformation through reconstruction).

17 So for example representations play a particular kind of role for Dennett's Popperian creatures, whose hypotheses die in their stead (Dennett, 1996, p. 88).

18 For an accessible introduction, see Schultz (2016) "Dopamine Reward Error Coding". For the seminal paper, see Schultz, Dayan, and Montague (1997). The history is explored in more detail in Colombo (2014).

19 The relevant version of the TD learning algorithm came from a series of papers by Richard Sutton in the late 1970s, while the original idea of using temporal differences goes back even further. See Sutton and Barto's reinforcement learning textbook (1998) for a brief history of the idea.

References

Barlow, H.B. (1961) 'Possible Principles Underlying the Transformation of Sensory Messages', in Rosenblith, W.A. (ed.) *Sensory Communication*. Cambridge, MA: MIT Press, pp. 217–234.

Barlow, H.B. (1972) 'Single Units and Sensation: A Neuron Doctrine for Perceptual Psychology?', *Perception*, 1 (4), pp. 371–394.

Bergstrom, C.T. and Rosvall, M. (2009) 'The Transmission Sense of Information', *Biology and Philosophy*, 28 (2), pp. 159–176.

Bialek, W., de Ruyter van Steveninck, R.R., and Tishby, N. (2007) 'Efficient Representation as a Design Principle for Neural Coding and Computation'. arXiv:0712.4381 [q–bio.NC].

Bolhuis, J.J. et al. (2012) 'Learning-Related Neuronal Activation in the Zebra Finch Song System Nucleus HVC in Response to the Bird's Own Song', *PLoS ONE*, 7 (7), e41556.

Burge, T. (2010) *Origins of Objectivity*. Oxford: Oxford University Press.

Carandini, M. and Heeger, D.J. (2012) 'Normalization as a Canonical Neural Computation', *Nature Reviews Neuroscience*, 13, pp. 51–62.

Carandini, M. et al. (2005) 'Do We Know What the Early Visual System Does?', *The Journal of Neuroscience*, 25 (46), pp. 10577–10597.

Churchland, M.M. et al. (2010) 'Cortical Preparatory Activity: Representation of Movement or First Cog in a Dynamical Machine?', *Neuron*, 68, pp. 387–400.

Colombo, M. (2014) 'Deep and Beautiful: The Reward Prediction Error Hypothesis of Dopamine', *Studies in History and Philosophy of Science Part C: Studies in History and Philosophy of Biological and Biomedical Sciences*, 45, pp. 57–67.

Dennett, D. (1996) *Kinds of Minds*. New York, NY: Basic Books.

Hardcastle, K. et al. (2017) 'A Multiplexed, Heterogeneous, and Adaptive Code for Navigation in Medial Entorhinal Cortex', *Neuron*, 94 (2), pp. 375–387.

Haugeland, J. (1993) 'Mind Embodied and Embedded', in Houng, Y.-H.H. and Ho, J. (eds.) *Mind and Cognition: 1993 International Symposium*. Taipei: Academica Sinica, pp. 233–267.

Hikosaka, O. (2010) 'The Habenula: From Stress Evasion to Value-based Decision-making', *Nature Reviews Neuroscience*, 11 (7), pp. 503–513.

Hubel, D.H. and Wiesel, T.N. (1959) 'Receptive Fields of Single Neurones in the Cat's Striate Cortex', *The Journal of Physiology*, 124 (3), pp. 574–591.

Ikeda, T. and Hikosaka, O. (2003) 'Reward-dependent Gain and Bias of Visual Responses in Primate Superior Colliculus', *Neuron*, 39 (4), pp. 693–700.

Kanwisher, N., McDermott J., and Chun, M.M. (1997) 'The Fusiform Face Area: A Module in Human Extrastriate Cortex Specialized for Face Perception', *The Journal of Neuroscience*, 17 (11), pp. 4302–4311.

Liu, X., Ramirez, S., and Tonegawa, S. (2014) 'Inception of a False Memory by Optogenetic Manipulation of a Hippocampal Memory Engram', *Philosophical Transactions of the Royal Society B: Biological Sciences*, 369, 20130142.

Ma, W.J. and Jazayeri, M. (2014) 'Neural Coding of Uncertainty and Probability', *Annual Review of Neuroscience*, 37, pp. 205–220.

Panzeri, S. et al. (2017) 'Cracking the Neural Code for Sensory Perception by Combining Statistics, Intervention, and Behavior', *Neuron*, 93 (3), pp. 491–507.

Ramsey, W.M. (2007) *Representation Reconsidered*. Cambridge, UK: Cambridge University Press.

Ramsey, W.M. (2016) 'Untangling Two Questions about Mental Representation', *New Ideas in Psychology*, 40, pp, 3–12.

Redgrave, P. and Gurney, K. (2006) 'The Short-Latency Dopamine Signal: A Role in Discovering Novel Actions?', *Nature Reviews Neuroscience*, 7 (12), pp. 967–975.

Rieke, F. et al. (1999) *Spikes: Exploring the Neural Code*. Cambridge, MA: The MIT Press.

Schultz, W. (2016) 'Dopamine Reward Prediction Error Coding', *Dialogues in Clinical Neuroscience*, 18 (1), pp. 23–32.

Schultz, W., Dayan, P., and Montague, R.R. (1997) 'A Neural Substrate of Prediction and Reward', *Science*, 275, pp. 1593–1599.

Shannon, C.E. (1948) 'A Mathematical Theory of Communication', *The Bell System Technical Journal*, 27, pp. 379–423, 623–656.

Shea, N. (2013) 'Naturalising Representational Content', *Philosophy Compass*, 8 (5), pp. 496–509.

Shenoy, K.V., Sahani, M., and Churchland, M.M. (2013) 'Cortical Control of Arm Movements: A Dynamical Systems Perspective', *Annual Review of Neuroscience*, 36, pp. 337–359.

Sprevak, M. (2013) 'Fictionalism about Neural Representations', *The Monist*, 96 (4), pp. 539–560.

Stachenfeld, K.L., Botvinick, M.M., and Gershman, S.J. (2017) 'The Hippocampus as a Predictive Map', *Nature Neuroscience*, 20 (11), pp. 1643–1653.

Sutton, R.S. and Barto, A.G. (1998) *Reinforcement Learning: An Introduction*. Cambridge, MA: MIT Press.

Wallis, J.D., Anderson, K.C., and Miller, E.K. (2001) 'Single Neurons in Prefrontal Cortex Encode Abstract Rules', *Nature*, 411 (6840), pp. 953–956.

Webb, B. (2006) 'Transformation, Encoding and Representation', *Current Biology*, 16, pp. R184–R185.

Wright, L. (1973) 'Functions', *Philosophical Review*, 82, pp. 139–168.

Wu, W. (2014) *Attention*. Abingdon, UK: Routledge.

22

COMPUTATION, CONSCIOUSNESS, AND "COMPUTATION AND CONSCIOUSNESS"

Colin Klein

Three preliminaries

Ms W

The Symphonie Philosophique reserves by ancient custom a chair for the viola de gamba. The current virtuosa, Ms W, is universally acclaimed for her work in other ensembles. Yet the symphony dropped early music from its repertoire many seasons ago. In her many appearances, Ms W has never played a note.

Subscribers differ on Ms W's aesthetic contributions. One group insists that her presence clearly enhances the aesthetic value of performances. As Miles Davis taught us, music is as much about the notes you don't play as the ones you do. Her presence gives the symphony far more *possibilities* against which the actual music can be juxtaposed, and thereby a richness and splendor that other ensembles cannot match. (The most breathless insist that if you couldn't play viola de gamba parts, you really hardly *count* as an orchestra at all.) Skeptics are more blunt. She does not add to the music. How could she? She does not play.

The core of this dispute is over the constitutive role of counterfactual properties. One side thinks that aesthetic value (whatever it is) depends both on what actually happens and on what *could have* happened. Aesthetic value is, on this picture, a *counterfactually loaded* property. Many goods are like this (Pettit, 2015). The other side thinks that aesthetic value is not counterfactually loaded, and that only the actual matters to the aesthetic. Many properties are also like this. Hence there's room for debate.

The question of whether a property is a counterfactually loaded one is behind many philosophical disputes. This piece will talk about an under-appreciated place where the conflict arises, and how it causes headaches for the computationalist about conscious experience.

The Action Max

When I was young, several unscrupulous companies offered a low-cost alternative to video game consoles. The Action Max came with a small light-gun setup and a VCR tape. I watched the commercials in breathless wonder: how could an ordinary VCR play video games? My parents were less interested in the answer, so I had to wait until I was an adult to learn what disappointment I had avoided. The Action Max played a tape of a thrilling space battle that you could shoot at. But it was just an ordinary VCR tape: nothing you did would make a difference to the outcome. The same ships would explode, the same dangers would be narrowly avoided, the same triumphal success awaited at the end.[1] Calling this a *video game* seems like a stretch. That is not a claim about what happens on the screen, or even how well the actual action matches up with the players intentions. Even if the movie exactly matched what a player *actually* did, there was no room for departure: differing inputs made no difference to what happened on the screen. What makes something a game is options and contingency, and the Action Max lacked those. *Being a video game*, in short, is a counterfactually loaded property.

Video games are a kind of physical computation, and the point holds true of computation more generally. Consider a humble Turing machine (TM). Call him Simon. Simon has a reasonably complex machine table that lets him reduce his input into its prime factors. Put Simon on some input τ and he'll click away merrily. Now suppose our unscrupulous Turing machine dealer offers a discount on a simpler model, Theodore. Theodore cuts costs: he does not have a machine table, and instead just has a tape recording that contains each transition that Simon would make on τ. Each change to the tape, each change of internal state indicator, each movement will be faithfully reproduced. Theodore will also factor τ, and just as fast as Simon does! Hardly a bargain, you protest. Given any input other than τ, Theodore will click along just the same. But computation must be counterfactually sensitive. Simon, and Simon alone, counts as implementing σ because he could do the right thing on *any* input. Theodore is not just worse than Simon; his lack of counterfactual sensitivity means he doesn't even count as computing in the first place.

Computation thus seems like a counterfactually loaded property. This is important for more than just the fight against shady Turing machine dealers. *Computationalism* about consciousness is the thesis that phenomenal properties supervene on computational ones – that is, that being the right kind of computer is enough to be conscious. Computationalism is exciting because it is a broad tent: brains compute, silicon does too, and so your laptop (it seems) could be just as conscious as you. A class of skeptical arguments pushes back by saying that computationalism is far *too* permissive, implausibly so. The molecular meanderings of buckets of water and stretches of brick can be mapped to the actual activity of a TM too (Searle, 1990; Putnam, 1991). Surely bricks aren't conscious, though!

Nor do they compute, goes the standard response. At a minimum, computing some function π requires that a system's activity *would have been* isomorphic to some abstract machine's for any of the inputs over which π is defined. Bricks don't seem to manage that. Attention to counterfactuals is thus necessary to avoid explosion. Which is all again by way of saying that computation is a counterfactually loaded notion. Two things can differ in computational status – in whether or what they are computing – without differing in what they're actually doing.

Anesthetics

What about consciousness? Start with things that remove it. The mechanism of action of inhalational anesthetics remains something of a scientific puzzle, especially given the ability of chemically inert gasses like xenon to (reversibly) remove consciousness at high concentrations. Most theories agree that interactions with the lipids in the neural membrane are crucial, as they alter the ability of the neuron to fire given appropriate stimulation (Frost, 2015). Here there is an important nit to pick. Anesthetics don't work *just* by changing membrane properties. For anesthetics affect all neurons indiscriminately (or let's suppose). What makes a difference is that neurons that would have fired are silenced. Effects on neurons that *wouldn't* have fired anyway (one might think) don't make a difference to consciousness. To knock you out, in other words, I only need to make the firing neurons quiet – the already quiet ones aren't making a difference to what you experience.

Indeed, that seems to be a quite general intuition not just about the loss of consciousness, but about the contents of consciousness altogether. A given episode of phenomenal experience supervenes (most think) on brain processes. That is to say, what you're aware of over an interval supervenes on the *actual activity* of the brain over that interval. Intuitively, neurons that are completely silent and inert over the interval can't make any contribution to what you're aware of.[2] This is to say very little about what 'activity' amounts to: the important thing is just that phenomenal awareness depends on what a system does, not on what it would do or might have done in other circumstances.

This is not a universally held thesis, but denying it forces you to say really odd things. Consider Tononi's influential Information Integration Theory of consciousness (IIT). Tononi is committed to the importance of a 'qualia space' (Tononi, 2004) or a 'cause–effect space' (Tononi and Koch, 2015) that traces out all of the possible informational states a system might be in. A system is a complex of different elements (such as neurons or neural columns) and "it is the activity state of all elements of the complex that defines a given conscious state, and both active and inactive elements count" (Tononi, 2004, p. 9). (He would, one imagines, be a supporter of Ms W's work.) Yet this is a very *weird* commitment. As Fekete and Edelman point in a nice discussion

> if silent units indeed contribute to a subject's phenomenal experience, cooling some of them reversibly (which would inactivate them without causing them to fire) would alter the experience. Having offered this prediction, Tononi stops short of explicitly addressing the crux of the problem: how can presently inactive – silent or silenced – units contribute to present experience? … It seems to us that making experience depend on a potentiality without explaining how it actually comes to pass falls short of completing the explanatory move.
>
> *(Fekete and Edelman, 2011, p. 813)*

That does seem to be the common intuition. Consciousness is an active, constructive process, and inactive units cannot add anything.

Of course, spelling out 'actual activity' brings more complications than one might expect. Let's put them aside. I assume that there is some intuitive distinction between the active and the inert, and that it would be surprising if the inert actually made a contribution to consciousness (however that is spelled out).

Maudlin's argument

Simple stories have led to a troubling conflict. Computation is counterfactually loaded: it depends in part on what could happen. Consciousness isn't: it depends only on what does happen. That mismatch seems like it ought to trouble the computationalist.

Tim Maudlin's (1989) "Computation and Consciousness" argues just that. Maudlin's argument remains relatively obscure, in part because the bulk of his paper is devoted to constructing an elaborate example that is easily misinterpreted. That is a shame, as the core argument is simple and powerful. The preliminaries above are there to bring out what I take to be the core of Maudlin's argument. I present it here in schematic form:

1   If computationalism is true, then there is some Turing machine π which, when run on input τ, is sufficient to have phenomenal experience.

2   Two things can differ in whether they implement π because of differences in wholly inert machinery.

3   Two things cannot differ in whether they are conscious because of differences in wholly inert machinery.

[Contradiction]

∴ Computationalism is false.

Premise 1 is meant to be a basic commitment of the computationalist, while premise 3 depends on the intuition sketched above. Premise 2 seems plausible insofar as computation is counterfactually loaded. But an ordinary TM like Simon may have no wholly inert machinery while processing τ – everything is active at some point during the run.

Maudlin's central innovation is a thought experiment designed to show how to make a TM *Olympia*, in which the counterfactuals are supported by wholly inert machinery. (Interested readers should consult his paper for details of the machines Olympia and Klara: I'll give a streamlined version here.) Return to Simon and Theodore. Let us suppose that Simon is configured to compute π on τ. 'No problem!' says the computationalist. 'Turing machines can be conscious!' Now Theodore apes what Simon does simply by following a pre-recorded sequence. Following a pre-recorded sequence seems like the sort of thing that isn't enough to be conscious. (In Maudlin's example, the corresponding machine simply sprays water from a hose.) 'No problem!' says the computationalist. 'That thing is too simple to be conscious. But it doesn't compute, either, and our thesis is about computation!'

Now the kicker. Consider a deluxe machine, Alvin. Alvin is a copy of Theodore with an extra sensor and a powered-down copy of Simon strapped on the back. On a run on τ, Alvin simply reads off of Theodore's tape as usual. If the input deviates from τ, however, the extra sensor switches off the Theodore-bits, powers up the Simon-bits, sets them in the appropriate way, and starts it running.[3]

Alvin is now counterfactually sensitive: he has all of the range of Simon. Hence, Maudlin claims, he computes π. But Alvin shows that premise 2 is correct: the difference between computing and not computing is in the inert bits of his machinery. Note that we could change Alvin to a non-computing thing by sticking a passive bit of insulation in the right spot and thereby prevent the Simon-copy from powering up. On a run on τ, Alvin's actual activity doesn't differ from the non-computing, non-conscious Theodore's – again, the added bits are all completely inert. If Theodore's simplistic activity isn't enough to be conscious, then Alvin's isn't either.

What to do? Giving up on premise 3 would be too strange. As Fekete and Edelman noted, it would be weird to think that we could be changed to zombies solely by (say) anesthetizing some nerves that weren't going to fire anyway. Giving up premise 2 won't work: counterfactuals are to distinguish the (computing) Alvin from the (non-computing) Theodore. More generally, as we noted in the discussion of the Action Max, computation seems to be a counterfactually laden notion. But that leaves only computationalism to abandon. Hence consciousness cannot depend on computation. The modal mismatch between their supervenience bases assures this.

A surprising conclusion, not in the least because it depends on what appear to be relatively lightweight assumptions. To be clear, I do not think Maudlin's argument succeeds. But I think that it has the feature of all beautiful thought experiments in philosophy: pushing back helps us clarify our assumptions. In the case of computationalism, it forces us to look at what seemed like a very simple and general thesis and constrain it in interesting ways.

Before moving on, it is worth distinguishing Maudlin's argument from a number of other arguments in the literature. Though it has interesting relationships to several other anti-computationalist arguments, it is *sui generis*. I think the reception of the argument has been blunted in part because many readers confuse it with one of these other, related arguments.

Maudlin's work bears an important relationship to various 'exploding implementation' arguments, which claim that any sufficiently complex object can implement any finite-state automaton (Searle, 1990; Putnam, 1991; Chalmers, 1996b; Bishop, 2009a; Bishop, 2009b). Maudlin's argument does not require exploding implementation to be true, however. Indeed, he presupposes (at least for the sake of argument) that appropriate counterfactual restrictions are sufficient to avoid explosions.

Olympia and Alvin may seem like instances of a 'funny implementation' strategy. Funny implementation arguments (such as Block's Chinese Nation (1978)) rely on intuitions that a non-standard implementation of a program couldn't possibly be conscious. Though Olympia has occasionally been taken this way (see e.g. Fekete and Edelman, 2011), I agree with Maudlin that the force is different. The argument is not merely that machines like Alvin look *strange*. Rather, the argument is that Theodore isn't conscious by the computationalist's own lights because he does not compute, and Alvin does not differ from Theodore in ways that ought to matter for consciousness. The problem is thus not with the oddness of the implementing machine, but its relationship to other machines that aren't conscious by anyone's lights.

The argument also bears an interesting relationship to some of Searle's (1980; 1990) critiques of computationalism. (This link is explored further by Bishop, 2009a.) Many of Searle's critiques can be read as expressing a concern over the fact that various conditions have to be in place for something to *count as* a computer. Yet it doesn't make sense to ask whether something 'counts as' conscious – either you are or you aren't. Searle's concerns tend to focus on the need for something with non-derivative intentionality to interpret something as a computer (which is in turn wrapped up with questions about the status of the symbols used by the computer, which is Searle's ultimate concern). Maudlin's argument is related, but more sparse. There is no issue here about the semantic interpretability of the symbols that Alvin uses. Even if all it takes to 'count as' a computer is counterfactual input sensitivity, that alone is enough to cause a mismatch between the demands of the phenomenal and the computational.

Consciousness, processes, and programs

There are many possible responses to Maudlin. Rather than catalog them individually,[4] I want to come at things from a slightly different angle.

Begin with an odd feature of Maudlin's argument. Computationalism, in my hand-waving introduction of the thesis, was a claim about *computation* broadly construed. Maudlin's argument, by contrast, reads computationalism more narrowly as the claim that some *Turing machine* can be conscious. Maudlin is explicit about the latter: his 'necessity condition' claims that computationalism "asserts that any conscious entity must be describable as a nontrivial Turing machine running a nontrivial program" (1989, p. 420). No defense is given of this. Presumably the idea is that TMs are universal, and that universal machines can compute whatever function you please. Hence TMs (despite their notoriously unwieldy nature) are as good a candidate for conscious experience as anything else.

Yet this embodies a substantial assumption. As Sprevak notes when discussing Searle, while a universal TM can compute any function that any other architecture can compute,

> ... it is not true that a universal computer can run any program. The programs that a computer (universal or otherwise) can run depend on that machine's architecture. Certain architectures can run some programs and not others. Programs are at the algorithmic level, and that level is tied to the implementation on particular machines.
>
> *(2007, p. 759)*

I think this is absolutely right. Computationalism could be formulated in terms of input–output functions. It needn't be, and it shouldn't be.

Let's flesh that out. Begin with some terminology. An *architecture* is a set of primitive operations and basic resources available for building computations (Pylyshyn, 1984, p. 93). The Turing machine architecture has as primitive operations (i) changing (or preserving) a single square of the tape, (ii) moving the head along the tape one square left or right, and (iii) changing state to one of a finite number of other states. A computational architecture specifies its primitive operations at a relatively high level of abstraction: we ought not to care what a TM tape is made of, or how long it takes the head to move to a new position. A *computational process*, as I use the term, is a temporally extended series of primitive operations. A *program* is a set of instructions to a machine which tell it how to generate a computational process in a context-sensitive way. The relationship between contexts and outputs defines the mathematical function that a machine computes.

Many different machines can compute the same mathematical function: this is the upshot of TM universality. But different architectures can do so in very different ways, because they have different ways of stringing together primitive operations. That is why, as Sprevak notes, we need to make clear whether computationalism is a thesis about mathematical functions (in which case we don't have to care about the architecture of our machine) or whether it is better expressed in terms of processes, architectures, or programs (in which case we do).

Consciousness can't depend on what function a machine computes. Sprevak (2007) gives several good arguments. Here is another. Take some computable function f; make it one that a TM takes many steps to perform. Any computable function can be a primitive in some other architecture: that is, one can posit a computational architecture that performs f as a single operation. Much of early chip design consisted in identifying useful functions that could be made into primitives: most computer architectures today have, for example, a primitive that does bit shifting, an operation which takes multiple steps on a TM. The Intel 8087 introduced primitive support for functions that approximated trigonometric functions, for example. From the point of view of that architecture, computing sines and cosines is a single operation, and so occurs in a single computational step.[5] Of course, the implementation of that primitive might be itself physically complex. That is irrelevant, just as the number of gears or wires or gallons that implement a single primitive in a TM is computationally irrelevant.

Return to consciousness. Take any mathematical function f_c, the computation of which is supposed to be enough for an extended bout of phenomenal experience. We can posit an architecture that has f_c as a computational primitive. But surely, executing a single primitive in a single computational step is not enough for conscious experience. From the computational point of view, there's no structure at all there. Hence there's no way to see how (for example) different elements of that conscious episode might change, because there's no structure in the computational supervenience base that could be changed.

Yet phenomenal experiences clearly have a combinatorial structure, and computationalists ought to say that this is mirrored by the combinatorial structure of the computations upon which it supervenes. Indeed, the combinatorial structure of computation is one of the things that makes computationalism so great in the first place.

The upshot is clear: phenomenal consciousness isn't a matter of what function you compute. It must depend on something more *computationally* fine-grained. That is not an abandonment of computationalism, though. It is a move from an implausible formulation to a more sensitive one.

The link between computational complexity and complexity of phenomenal experience also allows us to say something about a traditional objection to computationalism, usually attributed to Ned Block.[6] For any function you please, so long as it has a finite domain you can imagine a lookup table that computes the same function. The typical response is either to deny that sufficiently large lookup tables are physically possible (Dennett, 1998), or else to deny that lookup tables count as computations. The former feels unprincipled, and the latter would be surprising: lookup tables are widely used in computer programming, and play critical roles in lower-level programming (Duntemann, 2011, ch. 10).

Instead, we might point out that lookup tables are suspicious precisely because lookup requires a batch of information to be present as a computational primitive, and because lookup is usually envisioned as either a primitive operation or composed out of a small and repetitive handful of primitives. That mismatch between the demands of computation and of consciousness is what drives our intuition that simple lookups can't be sufficient for consciousness.

Input–output function is thus the wrong grain of analysis for consciousness. That's not a huge surprise: it's arguably the wrong grain of analysis for cognitive science as well (Pylyshyn, 1984). Instead, we should look to architectures and the processes that belong to them. Note that this doesn't (yet) require constraining consciousness to a particular architecture. Architectures themselves can be taxonomized. 'Turing machine' picks out a very general architecture which itself has many species depending on the number of symbols and states available. Different species of TM can differ in how they are most efficiently programmed as well – you can do things more quickly with numerous symbols than you can with just two, for example.

Higher-level taxonomy is also possible: there are important differences between architectures that process input serially from ones that have primitives that operate over the entire input at once.[7] Similarly, architectures differ in the primitive data structures available to them, the kinds and access parameters of memory available, and so on. Such concerns are far from ad hoc. Architecture is important because it places constraints on the time and space it would take to compute a particular mathematical function. These differences in computational complexity are the bread and butter of computer science (Aaronson, 2015). They may well matter for consciousness.

A final caveat before returning to Maudlin, I have talked about architectures and processes rather than *programs*. The relationship between a program and the process it gives rise to can be a complicated affair. I follow Cantwell-Smith in thinking that programs "would not be of much use unless they could be used to engender (not just to describe) computations. Programs, that is, are treated as much as *prescriptions* as *descriptions*" (1996, p. 36).[8] In *some* cases, programs simply specify a series of primitive operations to be performed. But that is typically only the case for very, very low-level languages. Higher-level languages are usually intended to be able to run on machines with very different primitive operations. They must be *compiled* before they specify a process in a particular architecture. Compilation is thus a complex relationship of *translation*.[9] In less familiar programming styles, a program may not even specify the temporal order of operations, leaving that to be determined by context (Klein, 2012). Because of cases like these, I think it is better to consider programs as a series of *directions* for building a computational process. Those directions must themselves be interpreted in order to actually build a process.[10]

If we don't distinguish programs and the processes they can give rise to after compilation, we can also generate additional, and unnecessary, versions of Maudlin's argument. Bishop (2009b), for example, gives several purported counterexamples to computation that rely on the fact that optimizing compilers might eliminate certain code paths. Similarly, we might note that compilers can speed execution by unrolling loops or by baking control logic into a simple lookup table. But that means that a good compiler might take a program that *appears* to specify a complex process and run it in an architecture where the complexity is packed into a single primitive.

Fair enough. That only shows that the computationalist ought to be wary of – or at least very, very careful about – formulating their thesis in terms of programs. It is the processes that computers run, and the computational processes that are built out of them, that are the appropriate grounds for a supervenience claim.

Alvin's true nature

If you buy all that, then it should now be pretty clear what the computationalist ought to say about machines like Olympia and Alvin. Both were claimed to be TMs on the basis of their actual and counterfactual similarity to what a TM would do. But there are other architectures that *emulate* TMs. Olympia and Alvin belong to one of those, I claim.

Consider a computational architecture $\mathcal{A}$, which has all of the primitive operations available to TMs and with one further complication. A machine in $\mathcal{A}$ is specified by a tuple $\langle p, i, j \rangle$, where p is an ordinary machine table, i is a privileged input (that is, a certain sequence of symbols which might appear as the initial state of the tape), and j is a sequence of sequences of changes to be performed, one sequence for each element of i. If such a machine is started on i, the lookup instruction will transform the tape according to a certain pre-determined sequence j. If the initial bits of the input match i and then diverge, a machine will transform the tape according to j up to the point where it diverges from i, and then switch back to running as per p. In the case where there are no initial bits of the input which match i, then p is run from the start.

One might specify the set of transitions j so as to match exactly what a TM running p on i would do. That is what Olympia and Alvin do. Yet this is not a general constraint on machines in $\mathcal{A}$. Some machines in $\mathcal{A}$ might change the tape in a way that no TM actually could – if p and j are sufficiently different, for example, there might be no single consistent machine table which would suffice to describe behavior of such machines.

This suggests that $\mathcal{A}$ machines are different in kind from TMs, even when they happen to act in similar ways. On Maudlin's view of computation, there is no space between 'acting like a Turing machine' and 'being a Turing machine'. The latter is just defined in terms of the former. But there's good reason to reject this notion, precisely because it can't distinguish between implementation and emulation. By contrast, the view of implementation I have advocated is one on which an architecture defines a set of *mechanisms* (Piccinini, 2007; 2015). These mechanisms have common spatiotemporal parts, each of which interacts causally. By those lights, Alvin and Olympia don't have the right set of parts interacting in the right way to implement a TM. Insofar as each has a dormant copy of a TM attached, that copy remains partially or fully dormant.

That still may not seem obvious. Here's another way to put the point. Upgrading Alvin to a machine that computed an entirely different function on i would be a trivial matter from the point of implementation: one would need to change only the sequence j. On the other hand, changing a TM to compute a different function can require arbitrarily many changes to the machine table. Finally, and most compellingly, $\mathcal{A}$ machines are strictly more powerful than TMs. An $\mathcal{A}$ machine can function as an Oracle machine, in Turing's parlance: on the special input i, *j* might (for example) transform the tape such that the *n*th square is a '1' if and only if the *n*th TM (under some enumeration) halts with *n* as input. Obviously, TMs can't calculate that. So the architecture $\mathcal{A}$ includes machines that cannot be TMs.[11]

From a programming perspective, recall, the architecture provides the functional primitives from which more complex processes must be built. This means that the basic operations defined by the computational architecture are also the *basic loci of intervention* upon a computational system. An architecture that provides both multiplication and addition as primitive operations can be directly intervened upon in a different way than one that provides only addition as basic and derives multiplication.

Considerations about computational architectures are explanatorily critical insofar as we take an interventionist stance on explanation. This is another important departure from accounts of computation that focus solely on isomorphism between machine tables and implementing machinery (Chalmers, 2011). Explanatory claims are claims about causal influence. Claims about causal influence require a well-defined sense in which one could manipulate the system in question from one state to another (Woodward, 2003, 115 ff.). To say that something belongs to a computational architecture, then, is to define the basic computational interventions that could be made upon it. That is what a mechanist approach to computation gives us.

Indeed, it's worth noting that a great number of responses to Maudlin and related arguments rely precisely on thinking about the causal structure of the implementing mechanism. Barnes (1991) focuses on the causal chain that leads from input to output. Klein (2008) argues that we ought to look to the dispositions that make true computational counterfactuals, and that these in turn must have their categorical basis in well-defined parts of the system. Bartlett (2012) complains that Klein doesn't provide a story about what counts as a well-defined part. Whatever the story, however, it seems like it ought to link into a more general mechanistic story – perhaps by appealing (for example) to the mutual manipulability of part and whole (Craver, 2007; Piccinini, 2015). So for example, in the case of Olympia, one could intervene on her water-buckets in ways that would cause tape transitions that no Turing machine would be capable of.

Yet it is clear that Alvin and Olympia do have different sets of parts to that of an ordinary TM. Since Alvin and Olympia don't have the right causal structure, they don't count as TMs. (This doesn't mean that TMs could actually be conscious, as per the argument above, but it's important to note that these guys aren't even in the running because they aren't TMs.) Further, the causal structure they *do* have puts them in a class of architectures that aren't a plausible candidate for consciousness. Those are claims about the causal structure of the machines. But then causal structure – how the spatiotemporal parts of the machines themselves are actually arranged and interact – is critical for determining whether a computing machine is conscious.[12]

The move to mechanism thus has what might be counterintuitive consequence. Suppose I emulate a Turing machine on my computer: that is, suppose I run a program that specifies a TM machine table and a tape, and displays what the transitions would be on some virtual tape. Does my computer thereby have a TM architecture? No.[13] Its spatiotemporal parts are just as they were when they left the factory. The primitive operations of the TM are implemented in some unknown but presumably sprawling and complicated way by the underlying architecture that my laptop actually has.

At best, then, say that my computer has a TM as a *virtual* architecture, running on top of the actual one. Because of the complex relationship between virtual architectures and actual ones, it may be difficult to disentangle which is which. Disentangle we must. For if the path we've been led down is the right one, then we computationalists must say something that is suspiciously close to what Searle (1980) says – there is no reason to think that a simulation of an architecture is sufficient for consciousness. Virtual machines, even the virtual machine that would arise from a simulation of my brain in all computationally relevant detail, are not the right kinds of thing to support conscious experience. The fact that a virtual machine has similar 'organizational invariants' (Chalmers, 1996a) to an actual architecture does not show that it is the same as a process that actually has that architecture.

Sprevak (2007) makes a similar argument about virtual machines. He claims that virtual machines do not, strictly speaking, run programs made for the virtualized architecture. Instead, virtual machines are better understood as "automated procedures for turning one program into another" (ibid., p. 762): that is, programs in the virtualized architecture are translated into specifications of programs for the implementing architecture. This translation process preserves input–output mappings and even certain properties of the implemented algorithm. But the actual running machine can use arbitrarily different primitives, in different ways, in order to instantiate that virtual machine.

The upshot of all of this has been to say that if (as Maudlin claims) computation depends on actual activity, then we ought to look at the actual activity of actual computing processes. The details of the computational activity matter, and those details may well place constraints on which architectures are actually sufficient for conscious experience. I think it is an open question about how strong those constraints might be. We might find, as classical philosophy of mind suggested, that the constraints are quite minimal. On the other hand, we may well find that the constraints on computational architectures are stronger than we had supposed. Ned Block notes that even abstract computational constraints might be difficult to satisfy if they are complex enough:

> In Walt Disney movies, teacups think and talk, but in the real world, anything that can do those things needs more structure than a teacup. We might call this the Disney Principle: that laws of nature impose constraints on ways of making something that satisfies a certain description. There may be many ways of making such a thing, but not just any old structure will do. It is easy to be mesmerized by the vast variety of different possible realizations of a simple computational structure ... But the vast variety might be cut down to very few when the function involved is mental, like thinking, for example, and even when there are many realizations, laws of nature may impose impressive constraints.
>
> (Block, 1997, p. 120)

The Disney Principle might end up restricting us to certain kinds of architectures. So for example, as I understand them, Fekete and Edelman (2011) argue that the only candidates for conscious experience are computational architectures that can be formulated in terms of continuous trajectories through a state-space (rather than successions of points in state-space). Yet the move to trajectories seems to require a phenomenally smooth, continuous transition between any two whole phenomenal states. That would, among other things, rule out *any* architecture that allows arbitrary transitions between states, or (it seems) architectures where the state-space is discrete rather than continuous. This would include TMs (see also Spivey (2007) for a similar argument). That seems to me to be *prima facie* implausible: if I am shown a sequence of disconnected images, it seems like my phenomenal state *does* make non-continuous transitions. Yet more subtle constraints along the same lines are not necessarily impossible, and would greatly restrict the space of potential implementers.

Hence Maudlin's argument, when seen in this light, is not a failure. Even if it does not take down computationalism *per se*, it may force important constraints on the computationalist thesis. Which things satisfy these constraints, and why, is ultimately a nontrivial empirical question.

Acknowledgments

Thanks to Peter Clutton, Stephen Gadsby, Annelli Janssen, Antonios Kaldas, and Mark Sprevak for thoughtful comments on an earlier draft, and to Sean Power for helpful discussion. Work on this paper was supported by Australian Research Council grant FT140100422.

Notes

1 There was a clever mechanism for tallying score if you shot at the right time. But the score had no effect on the actual gameplay.
2 This is something of a philosophical fiction. In an awake, conscious adult the whole brain is constantly active, and this high tonic level of activity appears to be a prerequisite for conscious experience (Raichle and Snyder, 2007). Further, while action potentials are discrete and distinct there is near-constant churn at the synapses, and balanced excitatory and inhibitory input can be neurocomputationally important even if it doesn't result in firing (Logothetis, 2008). Firing *delays* are also neurocomputationally important due to spike-timing-dependent plasticity and timing- and phase-dependent processing (Izhikevich, 2006). Further afield, insofar as the actual activity thesis requires a notion of *simultaneous* activity it is incompatible with special relativity. Whatever the supervenience base for conscious experience, it arguably ought to be something that is invariant across inertial reference frames (Power, 2010). The latter may seem especially *recherché*, but the easiest ways to avoid it – moving to causality or ordering rather than strict simultaneity – would require a careful rethink of the setup.
3 Part of the cleverness of Maudlin's example is to show how this switch function can be made using stuff that itself remains wholly inert on a run on the special input τ. I leave that as an exercise for the reader.
4 A task mostly done, albeit in a Maudlin-sympathetic way, by Bartlett (2012).
5 More or less. As you might expect, approximating transcendental functions in floating point is not for the faint of heart; see Ferguson et al. (2015).
6 From Block (1981). Though the lookup table arises as an objection to the Turing test – the link to phenomenal consciousness comes via a conflation with the Nation of China thought experiment from Block (1978).
7 Indeed, sufficiently exotic architectures can have surprising advantages over traditional architectures – Dewdney (1984) gives a delightful example of the speedups available in list sorting with analog computers that utilize dry spaghetti and a sufficiently large forklift.
8 Of course, not all computations involve running programs, and some computational processes (like those implemented in brains) weren't built by someone following a program. This has caused confusion in the past, but it's simply another reason not to put too much weight on programs as the unit of analysis. Instead, when a cognitive neuroscientist (say) gives something that looks like pseudocode but for the brain, we can say that it specifies instructions to build a model (given some implicit semantics) that is isomorphic to the brain in the relevant respects. In general, respecting the distinction between descriptions of models and descriptions of the world is the key to solving many puzzles about implementation (Klein, 2013).
9 Thanks to Peter Clutton for emphasizing this point to me.
10 'Interpretation' here is meant to be metaphysically lightweight: humans can interpret simple programs to build a machine, but the power of computers is that they can also interpret programs given in a suitable format.
11 For a full version of the argument, including examples of more subtle incompatibilities, see Klein (2015).
12 Of course, Alvin and Olympia both have Turing machines as proper parts, but that alone doesn't make something a Turing machine; to insist otherwise would be to commit the mereological fallacy (Bennett and Hacker, 2003). More formally, the notion of 'part' at play is a functional one, not a spatiotemporal one. The additional primitives available to them ensure that they have opportunities for manipulation which are quite different to those of ordinary TMs.
13 Assuming my computer is not actually a TM in the first place, or that its components are not assembled out of TMs, or so on. The argument that follows is not meant to show that a computer only ever belongs to one architecture, but rather that it can belong to more than one architecture only under very specific conditions involving the coincidence of spatiotemporal parts.

References

Aaronson, S. (2015) 'Why Philosophers Should Care about Computational Complexity', in Copeland, B.J., Posy, C., and Shagrir, O. (eds.) *Computability: Gödel, Turing, Church, and Beyond*. Cambridge, MA: MIT Press.

Barnes, E. (1991) 'The Causal History of Computational Activity: Maudlin and Olympia', *The Journal of Philosophy*, 88 (6), pp. 304–316.

Bartlett, G. (2012) 'Computational Theories of Conscious Experience: Between a Rock and a Hard Place', *Erkenntnis*, 76 (2), pp. 195–209.

Bennett, M.R. and Hacker, P.M.S. (2003) *Philosophical Foundations of Neuroscience*. Oxford: Blackwell.

Bishop, J.M. (2009a) 'A Cognitive Computation Fallacy? Cognition, Computations and Panpsychism', *Cognitive Computation*, 1 (3), pp. 221–233.

Bishop, M. (2009b) 'Why Computers Can't Feel Pain', *Minds and Machines*, 19 (4), pp. 507–516.

Block, N. (1978) 'Troubles with Functionalism', in Wade, C.S. (ed.) *Perception and Cognition: Issues in the Foundations of Psychology*, Minnesota Studies in the Philosophy of Science, vol. 9. Minneapolis, MN: University of Minnesota Press, pp. 261–325.

Block, N. (1981) 'Psychologism and Behaviorism', *The Philosophical Review*, 90 (1), pp. 5–43.

Block, N. (1997) 'Anti-Reductionism Slaps Back', in Tomberlin, J. (ed.) *Philosophical Perspectives: Mind, Causation, World*. Oxford: Wiley-Blackwell, pp. 107–133.

Cantwell-Smith, B. (1996) *On the Origin of Objects*. Cambridge, MA: The MIT Press.

Chalmers, D. (1996a) *The Conscious Mind: In Search of a Fundamental Theory*. New York, NY: Oxford University Press.

Chalmers, D. (1996b) 'Does a Rock Implement Every Finite-State Automaton?', *Synthese*, 108 (3), pp. 309–333.

Chalmers, D. (2011) 'A Computational Foundation for the Study of Cognition', *Journal of Cognitive Science*, 12, pp. 323–357.

Craver, C.F. (2007) *Explaining the Brain*. New York, NY: Oxford University Press.

Dennett, D. (1998) 'Can Machines Think?', in *Brainchildren: Essays on Designing Minds*. Cambridge, MA: MIT Press, pp. 3–30.

Dewdney, A.K. (1984) 'On the Spaghetti Computer and Other Analog Gadgets for Problem Solving', *Scientific American*, 250 (6), pp. 19–26.

Duntemann, J. (2011) *Assembly Language Step-by-Step: Programming with Linux*. New York, NY: John Wiley & Sons.

Fekete, T. and Edelman, S. (2011) 'Towards a Computational Theory of Experience', *Consciousness and Cognition*, 20 (3), pp. 807–827.

Ferguson, W. et al. (2015) 'The Difference Between x87 Instructions FSIN, FCOS, FSINCOS, and FPTAN and Mathematical Functions Sin, Cos, Sincos, and Tan', Intel Corporation. Available at: https://software.intel.com/en-us/articles/the-difference-between-x87-instructions-and-mathematical-functions (Accessed: October 5, 2016).

Frost, E.A.M. (2015) 'A Review of Mechanisms of Inhalational Anesthetic Agents', in Kaye, A.D., Kaye, A.M., Urman, R.D. (eds.) *Essentials of Pharmacology for Anesthesia, Pain Medicine, and Critical Care*. New York, NY: Springer, pp. 49–60.

Izhikevich, E.M. (2006) 'Polychronization: Computation with Spikes', *Neural Computation*, 18 (2), pp. 245–282.

Klein, C. (2008) 'Dispositional Implementation Solves the Superfluous Structure Problem', *Synthese*, 165 (1), pp. 141–153.

Klein, C. (2012) 'Two Paradigms for Individuating Implementations', *Journal of Cognitive Science*, 13 (2), pp. 167–179.

Klein, C. (2013) 'Multiple Realizability and the Semantic View of Theories', *Philosophical Studies*, 163 (3), pp. 683–695.

Klein, C. (2015) 'Olympia and Other O-Machines', *Philosophia*, 43 (4), pp. 925–931.

Logothetis, N.K. (2008) 'What We Can Do and What We Cannot Do with fMRI', *Nature*, 453, pp. 869–878.

Maudlin, T. (1989) 'Computation and Consciousness', *The Journal of Philosophy*, 86 (8), pp. 407–432.

Pettit, P. (2015) *The Robust Demands of the Good: Ethics with Attachment, Virtue, and Respect*. New York, NY: Oxford University Press.

Piccinini, G. (2007) 'Computing Mechanisms', *Philosophy of Science*, 74 (4), pp. 501–526.

Piccinini, G. (2015) *Physical Computation: A Mechanistic Account*. Oxford: Oxford University Press.

Power, S.E. (2010) 'Complex Experience, Relativity and Abandoning Simultaneity', *Journal of Consciousness Studies*, 17 (3–1), pp. 231–256.

Putnam, H. (1991) *Representation and Reality*. Cambridge, MA: MIT Press.

Pylyshyn, Z.W. (1984) *Computation and Cognition*. Cambridge, UK: Cambridge University Press.

Raichle, M.E. and Snyder, A.Z. (2007) 'A Default Mode of Brain Function: A Brief History of an Evolving Idea', *Neuroimage*, 37 (4), pp. 1083–1090.

Searle, J.R. (1980) 'Minds, Brains, and Programs', *Behavioral and Brain Sciences*, 3 (3), pp. 417–424.

Searle, J.R. (1990) 'Is the Brain a Digital Computer?', *Proceedings and Addresses of the American Philosophical Association*, 64 (3), pp. 21–37.

Spivey, M. (2007) *The Continuity of Mind*. New York, NY: Oxford University Press.

Sprevak, M.D. (2007) 'Chinese Rooms and Program Portability', *The British Journal for the Philosophy of Science*, 58 (4), pp. 755–776.

Tononi, G. (2004) 'An Information Integration Theory of Consciousness', *BMC Neuroscience*, 5 (42), pp. 1–22.

Tononi, G. and Koch, C. (2015) 'Consciousness: Here, There and Everywhere?', *Philosophical Transactions of the Royal Society of London B: Biological Sciences*, 370 (1668), pp. 117–134.

Woodward, J. (2003) *Making Things Happen*. New York, NY: Oxford University Press.

23

CONCEPTS, SYMBOLS, AND COMPUTATION

An integrative approach

Jenelle Salisbury and Susan Schneider

What is the nature of thought? Is there an important sense in which thinking is computational? Before answering these questions, one needs to distinguish the different senses in which thinking, and the brain, might turn out to be computational. So any claim that the brain is or is not computational should carefully specify the actual theory of computation that is in play (see Samuels; Stinson; Chemero and Faries, this volume).

In this chapter, we focus on one historically important approach to computationalism about thought. According to "the classical computational theory of mind" (CTM), thinking involves the algorithmic manipulation of mental symbols. Herein, we review CTM and the related language of thought (LOT) position, urging that the orthodox position, associated with the groundbreaking work of Jerry Fodor (1975), has failed to specify a key component: the notion of a mental symbol. Drawing from Schneider (2011), we identify a theory of symbols for LOT/CTM, leaving us with a LOT/CTM that is distinct from the orthodox view. Then, we use the theory of symbols to develop a new theory of concepts, *pragmatic atomism*.

Pragmatic atomism holds that concept individuation is determined by two features: a concept's symbol type and certain of its semantic features (namely, the concept's broad content). We urge that pragmatic atomism satisfies the desiderata that many believe a theory of concepts should satisfy, while being consonant with current psychological work on concepts. This two-tiered approach to concepts provides an integrative approach to the nature of thought, bringing the semantic and psychological elements of concepts together, and giving LOT symbols a key role in concept individuation. (Further, although we frame pragmatic atomism in terms of LOT, a similar theory of concepts could be framed by the connectionist as well.)

Understanding symbols, and how symbols relate to concepts, has never been as important as it is now. It is not just relevant to understanding whether, and in what sense, the biological brain is computational. There is also the increasing sentiment that the future of AI development will raise rich questions for computationalism. What is the space of possible intelligences? And how will the most successful AI systems work? Will they be hybrid systems, for instance, employing both deep learning/connectionist and symbolic resources (Schneider, 2011, ch. 1)? Further, can symbol mappings to underlying states of deep learning systems help make sense of the complex, and sometimes inscrutable computations of deep learning systems? *Inter alia*, this requires an antecedent understanding of what LOT's symbols are.

This being said, our discussion will proceed as follows. Section 1 provides background. In Section 2, we clarify the notion of a LOT symbol. In so doing, we advance an approach different from the orthodox, Fodorian LOT/CTM. We then put this notion of a symbol to work, devising a novel theory of concepts (Section 3).

1 Background

The language of thought (LOT) position is a leading approach to the computational nature of thought.[1] According to LOT, mental representation has a decidedly *symbolic*, language-like structure. Humans (and even certain non-human animals) think in a *lingua mentis*: an inner mental language that is different from any spoken, natural language. This language is computational in a sense of computation that is proprietary to the symbol processing tradition. More specifically, thinking is the algorithmic manipulation of mental symbols in the LOT (Fodor, 1975; Schneider, 2011).

The idea that there is a language of thought was originally developed by Jerry Fodor, who defended this hypothesis in his influential *The Language of Thought* (1975). Fodor drew from the work of Alan Turing, who had introduced the idea that symbol processing devices can think, a view which many in cognitive science are sympathetic to, yet which has nevertheless been a locus of controversy (Turing, 1950). The proposal that the mind is a kind of symbol processor, if correct, would provide an elegant explanation of the features of higher thought (e.g. systematicity, intentionality, and productivity). In this vein, Allen Newell and Herbert Simon suggested that psychological states can be understood in terms of an internal architecture that is like a digital computer (Newell and Simon, 1976).[2] Human psychological processes were said to consist in a system of discrete inner states (i.e. symbols) that are manipulated by a central processing unit (CPU). Sensory states served as inputs into the system, providing the "data" for processing according to the rules, and motor operations served as the outputs. This position, known as "Classicism" became the paradigm view in information processing psychology and computer science until the 1980s, when the competing connectionist or neural network view also gained traction. LOT grew out of this trend in information processing psychology to view the mind as a symbol processing device.

Nowadays, proponents of LOT do not take the analogy with the electronic digital computer too seriously, as the brain doesn't have a von Neumann architecture, i.e. the architecture that standard computers possess, which features a stored program and a serial, central processing unit (the CPU). Instead, proponents of LOT advance the following core features of LOT to explain the sense in which the brain is computational:

1 Cognitive processing consists in causal sequences of tokens (i.e. symbols) in the brain.

Thinking is a matter of the causal sequencing of tokens of mental representations that are ultimately realized by the brain. Thought is describable as a physical process, and further, as we shall see below, as a semantic and computational process as well. Further:

2 Mental representations have a combinatorial syntax and semantics.

A key feature of LOT is that its mental representations have a combinatorial syntax. A representational system has a combinatorial syntax when it employs a finite store of atomic representations, which can be combined to form compound representations, which can then be combined to form further compound representations. Relatedly, LOT holds that mental representations have a compositional semantics. That is, the meaning of compound representations formed by a system is a function of the meaning of its atomic parts and their syntactic structure. Further, the syntax and semantics will "stack up"; that is, formal languages allow for processes to be defined that are sensitive to the syntax of the language, while nevertheless respecting constraints on the semantics of the language (Fodor, 1975; Fodor and Pylyshyn, 1988; Pylyshyn, 1986; Fodor and McLaughlin, 1990). Finally:

3 Mental operations on internal representations are causally sensitive to the syntactic structure of the symbol.

Computational operations operate upon any token or string of symbol tokens that satisfy a certain structural description, and transform the token (or string) into another symbol (or symbol string) that satisfies another structural description. For instance, some system may employ an operation which recognizes any symbol token with the form "(R&Q)" and transforms it into a symbol of the form "(Q)". In addition to this, the structure of the symbolic representation corresponds to real physical structures in the brain such that the physical counterparts of the symbols, together with their structural properties, *cause* behaviors (Fodor and Pylyshyn, 1988, p. 99).

CTM and LOT both seek to answer the age-old question, "how could rational thought be realized by the brain?" The answer is that rational thought is a matter of the causal sequencing of symbol tokens in the brain. And further, these symbols, which are ultimately just patterns of matter and energy, possess both representational and causal properties. And the semantics will mirror the syntax. This means that a purely syntactical or formal causal relationship between symbols will preserve semantic relationships between them, accounting for the language-like features of thought. This yields the following picture of the nature of thought: thinking is symbol manipulation in which the symbols have an appropriate syntax and semantics.

Clearly, the notion of a "mental symbol" is doing a good deal of work in this approach to thought. Mental processing, on this account, is symbol manipulation. But what are mental symbols? And how would they relate to concepts? Because of the centrality of symbols to CTM/LOT, it is crucial that a clear notion of a symbol be developed. So, let us turn to this issue.

2 Mental symbols

Within the symbol processing/LOT tradition, there are three commonly agreed upon philosophical functions that symbols are supposed to play.

(i) Symbols are supposed to be ways of representing the world, or modes of presentation (MOPs).

Each symbol tokening by a person/system conforms to a way of representing entities in the world. By way of example, recall that the famous Greek orator, Cicero, had another name as well, "Tully". Suppose that one of Cicero's contemporaries didn't realize that the name "Tully" refers to Cicero. He has two modes of presentation (MOPs), or ways of representing Cicero. Perhaps, for instance, he associates the name "Tully" with a neighbor, and the name "Cicero" with a well-known man standing on a platform, speaking. According to LOT, he has two mental symbols (MOPs) for the same man. These two symbols amount to distinct modes of presentation of the same person (i.e. Cicero/Tully).

Philosophers of language often refer to these MOPs or ways of representing things as "guises", leaving it open what their precise nature is. Theories of narrow content in philosophy of mind, that is, theories that account for mental content using only the intrinsic properties of a system, sometimes take themselves to be providing accounts of MOPs (e.g. Block, 1998).

If symbols in the LOT are construed as MOPs, this means the relevant mental states will be at a level of grain suitable for capturing our way of conceiving the world; symbols are, in a sense, computational versions of what laypeople sometimes call one's inner "concept" or "notion".[3] In this vein, symbols must be fine grained enough to distinguish intuitively distinct representations that happen to co-refer (e.g. Cicero/Tully, groundhog/woodchuck). As Gottlob Frege's Hesperus/Phosphorus example demonstrated, one's ways of conceiving of an entity are distinct from the entity referred to; one may grasp a referent by means of certain of its features and yet be ignorant of others, as in our above example of Cicero.

Frege's point may inspire one to appeal to a semantics in which co-referring thoughts differ in their meanings. Alternatively, it may inspire a theory of thought in which distinct but co-referential thoughts only differ in their (non-semantic) cognitive significance. Importantly, because proponents of LOT generally appeal to a referential semantics, they tend to occupy this latter position (Fodor, 1994; Schneider, 2011). So for the standard LOT program, symbols *must* differentiate co-referring thoughts; meanings cannot do so.

(ii) Causal efficacy.

The LOT approach, as a computational theory of MOPs, takes theories of cognitive processing in cognitive science to supply the basis for an account of the causal production of thought and behavior. Whatever symbol tokens amount to in the brain, they should be causally efficacious: they should function causally to generate other mental states and behaviors. Relatedly, symbols should be able to function as causes in explanations of thought and behavior – including, importantly, explanations of the oft-cited productive and systematic nature of thought (Fodor, 1998; 2000).

(iii) Facilitate naturalism.

Third, symbols are essential tools for providing a naturalistic answer to the problem of intentionality. It seems that a thought (e.g. the belief that Australian wine is excellent, the desire to drink a cappuccino) can exhibit *intentionality*: it can be *directed at*, or about, something in the world. But how can this be? Naturalistic approaches to intentionality aim to integrate intentionality into the world that science investigates. They aim to show that there is nothing mysterious about mental phenomena. Metaphysically speaking, mental phenomena boil down to physical phenomena. In this vein, the LOT program answers the problem of intentionality by claiming that the intentionality of a thought, e.g. *the ocean is calm*, is a matter of a causal, and ultimately, physical, relationship between symbolic computational states and certain entities (e.g. the ocean, *being calm*). In the literature on mental content, there are various naturalistic theories of meaning or mental content that purport to specify the precise nature of this relationship. Such theories hold that symbols are "locked onto" properties or individuals of a certain type in virtue of standing in an appropriate nomic or causal relationship with the thing represented (Fodor, 1998; 2003; Schneider, 2011).

Historically, these three important features of symbols have had central import to the LOT/ CTM program. But is it plausible to venture that each of these roles is in fact *non-negotiable* for

LOT? We believe so. Recall that the original motivation behind the LOT program is to under-stand how it is possible for rational thought to be grounded in the brain. Considering this ambi-tion, (i) and (ii) are key: symbols in the LOT are meant to be the mental representations that fundamentally explain an individual's thinking and behavior. This cannot be done if the symbols are not causally efficacious or fail to be at a suitable level of grain. Indeed, (i) is of enhanced sig-nificance given that proponents of LOT generally hold that mental content is broad, so mental content cannot do the work of neo-Fregean MOPs. Turning to (iii), LOT/CTM is a naturalistic program; in order to find a place for thought in the natural world, an answer to the problem of intentionality is crucial. So, we are inclined to say that in order for the LOT program to succeed, mental symbols should play each of these roles.

Bearing in mind these roles, what are symbols? Schneider has argued that a certain approach to symbol natures is uniquely able to fill these rolls (2011). She canvases the alternative proposals for symbol natures, focusing on simple term types. "Simple term types" are the non-semantic correlates of concepts, which can undergo combinatorial operations in order to form com-plex expressions (e.g. "dog", "photon"). One option, favored by Fodor in his recent work, is a referentialist proposal; we will examine this now.

2.1 Fodor's referentialist proposal

At one point, Fodor claimed a symbol can be individuated by virtue of what it represents (Fodor, 2008). He proposed:

> (CD1) Two primitive symbol tokens are of the same symbol type if and only if they have the same broad content.

Theories of broad content take the basic semantic properties of thoughts to be reference and truth. The broad content of a predicate is just the property it refers to, and the broad content of a name is the individual named.

CD1 is problematic, however. First, it fails to deliver a notion of a symbol that facilitates naturalism (role iii), because it types symbols with respect to their broad contents, and such are semantic and intentional. This is problematic for LOT's naturalism. The proponent of LOT aims to naturalize the intentionality of thought by taking it to be a matter of a symbol's having a physically kosher non-semantic relationship to a property or thing in the world. This relation-ship is supposed to be non-semantic, for again, naturalism aims to explain mental phenomena in terms of non-semantic, non-intentional, and non-mentalistic phenomena that science ultim-ately explains. So given LOT's naturalism, symbols cannot be typed by their broad contents.

Second, bearing in mind that advocates of LOT generally envision symbols as being at a level of grain suitable to explain one's way of conceiving the world (role i), individuating symbols by their referential properties will not suffice. Consider that co-referential symbol tokens (e.g. #Hesperus#/#Phosphorus#) will be type identical, while functioning very differently in one's mental life. These tokens may play entirely different roles in bringing about subsequent thoughts and behaviors (Fodor, 1994; Schneider, 2005; Braun, 2001a; 2001b; Richard, 1990). This means that treating co-referential but cognitively distinct symbols (e.g. #Cicero#/#Tully#) as type identical will also lead to poor explanations of the causation of thought and behavior (role ii).

So, a referential manner of typing symbols will fail to deliver a notion of a symbol that plays any of the roles that we've claimed symbols are supposed to play in the LOT. Now, one might believe that the problems are all due to the fact that symbols are being typed referentially, rather than via some other form of semantic symbol individuation. Would typing symbols by their narrow contents avoid some of these problems? Assuming that one has a plausible theory of narrow content in hand, this would eliminate the second and third problems that affected CD1. However, the first problem that affected CD1 extends to any kind of semantic proposal; this is because any semantic proposal will appeal to non-naturalistically palatable facts when explaining what symbols are. Given the centrality of naturalism to the LOT program, this is a decisive reason to reject any semantic proposal. Let us now turn to a different sort of proposal: one that individuates symbols by the role they play in computation.

2.2 Computational role approaches

There are two basic types of computational role approaches to symbol individuation. They differ in terms of how the notion of computational role is understood. According to one view, the computational role of a symbol includes the *entire* computational role that the symbol is capable of playing in one's cognitive economy. That is, the symbol is individuated by all of the computational generalizations that involve the symbol, where such generalizations are not "folk" generalizations, but, in the spirit of *a posteriori* functionalism, are generalizations detailed by a completed computational account of our mental lives. Let us call such accounts "total computational role" accounts. The second type of proposal has a more restricted understanding of computational role: only *some* elements of the total role of the symbol are type-individuative. It is worth noting that both of these positions take the computational roles to specify the *causal powers* of the symbol, rather than merely specifying the actual causal profile of the symbol, given the circumstances the system encounters.

The second approach is a sort of "molecularism" about LOT symbol types. Molecularism about symbols holds that only certain causal relations in a symbol's total causal profile are type-individuative. Which causal connections matter? Typically, priority is given to the causal relations that have explanatory relevance to the system's behavior. Molecularists aim to type symbols such that when two systems token a given symbol in similar conditions, the systems are likely to think and behave in similar ways. For example, suppose that there is a population of "novices" who all share a bit of information about some natural kind. Suppose, for instance, a group of individuals all know that cats are a type of feline, but in addition, each person in the group associates a different experience with cats; one associates their favorite orange cat, Maurice, another thinks about how cats cause her allergy attacks, and so on. Now, the proponent of molecularism about symbols says certain features of the symbol are type individuative (e.g. *being feline*), but others are not (e.g. *causing allergy attacks*). Though the roles of the symbol in these individuals' cognitive economies are not identical, the molecularist holds that they share enough features for the thoughts to count as being the same symbol type.

Here, one may rightly press the molecularist to provide a more precise account of how to tell which computational roles are type-constitutive. A similar concern has been raised regarding molecularism about narrow content. In the mental content literature, Fodor and Lepore have charged that there seems to be no principled way to distinguish between those elements of conceptual or inferential role that are meaning constitutive from those that are not (Fodor and Lepore, 1992). Similar issues emerge for molecularism about symbol types, although the issues do not concern content individuation *per se*; instead, they involve symbol individuation.

Indeed, Murat Aydede has posed the following dilemma for the molecularist: insofar as a theory of symbols singles out only a select few symbol-constitutive computational relations as being constitutive of a symbol, the analysis will fail to distinguish cognitively distinct symbol types (Aydede, 1997). But if one builds more relations into the requirements for having a symbol of a given type, then it will be unlikely that different individuals will have symbols of the same type. For instance, suppose that the symbol #dog# is individuated by computational relations involving #canine# and #standardly four-legged#. Now suppose one individual has this symbol, because her system features these two computational relations, but she strongly associates #dog# with #flying# and #imaginary#. Would she really have the same notion of a dog as you and I? It is likely she would behave very differently toward dogs than we do, so are we really prepared to say that we all nonetheless share the same MOP or mental symbol? A natural reaction to this concern is to strengthen the requirement on having #dog# in various ways. The problem is that the more the requirement is strengthened, the less likely it is that different individuals will have symbols of the same type. Instead, different individuals will tend to have rather idiosyncratic mental symbols for dogs. This is a similar dilemma to that faced by conceptual role accounts of narrow content (Aydede, 1997).

In fact, upon reflection, LOT's classicist approach *requires* that primitive symbols be typed by their total computational roles. This is because LOT requires the syntactic structure of the symbol to be the only thing responsible for that symbol's computational role. Exchanging two type-identical symbols should result in a computationally indistinguishable system, which would not be the case if type-identical symbols could play distinct computational roles (Schneider, 2011, p. 114). Further, without this manner of symbol individuation, some cognitive processes would fail to supervene on symbols and the rules by which they are processed. This does not mesh with CTM's claim that cognitive processing *just is* the processing of mental symbols according to these rules.

Does typing symbols by their total computational roles allow them to play roles (i)–(iii) for symbols? It clearly allows symbols to play the role of neo-Fregean MOPs. Role (iii) is also satisfied, since symbols are typed non-semantically. Role (ii) is satisfied as well, for typing symbols by total computational role will completely capture a symbol's computational relationships with other symbols. This is important, because, as we explained, LOT symbols are meant to map directly onto the physical entities with structural properties that can explain the causal properties of the symbol (recall feature (3) from Section 1).[4]

One concern for the total computational role approach is that on such an account, mental symbols will be highly idiosyncratic. In our discussion of molecularism, we noted that the more computational relations one includes as being required to token a symbol of a given type, the less likely it is that two individuals will instantiate symbols of the same type. Total computational role approaches, since they include the entirety of a symbol's computational relations in a symbol's classification, mean that it is highly unlikely for two individuals (or even a single individual across time) to instantiate symbols of the same type.

However, we take the idiosyncratic nature of symbols to be a necessary evil. For recall role (i) for symbols: we need a way to differentiate between thoughts that co-refer. Considering those proponents of LOT who subscribe to a referential semantics (as many do), the meaning of a thought cannot play this role. So, on such an account, *symbols* would need to play the role of differentiating between co-referring thoughts. We've observed that even molecularism cannot accomplish this, and neither, more obviously, can a referentialist semantics. Typing symbols by total computational role, however, adequately captures this way in which thoughts can differ in their non-semantic cognitive significance.

Further, the idiosyncrasy of symbols is rather harmless, as it can be taken to be limited to the non-semantic dimension of thought. Co-referring symbols will share broad contents, and in this sense, thoughts are shared. In other words, even if two individuals do not token identical symbols, they still may be able to think about the same kinds of things and meaningfully converse with each other, in virtue of their having symbols with the same broad contents.

In fact, drawing from this manner of individuating symbols, there are further resources to account for meaningful communication and shared thought. On the view of *concepts* that we discuss in the following section, concepts can be shared. Schneider's theory of concepts draws from this total computational role approach to symbol individuation as well as from a referentialist semantics, an influential position on meaning held by many proponents of LOT as well as by direct reference theorists in philosophy of language.

3 Concepts: an ecumenical approach

The theory of symbols that we've defended will now be put to work to generate a theory of concepts. It is important to note that the term "concept" is a term of art, and the usage varies across disciplines and different theories of concepts. Broadly speaking, we take "concept" to mean one's way of thinking about some entity. Philosophical perspectives on concepts often emphasize concepts' semantic dimension, aiming to explain key features of thought such as intentionality, systematicity, productivity, and conceptual combination. Alternatively, psychological approaches to concepts tends to focus on how to understand humans' cognitive capacities for categorization, inference, learning, and understanding.

This is not to say the respective disciplines require distinct theories of concepts for different arenas of inquiry. Prinz's insightful book on concepts (2002), for example, argued that a single theory of concepts can encompass both kinds of explananda. Fodor, however, famously rejected understanding concepts in terms of psychological features such as categorization, inference, learning, and understanding. Fodor called his theory of concepts *conceptual atomism*, arguing that concepts are essentially what they refer to. He was opposed to any form of "concept pragmatism", where by "concept pragmatism" he meant any view which types concepts in terms of one's conceptual abilities, such as discrimination, recognition, and classification. Fodor regarded concept pragmatism as a "catastrophe of analytic philosophy of language and philosophy of mind in the last half of the Twentieth Century" (Fodor, 2003).

Instead, Fodor argued for what he called "Cartesianism" about concepts. On this picture, concepts are individuated by broad contents. What it is for an individual to have the concept POODLE is just for that individual to be able to think about poodles as such, that is, the class of poodles (Fodor, 2004, p. 31). This rejects any understanding of concept possession wherein what it is to have a concept involves knowledge of some kind (whether it be knowledge-how or knowledge-that).

Fodor's "Cartesianism" faces a host of problems, however (Prinz, 2002; Schneider, 2011). To begin with, Fodorian concepts are not suitable to play the role of neo-Fregean MOPs, as they are not sensitive to the role a concept plays in one's mental life. Relatedly, Fodor's view requires a radical revision of the understanding of concepts in psychology, which draws heavily from work on understanding, learning, inference, and categorization. Some might say that the difference is merely terminological – that psychologists working on "concepts" are just engaging in a different project from Fodor, and thus there is no substantial disagreement, just a verbal one. However, that is no reason to be unconcerned. If philosophers and psychologists use the same word, "concept", to refer to entirely different things, this impedes the possibility of progress through interdisciplinary cross-talk.

Additionally, Fodor's view on concepts is an outgrowth of LOT, which, as our discussion of symbols emphasized, actually gives MOPs a central role. Does the conceptual atomist have a way to incorporate MOPs in her theory? Perhaps her theory of LOT symbol individuation will enable her to account for MOPs by building symbol types into concept natures. However, this move would be inconsistent with Fodor's distaste for pragmatism. For consider that Fodor's conceptual atomist position includes two basic conditions:

(1) *Existence*: A primitive concept exists if and only if a primitive LOT symbol has broad content.
(2) *Identity*: Primitive concepts are identical if and only if they have the same broad content.

Condition (2) is too threadbare. As we've explained, broad content is insufficient to capture one's way of conceiving of the world. For example, this condition would classify co-referring primitive concepts as identical. We need a theory of concepts that taxonomizes concepts in a way that can capture their MOP types. The solution is an identity condition on concepts that requires that concepts be individuated by their symbol types, as well as their broad contents.[5] Identifying concepts partly by their symbol types, where symbols are understood as being individuated by their total computational roles, gives conceptual atomism a pragmatist dimension.

To underscore this, Schneider (2011) calls this view "pragmatic atomism". She urges that pragmatic atomism satisfies the primary desiderata for a theory of concepts. These desiderata include:

3.1 The intentionality requirement

A theory of concepts should be capable of explaining how thoughts represent or refer to entities in the world. Pragmatic atomism has resources to do this, at least when a specific theory of content is singled out. Once a proponent of pragmatic atomism supplements the theory with a theory of broad content, such as Fodor's asymmetric dependency theory, pragmatic atomism can attempt to explain intentionality (Fodor, 1987). Further, in keeping with LOT's interest in naturalism, semantic phenomena are ultimately explainable in non-intentional terms.

3.2 The publicity requirement

The publicity requirement says that our theory of concepts should explain how concepts can be shared between individuals and within the same individual over time. Without publicity, it is unclear how communication would be possible. Pragmatic atomism will be able to satisfy publicity and, importantly, it can do so despite the aforementioned fact that mental symbols turn out to be idiosyncratic. By considering the semantic dimension of concepts, and abstracting away from the symbol type, there's a sense in which different individuals can have the same concepts. By sharing contents, two individuals will be able to communicate meaningfully.

Since the identity condition for a concept includes not only a concept's broad content but the computational role, one might worry that two individuals cannot really precisely share a concept, since the associated symbols are different. However, this seems to be exactly the right result. Though two individuals can have a conversation about dogs on the understanding that they are talking about the same thing (i.e. that their concepts have the same broad content), it would be surprising if any two individuals think about dogs in *exactly* the same way. In this case, it would be a mistake to type their DOG concepts as completely identical. Importantly, though, we can still make sense of meaningful communication here, which is what matters for satisfying the publicity requirement. Interestingly, there may even be some degree of uncertainty as to whether an interlocutor's intended concept really *does* have the same broad content as your own, but this too is *prima facie* plausible: miscommunication is not uncommon.

3.3 *The compositionality requirement*

The compositionality requirement says that the content of complex symbols should be determined by the content of the primitive symbols, together with the syntactic relations between the primitive symbols. The aforementioned broad content dimension of concept individuation satisfies this condition. Can we also remain true to the classical position in which this compositional semantics "stacks up" with the combinatorial syntax of LOT symbols? Since we have argued that mental symbols should be typed by their total computational roles, this depends upon whether computational roles are compositional, which Schneider believes to be the case. This means that expressions can have complex computational roles that are fully determined by those of their constituents, including inherited dispositional properties of the constituents, such as being disposed to have a certain more complex role when combined with certain expressions.

3.4 *The MOP requirement*

This is the requirement that concepts be well-suited to play the role of neo-Fregean MOPs, in order to differentiate between co-referring concepts and in order to preserve intuitive notions of what having a concept amounts to. As discussed, this was a primary motivation for typing symbols in terms of their total computational roles. Since concepts are individuated partly by symbol types, this means that concepts can play the role of MOPs.

3.5 *The explanatory requirement*

Categorization abilities, according to pragmatic atomism, will be part of the computational role of the symbol, and therefore an essential part of a concept's nature. Pragmatic atomism is intended to be ecumenical, as the computational role dimension can be fleshed out through empirical work on concepts in psychology.

For example, consider the prototype theory, a leading psychological approach to the nature of concepts advanced by Eleanor Rosch (Rosch and Mervis, 1975; Murphy, 2004). The prototype view holds that concepts are stored as "summary representations" of sorts; humans encode a prototype of each type of object akin to a stored list of weighted features. Typicality judgments on this view are explained by closeness to the prototype, measured by statistical similarity.

Some object to the prototype view on the grounds that prototypes are not necessarily compositional and so cannot explain the systematic and productive nature of thought – for example, one's prototype for PET FISH may include features that are encoded in the prototype for neither PET nor FISH. Pragmatic atomism, however, is compatible with *both* the classical view and a version of the prototype view, subsuming their respective strengths and avoiding their weaknesses. On this view, experimental results of categorization will be features of the relevant symbols underlying computational roles. For example, consider the concept PET, for which the prototype includes the features one associates with pets on a graded continuum from most to least typical pets. Since classification of a percept as a pet requires a generalization, there must be some symbol that plays the requisite computational role to explain that generalization: that is, PET should be an individuatable mental symbol. Part of the computational role of this symbol is the way in which it figures in as a constituent of more complex expressions such as PET FISH so, on this understanding of prototypes, the symbols themselves compose, as well as the broad contents. There may be other concepts, like QUADRILATERAL, which play a more restrictive computational role, being more readily analyzable definitionally.

Both PET and QUADRILATERAL can be understood within the larger framework of pragmatic atomism because a concept's computational role includes the generalizations it enables one to make, the way in which it gets categorized, and the combinatorial operations the concept is able to undergo. Most importantly, this means the pragmatic atomist can incorporate psychological data on categorization abilities into her understanding of concept natures: it will provide insight into the computational roles of the relevant symbols.

Interestingly, pragmatic atomism is also compatible with the "theory–theory" view of concepts, which is sometimes taken to be an alternative to the prototype approach. According to the theory–theory view of concepts, concepts are analogous to scientific theories in that they are influenced by past knowledge and encode not just observable features, but also underlying causal mechanisms and ontological divisions (Murphy, 2004). The theory–theory captures explanatory relations and logical connections between concepts in a way that the prototype model is unable to do. While some take the theory–theory and the prototype view of concepts to be in opposition, it could be that some concepts are encoded as prototypes and some as theories.

The pragmatic atomist can remain neutral with respect to this debate – regardless of the way in which a concept's computational role is specified, it can still be the case that the concept's nature is determined by its broad content and symbol type. It is an advantage of the pragmatic atomist view that it does not run afoul of empirical evidence in psychology on the nature of concepts and categorization abilities. In fact, it provides an integrative way to understand how what looks to be oppositional data can all fit under a single theory of concept natures.

3.6 The scope requirement

The scope requirement is the idea that a theory of concepts should be able to account for all the concepts that we have. As our earlier discussion of the range of psychological theories indicates, Schneider can accommodate the range of concepts in her theory. Indeed, the pragmatic atomist can say that there is an important difference between perceptual concepts (e.g. RED), abstract concepts (e.g. JUSTICE), natural kind concepts (e.g. DOG), and so on, and yet all kinds of concepts fall under one larger theory of concepts.

3.7 The "innateness and learning" requirement

A theory of concepts should be compatible with leading work on innateness and learning. If there are no innate concepts, then the puzzle becomes explaining how the first concept is learned without there being any conceptual framework within which to place it. How do infants "break into" semantics for the first time? There are various conceptual atomist proposals to explain concept acquisition, including specifying the learning mechanisms that can explain concept acquisition without requiring innate concepts (Laurence and Margolis, 2002). Schneider argues that the same strategies for explaining concept learning available to traditional conceptual atomist views are also available to pragmatic atomist views on this matter (Schneider, 2011).

Conclusion

At the beginning of this chapter, we asked: what is the nature of thought? Is thinking computational? And we observed that before we can determine whether thinking is computational, we must first understand the different senses in which thinking, and the brain, may turn out to be computational. In the spirit of this, we've focused on spelling out one computational approach.

Because CTM/LOT claims that thinking involves the algorithmic manipulation of mental symbols, to understand CTM/LOT, it is important to know what symbols are. Not only is doing so crucial for better understanding the nature of thinking in biological systems, doing this can help us explore different kinds of AI systems, such as hybrid ones. In light of all this, we have identified a theory of symbols that LOT/CTM seems to require, one which differs significantly from the orthodox, Fodorian view.

Fodor vehemently opposed pragmatism, but we've urged that LOT and CTM require it. For pragmatism is at the heart of LOT's notion of a symbol. Pragmatic atomism holds that concept individuation is determined by a concept's symbol-type as well as its broad content. We argued that pragmatic atomism is an attractive view, satisfying the desiderata that many believe a theory of concepts should satisfy, while being consonant with current psychological work on concepts. This two-tiered approach to concepts thereby provides an integrative approach to the nature of thought, bringing the semantic and psychological elements of concepts together, and giving LOT symbols a key role in concept individuation.

Notes

1 Among the advocates of LOT are, for example, Alan Newell and Herbert Simon (1976), Jerry Fodor (1975; 1987; 1994), Brian McLaughlin (2008), Steven Pinker (1997), Gilbert Harman (1973), Gary Marcus (2001), Susan Schneider (2011), and Zenon Pylyshyn (1986).
2 However, see Aizawa (this volume) for a discussion of Newell and Simon's work that challenges this interpretation.
3 "Concept" is a term of art within cognitive science, however. We will return to "concepts" in Section 3. Proponents of LOT generally take concepts to be individuated by both broad content and symbol type, we explain.
4 Some (e.g. Prinz, 2002) worry, however, that if mental symbols are idiosyncratic, common psychological explanation between individuals will fail. Schneider (2011, ch. 6) offers four responses to objections of this kind, holding that explanation of thought and behavior is nevertheless possible.
5 Schneider develops her pragmatic atomism position in more detail in her (2011) study.

References

Aydede, M. (1997) 'Has Fodor Really Changed His Mind on Narrow Content?', *Mind and Language*, 12, pp. 422–458.
Block, N. (1998) 'Conceptual Role Semantics', in Craig, E. (ed.) *Routledge Encyclopedia of Philosophy*. Abingdon, UK: Routledge, pp. 242–256.
Braun, D. (2001a) 'Russelianism and Explanation', *Philosophical Perspectives*, 15, pp. 253–289.
Braun, D. (2001b) 'Russelianism and Prediction', *Philosophical Studies*, 105, pp. 59–105.
Fodor, J. (1975) *The Language of Thought*. Cambridge, MA: Harvard University Press.
Fodor, J. (1987) *Psychosemantics: The Problem of Meaning in the Philosophy of Mind*. Cambridge, MA: MIT Press.
Fodor, J. (1994) *The Elm and the Expert: Mentalese and Its Semantics*. Cambridge, MA: MIT Press.
Fodor, J. (1998) *Concepts: Where Cognitive Science Went Wrong*. Oxford: Oxford University Press.
Fodor, J. (2000) *The Mind Doesn't Work That Way: The Scope and Limits of Computational Psychology*. Cambridge, MA: MIT Press.
Fodor, J. (2003) *Hume Variations*. Oxford: Oxford University Press.
Fodor, J. (2004) 'Having Concepts: A Brief Refutation of the Twentieth Century', *Mind and Language*, 19 (1), pp. 29–47.
Fodor, J. (2008) *LOT 2: The Language of Thought Revisited*. Oxford: Oxford University Press.
Fodor, J. and LePore, E. (1992) *Holism: A Shoppers' Guide*. Oxford: Blackwell.
Fodor, J. and McLaughlin, B. (1990) 'Connectionism and the Problem of Systematicity', *Cognition*, 35 (2), pp. 183–205.

Fodor, J. and Pylyshyn, Z. (1988) 'Connectionism and Cognitive Architecture: A Critical Analysis', in Pinker, S. and Mehler, J. (eds.) *Connections and Symbols*. Cambridge, MA: MIT Press.

Harman, G. (1973) *Thought*. Princeton, NJ: Princeton University Press.

Laurence, S. and Margolis, E. (2002) 'Radical Concept Nativism', *Cognition*, 86, pp. 25–55.

Marcus, G.F. (2001) *The Algebraic Mind*. Cambridge, MA: MIT Press.

McLaughlin, B.P. (2008) 'Computationalism, Connectionism, and the Philosophy of Mind', in Floridi, L (ed.) *The Blackwell Guide to the Philosophy of Computing and Information*. Oxford: Blackwell, pp. 135–151.

Murphy, G. (2004) *The Big Book of Concepts*. Cambridge, MA: MIT Press.

Newell, A. and Simon, H.A. (1976) 'Computer Science as Empirical Inquiry: Symbols and Search', *Communications of the ACM*, 19 (3), pp. 113–126.

Pinker, S. (1997) *How the Mind Works*. New York, NY: Norton.

Prinz, J. (2002) *Furnishing the Mind: Concepts and Their Perceptual Basis*. Cambridge, MA: MIT Press.

Pylyshyn, Z. (1986) *Computation and Cognition*. London: MIT Press.

Richard, M. (1990) *Propositional Attitudes: An Essay on Thoughts and How We Ascribe Them*. Cambridge, UK: Cambridge University Press.

Rosch, E. and Mervis, C.B. (1975) 'Family Resemblances: Studies in the Internal Structure of Categories', *Cognitive Psychology*, 7, pp. 573–605.

Schneider, S. (2005) 'Direct Reference, Psychological Explanation, and Frege Cases', *Mind and Language*, 20 (4), pp 223–247.

Schneider, S. (2011) *The Language of Thought: New Philosophical Directions*. Cambridge, MA: MIT Press.

Turing, A.M. (1950) 'Computing Machinery and Intelligence', *Mind*, 49, pp. 433–460.

24

EMBODIED COGNITION

Marcin Miłkowski

Does embodied cognition clash with the computational theory of mind? The critics of computational modeling claim that computational models cannot account for the bodily foundation of cognition, and hence miss essential features of cognition. In this chapter, I argue that it is natural to integrate computational modeling with bodily explanations of cognition. Such explanations may include factors suggested by proponents of embodied cognition. Not only is there no conflict between embodied cognition and computationalism, but embodied cognition *alone* turns out to be fairly limited in its explanatory scope because it does not track proper invariant generalizations of all cognitive phenomena; some phenomena do not depend straightforwardly on embodiment alone but also on temperamental differences, individual learning history, cultural factors, and so on. This is why it works best when accompanied with other explanatory tools.

I first characterize embodied cognition, and the challenges inherent in understanding some non-trivial contribution of embodiment to the study of cognition. I argue that embodied cognition is best understood as a complex research tradition, rather than a single theory or hypothesis. Next, I shortly examine challenges to computationalism as posed by theorists of embodiment to show that theories of embodied cognition have non-trivial assumptions. Then, I turn to embodiment and robotics, to discuss a computational approach to neuroethology and morphological computation. The chapter is concluded with a sketch of the place of embodied computation in cognitive science.

1 Embodiment in cognitive science

Embodied cognition is a very broad term that covers many diverse approaches. They assume that the physical body of an agent is relevant to cognition, which essentially involves perception and action; in other words, cognition is not limited to the brain alone (Gibbs, 2006; Shapiro, 2011). This much has been accepted in diverse research frameworks, from embodiment in cognitive linguistics (Glenberg and Kaschak, 2002; Lakoff, 2012), through neoempiricism about concepts (Barsalou, 2008; Prinz, 2004), theories of "grounding" of language in gestural communication (Arbib, 2012; Rizzolatti and Arbib, 1998), neural reuse (Anderson, 2014), bodily formats of thought (Goldman, 2012), front-loaded phenomenology (Gallagher and Zahavi,

2008), to sensorimotor accounts of vision (O'Regan and Noë, 2001) and all kinds of cognition (Chemero, 2009; Gibson, 1986; Varela, Thompson, and Rosch, 1991).

Because of this variety of approaches, one may wonder whether the term *embodiment* actually means the same thing for them – it may have become, after all, systematically ambiguous. Another possible worry may be that the assumptions of embodied cognition are widely endorsed because they are trivial, and simply follow logically from the claim that cognition is a feature of biological physical systems. It was also argued that embodied cognition is theoretically vacuous when applied to most cognitive phenomena (Goldinger et al., 2016). I contend that embodied cognition is a research tradition rather than a theory, hypothesis, or list of hypotheses. As a research tradition, embodied cognition may avoid at least the first two of these worries, while there is a grain of truth in the last one: it is unlikely that embodied cognition will revolutionize cognitive science, and while it remains a progressive research tradition, it offers a fairly limited set of research heuristics that drive further empirical and theoretical work, rather than a grand theory of cognition. They are limited because bodily features of agents do not substantiate proper invariant generalizations concerning all kinds of cognitive phenomena.

The argument in this section will start from the proposal of Lawrence Shapiro to frame the significance of embodied cognition in terms of three separate hypotheses. While this sheds some light on this research tradition, in Section 1.2., I show that it does not demonstrate its novelty or driving forces, as this kind of approach minimizes at least some theoretical differences in embodied cognition. Moreover, it becomes difficult to show why embodied cognition is non-vacuous, while not offering a unified approach to all cognitive phenomena.

1.1 Defining embodiment

As Shapiro (2011, p. 68) argues, there are three ways to view the significance of embodied cognition: Conceptualization (e.g. Barsalou, 1999), Replacement (e.g. McBeath, Shaffer, and Kaiser, 1995), and Constitution (e.g. Clark, 2008). The hypothesis of Conceptualization states that "an organism's understanding of the world – the concepts it uses to partition the world into understandable chunks – is determined in some sense by the properties of its body and sensory organs" (Shapiro, 2011, p. 68). This hypothesis clearly has roots in the empiricist account of cognition. The defenders of the Replacement hypothesis "are convinced that the computational and representational tools that have for so long dominated standard cognitive science are in fact irremediably defective, and so must be abandoned in favor of new tools and approaches" (ibid., p. 68). Thus, this hypothesis is most radical in its rejection of computationalism. Finally, the Constitution hypothesis, as defended by Andy Clark in his extended mind thesis (Clark, 2003; Clark and Chalmers, 1998), claims that the body has a constitutive rather than merely causal role in cognition. In other words, the body does not only support the work of the cognitive system; instead, the cognitive system includes the body as its proper part.

The Constitution hypothesis does not exclude computational and representational explanations but is metaphysically most challenging, as it requires a substantive account of the difference between constitution and causation; otherwise, it may be argued that both metaphysical relationships are conflated (Adams and Aizawa, 2008). One simple solution would be to propose that constitution is a synchronic relationship while treating causation as diachronic (most theories of causation require that causes precede their effects anyway). Disentangling these matters is, however, quite difficult. Biological systems not only have multiple parts but also are constituted by multiple processes occurring at different time-scales. So, for example, while rods and cones are parts of the human eye, they also exert causal influence on retinal computation, and the light first causes them to respond, and then their response causes certain retinal computations. Constitutional relations cannot obtain by themselves, they require causal organization as well. The ensuing debate has shown that it is notoriously difficult to distinguish causal and constitutive relevance by relying on the scientific evidence (Barker, 2010; Sprevak, 2010b). Some philosophers have suggested that the mechanistic account of explanation, with its principled way of delineating mechanisms (Craver, 2007), could settle the debate (Kaplan, 2012; Walter, 2014). But others, albeit in a somewhat different context, claim that constitutional and causal relationships are undistinguishable under mechanistic assumptions (Leuridan, 2011). I wouldn't hold my breath to see this vexed issue settled in the near future. In what follows, then, I restrict myself to Conceptualization and Replacement.

1.2 *Triviality challenge and vacuity challenge*

Let us analyze the challenge that it is trivially true that cognition requires a cognitive agent to be embodied. Physicalism implies that the mind is constituted by, caused by, or otherwise closely dependent on physical bodily processes. Therefore, all physicalists should assume that the mind is embodied. Naturally, they would endorse the Conceptualization hypothesis. Even Jerry Fodor, criticized vehemently by defenders of embodied cognition, agrees that the organism's understanding of the world is determined in *some* sense by the properties of its body and sensory organs. How could it be otherwise? This is what his account of transduction of sensory energy to symbols states; although it is ridden with difficulties (as Fodor (1994, p. 113) readily admits), it is an attempt to specify this determination exactly.

Thus, Conceptualization does not help. Let us turn to Replacement: this thesis, in its anti-representational version and commitment to anti-computationalism, is indeed non-trivial. However, it is non-trivial not in virtue of the bodily nature of cognitive processes but thanks to its anti-representationalism, which remains controversial and, more importantly in this context, logically independent from the fact whether cognition is even physically embodied. Similarly, as I argue below, embodiment is not obviously incompatible with computationalism, so the Replacement claim is even more contentious – but again not because of the bodily nature of cognition.

In other words, neither the Conceptualization nor Replacement hypothesis make embodied cognition interesting. The Conceptualization hypothesis seems trivial, and the Replacement is purely negative, without real connection to embodiment.

To make matters worse, in a recent critique, another challenge has been stated; the authors claim that embodied cognition is "theoretically vacuous with respect to nearly all cognitive phenomena" (Goldinger et al., 2016, p. 961). To justify this harsh assessment, the critics of embodied cognition list twenty-nine phenomena from a standard cognitive psychology text-book, for example, priming effects, change blindness, Stroop interference, phoneme restoration, and selective attention. These phenomena, according to these critics, have not been elucidated at all by any empirical or theoretical work in embodied cognition.[1]

However, embodied cognition fares no worse than computationalism in this regard. Computationalism as such (in contrast to particular computational models) does not offer any detailed predictions or explanations for priming effects or phoneme restoration, or selective attention. This is because both embodied cognition and computationalism are not really specific *theories*; they are rather *research traditions* in cognitive science (Wołoszyn and Hohol, 2017).

The notion of a research tradition has been introduced by Larry Laudan (1978) to account for the historical development of science. Science, according to Laudan, is a problem-solving enterprise, and the historical dynamics of problem-solving cannot be fully captured by the notion of a *scientific research program*, introduced earlier by Imre Lakatos (1976). Scientific research programs remain historically immutable at their core, claims Lakatos. However, Laudan has shown that this is not the case even for examples cited by Lakatos. In Laudan's view, the core features of research traditions are the following: First, "every research tradition has a number of specific theories which exemplify and partially constitute it". Second, they exhibit "certain *metaphysical* and *methodological* commitments which, as an ensemble, individuate the research tradition and distinguish it from others". Third, traditions go through a number of formulations and usually have a long history (Laudan, 1978, pp. 78–79).

From this perspective, embodied cognition is not *defined* by abstract hypotheses discussed by Shapiro,[2] but is instead *exemplified* by and partially *constituted* by embodiment claims in cognitive linguistics, neoempiricism about concepts, accounts of "grounding" of language in gestural communication, or sensorimotor accounts of vision, and so on. Even if it is difficult to discern necessary and sufficient conditions of being a theory that exemplifies the tradition of embodied cognition, there is little doubt that the cited examples do exemplify it and bear a certain family resemblance to one another, even if they change over the course of history. Distilling *shared* basic claims of embodied cognition or the computational theory of mind from them may be useful for a philosophical debate but does not seem to be particularly productive for the empirical research guided instead by particular theories and successful research exemplars. The distilled claim may be even seen as an awkward abstract artifact of little use for practitioners, and may indeed seem trivial, also because individual theories and explanations of a given tradition remain in direct competition and may contradict one another – since the most controversial hypotheses will not be part of the shared, distilled claim. For example, only some proponents of embodiment claim that there is continuity between life and cognition (see Section 2.2 below).

The metaphysical and methodological commitments of embodied cognition make this research tradition distinct from other traditions in cognitive science. The metaphysical Constitution hypothesis cited by Shapiro is accepted by at least some proponents of embodied cognition (e.g. Clark, 2003). At least some methodological commitments can be seen in terms of fallible research heuristics. These heuristics help solve experimental and theoretical problems; for example, the gestural account of language is accompanied by the heuristic that one should investigate the motor areas of the brain in order to study linguistic communication. In particular, the research in embodied cognition has focused on a certain class of cognitive tasks for which sensory and motor processing or affective modulation is particularly relevant. Hence, its research heuristic is to investigate this kind of evolutionarily early processing before offering explanations in terms of mental representations.

In other words, the evaluation of embodied cognition should not focus on the triviality or novelty of individual hypotheses. It is usually impossible to disconfirm a research tradition by citing relative triviality of one of its metaphysical or methodological commitments. Research traditions are evaluated by looking at how progressive they are; that is how fast they develop and how adequately they solve their problems. The rate of progress, operationalized as the number of experimental studies published, remains impressive: yearly citations of "embodied cognition", according to Web of Science, have constantly risen from 109 in 2008 to 380 in 2015, and they occurred mostly in psychology and neuroscience (in contrast, the citations for "autopoiesis", have risen from twenty-two to forty-seven in the same period, and they are mostly in computer science, business or economics, and philosophy). While not all of the classical embodiment studies turned out to be replicable, such as the study that purported to show that hilarity of jokes depends on how one keeps a pen in one's mouth (Strack, Martin, and Stepper, 1988; cf. Wagenmakers et al., 2016), many results are already considered classical and theoretically plausible solutions of problems stated by cognitive science, for example the detailed study of why children fail to solve the A–not–B task in certain conditions (Thelen et al., 2001).

However, the question whether embodied cognition may address *all* cognitive phenomena in a theoretically fecund fashion seems to be answered in the negative. As critics rightly notice, the constituent theories of this tradition fail to discuss standard cognitive phenomena such as phoneme restoration or Stroop interference, and proponents of embodied cognition "selectively focus on a subset of domains that "work", while ignoring nearly all the bedrock findings that define cognitive science" (Goldinger et al., 2016, p. 961). In other words, critics are certain that embodied cognition will not "scale up" to all cognitive phenomena. Notice that, while computationalism cannot explain particular phenomena cited by Goldinger and colleagues, in particular phoneme restoration or Stroop interference, computational models can; however, there are no models related to embodied cognition that are even remotely relevant to these issues (but note that, as I have indicated before in note 1, change blindness is studied by proponents of embodied cognition).

The claim that not all cognitive phenomena could be explained by appealing to bodily or physiological processes has been defended already in the 1970s by Allen Newell and Herbert A. Simon:

> Man is the mirror of the universe in which he lives, all that he knows shapes his psychology, not just in superficial ways but almost indefinitely and subject only to a few basic constraints. ... The universe that man mirrors is more than his culture. It includes also a lawful physical universe, and a biological one – of which man's own body is not the least important part. ... But a *normal situation* is precisely one in which these biological limits are not exceeded ... the sensory and other biological limits [are] ... additional constraints upon behavior.
>
> *(Newell and Simon, 1972, p. 866)*

In other words, Newell and Simon claim that differences in cognitive performance cannot be explained by laws of physics or bodily factors *alone* because these may remain the same or vary without affecting cognitive performance at all. Although there are cases in which hunger, for example, arouses emotional response, and this, in turn, deteriorates cognitive performance, such simple causal relationships are rare, even if affective and cognitive processing are closely intertwined (Pessoa, 2014). Moreover, while there are known to be immense differences between individual people in cognitive abilities and temperament, similar differences are not known to exist in the sensory domain; most people are equally able in perceptual tasks. In short, we should not expect embodied cognition to scale up to all cognitive phenomena: cognitive capacities may vary while sensorimotor skills remain invariant.

Let me sum up the discussion in this section. The charge of triviality against embodied cognition is only to some extent true; indeed, at least the Conceptualization hypothesis is not novel or groundbreaking, while the non-trivial character of more radical proposals, such as Replacement, is logically independent from the issue of embodiment. But to say just this is to miss the fact that these hypotheses do not drive embodied cognition as a research tradition; the triviality is the feature of philosophical distillates of theories constituent for this tradition. It is misleading to frame embodied cognition as an isolated claim, a purported deep truth that illuminates cognitive research in all respects, as Goldinger and colleagues suggest in their critique. Embodied cognition is certainly not a silver bullet. It is a fruitful research tradition that attempts to discover bodily processes underlying cognitive capacities and behaviors.

327

Many proponents of embodied cognition indeed focus on phenomena that they find most interesting, while not offering explanations for all kinds of cognitive capacities. There are reasons to think embodied explanations will not deliver a unified theory of all cognition: bodily factors alone cannot explain various levels and structure of cognitive performance; instead, they must be complemented by factors that explain why people perform some tasks better or worse when bodily factors are kept invariant. The argument given by Newell and Simon, which underlies many criticisms of radicalizing the embodied approach to cognition, has never been rebutted. So, while it is undeniable that embodied cognition incites interesting empirical research, it may as well be true that it cannot work as the key to all aspects of cognition. At the same time, radical proponents of embodied cognition strive to show that in the future, it could indeed deliver *the* unificatory theory of cognition (or maybe even of life and cognition, see Section 2.2 below). In other words, one can distinguish radical and moderate embodied cognition by indicating the intended scope of their theoretical efforts; radicals think that all cognitive phenomena will be covered, and moderates contend that only some phenomena are explainable in the embodied fashion.

Moderate embodied accounts of cognition are rarely based on embodiment alone; most frequently, they also appeal to a large body of other research. In the next section, I argue that embodied approaches are not only compatible with computationalism but also implied by it. In addition, popular objections against computationalism point to claims of proponents of embodied cognition that are not at all trivial, though these may not be shared by all theories in this rich and varied research tradition.

2 Embodiment versus computation, or how embodiment offers non-trivial complementary perspectives

We can now start assessing the challenge of embodied cognition to the computational study of the mind. The computational theory of mind states that the mind is a computer of some kind. Herein, I assume the most generic reading of this claim, namely that computation is a necessary condition of cognition (even radical proponents of computationalism argue that it is sufficient only when computation is appropriately organized, e.g. Newell, 1980). The challenges described below have been stated as objections by various, sometimes radical, proponents of embodied cognition and can be filed under three major groups: (1) computation is abstract, cognition is not; (2) computers are not organisms; (3) computers ignore real-time, situated interaction. Although the challenges can be met, they also accentuate non-trivial contributions of embodied research tradition to the study of cognition.

2.1 Computation is abstract, cognition is not

Some proponents of embodied cognition claim that because symbols in computers are, in some sense, abstract and formal, computers – or at least computer programs – are abstract as well (Barrett, 2015; Barrett, Pollet, and Stulp, 2014; Lakoff, 1987). However, computers are physical, spatiotemporal devices, and these are not abstract in any straightforward sense. All attempts to account for the *physical* implementation of computation assume this much.

Moreover, many accounts of physical computation require showing a concrete causal structure responsible for it. For example, the mechanistic account of computation (Miłkowski, 2013; Piccinini, 2015) requires that the lowest level of organization of computational mechanisms bottom out in non-computational entities and processes whose causal organization is responsible for their computational properties. For biological systems, it means that a computational mechanism must be constituted or caused by some bodily process, or, simply, be *embodied*. The account rejects the idea of "computers all the way down" (or at least, it cannot be "the same computer all the way down", should one assume *pancomputationalism*, or the claim that everything is a computer of some kind). In other words, at least some accounts of concrete implementation of computation assume rather than contradict embodiment.

2.2 Computers are not organisms

Louise Barrett (2015), among others, presses the point that people are organisms and computers are not. But this is only true of typical electronic computers. A computer may be built of DNA strands (Zauner and Conrad, 1996), so it's definitely possible to have a biological computer. Why then suppose that organisms cannot be computers?

A more plausible way to spell out this objection is to say that biological brains, thanks to their unique biological nature, give rise to features necessarily absent in computers. In other words, features of life are somehow necessary and sufficient for cognition (Thompson, 2007), and this claim is typical for some defenders of embodiment (for a discussion, see Godfrey-Smith, 1994). Even if this is true, note that computationalism need not assume that computation is sufficient for cognition. Similarly, in response to claims that emotion cannot be abstracted from cognition (Thompson and Stapleton, 2009), one may acknowledge that mathematical models of computation do not account for all features of emotional processing. Computationalists might admit that embodiment actually is required for cognition to occur.

But this claim is interesting insofar as it points to an important theme in philosophical accounts of embodiment. Namely, it is claimed that *cognition* is essentially a normative notion, and that recognizing errors, learning by mistakes, and similar normatively evaluable tasks have to be undertaken by cognitive agents. Instead, however, of maintaining that epistemic normativity cannot be fully accounted for in a naturalistic fashion, as some critics of naturalized epistemology (Kim, 1988) did, defenders of embodied cognition claim that some account of biological function is both sufficient and necessary to account for epistemic normativity (Christensen and Bickhard, 2002). This theme is shared among multiple theories in the embodied research tradition; for example, theorists of mind–life continuity (Thompson, 2007), enactivism (Varela, Thompson, and Rosch, 1991) and biological self-organization (Deacon, 2012) endorse this position. If these claims are true, then artificial computational cognitive agents will never enjoy genuine cognitive normativity; their normativity will be derived only from their original biological creators. Nonetheless, it does not undermine the explanatory purchase of computation for non-artifactual, natural biological agents.

2.3 Computers ignore real-time, situated interaction

Researchers working in the research tradition of embodied cognition usually stress the importance of continuous bodily interaction with the environment and the time-pressured nature of some cognitive processes (Wilson, 2002). These two factors are, according to some, ignored by run-of-the-mill computational models. For example, Jerry Fodor, arguing for methodological solipsism (Fodor, 1980), appealed to computational accounts of cognition that, in his view, ignore both the environment and time pressures. In contrast, defenders of dynamical models of cognition, which are popular in the embodied cognition research community, stress that Turing machines do not appeal to real time; instead, they operate with the abstract notion of a computation step. There is no continuous time flow, just discrete clock ticks in a Turing machine (Bickhard and Terveen, 1995; Wheeler, 2005). This is true. But is this an objection to computationalism?

First, some models of computation specify the real-time duration of every computation step (Nagy and Akl, 2011), and such formalism could be assumed in a cognitive model. Second, the objection seems to confuse the formal model of computation with its physical realization, which surely operates in real time.

Moreover, in contrast to methodological solipsism, most theorists in cognitive science stressed the importance of accounting for timely environmental interaction. For example, one of the important research questions that a researcher must ask, according to David Marr (1982), when explaining a computational strategy of a cognitive system, is "Why is this strategy appropriate?" This can only be answered by appealing to features of the environment by which a strategy might be judged appropriate or inappropriate. The strategy must be also tractable and time-efficient for the agent in that environment (Frixione, 2001; Van Rooij, 2008).

Even more importantly, there is a critical evidential role of the environment in building computational models of cognition. It seems that one can fit too many computational models to physical processes occurring in cognitive systems if one ignores the environment. While this problem has been usually discussed as a merely conceptual charge against computationalism, it rears its ugly head in everyday practice. For example, it may be very difficult to decide what kind of computation is performed even by a mundane logical gate, or the device which is supposed to perform a logical operation such as conjunction (AND gate) or disjunction (OR gate). Suppose that low and high voltages correspond to logical truth-values. The problem is that the same physical device can be interpreted as an AND gate and an OR gate, depending on the interpretation of low and high voltages just because of truth tables for these operators (Shagrir, 2006, p. 409; Sprevak, 2010a). How should one decide such matters?

To do this, one could analyze the environment in which the computer is operating. Computational mechanisms are typically (though not always; cf. Miłkowski, 2013) parts of representational mechanisms, whose function may be to represent – among other things – the state of the physical environment of a biological organism. For this reason, to constrain the hypotheses about the overall computational structure of the cognitive system, one may suppose that it models its environment (Craik, 1967; Shagrir, 2010). So, computational hypotheses may be constrained by semantic hypotheses. For example, to explain a rat's capacity to navigate a maze, one may posit a computational mechanism of a cognitive map being constantly updated and reused for navigation, and use the research findings about the place cells in its hippocampus (Bechtel, 2016) to constrain hypotheses of possible computational architectures. This can then constrain possible mappings between, say, neural firing rates and their computational interpretation (cf. also Miłkowski, 2017).

Proponents of embodied cognition who embrace the Replacement hypothesis may not be particularly enthusiastic about accounting for the role of the environment in cognition in representational terms. Nevertheless, even if representational explanations are incompatible with programmatic anti-representationalism of some theorists of embodiment, they are part and parcel of most computational modeling. As we will see in the next section on the example of cricket phonotaxis, there may be interesting trade-offs between cognitive representing and embodied interaction and sensing. For moderate proponents of embodiment, in other words, a non-trivial line of research is open: namely, of finding out what kinds of interactions underlie cognitive capacities.

Let me sum up this short discussion of objections to computationalism, as posed by defenders of embodied cognition. The discussion shows that computational approaches are not logically incompatible with embodiment; on the contrary, the computational accounts usually assume physical embodiment, interaction with the environment and the need for tractable and prompt computation. Standard computational models are usually representational but, at least under some accounts of concrete computation, they need not be. Similarly, only some, usually radical, theories of embodied cognition assume anti-representationalism. In other words, embodied cognition may be deeply integrated with computational modeling, which may also appeal to contentful cognitive representations.

At the same time, by looking at challenges, we discovered that some topics, such as normativity, emotions, or self-organization, are of particular interest to theorists of embodiment. These topics might not be in the center of attention of cognitive science, as they are not usually in the purview of cognitive explanations, as Newell and Simon, cited in Section 1.2, rightly stress. For cognitive scientists, therefore, they may be of little interest. But they remain scientifically valid objects of research that require some explanation. In other words, our discussion so far hints that embodied cognition offers some value for cognitive science but also for other fields of research focusing on biological agency.

3 Non-trivial embodiment in cognitive robotics

In this section, I discuss how computational modeling can be fruitfully integrated with assumptions of moderate embodied cognition. These models may be the best answer to the triviality challenge so far, as they demonstrate non-trivial bodily capacities of robots that explain cognition in a biologically plausible way. Cognitive roboticists believe that the physical machinery of the robot can help explain cognitive processes in an integrated fashion (Morse et al., 2011). I discuss two issues related to these parts of the research tradition of embodied cognition: how robots may explain behavior and cognition and how the body computes morphologically. They do not exhaust the breadth of bodily contributions in robotics; for example, epigenetic robotics connects insights from developmental psychology and robotics (Lungarella et al., 2003), by stressing the development of sensorimotor control; others also stress the role of embodied emotions in the overall cognitive functioning of agents (Ziemke, 2008).

3.1 Computational modeling in neuroethology: the case of crickets

Neuroethology in biorobotics explains behavior of animals and their neurocognitive mechanisms by building robotic models. One important example is the study of phonotaxis, or the ability to track the source of sound in crickets (Webb, 1995). Barbara Webb and her collaborators have produced a series of increasingly realistic robotic models that explain how crickets can discover the sound source. However, what remained fairly invariant was the crucial component of the robot: the hearing organs. Instead of using a standard microphone, hearing organs were modeled physically as a special tube. Crickets have two pairs of ears connected with a tube that acts as a pressure-difference receiver. Sound reaches the external and internal surface of their eardrums, and in the case of the internal surfaces, it is filtered and delayed in the tracheal tubes. This delay allows for locating the sound source, and the sound remains out of phase on the side closer to the male cricket that makes the sound. The same solution was mimicked on a robot (see Webb, 2008, p. 10 for details). Other frequencies of the sound do not have to be filtered out by the cricket because it is the physical setup that makes the calling song frequency easier to localize – other frequencies are still audible but harder to locate. Simply, the cricket walks towards the sound to make it louder, and the direction is determined by the phase of the sound (see Figure 24.1).

This explanation has been cited by defenders of embodied cognition as an important case of the body replacing the need for neural computation (Clark, 2001, pp. 103–108). We can see

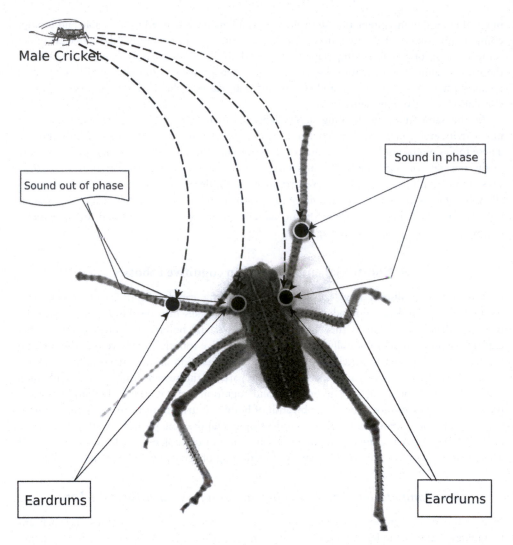

Male Cricket

Sound in phase

Sound out of phase

Eardrums

Eardrums

Figure 24.1 The female cricket has four eardrums, and the sound made by the male cricket is out of phase on the side of the female closer to the male. This makes the sound source easy to locate
Source: The image used in the picture was made by Tobias von der Haar, the whole diagram
© Marcin Miłkowski (2017)

how this happens: the physical morphology of the robot simply makes certain kinds of input information available, instead of processing it computationally. At the same time, the robot clearly has a (biologically plausible) spiking neural network that controls its behavior to replicate known ethological phenomena in crickets. In this case, the perceptual task for the cricket is essentially simplified by the shape of its sense organs. If one could replace the sense organ with a generic microphone and appropriate filtering software, the solution obtained would be much more computationally expensive, which is not biologically plausible for crickets. Let's imagine how this alternative cricket robot would work: it would have a standard microphone but it would require a much bigger neural network to perform the sound filtering task, and without four eardrums, it would need more processing to detect the direction of the sound source. Although one could build such a robot, this heavy processing is biologically implausible and inefficient. What evolution instead did was to "off-load" the processing to the body: the morphology of sensory organs enables more efficient computational processing.

In this robotic model, we can see that the approach of embodied cognition ceases to look trivial: the mainstream approach to computational modeling is to assume that the organism has some sensory organs, but inquiring into its physical morphology is not necessarily required. To build efficient robots, however, researchers must take the role of the body into account because it may ease the burden on the robot.

3.2 Morphological computation

Let us study morphology even more, as it has been cited as an important factor of embodiment. Proponents of embodiment in robotics have offered a new account of computation as involved in robotics and living organisms, called *morphological computation*. The term, however, is unclear. Rolf Pfeifer and Josh Bongard define morphological computation processes as the ones "performed by the body that otherwise would have to be performed by the brain" (Pfeifer and Bongard, 2007, p. 96). The definition suggests that morphological computation is functionally equivalent to the physical computation in the *brain*, or at least in the nervous system. But this equivalence may be misleading for some robots, and makes the definition too narrow. Robots may contain standard electronic computers, and such computers do not count as brains, so they could not perform any computation by their non-existent brains, and hence, no morphological computation, according to this definition. But there is no reason to suppose that the computational tasks of silicon computers in such robots could not be realized by physical parts of their bodies, for example by some mechanical gears as opposed to electronic parts. In a simple case, one could intuitively apply the above definition by replacing the term *brain* with the expression *electronic parts*. However, it is very difficult to make this distinction sufficiently systematic: there is nothing special about electric signals as opposed to gears and pulleys that could make theoretical difference for computation. After all, a fully functional computer may be made out of mechanical relays, gears, and pulleys. Thus, it's not clear what could replace the term *brain* in this definition to make it applicable in all possible cases.

In the subsequent debate, three kinds of morphological computation were distinguished: (1) morphology facilitating control; (2) morphology facilitating perception; (3) morphological computation proper (Müller and Hoffmann, 2017). In the first case, the morphology of the system facilitates its motor control. An example of this is the morphological control in a passive-dynamic walker (see Figure 24.2). This contraption walks naturally without any dedicated computational circuits.

However, as Müller and Hoffman argue, it is a stretch to call it computational at all – even if the mechanical control may be re-described in terms of information processing, there is no user of the information beyond immediate motor control. They argue that it makes passive walkers non-computational. Such robots do not have an output value that a "finite observer" could look up to discover the output of computation (for a similar argument, see Piccinini, 2015). This assumption is not universally shared by all computationalists; indeed, it may seem that a self-regulating system might operate autonomously without any need of requiring any observers and remain computational. An extreme example could be an active homing nuclear missile that could kill all biological observers – by relying on its internal computational structure.

The two other categories are decreasingly controversial: indeed, one can find real examples of how the physical shape of sensory receptors facilitates perception, for example in crickets

Figure 24.2 Three phases of the walk as executed by the passive-dynamic walker (built in the Nagoya Institute of Technology; see Ikemata, Sano, and Fujimoto, 2003) on a slanted surface. Instead of an electronic controller, the mechanical structure and gravity cause the simple robot to walk in a biologically plausible fashion
Source: Illustration © Marcin Miłkowski (2017)

(see Section 3.1 above). There are also possible hybrid architectures that use different physical media to jointly compute mathematical functions, and this is what constitutes morphological computation proper. Nowakowski (2017) argues that these hybrid architectures are the paradigmatic cases of morphological computation. In his view, such architectures involve at least two parts: one capable of performing computational operations by itself, and another usable only in connection with the proper computational part (think of an electronic computer connected to some non-standard physical medium). However, the existence of such hybrid architectures is not problematic for standard computationalism any more than the existence of vacuum tubes and different kinds of mechanical abaci.

Hybrid morphological computation is used to study the trade-offs between traditional computation and the uses of bodily structures to perform equivalent operations. By showing that some morphological structures obviate the need for extensive computational processing, one could argue that the role of the body in cognition is irreplaceable: while in principle, one could try to compensate for the missing morphology by adding more computational power, such compensations are not biologically plausible (for a similar point, see Dempsey and Shani, 2013).

Let me sum up this section. Robotics is one of the fields of cognitive science, beside experimental psychology, that contributes most to the research tradition of embodied cognition. It has to be stressed that among roboticists, there is no shared view on embodiment, so a common denominator among all of them would be necessarily quite diluted and trivial. However, their work on the role of the morphology in cognition has shown that cognitive processing might be avoided by designing the shape of robots in an appropriate fashion. This insight is far from trivial but it does not guarantee that morphology will be explanatorily relevant for all cognitive phenomena. In other words, robotics cannot prove that embodied cognition will "scale up" to cover such areas as abstract problem solving, phoneme restoration, or Stroop interference. But it certainly shows the promise of moderate embodied cognition.

4 Summary: the place of embodied computation in nature

Prima facie, the view that cognition is embodied seems to challenge the computational view on cognitive processing. In reality, the challenge is easy to meet, and generic computationalism is compatible even with radical embodied cognition. Physical computational systems are implemented by concrete non-computational mechanisms, for example bodily mechanisms in biological cognitive systems. Biological computational systems are engaged not only in computation; they also need energy for their functioning and biological kinds of organization are in some respects unlike artificial. It turns out that it is actually difficult to say why embodiment could even clash with computationalism, and finding non-trivial contributions of embodiment to cognitive explanations requires going beyond diluted formulations of embodied cognition.

Embodied cognition is particularly fruitfully linked with computationalism in domains such as robotics, including neuroethology and morphological computation, where physical features of robots may be explanatorily relevant for cognitive performance. It also plays an important role in studies of emotional contributions to cognition.

While embodied cognition remains a progressive research tradition, its role in cognitive science should not be exaggerated. The key problem is that it is unlikely that all cognitive phenomena might be systematically explained by relying merely on research heuristics of various approaches of embodiment; the features of the body and cognitive performance are not directly and linearly linked. In other words, in contrast to what radicals claim, embodied cognition is not – or at least not yet – a unified grand theory of all cognition. At the same time, moderate embodied cognition can complement traditional cognitive approaches by focusing the attention of researchers on evolutionarily early mechanisms. It is biologically implausible to presuppose that the nervous systems have evolved in isolation from the morphological and metabolic processes, and the proper study of cognitive computation must include processing in the peripheral nervous systems (in vertebrates) as well as close connections between affective, motor, and sensory systems. Thus, embodied cognition and computationalism are natural allies.

Acknowledgments

The work on this chapter was funded from National Science Centre research grant under the decision DEC-2014/14/E/HS1/00803. The author wishes to thank the volume editors, as well as Mateusz Hohol, Tomasz Korbak, Przemysław Nowakowski, Zuzanna Rucińska, Alfredo Vernazzani for their extensive comments to the previous drafts of this work.

Notes

1 This criticism seems too quick at least in some cases; for example, Ronald Rensink and Kevin O'Regan have studied change blindness extensively (Rensink, O'Regan, and Clark, 1997). For O'Regan, change blindness is evidence that traditional cognitivist approaches to vision are wrong-headed, and he offers a sensorimotor account of vision instead (O'Regan and Noë, 2001). Goldinger et al. seem to miss the point that the sensorimotor account predicts phenomena such as change blindness, which remain anomalous to approaches that assume that the function of vision is to produce a complete, detailed representation of the world, as David Marr (1982) assumed. However, there is indeed no specific embodiment-related explanation of change blindness.

2 Note that Shapiro (2007) stresses that embodied cognition is a research program; still, he insists that the hypotheses he mentions are research goals of this program.

References

Adams, F. and Aizawa, K. (2008) *The Bounds of Cognition*. Malden, MA: Blackwell.

Anderson, M.L. (2014) *After Phrenology: Neural Reuse and the Interactive Brain*. Cambridge, MA: MIT Press.

Arbib, M.A. (2012) *How the Brain Got Language: The Mirror System Hypothesis*. New York, NY: Oxford University Press.

Barker, M.J. (2010) 'From Cognition's Location to the Epistemology of Its Nature', *Cognitive Systems Research*, 11 (4), pp. 357–366.

Barrett, L. (2015) 'Why Brains Are Not Computers, Why Behaviorism Is Not Satanism, and Why Dolphins Are Not Aquatic Apes', *The Behavior Analyst*, 39 (1), pp. 9–23.

Barrett, L., Pollet, T.V., and Stulp, G. (2014) 'From Computers to Cultivation: Reconceptualizing Evolutionary Psychology', *Frontiers in Psychology*, 5, art. 867.

Barsalou, L.W. (1999) 'Perceptual Symbol Systems', *The Behavioral and Brain Sciences*, 22 (4), pp. 577–609.

Barsalou, L.W. (2008) 'Grounded Cognition', *Annual Review of Psychology*, 59, pp. 617–645.

Bechtel, W. (2016) 'Investigating Neural Representations: The Tale of Place Cells', *Synthese*, 193 (5), pp. 1287–1321.

Bickhard, M.H. and Terveen, L. (1995) *Foundational Issues in Artificial Intelligence and Cognitive Science: Impasse and Solution*. Amsterdam: Elsevier.

Chemero, A. (2009) *Radical Embodied Cognitive Science*. Cambridge, MA: MIT Press.

Christensen, W. and Bickhard, M.H. (2002) 'The Process Dynamics of Normative Function', *The Monist*, 85 (1), pp. 3–28.

Clark, A. (2001) *Mindware: An Introduction to the Philosophy of Cognitive Science*. Oxford: Oxford University Press.

Clark, A. (2003) *Natural-Born Cyborgs: Minds, Technologies, and the Future of Human Intelligence*. New York, NY: Oxford University Press.

Clark, A. (2008) *Supersizing the Mind*. Oxford: Oxford University Press.

Clark, A. and Chalmers, D.J. (1998) 'The Extended Mind', *Analysis*, 58 (1), pp. 7–19.

Craik, K. (1967) *The Nature of Explanation*. Cambridge, UK: Cambridge University Press.

Craver, C.F. (2007) *Explaining the Brain: Mechanisms and the Mosaic Unity of Neuroscience*. Oxford: Oxford University Press.

Deacon, T.W. (2012) *Incomplete Nature: How Mind Emerged from Matter*. New York, NY: W.W. Norton & Co.

Dempsey, L.P. and Shani, I. (2013) 'Stressing the Flesh: In Defense of Strong Embodied Cognition', *Philosophy and Phenomenological Research*, 86 (3), pp. 590–617.

Fodor, J.A. (1980) 'Methodological Solipsism Considered as a Research Strategy in Cognitive Psychology', *Behavioral and Brain Sciences*, 3 (1), pp. 63–73.

Fodor, J.A. (1994) 'Concepts: A Potboiler', *Cognition*, 50 (1–3), pp. 95–113.

Frixione, M. (2001) 'Tractable Competence', *Minds and Machines*, 11 (3), pp. 379–397.

Gallagher, S. and Zahavi, D. (2008) *The Phenomenological Mind*. New York, NY: Routledge.

Gibbs, R.W. (2006) *Embodiment and Cognitive Science*. Cambridge, UK: Cambridge University Press.

Gibson, J.J. (1986) *The Ecological Approach to Visual Perception*. Hove, UK: Psychology Press.

Glenberg, A.M. and Kaschak, M.P. (2002) 'Grounding Language in Action', *Psychonomic Bulletin and Review*, 9 (3), pp. 558–565.

Godfrey-Smith, P. (1994) 'Spencer and Dewey on Life and Mind', in Brooks, R. and Maes, P.-J. (eds.) *Artificial Life IV: Proceedings of the Fourth International Workshop on the Synthesis and Simulation of Living Systems*. Cambridge, MA: MIT Press, pp. 80–89.

Goldinger, S.D. et al. (2016) 'The Poverty of Embodied Cognition', *Psychonomic Bulletin and Review*, 23 (4), pp. 959–978.

Goldman, A.I. (2012) 'A Moderate Approach to Embodied Cognitive Science', *Review of Philosophy and Psychology*, 3 (1), pp. 71–88.

Ikemata, Y., Sano, A., and Fujimoto, H. (2003) 'Analysis of Stable Limit Cycle in Passive Walking', in *SICE 2003 Annual Conference* (IEEE Cat. No. 03TH8734), vol. 1, 117–122.

Kaplan, D.M. (2012) 'How to Demarcate the Boundaries of Cognition', *Biology and Philosophy*, 27 (4), pp. 545–570.

Kim, J. (1988) 'What Is "Naturalized Epistemology"?', *Philosophical Perspectives*, 2, pp. 381–405.

Lakatos, I. (1976) 'Falsification and the Methodology of Scientific Research Programmes', in Harding, S. (ed.) *Can Theories Be Refuted?* Dordrecht: Springer, pp. 205–259.

Lakoff, G. (1987) *Women, Fire, and Dangerous Things: What Categories Reveal about the Mind*. Chicago, IL: University of Chicago Press.

Lakoff, G. (2012) 'Explaining Embodied Cognition Results', *Topics in Cognitive Science*, 4 (4), pp. 773–785.

Laudan, L. (1978) *Progress and Its Problem: Towards a Theory of Scientific Growth*. Berkeley, CA: University of California Press.

Leuridan, B. (2011) 'Three Problems for the Mutual Manipulability Account of Constitutive Relevance in Mechanisms', *The British Journal for the Philosophy of Science*, 63 (2), pp. 399–427.

Lungarella, M. et al. (2003) 'Developmental Robotics: A Survey', *Connection Science*, 15 (4), pp. 151–190.

Marr, D. (1982) *Vision: A Computational Investigation into the Human Representation and Processing of Visual Information*. New York, NY: W.H. Freeman and Company.

McBeath, M.K., Shaffer, D.M., and Kaiser, M.K. (1995) 'How Baseball Outfielders Determine Where to Run to Catch Fly Balls', *Science*, 268 (5210), pp. 569–573.

Miłkowski, M. (2013) *Explaining the Computational Mind*. Cambridge, MA: MIT Press.

Miłkowski, M. (2017) 'The False Dichotomy between Causal Realization and Semantic Computation', *Hybris*, 38, pp. 1–21.

Morse, A.F. et al. (2011) 'The Role of Robotic Modelling in Cognitive Science', *New Ideas in Psychology*, 29 (3), pp. 312–324.

Müller, V.C. and Hoffmann, M. (2017) 'What Is Morphological Computation? On How the Body Contributes to Cognition and Control', *Artificial Life*, 23 (1), pp. 1–24.

Nagy, N. and Akl, S. (2011) 'Computations with Uncertain Time Constraints: Effects on Parallelism and Universality', in Calude, C. et al. (eds.) *Unconventional Computation*, LNCS vol. 6714. Berlin: Springer, pp. 152–163

Newell, A. (1980) 'Physical Symbol Systems', *Cognitive Science: A Multidisciplinary Journal*, 4 (2), pp. 135–183.

Newell, A. and Simon, H.A. (1972) *Human Problem Solving*. Englewood Cliffs, NJ: Prentice-Hall.

Nowakowski, P.R. (2017) 'Bodily Processing: The Role of Morphological Computation', *Entropy*, 19 (7), art. 295.

O'Regan, J.K. and Noë, A. (2001) 'A Sensorimotor Account of Vision and Visual Consciousness', *The Behavioral and Brain Sciences*, 24 (5), pp. 939–973.

Pessoa, L. (2014) *The Cognitive-Emotional Brain: From Interactions to Integration*. Cambridge, MA: MIT Press.

Pfeifer, R. and Bongard, J. (2007) *How the Body Shapes the Way We Think*. Cambridge, MA: MIT Press.

Piccinini, G. (2015) *Physical Computation: A Mechanistic Account*. Oxford: Oxford University Press.

Prinz, J.J. (2004) *Furnishing the Mind: Concepts and Their Perceptual Basis*. Cambridge, MA: MIT Press.

Rensink, R.A., O'Regan, J.K., and Clark, J.J. (1997) 'To See or Not to See: The Need for Attention to Perceive Changes in Scenes', *Psychological Science*, 8 (5), pp. 368–373.

Rizzolatti, G. and Arbib, M.A. (1998) 'Language within Our Grasp', *Trends in Neurosciences*, 21 (5), pp. 188–194.

Shagrir, O. (2006) 'Why We View the Brain as a Computer', *Synthese*, 153 (3), pp. 393–416.

Shagrir, O. (2010) 'Brains as Analog-Model Computers', *Studies in History and Philosophy of Science Part A*, 41 (3), pp. 271–279.

Shapiro, L. (2007) 'The Embodied Cognition Research Programme', *Philosophy Compass*, 2 (2), pp. 338–346.

Shapiro, L. (2011) *Embodied Cognition*. London and New York, NY: Routledge.

Sprevak, M. (2010a) 'Computation, Individuation, and the Received View on Representation', *Studies in History and Philosophy of Science Part A*, 41 (3), pp. 260–270.

Sprevak, M. (2010b) 'Inference to the Hypothesis of Extended Cognition', *Studies in History and Philosophy of Science Part A*, 41 (4), pp. 353–362.

Strack, F., Martin, L.L., and Stepper, S. (1988) 'Inhibiting and Facilitating Conditions of the Human Smile: A Nonobtrusive Test of the Facial Feedback Hypothesis', *Journal of Personality and Social Psychology*, 54 (5), pp. 768–777.

Thelen, E. et al. (2001) 'The Dynamics of Embodiment: A Field Theory of Infant Perseverative Reaching', *Behavioral and Brain Sciences*, 24 (1), pp. 1–34.

Thompson, E. (2007) *Mind in Life: Biology, Phenomenology, and the Sciences of Mind*. Cambridge, MA: Harvard University Press.

Thompson, E. and Stapleton, M. (2009) 'Making Sense of Sense-Making: Reflections on Enactive and Extended Mind Theories', *Topoi*, 28 (1), pp. 23–30.

Van Rooij, I. (2008) 'The Tractable Cognition Thesis', *Cognitive Science*, 32 (6), pp. 939–984.

Varela, F.J., Thompson, E., and Rosch, E.H. (1991) *The Embodied Mind: Cognitive Science and Human Experience*. Cambridge, MA: MIT Press.

Wagenmakers, E-J. et al. (2016) 'Registered Replication Report: Strack, Martin, & Stepper (1988)', *Perspectives on Psychological Science*, 11 (6), pp. 917–928.

Walter, S. (2014) 'Situated Cognition: A Field Guide to Some Open Conceptual and Ontological Issues', *Review of Philosophy and Psychology*, 5 (2), pp. 241–263.

Webb, B. (1995) 'Using Robots to Model Animals: A Cricket Test', *Robotics and Autonomous Systems*, 16 (2–4), pp. 117–134.

Webb, B. (2008) 'Using Robots to Understand Animal Behavior', in Brockmann, H.J. et al. (eds.) *Advances in the Study of Behavior*, vol. 38. Amsterdam: Elsevier, pp. 1–58.

Wheeler, M. (2005) *Reconstructing the Cognitive World*. Cambridge, MA: MIT Press.

Wilson, M. (2002) 'Six Views of Embodied Cognition', *Psychonomic Bulletin and Review*, 9 (4), pp. 625–636.

Wołoszyn, K. and Hohol, M. (2017) 'Commentary: The Poverty of Embodied Cognition', *Frontiers in Psychology*, 8. Available at: https://doi.org/10.3389/fpsyg.2017.00845.

Zauner, K.-P. and Conrad, M. (1996) 'Parallel Computing with DNA: Toward the Anti-universal Machine', in Voigt, H.-M. et al. (eds.) *Parallel Problem Solving from Nature – PPSN IV*, LNCS vol. 1141. Berlin: Springer, pp. 696–705.

Ziemke, T. (2008) 'On the Role of Emotion in Biological and Robotic Autonomy', *Bio Systems*, 91 (2), pp. 401–408.

25

TRACTABILITY AND THE COMPUTATIONAL MIND

Jakub Szymanik and Rineke Verbrugge

Introduction

Computational complexity theory, or in other words, the theory of tractability and intract-ability, is defined in terms of limit behavior. A typical question of computational complexity theory is of the form: As the size of the input increases, how do the running time and memory requirements of the algorithm change? Therefore, computational complexity theory, among other things, investigates the scalability of computational problems and algorithms, i.e. it measures the rate of increase in computational resources required as a problem grows (see, e.g., Arora and Barak, 2009). The implicit assumption here is that the size of the problem is unbounded. For example, models can be of any finite size, formulas can contain any number of distinct variables, and so on.[1]

Example 1: Satisfiability. The problem is to decide whether a given propositional formula is not a contradiction. Let ϕ be a propositional formula with $p_1, \ldots, p_n$ distinct variables. Let us use the well-known algorithm based on truth tables to decide whether ϕ has a satisfying valuation. How big is the truth table for ϕ? The formula has n distinct variables occurring in it and there-fore the truth table has 2^n rows. If $n = 10$, there are 1,024 rows; for $n = 20$, there are already 1,048,576 rows, and so on. In the worst case, to decide whether ϕ is satisfiable, we have to check all rows. Hence, in such a case, the time needed to find a solution is exponential with respect to the number of different propositional letters of the formula. A seminal result of computational complexity theory states that this is not a property of the truth-table method but of the inherent complexity of the satisfiability problem (Cook, 1971).

It is often claimed that, because complexity theory deals only with relative computational difficulty of problems (the question how the running time and memory requirements of problems increase relative to increasing input size), it does not have much to offer for cognitive and philosophical considerations. Simply put, the inputs we deal with in our everyday life are not of arbitrary size. In typical situations they are even relatively small, for example, a student in a typical logic exam may be asked to check whether a certain formula of length 18 is satisfiable. In fact, critics claim, computational complexity theory does not say how difficult it is to solve a given problem for a fixed size of the input. We disagree.

Even though in typical cognitive situations we are dealing with reasonably small inputs, we have no bounds on their size. Potentially, the inputs can grow without limit. Therefore, complexity theory's idealized assumption of unbounded input size is, like many idealized assumptions in the sciences, such as point-masses in Newtonian physics, both necessary in that it simplifies analysis of a complex world and convenient, because it results in characterizations of phenomena that balance simplicity of descriptions with empirical adequacy. As such, this idealization is justified on practical analytical grounds, whether it is true or not. Moreover, considering any input size, we avoid making arbitrary assumptions on what counts as a natural instance of the cognitive task. For example, such a general approach works very well for syntax, where the assumption that sentences in a natural language can be of any length has led to the development of generative grammar and mathematical linguistics (Chomsky, 1957).

Even though in each case of cognition we are dealing with inputs of a specific size, which in practice is limited, imposing *a priori* bounds on the input size would conflict with the generative nature of human cognition, that is, the idea that human minds can *in principle* yield cognitive outcomes such as percepts, beliefs, judgments, decisions, plans, and actions for an infinite number of situations. Moreover, in experimental practice, subjects usually do not realize the size of the model's universe in which they are supposed to solve some given problem, therefore, it often seems that they develop strategies (algorithms) for all possible sizes of universes. Still, we realize that many skeptics might not be satisfied with the above arguments. Therefore, in this chapter, after a brief introduction to computational complexity theory, we offer an overview of some interesting empirical evidence corroborating computational and logical predictions inspired by tractability considerations.

Theory of tractability

Philosophers are still discussing the precise meaning of the term "computation" (see e.g. Moschovakis, 2001; see also Shanahan, this volume). Intuitively, "computation is a mechanical procedure that calculates something". Formally speaking, the most widespread approach to capture computations is to define them in terms of Turing machines or an equivalent model. The widely believed Church-Turing Thesis states that everything that ever might be mechanically calculated can be computed by a Turing machine (see, e.g., Cooper, 2003, for an introduction to computability theory).

It has been quickly observed not only that there exist uncomputable problems but even that for some computable problems, effective algorithms appear not to exist, in the sense that some computable problems need too much of computational resources, like time or memory, to get an answer. As explained in the introduction, computational complexity theory investigates the amount of resources required and the inherent difficulty of computational problems. Practically speaking, it categorizes computational problems via complexity classes (see, e.g., Arora and Barak, 2009, for an introduction to complexity theory).

This chapter focuses on the distinction between tractable and intractable problems. The standard way to characterize this distinction is by reference to the number of steps a minimal Turing machine needs to use to solve a problem with respect to the problem size. Informally, problems that can be computed in polynomial time are called tractable; the class of problems of this type is called PTIME. The class of intractable problems, including those problems that require exponential time to be solved on a deterministic Turing machine, are referred to as NP-hard problems.[2] Intuitively, a problem is NP-hard if there is no "clever" algorithm for solving it, so NP-hard problems lead to combinatorial explosion.[3]

More formally, PTIME (or P) is the class of problems computable by deterministic Turing machines in polynomial time. NP-hard problems are problems that are at least as difficult as any of the problems belonging to the class of problems that can be computed by nondeterministic

Turing machines in polynomial time (NPTIME problems). NP-complete problems are NP-hard problems belonging to NPTIME, hence they are the most difficult problems among the NPTIME problems. It is known that P=NP if any NPTIME-complete problem is PTIME computable. However, whether P=NP is a famous open question. Almost all computer scientists believe that the answer is negative (Gasarch, 2012). Many natural problems are computable in PTIME, for instance, calculating the greatest common divisor of two numbers or looking something up in a dictionary. We already encountered the NP-hard problem of satisfiability in Example 1.

Using the two fundamental complexity classes PTIME and NPTIME Edmonds (1965) and Cobham (1965) proposed that the class of tractable problems is identical to the PTIME class. The thesis is accepted by most computer scientists (see, e.g., Garey and Johnson, 1990). The version of the Cobham-Edmonds Thesis for cognitive science is known as the P-Cognition Thesis (Frixione, 2001): *human cognitive capacities are constrained by polynomial time computability.*

However, Ristad (1993) and Szymanik (2010) have shown that natural language contains constructions of which the semantics is essentially NP-complete and Levesque (1988) has recognized the computational complexity of general logical reasoning problems like satisfiability to be NP-complete. In other cognitive domains, Tsotsos (1990) has shown that visual search is NP-complete. Therefore, the P-Cognition Thesis seems to be clearly too broad, excluding some non-polynomial problems with which the human mind can still deal. This does not need to mean that we should disregard these theories. Possibly the complexity of these theories may be just a result of over-specification, including certain instances of the problem that should be excluded from the realm of human cognitive capacity. To account for this problem, van Rooij (2008) proposed an alternative to the P-Cognition Thesis, the so-called Fixed-parameter Tractability Thesis. The idea here is to consider not only the size of the input but also other input parameters; then, intractability of some problems may come from a parameter which is in practice usually very small no matter the size of the whole input. Such problems should still be tractable for the human mind (see, e.g., Downey and Fellows, 1998, for an introduction to parameterized complexity theory).[4] In other words, if inputs have a certain structure, the problem becomes easy to solve.

Example 2. In the Traveling Salesman Problem, the input is a set of cities, distances between them, a point of departure, and a maximum route length. The computational problem is to decide whether there exists a route that starts and ends in the point of departure, visits all cities exactly once, and does not exceed the maximum route length. This problem is also known to be NP-complete, thus intractable (Karp, 1972). However, when the cities are aligned exactly on a circle, then the problem is obviously trivial to solve. Actually, it is even enough that relatively many cities are aligned on a circle to make the problem easy. This property can be parameterized, intuitively, by counting the number of cities inside the circle and the number of cities on the circle. The Traveling Salesman Problem is fixed-parameter tractable (Deıneko et al., 2006), meaning that all the intractability of the problem can be contained within the parameter, that is, the more cities are not located on the circle, the more intractable the problem becomes.

Complexity distinctions and logical descriptions

Many complexity distinctions can also be captured in descriptive terms via logic. The idea here is simple: we use logical languages to describe a computational problem in some minimal way. The simpler the description, the easier the problem. In other words, descriptive complexity deals with the relationship between logical definability and computational complexity. We replace the classic computational complexity question with the descriptive complexity question, i.e. the question: How difficult is it to describe the problem using some logic (see, e.g.,

Immerman, 1998)? In terms of our two basic computational classes PTIME and NPTIME, it is important to note that every problem that can be described by a first-order formula is computable in polynomial time. Moreover, the seminal result of descriptive complexity theory states: a problem is definable in the existential fragment of second-order logic if and only if it belongs to NP (Fagin, 1974).

Summing up, the idea behind capturing complexity of cognitive problems boils down to having a formal, in some sense minimal, computational or logical description of the cognitive problem. The hope is that this description captures inherent, intrinsic, combinatorial properties of the problem that are independent from particular descriptions. Such structural properties should correlate with human behavior; we will give some examples in the following sections. Next, we study complexity of such descriptions or models that should then also capture inherent cognitive complexity and lead to some (experimental) predictions or explanatory insights about the cognitive capacity in question.

In the next few sections, we give a personal selection of the outlined approach to study different aspects of cognition, namely Boolean categorization, semantic processing, and social reasoning. We will show several cases in which the P-Cognition Thesis fails but the Fixed-parameter Tractability Thesis comes to the rescue, while in one case of social reasoning, apparent levels of cognitive difficulty do not line up with levels of computational (standard or parameterized) complexity (see also van Rooij, 2008; Aaronson, 2013; Isaac, Szymanik, and Verbrugge, 2014, for more examples and discussion of complexity and the computational mind).

Boolean categorization

From infancy onwards, we learn to categorize objects, for example, into animate and inanimate, and we continue to learn new categories well into adulthood, for example, distinguishing between ale and lager beers. In particular, many of our new concepts are built from the old ones using Boolean relations, such as "and", "or", and "not". For instance, we know that "cousin" is a child of an uncle *or* aunt; "beer" is an alcoholic beverage usually made from malted cereal grain *and* flavored with hops, *and* brewed by slow fermentation; in basketball, "travel" is illegally moving the pivot foot *or* taking three or more steps without dribbling; "depression" is a mood disorder characterized by persistent sadness *and* anxiety, *or* a feeling of hopelessness *and* pessimism, *or* ... Therefore, an important question in psychology is how people acquire concepts. In order to approach that big question, one may try to consider the cognitive complexity of the process of acquisition, and ask: *Why are some concepts harder to acquire than others?*

Since the beginning of the experimental studies on categorization, it has been clear that some new concepts are easier to learn than others. For instance, intuitively, concepts depending on *and* are easier to learn than those depending on *or* (Bruner, Goodnow, and Austin, 1956).[5] Shepard, Hovland, and Jenkins (1961) have run a number of various experiments to study the acquisition of six different sorts of concepts based on three binary variables. Each concept was defined in a way to contain exactly four instances and four non-instances. In this way, the researchers created six novel concepts or categories. The experimental results showed a very robust complexity trend, which we describe below. Trying to explain Shepard and colleagues' finding, Feldman (2000) proposed to define their six concepts using Boolean propositional logic:

Concept I contains objects satisfying the following description: (not-a b c) or (not-a b not-c) or (not-a not-b c) or (not-a not-b not-c).

Concept II consists of the following instances: (a b c) or (a b not-c) or (not-a not-b c) or (not-a not-b not-c).

Concept III consists of the following instances: (a not–b c) or (not–a b not–c) or (not–a not–b c) or (not–a not–b not–c).

Concept IV consists of the following instances: (a not–b not–c) or (not–a b not–c) or (not–a not–b c) or (not–a not–b not–c).

Concept V consists of the following instances: (a b c) or (not–a b not–c) or (not–a not–b c) or (not–a not–b not–c).

Concept VI consists of the following instances: (a b not–c) or (a not–b c) or (not–a b c) or (not–a not–b not–c).

Shepard's complexity trend is: I < II < III, IV,V < VI. This means that subjects made the least errors (and took the least time) before they learnt concepts of type I, while they made the most errors (and took the longest time) before they learnt concepts of type VI.

Feldman's main insight was to propose that the Boolean complexity of a concept captures its cognitive difficulty in terms of errors made and time needed. Boolean complexity of the concept was defined as the length (expressed in terms of the number of literals, i.e. positive or negative variables) of the shortest Boolean formula logically equivalent to the concept.[6] For an easy example, the reader can check that the formula (a and b) or (a and not–b) or (not–a and b) can be succinctly and equivalently represented as (a or b), hence, its Boolean complexity is 2.

Computing the shortest descriptions for the six concepts we get:

I = not–a (complexity 1)
II = (a and b) or (not–a and not–b) (4)
III = (not–a and not–c) or (not–b and c) (4)
IV = (not–c or (not–a and not–b)) and (not–a or not–b) (5)
V = (not–a and not–(b and c)) or (a and (b and c)) (6)
VI = (a and ((not–b and c) or (b and not–c))) or (not–a and ((not–b and not–c) or (b and c))) (10).

Therefore, a prediction of cognitive difficulty based on Boolean complexity is consistent with Shepard's trend.

Based on this insight, Feldman also conducted experiments to provide a larger data set. He considered a generalization of the Shepard setting, an arbitrary Boolean concept defined by P positive examples over D binary features. For Shepard's six types, D was 3 and P was 4. Feldman (2000) experimentally studied seventy-six new Boolean concepts in a range of $D \in \{3,4\}$ and $2 \leq P \leq 4$. Boolean complexity accounts for 50 percent of variance in the extended dataset. One can therefore conclude that minimal description length predicts the cognitive difficulty of learning a concept.

Feldman's paper does not deal with the border of tractability and in-tractability directly, however, it uses a logical description and the prototypical complexity problem of satisfiability to successfully capture and explain the difficulty of a very crucial cognitive problem. As such, it is a beautiful and inspiring example of applying logic in cognitive science.

Still, one may object to logical models of categorization on the grounds of the P–Cognition Thesis by asserting that a theory based on the NP-hard satisfiability problem cannot be computationally plausible. One way out here would be to invoke the strategy suggested by the Parameterized Complexity Thesis, that is, instead of rejecting the whole model, one can point out that it probably overgeneralizes the cognitive capacity. In order to come closer to the real cognitive capacity, the mental representation language can be restricted to some tractable subset of Boolean logic. Examples are restrictions to only positive formulas, only Horn clauses,[7] or only constraints on pairs of variables, possibly only in conjunctive normal form (2-CNF). Such a restriction would make the model fixed-parameter tractable (see Samer and Szeider, 2009), where the parameters would reflect the "syntactic complexity" of the formula, corresponding to a mental representation.

The question of the underlying representation language for categorization may be asked more precisely within the use of machine learning techniques and Bayesian data analysis. Piantadosi, Tenenbaum, and Goodman (2016), using Bayesian concept learning models, ask precisely this question: Which representational system is the most likely, given human responses? Surprisingly, their analysis suggests that intractable fragments are better representation languages than the tractable fragment in terms of Horn clauses. However, the verdict is not yet final, because the authors look at slightly different categorization problems than Feldman and they do not consider other viable tractable representations. This is good news, because clearly there are still many interesting research opportunities in explaining and predicting the complexity of human categorization (see also Colombo, this volume).

Semantic processing

Probably the first serious applications of complexity theory beyond computer science are to be found in modern linguistics. Noam Chomsky started to view language from the computational perspective (Chomsky, 1965), proposing a computability hierarchy of various syntactic fragments of language. Chomsky's famous hierarchy of finite-state, context-free, context-sensitive, and recursive languages opened linguistics to many interactions with computer science and cognitive science. Let us remark at this point that Chomsky's approach is also asymptotic in nature. Even though the sentences we encounter are all of bounded length, he has assumed that they might be arbitrarily long. It was this assumption that directly led to the discovery of the computational model of language generation and the complexity hierarchy. This in turn was the source of the famous debate about how much of computational resources is needed to describe grammars of natural languages (see, e.g., Barton, Berwick, and Ristad, 1987). In other words, the computational approach provided us with methodological constraints on linguistic theories of syntax, as well as empirical predictions.

Already in the 1980s, researchers started to ask tractability questions about the grammatical formalism. Using computational complexity one could study whether a generative formalism is computationally plausible.

Computational complexity of parsing and recognition has become a major topic along with the development of computational linguistics (see, e.g., Barton, Berwick, and Ristad, 1987; Pratt-Hartmann, 2008). To give a very quick summary, the results show that even for relatively simple grammatical frameworks, some problems are intractable. For example, regular and context-free languages have tractable parsing and recognition problems. Already somewhat more complex formalisms, such as Lambek grammars, Tree-Adjoining grammars, Head-Driven Phrase Structure grammar, and context-sensitive grammars, all give rise to intractable problems.

Interestingly, there is also a prominent descriptive complexity spin-off from the grammatical research. Instead of using machine models (such as finite state machines, push-down automata, or Turing machines generating the language), one can specify grammars in terms of general constraints. A string (or a tree) is grammatical if and only if it satisfies the constraints. Naturally, such constraints can be expressed in logic, translating the problem of grammar complexity into the problem of *how much logic is needed to define the grammar*. This leads to some fundamental results: Büchi (1960) has shown that a language is definable by the so-called monadic fragment of second-order logic if and only if it is regular. McNaughton and Papert (1971) have proven that a set of strings is first-order definable if and only if it is star-free.[8] For readers who prefer modal logic to fragments of second-order logic, the following reformulation may seem more attractive: the temporal logic of strings captures star-free languages and propositional dynamic logic captures regular languages (see, e.g., Moss and Tiede, 2006).

More recently, complexity thinking has been applied to some issues in natural language semantics. The earliest results come from a book by Ristad (1993). He provides a complexity analysis of various formal approaches to the problem of dependencies in discourse, such as finding the proper referents for "she" and "her" in the sentences "Yesterday Judith visited Susan for a game of chess. She beat her although she played black". Ristad's conclusion is that this problem is NP-complete and therefore all good formalisms accounting for it and correctly resolving anaphora, should be at least as complex, i.e. NP-complete, but not more complex to avoid overgeneralizations. This very much resembles the argument from the Fixed-parameter Tractability Thesis, i.e. even though the general version of the problem is intractable, the hardness may come from a parameter that is usually very small in linguistic practice. However, as far as we know, to this day nobody has extended Ristad's analysis with new tools of parameterized complexity.[9]

One of the most prominent studies in semantic theory considers quantifier expressions such as "most", "some", or "many". Generalized quantifier theory has studied the descriptive complexity of quantifier meaning. It is well known, for instance, that the meaning of a quantifier like "most" is not definable in first-order logic (even if we restrict ourselves to finite universes) (see Peters and Westerståhl, 2006, for a systematic overview). Van Benthem (1986) started the work of characterizing quantifiers in terms of Chomsky's hierarchy and Szymanik (2010) draws a tractability/intractability border among natural language quantifier constructions. Interestingly, these distinctions turned out to predict cognitive difficulty of quantifier processing, as shown by Szymanik and Zajenkowski (2010) and Schlotterbeck and Bott (2013), respectively. Furthermore, computational complexity even has an impact on the distribution of lexical items in natural language, as recently observed by Szymanik and Thorne (2017) in the statistical analysis of English corpora. Obviously, there are still many open questions in this field, including both mathematical (e.g. parameterized analysis) and cognitive (e.g. modeling) questions (see Szymanik, 2016, for an overview).

Another prominent complexity problem in the semantic literature, pointed out already by Levesque (1988), is to account in a computationally tractable way for the process of linguistic inference: *does one given sentence follow from another given sentence?* This is important both for cognitive science considerations of how people reason and for natural language processing applications, like textual inference in search engines. The problem seems very hard, because inference in even such a simple formal system as Boolean propositional logic is already intractable. Hence, according to the P-Cognition thesis, standard logical systems must outstrip human reasoning capacities. One approach here, known as the Natural Logic Program, is to work bottom-up, formalizing in a computationally minimal way various fragments of natural language (see, e.g., Icard III and Moss, 2014, for an overview). Building on this idea, Pratt-Hartmann (2004) has provided a complexity characterization of reasoning problems in different language fragments. For instance, the satisfiability problem of the syllogistic fragment[10] is in PTIME as opposed to the fragment containing relative clauses,[11] which is NP-complete. These results have already motivated empirical work, both in cognitive modeling (Zhai, Szymanik, and Titov, 2015) and in linguistic analysis (Thorne, 2012).

Social reasoning

In this section we review some interesting puzzles and games in which it is useful for people to reason about one another's knowledge, beliefs, and intentions and we check the relevance of the P-Cognition Thesis and the Fixed-parameter Tractability Thesis for these tasks. The scope of possibilities turns out to be very varied.

Epistemic puzzles

The Muddy Children puzzle is a classical example of reasoning about other people's knowledge. Three children come home after playing outside. Their father says: "At least one of you has mud on your forehead". Then he asks the children: (I) "If you know for sure that you have mud on your forehead, please step forward". The children have common knowledge that their father never lies and that they are all sincere and perfect logical reasoners.[12] Each child can see the mud on the foreheads of the other two, but cannot see his or her own forehead. After the father asks (I) once, all three children remain standing in place. When their father asks the question a second time, however, all muddy children – in this case the two children b and c – respond by stepping forward, meaning that they know that they have mud on their foreheads. How could they have figured this out?

In epistemic logic, this puzzle is usually modeled using eight possible worlds, corresponding to the 2^3 different possible combinations of muddiness and cleanness of the three children a, b, c. For example, world $(0, 1, 1)$ would correspond to child a being clean and children b and c being muddy. Two worlds are joined by an accessibility edge for agent $i \in \{a, b, c\}$, if i cannot distinguish between the two worlds on the basis of his or her information. At successive states of the puzzle story, the agents' knowledge grows and more and more of these accessibility relations can be deleted, until the resulting possible worlds model only contains one world, namely the current real situation $(0, 1, 1)$ with three accessibility relations to itself only, for each agent a, b, c (see, e.g., van Ditmarsch, van der Hoek, and Kooi, 2007; Fagin et al., 1995).

For the above version of the muddy children puzzle with only three children, the solution based on possible worlds models as seen from the global perspective of the outside puzzle solver is elegant. However, it is hardly scalable, because a version of the puzzle with n children requires possible worlds models with 2^n worlds. Of course this is problematic in the context of the P-Cognition Thesis. It is intuitively implausible that actual human beings generate such exponential-sized models of all possible scenarios when they solve the muddy children puzzle for n children, because it is computationally intractable, requiring exponential time with respect to the number of agents. What is required here is a new local perspective, a study of reasoning about other agents' knowledge from the perspective of the agents involved. Such more local representations and epistemic logics are more cognitively plausible. Gierasimczuk and Szymanik (2011b; 2011a), based on results from the theory of general quantifiers, propose to use local representations for several variants of the muddy children puzzle for n agents. Surprisingly, the total size of the initial model that they need is only $2n + 1$. As a result, the proposed representation is exponentially more succinct than the standard dynamic epistemic logic approach (see, e.g., van Ditmarsch, van der Hoek, and Kooi, 2007) and their solution is tractable, bringing the puzzle into the realm of the P-Cognition Thesis. Dégremont et al. (2014) develop a general approach to local semantics for dynamic epistemic logics.

Theory of mind in story tasks

Theory of mind is the ability to reason about other people's mental states, such as their beliefs, knowledge, and intentions. Many studies appear to show that only when they are around four years of age do children learn that other people may have beliefs different than their own (but see the discussion on infants' precursors of theory of mind in McLeod and Mitchell, this volume).

Understanding that this ability can be applied recursively, such as in the second-order attribution "She doesn't know that I know that she wrote the anonymous Valentine card", starts even later, between five and seven years of age (Arslan, Hohenberger, and Verbrugge, 2017). Adults usually understand stories in which third-order theory of mind plays a role, but have difficulty answering questions at higher levels (Kinderman, Dunbar, and Bentall, 1998; Stiller and Dunbar, 2007). Theory of mind is often tested by asking experimental participants questions about stories starting from an initial situation, in which both the facts and the characters' first-order and second-order knowledge change a few times. The observer then needs to answer questions about a belief or knowledge statement of interest, such as "Does Ayla know that Murat knows that she moved the chocolate bar to the toy box?"

Recently, for the first time, this problem of dynamic knowledge update has been formalized on the basis of dynamic epistemic logic. Iris van de Pol, van Rooij, and Szymanik (2018) show that the problem, restricted to S5 models (in which the accessibility relations are reflexive, transitive, and symmetric) with a salient "real world", is PSPACE complete.[13] This is a surprisingly high level of complexity, considering that $P \subseteq NP \subseteq PSPACE$ and that most complexity theorists expect P and PSPACE to be different.[14] Even worse, it is not easy to prove parameterized tractability results for the belief update problem. Only if both the maximum number of events per update and the number of updates remain small, so that the final updated model remains small as well, does the dynamic belief update problem become fixed-parameter tractable (van de Pol, van Rooij, and Szymanik, 2018). Indeed it appears that in standard experimental false belief tasks, the number of actions and the number of events per action do stay small (Bolander, 2014), but that may not be the case for real-world belief update problems.

Perhaps most surprisingly, the order of theory of mind, corresponding to the modal depth of the formula that needs to be checked, does not play much of a role in the intractability of the dynamic belief update problem that participants in a false belief task need to solve: even for formulas of modal depth one, the problem remains intractable when the number of events per update or the number of updates grows large (van de Pol, van Rooij, and Szymanik, 2018). This contrasts with the literature showing that, all children learn first-order false belief tasks much earlier than second-order ones, even if the number of events per update and the number of updates remain the same (Arslan, Taatgen, and Verbrugge, 2017; Miller, 2009).

To move from first-order to second-order tasks, children have to keep separate the real situation (the chocolate in the toy box) both from Murat's belief about the chocolate and from Ayla's false belief about Murat's belief. Thus, they have to keep intermediate solutions in mind when asked a second-order question. It requires sophisticated complex memory skills to pass such a serial processing bottleneck. The serial processing bottleneck hypothesis (Verbrugge, 2009) is based on the finding that working memory acts as a bottleneck: people can only hold one chunk of information in working memory at a time (Borst, Taatgen, and van Rijn, 2010). This suggests that children need complex working memory strategies in order to process embedded beliefs in such a way that chunks of information can pass through the working memory bottleneck within that time threshold. It has indeed been shown that complex memory tasks (and not simple memory tasks) predict children's accuracy in second-order false belief tasks (Arslan, Hohenberger, and Verbrugge, 2017).

Strategic reasoning in dynamic games

Another surprise emerges when turning from how people apply theory of mind in false belief tasks to how they apply it in dynamic turn-taking games. It has been shown that children learn to apply second-order theory of mind in competitive dynamic games based on centipede-like

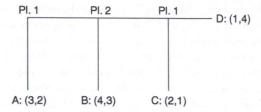

Figure 25.1 Game tree for a centipede-like game in which Player 1 chooses first; if she goes right, then Player 2 chooses, and if Player 2 also goes right, finally Player 1 chooses again. The pairs at leaves A, B, C, and D represent the payoffs of Player 1 and Player 2, respectively, if the game ends up there. Both players have the goal to gain an optimal individual pay-off for themselves. Therefore, the optimal move for Player 1 at the first decision point would be to go right, reasoning: "Player 2 *believes* that I *plan* to go down to C at my final decision point, which is not good for him, so he *plans* to move down to B, which is optimal for me"

game trees such as the one in Figure 25.1 only a few years after they have mastered second-order false belief tasks (Flobbe et al., 2008; Raijmakers et al., 2012) and even adults do not seem to be very good at such games (Hedden and Zhang, 2002). However, participants whose reasoning processes have been "scaffolded" by an intuitive presentation of the game or by step-wise training, which progresses from simple decisions without any opponent, through games that require first-order reasoning ("the opponent plans to go right at the next trapdoor"), to games that require second-order reasoning ("the opponent thinks that I plan to go left at the last trapdoor") learn to play the game almost perfectly (Goodie, Doshi, and Young, 2012; Meijering et al., 2011; Verbrugge et al., 2018).

Meijering et al. (2014) have constructed computational cognitive models to explain why people do not spontaneously start applying second-order theory of mind in competitive dynamic games. The model is based on the idea that theory of mind reasoning is effortful and that people first try out simpler strategies, only moving up a level of theory of mind when they lose too often, until they converge on a reasoning strategy that is "as simple as possible, as complex as necessary".[15] Their model turns out to fit the data of both the adults and the children of the earlier experiments (Meijering et al., 2011; Verbrugge et al., 2018; Flobbe et al., 2008).

All the centipede-like turn-taking games used in the experiments are most efficiently solved using backward induction, an inductive algorithm defined on a game tree (Osborne and Rubinstein, 1994). The backward induction algorithm tells us which sequence of actions will be chosen by agents that want to maximize their own payoffs, assuming common knowledge of rationality. Szymanik (2013) showed that backward induction is PTIME-complete with respect to the size of the game tree. So contrary to expectation, solving dynamic games is tractable and does comply with the P-Cognition Thesis, whereas solving false belief tasks does not.

Even though backward induction is the most efficient strategy, an eye-tracking study suggests that it is not necessarily the strategy that participants really use in centipede-like games; they seem instead to favor a form of "forward reasoning plus backtracking" and they look a lot at the decision points, not only at the payoffs at the leaves (Meijering et al., 2012). This reasoning strategy corresponds to the adagium "first try something simple that has worked in other contexts in the past" and is akin to causal reasoning, as in: "If I choose right, then what will my opponent do at the next decision point? Oh, he will choose left, but that's bad for me, so I better go left now to prevent it". Szymanik, Meijering, and Verbrugge (2013) and Bergwerff et al. (2014) have made computational models of the two reasoning strategies and have fit them to the participants' reaction time data, corroborating that the participants do use forward reasoning plus backtracking more than backward induction.

But which reasoning strategies do people actually use in specific games? Ghosh, Meijering, and Verbrugge (2014) and Ghosh and Verbrugge (2018) formulated a logical strategy language that can be turned into computational cognitive models and they used these models to rule out certain reasoning strategies based on the predictions on choices and reaction times from the simulations of the models' "virtual strategizers" in several variations of dynamic games, including ones with non-rational opponents (such as Ghosh et al., 2017). It would be interesting to apply these methods also to dynamic negotiation games, in which people also do not apply second-order theory of mind spontaneously, even though it leads to win–win solutions, but can be trained by a second-order theory of mind software opponent to do so (de Weerd, Verbrugge, and Verheij, 2017), as well as to cooperative games such as the Tacit Communication Game, where theory of mind is very useful to coordinate on signals but it is not clear whether people really apply it, although at least first-order theory of mind appears to be likely (van Rooij et al., 2011; Blokpoel et al., 2012; de Weerd, Verbrugge, and Verheij, 2015).

Conclusions

This book takes the computational perspective on cognition. In this chapter, we focus on the perspective of tractability: Is a specific cognitive task doable in general within a reasonable time and using reasonable memory space? A formal analysis of an information-processing task that takes tractability seriously generates empirical predictions, which can be tested by experiments. Using computational cognitive models, for example, in a cognitive architecture such as SOAR or ACT-R, leads to very precise predictions, for example, about reaction times and sequences of places on the screen where participants will look at certain moments during an experiment. The outcomes of these experiments may later feed back into revisions of the formal theory and the computational cognitive model.

It turns out that the P-Cognition Thesis, stating that human cognitive capacities are constrained by polynomial time computability, provides a fruitful lens for assessing cognitive tasks. Some well-known cognitive tasks, however, appear to be NP-complete. In that case, sometimes a more relaxed thesis, the Fixed-parameter Tractability Thesis, comes to the rescue. Some NP-complete tasks turn out to be fixed-parameter tractable: the intractability comes from the problem's deterministic time complexity being exponential in some parameters that are usually very small in practice, no matter the size of the input as a whole. Such problems should still be tractable for the human mind, in contexts where the "guilty" parameters can indeed be shown to be small. In other words, if the inputs have a helpful structure, the problem becomes tractable after all.

We have illustrated the cycle from complexity-theoretic analyses, through computational models and empirical results back to theory, by way of a number of specific examples in Boolean categorization, semantic processing in natural language, and social reasoning in story tasks, puzzles, and games. Many well-known tasks indeed turn out to be solvable in PTIME or can be shown to be fixed-parameter tractable by choosing an appropriate representation. Sometimes intuitions about which tasks are easy and which tasks are hard do not perfectly match with the complexity-theoretic analysis. For those cognitive tasks, the perceived complexity for the human mind may come from the required complicated working memory strategies, in which intermediate solutions need to be stored and correctly applied. In any case, when studying the computational mind, knowledge about tractability and fixed-parameter tractability proves to be an essential element of the cognitive scientist's toolbox.

Acknowledgments

The research of the first author leading to these results has received funding from the European Research Council under the European Union's Seventh Framework Programme (FP/2007–2013) / ERC Grant Agreement n. STG 716230 CoSaQ. The work of the second author on social cognition has been supported by Vici grant NWO-227-80-00.

Notes

1 Size of an input formula is often defined as its length in terms of number of symbols and size of a model is often defined as the number of elements of its universe. However, different contexts may require different definitions of the sizes involved.

2 In the context of this chapter we assume, like many computer scientists, that the open question whether P=NP has a negative answer; see the next paragraph for a precise explanation.

3 An example of combinatorial explosion happens when you try all valuations, that is, all combinations of truth values of the relevant propositional atoms, to find out whether a given formula is satisfiable (see Example 1).

4 Thus, an NP-hard problem may require time polynomial in the size of the input but exponential in a fixed parameter. For example, the satisfiability problem of Example 1 can be parameterized by the number of different atomic variables. A formula of size n with k atomic variables can be evaluated by checking all relevant valuations, which takes time of the order $n \times 2^k$. So for formulas that contain only three atomic variables, it appears to be tractable for people to check the satisfiability of quite long formulas.

5 One reason corresponds to the fact that $p \wedge q$ is true in just one of the four lines in a truth table while $p \vee q$ is true in three of them.

6 Interestingly, finding the shortest formula is intractable.

7 A Horn clause is a disjunction of literals in which at most one of the disjuncts is a (positive) propositional variable.

8 Regular star-free languages have Boolean operators like concatenation and union of two elements, but not the Kleene star (which allows any finite concatenation of elements of the language).

9 Szymanik (2016) gives another defense for Ristad's thesis in terms of inferential meaning and indirect computability.

10 The syllogistic fragment of first-order logic only contains sentences corresponding to "All As are B", "Some As are B", "Some As are not B" and "No As are B", where A and B are unary predicates.

11 In addition to the syllogistic fragment, this fragment also contains sentences such as "Every A who is not C is B".

12 Common knowledge means informally that all the children know, all the children know that they all know, and so on, *ad infinitum* (for more explanation and a formal definition see, for example, van Ditmarsch, Eijck, and Verbrugge, 2009).

13 It turns out that this is the same complexity class that was independently found for a similar problem, namely model checking in epistemic planning (Bolander et al., 2015).

14 The question P=?PSPACE remains a famous open problem, just like P=?NP.

15 The authors here use 'complex' informally in the sense of cognitively difficult.

References

Aaronson, S. (2013) 'Why Philosophers Should Care about Computational Complexity', in Copeland, J., Posy, C.J., and Shagrir, O. (eds.) *Computability: Turing, Gödel, Church, and Beyond*. Cambridge, MA: MIT Press, pp. 261–328.

Arora, S. and Barak, B. (2009) *Computational Complexity: A Modern Approach*, 1st ed. New York, NY: Cambridge University Press.

Arslan, B., Hohenberger, A., and Verbrugge, R. (2017) 'Syntactic Recursion Facilitates and Working Memory Predicts Recursive Theory of Mind', *PLoS ONE*, 12 (1), e0169510.

Arslan, B., Taatgen, N., and Verbrugge, R. (2017) 'Five-year-olds' Systematic Errors in Second-order False Belief Tasks Are Due to First-order Theory of Mind Strategy Selection: A Computational Modeling

Study', *Frontiers in Psychology: Cognitive Science*, 8 (275). Available at: https://doi.org/10.3389/fpsyg.2017.00275.

Barton, E.G., Berwick, R., and Ristad, E.S. (1987) *Computational Complexity and Natural Language.* Cambridge, MA: MIT Press.

Bergwerff, G. et al. (2014) 'Computational and Algorithmic Models of Strategies in Turn-based Games', in Bello, P. et al. (eds.) *Proceedings of the 36th Annual Conference of the Cognitive Science Society*, pp. 1778–1783.

Blokpoel, M. et al. (2012) 'Recipient Design in Human Communication: Simple Heuristics or Perspective Taking?', *Frontiers in Human Neuroscience*, 6 (253). Available at: DOI:10.3389/fnhum.2012.00253.

Bolander, T. (2014) 'Seeing Is Believing: Formalising False-belief Tasks in Dynamic Epistemic Logic', *CEUR Workshop Proceedings*, 1283, pp. 87–107.

Bolander, T. et al. (2015) 'Complexity Results in Epistemic Planning', *Proceedings IJCAI 2015*, pp. 2791–2797.

Borst, J.P., Taatgen, N.A., and van Rijn, H. (2010) 'The Problem State: A Cognitive Bottleneck in Multitasking', *Journal of Experimental Psychology: Learning, Memory, and Cognition*, 36 (2), pp. 363–382.

Bruner, J.S., Goodnow, J.J., and Austin, G.A. (1956) *A Study of Thinking.* New York, NY: Science Editions.

Büchi, J. (1960) 'Weak Second-order Arithmetic and Finite Automata', *Zeitschrift für Mathematische Logik und Grundlagen der Mathematik*, 6, pp. 66–92.

Chomsky, N. (1957) *Syntactic Structures.* The Hague: Mouton.

Chomsky, N. (1965) *Aspects of the Theory of Syntax.* Cambridge, MA: MIT Press.

Cobham, A. (1965) 'The Intrinsic Computational Difficulty of Functions', in Bar-Hillel, Y. (ed.) *Proceedings of the 1964 Congress for Logic, Methodology, and the Philosophy of Science.* Jerusalem: North-Holland Publishing, pp. 24–30.

Cook, S.A. (1971) 'The Complexity of Theorem-proving Procedures', *STOC '71: Proceedings of the Third Annual ACM Symposium on Theory of Computing.* New York, NY: ACM Press, pp. 151–158.

Cooper, B.S. (2003) *Computability Theory. Mathematical Series.* London: Chapman & Hall/CRC.

Dégremont, C., Kurzen, L., and Szymanik, J. (2014) 'Exploring the Tractability Border in Epistemic Tasks', *Synthese*, 191 (3), pp. 371–408.

Deineko, V.G. et al. (2006) 'The Traveling Salesman Problem with Few Inner Points', *Operations Research Letters*, 34 (1), pp. 106–110.

de Weerd, H., Verbrugge, R., and Verheij, B. (2015) 'Higher-order Theory of Mind in the Tacit Communication Game', *Biologically Inspired Cognitive Architectures*, 11, pp. 10–21.

de Weerd, H., Verbrugge, R., and Verheij, B. (2017) 'Negotiating with Other Minds: The Role of Recursive Theory of Mind in Negotiation with Incomplete Information', *Autonomous Agents and Multi-Agent Systems*, 31, pp. 250–287.

Downey, R.G. and Fellows, M.R. (1998) *Parameterized Complexity. Monographs in Computer Science.* New York, NY: Springer.

Edmonds, J. (1965) 'Paths, Trees, and Flowers', *Canadian Journal of Mathematics*, 17, pp. 449–467.

Fagin, R. (1974) 'Generalized First-order Spectra and Polynomial Time Recognizable Sets', in Karp, R. (ed.) *Complexity of Computation*, SIAM – AMS Proceedings, 7. Providence, RI: American Mathematical Society, pp. 43–73.

Fagin, R. et al. (1995) *Reasoning about Knowledge.* Cambridge, MA: MIT Press.

Feldman, J. (2000) 'Minimization of Boolean Complexity in Human Concept Learning', *Nature*, 407 (6804), pp. 630–633.

Flobbe, L. et al. (2008) 'Children's Application of Theory of Mind in Reasoning and Language', *Journal of Logic, Language and Information*, 17 (4), pp. 417–442.

Frixione, M. (2001) 'Tractable Competence', *Minds and Machines*, 11 (3), pp. 379–397.

Garey, M.R. and Johnson, D.S. (1990) *Computers and Intractability: A Guide to the Theory of NP-Completeness.* New York, NY: W.H. Freeman.

Gasarch, W.I. (2012) 'Guest Column: The Second P =?NP Poll', *SIGACT News*, 43 (2), pp. 53–77.

Ghosh, S., Meijering, B., and Verbrugge, R. (2014) 'Strategic Reasoning: Building Cognitive Models from Logical Formulas', *Journal of Logic, Language and Information*, 23 (1), pp. 1–29.

Ghosh, S. and Verbrugge, R. (2018) 'Studying Strategies and Types of Players: Experiments, Logics and Cognitive Models', *Synthese.* Available at: DOI: 10.1007/s11229-017-1338-7.

Ghosh, S. et al. (2017) 'What Drives People's Choices in Turn-taking Games, if Not Game-theoretic Rationality?', in Lang, J. (ed.) *Proceedings of the 16th Conference on Theoretical Aspects of Rationality and Knowledge*, pp. 265–284.

Gierasimczuk, N. and Szymanik, J. (2011a) 'Invariance Properties of Quantifiers and Multiagent Information Exchange', in Kanazawa, M. et al. (eds.) *Proceedings of 12th Meeting on Mathematics of Language*, 6878. Berlin: Springer, pp. 72–89.

Gierasimczuk, N. and Szymanik, J. (2011b) 'A Note on a Generalization of the Muddy Children Puzzle', in Apt, K.R. (ed.) *Proceedings of the 13th Conference on Theoretical Aspects of Rationality and Knowledge*. New York, NY: ACM Digital Library, pp. 257–264.

Goodie, A.S., Doshi, P., and Young, D.L. (2012) 'Levels of Theory-of-Mind Reasoning in Competitive Games', *Journal of Behavioral Decision Making*, 25 (1), pp. 95–108.

Hedden, T. and Zhang, J. (2002) 'What Do You Think I Think You Think?: Strategic Reasoning in Matrix Games', *Cognition*, 85 (1), pp. 1–36.

Icard III, T. and Moss, L. (2014) 'Recent Progress in Monotonicity', *Linguistic Issues in Language Technology*, 9, pp. 167–194.

Immerman, N. (1998) *Descriptive Complexity: Texts in Computer Science*. New York, NY: Springer.

Isaac, A., Szymanik, J., and Verbrugge, R. (2014) 'Logic and Complexity in Cognitive Science', in Baltag, A. and Smets, S. (eds.) *Johan van Benthem on Logic and Information Dynamics*, Outstanding Contributions to Logic, vol. 5. New York, NY: Springer, pp. 787–824.

Karp, R.M. (1972) 'Reducibility among Combinatorial Problems', in Miller, R.E. and Thatcher, J.W. (eds.) *Complexity of Computer Computations*. New York, NY: Plenum Press, pp. 85–103.

Kinderman, P., Dunbar, R., and Bentall, R.P. (1998) 'Theory-of-Mind Deficits and Causal Attributions', *British Journal of Psychology*, 89 (2), pp. 191–204.

Levesque, H.J. (1988) 'Logic and the Complexity of Reasoning', *Journal of Philosophical Logic*, 17 (4), pp. 355–389.

McNaughton, R. and Papert, S.A. (1971) *Counter-Free Automata*. MIT Research Monograph no. 65. Cambridge, MA: MIT Press.

Meijering, B. et al. (2011) 'I Do Know What You Think I Think: Second-order Theory of Mind in Strategic Games Is Not That Difficult', in *Proceedings of the 33rd Annual Meeting of the Cognitive Science Society*. Boston, MA: Cognitive Science Society.

Meijering, B. et al. (2012) 'What Eye Movements Can Tell about Theory of Mind in a Strategic Game', *PLoS ONE*, 7 (9), e45961.

Meijering, B. et al. (2014) 'Modeling Inference of Mental States: As Simple as Possible, as Complex as Necessary', *Interaction Studies*, 15 (3), pp. 455–477.

Miller, S.A. (2009) 'Children's Understanding of Second-order Mental States', *Psychological Bulletin*, 135 (5), p. 749.

Moschovakis, Y. (2001) 'What Is an Algorithm?', in Enquist, B. and Schmid, W. (eds.) *Mathematics Unlimited: 2001 and Beyond*. New York, NY: Springer, pp. 919–936.

Moss, L. and Tiede, H.J. (2006) 'Applications of Modal Logic in Linguistics', in Blackburn, P., van Benthem, J., and Wolter, F. (eds.) *Handbook of Modal Logic*, Studies in Logic and Practical Reasoning. Amsterdam: Elsevier Science, pp. 1031–1077.

Osborne, M.J. and Rubinstein, A. (1994) *A Course in Game Theory*. Cambridge, MA: MIT Press.

Peters, S. and Westerståhl, D. (2006) *Quantifiers in Language and Logic*. Oxford: Clarendon Press.

Piantadosi, S.T., Tenenbaum, J.B., and Goodman, N.D. (2016) 'The Logical Primitives of Thought: Empirical Foundations for Compositional Cognitive Models', *Psychological Review*, 123 (4), p. 392–424.

Pratt-Hartmann, I. (2004) 'Fragments of Language', *Journal of Logic, Language and Information*, 13 (2), pp. 207–223.

Pratt-Hartmann, I. (2008) 'Computational Complexity in Natural Language', in Clark, A., Fox, C., and Lappin, S. (eds.) *Computational Linguistics and Natural Language Processing Handbook*. New Jersey: Blackwell.

Raijmakers, M.E. et al. (2012) 'Children's Strategy Use When Playing Strategic Games', *Synthese*, 191 (3), pp. 355–370.

Ristad, E.S. (1993) *The Language Complexity Game*. Artificial Intelligence. Cambridge, MA: MIT Press.

Samer, M. and Szeider, S. (2009) 'Fixed-parameter Tractability', in Biere, A., Heule, M., and van Maaren, H. (eds.) *Handbook of Satisfiability*. Amsterdam: IOS Press, pp. 363–393.

Schlotterbeck, F. and Bott, O. (2013) 'Easy Solutions for a Hard Problem? The Computational Complexity of Reciprocals with Quantificational Antecedents', *Journal of Logic, Language and Information*, 22 (4), pp. 363–390.

Shepard, R.N., Hovland, C.I., and Jenkins, H.M. (1961) 'Learning and Memorization of Classifications', *Psychological Monographs: General and Applied*, 75 (13), pp. 1–42.

Stiller, J. and Dunbar, R.I. (2007) 'Perspective-taking and Memory Capacity Predict Social Network Size', *Social Networks*, 29 (1), pp. 93–104.

Szymanik, J. (2010) 'Computational Complexity of Polyadic Lifts of Generalized Quantifiers in Natural Language', *Linguistics and Philosophy*, 33 (3), pp. 215–250.

Szymanik, J. (2013) 'Backward Induction Is PTIME-Complete', in Grossi, D., Roy, O., and Huang, H. (eds.) *Proceedings of the Fourth International Workshop on Logic, Rationality and Interaction*, LNCS 8196. Heidelberg: Springer, pp. 352–356.

Szymanik, J. (2016) *Quantifiers and Cognition: Logical and Computational Perspectives*. Studies in Linguistics and Philosophy. New York, NY: Springer.

Szymanik, J., Meijering, B., and Verbrugge, R. (2013) 'Using Intrinsic Complexity of Turn-taking Games to Predict Participants' Reaction Times', in Knauff, M. et al. (eds.) *Proceedings of the 35th Annual Conference of the Cognitive Science Society*. Austin, TX: Cognitive Science Society, pp. 1426–1432.

Szymanik, J. and Thorne, C. (2017) 'Exploring the Relation of Semantic Complexity and Quantifier Distribution in Large Corpora', *Language Sciences*, 60, pp. 80–93.

Szymanik, J. and Zajenkowski, M. (2010) 'Comprehension of Simple Quantifiers. Empirical Evaluation of a Computational Model', *Cognitive Science: A Multidisciplinary Journal*, 34 (3), pp. 521–532.

Thorne, C. (2012) 'Studying the Distribution of Fragments of English Using Deep Semantic Annotation', in Bunt, H. (ed.) *Proceedings of the ISA8 Workshop*. SIGSEM.

Tsotsos, J. (1990) 'Analyzing Vision at the Complexity Level', *Behavioral and Brain Sciences*, 13 (3), pp. 423–469.

van Benthem, J. (1986) *Essays in Logical Semantics*. Dordrecht: Reidel.

van de Pol, I., van Rooij, I. and Szymanik, J., and (2018) 'Parametrized Complexity of Theory of Mind Reasoning in Dynamic Epistemic Logic', *Journal of Logic, Language and Information*. Available at: https://doi.org/10.1007/s10849-018-9268-4.

van Ditmarsch, H., Eijck, J.V., and Verbrugge, R. (2009) 'Common Knowledge and Common Belief', in Eijck, J.V. and Verbrugge, R. (eds.) *Discourses on Social Software*. Amsterdam: Amsterdam University Press, pp. 99–122.

van Ditmarsch, H., van der Hoek, W., and Kooi, B. (2007) *Dynamic Epistemic Logic*. Dordrecht: Springer.

van Rooij, I. (2008) 'The Tractable Cognition Thesis', *Cognitive Science: A Multidisciplinary Journal*, 32 (6), pp. 939–984.

van Rooij, I. et al. (2011) 'Intentional Communication: Computationally Easy or Difficult?', *Frontiers in Human Neuroscience*, 5 (0), pp. 1–18.

Verbrugge, R. (2009) 'Logic and Social Cognition: The Facts Matter, and So Do Computational Models', *Journal of Philosophical Logic*, 38 (6), pp. 649–680.

Verbrugge, R. et al. (2018) 'Stepwise Training Supports Strategic Second-order Theory of Mind in Turn-taking Games', *Judgment and Decision Making*, 13 (1), pp. 79–98.

Zhai, F., Szymanik, J., and Titov, I. (2015) 'Toward a Probabilistic Mental Logic for the Syllogistic Fragment of Natural Language', in Brochhagen, T., Roelofsen, F., and Theiler, N. (eds.) *Proceedings of the 20th Amsterdam Colloquium*, pp. 468–477.

PART IV

Applications

26

COMPUTATIONAL COGNITIVE NEUROSCIENCE

Carlos Zednik

Introduction

Computational cognitive neuroscience lies at the intersection of computational neuroscience, which aims to describe structures and processes in the brain through computational modeling and mathematical analysis, and cognitive neuroscience, which aims to explain behavior and cognition through the identification and description of neural mechanisms. Computational cognitive neuroscience invokes the descriptive tools of the former to achieve the explanatory aims of the latter: computational models and mathematical analyses are used to identify and describe not just any structures and processes in the brain, but just those structures and processes that constitute the mechanisms of behavior and cognition.

Like investigators in other branches of neuroscience, computational cognitive neuroscientists rely on neuroscientific measurement techniques such as single-cell recording, functional magnetic resonance imaging (fMRI), and electroencephalography (EEG). Much more so than their colleagues in other branches of the discipline, however, computational cognitive neuroscientists additionally invoke formal methods developed in theoretical disciplines such as artificial intelligence, machine learning, statistics, mathematical physics, and the science of complex systems. These formal methods contribute to the aims of computational cognitive neuroscience in at least two ways. For one, they allow researchers to describe mechanisms not merely as consisting of certain neural structures and processes, but also as possessing particular computational, dynamical, and/or topological properties. For another, these formal methods facilitate the task of discovering such mechanisms in the first place. For example, if an algorithm is known to be particularly effective for simulating behavior and cognition on a computer, it may inspire computational cognitive neuroscientists to look for implementations of similar algorithms in the brain.

This chapter provides a methodological overview of computational cognitive neuroscience, centering on a distinction between two widely used research strategies. On the one hand, *top-down* (or "reverse-engineering") strategies are used to infer, from formal characterizations of behavior and cognition, the function and structure of neural mechanisms. On the other hand, *bottom-up* strategies are used to identify and describe neural mechanisms and their formal properties, and to reconstruct their contributions to specific kinds of behavior and cognition. Although both research strategies simultaneously rely on neuroscientific measurement techniques and formal methods, they do so in markedly different ways. Moreover, both strategies can be used to understand cognitive systems at several different *levels of analysis* (Marr, 1982), and to thereby deliver *mechanistic explanations* of these systems' behavioral and cognitive capacities (Bechtel, 2008; Craver, 2007).[1]

In what follows, the top-down and bottom-up research strategies will be contrasted through a series of examples. These examples also illustrate the diversity of formal methods being used, including methods to approximate Bayesian inference, methods to characterize stochastic processes, artificial neural network models, and analytic techniques from graph theory, dynamical systems theory, and information theory. Each example shows how computational cognitive neuroscientists go about discovering and describing the mechanisms responsible for specific behavioral and cognitive phenomena. At the same time, these examples reveal the characteristic limitations of the top-down and bottom-up strategies. Thus, explanatory success in computational cognitive neuroscience may in fact require a bidirectional approach.

Starting with behavior: top-down strategies

One of the most widespread research strategies in computational cognitive neuroscience is a top-down (or "reverse-engineering") strategy inspired by David Marr's influential work on visual perception (Marr, 1982). Marr sought to understand the visual system by analyzing it at three distinct *levels of analysis* (see also Elber-Dorozko and Shagrir, this volume). At the *computational* level of analysis, he sought to answer questions about what the system is doing and why it is doing it. These questions are answered by specifying a mathematical function that describes the system's behavior, and by determining the extent to which this function reflects a relevant property or regularity in the environment (Shagrir, 2010). At the *algorithmic* level, Marr considered questions about how the system does what it does. These questions can be answered by specifying the individual steps of an algorithm for computing or approximating the mathematical function that describes the cognitive system's behavior. Finally, at the *implementational* level of analysis, Marr was concerned with questions about where in the brain the relevant algorithms are actually realized, by identifying individual steps of an algorithm with the activity of particular neural structures. By analyzing the visual system at all three levels of analysis, Marr sought to simultaneously describe the physical and computational properties of the mechanism responsible for visual perception (see also Bechtel and Shagrir, 2015; Piccinini and Craver, 2011; Zednik, 2017).

Although Marr deemed all three levels critical for the purposes of "completely understanding" a cognitive system (Marr, 1982, p. 4), he argued that the best way to develop such an understanding would be to begin by answering questions at the computational level and to work downwards:

> Although algorithms and mechanisms are empirically more accessible, it is the top level, the level of computational theory, which is critically important from an information-processing point of view. The reason for this is that ... an algorithm is likely to be understood more readily by understanding the nature of the problem being solved than by understanding the mechanism (and the hardware) in which it is embodied.
>
> *(Marr, 1982, p. 27; see also Dennett, 1994)*

Thus, Marr's top-down strategy involves using answers already available at higher levels of analysis to constrain the answers that might be given to questions at lower levels (Zednik and Jäkel, 2016). In other words, reverse-engineering is a matter of *inferring* the function and structure of mechanisms from (among others) prior characterizations of the behavioral and cognitive phenomena for which they are deemed responsible.[2]

Many past and present research efforts in computational cognitive neuroscience pursue this kind of reverse-engineering strategy. To this end, they often take as their starting point characterizations of behavior and cognition previously developed in disciplines such as cognitive psychology and psychophysics. Frequently, these characterizations take the form of statistical models of behavioral data. For example, the investigation of perceptual decision making introduced below aims to uncover the neural mechanisms responsible for the characteristic shape of response-time distributions in human subjects (Cao et al., 2016). Similarly, the studies of human categorization reviewed later in this section begin with a model in which the explanandum phenomenon is characterized as a form of Bayesian probabilistic inference (Anderson, 1991b; Sanborn, Griffiths, and Navarro, 2010). That said, computational-level characterizations of behavior and cognition need not be statistical; many reverse-engineers in computational cognitive neuroscience begin with characterizations of behavior and cognition as forms of information processing, in which inputs are deterministically transformed into outputs (e.g. Marr and Hildreth, 1980), or as dynamical trajectories through a multidimensional state-space with characteristic regions of stability and instability.

Investigators often have a choice to make about how to describe an explanandum phenomenon at the computational level. For example, an agent's reaching behavior might be characterized probabilistically, as the likelihood of reaching toward a particular target, but also dynamically, as a continuous trajectory through space and time. Such descriptive choices are not without consequence; the particular way in which a phenomenon is described can have a profound effect on the mechanisms that are likely to be discovered. This is because, given a formal characterization of the explanandum phenomenon at the computational level, the top-down strategy proceeds by identifying one or more algorithms with which to compute or approximate the mathematical function used in that characterization. Algorithms may be viewed as descriptions of the functional processes that contribute to a cognitive system's behavior: the component operations and functional organization of the mechanism responsible for that behavior (Zednik, 2017). Unfortunately, the identification of algorithms is often hampered by a considerable degree of uncertainty: many different algorithms serve to compute or approximate any particular mathematical function, and investigators are tasked with identifying the algorithm that is *actually* used by the relevant cognitive system, from among many algorithms that it might *possibly* use (Piccinini and Craver, 2011). In order to deal with this kind of uncertainty, many advocates of the top-down approach deploy *heuristics* to constrain the search space of possible alternatives (Simon, 1998; Zednik and Jäkel, 2016). Although fallible – the chosen heuristic might highlight an algorithm that is not actually implemented by the target system – these heuristics are instrumental for the purposes of efficiently formulating testable hypotheses at the algorithmic level of analysis.

One intuitive heuristic for formulating testable hypotheses at the algorithmic level is the *mirroring heuristic*. This heuristic is deployed whenever investigators assume that functional processes in the brain exhibit the same mathematical structure as the explanandum phenomenon under a particular formal characterization. The use of this heuristic ensures that the particular mathematical formalism that is invoked at the computational level has a direct influence on the hypotheses that will actually be considered at the algorithmic level. Perhaps the clearest recent example of the mirroring heuristic at work can be observed in recent efforts to motivate the *Bayesian coding hypothesis* (Knill and Pouget, 2004; Ma et al., 2006). Motivated by characterizations of behavior and cognition as forms of optimal probabilistic inference – in which sensory evidence is combined with prior beliefs in accordance with Bayes' rule

(Anderson, 1991a; Oaksford and Chater, 2001) – proponents of this hypothesis argue that neural mechanisms themselves implement probability distributions, and compute over them using (close approximations of) Bayes' rule (see also Colombo and Hartmann, 2015; Zednik and Jäkel, 2014).

Although the mirroring heuristic may be intuitive and easy to deploy, it is also potentially misleading. As has already been stated above, many different algorithms serve to compute or approximate any particular mathematical function. Thus, there is no reason to believe, from behavioral evidence alone, that the brain actually implements just the one algorithm that most accurately reflects the mathematical structure of the phenomenon being explained (see also Maloney and Mamassian, 2009). Moreover, in some cases the mathematical characterizations used at the computational level are such that the mirroring heuristic would yield algorithms that are psychologically or biologically implausible. For example, it is well-known that the generic algorithm for solving problems of optimal probabilistic inference via Bayes' rule is, in general, computationally intractable (Kwisthout, Wareham, and van Rooij, 2011). For this reason, the explanatory success of the top-down strategy is likely to depend on the use of heuristics more nuanced than mirroring.

One such heuristic may be the *tools-to-theories heuristic* (Gigerenzer, 1991). This heuristic is deployed whenever investigators assume that the algorithms implemented in the brain resemble an instrument, tool, or analytic technique that has previously been used to measure, study, or describe the behavioral or cognitive phenomenon being investigated. Notably, researchers in theoretical disciplines such as computer science, artificial intelligence, machine learning, and statistics have over time compiled a large portfolio of algorithms with which to compute or approximate many different mathematical functions in particularly efficient and/or reliable ways. Insofar as some of these functions resemble the ones that have been used to characterize behavior and cognition at the computational level, the tools-to-theories heuristic allows computational cognitive neuroscientists to exploit this portfolio for explanatory gains. As Griffiths et al. have remarked, "the best algorithms for approximating probabilistic inference in computer science and statistics" may be used as "candidate models of cognitive and neural processes" (Griffiths, Vul, and Sanborn, 2012, p. 264).

Consider a recent example, also from the recently-prominent Bayesian approach. Sanborn et al. (2010) advance the hypothesis that the mechanisms for categorization as described by Anderson (1991b) implement a *particle filtering* algorithm – a kind of *Monte Carlo sampling* that has been developed in machine learning to approximate optimal Bayesian inference. To this end, Sanborn et al. evaluate the performance of this algorithm relative to two alternatives: *Gibbs sampling* and Anderson's own *iterative algorithm*. Like particle filtering, these alternatives are also co-opted from applications in machine learning and artificial intelligence. Unlike particle filtering, however, Sanborn et al. demonstrate that these alternatives do not produce the kinds of order effects that are typically observed in human behavior. Therefore, they postulate that the particle-filtering algorithm is more likely than the two alternatives to correctly describe the operations of the mechanism for human categorization.

The tools-to-theories heuristic has also been used within a broadly dynamical approach. In a recent study on bistable perception, Cao et al. (2016) evaluate the relative merit of four different stochastic processes for explaining the characteristic "reversals" – spontaneous changes in the percept – that occur when human subjects encounter ambiguous stimuli such as the Necker cube. Each one of the *Poisson, Wiener, Ornstein-Uhlenbeck* and *generalized Ehrenfest* processes (for a review see Cox and Miller, 1977) are mathematical models previously used in disciplines such as statistical mechanics and telecommunications to predict e.g. the emission of particles from a radioactive source and the arrival of calls at a telephone exchange. In computational cognitive neuroscience, Cao et al. show that a generalized Ehrenfest process, unlike the others, reproduces the kind of short-tailed and scale-invariant distribution of reversals that is typically observed in human behavior. Thus, by starting from a detailed characterization of the relevant behavioral dynamics, and evaluating the relative ability of four well-understood stochastic processes to reproduce these dynamics, Cao et al. invoke the tools-to-theories heuristic to advance a testable algorithmic-level hypothesis, viz. that the neural structures involved in bistable perception implement a generalized Ehrenfest process.

In a reverse-engineering context, the mirroring and tools-to-theories heuristics are used to descend from the computational to the algorithmic level of analysis. But given a particular algorithm, investigators still face a question about how that algorithm is implemented in the brain. Answering this question is a matter of identifying the steps of the algorithm with the activity of specific neural structures in the brain, so as to answer a question about where in the brain the relevant functional processes are carried out (Bechtel and Richardson, 1993; Zednik, 2017). Sometimes, this kind of identification proceeds quite directly, by invoking neuroscientific measurement techniques such as single-cell recordings or fMRI to identify neural structures that exhibit patterns of activity that can be correlated with the ones posited by the algorithm. For example, in one particularly influential study of perceptual decision making, Newsome, Britten, and Movshon (1989) show that psychophysical judgments by macaque monkeys in a random-dot motion-detection task are well-correlated with concurrent single-cell recordings in area MT, and for this reason conclude that single MT-neurons themselves perform a kind of signal detection. More recently, proponents of the Bayesian coding hypothesis have sought to identify the location of probabilistic representations in the brain via fMRI imaging (see e.g. Vilares et al., 2012).

In many other cases, however, answering a question at the implementational level involves a considerable degree of speculation. Indeed, making an educated guess about which structure in the brain *might* implement a particular algorithm is perhaps the most common way in which proponents of the top-down strategy formulate testable hypotheses about where in the brain a particular process is carried out. Consider, for example, Marr and Hildreth's (1980) discussion of visual edge-detection, in which they speculate how the detection of "zero-crossings" might be implemented in area LGN:

> if an on-centre geniculate cell is active at location P and an off-centre cell is active at nearby location Q, then the value of $\nabla^2 G * I$ passes through zero between P and Q. Hence, by combining the signals from P and Q through a logical AND-operation, one can construct an operator for detecting when a zero-crossing segment (at some unknown orientation) passes between P and Q. By adding nonlinear AND-operations in the longitudinal direction, one can, in a similar way, construct an operator that detects oriented zero-crossing segments.
>
> *(Marr and Hildreth, 1980, pp. 208–209)*

Notably, Marr and Hildreth's appeal to AND-operations being implemented by geniculate cells is entirely speculative, being motivated by considerations of how the brain *might* detect zero-crossings rather than by actual knowledge of LGN. In a similarly speculative way, Pouget et al. (2013) outline several different ways in which the brain *might* represent probability distributions so as to underwrite the Bayesian coding hypothesis: the firing rate of a single neuron could directly code log-probabilities; a population of neurons with differing tuning curves may code a probability distribution by a basis function expansion; or the activity of pools of neurons might represent samples from a distribution. Finally, in the context of bistable perception, Cao et al.

(2016) suggest that the neural units most suited for implementing a generalized Ehrenfest process may be those that are assembled into so-called *attractor networks*, which are known to exist, but whose actual contribution to behavior and cognition remains unclear (Amit, 1995).

These examples show that, whereas proponents of the top-down approach in computational cognitive neuroscience have recourse to a wide array of algorithms with which to compute a particular function, they tend to be quite limited in their knowledge of how these algorithms are actually implemented in the brain. On the one hand, this observation gives credence to Marr's original suggestion that it is often easier to model an algorithm by considering what cognitive systems do, than by reflecting on the neural structures in which those algorithms are likely to be implemented. Indeed, as statistics, computer science, artificial intelligence, machine learning, and other theoretical disciplines provide an increasingly detailed understanding of the relative efficiency and degree of optimality of different algorithms, it seems likely that these disciplines' influence on the course of neuroscientific research will continue to grow. On the other hand, the examples reviewed here also show why the top-down approach may ultimately prove unsatisfying: although it has become relatively easy to formulate algorithmic-level hypotheses for a wide variety of phenomena, it remains difficult to know which of these hypotheses are actually true. It is in order to avoid this difficulty that, rather than begin with behavior and work their way down, many computational cognitive neuroscientists instead begin with the brain and work their way up.

Starting with the brain: bottom-up strategies

When Marr professed the benefits of the reverse-engineering approach, he could not have predicted the degree to which technological advances would eventually transform the bottom-up strategy into a viable alternative. Rather than infer the function and structure of neural mechanisms from characterizations of the phenomena being explained, bottom-up strategies in computational cognitive neuroscience aim to explain these phenomena by reproducing them in models and simulations that incorporate functional and structural details from several levels of brain organization.[3] As such, these strategies rely on single-cell recording, fMRI imaging, EEG and other neuroscientific measurement techniques that provide insight into the behavior, composition, and organization of mechanisms at the level of individual neurons, neural populations, and/or cortical columns and regions. Moreover, they invoke computational modeling methods and methods of mathematical analysis to illuminate the relevant mechanisms' statistical, dynamical, topological, and/or computational properties. Insofar as these techniques and methods can be used to discover and describe mechanisms, and to show how these mechanisms give rise to specific behavioral and cognitive phenomena, they yield mechanistic explanations of these phenomena (Bechtel, 2008; Craver, 2007).

Because the bottom-up strategy is driven by the insights provided by neuroscientific measurement techniques, this strategy tends to be most effective when the relevant techniques are most reliable. Among the most reliable measurement techniques is the single-cell recording, a measure of electrical activity at the level of individual nerve cells. At least since the 1950s, neuroscientists have appealed to the activity of single cells to explain the behavioral and cognitive capacities of whole organisms. This approach has been particularly influential in the domain of visual perception, in which *feature detector* cells have been discovered whose activity correlates with specific environmental features such as moving edges (Lettvin et al., 1959), oriented bars (Hubel and Wiesel, 1959), and (famously) bugs (Barlow, 1953). Motivated by these results, Horace Barlow advanced a *single neuron doctrine*, according to which the computational capacities of individual nerve cells suffice to explain an organism's perceptual abilities: "The subtlety and sensitivity of perception results from the mechanisms determining when a single cell becomes active, rather than from complex combinatorial rules of usage of nerve cells" (Barlow, 1972, p. 371).

Barlow's doctrine resonates even today. In an example briefly introduced above, Newsome et al. (1989) have found that recordings of individual MT neurons predict the performance of macaque monkeys in a random-dot motion-detection task. Motivated by this finding, the authors hypothesize that individual MT neurons solve the very same kind of signal-detection task that is solved by the monkey as a whole. Although it may be questioned whether correlations between the activity of single cells and the behavior of whole organisms are really all that significant (Stüttgen, Schwarz, and Jäkel, 2011), such correlations are still frequently appealed to in the context of the bottom-up approach in computational cognitive neuroscience: investigators attempt to explain the behavior of whole organisms by showing how that behavior can be reproduced by mechanisms at the level of individual neurons.

That said, it is fair to question whether the computational capacities of individual neurons suffice to explain behavioral and cognitive phenomena in general. Indeed, it is now a commonplace to assume that performance in a wide variety of tasks – especially tasks further removed from the sensorimotor periphery such as planning, reasoning, language learning, and attention – requires the computational capacities of neural networks (Yuste, 2015). Neural networks took center stage in computational cognitive neuroscience with the development of sophisticated *connectionist* modeling methods in cognitive science, in which networks of artificial "neural" units, arranged in layers and interconnected with weighted "synaptic" connections, are used to replicate various behavioral and cognitive capacities (see also Garson and Bruckner, this volume; and Stinson, this volume). Of course, early connectionists stressed the fact that their models were highly idealized, and that they should for this reason be considered "neurally inspired" rather than biologically plausible (Thorpe and Imbert, 1989). Nevertheless, many computational cognitive neuroscientists today rely on connectionist models that incorporate an ever-increasing degree of biological realism,[4] thus allowing them to view these models as plausible descriptions of the mechanisms responsible for specific behavioral and cognitive phenomena.

Consider a recent attempt to explain *C. elegans* klinotaxis, a form of goal-directed locomotion in which the nematode worm approaches a chemical source by way of a regular oscillatory motion. Beginning with a complete description of the *connectome* – a graphical representation of the *C. elegans* nervous system at the level of individual neurons (White et al., 1986) – Izquierdo and Beer (2013) derive a *minimal network* that includes only those chemosensory, motor, and inter-neurons that, due to graph-theoretical considerations, are deemed most likely to contribute to the production of klinotaxis. By inserting the minimal network into a simulated *C. elegans* body model, and in turn situating that body model within a simulated environment (see also Izquierdo and Lockery, 2010), Izquierdo and Beer artificially evolve network parameters suitable for the production of reliable and efficient klinotaxis. By comparing the klinotaxis produced in simulation to the klinotaxis produced in the real world, Izquierdo and Beer advance the hypothesis that the minimal network is "appropriate for the generation of testable predictions concerning how the biological network functions" (Izquierdo and Beer, 2013, p. 5). Indeed, in a subsequent study, Izquierdo, Williams, and Beer (2015) propose that some of the interneurons in the minimal network constitute "informational gates" through which chemosensory information is allowed to flow and thereby influence motor neuron activity, but only at specific moments in time. This "gating" is postulated to be a crucial feature of the mechanism for the oscillatory nature of *C. elegans* klinotaxis not only in simulation, but also in the real world (Zednik, 2018).

Of course, it is unclear whether Izquierdo and colleagues' approach will eventually scale up; investigators are still a long way away from having a comparable model of the *human* connectome (but cf. Sporns, 2012). Nevertheless, computational cognitive neuroscientists have made great progress in adding biological detail to many different connectionist models. For example, rather than deploy networks whose units exhibit a sigmoidal activation function, many investigators today deploy networks of spiking units which exhibit time-varying response profiles reminiscent of biological neurons (Maass, 1997). Moreover, many others deploy networks whose weights are determined by learning algorithms more biologically plausible than the backpropagation algorithm developed in the 1980s (see also Garson and Bruckner, this volume). Finally, reminiscent of the aforementioned work on *C. elegans* klinotaxis, some investigators no longer model generic neural network mechanisms, but rather aim to describe specific networks in well-defined areas of the brain (e.g. the hippocampus: Gluck and Myers, 1997). In general, insofar as connectionist models can be used to reproduce specific behavioral or cognitive capacities while incorporating an ever-increasing degree of biological realism, they deliver plausible mechanistic explanations of these capacities.

Connectionist models are traditionally viewed as describing networks of interconnected neurons. A different family of network models aims to describe networks of interconnected columns and regions, distributed across the brain as a whole (Sporns, 2011). Like other bottom-up approaches in computational cognitive neuroscience, the development of network models of this kind is grounded in knowledge of biological reality. Unfortunately, at this high level of brain organization, there is considerable disagreement about the reliability and informativeness of the measurement techniques that are used to acquire such knowledge. For example, there is still no agreed-upon method of individuating brain regions; investigators rely on a variety of *parcellation schemes* with which to identify individual network elements. Whereas some of these schemes may be quite principled – as when network elements are identified with Brodmann areas, themselves individuated on the basis of cytoarchitectural principles – other schemes are quite pragmatic, such as when network elements are identified with the location of electrodes in EEG recordings or with voxels in fMRI data. Similarly, investigators also rely on a variety of *connectivity schemes* for determining the extent to which any two network elements are connected. Whereas the elements of *structural* networks are connected anatomically, the elements of so-called *functional* networks have activity that is connected statistically, i.e. that is correlated over time. Most intriguingly, perhaps, the connections of *effective* networks correspond to the presumed causal interactions between network elements (Friston, 2011), often operationalized in terms of information-theoretic measures such as *Granger causality*. Not surprisingly, the use of such a wide variety of parcellation and connectivity schemes has led to the proliferation of whole-brain network models, with little certainty about how these models actually contribute toward specific explanatory goals (Craver, 2016; Miłkowski, 2016; Zednik, 2018). Thus, although bottom-up strategies at the level of the brain as a whole are grounded in an abundance of neuroscientific measurement data, it remains unclear to what extent this data constitutes genuine knowledge of the mechanisms responsible for behavior and cognition.

Although it remains unclear how this epistemological difficulty can be overcome, it is nevertheless worth understanding the way neuroscientific measurement data at the level of the brain as a whole can be analyzed using sophisticated mathematical and computational methods. These methods illuminate a particular network's topological, dynamical, and/or informational properties, and may also reveal potential interdependencies between different kinds of properties. In particular, graphs are frequently used to model a brain network's topology, and graph-theoretic techniques are used to identify the presence of e.g. hub nodes, modules, and motifs (Bullmore and Sporns, 2009). Moreover, the results of graph-theoretic analyses are increasingly deployed to constrain network models not unlike the connectionist models reviewed above. Although the units in these network models correspond to cortical columns or regions (or pragmatic-ally individuated fMRI voxels) rather than to individual neurons, they can similarly be used to simulate the relevant network's behavior, and to compare that behavior to the properties of a phenomenon of explanatory interest. This kind of comparison is greatly facilitated by information-theoretic measures that illuminate e.g. the flow of information through a network (Izquierdo, Williams, and Beer, 2015), as well as by dynamical systems theoretic techniques that characterize e.g. patterns of rhythmic oscillation, stable states, and bifurcations in the activity of individual network elements and/or in the behavior of the network as a whole (Uhlhaas et al., 2009). Perhaps the most interesting studies of this kind combine the insights of several different analytic techniques, thereby revealing dependencies between e.g. a network's topo-logical properties and its behavioral dynamics (e.g. Pérez et al., 2011), or between its dynamical and informational properties (Beer and Williams, 2015). Provided that computational cogni-tive neuroscientists are eventually able to overcome the epistemological difficulties associated with the identification of large-scale network mechanisms, these analyses of networks' formal properties are likely to deliver a detailed understanding of the way a network mechanism's behavior depends on its composition and organization. That is, they are poised to *show how* such mechanisms give rise to specific behavioral and cognitive phenomena (Craver, 2016; Zednik, 2014).

In general, these examples show that, no matter the level of brain organization, bottom–up strategies in computational cognitive neuroscience depend on the reliability and informative-ness of neuroscientific measurement techniques, as well as on the descriptive power of compu-tational modeling methods and methods of mathematical analysis. *Pace* Marr's concerns about the viability of the bottom-up approach, these techniques and methods render the bottom-up approach increasingly useful for uncovering the mechanisms for behavior and cognition. Indeed, insofar as they are grounded in knowledge of biological reality, bottom-up strategies are likely to be far more constrained than the top-down strategies discussed above. At the same time, bottom-up strategies have at least two characteristic limitations of their own.

For one, although bottom-up strategies are often more constrained than top-down alternatives, the descriptive power of the relevant mathematical and computational models still frequently exceeds the available knowledge of biological reality. This problem was widely acknowledged in the early days of the connectionist research program, but seems to have been mostly overcome due to the newfound ability to incorporate greater biological detail. That said, the same problem has once again come to the fore at the level of the brain as a whole. As illustrated by the lack of consensus about how to individuate the elements and connections of whole-brain networks, it has become relatively easy to identify and represent networks in the brain, but comparatively difficult to know which (aspects) of these networks should actually be cited in explanations of specific behavioral and cognitive phenomena. Indeed, commentators sometimes question the explanatory import of structural network modeling initiatives to map the *C. elegans* connectome, and Craver (2016) has recently denied that functional networks of pragmatically-individuated fMRI voxels should be viewed as explanations at all. Although these outright dismissals seem exaggerated – structural and functional network models might represent certain *aspects* of a mechanism, even if they do not represent the mechanism as a whole (Hochstein, 2016; Zednik, 2018) – bottom-up approaches in computational cognitive neurosci-ence are likely to properly get off the ground only when they are rooted in reliable knowledge of neurobiological reality.

For another, our ability to uncover neurobiological detail, and our ability to model that detail on a computer, may also often outstrip our ability to understand the mechanisms whose details are being modeled. Especially at the level of the brain as a whole, it is possible that computational models of network mechanisms remain *opaque* (Dudai and Evers, 2014). That is, these models may be no more easily analyzed and understood than the relevant mechanisms themselves. Although it remains unclear to what extent a model's intelligibility is related to its capacity to explain, this harks back to Marr's original suggestion that it may be easier to identify the computational workings of the brain by considering what it does, than by describing what it is made of. Of course, as the preceding examples show, bottom-up approaches do not only rely on computational models, but also invoke sophisticated mathematical techniques to analyze the dynamical, topological, and informational properties of the mechanisms being modeled. It remains to be seen whether these techniques are sufficiently illuminating to reveal the inner workings of even the most complex and large-scale brain mechanisms (see also Zednik, 2015).

Conclusion: toward a bidirectional approach?

Many research efforts in computational cognitive neuroscience can be viewed as instances of either the top-down or the bottom-up research strategy. Top-down (or reverse-engineering) strategies aim to infer the function and structure of neural mechanisms from prior descriptions of behavior and cognition. In contrast, bottom-up strategies seek to reproduce behavioral and cognitive phenomena in computational models that are grounded in knowledge of biological reality. Both strategies have distinct advantages, but also characteristic limitations. Whereas top-down strategies have recourse to a plethora of mathematical formalisms and computational algorithms co-opted from disciplines such as artificial intelligence, machine learning, and statistics, they still regularly bottom out in speculative proposals about how such algorithms might actually be implemented in the brain. In contrast, because bottom-up strategies take as their starting point actual neuroscientific measurement data, they are not similarly limited by this kind of speculation. Nevertheless, these strategies are often limited by insufficiently informative empirical data – especially at the level of the brain as a whole – and by computational models that may be no easier to understand than the mechanisms they are supposed to be models of.

In closing, it is worth considering the possibility that the characteristic limitations of the top-down and bottom-up strategies might eventually be overcome by adopting something akin to a *bidirectional* approach. Indeed, practicing scientists are not beholden to conceptual distinctions, and are free to adopt aspects of both research strategies simultaneously. In fact, many investigators do so already. For example, when proponents of reverse-engineering speculate about the possible neural implementations of a particular algorithm, they do not do so in a vacuum, but actually rely on what they already know about neurobiological reality to constrain their own speculative proposals. As the available knowledge of neural mechanisms increases, the frequency of unconstrained speculation in the context of the top-down approach decreases.

In a similar way, top-down considerations may enable researchers to overcome some of the characteristic limitations of the bottom-up approach. Theoretical disciplines such as artificial intelligence, machine learning, and statistics have not only developed a large portfolio of algorithms to be used as testable hypotheses, but have also developed sophisticated methods of mathematical analysis to understand how such algorithms actually work. For example, the popularity of *deep learning networks* in machine learning (Schmidhuber, 2014) has led to the development of analytic tools that can be used to understand different levels of representational abstraction in hierarchical networks (e.g. Montavon, Braun, and Müller, 2011). Although deep learning networks are generally considered biologically implausible because they, like early connectionist models, rely on backpropagation learning, it may be that some of the tools originally developed to understand the workings of deep learning networks can be co-opted to understand the computational capacities of hierarchical networks in the biological brain. In this way, a standard trick from the reverse-engineering toolbox – co-opting developments in theoretical disciplines such as machine learning – may even allow proponents of the bottom-up approach to overcome characteristic limitations such as opacity. More generally, therefore, it may be that the most fruitful research strategy for explanatory success in computational cognitive neuroscience is a bidirectional one.

Notes

1 It will be assumed that (many) computational cognitive neuroscientists aim to deliver mechanistic explanations in the sense recently explored in the philosophy of neuroscience (Bechtel, 2008; Craver, 2007), and that the use of formal methods is in no way antithetical to this aim (see also Bechtel and Shagrir, 2015; Piccinini and Craver, 2011; Zednik, 2017).
2 This top-down inference need not be completely unconstrained by low-level considerations, of course. Indeed, Marr himself often appealed to extant knowledge of neurological structures in addition to computational-level considerations. Nevertheless, as Marr's own words illustrate, it is characteristic of the top-down approach that the latter be weighted more heavily than the former.
3 Levels of organization should not be confused with levels of analysis. Whereas the former are individuated by the kinds of questions an investigator might ask about a particular cognitive system, the latter are individuated by constitution-relations within a mechanism (Bechtel, 2008; Craver, 2007). Insofar as many mechanisms are hierarchical it is often profitable to apply each one of the three levels of analysis at any single level of organization.
4 Many, but not all. Motivated in no small part by the finding that connectionist models with highly idealized and simplified "neural" units and connections are universal function approximators (Hornik, 1991), these models have become widespread in engineering disciplines such as artificial intelligence and machine learning (see e.g. Schmidhuber, 2014). Investigators working in these disciplines traditionally value computing power, efficiency, and optimality over biological realism.

References

Amit, D.J. (1995) 'The Hebbian Paradigm Reintegrated: Local Reverberations as Internal Representations', *Behavioral and Brain Sciences*, 18 (4), pp. 631–631.
Anderson, J.R. (1991a) 'Is Human Cognition Adaptive?', *Behavioral and Brain Sciences*, 14, pp. 471–517.
Anderson, J.R. (1991b) 'The Adaptive Nature of Human Categorization', *Psychological Review*, 98 (3), pp. 409–429.
Barlow, H.B. (1953) 'Summation and Inhibition in the Frog's Retina', *The Journal of Physiology*, 119 (1), pp. 69–88.
Barlow, H.B. (1972) 'Single Units and Sensation: A Neuron Doctrine for Perceptual Psychology?', *Perception*, 1 (4), pp. 371–394.
Bechtel, W. (2008) *Mental Mechanisms: Philosophical Perspectives on Cognitive Neuroscience*. New York, NY: Routledge.
Bechtel, W. and Richardson, R.C. (1993) *Discovering Complexity: Decomposition and Localization as Strategies in Scientific Research*. Cambridge, MA: MIT Press.
Bechtel, W. and Shagrir, O. (2015) 'The Non-Redundant Contributions of Marr's Three Levels of Analysis for Explaining Information-Processing Mechanisms', *Topics in Cognitive Science*, 7 (2), pp. 312–322.
Beer, R.D. and Williams P.L. (2015) 'Information Processing and Dynamics in Minimally Cognitive Agents', *Cognitive Science*, 39 (1), pp. 1–38.
Bullmore, E. and Sporns, O. (2009) 'Complex Brain Networks: Graph Theoretical Analysis of Structural and Functional Systems', *Nature Reviews Neuroscience*, 10 (3), pp. 186–198.
Cao, R. et al. (2016) 'Collective Activity of Many Bistable Assemblies Reproduces Characteristic Dynamics of Multistable Perception', *Journal of Neuroscience*, 36 (26), pp. 6957–6972.
Colombo, M. and Hartmann, S. (2015) 'Bayesian Cognitive Science, Unification, and Explanation', *The British Journal for the Philosophy of Science*, 68 (2), pp. 451–484.
Cox, D.R. and Miller, H.D. (1977) *The Theory of Stochastic Processes*. New York, NY: CRC Press.

Craver, C.F. (2007) *Explaining the Brain: Mechanisms and the Mosaic Unity of Neuroscience*. Oxford: Oxford University Press.

Craver, C.F. (2016) 'The Explanatory Power of Network Models', *Philosophy of Science*, 83 (5), pp. 698–709.

Dennett, D.C. (1994) 'Cognitive Science as Reverse Engineering: Several Meanings of "Top-Down" and 'Bottom-Up', *Logic, Methodology and Philosophy of Science*, 9, pp. 679–689.

Dudai, Y. and Evers, K. (2014) 'To Simulate or Not to Simulate: What Are the Questions?', *Neuron*, 84 (2), pp. 254–261.

Friston, K.J. (2011) 'Functional and Effective Connectivity: A Review', *Brain Connectivity*, 1 (1), pp. 13–36.

Gigerenzer, G. (1991) 'From Tools to Theories: A Heuristic of Discovery in Cognitive Psychology', *Psychological Review*, 98 (2), pp. 254–267.

Gluck, M.A. and Myers, C.E. (1997) 'Psychobiological Models of Hippocampal Function in Learning and Memory', *Annual Review of Psychology*, 48 (1), pp. 481–514.

Griffiths, T.L., Vul, E., and Sanborn, A.N. (2012) 'Bridging Levels of Analysis for Probabilistic Models of Cognition', *Current Directions in Psychological Science*, 21 (4), pp. 263–268.

Hochstein, E. (2016) 'One Mechanism, Many Models: A Distributed Theory of Mechanistic Explanation', *Synthese*, 193 (5), pp. 1387–1407.

Hornik, K. (1991) 'Approximation Capabilities of Multilayer Feedforward Networks', *Neural Networks*, 4, pp. 251–257.

Hubel, D.H. and Wiesel, T.N. (1959) 'Receptive Fields of Single Neurones in the Cat's Striate Cortex', *The Journal of Physiology*, 148 (3), pp. 574–591.

Izquierdo, E.J. and Beer, R.D. (2013) 'Connecting a Connectome to Behavior: An Ensemble of Neuroanatomical Models of C. Elegans Klinotaxis', *PLoS Computational Biology*, 9 (2), e1002890.

Izquierdo, E.J. and Lockery, S.R. (2010) 'Evolution and Analysis of Minimal Neural Circuits for Klinotaxis in Caenorhabditis Elegans', *Journal of Neuroscience*, 30 (39), pp. 12908–12917.

Izquierdo, E.J., Williams, P.L., and Beer, R.D. (2015) 'Information Flow through a Model of the C. Elegans Klinotaxis Circuit', *PLoS One*, 10 (10), e0140397.

Knill, D.C. and Pouget, A. (2004) 'The Bayesian Brain: The Role of Uncertainty in Neural Coding and Computation', *Trends in Neurosciences*, 27 (12), pp. 712–719.

Kwisthout, J., Wareham, T., and van Rooij, I. (2011) 'Bayesian Intractability is Not an Ailment that Approximation Can Cure', *Cognitive Science*, 35 (5), pp. 779–784.

Lettvin, J.Y. et al. (1959) 'What the Frogs Eye Tells the Frog's Brain', *Proceedings of the IRE*, 47 (11), pp. 1940–1951.

Ma, W.J. et al. (2006) 'Bayesian Inference with Probabilistic Population Codes', *Nature Neuroscience*, 9 (11), pp. 1432–1438.

Maass, Wo (1997) 'Networks of Spiking Neurons: The Third Generation of Neural Network Models', *Neural Networks*, 10 (9), pp. 1659–1671.

Maloney, L.T. and Mamassian, P. (2009) 'Bayesian Decision Theory as a Model of Human Visual Perception: Testing Bayesian Transfer', *Visual Neuroscience*, 26 (1), pp. 147–155.

Marr, D. (1982) *Vision: A Computational Investigation into the Human Representation and Processing of Visual Information*. Cambridge, MA: MIT Press.

Marr, D. and Hildreth, E. (1980) 'Theory of Edge Detection', *Proceedings of the Royal Society of London B: Biological Sciences*, 207 (1167), pp. 187–217.

Miłkowski, M. (2016) 'Explanatory Completeness and Idealization in Large Brain Simulations: A Mechanistic Perspective', *Synthese*, 193 (5), pp. 1457–1478.

Montavon, G., Braun, M.L., and Müller, K.-R. (2011) 'Kernel Analysis of Deep Networks', *Journal of Machine Learning Research*, 12 (September), pp. 2563–2581.

Newsome, W.T., Britten, K.H., and Movshon, J.A. (1989) 'Neural Correlates of a Perceptual Decision', *Nature*, 341 (6237), pp. 52–54.

Oaksford, M. and Chater, N. (2001) 'The Probabilistic Approach to Human Reasoning', *Trends in Cognitive Sciences*, 5 (8), pp. 349–357.

Pérez, T. et al. (2011) 'Effect of the Topology and Delayed Interactions in Neuronal Networks Synchronization', *PLoS One*, 6 (5), e19900.

Piccinini, G. and Craver, C. (2011) 'Integrating Psychology and Neuroscience: Functional Analyses as Mechanism Sketches', *Synthese*, 183 (3), pp. 283–311.

Pouget, A. et al. (2013) 'Probabilistic Brains: Knowns and Unknowns', *Nature Neuroscience*, 16 (9), pp. 1170–1178.

Sanborn, A.N., Griffiths, T.L., and Navarro, D.J. (2010) 'Rational Approximations to Rational Models: Alternative Algorithms for Category Learning', *Psychological Review*, 117 (4), pp. 1144–1167.

Schmidhuber, J. (2014) 'Deep Learning in Neural Networks: An Overview', 61, pp. 85–117.

Shagrir, O. (2010) 'Marr on Computational-Level Theories', *Philosophy of Science*, 77 (4), pp. 477–500.

Simon, H.A. (1998) 'Discovering Explanations', *Minds and Machines*, 8 (1), pp. 7–37.

Sporns, O. (2011) *Networks of the Brain*. Cambridge, MA: MIT Press.

Sporns, O. (2012) *Discovering the Human Connectome*. Cambridge, MA: MIT Press.

Stüttgen, M.C., Schwarz, C., and Jäkel, F. (2011) 'Mapping Spikes to Sensations', *Frontiers in Neuroscience*, 5, pp. 1–17.

Thorpe, S.J. and Imbert, M. (1989) 'Biological Constraints on Connectionist Modelling', in Pfiefer, R. et al. (eds.) *Connectionism in Perspective*. Amsterdam: North Holland, pp. 63–92.

Uhlhaas, P.J. et al. (2009) 'Neural Synchrony in Cortical Networks: History, Concept and Current Status', *Frontiers in Integrative Neuroscience*, 3, art. 17.

Vilares, I. et al. (2012) 'Differential Representations of Prior and Likelihood Uncertainty in the Human Brain', *Current Biology*, 22 (18), pp. 1641–1648.

White, J.G. et al. (1986) 'The Structure of the Nervous System of the Nematode Caenorhabditis Elegans', *Philosophical Transactions of the Royal Society London*, 314, pp. 1–340.

Yuste, R. (2015) 'From the Neuron Doctrine to Neural Networks', *Nature Reviews Neuroscience*, 16 (8), pp. 487–497.

Zednik, C. (2014) 'Are Systems Neuroscience Explanations Mechanistic?', in *Preprint Volume for Philosophy Science Association 24th Biennial Meeting*. Chicago, IL: Philosophy of Science Association, pp. 954–975.

Zednik, C. (2015) 'Heuristics, Descriptions, and the Scope of Mechanistic Explanation', in Wolfe, C.T., Huneman, P., and Reydon, T.A.C. (eds.) *Explanation in Biology*. New York, NY and London: Springer, pp. 295–318.

Zednik, C. (2017) 'Mechanisms in Cognitive Science', in Glennan, S. and Illari, P.M. (eds.) *The Routledge Handbook of Mechanisms and Mechanical Philosophy*. London: Routledge, pp. 389–400.

Zednik, C. (2018). 'Models and Mechanisms in Network Neuroscience', *Philosophical Psychology* (forthcoming).

Zednik, C. and Jäkel, F. (2014) 'How Does Bayesian Reverse-Engineering Work?', in Bello, P. et al. (eds.) *Proceedings of the 36th Annual Conference of the Cognitive Science Society*. Austin, TX: Cognitive Science Society, pp. 666–671.

Zednik, C. and Jäkel, F. (2016) 'Bayesian Reverse-Engineering Considered as a Research Strategy for Cognitive Science', *Synthese*, 193 (12), pp. 3951–3985.

27

SIMULATION IN COMPUTATIONAL NEUROSCIENCE

Liz Irvine

1 Introduction

In computational neuroscience the term 'model' is often used to capture simulations as well, but simulations have distinct features, and distinct epistemic uses. Models are static representations of a system, while simulations are dynamic: I follow Parker's (2009) definition of a simulation as "a time-ordered sequence of states that serves as a representation of some other time-ordered sequence of states [e.g. of the target system]" (p. 486). Simulations can be used to track the state of a system over time, where from a starting state at t_0, a program calculates the state of the system at t_1, and given these values, the program can calculate the next state of the system at t_2, and so on.

Simulations are used in computational neuroscience for a variety of reasons (see Stinson, this volume; Garson and Buckner, this volume). One of interest here is that simulation offers a way to investigate the internal functioning of a complex system without necessarily needing a lot of experimental data about that internal functioning. That is, unlike some standard approaches to simulation in other disciplines (Winsberg, 2010), simulations in neuroscience are often built without much background knowledge about the system they are (sometimes not very closely) trying to simulate.

A description of this is Corrado and Doya's 'model-in-the-middle' approach (Corrado and Doya, 2007; Corrado et al., 2009). They argue that investigating the process of decision making using standard methods in systems neuroscience is massively under-constrained. The standard method involves manipulating some variable of interest (e.g. visual input) and seeing what effect this has on other variables (e.g. motor action), and from there, trying to abstract away an account of decision making. With complex systems where it is not obvious what the relevant variables are, or how one would expect them to interact, this approach is deeply underdetermined by the available data.

Instead, with the 'model-in-the-middle' approach researchers make a reasonable guess about how the system works, build a simulation based on this guess, and then see if the decision variables and outputs in the simulation correlate with internal signals and the behaviors of the experimental subjects. If the simulation 'fits' the experimental data in various ways, then this provides evidence for the hypotheses instantiated in the simulation. In computational neuroscience, these hypotheses can concern abstract computational processes as well as mechanistic hypotheses about how certain computations are implemented.

In Section 2 below, I evaluate different types and different approaches to simulation in computational neuroscience, including small and large-scale simulations, and bottom-up and top-down approaches. Section 3 outlines what kind of explanations simulations can provide, including a brief discussion of mechanistic vs computational explanations. Section 4 briefly outlines some interesting benefits of computational simulations in this field to computer science, in the form of neuromorphic devices. Section 5 offers a short summary.

2 Types of simulation: large and small, bottom-up vs top-down

2.1 Small-scale simulation

Simulations are a key way to investigate brain function, and most simulations focus on small-scale 'local circuits' to investigate a specific cognitive function. These include simulations of sensory processing, decision making, motor control, and different types of learning and memory.

For example, reinforcement learning algorithms have been used to simulate learning and decision making. Reinforcement learning describes how agents should act over time in an uncertain environment in order to maximize long-term reward (see Colombo, this volume). Agents first recognize the present state of the environment, and then calculate and predict which action will deliver the highest expected reward using previous experience. The agent then performs the action, compares the predicted reward with the actual reward to get the 'reward prediction error', and then uses this to update its estimate of the reward values associated with particular actions. Reinforcement learning simulations can accurately predict real behavior of performing animals, and dopamine neurons in the basal ganglia circuit fire according to simulated reward prediction errors, suggesting that the simulations are fairly accurate depictions of the computational processes involved in learning and decision making (Corrado et al., 2009).

Another widespread type of simulation in computational neuroscience comes from the connectionist tradition. Briefly, connectionist simulations use principles of parallel and recurrent processing, and a set of learning rules to update connection weights between very simplified units, which represent acting neurons or groups of neurons. The same principles can be used to model a variety of specific behaviors, including word learning, perception, memory, concept formation, and reasoning (see Stinson (this volume); Garson and Buckner (this volume) for more detail; and Chemero and Faries (this volume); Danks (this volume); Hohwy (this volume) for alternative approaches).

In a review of the use of simulations in computational neuroscience, Sompolinksky (2014) states that most theories derived from simulation (particularly in the connectionist tradition) fall within a 'network paradigm'. Here, (relatively) simple and uniform simulated neurons connected via synaptic weights, whose activity is governed by (relatively) simple rules, provide explanations and predictions about core features of a local computational circuit. At least for these core features, adding extra levels of complexity and biological realism to these highly simplified and idealized simulated local circuits adds little in the way of predictive or explanatory power.

However, Sompolinsky argues that these simple simulations of local circuits are unlikely to scale up to offer explanations of higher-level cognitive abilities, for a number of reasons. One is that the network paradigm ignores the chemical soup that neurons function within, and which modulate and are modulated by neurons' electrical activity. Simulations of local circuits also ignore the complexity of different types of neurons and their patterns of connectivity. It seems likely that these biological details do make some difference to brain function at large scales (in any case, it would be puzzling if they do not). There are two other related reasons. The network paradigm ignores the active nature of perception; of sensory and cognitive systems seeking out information rather than being passive receivers of it. This is related to the more general point that focusing on local circuits and specific functions fails to capture the massive interconnectivity across the brain, and so the ways in which local circuits together contribute to the realization of many different functions.

Two different approaches to large-scale simulation that attempt to address some of these problems are reviewed below. One is a 'bottom-up' approach which attempts to address the problem of biological realism within simulations. The second is a 'top-down' approach which attempts to address the issue of whole-brain function across distributed local circuits.

2.2 Brain simulations: bottom-up

The Blue Brain project (http://bluebrain.epfl.ch/) is an example of a 'bottom-up' or data-driven approach to large-scale brain simulation, which has so far focused on building a biologically realistic simulation of a juvenile rat somatosensory cortex (though the eventual aim is to construct a whole brain). The simulation is based on the structure provided by neocortical columns, and closely simulates neural type, structure, position, connectivity, and electrical activity, to the level of individual neurons and synaptic connections. The simulation comprises computationally demanding algorithms, based on large databases of experimental data. The only features of the simulation that are programmed in are a biologically realistic density of different neuron types, and their typical connectivity and activity patterns, so whatever the simulation does from then on emerges from the total activity of the connected simulated neurons. This is what makes it a bottom-up simulation; the simulation is constructed from experimental evidence concerning low-level features of neural systems only, with no constraints from higher-level theory, such as general cognitive architecture or network properties of coalitions of neurons.

There are several reasons why one might take a bottom-up approach to brain simulation, and several things that one can do with such simulations. First, linked to the discussion above, such detailed simulations allow a better understanding of the roles of different types of neurons, layers, and connections between them, and so perhaps explain why there is such much complexity at this level. This is not possible with less biologically realistic models that use much simpler and more uniform simulated neurons.

Second, highly detailed models can make it possible to intervene on a (simulated) neural system in very specific ways, which can be used to corroborate and extend experimental findings. For example, Markram et al. (2015) varied tonic depolarization and calcium levels in a virtual brain slice (*in silico* experimentation), and found regular variations in neural firing synchrony. This was also found in *in vitro* experiments, and so this finding across both brain slices and simulated neocortical columns suggests that they had identified a "highly reproducible phenomenon, robust to biological and statistical variations in parameters [related to the microcircuit]" (p. 472). That is, the convergence of *in vitro* and *in silico* experimental data suggests that the findings in either condition were not artifactual, and hold over a wide range of neural microcircuits.

There are also downsides to such simulations. First, their very complexity makes it technologically difficult (to say the least) to simulate more than a tiny proportion of a brain at any one time. While this makes it possible to answer some questions about brain function, it misses out questions about overall brain function and control of behavior. Second, and relatedly, while clearly paying more attention to biological features of the brain, such data-driven models do not make contact with higher-level structural and functional characterizations of the brain, which again makes it difficult to connect these simulations to other levels of investigation. Third, their very complexity can also make it difficult to understand or explain exactly how neural phenomena unfold. The very practice of 'observing' the simulation and making sense of it is a massive technological and epistemic project in its own right.

2.3 Brain simulations: top-down

Another approach is a 'top-down' or hypothesis driven strategy. Here, simulations are not used to replicate the brain in vast detail, which are then manipulated to see how different parameters affect neural activity. Instead, the simulation embodies hypotheses about brain function, so 'running' the simulation and comparing its outputs and internal behavior to experimental data directly tests those hypotheses. To change the hypothesis, one changes the simulation, which can then be tested again.

Spaun (Eliasmith et al., 2012) is a well-known example of a top-down approach to brain simulation. Spaun uses functional accounts of the roles of different brain areas (e.g. visual, motor, prefrontal areas) to assign connection weights within simple simulated neural structures that represent these different brain areas. A key feature of Spaun is its three compression hierarchies over the domains of vision, action, and working memory. Information is compressed throughout the visual hierarchy as image-based encoding is transformed to feature-based encoding. Conversely, motor decisions are gradually decompressed from the selection of an action plan into the kind of high-dimensional encoding that is required for control of a multi-jointed arm. Given the neurally realized functional characteristics of the different simulated brain areas, and these compression/decompression routes, Spaun can link visual input (via an eye) to external behavior (via a physically modeled arm), and is capable of performing eight different visual, motor, and cognitive tasks. These features make Spaun an example of a 'top-down' simulation; what drives the construction of Spaun are experimentally informed hypotheses concerning high-level functional characterizations of brain areas.

Spaun is therefore rather different to the simulations provided by the Blue Brain project. Spaun is more coarse-grained, leaving out much biological detail, but this makes it possible to simulate the interactions between a range of brain areas and how they together perform a range of different tasks. Spaun is also aimed at answering rather different questions. Instead of trying to get an understanding of how fine-grained details of neural structures affect their functionality, the idea is to see how interconnected and functionally specified groups of neurons can generate flexible behavior. That is, the main aim of developing and testing a simulation like Spaun is to "propose a unified set of neural mechanisms able to perform [a range of tasks]" (Eliasmith et al., 2012, p. 1204).

This highlights the advantages of top-down simulations. First, they form complex and powerful tests of high-level hypotheses about overall brain function. Second, existing bodies of behavioral data and theory can be used to inform and test these hypotheses, and so they do not require extensive knowledge of neural structures and activity (which in some cases, we do not yet have). Third, their (relative) simplicity makes it possible to track the sources of inconsistencies between simulated and real data, so that it is possible to understand how and why the simulation is working (or failing to). Having epistemic access to the workings of the simulation is a major advantage of such an approach.

However, there are also some downsides. First, there is the obvious fact that Spaun is not biologically complete or particularly biologically realistic. There may be some features of neural activity or connectivity that are important for enabling flexible behavior that the simulation fails to capture. Second, Spaun is limited in its capacity to investigate brain development from juvenile to adult (which the Blue Brain project can, in principle), and although there is some task flexibility in Spaun, it is by no means as flexible as a 'real' human brain. Its findings then can only be partial.

2.4 *Different approaches, different aims*

There has been a vigorous debate on the appropriateness of both of these approaches to brain simulation (see e.g. Chi, 2016, for summary), but *if* the aim is to understand how brains generate complex behavior, then it is possible to argue that using (relatively) simple simulations to test hypotheses directly is an (more) efficient way of generating knowledge.

First, Spaun exemplifies the tendency in computational neuroscience toward top-down simulation, in which simpler and less biologically realistic simulations are used to test bundles of hypotheses about brain function. These constraints include on the one hand fairly easily accessible and plentiful behavioral data, and on the other hand, fairly inaccessible and less common neural data/recordings, all concerning an incredibly complex system. Getting the experimental data to even start building a simulation as complex as those developed in the Blue Brain project is a massive and on-going undertaking. Top-down simulation makes it possible to start answering questions and developing theories given what is available.

Second, hypotheses concerning the generation of complex behavior will themselves be fairly complex. Building complex hypotheses into a simulation makes it possible to test them in a way that no other method can offer. In particular, it makes it possible to test bundles of hypotheses together, and (somewhat easily) to change and re-test updated hypotheses. It is also possible to use top-down large-scale simulations to investigate the potential power of general computational principles or general organizational structures in explaining a range of behaviors.

Relatedly, it is (relatively) easier to understand a simple, top-down simulation than a complex bottom-up simulation, both when it seems to work, and perhaps more importantly when it fails to generate realistic looking outputs. Understanding a simulation like Spaun is easier both because the simulation contains simplifications (so there are fewer variables and activities to record and analyze), and because of its top-down nature. Researchers building the simulation have a good idea of how it fits together at the functional level precisely because this is a central feature of the simulation. Much of its behavior is emergent and unpredictable, but the general principles that are supposed to make it work are understood.

Testing hypotheses in a complex bottom-up simulation is harder, both because it is more complex (creating huge amounts of data to analyze) and because it is constructed 'blind' to functional or system-level properties, which themselves emerge from the low-level activity of the programmed parts. In this case, if the simulation fails to generate realistic looking outputs, it is far from obvious how to pinpoint the most causally relevant factors involved. There are techniques for getting a better understanding of some kinds of neural networks (e.g. deep visualization of deep neural nets, Yosinski et al., 2015), but techniques for visualizing Blue Brain, as a way to easily and visually identify causally relevant activity, are still under construction (Abdellah et al., 2015).

There are also questions about the epistemic value of adding more complexity or realism to simulations. As Winsberg (2010) discusses in depth, building simulations is a skill, and the epistemic value of a simulation depends in large part on the knowledge and skill sets of those building it. A researcher will (ideally) have a good idea of what can be left out of a simulation, what is crucial to include in detail, what short cuts can be taken in the programming, how to represent parts and activities in the simulation, and so on, given the specific epistemic aims of the simulation. The simplifications, idealizations, and so on in Spaun are directed at specific goals (i.e. testing specific hypotheses), and given these goals, it is reasonable to make certain widespread and sometimes extreme simplifications. These will affect the sort of conclusions that can be drawn from the simulation, but this in no way renders it epistemically inert. As McClelland (2009) writes: "Simplification is essential [for understanding], but comes at a cost, and real understanding depends in part on understanding the effects of the simplification" (p. 18). This is echoed in Trappenberg's (2009) textbook on computational neuroscience: "Modelling the brain is not a contest in recreating the brain in all its details on a computer. It is questionable how much more we would comprehend the functionality of the brain with such complex and detailed models" (p. 7). If understanding is the aim of simulation, then hypothesis–driven simulations should be favored.

Clearly though, there are idealizations, simplifications, and some things just left out of the Blue Brain simulations too. But as the purpose of this type of simulation is more of a multi-purpose exploratory and experimental tool, it appears to be less reasonable to make widespread simplifications, because it is not clear what specific properties might be relevant to a given behavior, and the creators of such a simulation presumably do not want to limit the kinds of conclusions that can be drawn from it in advance. Yet this may be the problem: a multi-purpose near replica of a complex system is almost as epistemically opaque as the original system. Constructing hypothesis–driven simulations makes it possible to simplify and idealize in specific and well-reasoned ways, and this in turn makes the performance of the simulation easier to understand, even if this limits the kinds of conclusions that can be drawn from it.

All this though is only relevant *if* the intended goal is to understand how brains generate complex behavior. The Blue Brain project produces other epistemic outputs though, including targeting questions in cellular/molecular neuroscience, generating an *in silico* experimental suite, and investigating links between genetics and cognition. Given these wide-ranging goals, the design of the Blue Brain project is clearly more appropriate than a top-down simulation. Different approaches to simulation must then be evaluated in terms of how well they can meet the epistemic goals of their designers, and top-down and bottom-up simulations may often be aimed at different goals, making them incomparable.

Building on this, the next section assesses the kinds of explanations that can be constructed by using computer simulations.

3 Simulations and computational explanations

It is natural to think that computer simulations in computational neuroscience generate computational explanations of the brain. However, things are not always so straightforward.

First, some philosophers working within the mechanistic approach to explanation have argued that computational explanations, as (somewhat) autonomous computational or functional level explanations, are not explanatory at all unless they fit into the mechanistic framework (Kaplan, 2011; Piccinini and Craver, 2011). Briefly, a mechanistic explanation of a phenomenon P is an explanation of how a system of spatially and temporally organized parts and activities together produce P (for review see Illari and Williamson, 2012). In particular, Kaplan (2011) has argued that to be explanatory at all, computational explanations must fit into the mechanistic framework by satisfying a 'model-to-mechanism-mapping' (3M) requirement:

> (3M) A model [or explanatory simulation] of a target phenomenon explains that phenomenon to the extent that (a) the variables in the model correspond to identifiable components, activities, and organizational features of the target mechanism that produces, maintains, or underlies the phenomenon, and (b) the (perhaps mathematical)

dependencies posited among these (perhaps mathematical) variables in the model correspond to causal relations among the components of the target mechanism.

(Kaplan, 2011, p. 347)

In this case, a simulation of purely computational processes that does not include any detail of how those processes are implemented in the brain may be predictive, but it is not explanatory. Further, a model or simulation that is more complete (detailed) is better than one that is less complete.

This obviously conflicts with the points about simplification and understanding raised above in discussion of Spaun, and blocks the possibility of non-mechanistically focused computational explanations of neural phenomena. These are taken in turn below.

3.1 Completeness

In contrast with Kaplan's suggestion that a more detailed mechanistic model is better than a less detailed one, and in line with the statements from neuroscientists themselves, Miłkowski (2016) has argued that idealization is an important feature of explanations gained from simulations. This is true not merely for practical reasons, but for reasons core to the mechanistic framework.

A core part of the mechanistic program is that mechanisms are mechanisms *for* generating a particular phenomenon, and so are individuated by functional capacities and/or explanatory targets. As a consequence of this, the only parts (and levels) that are necessary to include in a mechanism, and a mechanistic explanation, are those that are causally relevant to the explanatory target. In this case, idealizations and simplifications can be mechanistically appropriate, and indeed are regularly found in mechanistic explanations.[1]

In this case, Spaun can be seen as an idealized 'how–plausibly' mechanistic model of (some aspects of) cognitive flexibility. That is, it contains organized parts and activities that plausibly generate some degree of cognitive flexibility (at least the degree involved in shifting across the eight tasks that it can perform). This echoes the ideas outlined above: given the particular epistemic goal that Spaun is aimed at, its lack of biological realism is entirely acceptable.[2] If Spaun were aimed at a different explanatory target, it may not be plausible or sufficiently mechanistic, but this is the nature of mechanistic explanations in general.

With respect to the Blue Brain project, Miłkowski (2016) notes there is no obvious single and coherent explanatory target, but rather a wide series of questions that the Blue Brain project as a whole targets. Lacking a clear explanatory target, what the Blue Brain project amounts to therefore is not a single mechanistic model capable of providing a mechanistic explanation (for something), but a system for generating mechanistic simulations to test hypotheses. This echoes the points made above; that the Blue Brain project seems to have rather different epistemic aims than Spaun and other top-down simulations which are more driven towards testing potential explanations of specific phenomena. Perhaps more interestingly here, the lack of constraints from higher levels of description in generating the Blue Brain simulations make them mechanistically deficient: mechanisms are comprised of multiple levels of parts and activities. The strict bottom-up approach taken in the Blue Brain means that relevant levels are missed out, in as much as they cannot easily be identified within the simulation itself.

One aspect of top-down simulations (like Spaun) that a Kaplan-style approach gets right, however, is that while a simulation may generate outputs comparable to experimental data, it is not possible to claim that cognition actually works in the way suggested in the simulation; the simulation may or may not capture internal processes accurately. Only by specifying how the simulation is implemented, and then checking whether these details are in fact realized can this kind of simulation be said to accurately describe cognitive processes. This limits Spaun to giving 'how-plausibly' explanations. However, simulationists are generally open about this explanatory limitation on their approach.

3.2 Non-mechanistic computational explanations

There is clearly not enough space here to fully evaluate the mechanistic framework with respect to computational neuroscience (see other chapters in this part of the volume, and Chirimuuta, 2014; Irvine, 2015; Miłkowski, 2013; Piccinini, 2015; Rusanen and Lappi, 2007; Serban, 2015; Shagrir, 2010). One possibility is that, as above, computational explanations are a (possibly poor) species of mechanistic explanation, in which case there may be nothing distinctive about computational explanations, which should (ideally) be subsumed under a mechanistic framework. Another possibility is that computational explanations are a genuinely distinctive type of explanation, and so should not be subsumed or eliminated in favor of mechanistic explanations. The aims of researchers using top-down simulations in computational neuroscience suggests that computational explanations should be accepted as at least somewhat distinct from mechanistic explanation.

An initial move in this direction is to look to the kind of explanations provided by early connectionist simulations. These simulations were used to test the application of general computational principles concerning the effects of feedback learning algorithms on distributed knowledge representations to cognitive processes such as reading, acquisition of grammatical rules, and face recognition. One possible way in which the simulations themselves may have been counted as explanatory is that the simulations provided sketches of possible mechanisms, so were perhaps minimally mechanistically explanatory. However, this sharply contrasts with the expressed aims and conclusions from researchers at the time:

> We are striving for theories that explain phenomena in specific domains … in terms of more general principles concerning the representation of knowledge, its acquisition and use. … Modelling [simulating], on this view, is a way to both identify general principles and assess their validity.
>
> *(Seidenberg and McClelland, 1992, pp. 3–4).*

Here, it was the general principles that successful simulations were built from, not the simulations themselves, that were seen as explanatory (McClelland et al., 1987).

Looking more closely at the overall practice of using and constructing top-down simulations in computational neuroscience, it is apparent that the general principles instantiated in simulations are often based on computational templates borrowed from other disciplines (e.g. from statistics, economics, thermodynamics, AI). Computational templates are sets of equations or computational methods that are interpreted to generate models of particular phenomena, which here are often learning algorithms or general computational structures (Humphreys, 2002; 2004). These templates include reinforcement learning, Bayesian analysis, models of expected utility. Templates provide general principles which are interpreted and applied to target cognitive phenomena, and simulations based on these principles are subsequently tested and refined until they (if they can) provide satisfactory explanations of the target phenomena.

There are several related reasons why templates are commonly used in computational neuroscience. The first is that applying general computational templates to explain (neural) computational processes is epistemically efficient. Computational templates provide a ready-made set of algorithms and methods from which to build specific hypotheses about brain function. Relatedly, templates are tractable and usually well understood, which both makes it easier to apply them in new cases, and to tell whether their outputs will likely match behavioral data (Knuuttila, 2011). It also seems reasonable to assume that the brain is regulated by a set of common computational processes (e.g. compression algorithms, learning rules, etc.), in which case a template used to develop a simulation of visual perception may well be useful in developing a simulation of action or audition. In general, if the brain is seen as solving computational problems, then pre-existing computational templates developed in other fields that are known to solve similar problems can be imported and tested in a fairly straightforward way (for more discussion see Irvine, 2014).

Given this, at least some simulations function as 'proof of concept' that something like a particular template and the computational principles that it describes, captures the core computational principles that make the system able to do what it does. A simulation can test whether low-level decisions can be made in short time frames because they are governed by algorithms of sequential analysis (hypothesis testing where sampling is governed by a pre-defined stopping rule, see Gold and Shadlen, 2007), or that the brain can maximize reward in uncertain environments because it relies on reinforcement learning (Corrado et al., 2009), or whether performance degrades slowly in the face of damage because it uses parallel processing over distributed representations (McClelland et al., 1987). That is, simulations explain how a cognitive system solves a computational problem because it shows how it instantiates some common computational template (Shagrir, 2010).

Importantly, these explanations need not include any detail about how computational principles are implemented. The principles need to be implemented in the simulation in order to test whether they apply to a cognitive system, but having shown that the simulation fits with experimental data, it is the principles themselves, and not the simulation, that is explanatory. That they are used at all in a cognitive system can answer some important questions about cognition; how they are implemented answers others.

It is also possible that a simulation can offer both types of explanation at the same time (computational and mechanistic), and the more realistic the simulation, the more ways there are of checking that it does in fact describe real processes or merely has high predictive power. However, this does not mean that one type of explanation can be reduced to another (for more discussion, see references at the start of this section).

4 Contributions to computer science

Computer simulations, particularly those that are developed from pre-existing computational templates, make use of expertise from computer science in order to explain cognitive phenomena. However, the development of computer simulations can also contribute positively to computer science in several ways, reviewed below.

The Blue Brain project is a particularly good example of neuroscientists working with computer scientists and computer engineers (e.g. IBM, who supply the BlueGene supercomputer used in the project). Within the Blue Brain project, it is not only running the simulations that requires BlueGene, but also constructing the simulations in the first place. For example, Markram (2006) notes that the algorithm that determines the structural positions of neurons and connections between axons and dendrites is more computationally intense than running the resulting simulation. Complex software programs are required just to get the simulation to run across different processors. Writing in 2006, Markram stated that a million-fold increase of computer power was needed to simulate a whole brain at the level of detail then used to simulate a single neocortical column, but that algorithmic and hardware efficiencies could bring that down to manageable levels.

Colombo (2016) suggests that one possible way of developing efficient enough computers to run a detailed whole-brain simulation is to learn from existing simulations, and how they trade off features like execution time, processing capacity and energy consumption, compared to the brains they are trying to simulate. This is significant as energy consumption and heat production are pressing problems in moving beyond current levels of computer power. Taking inspiration from the properties of real brains and applying them to large-scale computer simulations of brains can be used to generate neuromorphic devices; computational devices that are modeled on brains and how they manage high computational efficiency. For example, the SpiNNaker chip and system (http://apt.cs.manchester.ac.uk/projects/SpiNNaker/project/) were developed in tandem with the Blue Brain project, and constitute a massively parallel architecture composed of billions of spiking (neuron-like) units. This can be used both to simulate neural networks but also has applications in robotics (where high computational power is needed from low power sources) and computer science more generally. In addition to the differences noted above, large-scale bottom-up simulations can therefore have significant impacts outside testing hypotheses about specific cognitive processes.

5 Summary

This chapter has reviewed the epistemic aims of different types of simulations in computational neuroscience, the epistemic advantages and disadvantages of each, and what kind of explanations they can offer. Top-down large-scale simulations may have the edge when it comes to providing explanations how brains generate complex behavior, but at least some bottom-up simulations have other epistemic goals as well, which they are better suited to. Simulations like Spaun can be argued to provide (idealized) 'how-plausibly' mechanistic explanations of high-level target phenomena (e.g. generation of flexible behavior). The BlueBrain simulation is not aimed at a specific explanatory target, so does not provide a mechanistic explanation, but does provide the means to test a range of mechanistic hypotheses. Finally, top-down simulations can also be seen as providing distinctive and non-mechanistic computational explanations by identifying the general computational principles by which a system operates. Beyond these explanatory goals, learning from the activity of simulation in computational neuroscience also opens possibilities to advance in other fields, including making possible the kind of computational power required to run more complex bottom-up simulations in the future.

Notes

1 As a special case of this, Levy and Bechtel (2013) outline how focusing on causal connectivity and leaving out aspects of mechanistic structure can also generate appropriate abstract mechanistic explanations.
2 It also appears that adding detail leads to no greater predictive power either; replacing simple neurons in Spaun's frontal cortex with more complex and biological realistic ones does not improve Spaun's performance (Chi, 2016).

References

Abdellah, M. et al. (2015) 'Physically-based in Silico Light Sheet Microscopy for Visualizing Fluorescent Brain Models', *BMC Bioinformatics*, 16 (11), p. S8.

Chi, K.R. (2016) 'Neural Modelling: Abstractions of the Mind', *Nature*, 531 (7592), pp. S16–S17.

Chirimuuta, M. (2014) 'Minimal Models and Canonical Neural Computations: The Distinctness of Computational Explanation in Neuroscience', *Synthese*, 191 (2), pp. 127–153.

Colombo, M. (2016) 'Why Build a Virtual Brain? Large-scale Neural Simulations as Jump Start for Cognitive Computing', *Journal of Experimental and Theoretical Artificial Intelligence*, 29 (2), pp. 361–370.

Corrado, G.S. and Doya, K. (2007) 'Understanding Neural Coding through the Model-based Analysis of Decision Making', *The Journal of Neuroscience*, 27 (31), pp. 8178–8180.

Corrado, G.S. et al. (2009) 'The Trouble with Choice: Studying Decision Variables in the Brain', in Glimcher, P.W. et al. (eds.) *Neuroeconomics: Decision Making and the Brain*. Cambridge, MA: Academic Press, pp. 463–480.

Eliasmith, C. et al. (2012) 'A Large-scale Model of the Functioning Brain', *Science*, 338 (6111), pp. 1202–1205.

Gold, J.I. and Shadlen, M.N. (2007) 'The Neural Basis of Decision Making', *Annual Review of Neuroscience*, 30, pp. 535–574.

Humphreys, P. (2002) 'Computational Models', *Philosophy of Science*, 69 (S3), pp. S1–S11.

Humphreys, P. (2004) *Extending Ourselves: Computational Science, Empiricism, and Scientific Method*. Oxford: Oxford University Press.

Illari, P.M. and Williamson, J. (2012) 'What Is a Mechanism? Thinking about Mechanisms across the Sciences', *European Journal for Philosophy of Science*, 2 (1), pp. 119–135.

Irvine, E. (2014) 'Model-based Theorizing in Cognitive Neuroscience', *The British Journal for the Philosophy of Science*, 67 (1), pp. 143–168.

Irvine, E. (2015) 'Models, Robustness, and Non-causal Explanation: A Foray into Cognitive Science and Biology', *Synthese*, 192 (12), pp. 3943–3959.

Kaplan, D.M. (2011) 'Explanation and Description in Computational Neuroscience', *Synthese*, 183 (3), pp. 339–373.

Knuuttila, T. (2011) 'Modelling and Representing: An Artefactual Approach to Model-based Representation', *Studies in History and Philosophy of Science Part A*, 42 (2), pp. 262–271.

Levy, A. and Bechtel, W. (2013) 'Abstraction and the Organization of Mechanisms', *Philosophy of Science*, 80 (2), pp. 241–261.

Markram, H. (2006) 'The Blue Brain Project', *Nature Reviews Neuroscience*, 7 (2), pp. 153–160.

Markram, H. et al. (2015) 'Reconstruction and Simulation of Neocortical Microcircuitry', Cell, 163 (2), pp. 456–492.

McClelland, J.L. (2009) 'The Place of Modeling in Cognitive Science', *Topics in Cognitive Science*, 1 (1), pp. 11–38.

McClelland, J.L. et al. (1987) *Parallel Distributed Processing*, vol. 2. Cambridge, MA: MIT Press.

Miłkowski, M. (2013) *Explaining the Computational Mind*. Cambridge, MA: MIT Press.

Miłkowski, M. (2016) 'Explanatory Completeness and Idealization in Large Brain Simulations: A Mechanistic Perspective', *Synthese*, 193 (5), pp. 1457–1478.

Parker, W.S. (2009) 'Does Matter Really Matter? Computer Simulations, Experiments, and Materiality', *Synthese*, 169 (3), pp. 483–496.

Piccinini, G. (2015) *Physical Computation: A Mechanistic Account*. Oxford: Oxford University Press.

Piccinini, G. and Craver, C. (2011) 'Integrating Psychology and Neuroscience: Functional Analyses as Mechanism Sketches', *Synthese*, 183 (3), pp. 283–311.

Rusanen, A.-M. and Lappi, O. (2007) 'The Limits of Mechanistic Explanation in Neurocognitive Sciences', in Vosniadou, S., Kayser, D., and Protopapas, A. (eds.) *Proceedings of the European Cognitive Science Conference 2007*. London: Taylor and Francis, pp. 284–289.

Seidenberg, M and McClelland, J. (1992) *Connectionist Models and Explanatory Theories in Cognition*, July 24. Available at: http://stanford.edu/~jlmcc/papers/PublicationFiles/MISC_manuscripts_Dates_Unknown/SeidenbergMcClellandXXConnectionistModelsandExplanatoryTheoriesinCognition.pdf (Accessed: July 24, 2016).

Serban, M. (2015) 'The Scope and Limits of a Mechanistic View of Computational Explanation', *Synthese*, 192 (10), pp. 3371–3396.

Shagrir, O. (2010) 'Marr on Computational-Level Theories', *Philosophy of Science*, 77 (4), pp. 477–500.

Sompolinsky, H. (2014) 'Computational Neuroscience: Beyond the Local Circuit', *Current Opinion in Neurobiology*, 25, xiii–xviii.

Trappenberg, T. (2009) *Fundamentals of Computational Neuroscience*. Oxford: Oxford University Press.

Winsberg, E. (2010) *Science in the Age of Computer Simulation*. Chicago, IL: University of Chicago Press.

Yosinski, J. et al. (2015) 'Understanding Neural Networks through Deep Visualization', *Deep Learning Workshop, 31st International Conference on Machine Learning*. Lille, France. Available at: http://arxiv.org/abs/1506.06579.

28

LEARNING AND REASONING

Matteo Colombo

1 Introduction

Learning consists in the acquisition of new psychological traits, including abilities, knowledge, and concepts. The improvement of some measure of performance when carrying out some task is the main source of evidence for learning. Reasoning consists in a change in view, where certain beliefs or intentions are taken to provide reasons for acquiring, retaining, dropping, or updating some other belief, or for acting in a certain way (Harman, 2008).

Learning and reasoning are prominent targets of research in computational cognitive science. Central questions include: On what kinds of innate knowledge and biases does learning rely? Does the human mind deploy multiple kinds of learning and reasoning systems? How are these learning and reasoning systems neurally realized? How do they interact? When are human learning and reasoning optimal or rational? This chapter will explore some of these questions in the light of recent advances in computational cognitive science such as the following two success stories.

First, the Google-owned artificial intelligence company DeepMind created a system called *deep Q-network* (DQN) that could learn how to play forty-nine different arcade games – including Pong, Pac-Man, and Space Invaders (Mnih et al., 2015). Starting with the same minimal body of built-in knowledge, and after about 924 hours training on each game, a deep Q-network learned how to play all forty-nine games. For more than half of the games, its performance was comparable to that of expert human gamers. Key to the network's versatile learning and human-level performance was the ability of deep Q-network to combine a model-free reinforcement learning algorithm, *Q-learning*, with a brain-inspired architecture that supported pattern recognition, *a deep convolutional neural network*.

Second, a computational system was developed within the *Bayesian* framework that could learn concepts associated with handwritten characters based on just a single example (Lake, Salakhutdinov, and Tenenbaum, 2015). This *Bayesian program learning* (BPL) system had the built-in knowledge that characters in writing systems consist of strokes, demarcated by the lifting of a pen, and that the strokes consist of sub-strokes, demarcated by points at which the pen's velocity is zero. Representing concepts as *probabilistic generative models*, its performance on a series of recognition, parsing, and generation tasks was indistinguishable from human behavior. Key to this system's performance was its ability to *recombine* its existing pieces of causal knowledge to construct hierarchical probabilistic models that *best explained* new observations.

In what follows, I will refer to these two cases to sketch a taxonomy of computational approaches to learning and reasoning (Section 2), and to discuss some implications for three issues. These three issues concern, first, the character of humans' innate cognitive architecture (Section 3); second, the distinction between two kinds of thinking: one fast and intuitive, the other slow and deliberative (Section 4); and third, the nature of rational behavior (Section 5).

2 An overview of computational approaches

This section distinguishes reinforcement learning from supervised, unsupervised, and Bayesian learning, and clarifies the functional significance of deep and hierarchical architectures.[1]

2.1 Reinforcement learning: model-based and model-free algorithms

Mnih et al.'s (2015) DQN learned how to master a wide range of video games by combining a deep learning architecture, a convolutional neural network, and a model-free reinforcement learning algorithm. *Reinforcement learning* (RL) is one of the most popular computational frameworks in machine learning and artificial intelligence. RL offers a collection of algorithms to solve the problem of learning what to do in the face of rewards and punishments, which are received by taking different actions in an unfamiliar environment (Sutton and Barto, 1998).

RL systems observe the current state of their environment and take an action – for example, DQN observes an array of pixels representing the current screen in the game it's playing. Then, it selects actions from a set of legal moves in the game – like 'move up', 'move right', or 'fire'. Actions produce rewards or punishments – for example, DQN receives a reward when the game score increases – and cause a transition from the current state to a new state in the environment.

Rewards and punishments can cause changes in behavior, as they serve as positive and negative reinforcers. The specific causal impact of rewards and punishments on behavior depends on their magnitude, which is specified by a scalar quantity that can be positive, negative, or zero.

Action selection is based on a value (or loss) function defined with respect to a *policy*, which is a mapping from each state and action to the probability of taking a certain action when in a certain state. Given a policy, a *value function* assigns values to either states or state-action pairs, and is updated on the basis of the rewards and punishments the system receives. Given the magnitude of rewards and punishments in a system's environment, the *value* of a state is the expected sum of future rewards (and punishments) that can be achieved by starting to act from that state in that environment under a certain policy. The system learns by pursuing the goal of maximizing its long-term cumulative reward – for example, maximizing its final score in a video game.

DQN implements a *model-free* reinforcement learning algorithm called "Q-learning" (Watkins and Dayan, 1992). Systems implementing model-free algorithms learn a value function that specifies the expected value of each pair of a current state of the environment and an action. Model-free learning algorithms learn the value function without building or searching any model of how an action might change the state of the environment. What drives learning is the *reward prediction-error* signal. This signal quantifies the difference between the predicted and currently experienced reward for a particular action in a particular environmental state, and it is used to update the value function.[2] Speaking to its neurobiological plausibility, a wealth of neurobiological evidence suggests that the phasic activity of dopaminergic neurons in the basal ganglia encode reward prediction-errors signals (Montague, Dayan, and Sejnowski, 1996; Colombo, 2014).

Systems implementing *model-based* algorithms build a model of the transition relations between environmental states under actions and the values associated with environmental states. This model may consist in a forward-looking decision tree representing the relationships between a sequence of states and actions, and their associated values. Model-based algorithms evaluate actions by searching through the model to find the most valuable action. In comparison to model-free computing, model-based computing produces more accurate and more flexible solutions to learning tasks. However, model-based computing is slow, and may not tractably solve complex reasoning and learning tasks.

2.2 Supervised and unsupervised learning

RL differs from both supervised and unsupervised learning. *Supervised learning* algorithms rely on an "external supervisor" that can supply the learner with the correct answer when learning. In supervised learning, for every input, the corresponding output is provided, and the learning algorithm seeks a function from inputs to the respective target outputs. For example, an algorithm for solving a classification task may rely on a training set of labeled examples, that is, a set of pairs consisting of some input (a certain example) and the correct output value (the right label to classify that example). After being trained on labeled examples, the behavior of the supervised learning system may generalize to solve the classification task for new, unlabeled examples. Thus, the main difference between RL and supervised learning is that RL algorithms, unlike supervised learning algorithms, pursue the goal of maximizing their expected reward without relying on a set of supervised instructions about input–output pairings.

Semi-supervised learning is a class of supervised learning, where a system learns by relying on both labeled and unlabeled training data. *Active learning* is a species of semi-supervised learning, where the system can actively query the "external supervisor" for the labeled outputs of the input data (or for the correct response to some problem) from which it chooses to learn. The advantage of active learning over supervised learning is that, for many tasks, providing the system with labeled input–output pairings is difficult and time-consuming; in these tasks, if the system could actively choose its input data and query the external supervisor for labeled outputs, its learning may be quicker and more efficient.

Unsupervised learning does not rely on an "external supervisor". In unsupervised learning, the system receives only a set of unlabeled input data. As no datasets about the corresponding outputs are provided, the learning algorithm seeks to find structure or hidden patterns in the input data. Popular unsupervised learning algorithms, like k-Means and hierarchical clustering algorithms, seek to cluster input data, where a cluster is a grouping of data that are similar between them and dissimilar to data in other clusters. Because unsupervised learning algorithms, unlike RL algorithms, do not rely on reward signals and do not pursue the goal of maximizing expected reward, RL differs from unsupervised learning too.

2.3 Convolutional neural networks and deep learning

DQN is a complex learning system consisting of two main sub-systems: a convolutional neural network and a model-free RL algorithm. *Convolutional neural networks* (LeCun et al., 1989) are a species of connectionist neural networks (see Garson and Buckner, this volume; Stinson, this volume) that make the assumption that their inputs are images. While every image can be represented as a matrix of pixel values, convolutional neural networks leverage two statistical properties of images: that local groups of pixel values are highly correlated (so as to form distinct local visual motifs), and that the local statistics of images are invariant to location (so that a certain motif can appear anywhere in an image) (LeCun, Bengio, and Hinton, 2015).

Leveraging these statistical properties of images, convolutional neural networks take arrays of data (e.g. pixel matrices) as inputs, pass them through a series of feed-forward processing stages (or "layers") to get an output. The output is the probability that, for example, the input image is a specific state in a video game. The convolutional network in the DQN learns these probabilities by extracting low-level features from input images, and then building up more abstract representations through a series of transformations carried out by multiple hidden layers of neurons. Low-level features extracted by the first layer might consist of dark and light pixels. The next layer might recognize that some of these pixels form edges. The next up the hierarchy might distinguish horizontal and vertical lines. Eventually, the network recognizes objects like trees and faces, and complex scenes like a video game frame.

The convolutional neural network in DQN has many layers, and can then be considered as having a "deep architecture". Inspired by the hierarchical organization of the visual cortex in the brain, a *deep learning architecture* is a multi-layer stack of nodes, whose processes can handle a large set of input data and extract progressively more abstract representations (Hinton, 2007). Recall that DQN takes as input screen pixels. Screen pixels implicitly contain the relevant information about the current state of the game, but the number of possible game states picked out by different combinations of screen pixels is *very* large. This is where deep learning helps. With greater "depth", that is, with many layers of neurons, the convolutional network in DQN can reliably and tractably recognize the current state of the environment from screen pixels.

2.4 Bayesianism: probabilistic models, conditionalization, and hierarchical hypotheses

Lake et al.'s (2015) Bayesian program learning system (BPL) can use one single example of a handwritten alphabetic character to successfully classify new characters, to generate new characters of the same type, and to generate new characters for a given alphabet. While Lake et al. (2015) took these successes to be evidence that BPL can learn *concepts*, BPL's performance depends on its capacity of constructing hierarchical probabilistic models that can explain central causal properties of handwriting under a Bayesian criterion.

Despite several important differences (Danks, this volume), BPL shares a common core structure with other Bayesian systems:[3] BPL aims at constructing an accurate model of a target data-generating process, where a *data-generating process* is the process, system, or phenomenon we want to learn about on the basis of the data it generates. For BPL, the handwriting of alphabetic characters is the generative process, and the data this process generates include sequences of pen strokes and raw images of characters.

To learn a model of the generative-process, the system assumes a space of hypotheses (a *generative model*) about what raw image and sequences of pen strokes are likely to be associated with what alphabetic character. BPL's hypotheses correspond to probability distributions defined by parameters – for example, by a mean μ and standard deviation σ. Because BPL's hypothesis space is *hierarchically* structured, it includes *over-hypotheses* about the values of the parameters defining the hypotheses at the level below – for example, over-hypotheses about the probability distribution of the values of parameters μ and σ. In turn, BPL's over-hypotheses correspond to probability distribution defined by hyper-parameters – for example, by hyper-parameters α and β.

BPL employs *Bayesian conditionalization* to compute an approximation of the posterior probability of each hypothesis, at each level in its hierarchical hypothesis space, in the light of observed raw images and sequences of pen strokes. Based on the hypotheses with the highest posterior probability, the system infers a specific alphabetic character – for example, an 'A'. BPL uses this inference to achieve human-level performance in a number of classification and generation tasks involving handwritten characters.

3 Learning and innateness[4]

This section makes two claims. First, the empirical successes of Bayesianism and deep learning vindicate *enlightened empiricism* as the correct way to understand the character of our innate cognitive architecture. Second, in contrast to deep learning approaches, Bayesianism displays learning as a rational inductive process of hypothesis-construction and testing, but this does not entail that "there is no such thing as learning a new concept" (Fodor, 1975, p. 95).

3.1 Nativism and empiricism

Contemporary nativists and empiricists agree that the acquisition of psychological traits depends on a certain amount of innate structure. The disagreement concerns the exact amount and character of this innate structure (Cowie, 1999, p. 26; Margolis and Laurence, 2013, p. 695). According to empiricists, the innate architecture of the mind includes few *general-purpose* (aka domain-general) *algorithms* for acquiring psychological traits. According to nativists, instead, the innate architecture of the mind includes many domain-specific algorithms or bodies of knowledge for acquiring new psychological traits, where *domain-specific algorithms* operate in a restricted class of problems in a specific psychological domain, and *domain-specific bodies of knowledge* are systems of mental representations that encode information about a specific subject matter such as physics and psychology, and that apply to a distinct class of entities and events (Spelke, 1994; Carey, 2011).

As nativism and empiricism admit of degrees, Cowie (1999, pp. 153–159) offers a more fine-grained taxonomy. She distinguishes between *Chomskyan Nativism*, *Weak Nativism*, and *Enlightened Empiricism*. In relation to language, *Chomskyan Nativism* is committed to three ideas: that learning a language requires bodies of knowledge specific to the linguistic domain (DS); that the bodies of knowledge specified in (DS) are innate (I);[5] and that the bodies of knowledge specified in (DS) as being required for language learning are the principles of a Universal Grammar (UG). *Weak Nativism* accepts (DS) and (I), but rejects (UG); *Enlightened Empiricism* accepts (DS), but rejects (I) and (UG). This taxonomy will be helpful for understanding how computational learning systems might be relevant for the nativism debate.

3.2 Bayesianism and deep learning vindicate enlightened empiricism

Deep learning neural networks and Bayesianism are not intrinsically anti-nativist. However, empirically successful Bayesian and deep learning neural models have two interesting consequences for the nativism debate. On the one hand, they show that the acquisition and developmental trajectory of psychological traits need *not* depend on a system of innate, domain-specific representations with combinatorial syntactic and semantic structure (a *language of thought*), which were once assumed to be essential, psychologically primitive (i.e. innate) ingredients of the human cognitive architecture (Fodor, 1975, 1981; Chomsky, 1980). On the other hand, empirically successful Bayesian and deep learning neural models vindicate enlightened empiricism.

Mnih et al.'s (2015) DQN shows that psychological traits such as the ability to play a video game can be acquired courtesy of three ingredients: a deep convolutional network for recognizing the current state of the game; a model-free RL algorithm searching for an optimal action-selection policy to maximize its expected score in the game; and inbuilt knowledge that input data are visual images and that only a specific set of actions can be taken in a certain game. Lake, Salakhutdinov, and Tenenbaum's (2015) BPL shows that acquiring new concepts of handwritten characters can be carried out by probabilistic algorithms that operate on hierarchical generative models and that exploit primitive representations of edges, and primitive non-propositional knowledge of general spatial and causal relations.

Learning how to play a video game, and learning new concepts of handwritten characters require learners' thoughts about video gaming, and about handwritten characters be constrained by knowledge that is specific to the target domains – respectively, by knowledge of which actions are most likely to yield a high score in a video game, and by knowledge of which pen strokes are most likely to constitute a handwritten character.

This domain-specific knowledge need not be built in. As the DQN was trained anew for each game, it acquired visual representations and decision policies specialized for each new game. BPL acquired concepts of handwritten characters by building them compositionally from primitive representations of edges and of causal and spatial relations. Edge representations were combined to make lines. Lines were combined according to certain spatial and causal relations. In turn, newly acquired representations of handwritten characters could be re-used to build new representations.

In summary, both Mnih et al.'s (2015) DQN and Lake et al.'s (2015) BPL can learn domain-specific constraints on future learning, on the basis of minimal bodies of innate knowledge and powerful general-purpose algorithms. To the extent that these two computational systems are representative of Bayesian and deep learning connectionist approaches, and are empirically successful, *enlightened empiricism* is the correct way of understanding the character of our innate cognitive architecture.

3.3 Is concept learning impossible for Bayesian systems?

Unlike connectionism, Bayesianism transparently displays learning as a rational inductive process of hypothesis-construction and testing. However, as Fodor famously argued, "[i]f the mechanism of concept learning is the projection and confirmation of hypotheses (and what else *could* it be), then there is a sense in which there is no such thing as learning a new concept" (1975, p. 95).

According to Fodor, one cannot acquire new concepts via hypothesis-testing because hypotheses are thoughts, and thoughts are constituted by concepts. So, hypothesis-testing presupposes concepts, which means that learning presupposes concepts. From this argument, it would follow that Bayesianism makes the very idea of learning all one's concepts incoherent.

In a sense, Fodor is right that Bayesian systems do not learn. After all, any Bayesian system assumes knowledge of a hypothesis space, which specifies the space of possible structures in the environment that could have generated input data. Each hypothesis in that space is defined as a probability distribution over the possible input data. The system acquires new psychological traits by searching and evaluating hypotheses in its hypothesis space. In this sense, Bayesian systems cannot acquire new psychological structures that were not built into their hypothesis space.

In a different sense, Fodor is wrong. Bayesian systems can acquire novel psychological structures. To understand how, we should distinguish between the *latent* and the *explicit* hypothesis space of a system (Perfors, 2012), and between *parametric* and *nonparametric* Bayesian models (Austerweil et al., 2015).

A system's *latent* hypothesis space consists of the system's representational resources. It defines the possible thoughts the system can have. The space of thinkable thoughts of biological systems might be determined by their brain's structural and functional patterns of connectivity (Park and Friston, 2013). The *explicit* hypothesis space consists of the representations available to the system for evaluation, manipulation, and inference. It defines the system's actual thoughts.

Two types of hypothesis spaces correspond to parametric and nonparametric models. *Parametric* models define the set of possible hypotheses with a fixed number of parameters. For example, the hypotheses might all be Gaussian distributions with a known variance, but unknown mean. Based on input data, the system acquires new psychological traits by estimating the mean of these Gaussians. *Nonparametric* models make weaker assumptions about the family of possible structures in the environment that could have generated input data. The number of parameters of a nonparametric model increases with the number of observed data. This allows for the acquisition of new psychological traits that need not have a fixed, predetermined shape.

Hierarchical Bayesian systems like Lake et al.'s (2015) BPL maintain multiple hypothesis spaces. At the highest level of the hierarchy, we find over-hypotheses concerning the shape of the hypotheses at the levels below (Gaussian, Dirichlet, Beta, etc.). Over-hypotheses are defined by psychologically primitive hyper-parameters that need not pick out any lexical concept – for example, if the system is using a beta distribution to model the distribution of the parameter μ of a Gaussian distribution at the level below, then α and β are parameters of an over-hypothesis, hence hyper-parameters. Hierarchical Bayesian systems can include both parametric and nonparametric hypothesis spaces. In hierarchical, nonparametric systems, the number of parameters is not fixed with respect to the amount of data, but it grows with the number of sensory data observed by the system.

During hypothesis testing, over-hypotheses in hierarchical Bayesian systems are compared and evaluated in the light of incoming data. Hyper-parameters that best fit the data lead to the generation of a class of hypotheses at the levels below. Specific hypotheses are constructed, and in turn evaluated in terms of their explanatory power over observed sensory data. As data flow into the system and tune hyper-parameters, new sets of representations become available at lower levels in the hierarchy.

The entire process of evaluation of different hypotheses at different levels in the hierarchy, and of construction of specific lower-level hypotheses allows the system to acquire novel psychological traits. These traits are not built into the systems, in the sense that they cannot be simply read off from the system's inbuilt hypothesis space (Kemp and Tenenbaum, 2008; Kemp, Perfors, and Tenenbaum, 2007).

Bayesian nonparametric hierarchical hypothesis testing need *not* involve psychologically primitive lexical concepts, and can lead to genuine conceptual learning. In this sense, Bayesian systems learn genuinely novel concepts: a richer system of representations can be acquired on the basis of a more impoverished one. This learning depends on a complex interplay of soft innate biases, environmental structure, and general-purpose mechanisms for hypothesis-testing and hypothesis-construction.

4 Reasoning beyond two systems

A popular distinction in the psychology and philosophy of reasoning is between intuition and deliberation. In social and cognitive psychology, this dichotomy is at the core of two-system theories of reasoning. These theories posit two kinds of reasoning systems in the human cognitive architecture, which are distinguished on the basis of two clusters of co-varying properties. System 1 is said to be fast, affective, autonomous, unconscious, effortless, it does not significantly engage working memory resources, and produces intuitive judgments. System 2 is said to be slow, cognitive, controlled, conscious, and effortful, it loads on working memory and produces deliberate judgments (Sloman, 1996; Kahneman, 2011; Evans and Stanovich, 2013). Samuels (2009, pp. 134–135) points out that if the human cognitive architecture comprises two reasoning systems, "there needs to be some way of distinguishing … a reasoning system from the rest of cognition so that there are plausibly just two reasoning systems". This section argues that advances in RL and Bayesianism in computational neuroscience are progressively eroding the distinction between two kinds of reasoning systems. RL and Bayesianism appeal to computational features on a continuum, allowing for several different kinds of reasoning systems and hybrid processes. There is no convincing case for an empirically supported distinction between just two reasoning systems.

4.1 RL and two reasoning systems

The distinction between model-free and model-based systems maps onto the distinction between System 1 and System 2 reasoning. To the extent that this mapping is plausibly grounded in computational, neural, and behavioral evidence, it would offer a promising way of carving out two reasoning systems in the human cognitive architecture. Here are three preliminary considerations in support of the mapping.

First, like System 1 reasoning, a model-free algorithm is typically fast, knowledge-sparse, and computationally frugal. A model-based algorithm is instead slower, knowledge-involving, and computationally expensive, similarly to System 2 reasoning. Second, the neural circuits that have been associated with System 1 and System 2 reasoning are roughly the same as those that have been associated with model-free and model-based RL. Like System 1 processing, model-free control has been associated with activity in a subcortical neural circuit comprising the striatum and its dopaminergic afferents. Like System 2 processing, model-based control has been associated with activity in the prefrontal cortex (Niv, 2009). Third, model-based systems underlie goal-directed behavior, which is typically said to be supported by System 2 processing. Model-free systems underlie habitual behavior, which is instead said to be supported by System 1 processing (Daw, Niv, and Dayan, 2005).[6]

In particular, Daw et al. (2005) proposed that activity in the prefrontal cortex is responsible for implementing model-based strategies, thereby supporting goal-directed behavior, whereas the dorsolateral striatum and its dopaminergic afferents would implement model-free strategies such as Q-learning, thereby supporting habitual behavior. These two systems would be "opposite extremes in a trade-off between the statistically efficient use of experience and computational tractability" (Daw, Niv, and Dayan, 2005, p. 1704). For Daw and collaborators, when the model-based and model-free strategies are in disagreement, the nervous system would rely on the relative accuracy of the evaluations of the two strategies to arbitrate between them. The relative accuracy of the two strategies depends on such factors as the amount of training (which increases accuracy in the model-free system) and the depth of search in the model (which requires heuristic approximations for making value estimates in deeper models, and consequently increases inaccuracy in the model-based system) (see also Keramati, Dezfouli, and Piray, 2011).

Despite the extraordinary fruitfulness of the model-based/model-free dichotomy, recent advances call into question the mapping between System 1 and model-free control, and between System 2 and model-based control. First, there are several intermediate modes of learning and reasoning between model-free and model-based control, which vary considerably in their algorithmic specification, representational formats, and computational properties. These intermediate modes of reasoning exhibit a combination of computational properties that crisscross the distinguishing clusters associated with System 1 and System 2 reasoning (Dolan and Dayan, 2013, p. 320; on this 'crossover' problem see also Samuels, 2009).

Second, the two neural pathways that have been associated with System 1/model-free reasoning and System 2/model-based reasoning are densely connected by cortico-basal ganglion loops, and span several parallel and integrative circuits that play several functional roles in reasoning, learning, decision making, and memory (Haber, 2003; Haruno and Kawato, 2006; Hazy, Frank, and O'Reilly, 2007).

In particular, one cannot maintain that dopaminergic activity is the signature feature of System 1/model-free processing. While initial findings suggested that the phasic firing of dopaminergic neurons reports the temporal difference reward prediction error featuring in model-free processing and underwriting several properties of System 1 processing, more recent studies indicate that sub-second dopamine fluctuations might actually encode a superposition of different prediction errors: reward prediction errors and counterfactual prediction errors (Kishida et al., 2016). Counterfactual prediction errors signal "how much better or worse than expected the experienced outcome could have been" had the agent performed a different action (ibid., p. 200; see also Doll, Simon, and Daw, 2012). Counterfactual error signals would speed up model-free learning, but would also be involved in mental simulation of alternative possible outcomes, which has been said to be a defining property of System 2 (Evans and Stanovich, 2013). This suggests that dopamine fluctuations in the striatum might implement hybrid forms of RL, involving aspects of both model-free and model-based computation.

Third and finally, a growing number of studies highlight that, in several reasoning tasks, people do not rely purely on either model-free or model-based control. Instead, they capitalize on aspects of both controllers at the same time: adaptive reasoners integrate the computational efficiency of model-free, habitual control with the flexibility of model-based, goal-directed control (Dezfouli and Balleine, 2013; Cushman and Morris, 2015). DQN, for example, does not purely rely on model-free control, but its reasoning integrates a Q-learning algorithm with stored *experience replay representations*; that is, during gameplay DQN can store in a replay memory representations of state-action-reward-state transitions, which it can use for reasoning and learning in an off-line mode. As Keramati et al. (2016, p. 12871) explain, "humans are equipped with a much richer repertoire of strategies, than just two dichotomous systems, for coping with the complexity of real-life problems as well as with limitations in their cognitive resources".

4.2 Approximate Bayes

Many believe that Bayesianism in cognitive science is committed to positing one general purpose reasoning algorithm, which consists of the Bayesian rule of conditionalization for computing posterior distributions. But the type of neurocomputational mechanism that might account for concept learning, categorization, causal reasoning and so on, cannot implement Bayesian conditionalization, because Bayesian conditionalization makes these learning and reasoning tasks intractable.

Almost all Bayesian computational systems, including Lake and colleagues' (2015) BPL, deploy a variety of algorithms that compute approximations of a target posterior distribution. For example, two Monte Carlo algorithms that have been used to solve category learning problems are Gibbs sampling and particle filtering (Sanborn, Griffiths, and Navarro, 2010). Both Gibbs sampler and particle filter algorithms are flexible, can successfully solve different types of problems, and are computationally less expensive than Bayesian conditionalization. They present important differences too. Perhaps, the most notable difference is that the particle filter algorithms are path dependent, while Gibbs samplers are not.

The Gibbs sampler assumes that all data are available at the time of learning and reasoning: if new data arrive over the course of processing of the Gibbs sampler, then the Gibbs sampler must start its processing anew, which makes it unsuitable for online, rapid, sequential learning and reasoning, whose trajectories may be constrained by evidence observed in the past. Instead, the particle filter algorithm assumes that data are collected progressively over time: posterior distributions are approximated by propagating samples, whose weights are updated as a function of incoming observations. Thus, the order in which different pieces of evidence are encountered has substantial effect on learning and reasoning underlain by particle filter algorithms.

Bayesian systems that compute approximations of target posterior distributions display computational features that straddle the System 1 vs System 2 distinction. Like Carruthers (2014, p. 199) and others (e.g. Kruglanski and Gigerenzer, 2011) have argued, "cognitive scientists would be well-advised to abandon the System 1/System 2 conceptual framework. The human mind is messier and more fine-grained than that". Reasoning is produced and supported by a hodgepodge of computationally diverse systems.

5 Computational (ir)rationality and optimality

Since the 1970s, psychologists Amos Tversky and Daniel Kahneman introduced the term 'cognitive bias' in psychology to describe the systematic and purportedly mistaken patterns of responses that characterize human judgment and decision making in many situations (Tversky and Kahneman, 1974). RL and Bayesian models, however, show a good fit (at least on the aggregate) with people's performance in a variety of psychophysical and cognitive tasks (Colombo and Hartmann, 2017; Niv, 2009), which has been taken to indicate "a far closer correspondence between optimal statistical inference and everyday cognition than suggested by previous research" (Griffiths and Tenenbaum, 2006, p. 771). So, there is an apparent tension between the finding that learning and thinking often instantiate "optimal statistical inference" and the observation that people are systematically biased, and often make errors in reasoning.

This final section puts this tension into sharper focus by asking two questions: How can RL and Bayesianism in computational cognitive neuroscience help us diagnose and assess instances of alleged irrationality? What challenges do computational approaches to rationality face?

5.1 Diagnosing (ir)rationality

To begin to address these two questions, two distinctions are helpful. The first distinction is between the *personal and the sub-personal* level of explanation (Dennett, 1969; Drayson, 2014). Explanation of people's behavior couched in terms of intentional mental states like beliefs, desires, preferences, expectations, and emotions is the paradigm case of explanation at the *personal* level. The contents of these mental states stand in logical and semantic relationships, and are easy to express in familiar propositional language. Explanation of behavior and cognitive functions couched in terms of parts or systems of cognitive agents – for example in terms of networks in the brain or of features of one's perceptual system – is at the *sub-personal* level.

The second distinction is between *constructivist and ecological* models of rationality (Gigerenzer, Todd, and the ABC Research Group, 1999; Smith, 2008). *Constructivist models* are built under the assumption that their target systems are designed to carry out well-defined functions in order to solve well-defined problems. Given this assumption, constructivist models embody some set of general norms that are used to justify the acceptance of the model, and to specify guidelines for building other general-purpose models of rational behavior. *Ecological models* of rationality are built on the assumption that their target systems display adaptive responses in certain environments. Given this assumption, ecological models embody some domain-specific strategy that agents can employ quickly and frugally to pursue some goal they care about when coping with a certain problem in a certain environment. Where constructivist models allow us to evaluate behavior and cognition against *norms* of rationality, ecological models allow us to evaluate behavior and cognition against *goals* (Polonioli, 2015).

Now, behavior that conforms to predictions based on Bayesian or RL models is often claimed to be 'optimal' or 'rational'. When these models are used in epistemology and decision theory, claims of optimality and rationality should be understood as *constructivist, personal*-level claims. Both Bayesianism and RL are in fact *normative* frameworks. Both embed norms of coherence for evaluating the rationality of people's beliefs and decisions.

RL agents aim to maximize the amount of reward they receive from interacting with the environment. While this aim coheres with the idea that rational behavior consists in maximizing expected utility, RL agents try to achieve this aim by learning and using an optimal policy that yields for each state (or state-action pair) visited by the agent the largest expected reward. Optimal policies in RL should respect a consistency condition defined by *Bellman's principle of optimality*. This principle expresses a relationship between the value of some initial state and the values of the states following from the initial one. It says that, in multi-stage problems, "an optimal policy has the property that whatever the initial state and initial decisions are, the remaining decisions must constitute an optimal policy with regard to the state resulting from the first decisions" (Bellman, 1954, p. 504). The basic idea is that a value function under an optimal policy can be decomposed into two parts: the immediate reward obtained from an action taken from an initial state, and the (discounted) value of the successor state. This condition makes it possible to construct RL algorithms that solve difficult multi-stage problems by breaking them down into simpler sub-problems.

Bayesianism in epistemology is committed to the ideas that people's beliefs come in degrees, that degrees of belief are probabilities, that people's degrees of belief at any given time ought to cohere with the axioms of the probability calculus, and that belief update ought to consist in transforming prior degrees of belief to posterior degrees of belief by conditionalizing on the evidence. Acceptance of such Bayesian models in epistemology depends on norms of epistemic rationality justified on the basis of a variety of considerations like Dutch book arguments and accuracy-based arguments (Hájek and Hartmann, 2010).

Taking a constructivist, personal-level approach, Tversky and Kahneman's (1974) work diagnoses that people are irrational when their beliefs do not conform to the epistemic norms embodied in Bayesianism. More recent studies in computational cognitive science, like Griffiths and Tenenbaum's (2006), take the same constructivist, personal-level approach; yet, unlike Tversky and Kahneman's, these studies are concerned with judgments about everyday phenomena, of which people may have extensive experience, and which might explain why people's judgments and behavior are sometimes found in line with Bayesian and RL norms of rationality (but see Marcus and Davis, 2013, for a criticism). In either case, RL and Bayesian models are used as a benchmark for rational behavior in a given task. If people's actual behavior falls short of the benchmark, then cognitive scientists may try to explain this discrepancy by tweaking the models including parameters that would reflect people's limitations in memory, attention, or some other cognitive resource (Zednik and Jäkel, 2016).

Many current Bayesian and RL models, however, do *not* target whole people. Mnih et al.'s (2015) DQN targeted perceptual, learning, and decision-making sub-systems. Lake et al.'s (2015) BPL targeted sensorimotor and learning sub-systems. As these types of models target parts of cognitive agents, they lie at the sub-personal level of explanation.

RL and Bayesian sub-personal models define the kind of computational problem faced by a target system and the function the system computes to solve the problem. This way, RL and Bayesian models can afford explanations of the *functional significance* of the behavior exhibited by some target sub-system in some information-processing task. How well the system is functioning is defined only with respect to a loss (or cost) function, which measures the cost associated with each combination of state of the environment and action taken by the system. A system is functioning optimally if its actions (or outputs) minimize expected loss.

Because optimality is defined only with respect to a system's environment and its loss function, the claim that a system functions (sub)optimally depends on correct modeling assumptions about the structure of its environment, on a correct identification of the system's available information and goal in that environment, and on a correct specification of the computational limitations of the system. This means that systems functioning in line with the predictions of a Bayesian or RL model may actually behave sub-optimally, when, for example, they have an incorrect representation of their environment.

5.2 Challenges towards an ecological computational rationality

The computational approaches discussed here are not properly grounded in ecological considerations. Properly grounding computational approaches in ecological considerations has several dimensions. *Time* is one of these dimensions. Learning and reasoning should be sensitive to the expected costs and values of computation under variable time constraints in a changing environment. DQN's training required 500 times more than the amount of time required by a human gamer to reach a similar performance.[7] By relying on a richer body of symbolic and sub-symbolic representations with compositional structure, BPL developed a capacity for one-shot learning with relatively less training, on around 150 different types of handwritten characters. The benefits of one-shot learning and, more generally, of making quick judgments by relying on computationally frugal heuristics that operate on richly structured representations often outweigh the costs of making sub-optimal judgments.

Flexibility is another dimension of ecological rationality. DQN requires re-training to play a novel game, or to pursue a new goal (e.g. 'Die as quickly as possible' instead of 'Make as many points as possible') in the same game. DQN cannot re-deploy knowledge gained in one game to play a new game or to pursue a new goal. BPL shows more flexibility, as it learns models of different classes of characters that can be re-deployed and recombined to adapt to new situations. While an ability for building models that show compositional structure seems necessary for flexible and timely reasoning, context-sensitive meta-reasoning and meta-learning systems supplement this ability that consider "the current uncertainties, the time-critical losses with continuing computation, and the expected gains in precision of reasoning with additional computation" (Gershman, Horvitz, and Tenenbaum, 2015, p. 275). Rather than aiming for optimal performance, the challenge becomes how to manage finite time, limited memory and attention, ambiguous data, and unknown unknowns to flexibly navigate a changing environment populated by other agents with different goals and abilities.

A third dimension of ecological rationality concerns the *tuning* between the informational and morphological structure of computational systems and the structure of their environment. While the idea is widespread that prior knowledge should be tuned to environmental statistics, "tuning an organism to its environment involves somewhat more than collecting statistics from the environment, interpreting them as the true priors, and endowing the organism with them" (Feldman, 2013, p. 23). Evolution need *not* put adaptive pressure on organisms to have true priors. It is an important challenge to sort between environments that may favor the evolution of true priors and environments where true priors are ecologically irrational and brittle.

Conclusion

This chapter has surveyed prominent computational frameworks that are used as a basis for analyzing and understanding biological learning and reasoning. After laying out a taxonomy of learning systems and clarifying the functional significance of deep connectionist architectures and hierarchically structured hypothesis spaces, the chapter has focus on three implications of computational approaches to learning and reasoning. It has argued that advances in computational cognitive science vindicate enlightened empiricism as the correct way of understanding the character of our innate cognitive architecture, and are progressively eroding the distinction between two kinds of reasoning systems, System 1 and System 2. The final section has put into sharper focus the complex relationship between rationality, optimality, and computational approaches.

Acknowledgments

I am grateful to Mark Sprevak, Felipe Romero, Andrea Polonioli, and Regina Fabry, who generously provided helpful comments on previous versions of this chapter.

Notes

1 For thorough overviews, readers may consult Mitchell (1997); Halpern (2005); Russell and Norvig (2009, Parts III–V); and Pearl (2009). Danks (2014a) and Wing (2006) are excellent, concise surveys of machine learning and computational thinking.
2 The basic insight is similar to the one informing Bush and Mosteller's (1951) pioneering work on animal learning: learning depends on error in prediction. As Rescorla and Wagner put it:

> Organisms only learn when events violate their expectations. Certain expectations are built up about the events following a stimulus complex; expectations initiated by the complex and its component stimuli are then only modified when consequent events disagree with the composite expectation.
>
> *(Rescorla and Wagner, 1972, p. 75)*

3 Not all Bayesian models are meant to make substantial claims about the mechanisms and representations underlying cognition and behavior. Some Bayesian models are meant to offer only an encompassing mathematical template that can be applied to a wide range of phenomena in order to provide computational-level analyses (Anderson, 1990) and/or in order to unify these phenomena without making commitments to underlying mechanisms and representations (Colombo and Hartmann, 2017; Danks, 2014b, ch. 8). Here I set aside questions about the psychological reality of Bayesian models (Colombo and Seriès, 2012). Rather, I assume that Bayesianism offers not only a mathematical template or computational-level analyses, but can also make substantial empirical claims about the nature of the mechanisms and representations underlying reasoning and learning (Pouget et al., 2013).
4 This section is based on Colombo (2017).
5 According to a prominent explication, innate psychological traits are *psychologically primitive*, which means that their acquisition cannot be explained by any adequate theory in cognitive science (Cowie, 1999; Samuels, 2002).
6 In the literature on computational neuroscience and animal learning goal-directed behavior "is defined as one that is performed because: (a) the subject has appropriate reason to believe it will achieve a particular goal, such as an outcome; and (b) the subject has a reason to seek that outcome" (Dayan, 2009, p. 213; Dickinson, 1985). Since the propensity of an agent to select a goal-directed action is sensitive to changes in the variables associated with conditions (a) and (b), goal-directed behavior is flexible. If

behavior is not affected by these two types of changes, then it is habitual, and is triggered by learned cues and associations.

7 As Lake et al. (2016) clarify, "DQN was trained on 200 million frames from each of the games, which equates to approximately 924 hours of game time (about 38 days), or almost 500 times as much experience as the human received".

References

Anderson, J.R. (1990) *The Adaptive Character of Thought*. Hillsdale, NJ: Erlbaum.

Austerweil, J.L. et al. (2015). 'Structure and Flexibility in Bayesian Models of Cognition', in Busemeyer, J.R. et al. (eds.) *Oxford Handbook of Computational and Mathematical Psychology*. Oxford: Oxford University Press, pp. 187–208.

Bellman, R. (1954) 'The Theory of Dynamic Programming', *Bulletin of the American Mathematical Society*, 60 (6), pp. 503–515.

Bush, R.R. and Mosteller, F. (1951) 'A Mathematical Model for Simple Learning', *Psychological Review*, 58, pp. 313–323.

Carey, S. (2011) 'The Origin of Concepts: A précis', *The Behavioral and Brain Sciences*, 34, pp. 113–123.

Carruthers, P. (2014) 'The Fragmentation of Reasoning', in Quintanilla, P., Mantilla, C., and Cépeda, P. (eds.) *Cognición social y lenguaje. La intersubjetividad en la evolución de la especie y en el desarrollo del niño*. Lima: Fondo Editorial de la Pontificia Universidad Católica del Perú, pp. 181–204.

Chomsky, N. (1980) *Rules and Representations*. New York, NY: Columbia University Press.

Colombo, M. (2014) 'Deep and Beautiful. The Reward Prediction Error Hypothesis of Dopamine', *Studies in History and Philosophy of Science Part C: Studies in History and Philosophy of Biological and Biomedical Sciences*, 45, pp. 57–67.

Colombo, M. (2017) 'Bayesian Cognitive Science, Predictive Brains, and the Nativism Debate', *Synthese*, pp. 1–22. Available at: DOI: 10.1007/s11229-017-1427-7.

Colombo, M. and Hartmann, S. (2017) 'Bayesian Cognitive Science, Unification, and Explanation', *The British Journal of Philosophy of Science*, 68, pp. 451–484.

Colombo, M. and Seriès, P. (2012) 'Bayes in the Brain: On Bayesian Modeling in Neuroscience', *The British Journal for Philosophy of Science*, 63, pp. 697–723.

Cowie, F. (1999) *What's Within? Nativism Reconsidered*. New York, NY: Oxford University Press.

Cushman, F. and Morris, A. (2015) 'Habitual Control of Goal Selection in Humans', *Proceedings of the National Academy of Science USA*, 112 (45), pp. 13817–13822.

Danks, D. (2014a) 'Learning', in Frankish, K. and Ramsey, W. (eds.) *Cambridge Handbook to Artificial Intelligence*. Cambridge, UK: Cambridge University Press, pp. 151–167.

Danks, D. (2014b) *Unifying the Mind: Cognitive Representations as Graphical Models*. Cambridge, MA: MIT Press.

Daw, N.D., Niv, Y., and Dayan, P. (2005) 'Uncertainty-based Competition between Prefrontal and Dorsolateral Striatal Systems for Behavioral Control', *Nature Neuroscience*, 8, pp. 1704–1711.

Dayan, P. (2009) 'Goal-directed Control and Its Antipodes', *Neural Networks*, 22, pp. 213–219.

Dennett D. (1969) *Content and Consciousness: An Analysis of Mental Phenomena*. London: Routledge & Kegan Paul.

Dezfouli, A. and Balleine, B.W. (2013) 'Actions, Action Sequences and Habits: Evidence that Goal-directed and Habitual Action Control are Hierarchically Organized', *PLoS Computational Biology*, 9, e1003364. Available at: DOI: 10.1371/journal.pcbi.100336.

Dickinson, A. (1985) 'Actions and Habits: The Development of Behavioural Autonomy', *Philosophical Transactions of the Royal Society of London, Series B, Biological Sciences*, 308, pp. 67–78.

Dolan, R.J. and Dayan, P. (2013) 'Goals and Habits in the Brain', *Neuron*, 80 (2), pp. 312–325.

Doll, B.B., Simon, D.A., and Daw, N.D. (2012) 'The Ubiquity of Model-based Reinforcement Learning', *Current Opinions in Neurobiology*, 22 (6), pp. 1075–1081.

Drayson, Z. (2014) 'The Personal/Subpersonal Distinction', *Philosophy Compass*, 9 (5), pp. 338–346.

Evans, J.S.B. and Stanovich, K.E. (2013) 'Dual-Process Theories of Higher Cognition Advancing the Debate', *Perspectives on Psychological Science*, 8 (3), pp. 223–241.

Feldman, J. (2013) 'Tuning Your Priors to the World', *Topics in Cognitive Science*, 5 (1), pp. 13–34.

Fodor, J.A. (1975) *The Language of Thought*. Cambridge, MA: Harvard University Press.

Fodor, J. (1981) 'The Present Status of the Innate Controversy', in *RePresentations*. Cambridge, MA: MIT Press, pp. 257–316.

Gershman, S.J., Horvitz, E.J., and Tenenbaum, J.B. (2015) 'Computational Rationality: A Converging Paradigm for Intelligence in Brains, Minds, and Machines', *Science*, 349 (6245), pp. 273–278.

Gigerenzer, G., Todd, P.M., and the ABC Research Group (1999) *Simple Heuristics That Make Us Smart*. New York, NY: Oxford University Press.

Griffiths, T.L. and Tenenbaum, J.B. (2006) 'Optimal Predictions in Everyday Cognition', *Psychological Science*, 17, pp. 767–773.

Haber, S.N. (2003) 'The Primate Basal Ganglia: Parallel and Integrative Networks', *Journal of Chemical Neuroanatomy*, 26 (4), pp. 317–330.

Hájek, A. and Hartmann, S. (2010) 'Bayesian Epistemology', in Dancy, J. et al. (eds.) *A Companion to Epistemology*. Oxford: Blackwell, pp. 93–106.

Halpern, J.Y. (2005) *Reasoning about Uncertainty*. Cambridge, MA: MIT Press.

Harman, G. (2008) *Change in View: Principles of Reasoning*. Cambridge, UK: Cambridge University Press.

Haruno, M. and Kawato, M. (2006) 'Heterarchical Reinforcement-Learning Model for Integration of Multiple Cortico-striatal Loops: fMRI Examination in Stimulus-Action-Reward Association Learning', *Neural Networks*, 19 (8), pp. 1242–1254.

Hazy, T.E., Frank, M.J., and O'Reilly, R.C. (2007) 'Towards an Executive without a Homunculus: Computational Models of the Prefrontal Cortex/Basal Ganglia System', *Philosophical Transactions of the Royal Society of London B: Biological Sciences*, 362 (1485), pp. 1601–1613.

Hinton, G.E. (2007) 'Learning Multiple Layers of Representation', *Trends in Cognitive Sciences*, 11 (10), pp. 428–434.

Kahneman, D. (2011) *Thinking, Fast and Slow*. New York, NY: Macmillan.

Kemp, C., Perfors, A., and Tenenbaum, J.B. (2007) 'Learning Overhypotheses with Hierarchical Bayesian Models', *Developmental Science*, 10 (3), pp. 307–321.

Kemp, C. and Tenenbaum, J.B. (2008) 'The Discovery of Structural Form', *Proceedings of the National Academy of Sciences*, 105 (31), pp. 10687–10692.

Keramati, M., Dezfouli, A., and Piray, P. (2011) 'Speed/Accuracy Trade-off between the Habitual and the Goal-directed Processes', *PLoS Computational Biology*, 7, e1002055. Available at: DOI:10.1371/journal.pcbi.1002055.

Keramati, M. et al. (2016) 'Adaptive Integration of Habits into Depth-limited Planning Defines a Habitual-Goal-directed Spectrum', *Proceedings of the National Academy of Sciences USA*, 113 (45), pp. 12868–12873.

Kishida, K.T. et al. (2016) 'Subsecond Dopamine Fluctuations in Human Striatum Encode Superposed Error Signals about Actual and Counterfactual Reward', *Proceedings of the National Academy of Sciences*, 113 (1), pp. 200–205.

Kruglanski, A.W. and Gigerenzer, G. (2011) 'Intuitive and Deliberative Judgements Are Based on Common Principles', *Psychological Review*, 118, pp. 97–109.

Lake, B.M., Salakhutdinov, R., and Tenenbaum, J.B. (2015) 'Human-Level Concept Learning through Probabilistic Program Induction', *Science*, 350 (6266), pp. 1332–1338.

Lake, B.M. et al. (2016) 'Building Machines That Learn and Think Like People', *Behavioral and Brain Sciences*, pp. 1–101. Available at: DOI:10.1017/S0140525X16001837.

LeCun, Y., Bengio, Y., and Hinton, G. (2015) 'Deep Learning', *Nature*, 521 (7553), pp. 436–444.

LeCun, Y. et al. (1989) 'Backpropagation Applied to Handwritten Zip Code Recognition', *Neural Computation*, 1, pp. 541–551.

Marcus, G.F. and Davis, E. (2013) 'How Robust Are Probabilistic Models of Higher-Level Cognition?', *Psychological Science*, 24 (12), pp. 2351–2360.

Margolis, E. and Laurence, S. (2013) 'In Defense of Nativism', *Philosophical Studies*, 165, pp. 693–718.

Mitchell, T.M. (1997) *Machine Learning*. New York, NY: McGraw-Hill.

Mnih, V. et al. (2015) 'Human-Level Control through Deep Reinforcement Learning', *Nature*, 518 (7540), pp. 529–533.

Montague, P.R., Dayan, P., and Sejnowski, T.J. (1996) 'A Framework for Mesencephalic Dopamine Systems Based on Predictive Hebbian Learning', *The Journal of Neuroscience*, 16 (5), pp. 1936–1947.

Niv, Y. (2009) 'Reinforcement Learning in the Brain', *Journal of Mathematical Psychology*, 53, pp. 139–154.

Park, H.-J. and Friston, K. (2013) 'Structural and Functional Brain Networks: From Connections to Cognition', *Science*, 342, pp. 579–587.

Pearl, J. (2009) *Causality: Models, Reasoning, and Inference*, 2nd ed. Cambridge, UK: Cambridge University Press.

Perfors, A. (2012) 'Bayesian Models of Cognition: What's Built in after All?', *Philosophy Compass*, 7 (2), pp. 127–138.

Polonioli, A. (2015) 'The Uses and Abuses of the Coherence–Correspondence Distinction', *Frontiers in Psychology*, 6, p. 507. Available at: DOI:10.3389/fpsyg.2015.00507.

Pouget, A. et al. (2013) 'Probabilistic Brains: Knowns and Unknowns', *Nature Neuroscience*, 16 (9), pp. 1170–1178.

Rescorla, R.A. and Wagner, A.R. (1972) 'A Theory of Pavlovian Conditioning: Variations in the Effectiveness of Reinforcement and Nonreinforcement', in Black, A.H. and Prokasy, W.F. (eds.) *Classical Conditioning II: Current Research and Theory*. New York, NY: Appleton Century Crofts, pp. 64–99.

Russell, S.J. and Norvig, P. (2009) *Artificial Intelligence: A Modern Approach*, 3rd ed. Upper Saddle River, NJ: Prentice Hall.

Samuels, R. (2002) 'Nativism in Cognitive Science', *Mind and Language*, 17, pp. 233–265.

Samuels, R. (2009) 'The Magic Number Two Plus or Minus: Some Comments on Dual-Processing Theories of cognition', in Evans, J and Frankish, K. (eds.) *In Two Minds: Dual Processes and Beyond*. Oxford: Oxford University Press, pp. 129–146.

Sanborn, A.N., Griffiths, T.L., and Navarro, D.J. (2010) 'Rational Approximations to Rational Models: Alternative Algorithms for Category Learning', *Psychological Review*, 117, pp. 1144–1167.

Sloman, S.A. (1996) 'The Empirical Case for Two Systems of Reasoning', *Psychological Bulletin*, 119, pp. 3–22.

Smith, V.L. (2008) *Rationality in Economics: Constructivist and Ecological Forms*. Cambridge, UK: Cambridge University Press.

Spelke, E. (1994) 'Initial Knowledge: Six Suggestions', *Cognition*, 50, pp. 431–445.

Sutton, R.S. and Barto, A.G. (1998) *Reinforcement Learning: An Introduction*. Cambridge, MA: MIT Press.

Tversky, A. and Kahneman, D. (1974) 'Judgment under Uncertainty: Heuristics and Biases', *Science*, 185, pp. 1124–1131.

Watkins, C.J. and Dayan, P. (1992) 'Q-learning', *Machine Learning*, 8 (3–4), pp. 279–292.

Wing, J.M. (2006) 'Computational Thinking', *Communications of the ACM*, 49 (3), pp. 33–35.

Zednik, C. and Jäkel, F. (2016) 'Bayesian Reverse-Engineering Considered as a Research Strategy for Cognitive Science', *Synthese*, 193 (12), pp. 3951–3985.

29

VISION

Mazviita Chirimuuta

Preamble: Is the eye like a camera?

In today's textbooks, and for centuries before now, it has been commonplace to explain the workings of the mammalian eye as being similar to those of a non-biological camera. The same principles of optics are exemplified in each kind of device, and it has tempted some to say that the eye *is* a fleshy, gelatinous, photographic machine. So from our vantage point it is surprising that before Kepler's discovery of the optical laws of image formation in the eye (living or dead) and *camera obscura*, this comparison was not readily available to early theorists of vision. Ibn al-Haytham ("Alhazen") was the first to apply inferentialist notions to the theory of vision, prefiguring Helmholtz and also current computational accounts. However, he did not explain the workings of the eye in terms of optical laws that hold across living, non-living and artifactual structures. His understanding of the eye presupposed capacities for the reception of Aristotelian *forms* that could only occur in an animate structure (Meyering, 1989, pp. 45–48).

The shift to taking the living eye, the eye of a dead animal, and an inert device, to be all relevantly similar to one another was significant in the history of science. Recognizing that the comparison was not always obvious helps us to make note of what is *dissimilar* about these systems: the living eye is highly mobile, and scientists now think that this is essential to understanding how vision works (Findlay and Gilchrist, 2003). Moreover, the habit of thinking of the eye as camera-like hampered scientists' efforts to understand how movement is integral to biological vision.

The moral of this story is that every useful analogy brings with it disanalogies which can mask important features of the target of investigation. Yet analogies like these are at the core of the models which scientists build in order to explain natural systems and mimic their functions. While it is misleading to say that the eye works *just like* a camera, or that both perform the same function of "seeing", the two systems illuminate each other. Building cameras has helped people better understand the optics of the eye, and knowledge of the eye inspired the invention of photographic cameras.

Computational models of vision are today's version of the camera model of the eye. And as I will show in this chapter, there has been a fruitful exchange between neuroscientists, psychologists, and computer scientists who study vision. The further question, to be considered at the end, is whether this work gives reason to think that vision is *fundamentally* computational.

Before then I will say something about what the computational approach to vision is, how it emerged historically, and how we should think about explanatory practice in this area of science.

The computational approach to vision

What computational vision is

Vision is a mental function that has been fairly successfully replicated in artificial intelligence. "Computational vision" often means visual AI or "machine vision". Beyond this, there are the fields of psychology and neuroscience which produce computational models of organic visual systems (Frisby and Stone, 2010). The visual system has been the point of origin and/or testing ground for many foundational concepts in computational neuroscience, such as the *receptive field*, *divisive normalization*, and *hierarchical processing*. Because vision is the most well-studied of all of the perceptual modalities, the computational theory of vision is one of the most advanced parts of the computational theory of mind.

This pre-eminence is the outcome of focused research since the 1960s on the combined challenges of reverse engineering animal visual systems, creating theoretical frameworks which specify the problem of vision, and developing adequate computational solutions. David Marr's book *Vision*, published posthumously in 1982, played a pivotal role in the story. It synthesized insights garnered over the previous two decades and presented a mathematical theory of visual function at each stage of the system from retinal input to object recognition. It also set an agenda for the subsequent three decades' research in vision science, not least because of the shortcomings of Marr's blueprints for artificial visual systems.

Neurons and seeing, feathers and flying

The popular account of Marr is that he successfully decoupled the computational approach from the neuroscience of vision, asserting the primacy of computational theory. In this context, the following passage from Marr is frequently quoted:

> trying to understand perception by studying only neurons is like trying to understand bird flight by studying only feathers: It just cannot be done. In order to understand bird flight, we have to understand aerodynamics; only then do the structure of feathers and the different shapes of birds' wings make sense.
>
> *(Marr, 1982, p. 27)*

The popular account needs to be revised. First, it is worth laying out its essentials. The starting point is Marr's *three levels of explanation*. Marr distinguished *computational, representational/algorithmic*, and *implementational* questions. The first task for the theory of vision is to understand seeing, in most abstract terms, as a computational problem. The second is to show how this problem can be solved using algorithms to transform incoming visual information (e.g. the 2D pixel array at the retina) into different representational formats (e.g. an edge array; a 3D model of objects in a scene). The implementation question – how a physical system like the brain actually runs the algorithm in order to solve the computational problem – is last, and seems trivial compared to the others. On this version of Marr, the conceptual heavy lifting of vision science is done by computational theoreticians, not experimental neuroscientists: scientific insight flows downwards from the heights of theory to the laboratory bench.

Thus it can be surprising to read that that *primal sketch*, Marr's proposal for the post-retinal stage of representation, was "inspired by findings about mammalian visual systems" (Marr and Hildreth, 1980, p. 188), and that Marr and his collaborators were actively working on computational models of simple cells in the early visual system (e.g. Marr and Ullman, 1981). In practice, Marr's research group at MIT pursued a many-pronged strategy which aimed to make progress at each level of explanation and attempted to use knowledge at any one level to constrain the problem space of the others. As Nishihara (2012, p. 1017) relates, "Marr wanted … to ground the study of AI in testable theories of the brain's function and architecture".

Levels of explanation versus levels of being

On the popular account, one often sees each of Marr's levels being associated with a particular kind of object of investigation, which has its own proprietary discipline: brains, neurons, and silicon chips for the implementational level; psychology and software engineering dealing with the representations and algorithms of the middle level; mathematics delivering the overarching computational theory. This way of carving out the levels meshes with the Fodor–Putnam tradition in the philosophy of mind. As an alternative to a reductive physicalism which identifies mental states with brain states, the non-reductive physicalism of this school starts with the notion that mental states can be multiply realized in systems which are physically completely different. Thus psychology (the science of mental representations and cognitive algorithms) will not undergo reduction to any science which deals just with the biological basis of mind (Fodor, 1974). Furthermore, because of the many-to-one relationship between neural state and cognitive function, psychology is understood as an autonomous discipline which is unconstrained by findings in neuroscience. These observations about the relations between the sciences of psychology and neuroscience also reinforce the functionalist thesis that the mind, though physical, is irreducible to the brain.

While I accept that the Marrian approach is a non-reductive one, I contend that it is misleading to assimilate it to the functionalist program in the ontology of mind (even if aspects of Marr's programme can be used in support of philosophical functionalism). My central point is that Marr's different levels of explanation are intended to be utilized in the study of *one* concrete system – the visual brain. Thus, the computational and algorithmic approaches are not proprietary to computer science and psychology,[1] but can also be different modes of explanation *within* neuroscience. This is, in effect, the position taken in theoretical neuroscience, when computational explanations are sought for the presence of specific features of neural systems, such as receptive field structures.[2]

The neurophysiologist Horace Barlow is an influential figure in this tradition of neuroscience, and it is interesting that in a paper which offers a computational explanation for the existence of inhibitory circuitry in the retina (lateral inhibition), he begins with a comparison with the case of flight, anticipating Marr's well known analogy:

> A wing would be a most mystifying structure if one did not know that birds flew. … [W]ithout understanding something of the principles of flight, a more detailed examination of the wing itself would probably be unrewarding. I think that we may be at an analogous point in our understanding of the sensory side of the central nervous system. We have got our first batch of facts from the anatomical, neurophysiological, and psychophysical study of sensation and perception, and now we need ideas about what operations are performed by the various structures we have examined. …
>
> It seems to me vitally important to have in mind possible answers to this question when investigating these structures, for if one does not one will get lost in a mass of irrelevant detail and fail to make the crucial observations.
>
> *(Barlow, 1961, p. 217)*

Barlow's point is that it pays to ask, "why?" questions of biological systems, concerning their function and adaptive value, and that these questions should be pursued amidst investigation into structures and mechanisms.[3]

We should think of Marr's computational-level questions as a sub-species of the biologist's functional questions.[4] This observation that computational-level questions can be raised in the investigation of neural systems themselves makes sense of the continued efforts of Marr and his colleagues within theoretical neuroscience. In contrast, the popular account, which employs a functionalist philosophy of mind and interprets the levels ontologically, precludes computational explanations of the brain itself. The point is just that the functionalist's association of the computational level with mental states and capacities abstracted away from neural hardware makes it hard to see how computational notions would be relevant to the brain, as opposed to the informational or mental states realized in it. My preferred account also makes sense of the uptake of Marr's distinction between levels of explanation within visual neuroscience today (Carandini, 2012). As Frisby and Stone (2012, p. 1042) write,

> A theory of vision should do more than identify a mechanism that could implement a given computation: it should also provide a functional (e.g. computational) reason why the computation was desirable in the first place. To some extent, Marr's call for a computational account of vision has been taken up in the nascent field of computational neuroscience, where fine-grained analysis of physiological data is commonly interpreted in terms of its functional significance.

In understanding the relationship between the different explanatory levels it is useful to import the concept of *perspectivism* from the philosophy of science. Theoretical frameworks (e.g. Newton's laws, Schrödinger's equation) define "perspectives" (i.e. classical mechanics, quantum mechanics) which are employed to develop models that are then tested against empirical data. As Giere (2006, p. 15) explains,

> general principles by themselves make no claims about the world, but more specific *models* constructed in accordance with the principles can be used to make claims about specific aspects of the world. And these claims can be tested against various instrumental perspectives. Nevertheless, all theoretical claims remain perspectival in that they apply only to aspects of the world and then, in part *because* they apply only to some aspects of the world, never with complete precision.[5]

Now in vision science – unlike physics, but like other parts of biology – theoretical frameworks are not usually defined by laws of nature; both working models and descriptions of mechanisms have a significant role to play (Machamer, Darden, and Craver, 2000). I suggest that we think of each of Marr's explanatory levels as characterizing kinds of perspectives that scientists use to approach the visual system. The implementational level aligns with a mechanistic perspective in which the goal is to develop detailed and realistic, causal descriptions of the visual brain. Bayesianism can be understood as a representational/algorithmic perspective. Given a clear computational definition of the task of vision as decision making under uncertainty, Bayesianism gives instructions as to how visual information is to be represented and processed in order to yield optimal decisions.

It is helpful to think back to our opening parable of the eye and the camera, and how choices of analogy can shape the direction of scientific research. The models and descriptions characteristic of any one explanatory level differ as to which comparisons they take to be relevant to understanding the target system. The computational and algorithmic perspectives invite comparisons between the biological visual system and a man-made computer which is said to perform the same function. Mechanistic perspectives, which look in detail at the nuts and bolts of the system, do not prompt such comparisons because from the point of view of physical implementation the biological and artifactual systems have little in common. No perspective, by itself, can give a complete view of the target system. Ideally the different perspectives should complement each other to give a richer explanation. The mutual inter-dependence of work at different levels is a note commonly struck in vision science. As Ullman writes,

> The study of the computations performed by the human visual system can … lead to new insights and to the development of new and better methods for analyzing visual information. At the same time, given the enormous complexity of the human visual system, a better theoretical understanding of the computations underlying the processing of visual information can supply useful guidelines for empirical studies of the biological mechanisms subserving visual perception.[6]

Marr's *Vision* realized?

Because of his tragically early death, David Marr might be thought of as a prophet who saw the promised land but never arrived there. He presented a vision of biologically inspired artificial systems which mimic the tasks that animals perform effortlessly using sight – avoiding obstacles while navigating through a cluttered environment, picking out useful items in a crowded scene. To an impressive degree, these problems have now been solved, though not in the ways that Marr thought they would be. Computationalism, of one kind or another, is now the dominant approach in vision research.[7] In this section I will discuss the merits of deep learning and Bayesian models. What these two strategies have in common is a basically statistical approach to the problem of vision. Through experience of masses of visual information, these models must learn whatever patterns there are in the dataset that facilitate reliable object recognition, for example. The solutions arrived at by statistical methods remain implicit – embedded in the weights of a connectionist network, or the probability distributions of a Bayesian model. In contrast, Marr's programme (like others in the classical "GOFAI" tradition) sought elegant, formal solutions to the problem, ones that could be written down as explicit instructions, such as those for analyzing a complex 3D object as a set of primitive solids.[8]

Deep learning and seeing machines

According to one analyst, there will be 10 million self-driving cars on the road by the year 2020 (Greenough, 2016). If this forecast is to be believed, AI will be driving the first major revolution in land transportation technology since the invention of the automobile. Artificial visual systems are obviously essential to the success of these vehicles. The "deep learning" AI (Talbot, 2015) which enables autonomous cars to see roads, lane markings, other cars, and pedestrians is the descendent of neurally informed network models of the early 1980s.[9]

Fukushima's (1980) "Neocognitron" was inspired by David Hubel and Torsten Wiesel's feed-forward, hierarchical description of the cat's visual cortex. The Neocognitron is a connectionist network in which units in different layers are said to perform computations analogous to the simple and complex cells of the brain. The model can be trained to perform pattern classification, for example, recognizing hand written numerals. In turn, the Neocognitron inspired other models such as the H-max model (Riesenhuber and Poggio, 1999), and LeNet (LeCun et al., 1995).

The "AlexNet" (Krizhevsky, Sutskever, and Hinton, 2012) is considered a landmark development in that it achieves human-level proficiency in the classification of objects presented in complex, real-world images.[10] Following training, the response profiles of the model's units in lower layers resemble the simple bar-like receptive fields of cells in the primary visual cortex. Similarly, Yamins et al. (2014) report that the units in the higher layers of their object recognition network have responses that accurately predict the responses of real neurons in the temporal cortex of the ventral stream.[11]

Yamins and diCarlo (2016, p. 356) argue that deep learning networks, trained to perform specific ecologically relevant tasks (such as object recognition) are one of the most important tools for understanding the sensory cortex. Their results do indeed indicate that there are intriguing, albeit broad, similarities between the solutions arrived at in nature, and those achieved in computational simulations – most obviously, the repetition of a simple "canonical" computation over many layers of a hierarchical system. But some caveats must be noted. Nguyen, Yosinski, and Clune (2015) showed that deep learning networks are, in their words, "easily fooled", giving high confidence classification responses to patterns which, to a human, look nothing like the actual object. For example, a panel of black and yellow horizontal stripes is confidently classified as an American school bus. Another intriguing weakness of these systems is revealed by "adversarial images". These are images with a few alterations in pixel values, such that they look like normal photographs to a human viewer but lead to gross errors in the artificial network's classification of them. While adversarial images may lead to real security vulnerabilities as such technologies are rolled out in day to day settings (Kurakin, Goodfellow, and Bengio, 2016), they also raise the question of whether artificial networks are solving the problem of image classification in a profoundly non-biological way.[12]

This is the inference made by Piekniewski et al. (2016), who also argue that the machine vision community faces a version of Moravec's paradox. Moravec (1988) wrote: "It is comparatively easy to make computers exhibit adult level performance on intelligence tests or playing checkers, and difficult or impossible to give them the skills of a one-year-old when it comes to perception and mobility".

In the case of machine vision, AlexNet has achieved adult-level performance in a task (i.e. the categorization of thousands of different kinds of objects) which would be beyond a human infant, or presumably any non-human animal. However, it has not yet been shown that artificial systems can solve basic sensory-motor coordination problems (like following a moving object in a complex, unpredictable environment) which year-old babies and all other animals do reliably.

Piekniewski et al. (2016) argue that a way forward is to make artificial networks more biologically realistic, by including feedback connections (which outnumber feedforward pathways in the sensory cortex) and lateral connectivity within network layers, so that both temporal and spatial context influence the computations in any one unit. Another more naturalistic feature of their work is that they train their network not with photographs but with videos, thus mimicking the continuous stream of sensory input that falls on the eyes. Their model does show good performance in tracking a single object, such as a green ball, recognizing its location in the frame over a variety of background colors, textures, and lighting conditions.

Bayesian brains and optimal solutions

Bayesianism is now one of the central approaches in the modeling of perceptual systems. It is a compelling manifestation of the inferentialist idea that perception is the process of drawing conclusions about states of affairs in the external world on the basis of limited sensory data which underdetermine their distal cause. While Marr emphasized the impoverishment of the external world information captured by the 2D projections onto the retina, Bayesians begin with the point that the data received by the visual system is noisy and ambiguous in a variety of ways, not least because of the stochastic nature of sensory transduction and neural transmission. Bayesian inference can provide optimal strategies for decision making under uncertainty. So it follows that it is at least theoretically interesting to compare the predictions of Bayesian models of the visual systems with the outputs of their biological counterparts.

While Bayesian models have come to the foreground really in the last twenty years, the essence and motivation for the approach was stated by Horace Barlow some decades earlier:

> Certain sensory events have occurred, and what one optimally needs are the probabil-
> ities of these events on certain hypotheses. For instance, if I enter my darkened home
> and come to the point where there is a swing door, I must decide whether to put out
> my hand and push it open or whether to walk straight on. The decision should be
> made partly on the basis of what I can see, but this information must be combined
> with the prior probabilities of the door being open or closed, and also the payoffs and
> penalties of the various outcomes; the survival value of walking through a closed door
> is obviously lower than it would be for the other possibilities. However, these are not
> sensory problems; what we need from our eyes is simply the probability of the sensory
> events occurring if the door is closed, and so on.
>
> *(Barlow, 1969, p. 878)*

The modeling of color constancy provides a useful example of the Bayesian approach.[13] Color vision is a useful guide to our surroundings because the color appearances of objects are relatively stable across changes in illumination, such that within a very broad range of lighting conditions at the breakfast table, we can tell whether our toast is burned or not, or if our juice is apple or cranberry, just by looking at the colors. However, the challenge of achieving constant color perception is set by the physics of light reflection and absorption. The wavelength of light reaching the eye after being reflected from the glass of juice is due both to the absorption-transmission profile of the liquid and the wavelength of incident light – which is quite different if coming from the sun through the window behind the table, or from an overhead bulb on a cloudy morning (see Figure 29.1a). On the Bayesian approach, color constancy is achieved when the visual system makes a correct inference about the reflectance profile of the object viewed, disambiguating it from the spectrum of the illumination. This is especially challenging because information loss occurs due to the broad, non-specific spectral sensitivity of the cones in the retina.

Figure 29.1b is a schematic of the Bayesian approach. The output of the Bayesian model is a guess (*hypothesis*) about what state of the world caused the sensory data. In the case of a color constancy model, the final hypothesis is a guess as to the reflectance profile of a colored object. Brainard and colleagues (2006) compared the output of their model with empirical data on the constancy of a simple array of tiles depicted under different illuminants and a good fit was achieved, though the authors note that the experimental conditions were not chosen specifically to test the model (ibid., p. 1277). A particularly intriguing comparison is that the model correctly predicts errors in color constancy judgments when the illumination is purple (Allred, 2012, p. 221). Because purple is an improbable color for lighting (has low prior probability) the Bayesian algorithm is biased towards inferring that the purple hue is a property of the object, not the illuminant. It would seem that the human visual system is biased in the same way.

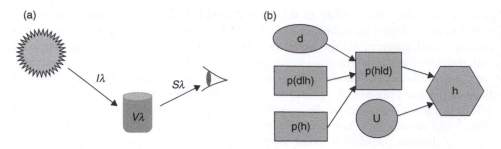

Figure 29.1 (a) The challenge of color constancy. The wavelength of the light incident on the eye ($S\lambda$) is a product of the wavelength of the ambient illuminating light ($I\lambda$) and the spectral absorption-transmission function of the glass of juice ($V\lambda$). Thus the proximal stimulus at the eye confounds the spectral properties of the perceived object and the illuminant. Color constancy is achieved if the visual system is able to disambiguate these two physical sources of color changes. (b) Schematic of Bayesian inference. The visual system receives uncertain sensory data (d) regarding conditions in the external world. In order to arrive at a correct hypothesis about external conditions (h), the optimal strategy is to calculate the posterior distribution, $p(h \mid d)$, from the likelihood distribution, $p(d \mid h)$, and prior $p(h)$, according to Bayes' theorem. The final hypothesis is calculated by weighting the posterior with a utility function, U

Bayesianism provides vision science with a powerful theoretical framework for understanding the computational task of vision, as well as flexible modeling tools. Its use has not been restricted to human visual capacities with, for example, Schloltyssek, Osorio, and Baddeley (2016) reporting that color perception in chicks can be described with a Bayesian model. Bayesian models have also been employed to explain individual and population responses of neurons, thus giving insights into how neurons might perform statistical computations (e.g. Beck et al., 2008). This holds out the promise that Bayesianism will be a comprehensive theoretical framework for investigation of both the psychophysics and neurophysiology of sensory perception.

Assuming, for the sake of argument, that the prophets of Bayesianism are right, and that the approach is unmatched in its scope and explanatory power, does this mean that the visual brain *is* Bayesian, that seeing *is* Bayesian inference?[14] Rescorla (2015) urges us to take a realist stance here, bolstered by the explanatory successes of Bayesian models. The claim is that the visual system approximately implements Bayesian inference, and that its inner states approximate to the representations of the probability distributions which feature in the models. As an alternative to realism, Rescorla only considers the instrumentalism of Colombo and Seriès (2012), where the models are interpreted as "tools for predicting, systematizing and classifying statements about people's observable performance" (ibid., p. 705).[15]

As an alternative both to realism and instrumentalism, I contend that we should be *perspectival realists* (Giere, 2006) and pluralists when interpreting Bayesian and other families of models in vision science. The idealized nature of Bayesian models – the fact that they make assumptions known to be false of biological systems, and posit intractable computations – is a fly in the ointment for realism. Rescorla (2015) bets on a de-idealizing trajectory of future research, where models eventually become more realistic descriptions of actual processes.

This optimism neglects the broader issues about the role of idealized models in science. It is instructive to compare Bayesian models with other optimality models used in biology. In brief, optimality models examine, in most general terms, the challenges and constraints imposed upon a biological system, and derive the theoretically optimal strategy for dealing with this situation. They are often highly abstract, describing none of the specifics of the concrete situation, and idealized in the sense of making assumptions known to be false (e.g. that there is an infinite breeding population). Batterman and Rice (2014) discuss Fisher's sex-ratio model in such terms, as a "minimal model" and a "caricature" of nature. Their idea is that the optimality model is applicable to natural populations because it stands in the same "universality class" of systems whose behavior converges on distinctive patterns of behavior. The systems within the same universality class are still fundamentally different in many other respects, most obviously physical constitution, but also regarding dispositions to perform other kinds of functions.

Now Bayesian models describe optimal solutions for perceptual decision making under uncertainty.[16] Real systems, to the extent that their behavior is accurately predicted by the model, fall within the same universality class as the model. But nothing within the Bayesian approach assumes that biological perceivers are always optimal, or that there are not radical differences between the strategies employed in nature, and described in the model. As Knill and Pouget (2004, p. 718) point out, departures from optimality are an important focus for research, and we know in advance that in a strict sense the brain is *not* Bayesian:

> an equally important challenge for future work is to find the ways in which human observers are not optimal. Owing to the complexity of the tasks, unconstrained Bayesian inference is not a viable solution for computation in the brain.

As I have argued elsewhere (Chirimuuta, 2017), the comparison between a neural system and a theoretical solution offers a *mathematical explanation* of why the system evolved to have the computational properties which are observed – for example, why sensory systems weight the impact of incoming data according to its uncertainty, or why neural populations might employ probabilistic representation. The mathematical theory of decision making gives *a priori* reason to think that Bayesian processing is relevant to biology, but it is just one perspective on a complex biological system.[17] This is how Griffiths et al. (2012, p. 421) make the point:

> Different theoretical frameworks, such as Bayesian modeling, connectionism, and production systems, have different insights to offer about human cognition, distributed across different levels of analysis. A connectionist model and a Bayesian model of the same phenomenon can both provide valuable information – one about how the brain might solve a problem, the other about why this solution makes sense – and both could well be valid.

Thus the corollary of perspectival realism is *pluralism* – the thesis that a number of different theoretical frameworks and modeling strategies should be employed to build a more well-rounded understanding of the natural system.[18]

To conclude, we can think again of the eye and the camera. The photographic camera, a man-made system with none of the complexity or evolutionary heritage of the eye does still instantiate the same optical laws which explain image formation on the retina. Likewise, simple and highly idealized models, in various theoretical traditions, capture some of the computational principles which are employed by the visual system and explain its capacities. Without doubt there is much still to be discovered, and the comparison between the visual brain and a computational model might come to be seen to future generations as both compelling and naïve as the camera model of the eye seems to us now.[19]

Notes

1 It might be asserted here that the computational approach is proprietary to computer science just because tools and ideas originally developed in that field were later employed to understand the brain.

In response I should point out that by "proprietary" I do not mean just to refer to the disciplinary source of the model. Many models and formal techniques used in special sciences originally came from elsewhere. People would not say that use of an optimality model from economics within evolutionary biology means that the biologist is 'doing economics'. Likewise, they should not think of a neuroscientist using an information-processing model as doing computer science or psychology.

2 Elsewhere I refer to this as *efficient coding explanation*, which I contrast with *mechanistic explanation* (Chirimuuta, 2014). See Sterling and Laughlin (2015) for an extensive (and opinionated) discussion of this approach.

3 It is worth making the comparison with Ernst Mayr's (1961) advocacy of non-reductive research strategies in biology, and emphasis on functional "why?" questions. Less well known is the neurologist Francis Walshe's (1961, p. 131) argument that progress in understanding the nervous system will only be made if reductionist strategies are employed in tandem with ones which foreground the function of the system:

> If we subject a clock to minute analysis by the methods of physics and chemistry, we shall learn a great deal about its constituents, but we shall not discover its operational principles, that is, what makes these constituents function as a clock. Physics and chemistry are not competent to answer questions of this order, which are an engineer's task.

I am not suggesting that it is any more than a coincidence that these three papers were published in 1961, but it does indicate that such ideas were "in the air" at the time. Note that Marr was a doctoral student in Horace Barlow's department, the Physiological Laboratory at Cambridge, before moving to MIT in 1977.

4 While Shagrir (2010) argues for the importance of "why?" questions in computational level explanations, he does not associate these with functional questions in biology more generally. Thus I go further than Shagrir (2010) in my proposal that we consider Marr and Barlow's theoretical work as part of a wide tradition of functional thinking in biology. See Chirimuuta (2018) for a more detailed presentation of this view.

5 Cf. Griffiths et al. (2012, p. 416) in their defense of Bayesian cognitive science: "A theoretical framework provides a general perspective and a set of tools for making models. ... Models are falsifiable, but frameworks are typically not".

6 Quotation from website available at: www.wisdom.weizmann.ac.il/~shimon/research.html (Accessed: October 14, 2016). See also Quinlan (2012, p. 1010), Warren (2012, p. 1054), Frisby and Stone (2012, pp. 1043–1044), Poggio (2012, p. 1017).

7 An exception is the *empirical paradigm* (Purves, Morgenstern, and Wojtach, 2015). See Orlandi (2014) for philosophical discussion.

8 See Warren (2012, p. 1055) on the limitations of Marr's programme in comparison with statistical approaches. The "noisiness" of input image data, and neural systems, is another important factor here. Warren (2012, p. 1057) writes that "Marr himself had little enthusiasm for probabilistic approaches because he felt that statistical machinery was not a substitute for the analysis of constraints and information that provides a firm basis for computational theory".

9 "Deep learning" refers to AI using artificial neural networks with very many hidden layers. See LeCun, Bengio, and Hinton (2015) for a useful review of kinds of networks and Garson and Bruckner (this volume).

10 The AlexNet was trained to associate 1.2 million human-labeled images with 1,000 different object classes. It was tested with 150,000 images and achieved a 37.5 percent top-1 error rate (network's estimate of most probable classification is incorrect) and 17.0 percent top-5 error rate (the correct answer does not appear amongst the network's selection of five most probable classifications). Networks are now reported to outperform humans in object recognition. See VanRullen (2017) for review and discussion.

11 The ventral stream is the portion of the visual system thought to be responsible for object recognition, and the temporal cortex is the end stage of the ventral pathway.

12 But see Yamins and DiCarlo (2016, p. 363). They speculate that it would be possible to create adversarial images to trick a human visual system if the individual's detailed neural circuitry were known.

13 See Allred (2012) for more of the scientific details discussed here and some useful reflections on different modeling strategies in vision science. See Kersten, Mamassian, and Yuille (2004) on the Bayesian approach to object perception, and Rescorla (2015) for a philosophy-oriented overview.

14 While the "prophet of Bayesianism" is intended to be a caricature, Rescorla (2015) argues something along these lines. And see Knill and Pouget (2004, p. 713) who infer the "Bayesian coding hypothesis" (that the brain houses probabilistic representations of sensory information) from the "Bayes optimality" of human performance in certain psychophysical tasks. Note that the Bayesian coding hypothesis is less contentious – and more specific – than the claim that biological perception is Bayesian inference.

15 Cf. Orlandi (2014, p. 88):

> although usefully described by a Bayesian framework, the visual system need not perform Bayesian inferences in any substantive sense. The system proceeds in rough accord with Bayesian norms. ... but this just means that the system acts *as if* it is a Bayesian observer.

16 In perceptual science, the optimal solution is usually cashed out as the answer given by an "ideal observer" – a hypothetical agent who extracts the most information ("signal") from the noisy data provided by the sensory system.

17 Cf. Frisby and Stone (2012, p. 1047): "This is not intended to imply that Bayes' theorem is a dominant feature of visual processing, but that, by virtue of being the only rational basis for inference under uncertainty, it is a necessary feature of visual information processing".

18 Another corollary is that the accuracy of models is only evaluable from *within* as perspective, not across perspectives (Giere, 2006). So I think perspectival realism, and not instrumentalism, gives the better account of this statement from Griffiths et al. (2012, p. 421):

> The ultimate test of these different theoretical frameworks will be not whether they are true or false, but whether they are useful in leading us to new ideas about the mind and brain, and we believe that the Bayesian approach has already proven fruitful in this regard.

19 I am much indebted to Joe Howse and to the editors of this volume for thoughtful and helpful comments on this chapter.

References

Allred, S. (2012) 'Approaching Color with Bayesian Algorithms', in Hatfield, G. and Allred, S. (eds.) *Visual Experiences: Sensation, Cognition, and Constancy*. Oxford: Oxford University Press.

Barlow, H.B. (1961) 'Possible Principles Underlying the Transformation of Sensory Messages', in Rosenblith, W.A. (ed.) *Sensory Communication*. Cambridge, MA: MIT Press.

Barlow, H.B. (1969) 'Pattern Recognition and the Responses of Sensory Neurones', *Annals of the New York Academy of Science*, 156, pp. 872–881.

Batterman, R. and Rice, C. (2014) 'Minimal Model Explanations', *Philosophy of Science*, 81 (3), pp. 349–376.

Beck, J.M. et al. (2008) 'Probabilistic Population Codes for Bayesian Decision Making', *Neuron*, 60, pp. 1142–1152.

Bowers, J. and Davis, C. (2012) 'Bayesian Just-So Stories in Psychology and Neuroscience', *Psychological Bulletin*, 138, pp. 389–414.

Brainard, D.H. et al. (2006) 'Bayesian Model of Human Color Constancy', *Journal of Vision*, 6, pp. 1267–1281.

Carandini, M. (2012) 'From Circuits to Behavior: A Bridge too Far?', *Nature*, 15 (4), pp. 507–509.

Chirimuuta, M. (2014) 'Minimal Models and Canonical Neural Computations: The Distinctness of Computational Explanation in Neuroscience', *Synthese*, 191, pp. 127–153.

Chirimuuta, M. (2017) 'Explanation in Neuroscience: Causal and Non-causal', *British Journal for the Philosophy of Science*. Available at: https://doi.org/10.1093/bjps/axw034.

Chirimuuta, M. (2018) 'Marr, Mayr, and MR: What Functionalism Should Now Be About', *Philosophical Psychology*, 31 (3), pp. 403–418.

Colombo, M. and Seriès, P. (2012) 'Bayes in the Brain: On Bayesian Modeling in Neuroscience', *British Journal for the Philosophy of Science*, 63, pp. 697–723.

Findlay, J. and Gilchrist, I. (2003) *Active Vision: The Psychology of Looking and Seeing*. Oxford: Oxford University Press.

Fodor, J.A. (1974) 'Special Sciences (Or: The Disunity of Science as a Working Hypothesis)', *Synthese*, 28, pp. 97–115.

Frisby, J.P. and Stone, J.V. (2010) *Seeing: The Computation Approach to Biological Vision*. Cambridge, MA: MIT Press.

Frisby, J.P. and Stone, J.V. (2012) 'Marr: An Appreciation', *Perception*, 41, pp. 1040–1052.

Fukushima, K. (1980) 'Neocognitron: A Self-organizing Neural Network Model for a Mechanism of Pattern Recognition Unaffected by Shift in Position', *Biological Cybernetics*, 36 (4), pp. 193–202.

Giere, R.N. (2006) *Scientific Perspectivism*. Chicago, IL: University of Chicago Press.

Greenough, J. (2016) '10 Million Self Driving Cars Will Be on the Road by 2020', *Business Insider*, June 15. Available at: www.businessinsider.com/report-10-million-self-driving-cars-will-be-on-the-road-by-2020-2015-5-6 (Accessed: October 14, 2016).

Griffiths, T.L. et al. (2012) 'How the Bayesians Got Their Beliefs (and What Those Beliefs Actually Are): Comment on Bowers and Davis', *Psychological Bulletin*, 138 (3), pp. 415–422.

Kersten, D., Mamassian, P., and Yuille, A. (2004) 'Object Perception as Bayesian Inference', *Annual Review of Psychology*, 55, pp. 271–304.

Knill, D.C. and Pouget, A. (2004) 'The Bayesian Brain: The Role of Uncertainty in Neural Coding and Computation', *Trends in Neurosciences*, 27, pp. 712–719.

Krizhevsky, A., Sutskever, I., and Hinton, G.E. (2012) 'ImageNet Classification with Deep Convolutional Neural Networks', *Advances in Neural Information Processing Systems*, 2, pp. 1097–1105.

Kurakin, A., Goodfellow, I., and Bengio, S. (2016) Adversarial Examples in the Physical World, arXiv pre-print, arXiv:1607.02533. Available at: https://arxiv.org/pdf/1607.02533v2.pdf.

LeCun, Y., Bengio, Y., and Hinton, G. (2015) 'Deep Learning', *Nature*, 521 (7553), pp. 436–444.

LeCun, Y. et al. (1995) 'Comparison of Learning Algorithms for Handwritten Digit Recognition', *International Conference on Artificial Neural Networks*, 60, pp. 53–60.

Machamer, P., Darden, L., and Craver, C.F. (2000) 'Thinking about Mechanisms', *Philosophy of Science*, 67, pp. 1–25.

Marr, D. (1982) *Vision: A Computational Investigation into the Human Representation and Processing of Visual Information*. San Francisco, CA: Freeman.

Marr, D. and Hildreth, E. (1980) 'Theory of Edge Detection', *Proceedings of the Royal Society of London B: Biological Sciences*, 207, pp. 187–218.

Marr, D. and Ullman, S. (1981) 'Directional Sensitivity and Its Use in Early Visual Processing', *Proceedings of the Royal Society B*, 211, pp. 151–180.

Mayr, E. (1961) 'Cause and Effect in Biology', *Science*, 134, pp. 1501–1506.

Meyering, T.C. (1989) *The Historical Roots of Cognitive Science*. Dordrecht: Kluwer.

Moravec, H. (1988) *Mind Children: The Future of Robot and Human Intelligence*. Cambridge, MA: Harvard University Press.

Nguyen, A., Yosinski, J., and Clune, J. (2015) 'Deep Neural Networks Are Easily Fooled: High Confidence Predictions for Unrecognizable Images', *IEEE Conference on Computer Vision and Pattern Recognition (CVPR)*, pp. 427–436.

Nishihara, H.K. (2012) 'Recollections of David Marr', *Perception*, 41, pp. 1027–1030.

Orlandi, N. (2014) *The Innocent Eye*. Oxford: Oxford University Press.

Piekniewski, F. et al. (2016) 'Unsupervised Learning from Continuous Video in a Scalable Predictive Recurrent Network', arXiv preprint, arXiv:1607.06854. Available at: https://arxiv.org/pdf/1607.06854v3.pdf.

Poggio, T. (2012) 'The Levels of Understanding Framework, Revised', *Perception*, 41, pp. 1017–1023.

Purves, D., Morgenstern, Y., and Wojtach, W.T. (2015) 'Perception and Reality: Why a Wholly Empirical Paradigm Is Needed to Understand Vision', *Frontiers in Systems Neuroscience*, November 18. Available at: http://dx.doi.org/10.3389/fnsys.2015.00156.

Quinlan, P. (2012) 'Marr's *Vision* 30 Years on: From a Personal Point of View', *Perception*, 41, pp. 1009–1012.

Rescorla, M. (2015) 'Bayesian Perceptual Psychology', in Matthen, M. (ed.) *The Oxford Handbook of Philosophy of Perception*. Oxford: Oxford University Press.

Riesenhuber, M. and Poggio, T. (1999) 'Hierarchical Models of Object Recognition in Cortex', *Nature Neuroscience*, 2 (11), pp. 1019–1025.

Schloltyssek, C., Osorio, D.C., and Baddeley, R.J. (2016) 'Color Generalization across Hue and Saturation in Chicks Described by a Simple (Bayesian) Model', *Journal of Vision*, 16 (8). Available at: DOI:10.1167/16.10.8.

Shagrir, O. (2010) 'Marr on Computational-level Theories', *Philosophy of Science*, 77 (4), pp. 477–500.

Sterling, P. and Laughlin, S.B. (2015) *Principles of Neural Design*. Cambridge, MA: MIT Press.

Talbot, D. (2015) 'CES 2015: Nvidia Demos a Car Computer Trained with "Deep Learning"' *MIT Technology Review*, January 6. Available at: www.technologyreview.com/s/533936/ces-2015-nvidia-demos-a-car-computer-trained-with-deep-learning/ (Accessed: October 14, 2016).

vanRullen, R. (2017) 'Perception Science in the Age of Deep Neural Networks', *Frontiers in Psychology*, 8 (142). Available at: DOI:10.3389/fpsyg.2017.00142.

Walshe, F.M.R. (1961) 'Contributions of John Hughlings Jackson to Neurology: A Brief Introduction to His Teachings', *Archives of Neurology*, 5, pp. 119–131.

Warren, W.H. (2012) 'Does This Computational Theory Solve the Right Problem? Marr, Gibson, and the Goal of Vision', *Perception*, 41, pp. 1053–1060.

Yamins, D.L.K and DiCarlo, J.J. (2016) 'Using Goal-driven Deep Learning Models to Understand Sensory Cortex', *Nature Neuroscience*, 19 (3), pp. 356–365.

Yamins, D.L.K. et al. (2014) 'Performance-optimized Hierarchical Models Predict Neural Responses in Higher Visual Cortex', *Proceedings of the National Academy of Science USA*, 111, pp. 8619–8624.

30

PERCEPTION WITHOUT COMPUTATION?

Nico Orlandi

Computationalism in the philosophy of mind is the view that mental processes, including perceptual processes, are computational. To assess the truth of this view, we need, first, some grasp of what computations are, and then some understanding of whether mental processes are computational in the relevant sense.

This chapter offers an overview of the notion of computation with a particular focus on how it applies in perceptual theory. Two prominent theories of perception, ecology and disjunctivism, are thought to be at odds with computationalism. The chapter aims to show that the incompatibility is only apparent by suggesting that the two theories are in tension only with a *semantic* way of individuating computation. Non-semantic understandings of computation are both theoretically plausible and in line with how the notion of computation is understood in computer science.

Section 1 presents a first take (the classical take) on the notion of computation and explains why, when this notion is applied to understanding perception, it would seem to produce a theory that is at odds with both ecology and disjunctivism. Section 2 argues that there is a syntactic way of understanding classical computation that dispels the incompatibility, but it also shows that we have little reason to accept Classicism (in both syntactic and semantic versions) when it comes to perception. Section 3 introduces two non-classical and non-semantic ways of understanding computation – minimalism and functionalism. Section 4 concludes by discussing how these theories relate to the common idea in cognitive science that computation is fundamentally a matter of information processing.

1 Perception and classical computation

To start understanding what computationalism in the philosophy of mind amounts to, it is useful to start from Marr's (1982) distinction between three different levels of analysis of a system: task, algorithmic, and physical-implementation levels. The *task* level identifies the goal of a given cognitive system or process. In perception, one recognized task is to explain how perceivers (and their brains) transform excitations at the sensory receptors (for example, projected light) into usable perceptions of the environment (for example, views of objects and properties in three dimensions). The task-level analysis specifies this input–output function, and it also involves an explanation of why this input–output function is appropriate. The latter explanation often appeals to ecological conditions. In a natural environment, a certain retinal input may have been repeatedly produced by a specific object. The visual system outputs a perception of the object in question because it is adequately adapted to reflect the environmental regularity between the object and the retinal stimulus.

The "algorithmic" level, by contrast, specifies *how* the system performs a given task. In the perceptual case, if we fix the task description given above, the algorithm specifies how the system derives percepts from retinal excitations. The algorithmic description identifies the intermediate steps between input and output.

One of Marr's crucial insights is that the same process described in task-level terms can be implemented, or realized, by a variety of different algorithms. Furthermore, an algorithm can be implemented by different neurophysiological or other physical processes (Marr's third level of analysis).[1] This means that, if we accept Marr's partition, for any given theory, we can wonder whether the theory specifies the task, algorithmic, or implementation levels, and models that are *prima facie* incompatible can be reconciled if viewed as implementations of one another.

Now, it is unfortunately not always advertised what level theory computationalism is, and we get weaker and stronger versions of the theory depending on the level we consider. Traditional computational views aspire to be theories of the *algorithmic* level (Fodor and Pylyshyn, 1981). Such theories specify *how* perceptual, and other cognitive processes are carried out. Marr, for example, appealed to a sequence of *representations* of various kinds – 2D representations that are intermediate between retinal input and 3D representations – as well as to rules governing the transition between representations. This way of understanding perceptual processing is essentially that of *classical computationalism*.

Classical computationalism (or Classicism) understands computations in a rather narrow, and *semantic* sense. Proponents of Classicism introduce two requirements that serve to define computations and to identify the types of computations that are useful as models of mental activity.

The main requirement of Classicism concerns the medium of computation. Classicism holds that computations are operations over representational states, so any computational process is *ipso facto* a process that involves representations (Fodor, 1975, p. 27; Pylyshyn, 1984). Later sections further discuss the notion of representation, but to give a concrete idea, digital computers typically use strings of 0s and 1s that can be assigned various meanings, and that are implemented in different types of electrical states of the computer (Piccinini and Scarantino, 2011, p. 26.)

A further requirement of Classicism concerns the kind of representations that should be used if computers aspire to be good models of the mind. Classicists think that computers are good explanatory tools for minds, only if the representations in the medium have a syntax that makes them akin to *linguistic symbols*. Like words of a language, symbolic representations can combine and re-combine to form strings that have a sentence-like form, being evaluable for truth and displaying genuine predication. The strings are not mere "lists of features" or "map-like" representations. Lists have no genuine linguistic structure since "any collection of items is a possible list" (Fodor and Pylyshyn, 1988, p. 34).[2]

Some early classicists also thought that a condition of computation concerns how it is carried out. A distinctive characteristic of computing systems is that they encode algorithms (Fodor, 1975, n. 15; Pylyshyn, 1984). "Encoding" is typically taken to mean that the algorithm is itself represented within the computational system (rather than the system simply conforming to what the algorithm says). In this way of understanding computation, the encoded algorithm is a causal antecedent of the system's behavior.

An algorithm, in this classical story, is an "effective, step-by-step procedure" to manipulate strings of representations and to "produce a result within finitely many steps" (Piccinini and Scarantino, 2011, p. 9).[3] In concrete computers, algorithms can be implemented in a similar way to how representations are implemented – e.g. in an electrical state of the computer (Piccinini, 2008a, p. 214.)

Other classicists – including Turing and Fodor in some articles (Fodor, 1968) – hold that a system can be a computer even if it doesn't explicitly represent its algorithm. Some Turing machines and some special purpose machines (such as arithmetic logic units) are built to conform to an algorithm without representing it. They can be *described* as following rules, or step-by-step procedures, but they do not instantiate any structure that encodes the rules (or the procedures). Because the requirement that they encode algorithms is controversial, what is more crucial to a classical understanding of computation is that computations happen over representational states that have a *language-like* format.

In the next section, we will look at the motivations for accepting this restrictive notion of computation. But going back to the case of perception, according to Marr and to early computationalists, the visual system performs computations in the sense of unconsciously transforming representations of light intensity into representations of three-dimensional objects in virtue of a set of rules (Fodor, 1988; Palmer, 1999; Rock, 1997; Ullman, 1980). This computational way of understanding perception is traditionally thought to be at odds with two prominent perceptual theories. The first theory is *ecology*, and the second is contemporary *naïve realism* or *disjunctivism*.

Ecological theories tend to clash with classical computationalism both in how they describe perception at the task level, and in how they understand it at the algorithmic level. When specifying the input–output function of perception, ecologists tend to reject the idea of perception as a *reconstructive* process – that is, as a process that gives observers a passive "view" of the world. The output of perceiving, according to ecologists, is action, and its input is a world of invariances that indicate the potential for action (Gibson, 1979).

As for the algorithmic level of description, "old-school" ecologists have often refused to specify how perception performs its action-guiding task (Gibson, 1979). This has been a source of criticism, since it is presumably a theorizer's task to understand the mechanism of perception (Marr, 1982). In general, ecologists admit that the brain has to "pick up" information about the environment, but they shy away from appeal to representational states of any kind.

According to ecologists, the perceptual process should be understood, *not* as the internal processing of representations, but as a process of engagement of a whole organism with the world. Observers derive a useful perception of objects from sensation by being physiologically attuned to the rich structure of the world, and by exploring it. Central importance is given to the ecological conditions that make perception possible – for example, to the regularities, in our world, between certain light intensities and certain objects. Classical Marrian views also had this focus, but they added an internal, representational process that ecologists think is unnecessary. In this sense, and in opposition to inferential accounts in perceptual psychology, Gibson remarked that perception is not computational.

While it is easy to see how ecology may be incompatible with computationalism as described so far, the case of disjunctivism is less obvious. Contemporary disjunctivism is not a theory about unconscious perceptual processing. It is rather a view of the nature of perceptual experience, or of conscious perception (Martin, 2003; Travis, 2004). One of the basic claims of disjunctivism is that having a perceptual experience consists in being directly related to mind-independent objects.

As it is, the view is silent concerning the kind of perceptual process that puts perceivers in direct contact with the environment. Such process may be, in some sense, computational.

But central to contemporary arguments for disjunctivism is the distinction between veridical experiences, on the one hand, and illusions and hallucinations, on the other. When a subject sees a three-dimensional object she is in a fundamentally different psychological state to that she is in when she hallucinates a three-dimensional object. The difference between the two is so fundamental, according to disjunctivism, that there is no *common factor* between the two types of states.

Now, the common factor, in this theory, has to be of a specific kind. Disjunctivists wouldn't deny, for example, that perception and illusion have something physiological in common (they both presumably involve neuronal firings). The common factor has to be such that it would make perception and illusion into psychological siblings. But this suggests why disjunctivism may be incompatible with computational models of perception as described so far (Burge, 2008).

Computational models tend to explain illusions in the same way in which they explain veridical perception (Palmer, 1999; Rock, 1983). In both instances, the brain processes representations and creates a percept that stands for distal elements (whether or not the elements are present). This suggests that there is a computational state in common between perception, illusion, and hallucination, and that this common state is representational. Further, this common element seems to be a very good candidate for the common factor that disjunctivists deny exists. The common representational element seems sufficient to specify what perceivers see both when they perceive, and when they hallucinate or have a visual illusion, making these different types of states psychologically akin to one another.

If this is true, there are reasons to presume that computationalism is incompatible with some prominent theories of perception. The remaining shows that this is not quite right.

2 Perception without classical computation

Why has computation been understood in this classical way? Part of the reason may have been that early computational devices had the features outlined by Classicism (Turing, 1950). Computers were initially symbolic. Each of the requirements, however, also has an independent *raison d'être*.

Appeal to representations has the important role of making computing systems *distinctive* from other physical systems. Computers are complex mechanical systems, but they are different from other complex mechanical systems, such as rocks and stomachs. One of the advantages of resorting to representations (and, in some cases, to encoded algorithms) to define computation is that this appeal restricts the number of systems that are able to compute, since it restricts it to the number of systems that are able to represent and follow procedures (Fodor, 1975, n. 15).

Further, computers that use symbols or representations are mechanical systems that, for all appearances, are sensitive to semantic elements. When one tells a computer to exit its current routine by entering a certain command to exit, the computer's behavior seems to be guided by the *content* of the command. It is the command *qua* "exit" command – that is, the command that *means* "exit" – that partly explains the computer's behavior.

This makes computers good models of the mind. Minds appear to be similarly sensitive to meaning. One of the recognized puzzles about mental activity is that mindful creatures seem to respond to reasons, rather than to mere causes. If we understand the mind on the model of a computer that uses internal representations, then we are able to explain how the behavior of mindful beings can be reason-responsive (Clark, 2000, p. 15; Fodor, 1975).

What is the advantage of thinking that the medium of computation is comprised of language-like representations? This feature of classical understandings of computation makes sense of two purported features of thought: productivity and systematicity.

Productivity consists in the fact that thinking agents, despite being finite, appear capable of producing novel thoughts in infinite number. Systematicity is, in turn, the fact that the ability to have certain thoughts is related to the ability to have certain others (Fodor and Pylyshyn, 1988).[4]

These features suggest that mental processes occur over states that have linguistic form. A potentially infinite number of new thoughts is produced by combining simple thoughts, or atomic symbols. If we think that mental representations are mere lists, then it is hard to see how finite beings could produce potentially infinite new thoughts.

A similar explanatory strategy is used in accounting for systematicity. The ability to have certain thoughts is related to the ability to have certain others because related thoughts have common constituents. The thought "Stephanie loves Paula" has the same semantic parts, and the same kinds of syntactic elements as the thought "Paula loves Stephanie", so Classicism predicts that an individual who is capable of entertaining one of these thoughts will also be able to entertain the others. If, however, we think that thoughts do not have linguistic parts, then we are not able to predict this systematicity. On the contrary, we should find punctate minds – minds that can only think one of these thoughts – as unsurprising.

Computationalism – classically understood – has then been regarded as the *only* plausible and scientifically respectable account of many aspects of the mind. According to a famous Fodorian argument, Classicism is the only option we have for explaining (in an even remotely plausible way) processes as different as decision making, concept acquisition, and perception (Fodor, 1975, pp. 28–42).

There are questions, however, both concerning Classicism as a good model of perception, and concerning the incompatibility between Classicism, on the one hand, and ecology and disjunctivism on the other.

A way to reconcile Classicism with ecological and disjunctivist views is to abandon its commitment to representations, and to adopt a purely *syntactic* understanding of the computations performed by classical computers (Stich, 1983). This approach would retain a basic classical model of perception, while getting rid of one of the defining claims of Classicism.

To get a sense of how this would work, it is useful to have a closer look at *digital* computers. As noted in the previous section, digital computers operate over digits. A digit is roughly a state that, in a system, can be reliably distinguished from other states and treated as the same in different contexts. Digits may be implemented by a voltage level or by a neuronal spike (Piccinini and Scarantino, 2011, p. 21; Piccinini, 2011; Piccinini and Scarantino, 2011, p. 7, p. 11).

At the abstract level, digits are typically labeled with numbers – 0s and 1s. The numbers, in turn, can be taken to refer to words of a language. This allows programmers to write – in abstract – how the computer should manipulate the digits. It is easy to assign both a specific meaning and a linguistic label to each of the digits. There is nothing mandatory, however, about this way of treating digits. Digits do not have to be regarded as standing for anything. There are digital computations that operate over strings that are not meaningful – for example, strings labeled as "r\%h@" (Piccinini and Scarantino, 2011, p. 12). So long as a system is properly described as operating in a regimented fashion over digits, then the system is computing digitally even if it does not represent at all (Piccinini, 2008a).

These considerations introduce the possibility of understanding computation in a non-semantic way. We will return to some non-semantic ways of understanding computation in the next section. Here, we should point out that an ecological view that is skeptical of representation is in a position to accept that perception is computational with respect to its syntax even if not to its semantics. Similarly, disjunctivists can concede that veridical perception and hallucination have a syntactic element in common while being fundamentally different states when it comes to semantic content. The semantic content of perception involves a mind-independent object, while the content of hallucination does not.

A syntactic version of Classicism may then be friendly to a variety of perceptual theories. But adopting it would still mean adopting an overly narrow idea of what computation is, and doing it without good reasons when it comes to perception. Perception does not seem to be a classical computation in either the semantic or syntactic sense.

To start seeing why this is the case, we should look at the motivations we have for accepting Classicism. They do not straightforwardly apply to perception. It is not obvious, for example, that perception is productive and systematic at all – and if perception has these features, the kind of productivity and systematicity that we find there, seems explainable without thinking of sensory and perceptual states as linguistically structured.

Productivity and systematicity are notions borrowed from linguistic analysis (Travieso, Gomila, and Lobo, 2014). Languages are productive and systematic. We are in principle able to produce infinitely many new sentences, and the ability to understand certain sentences is related to the ability to understand certain others. If we suppose that language is a mirror of thought – so that anything that we can say, we can also think – then we may accept that thought is productive and systematic.

It is a question, however, how to transfer these features to perception. It could be that perception displays the same basic structure and architecture of language and of thought, but this would seem to be the conclusion of an argument, not something that we can grant from the beginning.

Consider productivity first. As a generative capacity for producing potentially infinite new mental states, it is unclear in what sense it applies to perception. New perceptions are not produced by combining old perceptual or sensory states in new guises. New perceptions are rather produced by being responsive to the world, and by having new encounters with it.

Perceivers are typically able to discriminate "productive properties" – that is, properties such that, if one is capable of detecting them, then one is also capable of detecting novel stimuli that instantiate them (Fodor and Pylyshyn, 1981, pp 176–177). However, everyone grants that productive properties can be discriminated by systems that do not perform classical computations, and in fact by systems that are mere resonators to physical parameters (Fodor and Pylyshyn, 1981, p. 177). All it takes to be able to detect productive properties is to have, or acquire, the ability to respond in the same way to similar inputs.

Something similar can be said of systematicity. Like in the case of productivity, it is at first hard to understand what systematicity means in relation to perception. In the case of thought, systematicity manifests as the fact that the ability to have certain thoughts is related to the ability to have certain others. It is hard to see what the perceptual analogue of this is. Is it that the ability to see a three-dimensional cube is related to the ability to see a cube three-dimensional? It is dubious that there is any difference between these two states at the level of perceptual content.

The hurdle seems to be that, for us to understand systematicity in relation to perception, we would have to already accept that perceptual states have a certain form – for example, a form that resembles language and that involves predication and a subject–object structure. In that case, we could, speaking loosely, move the subject and the predicate around and account for why different perceptions are related. But this is not an assumption that we can freely make. Whether perception has syntactic and semantic parts is a debated issue. We can surely *describe* what we perceive with sentences and propositions, but this reflects the structure of perceptual *judgment*, not of perception *per se*.

Some have tried to understand systematicity by reference to amodal completion arguing that the capacity to see a circle occluded by a square, for example, comes in a bundle with the ability to see a square occluded by a circle (Aizawa, 2014). But, as it turns out, this does not generalize. There are instances where we can see one object occluded by another but not vice versa (Gomila, Travieso, and Lobo, 2014).

Perhaps a way to conceive of systematicity in perception is by reference to the phenomenon of perceptual *binding* (Malsburg, 1995; Treisman, 1996; O'Callaghan, forthcoming). There are different types of binding, but a relevant one consists in the capacity to bind together properties, such as shape and color. In this type of binding, the perceptual system, having neurons that selectively respond to shapes and colors binds them in different ways in different contexts.[5] One's capacity to see red and blue, and to see squares and triangles, subtends one's capacity to see red squares and blue triangles, but also to see red triangles and blue squares. Perceptual systematicity is then the fact that some basic perceptual competences make sense of why we are able to see, in different ways, scenes that have common constituents.

It is dubious that this type of systematicity requires linguistically structured representations. Accounts of how properties are bound together in perception typically appeal either to the role of selective attention – as features that are attended are processed as belonging together – or to signal-synchrony where groups of neurons are bound to each other by their synchronized activation (Treisman and Schmidt, 1982). Appeal to a subject predicate structure is unnecessary.

If this is true, then the usual considerations for supporting Classicism do not straightforwardly apply to the perceptual case. It is hard to make sense of productivity and systematicity at the perceptual level, and, when we do, we can explain these features without appeal to a language of thought.

As a matter of fact, the other main reason that Fodor presents for thinking that mental processes are computational is also not persuasive in the case of perception. Adopting a computational approach to the mind, and thinking that representations are an essential component of computation, is said to make sense of reason-responsiveness. Minds, like computers, appear to be sensitive to *content*.

Now, although reason-responsiveness is (again) a feature of higher-order cognition – as what one chooses, for example, is often sensitive to evidence – it does not seem to be a feature of perceptual processing. Perceptual processing is not properly sensitive to evidence (Kanizsa, 1985). Even recent Bayesian models of perception that describe the process as a rational operation of hypothesis formation and confirmation are often taken to be descriptions at the Marrian task level of analysis (Griffiths et al., 2012). When interpreted as models at the algorithmic level, they encounter problems, as many perceptual capacities appear to be non-Bayesian and guided by local, non-rational biases (Rahnev and Denison, 2016).

In perception, the brain does not seem to *conclude* that a three-dimensional object is present given sensory evidence. The brain seems to just be *attuned* to the presence of a three-dimensional object, where this attunement may involve organic adaptation that is not linguistic and rational – a fact that is hard to square with how Classicism conceives of mental processes. To see if we can rescue the computational idea in understanding perception, we need to move past Classicism.

3 Computation without representation

Classicism is an overly narrow way of understanding computation. Computations can happen without appeal to symbolic elements, without appeal to traditional algorithms, and without appeal to representations at all (Cummins, 1983, pp. 44–51; Rescorla, 2009a).

The development of different types of computational systems makes this clear. Artificial neural networks, or connectionist networks – both in their dated, and in their more recent "generative" instantiations (Sejnowski and Rosenberg, 1987; Hinton, 2007) – are systems that plausibly compute without crunching symbols, and without following step-by-step-procedures. It is indeed a substantive question whether networks represent at all.

Other chapters in this volume describe artificial neural networks, but the basic idea is that networks instantiate state transitions between input and output units that allow them to recognize and reproduce – and in this sense to *attune* to – specific environmental elements, without employing symbolic material.

In a network conceived for military submarines, the connectionist net learns to discriminate mine echoes from rock echoes at the bottom of the ocean (Gorman and Sejnowski, 1988; Poggio and Edelmann, 1990). One way to train the network is, roughly, as follows. Start with a net whose connection strengths between the units are set at random. Then expose the network to a large number of stimuli – a training set. Finally, adjust the network connections after each individual trial. Do so in order that the network's output would be closer to the desired response if it were exposed to the same input again.

A mine-detecting network, for instance, is exposed to a large number of echoes of mines and rocks, and then adjusted so as to minimize error. Error minimization consists in changing the connections and the level of activation of the units so as to get the network to output a certain vector whenever mines are present. After this sort of training, networks are typically able to detect mines, and also to "generalize". They are able to tell mines from rocks, not only in the training set, but also in novel instances.

Networks that perform tasks of this kind do not do so by following a procedure where the programmer breaks down into steps what to do at each stage. In fact, the programmer has generally little idea of what sonic features distinguish mine from rock echoes. The programmer would be unable to write a classical algorithm – a set of explicit rules concerning echoes – for the tasks performed by the network. When the programmer wants to change the way the network responds, she simply adjusts the strengths between the units without knowing, and without *needing* to know, what the strengths stand for.

Networks are then computing systems that, in some sense, conform to algorithms, but do not follow step-by-step procedures. Moreover, networks do not use symbolic representations (Fodor and Pylyshyn, 1988). Their internal states may be given a semantic interpretation – for example, a certain network activity may be taken to stand for various sonic properties. We can also *label* such sonic properties and internal states with linguistic symbols. But the symbols themselves are not what networks manipulate. Networks only instantiate evolutions of weights and activations.

This is a difference recognized by proponents of Classicism who tend to hold that the lack of symbolic elements makes networks either unable to explain mental activity, or mere instantiations of a classical architecture (Fodor and Pylyshyn, 1988). Networks, according to this line of reasoning, may be physical realizations (the third level in Marr's analysis) of classical computers in the brain.

Whether this is a fair criticism is a matter of dispute. Connectionist networks are typically described in fairly abstract terms, and they can be implemented in a variety of different ways making their status as mere implementations problematic.

Further, networks are types of computers that have been used as competitors of more classical set-ups. Unlike classical digital computers, networks are especially good at perceptual tasks, as they excel at pattern recognition. They can, among other things, recognize three-dimensional objects from two-dimensional views, turn written into spoken language, and recognize poorly written numbers. This speaks to their promise as models of perception.[6]

We can of course interpret networks as using representations even if the representations are not *symbolic*. The representations, in this case, would be given either by individual nodes, or they would be *distributed*. They would consist in a global state of the network that stands for something without coming packaged in symbols. Indeed, in some cases, it is relatively easy to give a semantic interpretation to the states of a network. A certain configuration of the input units, for example, can be seen to stand for certain sonic properties of mine echoes; and a given configuration of the output units can be regarded as standing for mine echoes themselves.

However, while such a semantic interpretation seems warranted, the question is whether it is *mandatory*. The issue is not that a semantic interpretation is in principle inappropriate. The issue is that it is in practice not needed to individuate the kinds of computations that networks perform.

To see this point, think, first, of the difficult case of the hidden units. In a network, it is not clear what environmental features, if any, the hidden units track. Hidden units do not respond individually to specific inputs. They may be tuned to specific features, but it is often hard to specify what these features are. Moreover, specifying what features the hidden units stand for is not *necessary* to think of the network as a computing system – or to understand how the network carries out its task (Ramsey, 1997; 2007). This point applies to input and output units as well. What a network programmer does is adjust the level of activation of the units to get the desired response. The concern is *not* with what *any* of the units stand for, but rather with how active they should be in order to produce the output vector that we want. So it seems that a semantic interpretation of the units is simply superfluous. Such an interpretation may be a nice, abstract way of describing the task that the network is performing, but it is not a good reflection of *how* the net is carrying out its task.

This introduces the possibility of using an argument that classicists use against connectionism to actually work *in favor* of connectionism. Connectionism can indeed be an implementation of Classicism, but that is because connectionism is a specification of the *algorithm* that the brain uses in performing different cognitive functions, while classical theories, such as Marr's, are rather abstract descriptions of the *task* level. Such theories do not commit to the existence of actual representational states in perceptual processing.

This type of approach would seem to be on point when it comes to recent Bayesian accounts of perception. Bayesians preserve the classicist metaphor of a perceptual inference where percepts are generated through a process of hypothesis formation and confirmation that roughly conforms to Bayes' theorem. However, it is not clear whether the Bayesian framework is a heuristic that helps describe the task level, rather than an account of the specific type of processing that perceptual systems perform. Task-level Bayesians need not, and often do not, commit to Bayesian algorithms, partly due to considerations of computational tractability (see, for example, Griffiths et al., 2012).

If this is true, then in the case of networks, we have a similar set of options as we had in the case of classical computers. We could understand classical computers as purely syntactic, and we can understand networks as similarly devoid of representational content. The difference between the two cases is not so much a difference in substance, but in how salient to us as enquirers the non-semantic option is. Because networks use no symbols they are less obviously using elements that have a semantic interpretation.

It is now time, then, to introduce non-semantic ways of individuating computation. There are two broad proposals for understanding computation without appeal to representation. The first proposal is *minimalism* (Chalmers, 2011). The second proposal is a *functionalist* and *mechanistic* proposal (Piccinini, 2015).[7]

According to minimalism, a system performs computations when the system's causal organization maps onto a computational description (Chalmers, 2011). In this view, the causal structure of the system mirrors the formal structure of the computation, where this mirroring means that the steps specified in the computational description correspond to the succession of steps that occur in the physical system.

It follows from minimalism that every system implements (at least) *one* computation because every physical system implements a finite state automaton with a single internal state (Chalmers, 2011, p. 5). This also means that, in this view, rocks are computational systems (Putnam, 1988).

To soften this negative result, minimalists appeal to the ideas of *complexity* and of *computational sufficiency* (Chalmers, 2011). Although all systems may perform *some* computations, not every system implements any given computation. Complex computations require fairly complex causal organizations such that very few physical systems – such as minds – implement them.

Minimalists argue, in particular, that the mapping of formal states onto physical states requires there to be a reliable, counterfactual-supporting connection between two (or more) states of the system. What this means is that for there to be a mapping it is not sufficient that, say, state *A* is followed by state *B* at one time. What is required is rather that the transition from *A* to *B* is reliable and counterfactual-supporting where, if the system were to be in state *A*, it would transit to state *B*. Complex computations that involve many such states are instantiated by only a small number of physical systems.

Additionally, complexity may not be *sufficient* for the interesting kinds of computations that we talk about in cognitive science. This is because not every system has the capacities that it has *in virtue* of instantiating a complex computation. Stomachs, for instance, may be fairly sophisticated computational systems. Instantiating a complex computation, however, is not sufficient for them to do what they do, and it is, in fact, quite irrelevant for the stomach to perform digestion. Certain chemical reactions are required. By contrast, the substantive hypothesis, in the case of perceptual systems and of minds, is that it is in virtue of instantiating a complex computation that the perceptual system has the capacities that it has.

A second proposal for individuating computation without appeal to representation is that a computational system is a particular kind of *functionally organized* system. As the name suggests, functionally organized systems are systems organized into components that have a certain function (Piccinini, 2007; 2011). Both traditional digital computers and connectionist networks have parts that are distinguished *not* by their physical properties, but by the job that they perform within the computer. They have input components, processing units and output components.

Additionally, computers are a special kind of functional mechanisms. They are distinctive because they manipulate states that persist through the computational process, and that are processed in virtue of certain properties of the states – for example, in virtue of their voltage level. That the states stand for something and represent is not needed to individuate the computation.

In this view, functional organization and the presence of states that persist through the process serve to restrict computations without appealing to semantic ideas. Rocks do not break down into parts that are individuated by the function they perform. Stomachs do not use states that persist through the process of digestion. Rocks and stomachs are derivatively not computational systems.

Minimalist and functionalist understandings of computation would seem to be friendly to both ecologists and to disjunctivists. If perception is computational just in the sense that a minimalist computational description is true of it, or just in the functionalist sense, then it is an open question whether it uses representations. It is also an open question whether there is a common factor of the relevant kind between perception, illusion, and hallucination.

4 Computation and information processing

Although in philosophy, the notion of computation has been traditionally understood as paired with the notion of representation, this is not generally true in cognitive science. Going back to the treatment by Neisser (1967), cognitive scientists tend to conceive of computation in terms of *information processing*, and it is a substantive question whether information is to be unpacked in a semantic way. The classic treatment of information by Shannon (1948) was explicitly statistical and quantitative (ibid., p. 379) having to do, roughly, with describing how a system can transmit a number of states $s_1, \ldots, s_n$ from a source to a destination.

Similarly, naturalistic accounts of information in philosophy of mind tend to think of it in causal or statistical terms (Fodor, 1987a; 1987b; Dretske, 1981). In the causal story, a certain pattern of neuronal firings carries information about an external quantity if it causally co-varies with it, or if it is consistently caused by it. In the statistical (and Shannon-inspired) story, the pattern carries information if its presence reduces uncertainty concerning the presence of the external quantity. In both of these stories, patterns of neuronal activity carry information about external elements. It is a further question, however, whether they also *represent* such external elements.

It is generally agreed that purely informational views of representational content are untenable (Dretske, 1991; Fodor, 1987a; 1987b; Burge, 2010; Ramsey, 2007; Piccinini and Scarantino, 2011). An informational state is not necessarily a representational state. Part of the reason for this claim is that information is as ubiquitous as causal co-variation, or as reduction of uncertainty. Representation, by contrast, is a more complex and distinctive notion. This is particularly true in the case of *mental* representation – something that is presumed to be one of the marks of the mental.

There is disagreement concerning what further features define mental representation, but there is broad consensus that mental representations are introduced to explain the behavior of complex organisms – for example, organisms that coordinate with absent and distal conditions. Informational states, by contrast, are found in systems whose behavior is explained simply in virtue of physiological responses to the world (Hubel and Wiesel, 1962). Human retinas and eye muscles function as they do partly in virtue of internal states that co-vary with the presence of light – as more light enters, the muscles contract. The behavior of eye muscles is often described as reactive and non-psychological. It may be guided by informational states, but not by representations. If we were to give a computational account of eye contraction we would plausibly describe something that processes information without using representations.

One could, of course, give a semantic interpretation of retinal states, thinking that they represent various light intensities, but this interpretation is not mandatory. To repeat a common theme of this chapter, we again have a choice to understand a system that processes information either as processing representations, or as processing vehicles that have certain causal and statistical properties.

If this is true, then there is no tension between minimalist and functionalist accounts of computation, and accounts that appeal to information processing (Rescorla, 2012). In the functionalist paradigm, for example, computational systems are functionally organized systems that process information without manipulating representations.

The compatibility of computationalism with disjunctivism and ecology is again on display. Ecologists do not deny that the brain needs to causally and statistically attune to the structure of the world in order for perception to be possible. By Gibson's own admission, perception involves information pick up. By using a non-semantic understanding of information, we can better understand Gibson's claim.

Similarly, disjunctivists can admit an informational and non-semantic common factor in perception, illusion, and hallucination. So long as such common factor is not sufficient to specify perceptual experience in the three cases – for example, it is not sufficient to specify the contents of the different experiences – it also does not constitute a problem for disjunctivists.

5 Conclusion

This chapter looked at three ways of individuating computation (semantic, minimalist, and functionalist), and showed how these different notions play out in perceptual theory. Although ecological and disjunctivist understandings of perception can be thought to be in tension with computational accounts, the chapter shows that, for some plausible ways of individuating computation, the tension is only apparent. Once we move past a representational gloss on computation, we open the door for a fairly non-committal reading of computational models of perception.

Acknowledgments

Thanks to Matteo Colombo and Mark Sprevak for comments on two drafts of this chapter.

Notes

1 To further complicate things, each of the levels can be gradually unpacked at different levels of specificity. So each level contains its nested sub-levels, but we won't focus too much on this complication.
2 There is a healthy literature on whether maps are, at base, linguistic representations (Fodor and Pylyshyn, 1988; see Rescorla, 2009a; 2009b). This literature focuses, in particular, on whether maps display genuine predication – one of the hallmarks of linguistic symbols. Plausibly, maps have some type of syntactic parts. The markers in a map can single out particulars in different ways. It is not obvious, however, that the markers function as genuine subjects and predicates in a way that would make maps akin to linguistic representations.
3 It is important not to confuse an algorithm as a procedure with the algorithmic level in Marr's analysis.
4 Strictly speaking, systematicity is the fact that the ability to have certain thoughts is *intrinsically* related to the ability to have certain others. Since it is not clear what "intrinsically" means in this context, we can work with a more generic definition.
5 Evidence from neuroscience suggests that in fact there are no specialized neurons that only pick up on colors or shapes. Neurons in sensory areas of the brain respond more or less to every input to which they are exposed. We leave this difficulty aside for present purposes.
6 Mathematically, anything that can be computed by a classical computer can also be computed by a connectionist network and vice versa. However, task demands, such as time efficiency and size of computational resources may favor modeling in one paradigm rather than the other. Classicism has encountered substantial difficulties in modeling and reproducing perceptual capacities.
7 See also Wilson (2004, ch. 7), and Haugeland (1998, pp. 231–237), for attempts to formulate non-standard accounts of computation.

References

Aizawa, K. (2014) 'Tough Time to Be Talking Systematicity', in Calvo, P. and Symons, J. (eds.) *The Architecture of Cognition: Rethinking Fodor and Pylyshyn's Systematicity Challenge*. Cambridge, MA: MIT Press, pp. 371–396.
Burge, T. (2008) 'Disjunctivism and Perceptual Psychology', *Philosophical Topics*, 33 (1), pp. 1–78.
Burge, T. (2010) *Origins of Objectivity*. Oxford: Oxford University Press.
Chalmers, D.J. (2011) 'A Computational Foundation for the Study of Cognition', *Journal of Cognitive Science*, 12 (4), pp. 323–357.

Clark, A. (2000) *Mindware: An Introduction to the Philosophy of Cognitive Science*. New York, NY: Oxford University Press.

Cummins, R. (1983) *The Nature of Psychological Explanation*. Cambridge, MA: MIT Press.

Dretske, F. (1981) *Knowledge and the Flow of Information*. Cambridge, MA: MIT Press.

Dretske, F. (1991) *Explaining Behavior: Reasons in a World of Causes*. Cambridge, MA: MIT Press.

Fodor, J.A. (1968) 'The Appeal to Tacit Knowledge in Psychological Explanation', *Journal of Philosophy*, 65 (20), pp. 627–640.

Fodor, J.A. (1975) *The Language of Thought*. Cambridge, MA: Harvard University Press.

Fodor, J.A. (1987a) *Psychosemantics*. Cambridge, MA: MIT Press.

Fodor, J.A. (1987b) 'Why Paramecia Don't Have Mental Representations', *Midwest Studies in Philosophy*, 10 (1), pp. 3–23.

Fodor, J.A. (1988) 'A Reply to Churchland's "Perceptual Plasticity and Theoretical Neutrality"', *Philosophy of Science*, 55 (2), pp. 188–198.

Fodor, J.A. and Pylyshyn, Z.W. (1981) 'How Direct Is Visual Perception? Some Reflections on Gibson's "Ecological Approach"', *Cognition: International Journal of Cognitive Science*, 9 (2), pp. 139–196.

Fodor, J.A. and Pylyshyn, Z.W. (1988) 'Connectionism and Cognitive Architecture: A Critical Analysis', *Cognition*, 28 (1), pp. 3–71.

Gibson, J. (1979) *The Ecological Approach to Visual Perception*. Boston, MA: Houghton Mifflin.

Gomila, A., Travieso, D., and Lobo, L. (2014) 'From Systematicity to Interactive Regularities: Grounding Cognition at the Sensorimotor Level', in Calvo, P. and Symons, J. (eds.) *The Architecture of Cognition: Rethinking Fodor and Pylyshyn's Systematicity Challenge*. Cambridge, MA: MIT Press, pp. 371–396.

Gorman, R.P. and Sejnowski, T.J. (1988) 'Analysis of Hidden Units in a Layered Network Trained to Classify Sonar Targets', *Neural Networks*, 1 (1), pp. 75–89.

Griffiths, T.L. et al. (2012) 'How the Bayesians Got Their Beliefs (and What Those Beliefs Actually Are): Comment on Bowers and Davis (2012)', *Psychological Bulletin*, 138 (3), pp. 415–422.

Haugeland, J. (1998) *Having Thought: Essays in the Metaphysics Of Mind*. Cambridge, MA: Harvard University Press.

Hinton, G.E. (2007) 'Learning Multiple Players of Representation', *Trends in Cognitive Science*, 11 (10), pp. 428–434.

Hubel, D.H. and Wiesel, T.N. (1962) 'Receptive Elds, Binocular Interaction and Functional Architecture in the Cat's Visual Cortex', *The Journal of Physiology*, 160 (1), pp. 106–154.

Kanizsa, G. (1985) 'Seeing and Thinking', *Acta Psychologica*, 59 (1), pp. 23–33.

Malsburg, C. (1995) 'Binding in Models of Perception and Brain Function', *Current Opinion in Neurobiology*, 5 (4), pp. 520–526.

Marr, D. (1982) *Vision: A Computational Investigation into the Human Representation and Processing of Visual Information*. New York, NY: Henry Holt and Co.

Martin, M. (2003) 'Sensible Appearances', in Baldwin, T. (ed.) *Cambridge History of 20th Century Philosophy*. Cambridge, UK: Cambridge University Press.

Neisser, U. (1967) *Cognitive Psychology*. Englewood Cliffs, NJ: Prentice Hall.

O'Callaghan, C. (forthcoming) 'Intermodal Binding Awareness', in *Sensory Integration and the Unity of Consciousness*. Cambridge, MA: MIT Press. Available at: http://ocallaghan.rice.edu//research/papers/ocallaghan-201x-Binding.pdf.

Palmer, S.E. (1999) *Vision Science: Photons to Phenomenology*, vol. 1. Cambridge, MA: MIT Press.

Piccinini, G. (2007) 'Computing Mechanisms', *Philosophy of Science*, 74 (4), pp. 501–526.

Piccinini, G. (2008a) 'Computation without Representation', *Philosophical Studies*, 137 (2), pp. 205–241.

Piccinini, G. (2011) 'Computationalism', in Margolis, E., Samuels, R., and Stich, S.P. (eds.) *Oxford Handbook of Philosophy and Cognitive Science*. Oxford: Oxford University Press, pp. 222–249.

Piccinini, G. (2015) *Physical Computation: A Mechanistic Account*. Oxford: Oxford University Press.

Piccinini, G. and Scarantino, A. (2011) 'Information Processing, Computation, and Cognition', *Journal of Biological Physics*, 37 (1), pp. 1–38.

Poggio, T. and Edelman, S. (1990) 'A Network That Learns to Recognize 3d Objects', *Nature*, 343 (6255), pp. 263–266.

Putnam, H. (1988) *Representation and Reality*, vol. 454. Cambridge, UK: Cambridge University Press.

Pylyshyn, Z. (1984) *Computation and Cognition*. Cambridge, UK: Cambridge University Press.

Rahnev, D. and Denison, R. (2016) *Suboptimality in Perception*. Available at: https://doi.org/10.1101/060194.

Ramsey, W.M. (1997) 'Do Connectionist Representations Earn Their Explanatory Keep?', *Mind and Language*, 12 (1), pp. 34–66.

Ramsey, W.M. (2007) *Representation Reconsidered*. Cambridge, UK: Cambridge University Press.

Rescorla, M. (2009a) 'Cognitive Maps and the Language of Thought', *The British Journal for the Philosophy of Science*, 60 (2), pp. 377–407.

Rescorla, M. (2009b) 'Predication and Cartographic Representation', *Synthese*, 169 (1), pp. 175–200.

Rescorla, M. (2012) 'How to Integrate Representation into Computational Modeling, and Why We Should', *Journal of Cognitive Science*, 13 (1), pp. 1–38.

Rock, I. (1983) *The Logic of Perception*. Cambridge, MA: MIT Press.

Rock, I. (1997) *Indirect Perception*. Cambridge, MA: MIT Press.

Sejnowski, T.J. and Rosenberg, C.R. (1987) 'Parallel Networks That Learn to Pronounce English Text', *Complex Systems*, 1 (1), pp. 145–168.

Shannon, C.E. (1948) 'A Mathematical Theory of Communication', *The Bell System Technical Journal*, 27, pp. 379–423.

Stich, S.P. (1983) *From Folk Psychology to Cognitive Science: The Case against Belief*. Cambridge, MA: MIT Press.

Travieso, D., Gomila, A., and Lobo, L. (2014) 'From Systematicity to Interactive Regularities: Grounding Cognition at the Sensorimotor Level', in Calvo, P. and Symons, J. (eds.) *The Architecture of Cognition: Rethinking Fodor and Pylyshyn's Systematicity Challenge*. Cambridge, MA: MIT Press, pp. 371–396.

Travis, C. (2004) 'The Silence of the Senses', *Mind*, 113 (449), pp. 57–94.

Treisman, A. (1996) 'The Binding Problem', *Current Opinion in Neurobiology*, 6 (2), pp. 171–178.

Treisman, A. and Schmidt, H. (1982) 'Illusory Conjunctions in the Perception of Objects', *Cognitive Psychology*, 14 (1), pp. 107–141.

Turing, A.M. (1950) 'Computing Machinery and Intelligence', *Mind*, 49, pp. 433–460.

Ullman, S. (1980) *Against Direct Perception*. Cambridge, UK: Cambridge University Press.

Wilson, R.A. (2004) *Boundaries of the Mind: The Individual in the Fragile Sciences-Cognition*. Cambridge, UK: Cambridge University Press.

31

MOTOR COMPUTATION

Michael Rescorla

Enjoying a bravura performance by a professional athlete or virtuoso musician, we marvel at the performer's skilled bodily motion. We are less apt to appreciate that relatively humdrum activities – such as walking, talking, riding a bicycle, tying shoelaces, typing, using silverware, or pouring milk into a cup without spilling – already require impressive control over one's motor organs. The ease with which we execute these activities belies their difficulty, as evidenced by our current inability to build robots that match human performance. During the course of each day, a typical adult achieves myriad goals through an extraordinary range of dexterous bodily motions. How do humans manage to achieve their goals by exerting such refined control over their motor organs?

Sensorimotor psychology, the scientific study of motor control, emerged from Hermann von Helmholtz's (1867) pioneering investigations and assumed its modern form in the work of Nikolai Bernstein (1923; 1930; 1967). Building on insights of Helmholtz and Bernstein, contemporary sensorimotor psychologists have convincingly established that human motor control involves sophisticated unconscious computations that mediate between cognition and bodily motion. The present entry will discuss basic aspects of motor computation, along with some implications for philosophy of mind.

From intentions to motor commands

Suppose I form an intention to do something – say, to push an elevator button with my right index finger. My motor system must transform the intention into a sequence of suitable motor commands. How does this transformation work? How does my motor system select commands that promote my goal? Bernstein first highlighted a *redundancy problem* that bedevils the transformation of intentions into motor commands. There are innumerable ways the motor system might achieve some goal. For example, there are many trajectories my finger might take to reach the elevator button and many muscle activations that would achieve a given trajectory. The motor system must choose rapidly from among these infinitely many options.

Bernstein decisively advanced research into the redundancy problem with a pivotal discovery: the movement details through which an agent completes a motor task vary considerably across trials in certain characteristic ways. In particular, performance across trials varies far less along task-relevant dimensions than task-irrelevant dimensions. For example, suppose the task is to aim a laser pistol at a target. Joint configurations in the arm can fluctuate widely even as the agent maintains a fixed aim. Scholz, Schöner, and Latash (2000) found that fluctuations in joint angle that affect how well the pistol aims at the target are much smaller than fluctuations that have no such effect. In a similar vein, Todorov and Jordan (2002) studied a task where the subject moved her hand through a sequence of five widely spaced targets arranged in a plane. Hand trajectories varied much more between the targets than near the targets, reflecting the fact that hand position between targets was task-irrelevant. The scientific literature conclusively shows that a large disparity between task-relevant variation and task-irrelevant variation occurs within a wide range of motor activities (Todorov and Jordan, 2002), such as postural control, walking, talking, skiing, writing, reaching, and bimanual coordination. Any adequate theory of motor control must explain the disparity.

Optimal feedback control

Sensorimotor psychologists have explored various theoretical frameworks for explaining motor control (Rosenbaum, 2002). The most empirically successful is *optimal feedback control* (OFC). This framework uses *optimal control theory*, a mathematical approach to decision making that has been extensively developed in engineering and statistics (Stengel, 1986). The basic idea behind OFC is that the motor system selects motor commands that are in some sense optimal (or near-optimal) with respect to one's current goal. Researchers begin with a normative model delineating how an idealized decision maker would accomplish the goal. They then investigate how well the normative model fits actual human performance.

The central construct of optimal control theory is a *cost function*, which measures the desirability of issuing a motor command under the assumption that certain environmental conditions obtain. The cost function quantifies various performance criteria. Some of the performance criteria are task-independent (e.g. minimizing expenditure of energy). Some are task-dependent and reflect the goal being pursued (e.g. that I move the tip of my index finger to a specific location; or that I walk to the other end of a room; or that I pick up a nearby ball). Optimal motor commands are those that minimize expected costs. Thus, "optimality" is relative to a cost function. An *optimal controller* selects motor commands that are optimal given the current cost function. Depending on the details, more than one motor command may be optimal.

OFC uses optimal control theory to illuminate how the motor system solves Bernstein's redundancy problem (Scott, 2004; Todorov, 2004; Todorov and Jordan, 2002). The crucial insight is that the motor system selects certain motor commands over the infinitely many alternatives because the selected commands are "better" according to well-defined performance criteria. The selected commands minimize (or nearly minimize) expected costs. OFC elaborates this insight into detailed normative models describing how the human motor system *should* choose motor commands (given certain performance criteria). These models are pressed into service as psychological descriptions of human motor computation, yielding testable predictions. In many cases, researchers have validated the predictions. A well-confirmed optimal control model of a motor task provides satisfying explanations for key aspects of human performance.

A crucial plank of OFC is the *minimal intervention principle*, articulated by Todorov (2004). When I pursue a goal, factors such as motor noise or external interference frequently perturb my bodily trajectory. It is not a good idea to correct each perturbation, because every correction expends energy. An optimal controller corrects only those perturbations that are task-relevant. Hence the minimal intervention principle, which enjoins: "make no effort to correct deviations away from average behavior unless those deviations interfere with task performance" (Todorov,

2004, p. 911).The minimal intervention principle directs the controller to tolerate perturbations so long as they do not interfere with the task.

The minimal intervention principle is a norm. It decrees how motor processing *should* operate. OFC postulates that there are numerous cases where the motor system conforms (at least approximately) to this norm. In such cases, the motor system pursues a task goal rather than enforcing a predetermined movement plan that effectuates the goal. As the task unfolds, the motor system chooses motor commands that optimally (or near-optimally) promote the goal. Perturbations from the average trajectory may occur, but the motor system only corrects perturbations that impede task completion. Motor activity optimizes relatively abstract performance criteria, rather than implementing a pre-specified sequence of bodily movements. OFC develops these ideas into mathematically detailed, empirically successful models of specific motor tasks (Haith and Krakauer, 2013;Wolpert and Landy, 2012).

By invoking the minimal intervention principle, OFC achieves several notable explanatory successes:

- OFC explains the striking disparity noted above between task-relevant and task-irrelevant variation across trials. If a controller corrects task-relevant deviations but leaves task-irrelevant deviations uncorrected, then task-irrelevant deviations accumulate so that bodily movements vary far more along task-irrelevant dimensions.
- OFC illuminates how the motor system responds to experimentally-induced perturbations of bodily motion.The minimal intervention principle dictates that the motor system should preferentially correct task-relevant perturbations, and this is indeed what happens in numerous motor tasks (Crevecoeur, Cluff, and Scott, 2014). For example, Nashed, Crevecoeur, and Scott (2012) studied subjects performing two slightly different tasks: reaching rapidly either to a small circular target or to a long horizontal bar. In random trials, an unexpected mechanical perturbation disrupted hand trajectory along the horizontal direction. In the circular target task, the motor system responded by correcting course back towards to the target. Corrective motions began as early as 70 ms after the perturbation – strong evidence that they were automatic and not generated voluntarily. In the horizontal bar task, the motor system did not correct the perturbation, because it could still accomplish the goal (reaching the horizontal bar) without any course correction.Thus, the task goal decisively influenced how the motor system responded to mechanical perturbations. Perturbations were corrected only when they affected the goal, as dictated by the minimal intervention principle.

These successes exemplify the fruitful nexus between normative evaluation and psychological explanation made possible by OFC.

OFC differs significantly from virtually all rival theories of motor control. Rival theories usually enshrine the *desired trajectory hypothesis*, which postulates a rigid division between motor planning and motor execution: the motor system first chooses a detailed movement plan, and it then tries to implement the chosen plan. From the perspective of OFC, this rigid division is non-optimal. No matter how sensible some predetermined detailed movement plan may initially seem, enforcing it will waste energy by correcting task-irrelevant deviations. According to the minimal intervention principle, the motor system should not solve Bernstein's redundancy problem in advance of executing the motor task. It should instead solve the redundancy problem *on-line*, selecting motor commands in furtherance of the task goal as the task unfolds. The desired trajectory hypothesis does not explain why motor processing preferentially corrects task-relevant perturbations, nor does it explain why performance varies more along task-irrelevant dimensions than task-relevant dimensions. Thus, the desired trajectory hypothesis looks unpromising. Nevertheless, it has recently attracted high-profile advocates in the scientific (Friston, 2011) and philosophical (Clark, 2015; Hohwy, 2014) communities. These authors do not say how they hope to explain the asymmetry between task-relevant and task-irrelevant variation – a fundamental aspect of motor control that looks incompatible with their favored approach and that OFC easily explains.

Estimating environmental state

Environmental conditions are highly relevant to task performance. If my goal is to walk across the room and pick up a ball, then relevant factors include the ball's location, its size, its weight, the presence of any obstacles, my own current bodily configuration, and so on. To choose appropriate motor commands, the motor system takes these and other factors into account. However, motor processing cannot directly access environmental conditions. It can access the environment only by way of sensory stimulations, including stimulations of the retina, the inner ear, muscle spindles, and so on. The motor system must use sensory stimulations to *estimate* environmental state.

Here we encounter a striking commonality between motor control and perception. I can consciously perceive certain properties of my environment, such as the shapes, colors, sizes, and locations of nearby objects. But perceptual processing cannot directly access these environmental properties. The perceptual system must estimate environmental conditions based upon sensory stimulations. Helmholtz (1867) postulated that it does so through an *unconscious inference*. In response to proximal sensory input, the perceptual system forms a "best hypothesis" regarding which environmental conditions caused that proximal input. Contemporary sensorimotor psychologists adapt Helmholtz's approach to explain how motor processing estimates environmental conditions. Sensorimotor psychology postulates that the motor system executes an unconscious inference from sensory stimulations to estimates of environmental state. The motor system chooses "best hypotheses" regarding the environmental causes of sensory stimulations. It consults the chosen hypotheses when selecting motor commands that promote the current task goal.

Recently, perceptual and sensorimotor psychologists have elucidated unconscious inference in terms of *Bayesian decision theory*, which is a mathematical framework for modeling reasoning and decision making under uncertainty. Bayesian agents handle uncertainty by assigning *subjective probabilities* to hypotheses. The probabilities are "subjective" because they reflect the agent's own psychological degree of confidence rather than objective probabilities out in the world. A Bayesian agent begins with initial subjective probabilities (called *priors*) and then revises those initial probabilities in light of new evidence. Precise Bayesian norms dictate how the agent should revise her probabilities in light of new evidence.[1] As applied within sensorimotor psychology, the basic idea is that the motor system assigns probabilities to hypotheses regarding environmental conditions that are relevant to the current task. Ongoing sensory stimulation causes constant revision of these probabilities, in rough conformity to Bayesian norms. Hence, the motor system estimates environmental conditions through an unconscious Bayesian inference. When transforming intentions into motor commands, motor processing selects commands that minimize expected cost – i.e. the cost one expects to incur, given current probabilities. Bayesian modeling of motor estimation has proved extremely successful and is an important component of the overall OFC framework (Shadmehr and Mussa-Ivaldi, 2012; Wolpert, 2007).

A pervasive challenge facing sensorimotor estimation is *sensory delay*. Motor control requires rapid on-line selection of motor commands, but sensory signals take a while to reach the brain. To overcome sensory delay, the motor system anticipates how its own commands are likely to impact environment state (Wolpert and Flanagan, 2009). For each motor command sent to the musculature, the brain produces an *efference copy*. Using efference copy, the motor system predicts likely consequences of its own commands (Miall and Wolpert, 1996). Basically, the motor system begins with its current estimate of environmental state and then extrapolates forward using efference copy. The result: a new environmental state estimate that is correctable by future sensory signals but that can guide motor control until such signals arrive.

Challenges for optimal feedback control

OFC has been successfully applied to various relatively simple motor tasks, such as reaching, pointing, aiming, and so on. It has also been successfully applied to at least one fairly complex task involving the whole body (Stevenson et al., 2009): balancing on a snowboard. An important agenda item for sensorimotor psychology is to apply OFC to more complex real-world tasks, such as riding a bicycle or playing a musical instrument.

A significant hurdle here is that Bayesian inference and expected cost minimization are, in general, computationally intractable. Aside from a few simple cases, a physical system with limited computational resources cannot update probabilities in precise conformity to Bayesian norms, nor can it minimize expected cost with complete precision. A version of this problem arises for all fields that employ Bayesian decision theory, including engineering, statistics, and artificial intelligence. The standard solution is to investigate algorithms through which a physical system can efficiently *approximate* Bayesian inference and expected cost minimization. Sensorimotor psychologists have explored computationally tractable approximation schemes tailored to the human motor system, with excellent results (e.g. Li, Todorov, and Pan, 2004; Todorov, 2009). Future research will presumably deploy these and perhaps other as-yet-undiscovered approximation schemes so as to model a range of motor tasks.

Another important agenda item is to illuminate the *neurophysiological processes* through which the motor system implements (or approximately implements) computations postulated by OFC models. How exactly does the brain encode an assignment of subjective probabilities to hypotheses? How does it encode a cost function? Through what neural processing does it update subjective probabilities and select optimal (or near-optimal) motor commands? We do not know the answers to these questions, although recent research offers some intriguing suggestions (e.g. Denève, Duhamel, and Pouget, 2007; DeWolf and Eliasmith, 2011).

With so many questions left unanswered, OFC at present hardly constitutes a complete theory of human motor computation. Even in its current incomplete state, OFC offers powerful explanations for a range of motor phenomena.

Motor control as unconscious inference and decision making

I favor a broadly *scientific realist* perspective: when a scientific theory is explanatorily successful, this gives us a *prima facie* reason to accept that the theory is at least approximately true. I apply the scientific realist perspective to sensorimotor psychology: OFC models are explanatorily successful, far more so than rival theories, so we have strong *prima facie* reason to regard them as at least approximately true. I do not say that we should regard a successful OFC model as true in every detail. For example, current models often use priors that reflect a highly simplified dynamics for the human body. They do this for reasons of analytical tractability, not because there is any independent reason to think that the motor system employs these precise priors. A more accurate model would presumably use more psychologically realistic priors. While we should not accept that current OFC models are precisely true in every detail, we should accept in broad strokes the picture of motor computation that they embody. More specifically:

- The motor system assigns subjective probabilities to hypotheses regarding environmental conditions. It updates those probability assignments in response to sensory stimulations and efference copy. Transitions between probability assignments conform, at least approximately, to Bayesian norms.
- When pursuing a motor task, the motor system encodes a cost function that reflects the goal being pursued. As the task unfolds, the motor system selects motor commands that are near-optimal in light of the cost function and current subjective probabilities.

I defend my realist perspective at length in (Rescorla, 2016). For an opposing *instrumentalist* viewpoint on Bayesian modeling, see (Colombo and Seriès, 2012). For helpful comparison of the realist and instrumentalist viewpoints, see (Sprevak, 2016).

Assuming a realist interpretation of OFC modeling, motor control results from subpersonal mental processes similar in key respects to high-level conscious inference and decision making. The processes fall under (and approximately conform to) the same Bayesian norms that govern inference and decision making by agents. However, the processes are executed not by the person herself but rather by her subsystems. They are *subpersonal*. Except in very unusual cases, the *person* does not consciously choose a detailed movement plan. She is not aware of specific motor commands relayed to her musculature. She does not consciously access the environmental state estimates that inform selection of motor commands. She simply sets a goal (e.g. *pick up that nearby ball*) and lets her motor system do the rest.

One important consequence of the realist viewpoint is that volitional bodily motion results from highly sophisticated computations executed by the motor system. The computations are subpersonal and inaccessible to consciousness, but they approximately implement personal-level rational norms that have been extensively studied within engineering, statistics, robotics, and artificial intelligence. Unconscious Bayesian inference and decision making mediate the transition from intentions to motor commands.

Motor learning

Improvements in motor performance are crucial to the refined control that we exert over our bodies. When I master a new motor skill, such as playing the clarinet or hitting a ball with a tennis racket, many changes occur in my motor processing. Even everyday activities such as walking or talking require extensive practice for their mastery. Compensatory adjustments in motor control are also needed when my body changes over the short term (e.g. through fatigue or injury) or the long term (e.g. through development or aging) and when the external environment changes (e.g. walking on pavement versus walking through mud). Any change in motor control that improves task performance is called *motor learning*. This rubric covers the acquisition of new motor skills and also improved performance in previously learned activities (Haith and Krakauer, 2013).

Scientific research mainly studies a specific type of motor learning called *adaptation*. During adaptation, the motor system corrects a disruption of some previously mastered activity. In a seminal experiment, Helmholtz instructed subjects to reach to a target, which they did quite easily. He then equipped the subjects with prism lenses that shifted the visual field to the left or right. Subjects initially missed the target, but they quickly adapted and learned to reach the target. Upon removal of the prism lenses, subjects once again failed at the reaching task, although they quickly re-adapted. Helmholtz's prism experiment vividly illustrates the speed and efficiency with which the motor system responds to ever-changing conditions (in this case, a perturbation of visual input). It is well-established that adaptation mainly involves subpersonal processes rather than conscious correction by the subject erself. Although subjects sometimes realize that conditions have changed and try to compensate accordingly, adaptation by the motor system proceeds in relative independence from high-level conscious thought (Mazzoni and Krakauer, 2006; Shadmehr and Mussa-Ivaldi, 2012, pp. 187–192).

Sensorimotor psychologists have extensively investigated the subpersonal mental activity that underlies adaptation. A key finding is that adaptation, like motor control itself, involves sophisticated computations that draw upon available sensory information. When sensory prediction error occurs (e.g. my hand does not reach the visual target as expected), the motor system cannot directly pinpoint what caused the error. Instead, it must estimate what caused the error. Bayesian decision theory provides models that dictate how to solve this estimation problem (Shadmehr and Mussa-Ivaldi, 2012, pp. 192–212). Researchers have applied Bayesian modeling to several adaptation paradigms, sometimes with striking explanatory success.

To illustrate, suppose we perturb hand movements during a reaching task by applying an external force field to the hand. Motor performance quickly adapts, so that the subject reaches the target despite the perturbing force field. Surprisingly, though, force field adaptation does not merely change the mapping from sensory estimates to motor commands. It also changes subpersonal sensory estimates themselves (Haith et al., 2009). Repeated exposure to an external force field on the right hand causes a shift in visual and proprioceptive estimates of the hand's position. Due to this shift, estimates of hand position become markedly less accurate. Thus, force field adaptation generates a *sensorimotor illusion*. The illusion is puzzling, because visual and proprioceptive input agree even in the presence of the external force field. Why should visual and proprioceptive estimation change when no discrepancy between them occurs?

A plausible answer is that the sensorimotor illusion reflects a "credit assignment" problem. Sensory prediction error might arise from perturbed motor execution (e.g. an external force field), perturbed sensory input (e.g. prism lenses), or some combination thereof. The Bayesian strategy is to divide the credit for prediction error between motor execution and sensory estimation, taking into account the reliability of all relevant information sources (Haith et al., 2009). A Bayesian estimator will attribute the prediction error partly to sensory miscalibration, even though the error actually arises entirely from an external force field. Thus, the sensorimotor illusion does not manifest some underlying defect in sensorimotor processing. Rather, it reflects the motor system's ongoing effort to estimate environmental conditions based upon ambiguous sensory cues.

This example illustrates two important points: first, motor learning involves sophisticated subpersonal computations that share many notable properties with high-level reasoning; second, Bayesian modeling illuminates these computations by isolating norms to which they (approximately) conform.

Mental representation as explanatorily central

Sensorimotor psychology has significant implications for longstanding debates about the nature of the mind.

Philosophers traditionally regard the mind as a *representational organ*. On the traditional picture, mental states represent the world, and representational properties of mental states are vital for understanding how the mind works. Contemporary philosophers often develop this picture by linking representation to *veridicality-conditions* – conditions for veridical representation of the world. To illustrate:

- Beliefs are the sorts of things that can be true or false. My belief *that Emmanuel Macron is French* is true if Emmanuel Macron is French, false if he is not.

- Perceptual states are the sorts of things that can be accurate or inaccurate. My perceptual experience *as of a red sphere before me* is accurate only if a red sphere is before me.
- Intentions are the sorts of things that can be fulfilled or thwarted. My desire *to eat chocolate* is fulfilled only if I eat chocolate.

Beliefs have truth-conditions, perceptual states have accuracy-conditions, and intentions have fulfillment-conditions. Truth, accuracy, and fulfillment are species of veridicality. It is widely agreed that veridicality-conditions are vital for understanding belief, perception, intention, and many other mental states (Burge, 2010, p. 9; Fodor, 1987, pp. 10–11).

The traditional emphasis upon mental representation encounters periodic resistance among philosophers and psychologists. Some authors castigate mental representation as a scientifically unrespectable notion that should be expunged from serious theorizing (e.g. Chemero, 2009; Quine, 1960; Skinner, 1938; van Gelder, 1992). In response, *representationalists* maintain that representational discourse is both legitimate and scientifically indispensable. Fodor (1975; 1987) develops the representationalist viewpoint. He argues that current cognitive science offers impressive representational explanations whose benefits are not replicable within a non-representational framework. Burge (2010) argues similarly, focusing especially upon the role that mental representation plays within perceptual psychology.

Sensorimotor psychology provides strong support for representationalism. The science seeks to explain how motor activity transforms intentions into motor commands that promote fulfillment of those intentions. An intention's fulfillment-condition plays a key role in explaining the motor commands that it triggers. In particular, the fulfillment-condition helps explain why a particular cost function is operative in a given motor task. For example, if I intend to move my index finger to some target, then the cost function assigns lower cost to outcomes where my finger reaches the target. If I intend to move my hand through five widely spaced targets, then the cost function assigns lower cost to outcomes where my hand moves through those targets. More generally, the intention operative in a motor task helps determine the cost function that the motor system employs when computing minimal (or near-minimal) expected costs. This explanatory strategy presupposes personal-level intentions with fulfillment-conditions. We cite the condition under which an intention is fulfilled (e.g. that my finger reaches the target) to explain which cost function the motor system deploys.

The science also invokes veridicality-conditions when characterizing subpersonal computations. According to current Bayesian models, the motor system estimates environmental conditions by updating subjective probabilities $p(h)$ assigned to hypotheses h. Each hypothesis h represents the environment as being a certain way. For example, h might represent the size of an object, or it might represent the current configuration of one's body. h is veridical just in case the environment is as h represents it. The cost function $c(h, u)$ measures the desirability of issuing motor command u in situations where h is veridical. Detailed explanatory generalizations describe (a) how sensory input and efference copy influence reallocation of subjective probabilities over hypotheses; (b) how subjective probabilities along with the cost function inform selection of motor commands. Generalizations of types (a) and (b) cite veridicality-conditions. To illustrate, suppose the cost function rewards placing my index finger at a target. Then a different motor command will result when the Bayesian estimator treats it as likely that my finger is left of target than when the Bayesian estimator treats it as likely that my finger is right of target. A type (b) generalization rigorously captures this pattern by citing veridicality-conditions of hypotheses, e.g. by adducing whether hypothesis h represents my finger as left or right of target. In this manner, our current best sensorimotor psychology assigns a central explanatory role to representational aspects of subpersonal motor computation.

Over the past century, many scientists have tried to explain motor control in non-representational terms (e.g. Chemero, 2009; Kelso, Dumas, and Tognoli, 2013). These attempts have proved far less explanatorily successful than representational theories. In particular, anti-representationalists have not successfully explained Bernstein's fundamental observation that motor performance displays more variability along task-irrelevant dimensions than task-relevant dimensions. Indeed, it is unclear whether one can so much as state this explanandum in non-representational terms, since the task-relevant/task-irrelevant distinction presupposes a *goal* represented and pursued by the subject.

Anti-representationalists often insist that, even when a scientific explanation invokes mental representation, we can recast the explanation in non-representational terms while replicating any benefits that it offers. They claim that we can purge representational locutions from cognitive science without explanatory loss (e.g. Field, 2001; Stich, 1983).

I think that we should regard such claims quite warily. We cannot usually purge a science of its central notions while preserving its explanatory achievements. Physicists cannot renounce forces while offering anything resembling the explanations offered by Newtonian physics. Biologists cannot renounce genes while preserving anything resembling modern genetics. Similarly, anti-representationalists have given us little reason to suspect that we can purge cognitive science of representational mental states while preserving its explanatory achievements. For further defense of a representationalist perspective on sensorimotor psychology, see (Rescorla, 2016). For a kindred representationalist analysis of perceptual psychology, see (Rescorla, 2015).[2]

Future directions

We are only beginning to understand motor control in humans and other animals. To conclude, I highlight a few areas where further scientific or philosophical inquiry is needed. In several cases, these areas are under active investigation.

Computational architecture

The motor system and the perceptual system both estimate environmental state. How does sensorimotor estimation relate to perceptual estimation? This question has generated considerable controversy (e.g. Briscoe, 2008; Milner and Goodale, 1995; Schenk, Franz, and Bruno, 2011). A less widely discussed question concerns the extent to which high-level cognition influences motor control. Intentions crucially influence motor processing by influencing the cost function. Beliefs, desires, and other mental states influence the cost function *by way of* influencing intentions. To what extent can higher-level mental states influence motor activity without mediation by intentions? For example, to what extent can conscious beliefs influence subpersonal estimation by the motor system? Such questions relate to longstanding debates about the *modularity* of perception sparked by Fodor's (1983) famous discussion.

Format and content

I have argued that motor control features subpersonal representational mental states: probability assignments to hypotheses that have veridicality-conditions. We would like to understand the format and content of the hypotheses. Are they propositional? Conceptual? Do they involve something like imagistic or map-like representation? How do they bear upon standard philosophical theories of representational content, such as Fregean thoughts or Russellian propositions? Further investigation would illuminate the underpinnings of sensorimotor psychology. It would also enhance philosophical discussion of representational content with an expanded diet of scientifically important examples.

Subpersonal subjective probability

What is it to assign a subjective probability to a hypothesis? This question is basic for Bayesian decision theory. Philosophers have made several attempts to answer the question in a non-trivial way, without much visible success (Erikkson and Hájek, 2007). Existing proposals tend to emphasize sophisticated personal-level activities, such as gambling or linguistic communication. The motor system does not engage in such activities. Thus, it seems doubtful that existing proposals shed much light on subjective probability as it figures in motor computation. A major philosophical task is to elucidate the subjective probabilities employed by the motor system and to clarify how exactly they resemble the personal-level subjective probabilities emphasized by traditional philosophical inquiry. Can we provide an analysis of subjective probability that applies equally well to the personal and subpersonal levels?

Intention

The nature of intention is a central topic for philosophy of mind and philosophy of action. Discussion usually focuses upon the role that intention plays within practical reasoning. The basic strategy is to explore how intention interfaces with belief, desire, planning, instrumental reasoning, and other high-level facets of human psychology. A complementary strategy, pursued recently by Pacherie (2000; 2006), is to explore how intention interfaces with motor control. Fulfilling an environment-directed intention requires a capacity to control one's motor organs in appropriate ways. Accordingly, one might hope to illuminate environment-directed intentions by studying how they engage subpersonal motor processing. A potential benefit of this complementary strategy is that sensorimotor psychology is far better developed than the science of high-level propositional attitudes, so that it arguably provides a sounder basis for philosophical inquiry.

These are just a few research avenues suggested by sensorimotor psychology. There are many additional avenues that I have not addressed. Given the central role that motor control plays within our mental lives, the foundations and ramifications of sensorimotor psychology merit thorough scrutiny by the philosophical community.

Acknowledgments

I am grateful to Matteo Colombo and Mark Sprevak for comments that improved this entry.

Notes

1 For general discussion of Bayesian modeling in cognitive science, see Colombo and Hartmann (2017).
2 I have argued that explanations offered by sensorimotor psychology cite representational properties of mental states. However, some representational properties are far more relevant than others to the explanation of bodily motion. Context-dependent representational properties are usually much less relevant

than context-invariant representational properties. For example, suppose I perceive a marble on the floor and form an intention to grab *that* marble. My intention is fulfilled only if I grab that particular marble. My intention's fulfillment-condition depends upon the specific marble represented by the intention. But the specific marble does not seem explanatorily relevant to explaining which motor commands my motor system issues. The marble could have been replaced by a qualitatively indistinguishable duplicate, and this change does not seem relevant to explaining my bodily motion. Likewise, the marble's specific spatio-temporal location does not seem explanatorily relevant. What seems relevant is rather the marble's *location relative to me*, e.g. its location as described by some egocentric coordinate system. I might have represented a different spatio-temporal location but the same location relative to me (if I myself had had a different location), and this change does not seem relevant to explaining my bodily motion. These issues merit extensive further discussion. For present purposes, I must set them aside.

References

Bernstein, N. (1923) 'Studies on the Biomechanics of Hitting Using Optical Recording', *Annals of the Central Institute of Labor*, 1, pp. 19–79.

Bernstein, N. (1930) 'A New Method of Mirror Cyclographie and Its Application Towards the Study of Labor Movements during Work on a Workbench', *Hygiene, Safety and Pathology of Labor*, 56, pp. 3–11.

Bernstein, N. (1967) *The Coordination and Regulation of Movements*. Oxford: Pergamon.

Briscoe, R. (2008) 'Another Look at the Two Visual Systems Hypothesis: The Argument from Illusion Studies', *Journal of Consciousness Studies*, 8, pp. 3–62.

Burge, T. (2010) *Origins of Objectivity*. Oxford: Oxford University Press.

Chemero, A. (2009) *Radical Embodied Cognitive Science*. Cambridge, MA: MIT Press.

Clark, A. (2015) *Surfing Uncertainty*. Oxford: Oxford University Press.

Colombo, M. and Hartmann, S. (2017) 'Bayesian Cognitive Science: Unification and Explanation', *The British Journal for the Philosophy of Science*, 68, pp. 451–484.

Colombo, M. and Seriès, P. (2012) 'Bayes in the Brain: On Bayesian Modeling in Neuroscience', *British Journal for the Philosophy of Science*, 63, pp. 697–723.

Crevecoeur, F., Cluff, T., and Scott, S. (2014) 'Computational Approaches for Goal-Directed Movement Planning and Execution', in Gazzaniga, M. and Mangun, G. (eds.) *The Cognitive Neurosciences*. Cambridge, MA: MIT Press.

Denève, S., Duhamel, J.R., and Pouget, A. (2007) 'Optimal Sensorimotor Integration in Recurrent Cortical Networks: A Neural Implementation of Kalman Filters', *The Journal of Neuroscience*, 27, pp. 5744–5756.

DeWolf, T. and Eliasmith, C. (2011) 'The Neural Optimal Control Hierarchy for Motor Control', *The Journal of Neural Engineering*, 8 (6), 065009.

Erikkson, L. and Hájek, A. (2007) 'What Are Degrees of Belief?', *Studia Logica*, 86, pp. 183–213.

Field, H. (2001) *Truth and the Absence of Fact*. Oxford: Oxford University Press.

Fodor, J. (1975) *The Language of Thought*. New York, NY: Thomas Y. Crowell.

Fodor, J. (1983) *The Modularity of Mind*. Cambridge, MA: MIT Press.

Fodor, J. (1987) *Psychosemantics*. Cambridge, MA: MIT Press.

Friston, K. (2011) 'What Is Optimal about Motor Control?', *Neuron*, 72, pp. 488–498.

Haith, A. et al. (2009) 'Unifying the Sensory and Motor Components of Sensorimotor Adaptation', in Koller, D. et al. (eds.) *Advances in Neural Information Processing Systems 21*, New York, NY: Curran Associates, pp. 593–600.

Haith, A. and Krakauer, J. (2013) 'Theoretical Models of Motor Control and Motor Learning', in Richardson, M., Riley, M., and Shockley, K. (eds.) *Progress in Motor Control VII: Neural Computational and Dynamic Approaches*. New York, NY: Springer, pp. 7–28.

Hohwy, J. (2014) *The Predictive Mind*. Oxford: Oxford University Press.

Kelso, J., Dumas, G., and Tognoli, E. (2013) 'Outline of a General Theory of Behavior and Brain Coordination', *Neural Networks*, 37, pp. 120–131.

Li, W., Todorov, E., and Pan, X. (2004) 'Hierarchical Optimal Control of Redundant Biomechanical Systems', *Proceedings of the 26th Annual International Conference of the IEEE Engineering in Medicine and Biology Society*. San Francisco, September 1–5. Piscataway, NJ: IEEE.

Mazzoni, P. and Krakauer, J. (2006) 'An Implicit Plan Overrides an Explicit Strategy during Visuomotor Adaptation', *Journal of Neuroscience*, 26, pp. 3642–3645.

Miall, R.C. and Wolpert, D. (1996) 'Forward Models for Physiological Motor Control', *Neural Networks*, 9, pp. 1265–1279.

Milner, A. and Goodale, M. (1995) *The Visual Brain in Action*. Oxford: Oxford University Press.

Nashed, J., Crevecoeur, F., and Scott, S. (2012) 'Influence of the Behavioral Goal and Environmental Obstacles on Rapid Feedback Responses', *Journal of Neurophysiology*, 108, pp. 999–1009.

Pacherie, E. (2000) 'The Content of Intentions', *Mind and Language*, 15, pp. 400–432.

Pacherie, E. (2006) 'Towards a Dynamic Theory of Intentions', in Pockett, S., Banks, W., and Gallagher, S. (eds.) *Does Consciousness Cause Behavior? An Investigation of the Nature of Volition*. Cambridge, MA: MIT Press, pp. 145–167.

Quine, W. V. (1960) *Word and Object*. Cambridge, MA: MIT Press.

Rescorla, M. (2015) 'Bayesian Perceptual Psychology', in Matthen, M. (ed.) *The Oxford Handbook of the Philosophy of Perception*. Oxford: Oxford University Press.

Rescorla, M. (2016) 'Bayesian Sensorimotor Psychology', *Mind and Language*, 31, pp. 3–36.

Rosenbaum, D. (2002) 'Motor Control', in Pashler, H. and Yantis, S. (eds.) *Stevens' Handbook of Experimental Psychology*, vol. 1, 3rd ed. New York, NY: Wiley, pp. 315–340.

Schenk, T., Franz, V., and Bruno, N. (2011) 'Vision-for-Perception and Vision-for-Action: Which Model Is Compatible with the Available Psychophysical and Neuropsychological Data?', *Vision Research*, 51, pp. 812–818.

Scholz, J., Schöner, G., and Latash, M. (2000) 'Identifying the Control Structure of Multijoint Coordination during Pistol Shooting', *Experimental Brain Research*, 135, pp. 382–404.

Scott, S. (2004) 'Optimal Feedback Control and the Neural Basis of Volitional Motor Control', *Nature Reviews Neuroscience*, 5, pp. 532–546.

Shadmehr, R. and Mussa-Ivaldi, S. (2012) *Biological Learning and Control*. Cambridge, MA: MIT Press.

Skinner, B. F. (1938) *The Behavior of Organisms*. New York, NY: Appleton-Century-Crofts.

Sprevak, M. (2016) 'Philosophy of the Psychological and Cognitive Sciences', in Humphrey, P. (ed.) *The Oxford Handbook of Philosophy of Science*. Oxford: Oxford University Press.

Stengel, R. (1986) *Optimal Control and Estimation*. New York, NY: Dover.

Stevenson, I. et al. (2009) 'Bayesian Integration and Non-Linear Feedback Control in a Full-Body Motor Task', *PLOS Computational Biology*, 5, e1000629.

Stich, S. (1983) *From Folk Psychology to Cognitive Science*. Cambridge, MA: MIT Press.

Todorov, E. (2004) 'Optimality Principles in Sensorimotor Control', *Nature Neuroscience*, 7, pp. 907–915.

Todorov, E. (2009) 'Stochastic Optimal Control and Estimation Methods Adapted to the Noise Characteristics of the Sensorimotor System', *Neural Computation*, 17, pp. 1084–1108.

Todorov, E. and Jordan, M. (2002) 'Optimal Feedback Control as a Theory of Motor Coordination', *Nature Neuroscience*, 5, pp. 1226–1235.

van Gelder, T. (1992) 'What Might Cognition Be, If Not Computation?', *Journal of Philosophy*, 92, pp. 345–381.

von Helmholtz, H. (1867) *Handbuch der Physiologischen Optik*. Leipzig: Voss.

Wolpert, D. (2007) 'Probabilistic Models in Human Sensorimotor Control', *Human Movement Science*, 26, pp. 511–524.

Wolpert, D. and Flanagan, J. R. (2009) 'Forward Models', in Bayne, T., Cleeremans, A., and Wilken, P. (eds.) *The Oxford Companion to Consciousness*. Oxford: Oxford University Press, pp. 294–296.

Wolpert, D. and Landy, M. (2012) 'Motor Control Is Decision-making', *Current Opinion in Neurobiology*, 22, pp. 1–8.

32

COMPUTATIONAL MODELS OF EMOTION

Xiaosi Gu

The best and most beautiful things in the world cannot be seen or even touched. They must be felt with the heart.

(Helen Keller)

Introduction

Helen Keller not only precisely described the powerful role of emotion in our human existence, but also presented a challenge to the scientific investigation of emotion – its subjectivity, the fact that it cannot be "seen" or "touched". Emotion is much more difficult for researchers to study in laboratory settings due to its subjective nature. Despite its long history, compared to the studies of vision, audition, memory, and many other mental processes, emotion research still faces several major challenges. These challenges include: (1) the definition of emotion is imprecise and many related terms (e.g. affect, feeling, mood) are used interchangeably; (2) there is profound inconsistency between subjective reports of emotion and objective measures such as functional magnetic resonance imaging (fMRI) or electroencephalogram (EEG); and (3) existing analyses are largely correlational and lack mechanistic or computational approaches. While the first two issues are also critical in understanding the true nature of emotion, the current chapter will focus on the third problem and rely on commonly accepted definitions and experimental measurements of emotion. Furthermore, this chapter will not serve the purpose of an exhaustive review of emotion as has been done elsewhere (e.g. see Dalgleish, 2004; Davidson and Irwin, 1999; LeDoux, 2000; Phelps, 2006). Instead, I will focus on computational theories of emotion.

What is emotion?

Emotion is a multifaceted construct. While the exact definition of emotion still remains controversial, most researchers agree that there are at least two layers to what is commonly accepted as an emotion. Figure 32.1a represents a simplified definition of emotion illustrated as a Russian doll. "Core" emotion, often equated with the term *affect*, is the subjective *feeling* aspect of emotion. Naturally, this *core affect* component of emotion is the most difficult to measure due to its subjectivity. The "outer" layer of emotion includes cognitive, behavioral, and physiological processes involved in what is termed a *prototypical emotional episode*, such as attention directed toward the stimulus, overt behavior, cognitive appraisal, autonomic responses (Russell and Barrett, 1999). This outer layer has been the most studied aspect of emotion, due to its objectivity.

The distinction between the two layers of subjectivity vs objectivity can be further illustrated in the following example. Say you present a clip from the movie *Titanic* to induce sadness in your study participants. You can measure physiological responses from the body, such as skin conductance, or record facial expressions of your participants, associated with sadness. These measures, however, do not necessarily represent how your participants are actually feeling, the subjective aspect of emotion. This dichotomous "Russian doll" framework is obviously a simplified definition of emotion. Nevertheless, Figure 32.1a captures the main ingredients involved in an emotional event/process and has served as the basic framework for emotion research for decades (Russell and Barrett, 1999).

A cognitivist tradition of emotion research

As defined above, cognition is an integral part of emotional processes (Figure 32.1a). Indeed, the scientific inquiry into the nature of emotion has had a strongly cognitivist tradition since ancient Greece, if not earlier. For instance, Aristotle considers emotions as "those things that cause people to change their minds in respect of their judgments and are accompanied by pleasure and pain" (Aristotle, 350 BC). In other words, he thinks that emotions need to have an effect on actions and choices. Aristotle also argues that the feeling aspect of emotion stems from human cognitive capacity, and that emotions, feelings, and cognition are highly correlated. This view emphasizes the interaction between emotion and cognitive systems, and the behavioral consequence of emotion. Thus, the Aristotelian approach lays the foundation for the cognitivist tradition of emotion research (see, for a sample of papers, Gu, Liu et al., 2013; Lazarus, 1991; LeDoux, 1989; Oatley and Johnson-Laird, 1987; Ochsner and Gross, 2005; Pessoa, 2008; Pezzulo, Barca, and Friston, 2015; Roseman, 1984; Schachter and Singer, 1962).

Another benefit of focusing on the cognitive and behavioral aspects of emotion is that it makes it much easier for experimentalists later on to be able to operationalize emotion, as we have seen in the history of emotion research. Typical emotion paradigms and tasks such as those involving the recognition of facial emotion (Pessoa, 2008; Phelps, 2006) heavily rely on cognitive systems of decision making and judgment. As subjective feelings are not directly measurable (other than self-report), the majority of studies depend on some sort of objective indices such as reaction time or accuracy as outcome measures of emotion. Physiological measures such as skin conductance response, heart rate, or pupil diameter are also commonly used, to index autonomic arousal associated with emotional responses. With the emergence of brain imaging, new methods such as fMRI are now widely used as objective measures for mental states including emotion. The neural circuits involved in emotion will be discussed in detail in the sections below. However, researchers are beginning to realize that neither physiological or brain imaging measures can provide *unique* indices for emotion. On the contrary, it has become clearer that emotional and cognitive processes are inseparable, behaviorally and neurally (for two recent arguments on this issue, see Gu, Liu et al., 2013; Pessoa, 2008).

Embodied emotions: the role of bodily responses

Bodily responses are another important aspect of a *prototypical emotional episode* (Figure 32.1a). Most textbooks start their introduction of emotion with the James-Lange and Cannon-Bard theories of emotion, which center their discussions on the relationship between bodily responses and emotional feelings. Contrary to the folk notion that bodily responses follow emotional feelings (e.g. "I perceive fear therefore my heart races"), William James and Carl Lange proposed that bodily responses, including physiological responses of the muscles, skin, and viscera, precede conscious emotional feelings (e.g. "my heart races therefore I perceive fear") (James, 1884; Lange and James, 1922). This embodied view of emotion was challenged by several experimental findings. For example, physiological responses of the body could happen more slowly than human subjects' reports of changed feelings. Thus, Walter Cannon and his student Philip Bard proposed what is now called the Cannon-Bard theory of emotion, which suggests that physiological responses of the body and subjective experiences of emotion can occur simultaneously and independently from each other (Bard, 1928; Cannon, 1927). In other words, physiological signals coming from the body are not necessarily the cause or consequence of subjective feelings of emotion.

As emotion researchers turned to investigate the neural circuits involved in emotion, the controversy on embodied emotion was forgotten by the research community for several decades, until researchers such as Antonio Damasio (Bechara et al., 1996; Damasio, 2008) and Bud Craig (2002; 2009) brought it back to the spotlight of scientific research. Primarily based on findings of impaired physiological responses and abnormal behavior in patients with certain brain lesions, Damasio and colleagues proposed the "somatic marker" hypothesis, which suggests that bodily signals associated with emotion, or "somatic markers", can influence behavior at multiple levels (Adolphs et al., 1994; Bechara et al., 1996; Damasio, Vanhoesen, and Vilensky, 1981; Eslinger and Damasio, 1985; Tranel and Damasio, 1994). This "somatic marker" is hypothesized to be located in the ventromedial prefrontal cortex (vmPFC). While this hypothesis has been criticized for several shortcomings (Maia and McClelland, 2004), it does bring an important point back – that bodily responses are an essential part of emotion and even consciousness and selfhood. We shall see later how this idea influenced computational models of interoception (i.e. the sense of the physiological states of the body).

Neural circuits involved in emotion

Starting from the 1930s, researchers turned to ask the question of how emotion was implemented in the brain. The first attempt was made by James Papez who proposed that a neural circuit including the hypothalamus, the anterior thalamus, the cingulate cortex, and hippocampus, and the fornix, was the basis for emotional experience (Papez, 1937). Paul MacLean formalized Papez's idea and coined the term *limbic system* (MacLean, 1952). In MacLean's limbic system, the amygdala and several other regions are also critical for emotional experience. Papez's and MacLean's ideas, however, were challenged almost immediately after they were proposed, as studies in the 1950s showed that lesions in limbic regions such as the hippocampus caused memory deficits rather than emotional disturbances (Scoville and Milner, 1957).

With the emergence of brain imaging tools in the 1990s, researchers began the investigation of emotional brain regions using functional neuroimaging (George et al., 1993; Pardo, Pardo, and Raichle, 1993). Many of these studies confirmed the involvement of several limbic and paralimbic regions in emotion (for a meta-analysis, see Phan et al., 2002). Some of the key regions involved in emotion are shown in Figure 32.1b. These early studies mostly rely on the idea of *functional localization*, which considers brain regions as specialized for different mental functions such as emotion, memory, and attention (Friston, 2002). Using positron emission tomography (PET), George and colleagues found activation in the anterior cingulate cortex and inferior frontal gyrus during an emotion recognition paradigm (George et al., 1993). Also using PET, Pardo and colleagues employed an emotion generation paradigm where healthy participants were asked to experience sadness; the authors reported inferior and orbitofrontal

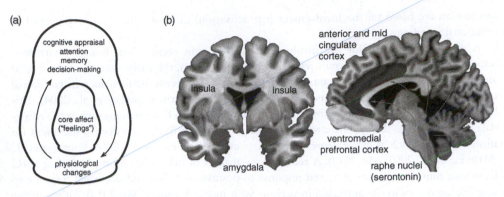

Figure 32.1 (a) Definition of emotion: a Russian doll model. Emotion involves both a core affect component (also called feelings) and cognitive, behavioral, and physiological responses. (b) Neural circuits that have been reported to subserve emotion include at least: the amygdala, insula, ventromedial prefrontal cortex, and anterior and mid cingulate cortex. In addition, cells in the raphe nuclei in the brainstem produce serotonin and projects to various brain regions

activation related to the sadness experience (Pardo, Pardo, and Raichle, 1993). These two earliest studies set the tone for the functional neuroimaging research of emotion later, as emotion recognition and emotion generation became the two most popular types of paradigms. These studies also led to a surge in the number of PET and fMRI studies on emotion in the late 1990s and 2000s and the birth of the new field *affective neuroscience* (for review and meta-analysis, see Fusar-Poli et al., 2009; Lindquist et al., 2012; Murphy, Nimmo-Smith, and Lawrence, 2003; Phan et al., 2002).

As the neuroimaging field moved toward a *functional integration* view of the brain (Friston, 2002), researchers in affective neuroscience started to realize that the so-called *emotion network* may not subserve emotional functions exclusively. Instead, many of the brain regions considered to be specialized for emotion are involved in many other mental processes such as attention, learning, memory, and decision making. The anterior cingulate cortex (ACC) is a good example. Early on, the ACC, especially the rostral part of the ACC (rACC) was considered a brain region specialized for emotion (Bush, Luu, and Posner, 2000). More recently, however, evidence suggests that this segregation model is no longer tenable, and that different streams of information, cognitive or emotional, converge in overlapping regions within the ACC (Shackman et al., 2011). Moreover, with the emergence of new methods such as multivariate pattern analysis (Krishnan et al., 2016; Sinha and Parsons, 1996), it is becoming clear that patterns of neural activations, rather than isolated brain regions *per se*, encode different aspects of emotional processing. This is a fast-growing field with great promise and potential.

Serotonin and emotion

Another important topic in affective neuroscience is to understand the neurotransmitters involved in emotions, which would have significance for developing pharmacological treatments for mood disorders. Serotonin, or 5-hydroxytryptamine (5-HT), has been proposed to be one of the main neurotransmitters subserving emotion. Serotonin is released by neurons in the raphe nuclei in the brainstem and is then sent to a wide range of brain regions including the hippocampus, basal ganglia, thalamus, hypothalamus, and cortex (Figure 32.1b). Serotonin is not directly measurable in healthy human volunteers. Thus, most studies claiming a role of serotonin in emotion are based on the involvement (e.g. activation) of serotonin-containing regions in emotional paradigms.

A stronger argument for the involvement of serotonin comes from human pharmacological studies. Selective serotonin reuptake inhibitor (SSRI), the main ingredient for typical antidepressants, can increase synaptic serotonin level and improve performance in emotional tasks in healthy volunteers (Harmer, Mackay et al., 2006; Harmer, Shelley et al., 2004). This behavioral effect is also paralleled by changes in activity level in brain regions such as the amygdala (Murphy et al., 2009). These results support the use of SSRI as an effective treatment for mood disorders such as major depression (Bellani et al., 2011; Fales et al., 2009; Fournier et al., 2010; Fu et al., 2007; Ma, 2014). A recent meta-analysis of neuroimaging studies using SSRI treatment found consistent increased response to positive emotions and decreased response to negative emotions in the amygdala in patients with mood disorders (Ma, 2014). Although the clinical efficacy of antidepressants remains controversial (Fournier et al., 2010; Kirsch et al., 2008), the combination of neuroimaging and pharmacology provides an important approach to uncover the mechanism of serotonergic actions in emotional processes.

It is worth noting that other than serotonin, dopamine has also been heavily involved in emotion (Cools, Nakamura, and Daw, 2011; Guitart-Masip et al., 2014). Recent theories suggest that both dopamine and serotonin encode both emotional valence and action. Specifically, dopamine encodes "go-for-reward" responses, whereas serotonin encodes response inhibition when the stimulus is negative (Cools, Nakamura, and Daw, 2011; Guitart-Masip et al., 2014). The intricate relationship between neurotransmitters and emotion remains to be investigated.

Existing computational models of emotion

The literature reviewed so far has laid important foundation for computational modeling of emotion, the work I am going to review in this section. Compared to the vast body of work on emotion from psychology and neuroscience, the literature on computational mechanisms of emotion is relatively small. However, it is a fast-growing field with already fruitful results, as we shall see next.

Affective computing

What is the purpose of trying to come up with computational models of emotion? It is not just for the curiosity of scientists, but also has great utility for the artificial intelligence (AI), computer science, and robotics communities, as whether we *can* design computers with emotions largely depends on a well-defined computational model of emotion. Although there is some debate regarding whether we *need* emotional computers (Minsky, 2007), researchers generally agree that having emotions could make computers more human-like (e.g. more empathetic). *Affective computing*, a hybrid field built on principles from computer science, cognitive science, and psychology, has attracted much attention (Marsella, Gratch, and Petta, 2010; Minsky, 2007) since the term was coined in the late 1990s (Picard and Picard, 1997). One of the main goals of this area is to build artificial computing machines that can recognize and even express emotions, with the hope that such progress can improve machine intelligence (e.g. imagine a smartphone that can detect your emotions). It is noteworthy that both emotion recognition and expression belong to the outer layer of our Russian doll model of emotion (Figure 32.1a), and that the "core affect" part has not yet been included in the discussion.

One main line of work in affective computing is to use objective measures, such as skin conductance and electromyogram (i.e. electrical activities of facial muscles), to predict emotions.

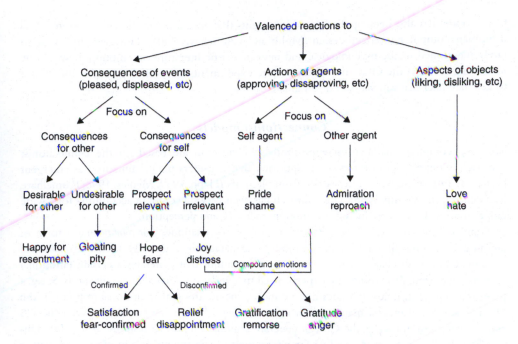

Figure 32.2 The OCC model of emotion. Emotion is considered the valenced reactions to an external event or situation that is perceived as good or bad to oneself or to another person
Source: Adapted from Ortony, Clore, and Collins (1990)

For instance, Picard and colleagues recorded electromyogram, blood volume pressure, skin conductance, and respiration in one subject over thirty days (Picard, Vyzas, and Healey, 2001). The authors then developed pattern recognition algorithms that achieved 81 percent classification accuracy for the eight emotions tested in this subject (anger, hate, grief, platonic love, romantic love, joy, reverence, neutral). Bartlett and colleagues used spontaneous facial actions recorded in videos and also machine learning algorithms to predict emotion. These authors were able to achieve 93 percent accuracy with the best performing algorithm in a real-time setting (Bartlett et al., 2005). These machine learning algorithms could be valuable for developing "smarter" commercial products that can detect or even express emotions. For example, imagine a smartphone that can detect your mood by facial expressions captured by the phone camera. Your phone can then suggest places to go (e.g. suggest parties/bars when you are happy or quiet places to go when you are feeling blue) or assemble a music playlist for your particular mood at the moment.

Compared to the thriving area of AI emotion recognition, to actually build a computational model of emotion, however, has been deemed much more difficult (Marsella, Gratch, and Petta, 2010). One model, which is still widely acknowledged and used today, is called the OCC model, named after its inventors Ortony, Clore, and Collins (1990). The OCC model (Figure 32.2) is essentially a cognitive model of emotion. It considers emotion as a result of valenced response subsequent to the cognitive appraisal of a stimulus as being harmful or beneficial to the agent. As illustrated in Figure 32.2, this model is able to describe the mechanisms of many emotions, including some complex ones such as disappointment or admiration. The OCC model has been very successful in many areas. For example, it has been used to account for users' emotional responses to consumer products in product design (Desmet and Hekkert, 2002). The

OCC model has also been applied to design agents that are more emotional and more social in human–computer interface design (Moldt and von Scheve, 2001). However, this model is rarely mentioned in the psychological and neuroscientific literature on emotion. It would be interesting to see if the OCC model can inspire experiments in psychology and neuroscience to generate data that can validate or invalidate the model.

Connectionist models

The first computational neuroscience models of emotion are based on the connectionist approach. Connectionism refers to an approach that considers mental functions as emergent properties of interconnected networks of simple units (Hebb, 1949; Medler, 1998; Rumelhart, McClelland, and Group, 1988). This approach has been very successful in accounting for a wide range of mental functions, including emotion, memory, and perception.

Connectionist approaches towards emotion typically examines *fear conditioning*, a form of emotional learning. In a typical fear conditioning paradigm (Figure 32.3a), an *unconditioned stimulus* (US; e.g. an electrical shock) is a natural stimulus that generates a certain emotional response (e.g. arousal) without any experimental manipulation. A *conditioned stimulus* (CS; e.g. a tone) is a neutral stimulus that does not naturally generate the same emotional response as the US. The key experimental manipulation is *conditioning*, which is the pairing between the US and CS. After conditioning, the CS can generate a similar emotional response to the US. This paradigm has been the gold standard for neuroscience experiments on emotion and learning and has generated fruitful results over the past few decades (for a sample of papers, see Delgado et al., 2008; LaBar et al., 1998; LeDoux, 2000; Schiller et al., 2010).

One key finding from these studies is the involvement of amygdala in emotion. An exemplar connectionist model of how emotion is processed in the amygdala and its associated neural regions is shown in Figure 32.3b (adapted from Armony et al., 1997). In this simplified connectionist model of fear conditioning, an auditory CS is first processed by the auditory part of the thalamus and then by the auditory cortex. The information is then passed to the amygdala through one cortical pathway and one subcortical pathway. According to this model, each brain region is a module of non-linear input–output transformation, consisting of mutually inhibitory units (i.e. the dots within each region shown in Figure 32.3b). The connections between brain regions/activation units are assumed to be feedforward and excitatory. In addition, each unit exerts inhibitory self-connection. The input pattern represents auditory tones of varying frequencies. The response of each unit to the input can be considered as the time-averaged firing rate of a neuron calculated using a soft competitive learning rule. After conditioning, each unit develops a *receptive field*. In other words, each unit only responds to a subset of input patterns associated with a *best frequency*.

Despite its simplicity, the connectionist model, which is built on the principles of Hebbian learning and lateral inhibition, provides a quantitative and biologically realistic framework to account for a wide range of experimental findings. For example, one empirical finding from the animal literature is that, after conditioning, the frequency of the CS becomes the best frequency, a finding that is predicted by the connectionist model (Armony et al., 1997). The model also makes new predictions that can be tested in the laboratory. For example, previous studies suggest that removing auditory cortical input to the amygdala would cause fear responses to generalize stimuli other than the CS. However, the model predicts that lesion in the auditory cortex should not affect the gradient of stimulus generalization, a prediction that contradicts existing hypotheses but is supported by more recent data from lesioning the rat auditory cortex (Armony et al., 1997). This suggests that a connectionist approach could be highly valuable to emotion research.

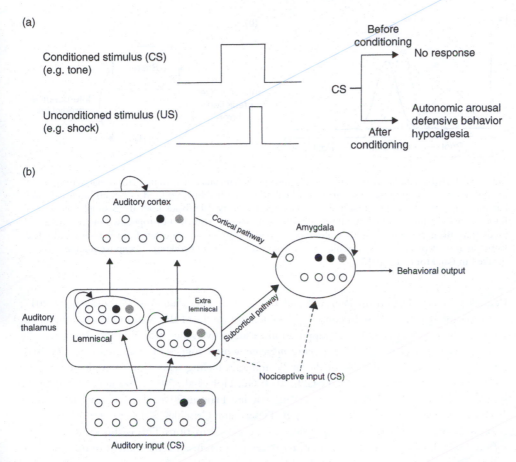

Figure 32.3 Connectionist approach to emotion. (a) A typical fear-conditioning paradigm involves a conditioned stimulus (CS) such as tone, and an unconditioned stimulus such as shock. After conditioning (i.e. pairing the CS with US), the CS can generate emotional responses such as arousal. (b) A simplified neural network model of fear conditioning and amygdala function. Each brain region is a non-linear module with mutually inhibitory units. White represents zero activation and black represents maximum activation. Connections between modules are feedforward and excitatory
Source: Adapted from Armony et al. (1997)

Bayesian models of emotion

An emerging topic in the computational neuroscience of emotion is Bayesian models, whose principle can be described as follows (Figure 32.4a):

Bayesian models take into account the probabilistic nature of the world, and have been successful in accounting for a wide range of cognitive and neural phenomena such as perception, learning, and memory (for a sample of papers, see Doya, 2007; Friston, 2010; Knill and Pouget, 2004; Moutoussis, Fearon et al., 2014). This leads to the *Bayesian brain hypothesis*, which suggests that the human brain represents sensory information in the form of probabilistic distribution (Colombo and Seriès, 2012; Knill and Pouget, 2004). With the rising of the new field of computational psychiatry, Bayesian approaches have also proved to be successful in explaining aberrant perception and cognition in many psychiatric disorders such as schizophrenia (Moutoussis,

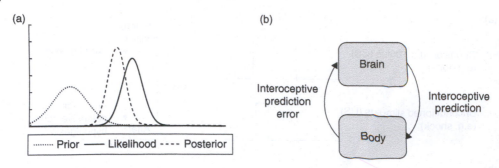

Figure 32.4 (a) Bayesian updating rule. In a Bayesian brain, mental states such as emotional states, are formulized in terms of probabilistic *posterior* distributions (dashed line) updated in a continuous fashion based on *prior* distribution (dotted line) and likelihood/sensory data (black line). (b) A simplified interoceptive inference model of emotion. Bodily responses are regulated by top-down interoceptive predictions from the brain. The brain also receives bottom-up prediction errors from the body to update its predictions. A possible neural architecture within the brain that encodes interoceptive inference is detailed in Gu, Hof et al. (2013)

Bentall et al., 2011), autism (Pellicano and Burr, 2012), and addiction (Gu and Filbey, 2017; Schwartenbeck et al., 2015). In contrast to the fruitful results of Bayesian models in other areas of neuroscience and psychology, its application to subjective states such as emotion is rare.

One such model is called *interoceptive inference*, which suggests the approximate Bayesian inference of physiological states of the body underlies feeling states (for a sample, see Barrett and Simmons, 2015; Gu and FitzGerald, 2014; Gu, Hof et al., 2013; Pezzulo, 2014; Pezzulo, Rigoli, and Friston, 2015; Seth, 2013; 2014; Seth and Friston, 2016; also see a special issue in *Philosophical Transactions of the Royal Society B*: Tsakiris and Critchley, 2016). Under this Bayesian framework, the brain actively tries to infer the causes of sensations. This is also known as *active inference*, which is one way of implementing Bayesian inference. In the context of interoceptive inference, emotions can be considered as beliefs about bodily or interoceptive states. The mismatch between one's prediction and the actual interoceptive signal contributes to an "interoceptive prediction error" signal that is used to update future beliefs. This model is rooted in the longstanding debate about the relationship between bodily signals and subjective experience, the center of debate between James-Lange and Cannon-Bard theories as introduced earlier. While these early theories try to determine a one-directional relationship between bodily responses and subjective experience, a fundamental difference in the interoceptive inference model is that it suggests brain–body relationship can be a two-way street. This area has undergone substantial theoretical developments over the past few years. We shall look forward to empirical results that can validate or disprove this model in the next few years. For instance, this model predicts that emotional impairments should exist in people with deficits in the processing of bodily signals (i.e. due to less precise sensory data) and emotional function could improve in individuals with better interoceptive accuracy (i.e. due to more precise sensory data; such as reported in Barrett et al., 2004). This model also predicts that strategies that can help individuals interpret bodily signals correctly should also be able to help with emotional functions. For example, psychotherapy that can re-interpret the emotional content and meaning of increased heart rate should help individuals with panic attacks.

Related to the active inference framework, Joffily and Coricelli proposed a definition of emotional valence as the negative rate of change of *free energy* over time (Joffily and Coricelli, 2013). Free energy is an information theory measure that limits the surprise on sampling some data, given a generative model (Friston, 2010; Friston, Kilner, and Harrison, 2006). By defining emotional valence as the negative rate of change of free energy over time and also taking into account the second time-derivative of free energy, the authors provided a computational account for seven emotions – happiness, unhappiness, hope, fear, surprise, relief, and disappointment. Under this framework, an important function of emotional valence is to regulate the learning rate of the causes of sensory inputs. For example, this model predicts that when sensation violates expectation, valence is negative and increases learning rate (and vice versa). Compared to the interoceptive inference model, this free energy model of emotion mostly focuses on the relationship between emotional valence, learning, and sensations, rather than the relationship between emotional feelings and bodily states. More empirical data (e.g. using sensory learning paradigms) is needed to validate its model predictions.

There has been one fMRI study that directly applied Bayesian modeling to quantify subjective feelings (Xiang, Lohrenz, and Montague, 2013). Participants were asked to rate how happy they felt about a monetary offer they received at the moment using a nine-point scale while being scanned. Using a Bayesian observer model, the authors found that feeling prediction errors were encoded in the nucleus accumbens, vmPFC, and posterior cingulate, whereas feeling variance prediction errors were computed in bilateral anterior insula. To date, this was still the first fMRI study to utilize the Bayesian framework to model subjective feelings directly and more studies are needed in this line of research to echo such effort.

Neuroeconomic models of emotion

Lastly, recent studies investigating the neural basis of value-based decision making, a field termed *neuroeconomics*, are also starting to address the questions of how emotions are encoded in the human brain. This line of work has its root in early reinforcement learning theories of emotion (Gray, 1981; Rolls, 1990), which consider emotions as states caused by reinforcing stimuli. In Edmund Rolls' model, for example, emotion can be expressed as the result of a reinforcement signal (Rolls, 1990). The advantage of this framework is that emotion can then be manipulated and measured objectively – by changing the quantities of the reinforcer. This principle serves as the premise of almost all decision-theoretic studies on emotion, which usually involve an economics task with manipulation of a certain reinforcer (e.g. money, food)

The Fehr-Schmidt model, which originated in behavioral economics, is one of the most influential models in this domain (Fehr and Schmidt, 1999). In this model, individuals are not exclusively self-interested as assumed by classic economic models. Instead, people care about inequity. When unfairness is directed at oneself, that individual will have feelings of "envy"; when unfairness is directed at another person, the individual will develop feelings of "guilt". This model is not only seminal in behavioral economics, but also has inspired a growing field of neuroeconomic research (Chang et al., 2011; de Quervain et al., 2004; Gu, Wang et al., 2015; Krajbich et al., 2009; Spitzer et al., 2007; Xiang, Lohrenz, and Montague, 2013). It is noteworthy that in most studies using the Fehr-Schmidt model, these feelings are implicit and "hidden" states inferred from overt choice behaviors, and that it remains unclear if these estimated parameters are actually correlated with subjective reports of feelings.

Social exchange paradigms are commonly used to test the Fehr-Schmidt model. One such example is the Ultimatum Game (UG). In the UG (Figure 32.5), two partners – one proposer and one responder – jointly decide the outcome of a simple economic exchange. First, the proposer decides how much money to give to the responder (e.g. $2 out of a total of $10). Then, the responder decides whether to accept the proposal (e.g. $2). If she accepts, they divide the money according to the proposal and the payoff is [$8, $2] for proposer and responder. If she

Figure 32.5 The Ultimatum Game as an example of neuroeconomic approach to emotion. In this game, the proposer first decides on an amount to send to the responder (e.g. $2 out of a total of $10). The responder than decides whether to accept (which leads to a [$8, $2] payoff to the proposer and responder) or reject (which leads to a [$0, $0] payoff) the proposal. This paradigm is often used in conjunction with the Fehr-Schmidt model to quantify emotion during social exchange

rejects, however, they both receive nothing. In most experiments using the UG, the subject plays the role of the responder (Crockett et al., 2008; Gu, Wang et al., 2015; Harle and Sanfey, 2007; Sanfey et al., 2003). According to the Fehr-Schmidt model, we can represent the responder's utility function as the following:

$$U(x_i) = x_i - \alpha \max\{y_i - x_i, 0\} - \beta \max\{x_i - y_i, 0\}$$

Here x_i and y_i denote the payoff of the responder and the proposer on trial i, respectively. α represents the sensitivity to disadvantageous inequity, or "envy"; β represents the sensitivity to advantageous inequity, or "guilt". Using a computational model based on this Fehr-Schmidt utility function and ultimatum, dictator, and trust games (the last two are social exchange games closely related to the UG), Krajbich and colleagues reported diminished sense of "guilt", but normal levels of "envy", in a group of patients with damage to the vmPFC. The authors concluded that the vmPFC is critical for encoding guilt during social exchange. It is worth noting that many of these neuroeconomic studies do not directly measure subjects' actual feelings. Instead, they use a decision theoretic approach towards emotion and consider emotion to be the result of values and decisions.

A few recent studies have directly measured and modeled subjective feelings (Eldar and Niv, 2015; Rutledge et al., 2015). For example, Rutledge and colleagues directly recorded participants' subjective reports of happiness on a continuous visual scale during a gambling task (Rutledge et al., 2015). In this study, happiness is constructed as a function of certain rewards, expected values of chosen gambles, and reward prediction errors. The authors found that the momentary happiness was explained by the combined influence of recent reward expectations and reward prediction errors, but not by current task earnings. The authors also reported that activations in ventral striatum and anterior insula were associated with happiness rating. Eldar and Niv used a similar approach of measuring mood during a decision-making task and found that mood can also influence value-based decision making, in addition to being influenced by value signals (Eldar and Niv, 2015). Taken together, these studies represent a critical step forward in the area of neuroeconomics to consider emotion as an important aspect of mental function that can be modeled computationally.

Conclusion and future directions

Over the past few decades, there have been considerable developments in the field of computational modeling of emotion. Most of these developments come from artificial intelligence, connectionism, Bayesian modeling, and neuroeconomics. The ideas are deeply rooted in the cognitivist tradition of emotion research as well as the embodied view of emotion. The majority of existing models focus only on the outer layer of our Russian doll definition of emotion (cognitive, behavioral, physiological) and only a handful directly model the core affect aspect. Clearly, there are still many knowledge gaps to fill. For example,

- How can we, as neuroscientists and psychologists, benefit from models of emotion from affective computing and AI?
- The amygdala is not the only region involved in emotion. How do we use the connectionist approach to study other neural circuits involved in emotion?
- Other than neuroeconomic paradigms, can we develop other perceptual and cognitive paradigms that operationalize emotion?
- What measures and models best capture the *core affect* component of emotion?

Answers to these questions will significantly improve our understanding of the mechanisms underlying emotion, a topic that we still know so little about after centuries of research. Lastly, empirical evidence is urgently needed to validate or invalidate the models reviewed in this chapter. I hope that this chapter can encourage and also serve as a reference for researchers who are enthusiastic about this topic.

References

Adolphs, R. et al. (1994) 'Impaired Recognition of Emotion in Facial Expressions Following Bilateral Damage to the Human Amygdala', *Nature*, 372 (6507), pp. 669–672.

Aristotle. (350 BC) Rhetoric.

Armory, J.L. et al. (1997) 'Computational Modeling of Emotion: Explorations through the Anatomy and Physiology of Fear Conditioning', *Trends in Cognitive Sciences*, 1 (1), pp. 28–34.

Bard, P. (1928) 'A Diencephalic Mechanism for the Expression of Rage with Special Reference to the Sympathetic Nervous System', *American Journal of Physiology – Legacy Content*, 84 (3), pp. 490–515.

Barrett, L.F., and Simmons, W.K. (2015) 'Interoceptive Predictions in the Brain', *Nature Reviews Neuroscience*, 16, pp. 419–429.

Barrett, L.F. et al. (2004) 'Interoceptive Sensitivity and Self-Reports of Emotional Experience', *Journal of Personality and Social Psychology*, 87 (5), pp. 684–697.

Bartlett, M.S. et al. (2005) 'Recognizing Facial Expression: Machine Learning and Application to Spontaneous Behavior', *IEEE Computer Society Conference on Computer Vision and Pattern Recognition*, San Diego, June, 20–25. Piscataway, NJ: IEEE.

Bechara, A. et al. (1996) 'Failure to Respond Autonomically to Anticipated Future Outcomes Following Damage to Prefrontal Cortex', *Cerebral Cortex*, 6 (2), pp. 215–225.

Bellani, M. et al. (2011) 'The Effects of Antidepressants on Human Brain as Detected by Imaging Studies: Focus on Major Depression', *Progress in Neuropsychopharmacology and Biological Psychiatry*, 35 (7), pp. 1544–1552.

Bush, G., Luu, P., and Posner, M.I. (2000) 'Cognitive and Emotional Influences in Anterior Cingulate Cortex', *Trends in Cognitive Sciences*, 4 (6), pp. 215–222.

Cannon, W.B. (1927) 'The James-Lange Theory of Emotions: A Critical Examination and an Alternative Theory', *The American Journal of Psychology*, 39 (1/4), pp. 106–124.

Chang, L.J. et al. (2011) 'Triangulating the Neural, Psychological, and Economic Bases of Guilt Aversion', *Neuron*, 70 (3), pp. 560–572.

Colombo, M. and Seriès, P. (2012) 'Bayes in the Brain: On Bayesian Modelling in Neuroscience', *The British Journal for the Philosophy of Science*, 63 (3), pp. 697–723.

Cools, R., Nakamura, K., and Daw, N.D. (2011) 'Serotonin and Dopamine: Unifying Affective, Activational, and Decision Functions', *Neuropsychopharmacology*, 36 (1), pp. 98–113.

Craig, A.D. (2002) 'How Do You Feel? Interoception: The Sense of the Physiological Condition of the Body', *Nature Reviews Neuroscience*, 3 (8), pp. 655–666.

Craig, A.D. (2009) 'How Do You Feel – Now? The Anterior Insula and Human Awareness', *Nature Reviews Neuroscience*, 10 (1), pp. 59–70.

Crockett, M.J. et al. (2008) 'Serotonin Modulates Behavioral Reactions to Unfairness', *Science*, 320 (5884), p. 1739.

Dalgleish, T. (2004) 'The Emotional Brain', *Nature Reviews Neuroscience*, 5 (7), pp. 583–589.

Damasio, A. (2008) *Descartes' Error: Emotion, Reason and the Human Brain*. New York, NY: Random House.

Damasio, A.R., Vanhoesen, G.W., and Vilensky, J. (1981) 'Limbic-Motor Pathways in the Primate: A Means for Emotion to Influence Motor Behavior', *Neurology*, 31 (4), p. 60.

Davidson, R.J., and Irwin, W. (1999) 'The Functional Neuroanatomy of Emotion and Affective Style', *Trends in Cognitive Science*, 3 (1), pp. 11–21.

Delgado, M.R. et al. (2008) 'Neural Circuitry Underlying the Regulation of Conditioned Fear and Its Relation to Extinction', *Neuron*, 59 (5), pp. 829–838.

de Quervain, D.J. et al. (2004) 'The Neural Basis of Altruistic Punishment', *Science*, 305 (5688), pp. 1254–1258.

Desmet, P.M. and Hekkert, P. (2002) 'The Basis of Product Emotions', in Green, W.S. and Jordan, P, *Pleasure with Products, beyond Usability*. London: Taylor & Francis, pp. 60–68.

Doya, K. (2007) *Bayesian Brain: Probabilistic Approaches to Neural Coding*. Cambridge, MA: MIT Press.

Eldar, E. and Niv, Y. (2015) 'Interaction between Emotional State and Learning Underlies Mood Instability', *Nature Communications*, 6, 6149, pp. 1–9.

Eslinger, P.J. and Damasio, A.R. (1985) 'Severe Disturbance of Higher Cognition after Bilateral Frontal Lobe Ablation: Patient EVR', *Neurology*, 35 (12), p. 1731.

Fales, C.L. et al. (2009) 'Antidepressant Treatment Normalizes Hypoactivity in Dorsolateral Prefrontal Cortex during Emotional Interference Processing in Major Depression', *Journal of Affective Disorders*, 112 (1–3), pp. 206–211.

Fehr, E. and Schmidt, K.M. (1999) 'A Theory of Fairness, Competition, and Cooperation', *The Quarterly Journal of Economics*, 114 (3), pp. 817–868.

Fournier, J.C. et al. (2010) 'Antidepressant Drug Effects and Depression Severity: A Patient-Level Meta-analysis', *Journal of the American Medical Association*, 303 (1), pp. 47–53.

Friston, K. (2002) 'Beyond Phrenology: What Can Neuroimaging Tell Us about Distributed Circuitry?', *Annual Review of Neuroscience*, 25, pp. 221–250.

Friston, K. (2010) 'The Free-Energy Principle: A Unified Brain Theory?', *Nature Reviews Neuroscience*, 11 (2), pp. 127–138.

Friston, K., Kilner, J., and Harrison, L. (2006) 'A Free Energy Principle for the Brain', *Journal of Physiology Paris*, 100 (1–3), pp. 70–87.

Fu, C.H. et al. (2007) 'Neural Responses to Happy Facial Expressions in Major Depression Following Antidepressant Treatment', *American Journal of Psychiatry*, 164 (4), pp. 599–607.

Fusar-Poli, P. et al. (2009) 'Functional Atlas of Emotional Faces Processing: A Voxel-based Meta-analysis of 105 Functional Magnetic Resonance Imaging Studies', *Journal of Psychiatry and Neuroscience*, 34 (6), pp. 418–432.

George, M.S. et al. (1993) 'Brain Regions Involved in Recognizing Facial Emotion or Identity: An Oxygen-15 PET Study', *Journal of Neuropsychiatry and Clinical Neurosciences*, 5 (4), pp. 384–394.

Gray, J. (1981) 'Anxiety as a Paradigm Case of Emotion', *British Medical Bulletin*, 37 (2), pp. 193–197.

Gu, X. and Filbey, F. (2017) 'A Bayesian Observer Model of Drug Craving', *Journal of the American Medical Association Psychiatry*, 74 (4), pp. 419–420.

Gu, X. and FitzGerald, T.H. (2014) 'Interoceptive Inference: Homeostasis and Decision-making', *Trends in Cognitive Science*, 18 (6), pp. 269–270.

Gu, X., Hof, P.R. et al. (2013) 'Anterior Insular Cortex and Emotional Awareness', *Journal of Comparative Neurology*, 521 (15), pp. 3371–3388.

Gu, X., Liu, X. et al. (2013) 'Cognition-Emotion Integration in the Anterior Insular Cortex', *Cerebral Cortex*, 23 (1), pp. 20–27.

Gu, X., Wang, X. et al. (2015) 'Necessary, yet Dissociable Contributions of the Insular and Ventromedial Prefrontal Cortices to Norm Adaptation: Computational and Lesion Evidence in Humans', *Journal of Neuroscience*, 35 (2), pp. 467–473.

Guitart-Masip, M. et al. (2014) 'Action versus Valence in Decision Making', *Trends in Cognitive Science*, 18 (4), pp. 194–202.

Harle, K.M. and Sanfey, A.G. (2007) 'Incidental Sadness Biases Social Economic Decisions in the Ultimatum Game', *Emotion*, 7 (4), pp. 876–881.

Harmer, C.J., Mackay, C.E. et al. (2006) 'Antidepressant Drug Treatment Modifies the Neural Processing of Nonconscious Threat Cues', *Biological Psychiatry*, 59 (9), pp. 816–820.

Harmer, C.J., Shelley, N.C. et al. (2004) 'Increased Positive versus Negative Affective Perception and Memory in Healthy Volunteers Following Selective Serotonin and Norepinephrine Reuptake Inhibition', *American Journal of Psychiatry*, 161 (7), pp. 1256–1263.

Hebb, D.O. (1949) *The Organization of Behavior: A Neuropsychological Theory*. Abingdon, UK: Psychology Press.

James, W. (1884) 'What Is an Emotion?', *Mind*, 9 (34), pp. 188–205.

Joffily, M. and Coricelli, G. (2013) 'Emotional Valence and the Free-Energy Principle', *PLoS Computational Biology*, 9 (6), e1003094.

Kirsch, I. et al. (2008) 'Initial Severity and Antidepressant Benefits: A Meta-analysis of Data Submitted to the Food and Drug Administration', *PLoS Medicine*, 5 (2), e45.

Knill, D.C. and Pouget, A. (2004) 'The Bayesian Brain: The Role of Uncertainty in Neural Coding and Computation', *Trends in Neurosciences*, 27 (12), pp. 712–719.

Krajbich, I. et al. (2009) 'Economic Games Quantify Diminished Sense of Guilt in Patients with Damage to the Prefrontal Cortex', *Journal of Neuroscience*, 29 (7), pp. 2188–2192.

Krishnan, A. et al. (2016) 'Somatic and Vicarious Pain Are Represented by Dissociable Multivariate Brain Patterns', *eLife*, 5, e15166.

LaBar, K.S. et al. (1998) 'Human Amygdala Activation during Conditioned Fear Acquisition and Extinction: A Mixed-Trial fMRI Study', *Neuron*, 20 (5), pp. 937–945.

Lange, C.G. and James, W. (1922) *The Emotions*, vol. 1. Philadelphia, PA: Williams & Wilkins.

Lazarus, R.S. (1991) 'Progress on a Cognitive-Motivational-Relational Theory of Emotion', *American Psychologist*, 46 (8), pp. 819–834.

LeDoux, J.E. (1989) 'Cognitive-Emotional Interactions in the Brain', *Cognition and Emotion*, 3 (4), pp. 267–289.

LeDoux, J.E. (2000) 'Emotion Circuits in the Brain', *Annual Review of Neuroscience*, 23, pp. 155–184.

Lindquist, K.A. et al. (2012) 'The Brain Basis of Emotion: A Meta-analytic Review', *Behavioral and Brain Sciences*, 35 (3), pp. 121–143.

Ma, Y. (2014) 'Neuropsychological Mechanism Underlying Antidepressant Effect: A Systematic Meta-analysis', *Molecular Psychiatry*, 20, pp. 311–319.

MacLean, P.D. (1952) 'Some Psychiatric Implications of Physiological Studies on Frontotemporal Portion of Limbic System (Visceral Brain)', *Electroencephalography and Clinical Neurophysiology*, 4 (4), pp. 407–418.

Maia, T.V. and McClelland, J.L. (2004) 'A Reexamination of the Evidence for the Somatic Marker Hypothesis: What Participants Really Know in the Iowa Gambling Task', *Proceedings of the National Academy of Sciences of the USA*, 101 (45), pp. 16075–16080.

Marsella, S., Gratch, J., and Petta, P. (2010) 'Computational Models of Emotion', *A Blueprint for Affective Computing: A Sourcebook and Manual*, 11 (1), pp. 21–46.

Medler, D.A. (1998) 'A Brief History of Connectionism', *Neural Computing Surveys*, 1, pp. 18–72.

Minsky, M. (2007) *The Emotion Machine: Commonsense Thinking, Artificial Intelligence, and the Future of the Human Mind*. New York, NY: Simon and Schuster.

Moldt, D. and von Scheve, C. (2001) 'Emotional Actions for Emotional Agents', *AISB'01 Symposium on Emotion, Cognition, and Affective Computing*. University of York, March 21–24. AISB Press.

Moutoussis, M., Bentall, R.P. et al. (2011) 'Bayesian Modelling of Jumping-to-Conclusions Bias in Delusional Patients', *Cognitive Neuropsychiatry*, 16 (5), pp. 422–447.

Moutoussis, M., Fearon, P. et al. (2014) 'Bayesian Inferences about the Self (and Others): A Review', *Consciousness and Cognition*, 25, pp. 67–76.

Murphy, F.C., Nimmo-Smith, I., and Lawrence, A.D. (2003) 'Functional Neuroanatomy of Emotions: A Meta-analysis', *Cognitive, Affective and Behavioral Neuroscience*, 3 (3), pp. 207–233.

Murphy, S.E. et al. (2009) 'Effect of a Single Dose of Citalopram on Amygdala Response to Emotional Faces', *British Journal of Psychiatry*, 194 (6), pp. 535–540.

Oatley, K. and Johnson-Laird, P.N. (1987) 'Towards a Cognitive Theory of Emotions', *Cognition and Emotion*, 1 (1), pp. 29–50.

Ochsner, K.N. and Gross, J.J. (2005) 'The Cognitive Control of Emotion', *Trends in Cognitive Science*, 9 (5), pp. 242–249.

Ortony, A., Clore, G.L., and Collins, A. (1990) *The Cognitive Structure of Emotions*. Cambridge, UK: Cambridge University Press.

Papez, J.W. (1937) 'A Proposed Mechanism of Emotion', *Archives of Neurology and Psychiatry*, 38 (4), pp. 725–743.

Pardo, J.V., Pardo, P.J., and Raichle, M.E. (1993) 'Neural Correlates of Self-induced Dysphoria', *American Journal of Psychiatry*, 150 (5), pp. 713–719.

Pellicano, E. and Burr, D. (2012) 'When the World Becomes "Too Real": A Bayesian Explanation of Autistic Perception', *Trends in Cognitive Sciences*, 16 (10), pp. 504–510.

Pessoa, L. (2008) 'On the Relationship between Emotion and Cognition', *Nature Reviews Neuroscience*, 9 (2), pp. 148–158.

Pezzulo, G. (2014) 'Why Do You Fear the Bogeyman? An Embodied Predictive Coding Model of Perceptual Inference', *Cognitive, Affective and Behavioral Neuroscience*, 14 (3), pp. 902–911.

Pezzulo, G., Barca, L., and Friston, K.J. (2015) 'Active Inference and Cognitive-Emotional Interactions in the Brain', *Behavioral and Brain Sciences*, 38, e85.

Pezzulo, G., Rigoli, F., and Friston, K. (2015) 'Active Inference, Homeostatic Regulation and Adaptive Behavioural Control', *Progress in Neurobiology*, 134, pp. 17–35.

Phan, K.L. et al. (2002) 'Functional Neuroanatomy of Emotion: A Meta-analysis of Emotion Activation Studies in PET and fMRI', *Neuroimage*, 16 (2), pp. 331–348.

Phelps, E.A. (2006) 'Emotion and Cognition: Insights from Studies of the Human Amygdala', *Annual Review of Psychology*, 57, pp. 27–53.

Picard, R.W. and Picard, R. (1997) *Affective Computing*, vol. 252. Cambridge, MA: MIT Press.

Picard, R.W., Vyzas, E., and Healey, J. (2001) 'Toward Machine Emotional Intelligence: Analysis of Affective Physiological State', *IEEE Transactions on Pattern Analysis and Machine Intelligence*, 23 (10), pp. 1175–1191.

Rolls, E.T. (1990) 'A Theory of Emotion, and Its Application to Understanding the Neural Basis of Emotion', *Cognition and Emotion*, 4 (3), pp. 161–190.

Roseman, I.J. (1984) 'Cognitive Determinants of Emotion: A Structural Theory', in Shaver, P (ed.) *Review of Personality and Social Psychology*. Beverley Hills, CA: Sage, pp. 11–36.

Rumelhart, D.E., McClelland, J.L., and Group, P.R. (1988) *Parallel Distributed Processing*, vol. 1. Piscataway, NJ: IEEE.

Russell, J.A. and Barrett, L.F. (1999) 'Core Affect, Prototypical Emotional Episodes, and Other Things Called Emotion: Dissecting the Elephant', *Journal of Personality and Social Psychology*, 76 (5), pp. 805–819.

Rutledge, R.B. et al. (2015) 'Dopaminergic Modulation of Decision Making and Subjective Well-Being', *Journal of Neuroscience*, 35 (27), pp. 9811–9822.

Sanfey, A.G. et al. (2003) 'The Neural Basis of Economic Decision-making in the Ultimatum Game', *Science*, 300 (5626), pp. 1755–1758.

Schachter, S. and Singer, J.E. (1962) 'Cognitive, Social, and Physiological Determinants of Emotional State', *Psychological Review*, 69 (5), pp. 379–399.

Schiller, D. et al. (2010) 'Preventing the Return of Fear in Humans Using Reconsolidation Update Mechanisms', *Nature*, 463 (7277), pp. 49–53.

Schwartenbeck, P. et al. (2015) 'Optimal Inference with Suboptimal Models: Addiction and Active Bayesian Inference', *Medical Hypotheses*, 84 (2), pp. 109–117.

Scoville, W.B. and Milner, B. (1957) 'Loss of Recent Memory after Bilateral Hippocampal Lesions', *Journal of Neurology, Neurosurgery and Psychiatry*, 20 (1), pp. 11–21.

Seth, A. (2013) 'Interoceptive Inference, Emotion, and the Embodied Self', *Trends in Cognitive Sciences*, 17 (11), pp. 565–573.

Seth, A.K. (2014) 'The Cybernetic Bayesian Brain', in Metszinger, T. and Windt, J.M. (eds.) *Open MIND*. Frankfurt am Main: MIND Group.

Seth, A.K. and Friston, K.J. (2016) 'Active Interoceptive Inference and the Emotional Brain', *Philosophical Transactions of the Royal Society B*, 371 (1708), 20160007.

Shackman, A.J. et al. (2011) 'The Integration of Negative Affect, Pain and Cognitive Control in the Cingulate Cortex', *Nature Review Neuroscience*, 12 (3), pp. 154–167.

Sinha, R. and Parsons, O.A. (1996) 'Multivariate Response Patterning of Fear and Anger', *Cognition and Emotion*, 10 (2), pp. 173–198.

Spitzer, M. et al. (2007) 'The Neural Signature of Social Norm Compliance', *Neuron*, 56 (1), pp. 185–196.

Tranel, D. and Damasio, H. (1994) 'Neuroanatomical Correlates of Electrodermal Skin-Conductance Responses', *Psychophysiology*, 31 (5), pp. 427–438.

Tsakiris, M. and Critchley, H. (2016) 'Interoception beyond Homeostasis: Affect, Cognition and Mental Health', *Philosophical Transactions of the Royal Society B: Biological Sciences*, 371 (1708), pp. 1–6.

Xiang, T., Lohrenz, T., and Montague, P.R. (2013) 'Computational Substrates of Norms and Their Violations during Social Exchange', *Journal of Neuroscience*, 33 (3), pp. 1099–1108.

33

COMPUTATIONAL PSYCHIATRY

Stefan Brugger and Matthew Broome

Introduction

Inspired by the explanatory power of computational modeling in basic cognitive neuroscience (Schultz et al., 1997; Behrens et al., 2007; Rao and Ballard, 1999; Dayan and Daw, 2008) researchers in the field of computational psychiatry aim to characterize mental disorder in terms of differences in information processing, specified explicitly and precisely in mathematical terms. In this chapter, we illustrate the power of this diverse emerging field using examples drawn from computational investigations of schizophrenia. In focusing on applications of the computational approach to the mind, our outlook will be somewhat more empirical than other, more theoretical chapters in this volume. We focus on two main approaches within computational psychiatry: reinforcement learning (Sutton and Barto, 1998) and predictive processing (Friston and Kiebel, 2009). Finally, we consider whether computational approaches can offer a plausible philosophical account of delusions.

Reinforcement learning refers to a family of approaches, currently popular in machine learning, which grew out of classical work on operant conditioning in the behaviorist tradition (Skinner, 1938), in which agents receive rewards that depend probabilistically on their behavior and learn by trial and error which behavior maximizes accumulated reward. Predictive processing is a framework in which all brain, nervous-system, and even whole-organismal function is conceived as acting to predict upcoming sensory signals as accurately as possible. It should be noted that reinforcement learning and predictive processing by no means encompass the range of techniques of computational psychiatry; nor are they incompatible: indeed, recent theoretical work in the predictive processing paradigm has focused on implementing schemes from decision theory and reinforcement learning (Friston, Daunizeau, and Kiebel, 2009; Friston et al., 2016). Indeed, the notion of prediction error is prominent in both paradigms. However, before we assess the application of these approaches to schizophrenia, we begin with a few general remarks about the field of computational psychiatry.

A computational psychiatrist seeking to model a psychopathological phenomenon of interest – hallucinations, anhedonia, anxiety, impulsiveness, delusions – and a number of mental functions wherein the putative abnormality is thought to lie – emotion, motivation, learning, decision making, reasoning, perception – asks the question: what problems are these functions involved in solving? What computations should an organism use to solve these problems in an *optimal* manner? The relevant notion of optimality has two elements: epistemic and pragmatic. By epistemic optimality, we mean simply the sense that a solution is 'correct', and results in adaptive behavior. Pragmatic optimality on the other hand refers to computational tractability – the need for a problem to be solved in reasonable time – there is thus an accuracy/complexity trade-off. This is the concept of bounded rationality (Simon, 1972; Dayan, 2014).

A computational model is then constructed to describe the problem, and the problem-solving process, in a mathematically rigorous way, allowing specific predictions as to the nature of the computational aberration underlying the clinical phenomenon. Problems and their computational solutions are drawn from a wide variety of sources, including engineering, economics, psychology, cybernetics, machine learning, and statistical science (Maia and Frank, 2011; Huys et al., 2015; Kishida, King-Casas, and Montague, 2010; Montague et al., 2012). This interdisciplinary eclecticism is, in our view, a key strength of the field, allowing mental function and dysfunction to be characterized with a breadth and depth as never before. Furthermore, selection between models need not be completely arbitrary as techniques exist for comparing the goodness-of-fit of competing behavioral and neural models (Stephan et al., 2009).

Computational psychiatry, like cognitive neuropsychiatry (Halligan and David, 2001), is explicitly normative, in that it seeks to describe psychopathology in terms of aberration from 'normal' cognition. However, unlike cognitive neuropsychiatry, in computational psychiatry there is a second, deeper source of normativity. Psychopathology is no longer solely defined in terms of deviations from healthy cognition, but also from 'optimal' cognition, as defined by (bounded) optimal solutions to computational problems. Note that we do not (although in practice many do) equate the two sources of normativity: a population manifesting psychopathology may solve a computational problem more accurately, although this may be sub-optimal from the perspective of individual survival and wellbeing. The absence of optimism-biases in depression (Sharot, 2011; Korn et al., 2014) and the reduction of the positive self-referential bias in social anxiety (Button et al., 2015; Button et al., 2012) are two examples of such a dissociation. Finally, there is much about brain function that remains mysterious, so computational psychiatry must develop hand-in-hand with basic computational neuroscience; findings in each discipline informing developments in the other. This pattern of 'co-production' of basic and clinical science is a common one, reminiscent of the interdependence in the development of cognitive and clinical neuropsychology (Shallice, 1988).

Reinforcement learning

Reward prediction error and dopamine

It is possible to model a diverse range of psychopathology in terms of alterations in learning of associations between stimuli and rewarding or aversive outcomes. These alterations are typically investigated in laboratory tasks in which participants aim to win monetary rewards, or avoid punishments, such as loss of reward or even mild electric shocks, by learning associations between such outcomes and otherwise innocuous stimuli. A key element of such tasks is that the stimulus-reward associations are *probabilistic* – such that on some occasions, a usually-rewarding stimulus may go unrewarded, and a usually non-rewarding stimulus may lead to a reward. For example, a subject may learn that blue circles are rewarded more often than red squares, so will tend to select these stimuli in order to maximize reward. Thus, a *reward-value* or *reward-expectation* for each stimulus is learned – the magnitude of the reward associated with the stimulus, multiplied by the probability of receiving the reward. So the reward-value of a stimulus that pays out £1 with a probability of 0.7 would be £0.70. The extent to which subjects change their estimation of the reward value of a stimulus in response to an error in their predictions about it is termed the learning rate. Thus, under a simple computational model (Sutton and Barto, 1998; Rescorla and Wagner, 1972):

$$v_{n+1} = v_n + \alpha\delta_n$$

$$\delta_n = r_n - v_n$$

Where v_n corresponds to the reward value of the stimulus on the nth trial, δ_n is the *reward prediction error* (RPE), the difference between reward value v_n and actual reward received r_n, and α is the learning rate (the extent to which subjects update v_n in response to RPE). Thus, in the limiting case where a stimulus is rewarded with a probability 1, v_n tends towards r_n as learning progresses. Models such as this may be fitted to the choices made by human subjects and parameters compared between groups of participants, such as patients and healthy controls.

How might such an approach be of interest to schizophrenia research? Schizophrenia is a disorder with three main clusters of symptoms. These include positive psychotic symptoms, such as hallucinations (typically auditory – 'hearing voices') and delusions (strongly held beliefs which are impervious to counter-evidence), and negative symptoms, emotional and motivational deficits such as anhedonia (inability to experience pleasure) and avolition (reduced motivation to perform activities). Patients with schizophrenia also frequently experience a marked cognitive dysfunction, with deficits in working and long-term memory and attentional processes.

So, what is the link to reward learning? Positive psychotic symptoms tend to respond to treatment with antipsychotic medications, which – for the most part – work by blocking dopamine D2 receptors. The dopamine system is known to be hyperactive in schizophrenia, particularly the mesolimbic dopamine system (Howes et al., 2012; Howes et al., 2013) – a system of dopaminergic projections running from the midbrain to the ventral striatum. Phasic fluctuations in the firing rate of these dopaminergic projections have been shown to bear a remarkable resemblance to RPEs generated under a temporal difference learning model (Schultz et al., 1997), leading to the characterization of striatal dopamine release as a 'teaching signal' (Schultz, 1998), with increased release indicating unpredicted reward. This drives the learning of new associations to better predict the future occurrence of reward.

An early study utilizing this approach in patients with psychosis is that of Murray and colleagues (Murray et al., 2008). Subjects chose between pairs of stimuli under two conditions: in the first, stimuli were differentially (probabilistically) associated with a monetary reward (as above); in the second, the differential association was with the presentation of an additional, non-rewarding stimulus. In computational psychiatry, such tasks are often carried out while subjects undergo some form of neuroimaging such as functional magnetic resonance imaging (fMRI). Parameters derived from a learning model fitted to each subject's behavioral responses may then be used as parametric regressors in analysis of the blood oxygen level-dependent (BOLD) fMRI signal ("model-based fMRI"). This procedure, frequently adopted with trial-by-trial RPE, allows for the localization of brain regions whose activity mirrors the trial-by-trial variation in these parameters. It also allows the strength of that association – the magnitude of the brain response to RPE – to be quantified and compared between individuals or groups.

Murray and colleagues found that, relative to controls, patients exhibited a diminished BOLD response to RPE in the rewarding condition, but an *enhanced* response (and faster relative reaction time) to prediction errors in the non-rewarding condition. The loci of these differential BOLD responses included the dopaminergic midbrain and the ventral striatum: the mesolimbic system, known to be hyperactive in schizophrenia. How does this relate to delusions and hallucinations? The presence of a prediction error signal in the absence of reward suggests that the brain is not filtering relevant (rewarding) from non-relevant stimuli – it is not effectively 'gating' stimuli (interpreted in the widest sense: thoughts, internal speech, other percepts) (Maia and Frank, 2017). And since prediction error drives learning, patients develop new – delusional – associations. This account has close parallels with another account of the role of dopamine in schizophrenia – that of aberrant (incentive) salience (Berridge and Robinson, 1998; Kapur, 2003). According to the salience model, dopamine release acts as an indicator of the importance of a stimulus, and the extent to which it demands attention and explanation (see Colombo (2014) for a further exploration of the differences between – and relative merits of – the RPE and incentive salience accounts of dopamine). It is worth noting that proponents of this theory argue that dopamine signals both 'positive' (i.e. reward-related) and 'negative' (punishment-related) salience. Thus, or so it is argued, dysregulated phasic dopamine release results in the attribution of aberrant salience to both reward-associated and aversive stimuli (Kapur, 2003). This is an important distinction, as the positive symptoms of psychosis, at least in those seen by services, generally (but not exclusively) relate to aversive beliefs and experiences (e.g. paranoid or persecutory delusions, derogatory auditory verbal hallucinations). We will return to this distinction later.

Striatal dopamine synthesis capacity has been found to be inversely correlated with BOLD response to RPE both in patients and in healthy subjects (Schlagenhauf et al., 2013; Boehme et al., 2015). Methamphetamine administration, which triggers dopamine release as well as activating dopamine receptors directly, also reduces striatal BOLD response to RPE (Bernacer et al., 2013). Thus, increased dopamine release, unrelated to reward, appears to reduce the signal-to-noise ratio of the RPE-related signal. In terms of salience, this leads to the erroneous attribution of salience to irrelevant stimuli (Kapur, 2003; Boehme et al., 2015), and/or reduced attribution of salience to relevant (reward-signaling) stimuli (Roiser et al., 2009; Smieskova et al., 2015).

Heterogeneity: model-based vs model-free learning

We now consider a more complex task involving contingency reversals (Schlagenhauf et al., 2014). Pairs of stimuli with different reward-contingencies (high probability of reward vs low probability of punishment; low probability of reward vs high probability of punishment) are presented sequentially; with subjects learning the appropriate choice for each pair to maximize reward and minimize punishment. However, the stimulus-reward contingencies are reversed within each pair one or more times over the course of the task, such that in order to maximize reward subjects must learn new associations as the task progresses. The learning process may now be described in a more complex manner, explicitly modeling changing beliefs as to the stimulus with higher reward value. This is "model-based" learning (Sutton and Barto, 1998). Unlike the "model-free" learning described previously, in which reward values – and subject choices – change gradually over time, when beliefs about the reward contingencies change, stimulus choices also change immediately in line with updated belief. People appear to make decisions employing a combination of both strategies (Wunderlich, Dayan, and Dolan, 2012), with contributions from each weighted according to factors including predicted accuracy (Daw, Niv, and Dayan, 2005), and (intriguingly) dopaminergic tone (Wunderlich, Smittenaar, and Dolan, 2012). Patients' performance was significantly poorer than that of controls, and consistent with the findings of Murray and colleagues (Murray et al., 2008), patients displayed a reduced ventral striatal BOLD response to model-free RPE. They also displayed reduced BOLD response signature of the model-based approach in this region. This latter technique, which fit the behavioral data better than the simpler RW approach for most subjects, also revealed a significantly increased 'tendency to switch' in the patient group, consistent with the

idea of increased sensory or cognitive noise resulting in a reduced value of additional information sampling (Moutoussis et al., 2011). Thus, patients displayed deficits in neural correlates of
both model-free *and* model-based reinforcement learning systems.

However, schizophrenia is a highly clinically and neurobiologically heterogeneous disorder
(Brugger and Howes, 2017). The patient group of Schlagenhauf et al. displayed a curious
heterogeneity in their employment of model-based learning, with this approach proving
a very poor fit (i.e. no better than chance) to the behavioral data for the subset of patients
with most severe positive symptoms. Furthermore, while both controls and the remaining
patients displayed a *prefrontal* signature of the model-based approach, this was abolished in
the severely affected patient subset. This finding has been replicated (Culbreth et al., 2016),
and may be related to a general cognitive impairment in the disorder, such as deficits in
working memory (Collins et al., 2014). A heterogeneous picture thus emerges: all patients
show reduced model-based and model-free striatal BOLD responses; a subgroup of patients
(with less severe symptoms) maintain *prefrontal* model-based BOLD responses. However, the
most severely affected patients do not appear to make use of a model-based strategy at all (as
indicated by the poor fit of these models) and are only able to utilize the simpler model-free
strategy. However, this account leaves some unanswered questions. If higher striatal dopamine biases striatal responses towards model-based learning in healthy subjects (Wunderlich,
Smittenaar, and Dolan, 2012), why do we see the abolition of the striatal model-based neural
signature in patients? It may be that there is a 'sweet-spot' for model-based learning, requiring
just enough dopamine (but not too much). Alternatively, it is possible that other abnormalities, such as cortical *hypodopaminergia* (Slifstein et al., 2015), NMDA receptor hypofunction
(Coyle, 2012), or other abnormalities in excitatory-inhibitory balance (Merritt et al., 2016;
Frankle et al., 2015) explain this deficit. The same may be true for subgroup differences in
cortical model-based learning signatures. There is certainly evidence for differential path-
ologies in schizophrenia (Egerton et al., 2012; Demjaha et al., 2014), but the relationship
with reinforcement learning deficits has not been established. Ultimately it is likely that any
explanation involves a number of factors (Reddy et al., 2016) operating at different levels of
analysis (Marr and Poggio, 1976).

Reward vs punishment: negative symptoms

In contrast to the wealth of findings of abnormal model-free reinforcement learning in the context of reward (Radua et al., 2015), patients with schizophrenia do not appear to differ greatly
from healthy controls in performance on loss-avoidance tasks (Waltz et al., 2007), and BOLD
responses RPE on such tasks appear unimpaired (Reinen et al., 2016). In a cleverly designed
study, Gold and colleagues (Gold et al., 2012) asked whether this performance asymmetry
might reflect the domination of a simpler, less flexible form of model-free RL than those we
have discussed thus far. They contrasted a model-free learning algorithm as previously described
(Watkins and Dayan, 1992), with a simpler algorithm, the so-called actor-critic model. A variety
of implementations of actor-critic learning have been proposed (Joel, Niv, and Ruppin, 2002),
but all share the feature that it is only the strength of association between stimulus and (positive)
RPE which is learned by the 'critic', rather than stimulus reward values itself. In effect, actor-
critic models learn to distinguish options that lead to better-than-average rewards from those
that lead to worse-than-average rewards but cannot compare the values of rewards directly. In
the task of Gold et al., subjects learned probabilistic associations between two pairs of stimuli.
In the first pair, one stimulus was weakly associated with monetary reward; the other strongly
associated with no reward. In the second pair, one stimulus was strongly associated with loss

of previously earned reward; the other strongly associated with safeguarding of such reward. Following learning, stimulus pairs were rearranged and subjects asked to pick from the new pairings.

Patients with severe negative symptoms – such as anhedonia (reduced or absent experience of pleasure), emotional blunting, and avolition (reduced motivation) – exhibited a selective deficit for learning stimulus-reward associations, but retained unimpaired loss-avoidance learning. Conversely, healthy controls exhibited greater accuracy in learning from rewards than from losses. Patients with low negative symptoms exhibited an intermediate pattern, with similar accuracy across conditions. The actor-critic model provided a better fit to behavior in the high negative symptom group relative to the other groups. Most notably, as predicted by this model, when stimuli were arranged into new pairs, only this group of patients failed to select the weakly rewarding stimulus over the strongly-safeguarding stimulus, despite the higher reward value of the former. This suggests that the dysfunction associated with negative symptoms is not (only) a reduced processing of RPE but (also) a failure to represent stimulus reward values. Neuroimaging correlates of such dysfunction have been reported (Gradin et al., 2011; Waltz et al., 2010). The relevance to negative symptoms, such as anhedonia, is clear. As Gold et al. state: "This is a reinforcement learning formula for avolition: patients are better able to learn actions that lead to the avoidance of punishing outcomes than they are to learn actions that lead to positive outcomes".

We now return to the aberrant salience hypothesis of schizophrenia. Recall that under this framework, rather than RPE, dopamine simply signals the motivational salience of a stimulus, regardless of valence (Berridge and Robinson, 1998). Thus, striatal hyperdopaminergia drives associative learning relating to aversive (as well as rewarding) stimuli, leading to symptoms such as paranoid or persecutory delusions, or derogatory auditory verbal hallucinations (Kapur, 2003). However, there is good evidence that dopamine release in the striatum does more than signal prediction error, reward-related or otherwise. Stimuli are processed by the brain in a distributed and hierarchical fashion, with computationally simpler processing reaching completion prior to more demanding processing (Schultz, 2016a; Hillyard, Teder-Sälejärvi, and Münte, 1998). Recent work on the temporal dynamics of dopamine neuron firing suggests that stimulus-driven increases in firing follow a multiphasic pattern, with an early peak that correlates with basic stimulus intensity, followed by a second, larger reward-related peak – or trough, in the case of less-than-predicted reward or loss – conveying more complex, RPE-related information (Fiorillo, Song, and Yun, 2013). (The difference in latency is more readily apparent with stimuli which require lengthier basic sensory processing prior to evaluation of their reward value (Nomoto et al., 2010).) The size of this early peak is modulated by reward *potential*, which depends on a number of factors related to the prior probability that the stimulus will convey reward-related information. These include intensity (a loud noise elicits greater response than a quiet noise), novelty (a stimulus with unexpected basic sensory properties elicits a greater response than a frequently occurring one), as well as the reward-density of the environment (an identical stimulus elicits a greater response in environments where reward frequently occurs) (Schultz, 2016a; Fiorillo et al., 2013; Kobayashi and Schultz, 2014).

Schulz argues that this transitory early peak explains the apparent dopamine response to aversive stimuli. Thus, rather than signaling salience (regardless of valence), the striatal dopamine release seen in response to aversive stimuli is in fact the early response to the (sensory or physical) magnitude of a stimulus, which occurs prior to reward-related information becoming available, with later dopamine release in response to RPE. Indeed, recent work has demonstrated that negative or aversive RPE is signaled by another brain region, the lateral habenula, whose neurons are largely non-dopaminergic (Lawson et al., 2014; Hong et al., 2011). Thus, argues

Schultz, the hypothesis that aberrant salience in schizophrenia is driven by exaggerated dopaminergic signaling "can probably now be laid to rest" (Schultz, 2016b).

However, it is possible that the balance in dopamine's different roles is upset in psychosis. We know that ventral striatal activity in response to RPE is reduced in schizophrenia, but what about response to expected rewards? Morris and colleagues (Morris et al., 2012) used a reinforcement learning paradigm similar to many of the ones examined previously, modeling subject responses to expected and unexpected rewards, and expected and unexpected omissions of reward. As well as blunted responses to both unexpected rewards (reduced RPE signal), and unexpected omissions (reduced negative RPE signal), they found exaggerated ventral striatal responses to expected rewards (excessive activation) and also to expected omissions (excessive *deactivation*). This shows that the finding of a reduced prediction error signal, often straightforwardly attributed to reduced response to unpredicted reward, can in fact be attributed to both this and an *increased* baseline response to accurately predicted rewards, consistent with much work on failures of sensory mismatch processing in schizophrenia (Neuhaus et al., 2013; Umbricht and Krljes, 2005). It is to computational work relating to this phenomenon – of increased prediction error signaling in general (i.e. unrelated to the reward associated with a stimulus) – to which we now turn.

Predictive processing: delusions and hallucinations

The notion of prediction, and the signaling of errors of prediction, is central to a family of computational approaches to brain function that radically reconceptualize the processes of perception, action, belief formation, and learning – Predictive Processing (PP) (Clark, 2016; Hohwy, 2015). PP belongs to the 'Bayesian brain' tradition, a family of approaches to brain function premised on the assumption that the brain represents beliefs about the world (and their uncertainty) using probability distributions, which are updated according to the rules of (approximate) Bayesian inference (Dayan and Hinton, 1996; Knill and Pouget, 2004). Within the PP framework, the goal of the brain is to minimize the differences between predicted and actual sensory input (Friston, 2005; Friston, 2009). It does this by constructing a hierarchical generative model of the (hidden) causes of this input, which is continuously updated to minimize its prediction error. According to PP, populations of neurons combine predictions, transmitted from hierarchically higher populations, with signals derived from the sensory data transmitted from below. This yields a *prediction error*, which is transmitted back up the hierarchy to modify higher-level expectations. The activities of the neuronal populations at the intermediate level are themselves modified by ascending prediction errors from the levels below, and so on, right down to the level of the sensory transducers. In contrast to the traditional account of perception as (hierarchical) bottom-up feature-detection, in this implementation of a predictive coding scheme (Rao and Ballard, 1999), perception arises from this dynamic interaction of top-down prediction and bottom-up prediction error.

Thus, imagine I am awoken in the night by a loud noise. Under the empiricist, traditional model, vibrations of basilar membrane in the Organ of Corti are transduced by inner hair cells into electrical signals corresponding to the contributions of different frequencies to the incoming sound. These electrical signals are transmitted via subcortical nuclei, where binaural computations enable localization of the signal in space, to the primary auditory cortex, where individual frequencies are processed, and on to other regions of the brain where detection of speech, music perception, and other high-level features occurs. Thus, at the top of this processing hierarchy, the perception of a baby crying, or of music from a passing car, is assembled from lower-level auditory information. Now, consider the PP account: my brain immediately attempts to predict the cause of this sudden awakening. From experience (priors), the most likely cause is the cry of my hungry six-month-old daughter. Signals corresponding to this expectation descend the hierarchy and this is what I initially perceive. But wait! At the lowest level of the hierarchy, predictions of inner hair cell activity engendered by this expectation differ markedly from their actual activities. Thus a prediction error is generated, which "carries the news" (Clark, 2016) progressively up the cortical hierarchy. Thus my percept changes – I realize that I was mistaken: a car playing loud music has just passed by our house, and it is not my daughter crying. I breathe a sigh of relief and return to sleep.

However, it remains to be specified exactly where in the hierarchy a prediction should be updated in response to a prediction error. The solution adopted by PP is that predictions are updated in proportion to their relative uncertainty, and in inverse proportion to the uncertainty in the prediction error. Thus, if I am highly certain that there are no cars outside (perhaps because I am staying in a remote mountain area without roads), and the sound is quite clearly that of a baby, I might update my belief as to the current location of the baby. However, if I am less certain in my beliefs about the absence of cars (say I am in a less remote environment), and the noise itself is rather more indistinct, I may leave unchanged my belief about the location of the baby and instead update my belief about the presence of the passing car. In PP, the precision (inverse of uncertainty) of a prediction is theorized to correspond to the synaptic gain of the neural units encoding the prediction (Feldman and Friston, 2010). It is here that the putative inferential deficit in schizophrenia is hypothesized to occur, with a variety of neurotransmitter and receptor abnormalities bestowing abnormally high precision on prediction errors at lower relative to higher levels of the hierarchy (Adams et al., 2013; Adams, Brown, and Friston, 2015; Adams, Huys, and Roiser, 2015). In addition to the role of striatal hyperdopaminergia in increasing the precision of low-level prediction errors, they point to further abnormalities linked to reduced high-level (prefrontal) precision. These may include inhibitory interneuron (Gonzalez-Burgos and Lewis, 2012; Volman, Behrens, and Sejnowski, 2011; Nakazawa et al., 2012) and NMDA receptor hypofunction (Olney and Farber, 1995; Corlett et al., 2011), as well as *reduced* prefrontal dopamine release (Slifstein et al., 2015). Frith and Friston (2013) demonstrate how such an imbalance may lead to a failure of inference with the following memorable analogy:

> Consider what might happen if something goes wrong with the fancy system in my car that signals problems. In particular, assume that an error warning light is unduly sensitive to fluctuations in the engine's performance from normal levels. This would correspond to a pathologically highly precision at the sensory level, leading to a dashboard warning light that is almost continuously illuminated. I am led to falsely believe that there is indeed something wrong with the engine. I take my car to the garage and they report that nothing is wrong. However, the light is still on and keeps on signaling an error. So, this leads me to falsely believe that the garage is incompetent. I report them to the "good garage guide" who investigate and conclude that the garage is not incompetent. Now I believe that the "good garage guide" is corrupt.
>
> *(Frith and Friston, 2013)*

Adams et al. (2013) argue that a number of phenomena associated with schizophrenia, including delusions and hallucinations, but also catatonia and subtle neurological abnormalities (Chan et al., 2010) are manifestations of this same underlying imbalance of precision. They built a computational simulation of a neurobiologically plausible predictive coding scheme and exposed it to various stimuli, reproducing classical electrophysiological effects such as P300 and mismatch negativity EEG components. They then modeled the hypothesized 'trait' deficits in schizophrenia by reducing the precision of prediction errors at higher levels of the model. The resulting simulations reproduced differences in mismatch negativity and P300, as well as abnormalities of oculomotor smooth pursuit (of partially-occluded stimuli) seen in the disorder (O'Driscoll and Callahan, 2008). Furthermore, this 'lesioned' model also reproduced a performance *advantage* seen in patients (Hong, Avila, and Thaker, 2005) in tracking *unpredictably* moving stimuli.

Most interestingly of all, Adams et al. endowed their predictive coding simulation with active inference (Friston et al., 2010) – motor control under PP. In contrast to the classical formulation, where movement results from the issue of motor commands, in active inference movement is achieved by a prediction of the proprioceptive consequences of movement (Adams, Shipp, and Friston, 2013). These predictions elicit sensory prediction errors indicative of the fact that the movement has not (yet) occurred. In active inference, instead of updating the prediction in response to the error, reflex arcs are activated to update the state of the world in order to eliminate the prediction errors. Thus, movement itself is just a special case of prediction-error minimization, in which – instead of updating the prediction – the state of the world itself is changed. However, in order for this to occur, the precision of proprioceptive prediction errors must be temporarily down-weighted, to allow the prediction of movement to predominate. This, argue proponents of PP, provides a principled explanation for sensory attenuation (Blakemore et al., 2000; Brown et al., 2013) – the phenomenon in which self-produced stimuli are perceived as less intense than identical externally produced stimuli. This is the basis of the force-matching illusion: wherein subjects endeavor to produce a force equal in magnitude to one externally applied to them. Subjects invariably over-estimate the force required – due to attenuation of the sensations arising from self-produced movement (Shergill, 2003). However, patients with schizophrenia with prominent positive symptoms do not experience the force-matching illusion (Shergill et al., 2005). This absence of sensory attenuation of self-produced stimuli has been hypothesized to be involved in the etiology of delusions of control and auditory hallucinations (Pynn and DeSouza, 2013; Shergill, White et al., 2014; Ford et al., 2007; Lemaitre, Luyat, and Lafargue, 2016).

Adams et al. reproduced the force-matching illusion using their active inference simulation. To model schizophrenia, they then 'lesioned' the model by reducing its ability to attenuate the precision of sensory prediction errors. The result was that the model produced no action at all in response to external force. The reason for this is clear: without sensory attenuation, the prediction of movement is updated to reflect (actual) lack of movement – the highly precise sensory prediction error predominates. Adams et al. suggest that this provides a principled account of features of the catatonic state, arguing:

> Because there are no predictions about proprioceptive changes, there is a consequent akinesia. This state is reminiscent of the catatonic symptoms of schizophrenia such as immobility, mutism, catalepsy and waxy flexibility, in which the patient may maintain a fixed posture for a long time, even though (in the case of waxy flexibility) their limbs can be moved easily by someone else.
>
> *(Adams et al., 2013)*

However, the majority of patients with schizophrenia do not experience catatonia. The reason for this, argue Adams et al., is a compensatory increase in the precision of the prediction of the proprioceptive consequences of movement (technically an increase in the precision of high-level prediction errors), such that this is now more precise than the low-level sensory prediction errors, with resultant movement fulfilling the prediction. According to this model, high- and low-level prediction errors are excessively precise relative to those at intermediate levels of the hierarchy. It is here that this thus far highly speculative account gains a degree of face validity. In addition to allowing movement, this instance of the model – with increased precision at both high and low levels – does not display the force-matching illusion. This is because it still has access to high-precision information about its present proprioceptive state, enabling the accurate estimation of the force it applies. However, the model makes a bizarre inference: it infers the presence of an external force acting in opposition to its own movement-inducing prediction. Adams et al. state:

> The reason for this false inference or delusion is simple: action is driven by proprio-
> ceptive prediction errors that always report less force than that predicted. However,
> when these prediction errors are very precise they need to be explained – and can
> only be explained by falsely inferring an opposing exogenous force … This false infer-
> ence could be interpreted as a delusion.
>
> *(Adams et al., 2013)*

This then is the PP account of delusions of control. A similar two-stage story may be constructed for the phenomena of thought blocking and thought insertion: a failure of sensory attenuation permitting inner or imagined speech acts (Gregory, 2016) that is overcome by increased preci-sion at a higher level, leading to the inference that the thought was externally caused. We can construct an analogous account of auditory verbal hallucinations: as misattributed inner or imagined speech, whereby failure of sensory attenuation (Ford et al., 2007) and compensatory increase in high-level precision leads to the inference of an external speaker (Shergill, Brammer et al., 2014).

Delusions explained?

Finally, we consider whether a predictive processing account is able to successfully account – in principle – for the formation and maintenance of delusions. A number of authors in recent years have proposed increased prediction error concerning normally well-predicted (including self-generated) stimuli as an alternative to the influential two-factor account of delusion (Coltheart, 2007). According to the two-factor account, two distinct deficits are required in order for a delusional belief to develop. The first, responsible for the content of the delusion, is an abnormal experience or perception, while the second is a deficit in the reasoning process leading to the adoption and maintenance of a delusional explanation of this experience (Coltheart, 2007). For example, in the classical application of this theory to the Capgras delusion, the first factor is the lack of affective response to a familiar face (Ellis et al., 1997), for example of a loved one. The second is an error of reasoning that allows an implausible belief – in this case that the person has been replaced by an imposter – to be adopted (Ellis and Young, 1990; Coltheart, 2007). The two-factor theory is often contrasted to the earlier theories in which the delusional belief is a rational explanation of a profoundly unusual perceptual experience (Maher, 1974).

One consequence of adopting a PP approach to brain function is that the dualism between 'lower' perceptual states and 'higher' intentional states (such as beliefs and desires), breaks down. Under PP, all such states are hierarchically arranged hypotheses about the most probable causes of the activity of sensory transducers. Following Helmholtz, perception is thus a variety of infer-ence and not a special category cognitive process of its own. The idea here is that aberrations of belief formation at multiple levels of the cerebral hierarchy (both at 'lower' perceptual levels and at levels involving 'higher' intentional states) are explicable by the same kinds of abnormalities of probabilistic inference (Adams et al., 2013). Thus, rather requiring two separate deficits, as under the two-factor account, the process of delusion-formation under PP corresponds to a single kind of deficit in the hierarchical cascade of inference about upcoming sensory input (Corlett and Fletcher, 2015; Fletcher and Frith, 2009). The delusion itself is a high-level belief of unusual precision, formed in response to abnormally precise sensory prediction errors (Adams et al., 2013; Corlett et al., 2007).

Does the PP/prediction error account of delusions succeed in reducing the two-factor account into a single deficit, in which a second "coincidental" (Fletcher and Frith, 2009) explanatory factor is not required? Two objections to this claim have been proposed (Miyazono, Bortolotti, and Broome, 2015). The first uses the Capgras delusion – the belief that a physically identical imposter has replaced a close family member or friend – as an instructive example, and is the familiar dissociation argument against the plausibility of a one-factor account of the delusion (Davies et al., 2001; Coltheart, Langdon, and McKay, 2011; Coltheart, 2007). People who have sustained damage to regions of the ventromedial prefrontal cortex (VMPFC) also fail to show an affective response to familiar faces (Tranel, Damasio, and Damasio, 1995). However, they do not go on to develop the Capgras delusion. If, as argued by Corlett (Corlett et al., 2010), the Capgras delusion arises in reaction to affective prediction errors elicited by this profoundly unexpected lack of affective response, then it should not be possible to dissociate the two phenomena. Miyazono et al. note one potential response to this line of argument: that the magnitude of the prediction errors in such cases may not have reached the threshold for delusion development (Miyazono et al., 2015; McKay, 2012). We may elaborate on this explanation by suggesting that in such circumstances it is not the magnitude *per se* but rather the *precision* of the prediction errors that lead to the development of the delusion. Patients who have sustained structural damage to the VMPFC will nevertheless have an intact system for the setting of synaptic gain, without the numerous physiological abnormalities associated with schizophrenia and (*ex hypothesi*) other sufferers of the Capgras delusions. While the experience may be a highly unusual and distressing one, eliciting prediction errors of some magnitude, it will not be able to completely overpower other beliefs as to the plausibility of imposter-replacement. The prediction errors will eventually be largely explained away, perhaps through the adoption of new (non-delusional) beliefs concerning the effects of head injury. However, in cases where a delusion develops, alteration of precision which exerts a multiplicative effect, will ensure small residual prediction errors will continue to exert a large influence over the inference process, leading (or so the theory goes) to delusion formation.

This brings us to the second objection to the PP account of delusions. This is that of delusion maintenance. One candidate for the second factor in the two-factor delusions is something akin to a confirmation bias – a selective disregard of new evidence. This bias would clearly explain the fixity of delusional beliefs, once formed. However, under the PP account a delusional belief should never reach fixity. Aberrant prediction error signalling does not cease once a delusion is adopted. However, prediction errors now indicate that the model of the world incorporating the delusion is incorrectly updated. Thus, it seems that a delusion should never achieve fixity and should be a series of different beliefs, none held with particular strength or duration. Miyazono

It is hypothesised, in the theory, that prediction-error signals are impaired with delusions. This presumably does not suddenly come to an end once a delusional hypothesis is adopted [as the neurobiological abnormality remains other words, prediction-error signals will remain excessive even after the adoption of delusional hypotheses. But this seems to predict that delusions, after adoption, will be unstable instead of firmly maintained.

(Miyazono et al., 2015, pp. 42–43)

This picture fits much better with descriptions of the early phases of the development of delusions – the *trema* or delusional mood of Conrad, rather than the *apophony* (Conrad, 2012). However, this argument conflates the *magnitude* of a prediction error with its *precision*. We must note that, in the case of the Capgras delusion at least, prediction errors are not occurring at random: they all relate to the same phenomenon: the lack of an emotional response to familiar faces. The new (delusional) high-level belief reflects this. We have argued that the reason not all people with VMPFC damage (and consequent reduced emotional response to familiar faces) develop the Capgras delusion is that the factor driving its development is not the presence of prediction errors of excessive magnitude *per se*, but rather the neurobiological abnormalities determining their (excessive) precision. So, once the delusional belief has been fully adopted, the magnitude of the prediction errors drops to zero, even if the underlying pathophysiology remains unchanged. Were the individual to, for whatever reason, start to entertain an alternative explanation, highly precise prediction errors to that alternative high-level belief would once again be generated, leading to a re-adoption of the delusional explanation.

Can an analogous argument apply to other types of delusion? Let us consider delusions of control – the belief that one's thoughts, feelings, or actions are controlled by an outside force or agency. Here, if we accept the active inference account of motor action, the primary deficit is a failure of the normal attenuation of sensory prediction errors that allow proprioceptive predictions to drive action, which is overcome by a compensatory increase in precision of the (proprioceptive) prediction. Recall that precision is simply the inverse of the variance of a probability distribution, and quantifies the degree of certainty in a prediction (or, indeed, prediction error). What does it mean to say that we have absolute certainty (i.e. a high precision prediction) that an event or upcoming movement will occur? If this is a voluntarily willed action, there is always the possibility that we could decide not to act. But this possibility does not arise if our actions (or thoughts) are being controlled by an outside agency. Thus, according to PP, this delusional high-level belief is formed as a consequence of unduly precise prediction-error signaling in the context of action. This is analogous to the case of the Capgras delusion: prediction errors occur not because of a lack of emotional response to familiar faces, but simply because the prediction that drives movement is, in a sense, fictive (with respect to the present state of the body) (Friston et al., 2012). As in cases where the Capgras delusion develops, and perhaps due to similar neurobiological dysfunction, they are unduly precise. And finally, the resulting high-level belief is driven not by the need to explain away these prediction errors but by the necessity of movement. However, the overly-precise sensory prediction errors continue to occur once the delusional belief comes into existence. Should they not lead to this belief being replaced by a succession of others? The answer is clearly 'no': the belief accords perfectly with the prediction errors. Voluntary movement still occurs; attenuation of sensory prediction error does not: this accords perfectly with the belief that movement is externally controlled. The prediction errors support the maintenance of the delusional belief, which explains the persistence of (precise) prediction errors during voluntary movement.

Conclusion

We have presented a brief and by no means exhaustive sketch of the diversity of approaches of computational psychiatry. We have surveyed model-based and model-free approaches to reinforcement learning deficits in schizophrenia and examined the central role of dopamine in these processes, and how abnormalities in the dopamine system in schizophrenia are linked to these deficits. We have considered the asymmetry of learning to maximize reward and learning to avoid punishment, and the link to negative symptoms associated with schizophrenia, particularly apathy and amotivation. We then considered the developing framework of predictive processing and explored the way in which it radically reimagines perception and action, and how the insights of this predictive processing may provide a unifying framework for understanding the disparate perceptual, neuropsychological, and doxastic abnormalities in schizophrenia. Finally, we have considered the potential of the predictive processing account to provide a full conceptual account of the emergence and the maintenance of delusions, arguing that at least some delusions are explicable under this framework (e.g. the Capgras delusion, delusions of control).

References

Adams, R.A., Brown, H.R., and Friston, K.J. (2015) 'Bayesian Inference, Predictive Coding and Delusions', *Avant*, 5 (3), pp. 51–88.

Adams, R.A., Huys, Q.J.M., and Roiser, J.P. (2015) 'Computational Psychiatry: Towards a Mathematically Informed Understanding of Mental Illness', *Journal of Neurology, Neurosurgery, and Psychiatry*. Available at: DOI:10.1136/jnnp-2015-310737.

Adams, R.A., Shipp, S., and Friston, K.J. (2013) 'Predictions Not Commands: Active Inference in the Motor System', *Brain Structure and Function*, 218 (3), pp. 611–643.

Adams, R.A. et al. (2013) 'The Computational Anatomy of Psychosis', *Frontiers in Psychiatry*, 4, art. 47.

Behrens, T.E.J. et al. (2007) 'Learning the Value of Information in an Uncertain World', *Nature Neuroscience*, 10 (9), pp. 1214–1221.

Bernacer, J. et al. (2013) 'Methamphetamine-induced Disruption of Frontostriatal Reward Learning Signals: Relation to Psychotic Symptoms', *American Journal of Psychiatry*, 170 (11), pp. 1326–1334.

Berridge, K.C. and Robinson, T.E. (1998) 'What Is the Role of Dopamine in Reward: Hedonic Impact, Reward Learning, or Incentive Salience?', *Brain Research Reviews*, 28 (3), pp. 309–369.

Blakemore, S.-J. et al. (2000) 'Why Can't You Tickle Yourself?', *NeuroReport*, 11 (11), pp. R11–R16.

Boehme, R. et al. (2015) 'Aberrant Salience Is Related to Reduced Reinforcement Learning Signals and Elevated Dopamine Synthesis Capacity in Healthy Adults', *Journal of Neuroscience*, 35 (28), pp. 10103–10111.

Brown, H. et al. (2013) 'Active Inference, Sensory Attenuation and Illusions', *Cognitive Processing*, 14 (4), pp. 411–427.

Brugger, S.P. and Howes, O.D. (2017) 'Heterogeneity and Homogeneity of Regional Brain Structure in Schizophrenia: A Meta-analysis', *JAMA Psychiatry*, 74 (11), pp. 1104–1111.

Button, K.S. et al. (2012) 'Social Inference and Social Anxiety: Evidence of a Fear-congruent Self-referential Learning Bias', *Journal of Behavior Therapy and Experimental Psychiatry*, 43 (4), pp. 1082–1087.

Button, K.S. et al. (2015) 'Fear of Negative Evaluation Biases Social Evaluation Inference: Evidence from a Probabilistic Learning Task', *PLoS ONE*, 10 (4). Available at: DOI:10.1371/journal. pone.0119456.

Chan, R.C.K. et al. (2010) 'Neurological Soft Signs in Schizophrenia: A Meta-analysis', *Schizophrenia Bulletin*, 36 (6), pp. 1089–1104.

Clark, A. (2016) *Surfing Uncertainty: Prediction, Action, and the Embodied Mind*. Oxford: Oxford University Press.

Collins, A.G.E. et al. (2014) 'Working Memory Contributions to Reinforcement Learning Impairments in Schizophrenia', *The Journal of Neuroscience*, 34 (41), pp. 13747–13756.

Colombo, M. (2014) 'Deep and Beautiful: The Reward Prediction Error Hypothesis of Dopamine', *Studies in History and Philosophy of Science Part C: Studies in History and Philosophy of Biological and Biomedical Sciences*, 45 (1), pp. 57–67.

Coltheart, M. (2007) 'Cognitive Neuropsychiatry and Delusional Belief', *Quarterly Journal of Experimental Psychology*, 60 (8), pp. 1041–1062.

Coltheart, M., Langdon, R., and McKay, R. (2011) 'Delusional Belief', *Annual Review of Psychology*, 62 (1), pp. 271–298.

Conrad, K. (2012) 'Beginning Schizophrenia: Attempt for a Gestalt-Analysis of Delusion', in Broome, M.R. et al. (eds.) *The Maudsley Reader in Phenomenological Psychiatry*. Cambridge, UK: Cambridge University Press, pp. 158–164.

Corlett, P.R. and Fletcher, P.C. (2015) 'Delusions and Prediction Error: Clarifying the Roles of Behavioural and Brain Responses', *Cognitive Neuropsychiatry*, 20 (2), pp. 95–105.

Corlett, P.R. et al. (2007) 'Disrupted Prediction-Error Signal in Psychosis: Evidence for an Associative Account of Delusions', *Brain*, 130 (9), pp. 2387–2400.

Corlett, P.R. et al. (2010) 'Toward a Neurobiology of Delusions', *Progress in Neurobiology*, 92 (3), pp. 345–369.

Corlett, P.R. et al. (2011) 'Glutamatergic Model Psychoses: Prediction Error, Learning, and Inference', *Neuropsychopharmacology*, 36 (1), pp. 294–315.

Coyle, J.T. (2012) 'NMDA Receptor and Schizophrenia: A Brief History', *Schizophrenia Bulletin*, 38 (5), pp. 920–926.

Culbreth, A.J. et al. (2016) 'Reduced Model-Based Decision-Making in Schizophrenia', *Journal of Abnormal Psychology*, 125 (6), pp. 777–787.

Davies, M. et al. (2001) 'Monothematic Delusions: Towards a Two-Factor Account', *Philosophy, Psychiatry, and Psychology*, 8 (2), pp. 133–158.

Daw, N.D., Niv, Y., and Dayan, P. (2005) 'Uncertainty-based Competition between Prefrontal and Dorsolateral Striatal Systems for Behavioral Control', *Nature Neuroscience*, 8 (12), pp. 1704–1711.

Dayan, P. (2014) 'Rationalizable Irrationalities of Choice', *Topics in Cognitive Science*, 6 (2), pp. 204–228.

Dayan, P. and Daw, N.D. (2008) 'Connections between Computational and Neurobiological Perspectives on Decision Making', *Cognitive, Affective, and Behavioral Neuroscience*, 8 (4), pp. 429–453.

Dayan, P. and Hinton, G.E. (1996) 'Varieties of Helmholtz Machine', *Neural Networks*, 9 (8), pp. 1385–1403.

Demjaha, A. et al. (2014) 'Antipsychotic Treatment Resistance in Schizophrenia Associated with Elevated Glutamate Levels but Normal Dopamine Function', *Biological Psychiatry*, 75 (5), pp. e11–e13.

Egerton, A. et al. (2012) 'Anterior Cingulate Glutamate Levels Related to Clinical Status Following Treatment in First-Episode Schizophrenia', *Neuropsychopharmacology*, 37 (11), pp. 2515–2521.

Ellis, H.D. and Young, A.W. (1990) 'Accounting for Delusional Misidentifications', *British Journal of Psychiatry*, 157 (2), pp. 239–248.

Ellis, H.D. et al. (1997) 'Reduced Autonomic Responses to Faces in Capgras Delusion', *Proceedings of the Royal Society B*, 264 (1384), pp. 1085–1092.

Feldman, H. and Friston, K.J. (2010) 'Attention, Uncertainty, and Free-Energy', *Frontiers in Human Neuroscience*, 4, art. 215.

Fiorillo, C.D., Song, M.R., and Yun, S.R. (2013) 'Multiphasic Temporal Dynamics in Responses of Midbrain Dopamine Neurons to Appetitive and Aversive Stimuli', *The Journal of Neuroscience*, 33 (11), pp. 4710–4725.

Fletcher, P.C. and Frith, C.D. (2009) 'Perceiving Is Believing: A Bayesian Approach to Explaining the Positive Symptoms of Schizophrenia', *Nature Reviews Neuroscience*, 10 (1), pp. 48–58.

Ford, J.M. et al. (2007) 'Synch before You Speak: Auditory Hallucinations in Schizophrenia', *American Journal of Psychiatry*, 164 (3), pp. 458–466.

Frankle, W.G. et al. (2015) 'In Vivo Measurement of GABA Transmission in Healthy Subjects and Schizophrenia Patients', *American Journal of Psychiatry*, 172 (11), pp. 1148–1159.

Friston, K. (2005) 'A Theory of Cortical Responses', *Philosophical Transactions of the Royal Society of London B*, 360 (1456), pp. 815–836.

Friston, K. (2009) 'The Free-Energy Principle: A Rough Guide to the Brain?', *Trends in Cognitive Sciences*, 13 (7), pp. 293–301.

Friston, K., Daunizeau, J., and Kiebel, S.J. (2009) 'Reinforcement Learning or Active Inference?', *PLoS ONE*, 4 (7), art. e6421.

Frith, C. and Friston, K. (2013) 'False Perceptions and False Beliefs: Understanding Schizophrenia', in Battro, A.M., Dehaene, S., Sánchez Sorondo, M., and Singer, W.J. (eds.) *Neuroscience and the Human Person: New Perspectives on Human Activities*. Vatican City: The Pontifical Academy of Sciences, pp. 134–149.

Friston, K. and Kiebel, S. (2009) 'Predictive Coding under the Free-Energy Principle', *Philosophical Transactions of the Royal Society B*, 364 (1521), pp. 1211–1221.

Friston, K.J. et al. (2010) 'Action and Behavior: A Free-Energy Formulation', *Biological Cybernetics*, 102 (3), pp. 227–260.

Friston, K. et al. (2012) 'Perceptions as Hypotheses: Saccades as Experiments', *Frontiers in Psychology*, 3, art. 151.

Friston, K. et al. (2016) 'Active Inference and Learning', *Neuroscience and Biobehavioral Reviews*, 68, pp. 862–879.

Gold, J.M. et al. (2012) 'Negative Symptoms and the Failure to Represent the Expected Reward Value of Actions: Behavioral and Computational Modeling Evidence', *Archives of General Psychiatry*, 69 (2), pp. 129–138.

Gonzalez-Burgos, G. and Lewis, D.A. (2012) 'NMDA Receptor Hypofunction, Parvalbumin-Positive Neurons, and Cortical Gamma Oscillations in Schizophrenia', *Schizophrenia Bulletin*, 38 (5), pp. 950–957.

Gradin, V.B. et al. (2011) 'Expected Value and Prediction Error Abnormalities in Depression and Schizophrenia', *Brain*, 134 (6), pp. 1751–2764.

Gregory, D. (2016) 'Inner Speech, Imagined Speech, and Auditory Verbal Hallucinations', *Review of Philosophy and Psychology*, 7 (3), pp. 653–673.

Halligan, P.W. and David, A.S. (2001) 'Cognitive Neuropsychiatry: Towards a Scientificpsychopathology', *Nature Reviews Neuroscience*, 2 (3), pp. 209–215.

Hillyard, S.A., Teder-Sälejärvi, W.A., and Münte, T.F. (1998) 'Temporal Dynamics of Early Perceptual Processing', *Current Opinion in Neurobiology*, 8 (2), pp. 202–210.

Hohwy, J. (2015) *The Predictive Mind*. Oxford: Oxford University Press.

Hong, L.E., Avila, M.T., and Thaker, G.K. (2005) 'Response to Unexpected Target Changes during Sustained Visual Tracking in Schizophrenic Patients', *Experimental Brain Research*, 165 (1), pp. 125–131.

Hong, S. et al. (2011) 'Negative Reward Signals from the Lateral Habenula to Dopamine Neurons Are Mediated by Rostromedial Tegmental Nucleus in Primates', *Journal of Neuroscience*, 31 (32), pp. 11457–11471.

Howes, O.D. et al. (2012) 'The Nature of Dopamine Dysfunction in Schizophrenia and What This Means for Treatment', *Archives of General Psychiatry*, 69 (8), pp. 776–786.

Howes, O.D. et al. (2013) 'Midbrain Dopamine Function in Schizophrenia and Depression: A Post-mortem and Positron Emission Tomographic Imaging Study', *Brain*, 136 (11), pp. 3242–3251.

Huys, Q.J.M. et al. (2015) 'Decision-Theoretic Psychiatry', *Clinical Psychological Science*, 3 (3), pp. 400–421.

Joel, D., Niv, Y., and Ruppin, E. (2002) 'Actor-Critic Models of the Basal Ganglia: New Anatomical and Computational Perspectives', *Neural Networks*, 15 (4–6), pp. 535–547.

Kapur, S. (2003) 'Psychosis as a State of Aberrant Salience: A Framework Linking Biology, Phenomenology, and Pharmacology in Schizophrenia', *American Journal of Psychiatry*, 160 (1), pp. 13–23.

Kishida, K.T., King-Casas, B., and Montague, P.R. (2010) 'Neuroeconomic Approaches to Mental Disorders', *Neuron*, 67 (4), pp. 543–554.

Knill, D.C. and Pouget, A. (2004) 'The Bayesian Brain: The Role of Uncertainty in Neural Coding and Computation', *Trends in Neurosciences*, 27 (12), pp. 712–719.

Kobayashi, S. and Schultz, W. (2014) 'Reward Contexts Extend Dopamine Signals to Unrewarded Stimuli', *Current Biology*, 24, pp. 56–62.

Korn, C.W. et al. (2014) 'Depression Is Related to an Absence of Optimistically Biased Belief Updating about Future Life Events', *Psychological Medicine*, 44 (3), pp. 579–592.

Lawson, R.P. et al. (2014) 'The Habenula Encodes Negative Motivational Value Associated with Primary Punishment in Humans', *Proceedings of the National Academy of Sciences*, 111 (32), pp. 11858–11863.

Lemaitre, A.-L., Luyat, M., and Lafargue, G. (2016) 'Individuals with Pronounced Schizotypal Traits Are Particularly Successful in Tickling Themselves', *Consciousness and Cognition*, 41, pp. 64–71.

Maher, B.A. (1974) 'Delusional Thinking and Perceptual Disorder', *Journal of Individual Psychology*, 30 (1), pp. 98–113.

Maia, T.V. and Frank, M.J. (2011) 'From Reinforcement Learning Models to Psychiatric and Neurological Disorders', *Nature Neuroscience*, 14 (2), pp. 154–162.

Maia, T.V. and Frank, M.J. (2017) 'An Integrative Perspective on the Role of Dopamine in Schizophrenia', *Biological Psychiatry*, 81 (1), pp. 52–66.

Marr, D.C. and Poggio, T. (1976) *From Understanding Computation to Understanding Neural Circuitry*. MIT AI Memo 357.

McKay, R. (2012) 'Delusional Inference', *Mind and Language*, 27 (3), pp. 330–355.

Merritt, K. et al. (2016) 'Nature of Glutamate Alterations in Schizophrenia: A Meta-analysis of Proton Magnetic Resonance Spectroscopy Studies', *JAMA Psychiatry*, 73 (7), pp. 1–10.

Miyazono, K., Bortolotti, L., and Broome, M.R. (2015) 'Prediction-Error and Two-Factor Theories of Delusion Formation', in Galbraith, N. (ed.) *Aberrant Beliefs and Reasoning*. London: Psychology Press, pp. 34–54.

Montague, P.R. et al. (2012) 'Computational Psychiatry', *Trends in Cognitive Sciences*, 16 (1), pp. 72–80.

Morris, R.W. et al. (2012) 'Disambiguating Ventral Striatum fMRI-related Bold Signal during Reward Prediction in Schizophrenia', *Molecular Psychiatry*, 17 (3), pp. 280–289.

Moutoussis, M. et al. (2011) 'Bayesian Modelling of Jumping-to-Conclusions Bias in Delusional Patients', *Cognitive Neuropsychiatry*, 16 (5), pp. 422–447.

Murray, G.K. et al. (2008) 'Substantia Nigra/Ventral Tegmental Reward Prediction Error Disruption in Psychosis', *Molecular Psychiatry*, 13 (3), pp. 267–276.

Nakazawa, K. et al. (2012) 'GABAergic Interneuron Origin of Schizophrenia Pathophysiology', *Neuropharmacology*, 62 (3), pp. 1574–1583.

Neuhaus, A.H. et al. (2013) 'Evidence for Impaired Visual Prediction Error in Schizophrenia', *Schizophrenia Research*, 147 (2), pp. 326–330.

Nomoto, K. et al. (2010) 'Temporally Extended Dopamine Responses to Perceptually Demanding Reward-Predictive Stimuli', *Journal of Neuroscience*, 30 (32), pp. 10692–10702.

O'Driscoll, G.A. and Callahan, B.L. (2008) 'Smooth Pursuit in Schizophrenia: A Meta-analytic Review of Research since 1993', *Brain and Cognition*, 68 (3), pp. 359–370.

Olney, J.W. and Farber, N.B. (1995) 'Glutamate Receptor Dysfunction and Schizophrenia', *Archives of General Psychiatry*, 52 (12), pp. 998–1007.

Pynn, L.K. and DeSouza, J.F.X. (2013) 'The Function of Efference Copy Signals: Implications for Symptoms of Schizophrenia', *Vision Research*, 76, pp. 124–133.

Radua, J. et al. (2015) 'Ventral Striatal Activation during Reward Processing in Psychosis', *JAMA Psychiatry*, 72 (12), pp. 1243–1251.

Rao, R.P.N. and Ballard, D.H. (1999) 'Predictive Coding in the Visual Cortex: A Functional Interpretation of Some Extra-classical Receptive-field Effects', *Nature Neuroscience*, 2 (1), pp. 79–87.

Reddy, L.F. et al. (2016) 'Probabilistic Reversal Learning in Schizophrenia: Stability of Deficits and Potential Causal Mechanisms', *Schizophrenia Bulletin*, 42 (4), pp. 942–951.

Reinen, J.M. et al. (2016) 'Motivational Context Modulates Prediction Error Response in Schizophrenia', *Schizophrenia Bulletin*, 42 (6), pp. 1467–1475.

Rescorla, R.A. and Wagner, A.R. (1972) 'A Theory of Pavlovian Conditioning: Variations in the Effectiveness of Reinforcement and Nonreinforcement', *Classical Conditioning II: Current Research and Theory*, 21 (6), pp. 64–99.

Roiser, J.P. et al. (2009) 'Do Patients with Schizophrenia Exhibit Aberrant Salience?', *Psychological Medicine*, 39 (2), pp. 199–209.

Schlagenhauf, F. et al. (2013) 'Ventral Striatal Prediction Error Signaling Is Associated with Dopamine Synthesis Capacity and Fluid Intelligence', *Human Brain Mapping*, 34 (6), pp. 1490–1499.

Schlagenhauf, F. et al. (2014) 'Striatal Dysfunction during Reversal Learning in Unmedicated Schizophrenia Patients', *NeuroImage*, 89, pp. 171–180.

Schultz, W. et al. (1997) 'A Neural Substrate of Prediction and Reward', *Science*, 275 (5306), pp. 1593–1599.

Schultz, W. (1998) 'Predictive Reward Signal of Dopamine Neurons', *Journal of Neurophysiology*, 80 (1), pp. 1–27.

Schultz, W. (2016a) 'Dopamine Reward Prediction-Error Signalling: A Two-Component Response', *Nature Reviews Neuroscience*, 17 (3), pp. 183–195.

Schultz, W. (2016b) 'Dopamine Reward Prediction Error Coding', *Dialogues in Clinical Neuroscience*, 18 (1), pp. 23–32.

Shallice, T. (1988) *From Neuropsychology to Mental Structure*. Cambridge, UK: Cambridge University Press.

Sharot, T. (2011) 'The Optimism Bias', *Current Biology*, 21 (23), pp. R941–R945.

Shergill, S.S. (2003) 'Two Eyes for an Eye: The Neuroscience of Force Escalation', *Science*, 301 (5630), p. 187.

Shergill, S.S. et al. (2005) 'Evidence for Sensory Prediction Deficits in Schizophrenia', *The American Journal of Psychiatry*, 162 (12), pp. 2384–2386.

Shergill, S.S., Brammer, M.J. et al. (2014) 'Engagement of Brain Areas Implicated in Processing Inner Speech in People with Auditory Hallucinations', *The British Journal of Psychiatry*, 182 (6), pp. 525–531.

Shergill, S.S., White, T.P. et al. (2014) 'Functional Magnetic Resonance Imaging of Impaired Sensory Prediction in Schizophrenia', *JAMA Psychiatry*, 71 (1), pp. 28–35.

Simon, H. (1972) 'Theories of Bounded Rationality', *Decision and Organization*, 1 (1), pp. 161–176.

Skinner, B.F. (1938) *The Behavior of Organisms: An Experimental Analysis*. New York, NY: Appleton-Century-Crofts.

Slifstein, M. et al. (2015) 'Deficits in Prefrontal Cortical and Extrastriatal Dopamine Release in Schizophrenia: A Positron Emission Tomographic Functional Magnetic Resonance Imaging Study', *JAMA Psychiatry*, 72 (4), pp. 316–324.

Smieskova, R. et al. (2015) 'Modulation of Motivational Salience Processing during the Early Stages of Psychosis', *Schizophrenia Research*, 166 (1–3), pp. 17–23.

Stephan, K.E. et al. (2009) 'Bayesian Model Selection for Group Studies', *NeuroImage*, 46 (4), pp. 1004–1017.

Sutton, R.S. and Barto, A.G. (1998) *Reinforcement Learning: An Introduction*. Cambridge, MA: MIT Press.

Tranel, D., Damasio, H., and Damasio, A.R. (1995) 'Double Dissociation between Overt and Covert Face Recognition', *Journal of Cognitive Neuroscience*, 7 (4), pp. 425–432.

Umbricht, D. and Krljes, S. (2005) 'Mismatch Negativity in Schizophrenia: A Meta-analysis', *Schizophrenia Research*, 76 (1), pp. 1–23.

Volman, V., Behrens, M.M., and Sejnowski, T.J. (2011) 'Downregulation of Parvalbumin at Cortical GABA Synapses Reduces Network Gamma Oscillatory Activity', *Journal of Neuroscience*, 31 (49), pp. 18137–18148.

Waltz, J.A. et al. (2007) 'Selective Reinforcement Learning Deficits in Schizophrenia Support Predictions from Computational Models of Striatal-Cortical Dysfunction', *Biological Psychiatry*, 62 (7), pp. 756–764.

Waltz, J.A. et al. (2010) 'Abnormal Responses to Monetary Outcomes in Cortex, but Not in the Basal Ganglia, in Schizophrenia', *Neuropsychopharmacology*, 35 (12), pp. 2427–2439.

Watkins, C.J.C.H. and Dayan, P. (1992) 'Technical Note: Q-Learning', *Machine Learning*, 8 (3), pp. 279–292.

Wunderlich, K., Dayan, P., and Dolan, R.J. (2012) 'Mapping Value Based Planning and Extensively Trained Choice in the Human Brain', *Nature Neuroscience*, 15 (5), pp. 786–791.

Wunderlich, K., Smittenaar, P., and Dolan, R.J. (2012) 'Dopamine Enhances Model-based over Model-free Choice Behavior', *Neuron*, 75 (3), pp. 418–424.

34

COMPUTATIONAL APPROACHES TO SOCIAL COGNITION

John Michael and Miles MacLeod

1 Introduction

In order to successfully navigate the physical world and to flourish as a biological agent, it is very useful to acquire information about what is in one's environment. If you don't want to walk off a cliff or run into a tree, you would do well to check what is in front of you before you step. And if you don't want to starve to death, then it behooves you to find out where there is something to eat. For highly social species such as we humans are, it is also very useful to acquire information about other agents in one's environment. After all, we need to be able to anticipate and adapt to others' behavior, to coordinate with them, to learn from them, to choose appropriate cooperation partners and to appropriately calibrate our degree of commitment to joint activities. It is therefore no surprise that we have developed sophisticated social-cognitive abilities that enable us to detect agents in our environment and to track a great many features of them – ranging from their bodily features, such as size, age, gender, and attractiveness, to social-relational features such as social status and group membership, to mental features such as preferences (Michael and Christensen, 2016), intentions (Sartori, Becchio, and Castiello, 2011), beliefs (Apperly and Butterfill, 2009; Michael, Christensen, and Overgaard, 2013), desires (Rakoczy, Warneken, and Tomasello, 2008; Steglich-Petersen and Michael, 2015), emotions (Tamietto and de Gelder, 2010), and personality traits (Westra, 2017).

In recent decades, there has been a great deal of research in the cognitive sciences into the psychological mechanisms underpinning these various social-cognitive abilities. Much of this research has been devoted to the attempt to explain how we identify and reason about our own and others' mental states (which is often referred to, tongue-in-cheek, as "mindreading"). Of course, mindreading is not all that goes into social cognition – evaluating bodily and social-relational features, as noted already, is also important. Nevertheless, mindreading has been seen to be sufficiently foundational to social cognition in humans[1] that a theory of mindreading may constitute the centerpiece of a computationalist account of social cognition research.

Accordingly, the search for a general theory of mindreading has been a main project in social cognition research since at least the 1970s. Lately, though, many researchers have become frustrated with this project, and questioned the prospects of a unified computational theory of mindreading. In spite of this, the emergence of the Prediction Error Minimization (PEM) framework (Hohwy, 2013; Clark, 2013; Friston, 2013; Friston et al., 2013) has raised hope in some quarters that a unified account may be attainable after all (de Bruin and Michael, under review; Westra, 2017; Koster-Hale and Saxe, 2013; Baker et al., 2017). The PEM framework organizes cognition as a hierarchy of models of causal relations at different levels of generality. PEM conceptualizes learning as a process of Bayesian inference in response to prediction errors.[2] There is much ongoing debate about what the appropriate level is at which to situate explanations generated by the PEM framework. In particular, it is not entirely clear whether they are best interpreted as abstract models which specify the relevant formal properties of psychological mechanisms, or as hypotheses about the psychological mechanisms themselves (Colombo and Hartmann, 2015; Colombo and Wright, 2017). This chapter will contribute to this ongoing debate by considering how best to interpret PEM models in the case of social cognition and in particular mindreading. We will first suggest that PEM is promising as a general *computational* account in Marr's sense, i.e. as an abstract account of the formal properties of the psychological mechanisms that carry out social cognition and in particular mindreading. PEM in this sense is compatible with multiple different accounts of the representations and algorithms which the brain actually uses to carry out social cognition and in particular mindreading.

In Section 2, we will very briefly recapitulate the trajectory of mindreading research in recent decades, and consider some recent developments that have grown out of the frustration with earlier theories. In Section 3, we take a step back and ask how theories and models in social cognition research may be evaluated along three dimensions corresponding to the three levels of analysis proposed by Marr (1975; Marr and Poggio, 1977): computational, algorithmic, and implementational. In Section 4, we will consider how a PEM framework may be used to provide structure and direction for research on mindreading in particular and possibly of social cognition generally.

2 The mindreading debate[3]

The term "mindreading" (other terms, notably "theory of mind" and "mentalizing", have been used to refer to the same explanandum) is taken to refer, in the words of Goldman and Sripada, to "the capacity to identify the mental states of others, for example, their beliefs, desires, intentions, goals, experiences, sensations and also emotion states" (2005, p. 193). In other words, the term "mindreading" picks out our perfectly ordinary ability to understand others as having mental states of various sorts, including emotions, sensations, beliefs, desires, intentions, goals, etc.

Most research on mindreading in the cognitive sciences has been devoted to the question of how we accomplish this – that is, it has investigated the nature of the representations and algorithms that enable us to mindread. In the 1980s and 1990s two well-known families of positions dominated the mindreading debate, the basic ideas of which may be outlined as follows:

Theory Theory (TT): we mindread by utilizing a rich body of information about mental states and how they are connected with other mental states, with observable behavior, and with the environment. This body of information is either:

(a) A "theory" that is formed on the basis of observation, testing, and learning more generally (e.g. Gopnik and Wellman, 1992); or:
(b) Contained in a "module" that is activated at some point in development (e.g. Leslie, 1994; see also Baron-Cohen et al., 1995).

Simulation Theory (ST): we mindread by putting ourselves in other people's "shoes", using our own mind to work out what we would do, think, or feel in their situation – and then attributing those intentions, thoughts, or emotions to those other people (e.g. Goldman, 1989; Gordon, 1986).

To see how TT and ST accounts of mindreading differ, consider the following simple example. You have been informed that your friend Barbara's wallet has been stolen. When you run into her, you notice that she is frowning, and so you conclude that she is angry. How did you arrive at that conclusion? According to (a simplified version of) TT, you connected the information about the theft and the visual information about her frowning with stored general information about people, of something like the following kind: *ceteris paribus*, people who have suffered an injustice tend to be angry; *ceteris paribus*, people who frown tend to be angry. Together, the information about this particular case and the stored "theoretical" information allow you to infer that your friend Barbara is angry. A simplified version of ST, on the other hand, would maintain that you used the visual and other information about the particular case in a different way. Instead of connecting this with general assumptions about people and what makes them angry, you imagine how you would feel if someone had stolen your wallet (or how you would feel if you were frowning like Barbara) and then attribute the result of this "simulation" to her.

Clearly, both the example and the sketches of explanations are highly simplified. Nevertheless, they serve to illustrate how explanations can be derived from TT and ST – i.e. these accounts suggest that we attribute mental states to others either by applying stored general information about mental states and how they are connected with other mental states, behavior, etc. (TT), or by simulating with our own mind what the target might be going through (ST).

Despite nearly thirty years of intense debate, however, neither TT nor ST has established itself as a general framework for social cognition. And indeed, both theories have been subjected to harsh criticism of late – both on empirical and on theoretical grounds. Apperly (2011), for example, has argued forcefully that either theory can accommodate the existing data equally well, and that it is therefore not possible to adjudicate between them on the basis of the available evidence. As a result of the apparent failure of TT and ST to establish a unified theory of mindreading – a theory which would account for all mindreading phenomena – most researchers in the field have either put aside their search for a general theory, or else embraced a *non-unifying* theory, such as a dual-systems theory (e.g. Apperly and Butterfill, 2009; Bruin and Newen, 2014), or a pluralistic theory that postulates a wide range of mechanisms (Fiebich and Coltheart, 2015). One reason for the failure of previous attempts to develop a unified theory of mindreading may be that the explanandum itself has not been sufficiently well circumscribed. What, after all, does it mean to "identify" one's own or others' mental states? While there is a perfectly clear answer to this question in the context of a lab experiment in which the task is to report on one's own or someone else's mental state, we rarely have to perform such tasks in everyday life. Indeed, we rarely have to perform such tasks even in lab experiments investigating mindreading. Even in the classic explicit false-belief task, for example, children are asked where the agent is going to search, not where s/he believes an object to be located. The rationale of course is that the child will need to identify the agent's mental state in order to give the correct response to the test question, and that success on the task therefore depends on (somehow or other) identifying the agent's false belief. Unfortunately, however, this remains vague as long as we lack an agreed-upon theory of what beliefs and other mental states are. As a result, researchers have had to rely on intuitions and everyday folk psychology in thinking about their explanatory target.

In the remainder of this chapter, we will be exploring how a computational perspective can be useful in addressing this problem. First, let us take a small step back and recall David Marr's (1982) influential tripartite distinction, which, as we shall see, may help to provide the structure we need to move forward.

3 Three levels of social cognition

In Chapter 1 of *Vision*, David Marr (1982; Marr, 1975; Marr and Poggio, 1977; Gu, this volume; Chirimuuta, this volume; Rescorla, this volume; Broome and Brugger, this volume) distinguishes following "three levels at which any machine carrying out an information-processing task must be understood":

- *Computational*: What is the problem that is to be solved, and what is the logic of the strategy by which it can be solved?
- *Algorithmic*. What cognitive processes carry out the computations? In particular, what representations feature in the computational processes carrying out the function, and what algorithm(s) are used in the transformation from inputs to outputs?
- *Implementational*: How are these representations and algorithms realized physically in the brain? (Marr, 1982, p. 25)

To illustrate, Marr applies this distinction to the levels at which a cash register may be analyzed.[4] At the *computational* level, "what [the cash register] does is arithmetic, so our first task [in understanding its workings] is to master the theory of addition" (Marr, 1982, p 22). At the algorithmic level, "we might choose Arabic numerals for the representations, and for the algorithm we could follow the usual rules about adding the least significant digits first and 'carrying' if the sum exceeds 9" (ibid., p. 23). At the implementational level, we must develop an account of the neural processes supporting these representations and algorithms.

With this tripartite distinction in hand, let us turn our attention back to the mindreading debate and to social cognition research more broadly. The accounts of mindreading that were briefly reviewed in Section 2 are best understood as attempts to specify the representations and processes at the algorithmic level that underpin the capacity to mindread. But how are we to evaluate whether such accounts are successful? As noted already, it appears that we need an account of what these processes and representations are actually doing, i.e. we need a computational-level account. Such an account might serve to constrain and structure hypotheses about the algorithmic level, and thereby spur progress in resolving the issues that have proven so vexing in the mindreading literature so far.

In the next section, we will consider a theoretical approach which has recently been emerging and which may prove useful in this regard. Specifically, we will be considering the PEM framework, which has ignited hope in some quarters of new cognitive neuroscience and computational modeling that a unifying theory might be possible after all. Indeed, one of the key selling points of the PEM framework is its ability to integrate a broad range of findings into a single coherent framework. De Bruin and Michael (under review; see also de Bruin and Michael, 2017; Westra, 2017; Koster-Hale and Saxe, 2013; Baker et al., 2017) suggest that PEM may be able to provide a unifying theoretical framework for the study of social cognition, which elegantly synthesizes existing data from social cognition research and raises fruitful new questions for further investigation, such as whether and how individuals hierarchically classify social causes.

Interestingly, PEM can also be seen as an account of the algorithms and representations that the brain actually uses in order to carry out the computations underpinning mindreading and other forms of social cognition. Indeed, some researchers (Hohwy, 2013; Clark, 2013; Friston, 2013; Friston et al., 2013) are optimistic about the PEM framework not only as a computational-level account but also as an account of how the brain actually works (i.e. at least as an account of the algorithmic level) and possibly even as an account of the implementational level. We will not take a position here on this question (see Colombo and Hartmann, 2015; Colombo and Wright, 2017). Instead, we will attempt to flesh out the idea that PEM may provide a computational-level account of mindreading, and possibly even of social cognition in general. In so doing, it will be important to keep in mind that such a computational-level account is compatible with multiple different algorithm-level accounts of mindreading.

4 Bayes at the computational level: the Bayesian predictive processing framework

Bayesian computational models of cognition

A starting point for PEM as a computational-level account of cognition in general is to identify the general problem that the brain solves as *anticipating incoming sensory, proprioceptive and interoceptive input*. The general logic of the strategy for solving this problem is to construct models of the possible causes of those inputs.[5] These models generate predictions about likely inputs at any given time, which can then be compared to actual inputs. If the discrepancy between predicted and actual inputs – i.e. the prediction error – is small, then there may be no need to revise the model that gives rise to the prediction. If, on the other hand, the prediction error is large, then it is likely that the model fails to explain the causes of the inputs, and therefore must be revised. Revisions proceed via Bayesian inference, taking the prior distribution of probabilities into account as well as the new (unpredicted) input. To see how this works, consider the following toy example: you are lying in your bed on Christmas Eve and listening to the sound of a tree next to your window creaking under the weight of the snow. As the wind picks up, you expect that the bough may brush up against the house, and anticipate the sound that this would produce. But suddenly, you hear something unexpected, namely what sounds a lot like a pack of reindeer scampering about on the roof. Insofar as you were not expecting this, your world-model did not include anything on the roof that would produce such noises. As a result, you are now confronted with a prediction error that needs to be explained away. In order to do this, you quickly identify some candidate hypotheses, or models:

Model 1 (M1): Santa has landed on your roof.
Model 2 (M2): There are squirrels on the roof.

What you now want to do is to rank these models in terms of their posterior probability. To do this, you will first need to work out the *likelihood* of the input you are receiving under each model, and you will need to assign each model a *prior probability*. The *likelihood* is the probability of the sensory outcome (i.e. the sounds you are hearing), given a value for the parameter picking out an environmental cause. Let's assume that the sound on the roof really sounds like reindeer. M1 therefore has a very high likelihood. This means that if M1 is true, then this is exactly the input you would expect. M2 has a lower likelihood, since the noises don't really sound quite as you would expect from squirrels on the roof. If you only took the likelihood into account, then, you would wind up favoring M1. But you also need to consider the *prior probability*, which is your subjective estimate of how probable that model is independent of the sensations you are currently observing. M1, of course, is extremely improbable, whereas M2 is fairly probable. For each model, you would then plug these probabilities into *Bayes' Theorem*:

$$P(m \mid e) = P(e \mid m) \ P(m) / \ P(e)$$

$P(m \mid e)$ is the posterior probability of the model; $P(e \mid m)$ is the probability of the evidence, given the model (likelihood); $P(m)$ is the prior probability of the model and $P(e)$ is the probability of observing the evidence independently of the model. Presumably, this will reveal that M2 provides the best explanation for the data, and you will adopt M2. Now, the evidence has been explained away and need not trouble you further as you settle in for a long winter slumber.[6]

One other very important aspect of the PEM framework is that the models of the world that enable the brain to predict inputs are organized in a *hierarchy*. At the lowest level of the hierarchy, the brain must encode such features as surfaces, edges, and colors. At a hierarchically superordinate level, these low-level features are grouped together into objects, while even further up the hierarchy these objects are grouped together as components of larger scenes involving multiple objects.

To illustrate this, let us consider a new toy example. When you see a red cup moving leftward across your visual field, the red surface will typically move in concert with the edges, i.e. the changes in the inputs pertaining to the locations of the edges and the red surfaces will be correlated. In order to draw upon such regularities in anticipating inputs, the brain, at a hierarchical level that is superordinate to the representation of such low-level features as surfaces and edges and colors, represents the cup as an object. Moreover, to anticipate changes over longer timescales, superordinate models embed this object into larger scenes, such as tea parties, and thereby generate predictions pertaining to objects and overall scenes in a context-dependent fashion (rather than low-level features such as edges, surfaces, and colors). Thus, by embedding the cup into a model of a tea party, it will become possible to predict roughly in what ways the cup will be moved, by whom, and where to. On the other hand, since we also lose detail and precision as we move up the hierarchy, lower hierarchical levels are still required in order to make specific predictions.

Modeling more abstract features of the world helps to reduce uncertainty because it introduces causal structure, which enables you to interpret statistical regularities and more flexibly to predict events in novel circumstances and over longer timescales. Cups retain their shapes for years or even centuries, as do the social norms governing behavior at tea parties. But whereas hierarchical models reduce uncertainty, prediction errors will always occur (even if one expects tea cups, for example, to be placed on tables, to be filled with tea, etc., one will generally not know *precisely* when and where). How, then, does the brain deal with the inevitable prediction errors? The basic mechanism is as follows: when a prediction error exceeds a given threshold, the model giving rise to the prediction must be revised, so an error signal is sent up to the immediately superordinate model, which is accordingly revised. New predictions are thereby generated and sent back down the hierarchy, where they are tested against new inputs. The process is repeated continuously, and in this manner the brain minimizes average long-term prediction error.

So far, this is a computational description of how the brain goes about solving the problem of anticipating sensory, proprioceptive, and interoceptive input. An important point to emphasize is that describing things this way does not commit one to thinking that the brain actually represents Bayes' theorem or carves up the hierarchical levels as we would as scientists. One could think this, of course; and if one did, one would be committing to the idea of PEM at the algorithmic level. But one might also think that the algorithms and representations used by the brain approximate PEM models by some other means. If so, PEM models would be useful in formulating the explanandum to be addressed by models of the algorithmic level – i.e. theorizing about the algorithmic level would be informed and constrained by PEM models at the computational level.

Having laid out the basic concepts of the PEM framework, let us now consider how they might be applied in the study of mindreading in particular and social cognition more generally. We will proceed in two steps: first characterizing the task with which the need for social cognition presents the brain, and then attempting to articulate the strategy with which the brain solves the problem of social cognition.

Prediction error minimization and social cognition: the task

In characterizing the task of social cognition from within a PEM framework, one might start out from the observation that other people are a particular kind of cause of sensory input on a par with coffee cups. Just as it is sometimes helpful in reducing uncertainty about the behavior of edges and surfaces and colors to model objects, such as coffee cups as the bearers of those lower-level features, it is also sometimes useful to model other people.

Indeed, the differences between other people and coffee cups such as objects are at least as important as the similarities. Starting at the bottom-level of the hierarchy, other people can already be distinguished from non-agentive objects on the basis of low-level features such as faces (Haxby, Hoffman, and Gobbini, 2002), eyes (Haxby, Hoffman, and Gobbini, 2000), gaze direction (Teufel et al., 2009), and emotional expressions (Tamietto et al., 2009). The detection of these features makes it possible to bring a whole set of expectations to bear that are specific to agents in contrast to non-agentive objects. To focus for a moment just on the example of eyes, there is a very deep-seated expectation that one will learn something useful by following others' gaze direction. Gaze following occurs by six months at the latest (Senju and Csibra, 2008), and Hood, Willen, and Driver (1998) have even found evidence for it in two-and-a-half-month-olds. And if the eyes happen to be directed at oneself, then the other person will be able to acquire information about one's emotions from one's facial expressions and posture, to track the direction of one's gaze and to anticipate one's movements. Moreover, it is likely that she will initiate certain actions directed toward one. Thus, it should come as no surprise that eye contact consistently elicits a relatively strong reaction, as evinced, for example, by galvanic skin response, electroencephalogram activity (Nichols and Champness, 1971; Gale et al., 1975), and the activation of specific motivational brain systems (Hietanen et al., 2008). In fact, the importance of eye contact is so fundamental and pervasive that even newborns are sensitive to it: Farroni and colleagues, for example, found that two- to five-day-old newborns looked longer and more frequently at a photograph of a face whose eyes were facing directly to them than a different image of the same face with the eyes facing away (Farroni et al., 2002).

Human bodies not only look different from coffee cups, they are also subject to characteristic regularities governing their movements that do not apply to objects in general. Thus, by hypothesizing the presence of a human body, it is possible to draw upon a whole set of expectations about how human bodies move around in space. For example, human bodies are subject to biomechanical laws, and typically move about in an efficient goal-directed manner. If a person is walking across the room and passes behind a barrier, the default prediction is that they will continue along the same path and re-appear on the other side of the barrier moving at the same speed.

Moving up to a hierarchically superordinate level, the brain also embeds human bodies into models of larger situations, thereby making it possible to draw upon knowledge about what behavior is likely in light of contextual factors. For example, a prediction with high prior probability is that people turn toward objects that suddenly appear or suddenly emit bright lights (Pelphrey et al., 2003). Moreover, by representing other people as actors within situations, it is possible to appeal to situational regularities that derive from the fact that people's behavior, unlike that of coffee cups and clouds, is governed by various kinds of norms and conventions. Social and moral norms, for example, make it highly unlikely that people will run up and kiss strangers, strangle cats in public squares, or drive their cars on the left side of the road (unless they happen to be in one of the countries in which conventions dictate that they do so). Sensitivity towards these norms already emerges in early ontogeny. Developmental studies show that when infants begin to imitate the actions of adults, they do not merely re-enact the idiosyncratic act of individuals, but rather learn something about the general form of the action, and how normative dimensions of appropriate and inappropriate performance structure it. For example, when two-year-old infants see someone use a novel object systematically in an instrumental way, they use the object in similar ways themselves later on, and only for this purpose. What is more, they expect other people to do so as well (Casler and Kelemen, 2005). In a series of studies, Rakoczy and colleagues demonstrated that, in addition to respecting social norms, infants also enforce them on third parties. Not only do they protest at norm violations, but they also try to alter the norm transgressor's behavior, for instance, by teaching the "right" way to do it (Rakoczy, 2008; Raoczy, Warneken, and Tomasello, 2008).

An interesting though slightly more controversial question is whether these norms can be said to be *rational*, in the sense that people tend to choose the most efficient means available in order to achieve their goals. There is evidence that infants and adults expect that objects which appear to move about in a goal-directed fashion (such as geometrical shapes on a computer screen) tend to choose the most direct paths available toward their goals, and will change course when more direct routes become available (Csibra et al., 1999; Gergely and Csibra, 2003). Another illustration is the phenomenon of rational imitation, in which infants imitate only those features of an action that are relevant to the goal, which is present at around fourteen months (Gergely, Bekkering, and Kiraly, 2002; however, see also Paulus et al., 2011). In other words, it seems that infants already have a tendency to bring norms of rationality to bear in interpreting the movements of other people – and even of non-human shapes as long as those shapes exhibit agent-like features such as self-propelled motion (Csibra, 2008; Bíró and Leslie, 2007; Bíró, Csibra, and Gergely, 2007). The crucial thing to point out is that these kinds of regularities can only be captured by appealing to features that are unique to agents: namely their goals. In a PEM framework, what this means is that we represent others' minds as hidden causes of observable events, and in fact as a hidden causes of a unique kind insofar as they are causes that, like us, employ hierarchical models in order to reduce their own prediction error (Daunizeau et al. 2010a; 2010b).

Moving still further up the hierarchy, there are also psychological features that are unique to specific agents and which persist over longer time scales, such as their preferences. Thus, agents can be expected to act in ways that are consistent with their specific preferences. A study by Woodward (1998) showed that infants take prior actions into account when attributing goals. In this study five-month-old infants were first habituated to an event in which an agent reached for toy A in an array of two toys, A and B. The locations of the toys were then reversed and the agent reached either for toy A at the new location, or for toy B at the original location. The main finding was that the infants looked longer when the agent reached for toy B, suggesting that they interpreted the goal of the reaching in the habituation phase as being the object rather than the location, and expected in the test trial that the reaching would have the same goal. In a more recent study based upon the same paradigm, Cannon and Woodward (2012) found convergent evidence by measuring eleven-month-old infants' predictive eye movements rather than looking time.

Similarly, the ascription of specific beliefs and desires to individual agents makes it possible to exploit regularities that can span quite long time scales. If an agent believes that the object she desires is at one location, she is likely to seek it there regardless of whether it really is still there, and indeed even if it happens to have been transferred years ago to some other location. Recent findings in developmental psychology suggest very strongly that infants are able to anticipate such regularities by the second year of life (Baillargeon, Scott, and He, 2010; Butterfill and Apperly, 2013), and perhaps even by six to seven months (Kovács, Téglás, and Endress, 2010; Southgate and Vernetti, 2014). And when, in experimental settings in which false belief scenarios are implemented, this type of pattern is broken, children tend to look longer at the scene, suggesting that their expectation has been violated (i.e. there has been a prediction error).[7]

In predicting other people's behavior, it is important not only to keep track of their mental states at a given time but also to draw upon information about features obtaining across longer time scales – i.e. personality traits and reputation, such as the degree to which they are trustworthy, lazy, prone to temper tantrums, etc. (Moutoussis et al., 2014). For example, there is evidence that people use information about other people's reputation (i.e. gossip) in order to generate expectations about how cooperative those people will be in economic games, and to calibrate their own behavior accordingly (Sommerfield et al., 2007).

Prediction error minimization and social cognition: the logic of the strategy

Having provided a sketch of the hierarchy of the worldly causes with which social cognition must somehow deal, the question arises how models at different levels of this hierarchy may reciprocally constrain each other via Bayes' theorem. To see how this might work, let us consider another toy example. Your friend produces a facial expression which looks a bit like a frown. This is surprising given that it has just been announced that Donald Trump, Mike Pence, Viktor Orban, and Recep Erdogan have all drowned in the water hazard at the seventh hole of Trump's golf course in Florida, and your friend is a reasonable and ethically minded human being. To explain away this surprising input you will have to consider various alternative models. Perhaps your friend is not as reasonable or ethical as you thought? Or perhaps she has some mistaken beliefs about who these people are? Or perhaps she simply misheard the news? The PEM framework suggests that in cases like this, you won't just cast about willy-nilly for an explanation but that the process of revision will proceed up the hierarchy one level at a time. Specifically, you will first try to explain away the prediction error by revising the model one hierarchical level up from the model of her facial expressions, and then move up one level further if this is not successful, and so on.

But which model is one level up from the model of her facial expressions? What is higher up – personality traits or beliefs? In the previous subsection, we sketched a rough overview of the hierarchy of causes modeled by social cognition, but this was only a very rough starting point based largely upon armchair reflection. An important task for researchers applying PEM to social cognition is to develop more specific models of how the hierarchy of social causes can be modeled. How many levels should such a hierarchy of social causes optimally include? Where should the gaps be between the levels? What should be represented at each level?

At this point, it becomes apparent that PEM as a computational-level project must work hand in hand with research at the algorithmic level and the implementational level. This is because we must distinguish between an objectively accurate model of the hierarchy of social causes, on the one hand, and the way in which the human brain models the hierarchy of social causes, on the other. Presumably the latter is of interest to those of us who would like to understand how humans and other species *actually* perform mindreading specifically and social cognition more generally. And this will depend on such factors as the relative cost of different computations for the brain, and the relative overall efficiency of different architectures (i.e. social cognition is just a subset of the tasks performed by the brain).

In carrying out this project, we should keep an open mind about the possibility that the optimal way of modeling such a hierarchy of social causes may differ greatly from everyday intuitions or scientific models of those same causes. Nevertheless, an intuitive sketch like the one that we have offered can provide a useful starting point in constructing more specific models which can then be refined in light of empirical evidence. Baker et al. (2017) take such an approach in constructing a model of how agents can perform mindreading by modeling the relationship among beliefs, desires, and perceptions. They make the plausible assumption that an agent engaged in mindreading will assume that the target agent is rational, i.e. that she will form the beliefs that she should on the basis of the perceptual input available to her, that she will perform the actions she should given her beliefs, desires, and perceptual input, etc. And from here they develop a more precise model of how the mindreading agent draws upon a model of the target agent's beliefs and desires and perceptions to generate predictions about her behavior. They then show that this model can be used to predict participants' responses to questions about how probable it is that target agents in simple scenarios have particular beliefs or desires, etc. In doing so, Baker and colleagues are able to refine their model within this framework to make it predictively powerful. But it is important to note that this does not yet automatically make it into an algorithmic-level account of how the brain performs mindreading. It *can* be interpreted that way, but it can also be interpreted as a computational-level account which leaves open what the algorithms and representations are that the brain actually utilizes. And indeed, when developing algorithmic-level accounts, it may sometimes be necessary to improve predictive power by departing more radically from everyday intuitions. For example, it may be that in some contexts, some kinds of representations of beliefs may be representationally segregated from each other, and thus not integrated in an optimal fashion. In fact, two-systems theories of belief reasoning, such as that espoused by Butterfill and Apperly (2013), suggest that this may be the case.[8]

A different source of divergence from optimality may arise from the way in which representations of social causes are distributed along the hierarchy. If there is information present at a high level of the hierarchy that should in principle influence predictions that are made at a very low level of the hierarchy, it may nevertheless fail to do so if there is no pathway between the two models. If prediction errors do not propagate up the hierarchy to reach the high-level model in which the information is encoded, then it may not be able to propagate back down to penetrate the low-level model in question. This type of divergence from optimality may be one source of testable predictions, which can hopefully be formulated and tested as further progress is made in articulating algorithmic-level models specifying how information about social causes is distributed along the hierarchy.

5 Conclusion

PEM offers a theoretically rich unifying computationalist account of mindreading in particular and social cognition more generally, indicating the potential productivity of such accounts in the social realm. In the spirit of Marr's stipulation that computational theories should be explanatory at their level but also provide constraints which can inform lower-level investigations, PEM has the potential to constitute a genuine advance in current social cognition research. As noted, PEM may also provide an algorithmic-level account, but it need not do so in order to be a fruitful resource.

Notes

1 For recent findings providing evidence of mindreading in non-human primates and in corvids, see Krupenye et al. (2016); and Bugnyar, Reber, and Buckner (2016), respectively.
2 There are many heterogeneous approaches emphasizing the importance of prediction error minimization. Some, but not all, conceptualize prediction error minimization as a process of Bayesian inference. Clark (2015) has advocated the use of the more general term 'predictive processing' as an umbrella term that does not imply Bayesian inference. In the following, our focus will be on Bayesian versions (Friston, 2013).
3 The following summary of the mindreading debate is adapted from Overgaard and Michael (2015, pp. 2–3)
4 For further discussion of this example and of Marr's three levels, see McClamrock (1991).
5 Some versions of the predictive processing framework incorporate model-free reinforcement learning systems which, rather than using Bayesian inference to generate a hierarchy of world-models,

> draw on experience to learn action values directly, without building and searching any explicit model of the environment. What drives learning and action selection in model-free algorithms is a reward prediction-error, which reinforces successful actions without relying on explicit knowledge about state transitions or reward structure of the environment.
>
> *(Colombo, 2014, p. 81; cf. Clark, 2015)*

In the following, we will be considering accounts based on the idea that the revision of models proceeds via Bayesian inference.
6 It is worth noting that in this case there is no need for revision of the probabilities of models, so learning does not occur.
7 Many other measures apart from looking time have also been used. For reviews, see Baillargeon, Scott, and He (2010) and Christensen and Michael (2015). Much has been made of the discrepancy between these findings, on the one hand, and the failure of three-to-four-year-old children to succeed at false belief tasks in which they are asked verbally to predict where an agent with a false belief is likely to search for the object in question (Wimmer and Perner, 1983; Wellman, Cross, and Watson, 2001; Butterfill and Apperly, 2013). Attempts to account for this puzzle have ranged from denial that the data really does reveal a sensitivity to belief states on the part of infants (Heyes, 2014; Perner and Ruffman, 2005), to arguments that the infants do represent beliefs *per se* but have specific difficulties with various task demands arising in explicit verbal versions (Baillargeon, Scott, and He, 2010) to something in between (Apperly and Butterfill, 2009; De Bruin and Newen, 2014). Resolving this puzzle is an important desideratum for current and future research.
8 For critical discussion, see Christensen and Michael (2015); Michael and Christensen (2016).

References

Apperly, I.A. (2011) *Mindreaders: The Cognitive Basis of "Theory of Mind"*. New York, NY: Psychology Press.
Apperly, I.A. and Butterfill, S.A. (2009) 'Do Humans Have Two Systems to Track Beliefs and Belief-like States?', *Psychological Review*, 116 (4), pp. 953–970.
Baillargeon, R., Scott, R.M., and He, Z. (2010) 'False-belief Understanding in Infants', *Trends in Cognitive Sciences*, 14 (3), pp. 110–118.
Baker, C.L. et al. (2017) 'Rational Quantitative Attribution of Beliefs, Desires and Percepts in Human Mentalizing', *Nature Human Behaviour*, 1 (4), 0064, pp. 1–10.
Baron-Cohen, S. et al. (1995) 'Are Children with Autism Blind to the Mentalistic Significance of the Eyes?', *British Journal of Developmental Psychology*, 13 (4), pp. 379–398.

Bíró, S., Csibra, G., and Gergely, G. (2007) 'The Role of Behavioral Cues in Understanding Goal-directed Actions in Infancy', *Progress in Brain Research*, 164, pp. 303–323.

Bíró, S. and Leslie, A.M. (2007) '"Infants" Perception of Goal-directed Actions: Development through Cuebased Bootstrapping', *Developmental Science*, 10, pp. 379–398.

Bugnyar, T., Reber, S.A., and Buckner, C. (2016) 'Ravens Attribute Visual Access to Unseen Competitors', *Nature Communications*, 7, art. 10506.

Butterfill, S.A. and Apperly, I.A. (2013) 'How to Construct a Minimal Theory of Mind', *Mind and Language*, 28 (5), pp. 606–637.

Cannon, E.N. and Woodward, A.L. (2012) 'Infants Generate Goal-based Action Predictions', *Developmental Science*, 15 (2), pp. 292–298.

Casler, K. and Kelemen, D. (2005) 'Young Children's Rapid Learning about Artifacts', *Developmental Science*, 8 (6), pp. 472–480.

Christensen, W. and Michael, J. (2015) 'From Two Systems to a Multi-Systems Architecture for Mindreading', *New Ideas in Psychology*, 40, pp. 48–64.

Clark, A. (2013) 'Whatever Next? Predictive Brains, Situated Agents, and the Future of Cognitive Science', *Behavioral and Brain Sciences*, 36 (3), pp. 181–204.

Clark, A. (2015) *Surfing Uncertainty: Prediction, Action, and the Embodied Mind*. Oxford: Oxford University Press.

Colombo, M. (2014) 'Two Neurocomputational Building Blocks of Social Norm Compliance', *Biology and Philosophy*, 29 (1), pp. 71–88.

Colombo, M. and Hartmann, S. (2015) 'Bayesian Cognitive Science, Unification, and Explanation', *The British Journal for the Philosophy of Science*, 68 (2), pp. 451–484.

Colombo, M. and Wright, C. (2017) 'Explanatory Pluralism: An Unrewarding Prediction Error for Free Energy Theorists', *Brain and Cognition*, 112, pp. 3–12.

Csibra, G. (2008) 'Goal Attribution to Inanimate Agents by 6.5-Month-Old Infants', *Cognition*, 107, pp. 705–717.

Csibra, G. et al. (1999) 'Goal Attribution without Agency Cues: The Perception of "Pure Reason" in Infancy', *Cognition*, 72, pp. 237–267.

Daunizeau, J. et al. (2010a) 'Observing the Observer (I): Meta-Bayesian Models of Learning and Decision-Making', *PLoS ONE*, 5 (12), e15554.

Daunizeau J. et al. (2010b) 'Observing the Observer (II): Deciding When to Decide', *PLoS ONE*, 5 (12), e15555.

de Bruin, L. and Michael, J. (2017) 'Prediction Error Minimization: Implications for Embodied Cognition and the Extended Mind Hypothesis', *Brain and Cognition*, 112, pp. 58–63.

de Bruin, L. and Michael, J. (under review) 'Prediction Error Minimization as a Framework for Social Cognition Research'.

de Bruin, L. and Newen, A. (2014) 'The Developmental Paradox of False Belief Understanding: A Dual-System Solution', *Synthese*, 191 (3), pp. 297–320.

Farroni, T. et al. (2002) 'Eye Contact Detection in Humans from Birth', *Proceedings of the National Academy of Sciences*, 99 (14), pp. 9602–9605.

Fiebich, A. and Coltheart, M. (2015) 'Various Ways to Understand Other Minds: Towards a Pluralistic Approach to the Explanation of Social Understanding', *Mind and Language*, 30 (3), pp. 235–258.

Friston, K. (2013) 'Life As We Know It', *Journal of the Royal Society Interface*, 10 (86), 20130475.

Friston, K. et al. (2013) 'The Anatomy of Choice: Active Inference and Agency', *Frontiers in Human Neuroscience*, 7, art. 598.

Gale, A. et al. (1975) 'EEG Correlates of Eye Contact and Interpersonal Distance', *Biological Psychology*, 3 (4), pp. 237–245.

Gergely, G., Bekkering, H., and Kiraly, I. (2002) 'Rational Imitation in Preverbal Infants', *Nature*, 415 (6873), p. 755.

Gergely, G. and Csibra, G. (2003) 'Teleological Reasoning in Infancy: The Naïve Theory of Rational Action', *Trends in Cognitive Sciences*, 7, pp. 287–292.

Goldman, A.I. (1989) 'Interpretation Psychologized', *Mind and Language*, 4 (3), pp. 161–185.

Goldman, A.I. and Sripada, C.S. (2005) 'Simulationist Models of Face-based Emotion Recognition', *Cognition*, 94 (3), pp. 193–213.

Gopnik, A. and Wellman, H.M. (1992) 'Why the child's theory of mind really is a theory', *Mind and Language*, 7 (1–2), pp. 145–171.

Gordon, R.M. (1986) 'Folk Psychology as Simulation', *Mind and Language*, 1 (2), pp. 158–171.

Haxby, J.V., Hoffman, E.A., and Gobbini, M.I. (2002) 'Human Neural Systems for Face Recognition and Social Communication', *Biological Psychiatry*, 51, pp. 59–67.

Heyes, C. (2014) 'False Belief in Infancy: A Fresh Look', *Developmental Science*, 17 (5), pp. 647–659.

Hietanen, J.K. et al. (2008) Seeing Direct and Averted Gaze Activates the Approach–Avoidance Motivational Brain Systems. *Neuropsychologia*, 46(9), 2423–2430.

Hohwy, J. (2013) *The Predictive Mind*. Oxford: Oxford University Press.

Hood, B.M., Willen, J.D., and Driver, J. (1998) 'Adult's Eyes Trigger Shifts of Visual Attention in Human Infants', *Psychological Science*, 9 (2), pp. 131–134.

Koster-Hale, J. and Saxe, R. (2013) 'Theory of Mind: A Neural Prediction Problem', *Neuron*, 79 (5), pp. 836–848.

Kovács, Á.M., Téglás, E., and Endress, A.D. (2010) 'The Social Sense: Susceptibility to Others' Beliefs in Human Infants and Adults', *Science*, 330 (6012), pp. 1830–1834. Available at: DOI:10.1126/science.1190792.

Krupenye, C. et al. (2016) 'Great Apes Anticipate That Other Individuals Will Act According to False Beliefs', *Science*, 354 (6308), pp. 110–114.

Leslie, A.M. (1994) 'Pretending and Believing: Issues in the Theory of ToMM', *Cognition*, 50 (1–3), pp. 211–238.

Marr, D. (1975) 'Approaches to Biological Information Processing', *Science*, 190, pp. 875–876.

Marr, D. (1982) *Vision: A Computational Approach*. San Francisco, CA: Freeman & Co.

Marr, D. and Poggio, T. (1977) 'From Understanding Computation to Understanding Neural Circuitry', *Neurosciences Research Program Bulletin*, 15, pp. 470–488.

McClamrock, R. (1991) 'Marr's Three Levels: A Re-evaluation', *Minds and Machines*, 1 (2), pp. 185–196.

Michael, J. and Christensen, W. (2016) 'Flexible Goal Attribution in Early Mindreading', *Psychological Review*, 123 (2), pp. 219–227.

Michael, J., Christensen, W., and Overgaard, S. (2013) 'Mindreading as Social Expertise', *Synthese*, pp. 1–24. Available at: DOI:10.1007/s11229-013-0295-z.

Moutoussis, M. et al. (2014) 'A Formal Model of Interpersonal Inference', *Frontiers in Human Neuroscience*, 25 (8), art. 160.

Nichols, K.A. and Champness, B.G. (1971) 'Eye Gaze and the GSR', *Journal of Experimental Social Psychology*, 7 (6), pp. 623–626.

Overgaard, S. and Michael, J. (2015) 'The Interactive Turn in Social Cognition Research: A Critique', *Philosophical Psychology*, 28 (2), pp. 160–183.

Paulus, M. et al. (2011) 'Imitation in Infancy: Rational or Motor Resonance', *Child Development*, 82, pp. 1047–1057.

Pelphrey, K.A. et al. (2003) Brain Activation Evoked by Perception of Gaze Shifts: The Influence of Context. *Neuropsychologia*, 41(2), 156–170.

Perner, J. and Ruffman, T. (2005) 'Infants' Insight into the Mind: How Deep?', *Science*, 308 (5719), pp. 214–216.

Rakoczy, H. (2008) 'Taking Fiction Seriously: Young Children Understand the Normative Structure of Joint Pretend Games', *Developmental Psychology*, 44 (4), pp. 1195–1201.

Rakoczy, H., Warneken, F., and Tomasello, M. (2008) 'The Sources of Normativity: Young Children's Awareness of the Normative Structure of Games', *Developmental Psychology*, 44 (3), pp. 875–881.

Sartori, L., Becchio, C., and Castiello, U. (2011) 'Cues to Intention: The Role of Movement Information', *Cognition*, 119 (2), p. 242–252.

Senju, A. and Csibra, G. (2008) 'Gaze Following in Human Infants Depends on Communicative Signals', *Current Biology*, 18 (9), pp. 668–671.

Sommerfeld, R.D. et al. (2007) 'Gossip as an Alternative for Direct Observation in Games of Indirect Reciprocity', *Proceedings of the National Academy of Sciences USA*, 104 (44), pp. 17435–17440.

Southgate, V. and Vernetti, A. (2014) 'Belief-based Action Prediction in Preverbal Infants', *Cognition*, 130 (1), pp. 1–10.

Steglich-Petersen, A. and Michael, J. (2015) 'Why Desire Reasoning Is Developmentally Prior to Belief Reasoning', *Mind and Language*, 30 (5), pp. 526–549.

Tamietto, M. and De Gelder, B. (2010) 'Neural Bases of the Non-conscious Perception of Emotional Signals', *Nature Reviews Neuroscience*, 11 (10), pp. 697–709.

Tamietto, M. et al. (2009) 'Unseen Facial and Bodily Expressions Trigger Fast Emotional Reactions', *Proceedings of the National Academy of Science U.S.A.*, 106, pp. 17661–17666.

Teufel, C. et al. (2009) 'Social Cognition Modulates the Sensory Coding of Observed Gaze Direction', *Current Biology*, 19 (15), pp. 1274–1277.

Wellman, H.M., Cross, D., and Watson, J. (2001) 'Meta-Analysis of Theory-of-Mind Development: The Truth about False Belief', Child Development, 72 (3), pp. 655–684.

Westra, E. (2017) 'Stereotypes, Theory of Mind, and the Action–Prediction Hierarchy', *Synthese*, pp. 1–26.

Wimmer, H. and Perner, J. (1983) 'Beliefs about Beliefs: Representation and Constraining Function of Wrong Beliefs in Young Children's Understanding of Deception', *Cognition*, 13 (1), pp. 103–128.

Woodward, A.L. (1998) 'Infants selectively encode the goal object of an actor's reach', *Cognition*, 69 (1), 1–34.

35

COMPUTATIONAL THEORIES OF GROUP BEHAVIOR

Bryce Huebner and Joseph Jebari

Repeated interactions between animals can generate stable patterns of collective behavior (Couzin, 2009). For example, colonies of eusocial insects can make collective decisions about where to build their nests, and where to forage (Reid et al., 2015; Sasaki et al., 2013; Seeley, 1995; 2010). And people working together develop the skills that are required to fly commercial airplanes, and to navigate modern naval vessels (Hutchins, 1995a; 1995b). In each of these cases, and in many others as well, computational models have provided useful insights about the nature and structure of group-level behavior; and some philosophers have suggested that such models provide a plausible foundation for thinking about collective mentality. But while group structure often impacts individual computations, and shapes individual mentality, it is substantially less clear whether these group-level computations ever yield forms of group-mindedness. By looking to coordination dynamics, we can begin to understand how the strength of informational relations between the components of distributed systems can stabilize collective behavior (Anderson, Richardson, and Chemero, 2012). But it is more difficult to say when such relations yield collective mentality.

In addressing the issue of collective mentality, some philosophers have adopted a dynamical approach. They have focused on patterns of self-organization, and argued that collective mentality requires neither collective computation nor collective mental representation (Palermos, 2016). Others have focused on the ways that group members acquire, store, transmit, and manipulate information as they perform collaborative tasks; they hold that collective mentality emerges as a result of informational transactions, which can occur even in the absence of collective mental representations (Theiner, 2013; 2014). And still others have suggested that we should only posit collective mentality "where no subsystem is capable of producing an authoritative representation and where the representations of multiple subsystems can be coordinated and integrated to yield flexible, goal-directed system-level behavior" (Huebner, 2014, p. 14). Stepping back from these disagreements, we can begin to see substantial overlap between 'pure' cases of dynamic coordination and more complex forms of coordination that depend on mental representations and informational relations (cf., Dale et al., 2013). And from this perspective, it becomes possible to discern cases that don't fit nicely within any of these perspectives, but which seem to play a role in biologically significant forms of cooperative behavior. Our aim in this paper is to clarify the variety of different ways in which individual and collective computations unfold in cooperative contexts. While we offer some reflections along the way, our aim is not to establish where collective mentality occurs; instead, we hope to clarify the variety of different ways in which a computational approach can be used to understand collective behavior, and the possibility of collective mentality.

Throughout the paper, we treat dynamic forms of coordination as physical computations, which are best modeled using differential equations (Piccinini and Scarantino, 2011). This is consistent with the rapidly expanding empirical literature on collective behavior, which often appeals to dynamical computations without specifying what is represented – or whether anything is. We believe that many of these collective computations are likely to occur in the absence of group-level representations (cf., Piccinini, 2008). And for this reason, we adopt a mechanistic account of computation that requires: (1) a functional mechanism that processes variables that can change states, (2) in accordance with rules that map inputs to outputs, (3) in ways that are sensitive to the properties of these variables and to differences between different portions of them (Piccinini and Bahar, 2013, p. 458; Piccinini and Scarantino, 2011, p. 10). By paying attention to the precise nature of the computations that have been posited to explain different kinds of group behavior, we hope to show that there is a continuum between minimal forms of coordination – such as synchronous flashing in fireflies – and maximal forms of coordination – such as collective decision making on the basis of distributed sources of information.

Individual computations

Let's begin with the form of dynamic updating that allows some colonies of fireflies to synchronize their flashing behavior. Individual fireflies flash to attract mates. But in one colony in the Great Smoky Mountains, stable patterns of synchronization reliably emerge for two weeks each summer. Each insect functions as an intrinsic oscillator that tracks the distribution and frequency of nearby flashes, and adjusts its rate and frequency of flashing against the observed value (Ramírez-Ávila, Guisset, and Deneubourg, 2003, p. 255). Individuals flash within a fixed period (965 ± 90 ms); but if another firefly flashes within the first 840 ms of a cycle, this will inhibit the upcoming flash, and cause a one second delay before the next one; and if an insect flashes within the last 160 ms of this period, the next flash will occur normally, and subsequent flashes will advance to synchronize with observed flashes (Buck et al., 1981). This pattern of individual updating yields coordinated collective behavior. At the beginning of the night, flashing is chaotic; but order emerges as each firefly tracks the locally observable firing patterns, and uses this information to update its own behavior (Mirollo and Strogatz, 1990). As the night goes on, one or two individuals will produce one or two flashes, triggering synchronized flashing in every member of a colony. In most cases, a "burst of five to eight species-specific flashes is produced, and then group flashing abruptly ends" (Moiseff and Copeland, 1994, p. 403); but after a brief period of inactivity the process repeats.

We contend that this is a relatively pure case of dynamical updating, which occurs in the absence of mental representations. Individual fireflies act as functional mechanisms (intrinsic oscillators), which track nearby flashes, and mechanically adjust their behavior in ways that yield stable patterns of coordinated behavior. Since these insects are functioning as intrinsic oscillators, the behavior of nearby insects will become dynamically coupled. Finally, the emergence of synchrony yields a transition from a collection of independent and randomly flashing individuals, to a well-ordered system with stable collective dynamics.

Significantly, this means that individual behavior sustains group-level coordination because individuals update their behavior in light of the behavior of other group members. But while this allows groups of fireflies to function as coordinated systems, the resulting patterns of emergent behavior play no further computational role in the unfolding of individual or collective behavior. None of the individuals tracks the emergent state of the system; instead, each insect changes its behavior in response to flashes that occur nearby. Moreover, the group doesn't track any changes in internal or external variables, and it doesn't update its state in ways that are sensitive to the properties of such variables, or to differences in their portions. Nonetheless, coordinated behavior bubbles-up through patterns of individual behavior, yielding interesting group-level stabilities. We claim that this kind of dynamic, group-level behavior is sustained by individual computations that occur in the absence of representations, and that only the most minimal form of group-level computations is being carried out. Put differently, synchronously flashing fireflies reveal the power of simple tracking mechanisms for creating and sustaining stable patterns of collective behavior.

This point is more significant than it might initially seem, as humans and other animals often "'dance' like fireflies" (Schmidt and Richardson, 2008, p. 287), taking perceptually available information as input to behavioral oscillatory systems that facilitate behavioral entrainment. A well-known dynamical model (the HKB-model) explains how such ordered states emerge, why they stabilize, and why shifts occur between different coordinative states (Kelso, 2008). For example, people can wag their fingers in parallel at low frequencies; but increasing the speed of this movement triggers a switch to an anti-parallel pattern of movement. Something similar appears to hold across a wide range of interpersonal phenomena, where each person's behavior constrains the activity of the other, and each person allows their activity to be so constrained (Walton, Richardson, and Chemero, 2014, p. 12). Through this process, people draw one another into robust patterns of coordination. For example, in the context of improvisational jazz, musicians are "constrained by the sonic and kinesthetic results of the activities of the other improvisers", and their coordinated interactions yield a musical system that is constituted by the improvisers and their ongoing patters of interaction (Walton, Richardson, and Chemero 2014, p. 19).

There is good reason to believe that dynamical updating of this sort is "a universal self-organizing strategy that occurs at multiple scales of nature" (Schmidt and Richardson, 2008, p. 285). And we contend that it is driven by a minimal form of collective computation: rhythmic oscillations become synchronized through dynamic coupling between individuals, yielding group-level regularities that accord with the HKB-model. Across many cases, individuals can reasonably be seen as components in computational systems, which track changes in each other's states, and update their behavior in accordance with behavioral rules that are sensitive to such changes. But many kinds of mutual alignment require more robust forms of information processing, which go beyond oscillatory resonance. Colonies of insects, schools of fish, flocks of birds, and herds of mammals often move together as groups, as individuals adjust their behavior in light of the observed behavior of nearby organisms. And behavioral alignment emerges as individuals adjust their behavior in light of "locally acquired cues such as the positions, motion, or change in motion, of others" (Couzin, 2009, p. 36). And as we argue in the next section, this is true even where nothing is represented by the group.

Group-level information processing

Individuals within a school, a flock, or a herd typically adjust their direction of travel to avoid isolation, and these adjustments reliably scale to yield stable forms of collective behavior. But in some cases, animals also exploit the information about unobserved resources or predators that is embodied in the movement decisions of nearby neighbors, treating observed directional changes as evidence of a biological salient object or event (Kao et al., 2014). Where the location of resources and predators is known to a subset of a population, naïve individuals who track the movement of nearby neighbors, and treat their behavior as information about inaccessible features of the local environment, expand their 'effective range' of perception (Couzin, 2007, p. 715). And where animals adjust their willingness to commit to a course of action in light of the number of committed animals, this can generate cohesive forms of group-level behavior that reduce the cost of seeking new information for all individuals (Hein et al., 2015; Sumpter et al., 2008, p. 1775).

Understanding these kinds of phenomena doesn't require adding much to the form of dynamical updating that we discussed in the previous section. But particular forms of information processing are important to the kind of computational phenomena that occurs in these kinds of cases. Individuals adjust their direction of travel, using simple behavioral rules that map inputs to outputs, in ways that are sensitive to the movements of others and to differences in the distribution of such movements. But just as importantly, they treat observed behavior as a source of natural information that provides evidence about the presence of resources and predators. Consequently, these behavioral adjustments often cascade through a group, allowing each animal to update its own decisions in ways that are sensitive to the group's overall informational state. As animals move toward a foraging location, or away from a predator, they provide a signal that can be interpreted by others as behaviorally relevant. And as individual animals change their state in light of this information, using simple interaction rules to map the distribution and value of observed movements onto behavioral outputs, their behavior constitutes a signal for further observation. To understand these kinds of collective behavior, it is thus necessary to examine both the behavioral rules that are employed by individuals, as well as the sensitivity to the information encoded in observed behavior.

Consider the way that colonies of Olive baboons make decisions about where and when to forage. These baboons are "most likely to follow when there are many initiators with high agreement. However, when agreement is low, having more concurrent initiators decreases the likelihood that a baboon will follow anyone" (Strandburg-Peshkin et al., 2015, p. 1361). Within colonies, group-level cascades of information help individuals make decisions that will guide them toward preferable foraging locations, while reducing the cost of leaving the group to seek new information. The decision an individual makes thus depends on the decisions that others are making; and since all individuals adjust their decisions in light of the changes in group-level properties, these shifts can be seen as inputs into a parallel processing algorithm that reliably moves the group toward consensus (Sumpter and Pratt, 2009, p. 743). Here, as in many different species, a simple "quorum-response" rule is used to effectively integrate multiple sources of information about a course of action; uninformed and misinformed individuals then correct their behavior in light of group-wide behaviors; and since individuals raise their decision thresholds as group size increases, being in a larger group improves the accuracy of such decisions (Sumpter et al., 2008, p. 1776). Where this pattern of tracking and updating occurs in the context of a relatively stable group, it yields a group-based computational process, where small changes in individual states yield large changes in group-level behavior, and where cascades of biologically significant information – embodied in the prevalence and distribution of movement decisions – lead individual preferences to converge on the best available option, in ways that would otherwise be impossible (Sumpter and Pratt, 2009).

Similarly, consider the case of predator avoidance in Golden Shiners, which emerge as individual fish adjust their speed and direction to align with their nearest-neighbors (Berdahl et al., 2013). Golden Shiners are skittish, and they often display spontaneous avoidance behavior in the absence of predators – but crucially, the effect of this behavior is dampened in schools (Rosenthall et al., 2015). Within a school, fish respond to the avoidance displays of any fish they can see. And since few fish will see the spontaneous avoidance behavior of a single fish, skittishness only triggers a limited response in the school. By contrast, the presence of a predator leads multiple fish on the same edge of a school to produce simultaneous avoidance signals. This yields a threat signal that cascades through the school, as each fish will observe several simultaneous avoidance displays. Where this occurs, the information that is embodied in predator avoidance triggers group-wide avoidance behavior, as the information cascades through the entire school. The important thing to notice, here, is that informational signals are amplified by parallel patterns of behavioral resonance. And information processing cascades occur when "the growing number of adherents to an option increases its attractiveness to undecided animals" (Sumpter and Pratt, 2009, p. 745). Likewise, informational signals are dampened by behavioral dissonance, and negative feedback prevents uninformed individuals from guiding group-level behavior.

In each of these cases, adjustments to individual behavior unfold dynamically in real-time, and they are sensitive to the value of food resources, and to the presence or absence of predators. But as with the cases we addressed above, the most salient computations are those that are carried out by individuals. Each animal adjusts its behavior in light of its own observations, with patterns of mutual adjustment yielding a computational process that governs group-level behavior. As information cascades through a group, this generates successful forms of individual and collective behavior – without individuals needing to know that a collective computation is occurring. But here, we think it is substantially less clear whether these group-based computations yield collective mentality. Perhaps colonies of baboons and schools of fish should be treated as cognitive systems, as they are carrying out classically cognitive tasks (i.e. avoiding predators, and finding foraging patches), and they are doing so in a way that depends on integrated networks of computational processes. Or perhaps the individuals are carrying out these cognitive tasks, by tracking the distributed computation that is being carried out by the group; on this latter approach, each animal is looking for the best foraging option, and their success depends on using the information that other animals have broadcast. Of course, acting in the context of a group is a good way to succeed in this task – and it may be the only biologically feasible way for such organisms to track preferable food sources and dangerous predators.

In general, we prefer this second approach, which focuses on the ways that individuals use the information embodied in the structure of the group. There are likely to be many cases where aggregate success depends on the independence of decision-makers (Surowiecki, 2005). And in such cases, tendencies toward local control should be preserved, even in species where collective action is common. More importantly, where consensus is reached too rapidly, informational cascades can often generate forms of groupthink, and "when individuals sense too much of the group, the result is a filtering of the local influences and an averaged (compromised) collective response" (Leonard et al., 2012, p. 232). Consequently, it is biologically plausible that individual-level computations will tend to retain a high degree of salience in many cases, as they are necessary to prevent group-level processing from repeatedly leading to sub-optimal decisions (Torney et al., 2015). But there are cases where the properties of a network become just as important as individual computations, and in the remainder of this chapter, we turn to forms of collective behavior where this seems to be the case.

Network structure and informational processing

Simple responses to the position and motion of others produce many forms of group-level behavior. But in well-organized groups, network structure, as well as flows of information, and relations of independence and interdependence can play critical roles in individual and group-level computations (Derex and Boyd, 2016). In some groups, individuals learn to track the network structure of the group they belong to; and this can open up novel individual strategies, which in turn transform the structure of the group. This kind of computational phenomena is complex, but it is pervasive. And to see what it amounts to, it will help to work through a particular case in detail. Here, we consider the way that pigtailed macaques track and maintain stable dominance hierarchies.

A smart animal should only compete for resources if their chance of winning is high – otherwise they should acquiesce. However, in competitive colonies, such decisions are often made under conditions of uncertainty: success is subject to numerous environmental factors, and immediate past successes or failures are often unreliable predictors of future outcomes. To solve this problem, pigtailed macaques have arrived upon an ingenious strategy for collectively determining the "temporally stable factors that predict who will be the winner on average" (Flack, 2012, p. 1804). Over the course of repeated dyadic and polyadic conflicts, macaques generate information about their relative fighting ability, as the less adept fighters are sure to lose more often over multiple bouts. After losing numerous fights, a monkey will begin signaling submission by baring its teeth toward the previous winner. This shift to subordination signaling consolidates the information generated by the fights, and communicates a general willingness to acquiesce, functioning as a kind of contract that allows the macaques to interact without fighting. So through repeated interactions, these monkeys are able to compute a measure of relative fighting ability and encode it in a subordination signal; and when these signals are expressed across multiple overlapping pairs of monkeys, they generate a subordination signaling network, whose overall structure encodes the dominance hierarchy of the group. Thus, while noisy signals are produced by the result of any single competition, the integration of these signals into a larger network of mutually adjusted responses produces a stable hierarchy organized according to a robust measure of relative fighting ability.

What is the nature of the computation that occurs in this case? As with the golden shiners, the interactions between colony members have the function of producing a robust measure of a biologically salient value: relative fighting ability. Moreover, the distributed nature of this process allows for the emergence of a stable collective order. But unlike the cases we have examined thus far, this subordination signaling network allows each macaque to locate its position within the larger group structure, by determining its own rank within the dominance hierarchy (Flack and Krakauer, 2006). Each macaque can estimate its social power, as well as its position in the hierarchy, by tracking the number of monkeys that signal subordination to them, and the frequency with which they do so. And by integrating over this information, each macaque can obtain a reliable estimate of how much power it has within the group. Thus, the subordination signaling network gives the individual macaques access to the output of multiple parallel competitions – they not only acquire a position in the hierarchy, they also obtain knowledge of that position.

To summarize, individual monkeys continually generate information about relative fighting ability, and encode that information through their patterns of signaling behavior within the subordination network. By tracking their history of agonistic interactions, they can determine the likelihood they will win in a fight against a given conspecific and then use the resulting representations to decide when to signal subordination, and to whom. Since multiple monkeys are doing this in parallel, this yields multiple interaction networks, with individual monkeys as nodes, and fights and subordination signals as edges (i.e. the connections between the nodes). Within these networks, altercations constitute physical computations, which collectively determine the dominance relations within the colony. Once stabilized, these dominance relations are encoded as constitutive features of the subordination signaling network; and in this context, individual monkeys can use the information encoded in the subordination signaling network to infer their own location within the hierarchy (Flack and Krakauer, 2006, E93). This is possible because each macaque can average over multiple signals to accurately measure its position in the colony and track its social power.

In this way, these monkeys become able to "see" the output of the computations that are occurring across the colony and use this information to guide colony-relevant actions, making it possible to feed the output of the collective process back into the dynamics of the process. As Jessica Flack and her colleagues (2006) argue, the computations carried out within this signaling network guide forms of individual decision making that make new and valuable forms of social decision making possible. Specifically, the ability to determine one's own position in the overall hierarchy increases the stability and cohesiveness of the group by allowing for a form of policing, where dominant macaques monitor the behavior of their group-mates, and intervene in conflicts that would destabilize the group. Such interventions are generally risky, making this kind of policing biologically unlikely. However, since these monkeys can reliably evaluate their own power within a group, dominant monkeys can engage in policing behavior with minimal risk of being harmed; for after all, the dominance hierarchy ensures that other monkeys will acquiesce to them. This form of policing stabilizes the network structure that allows policing to occur, and this means that the stability of the group structure is both the cause and the effect of effective policing. As a result, colonies where policing occurs are larger, and they have higher rates of partner diversity, as well as increased possibilities for forms of socially contagion and cooperation; by contrast, colonies without policing have high rates of conflict, yielding less integrated groups, with less stable social interactions (Flack et al., 2006).

Similar forms of computational phenomena are ubiquitous within human groups; and the expressive power of language allows us to exchange signals about an indefinitely large class of topics, far beyond considerations of social dominance. Humans can identify useful environmental stabilities that can be signaled, and they can establish robust network structures that are capable of processing collective information about these stabilities (Barkoczi and Galesic, 2016). This yields a kind of social learning that can contribute to individual- and group-level performance by providing a way to diffuse successful strategies through a communication network (e.g. Apicella et al., 2012; Hill et al., 2011; Rand, Arbesman, and Christakis, 2011). However, in complex adaptive environments, communities of social learners risk settling on locally optimal strategies, while being unable to successfully explore superior strategies; and whether the most successful strategy can be identified and spread across a network largely depends on the structure of the network and the social learning rule used by the agents (Derex and Boyd, 2016).

This brings us to an intriguing fact about human sociality: where multiple agents execute a social learning routine in parallel, it is possible for a network of interacting agents to efficiently search for the best strategy, in ways that go beyond what would be possible for a lone individual (Derex and Boyd, 2016). This happens as individual agents repeatedly sample the group-level process to identify better strategies, and use these strategies as the basis for further individual search. When superior strategies are found individually, these feed back into the group-level computational process, ratcheting up the overall performance of the network. This is possible because the agents are embedded in a signaling network that allows other agents to communicate both the strategy they are using and its value. A focal agent can then integrate over the signals they receive, to infer the relative value of their own strategy, and this in turn can guide decision making. Although the integration algorithm is different from the one that undergirds macaque policing, it yields a similar type of phenomena: an agent uses their position in a signaling network to infer their own position with respect to that network, and uses this information to guide their own individual decisions. The outcome of these individual decisions then feeds back into the signaling network, altering the dynamics of the collective computation.

This process creates complex computational processes that are optimized by striking a balance between independence and interdependence; and this capacity provides a foundation for a more robust form of collective decision making, which we examine in the next section (List, Elsholtz, and Seeley, 2008).

Decisions

Identifying cases of group-level cognition is, at least in part, "a matter of determining how a cognitive system at a higher level can subsume cognitive systems at a lower level, and how the systems at multiple levels can strengthen rather than diminish one another" (Goldstone and Theiner, 2017). Thus far, we've argued that dynamic forms of coupled processing allow animals to engage in flexible and adaptive forms of behavior; but do coupled systems ever "instantiate cognitive mechanisms in virtue of which a variety of systems perform important cognitive functions associated with flexible, adaptive, and intelligent behavior" (Goldstone and Theiner, 2017)? In a recent paper, Rob Goldstone and Georg Theiner (2017) have argued that diffusion-based computations facilitate the accumulation of evidence, and generate rapid and accurate decisions; they also contend that the computational processes that allow individuals to make perceptual decisions under uncertainty are realized in the decision making of social insect colonies. In each case, interacting populations use competitive algorithms, arriving at decisions when one population exceeds an uncertainty threshold, which is adjusted in light of the salience of speed and accuracy (Marshal et al., 2011). We think that Goldstone and Theiner are on the right track.

Colonies of ants and honeybees are often able to function as "parallel information-processing systems capable of intricate collective decision making during essential tasks such as foraging, moving home or constructing a nest" (Couzin, 2009, p. 39). In each case, collective decisions arise through a process that parallels the winner-take-all algorithms that are used to explain how the visual system categorizes objects (Riesenhuber and Poggio, 1999), or by forms of diffusion-based processing that yield rapid and accurate perceptual decisions (Marshal et al., 2011). By enhancing the activity of some computational units (here, ants or honeybees), while inhibiting or suppressing the activity of others, responses can be pooled in ways that will achieve an accurate representation of the biologically salient features of an object (here a foraging location or a nest site). Consequently, decisions are reached that are relevant to group-level behavior by way of the friendly competition between group members.

One of the clearest examples of this kind of phenomena occurs when a honeybee hive splits. Scouts carry out a random search for a new nest site, evaluating each alternative in terms of "cavity volume, entrance height, entrance area, entrance direction, entrance position relative to the cavity floor, and presence of combs from a previous colony" (Seeley and Buhrman, 1999, p. 31). Few bees visit more than one site, but the colony settles on a decision by representing the variety of different options and selecting among them. Each option is evaluated in terms of its attributes (as listed above), and the group's choice is typically optimal with respect to the value of each attribute for colony survival and reproduction (Seeley and Buhrman, 1999). When scouts return to the hive, they dance in support of the site they visit, using a waggle dance that varies in intensity as a function of the quality of the site. Few scouts dance in support of more than one site; and "most bees that dance initially for a site other than the ultimately chosen site terminate their dancing for this site by ceasing their dancing altogether, not by switching their dancing to the chosen site" (Seeley and Buhrman, 1999, p. 30). Some bees that dance for the ultimately chosen site stop before consensus is reached; but in general, scouts who find a preferable site tend to recruit others to inspect the same site; and the increasing levels of recruitment to a site further increase support for that site (List, Elsholtz, and Seeley, 2008; Seeley et al., 2012). Decisions are thus made by "quorum", with colonies settling on a preferred alternative as soon as there is sufficient support for it (Seeley and Visscher, 2003). Importantly, their "independence in assessing the various sites' quality and their interdependence through communication are both necessary and sufficient for the reliability of the bees' decision process" (List, Elsholtz, and Seeley, 2008, p. 758).

A similar consensus-based algorithm is used by ants to compare multiple potential nest sites, which differ with respect to cavity volume, interior dimness, and entrance size (Pratt et al., 2002; Sasaki et al., 2013). But more intriguingly, when army ants build bridges to create a shortcut in a foraging trail, for example, they make adjustments to the length of the bridge in response to the flow of traffic across their bodies (Reid et al., 2015, p. 15114). As traffic decreases, ants abandon their position; and as traffic increases, ants are recruited to the bridge. But bridge expansion will often stop before the maximum foraging shortcut has been achieved. This phenomenon is interesting because no individual can represent the costs and benefits to the colony – yet the variations in recruitment underwrite a form of parallel information processing that is sensitive to "the diminishing returns of shortening the trail to avoid the cost of locking up an increasing number of workers in the structure" (Reid et al., 2015, p. 15116).

The important thing to notice about these two cases is that both group-level computations, and group-level representations, play a critical role in the production of collective behavior. In contrast to the cases that we have discussed above, the individuals are serving as nodes in an integrated computational network that solves a group-relevant task. Individual bees observe informationally rich dances, and adjust their behavior in light of what they perceive; but *the colony* chooses the best nest site, for a large range of parameter conditions, by aggregating over individual patterns of behavior. Likewise, individual ants join or abandon their position in a bridge, in a way that is sensitive to the number of ants currently using the bridge; but the colony determines the optimal bridge length for successful hunting. While an account of the independent decisions of individual animals would be interesting, it is only by understanding the trade-off between independence and interdependence that we can understand what these colonies are doing, and why (cf. List, Elsholtz, and Seeley, 2008)

There have been speculative extensions of these types of models to human decision making. For example, John Dyer and colleagues (2008) have argued that the motion of crowds is likely to be driven by a computational process like this. But while there is a computation at the group level according to his account, the relevant forms of motion guidance aren't used by the group for any group-relevant ends. Bryce Huebner (2014, 69 ff.) has suggested that a stock market could display computational properties that were best modeled in terms of a competitive algorithm; but he worries that all of the relevant representations would be used for individual decision making, not for any sort of collective decision making. And Bernard Grofman and Scott Feld (1988) have argued that democratic group decisions could arise through a process of Condorcet aggregation (using a process of recruitment like the one suggested by List, Elsholtz, and Seeley, 2008). But here too, there is little evidence that successful democratic decision making relies on these specific kinds of computations.

Against this backdrop, it is worth asking what other kinds of system-level computations might lead to the production of group-level behavior in human groups, and whether any of these might yield stable forms of collective mentality. Much of the existing research on distributed cognition has focused on the ways that representations are passed between small numbers of people to yield higher-level regularities. For example, research on collaborative retrieval (Harris et al., 2011; 2014; Harris, Barnier, and Sutton, 2013; Michaelian and Sutton, 2013) and transactive memory (for reviews, see Ren and Argote, 2011; Theiner, 2013) has examined the ways that groups of two or three people broadcast and receive semantic information to one another. These projects often proceed at a relatively high level of abstraction; and as Matteo Colombo (2015) suggests, emerging research on hierarchical Bayesian algorithms may offer an interesting, biologically plausible model of collective learning and agency that can be used to flesh out these proposals. But at present, this suggestion remains quite speculative.

One way of moving forward on this speculative suggestion is to examine cases of top-top cognition. As Andreas Roepstorff and Chris Frith (2004) argue, we are able to communicate with one another (both linguistically and non-linguistically), in ways that allow us to draw one another into patterns of mutual alignment. Where this process is successful, it does seem to yield shared representations of a situation or an event, and there is some recent evidence that these similarities are grounded in patterns of overlapping neural activity (Clark, 2015, pp. 286–287; Friston and Frith, 2015; Gallotti, Fairhurst, and Frith, 2017; Dikker et al., 2017). Perhaps this is a way of linking the top-level structures of multiple interacting agents, and perhaps this allows for the possibility of treating people as computational nodes in an integrated computational network. At present, this remains a theoretically interesting possibility, which is only beginning to be demonstrated empirically – but it does recommend a fruitful path for future exploration, which we examine in the final section of this paper.

A speculative conclusion

It would be incredibly interesting if human forms of collective mentality were implemented by powerful forms of machine learning, such as hierarchical Bayesian algorithms. But which algorithms produce collective mentality, and whether they are the same kind across forms of biological cognition, are open empirical questions. We contend that mentality is likely to emerge wherever self-organizing systems achieve enough unity and stability to process information that is relevant to group-level ends, and to adjust group-level behavior in accordance with a group's representation of the world. This can be achieved in many different ways, and this is why we refrain from making claims about the class of algorithms and the kinds of representations that are necessary for collective mentality. We are unaware of cases where group-level cognitive capacities have been shown to depend on hierarchical Bayesian algorithms, but ants and honeybees do exhibit forms of collective mentality implemented by consensus algorithms and winner-take-all algorithms. And while it would be premature to attempt to pull all forms of collective mentality under the hierarchical Bayesian umbrella, there are interesting questions in this vicinity.

Collective behavior of various sorts is ubiquitous in human life. For as long as we have been human, we have been immersed in a integrated network of interaction, which is integral to the human phenotype, and to the possibility of human lifeways (cf. Jebari and Huebner, in press); furthermore, there is good reason to believe that our ability to flexibly exploit the forms of collective computation that are carried out within this network structure are central to our capacity to sustain increasingly complex social systems and acquire increasingly complex understandings of the world (Dedeo, 2013; Goldstone and Theiner, 2017). One of the major attractions of the hierarchical Bayesian framework in computational neuroscience is that it promises to unify within a single framework the mosaic of algorithms that have been proposed to explain neural function. And one tantalizing possibility is that something similar could be achieved with respect to human social systems. As we noted in the previous section, the research investigating the nature of human collective computation has been largely exploratory, emphasizing the vast array of different (and perhaps complementary) mechanisms that plausibly undergird the various dimensions of human sociality. We believe the question of unification should be taken up more seriously; it is possible that there is a universal algorithm that characterizes the basic processing structure of all human social systems – and it may be a hierarchical Bayesian process, or something like it. If this were established, it would revolutionize sociology, political science, and public policy. And recent empirical results suggest a way of moving forward on this approach to collective computation.

We already know that human social systems preserve certain network properties across scales, and that this is a feature of human social organization (Derex and Boyd, 2015; 2016; Salali et al., 2016). Analyzing a range of data involving multiple different measures of social network structure, Wei-Xing Zhou and colleagues (2005) have found that social networks across the developed world observe a hierarchical fractal-like scaling ratio, with units at each level of analysis constituted by approximately four units from the level below. Specifically, they show that small groups composed of approximately four closely-associated individuals tend to associate with approximately three other groups of similar size, forming larger, more loosely associated groups. Larger groups then associate with approximately three similarly structured groups, etc. If they are right that various human groups conform to this scaling property, this would suggest that human social systems tend to form self-similar structures at multiple levels of organization.

This scaling property has been confirmed in the social organization of contemporary hunter-gatherers (Hamilton et al., 2007) as well as in online multiplayer games (Fuchs, Sornette, and Thurner, 2014) indicating that it may be a universal feature of human sociality. Perhaps this kind of structure may have developed to deal with the demands of maintaining efficient resource and information exchange (Hamilton et al., 2007), and to preserve collective adaptability in the face of changing environments (Flack et al., 2013). If basic forms of human sociality are adapted to this structure, in a way that parallels the phenomena in macaques that we discussed above, then perhaps the ability to exploit the information that is encoded in the dynamics of social inter-action may prove to be an essential feature of efficient information processing across human groups. If this is right, then hierarchical network structure may function analogously to a hier-archical neural network, with information acquired at the individual level being aggregated and refined as it spreads through the network. Put differently, something like the following might be the case: network structure may provide constraints on the flow of information through human groups of various sizes; patterns of informational exchange within these structures may then yield local sources of knowledge, which can be fed upward through the group (using an aggregation function that strikes a balance between independence and interdependence); finally the information encoded in these aggregated signals may feed downward into individual-level computations, allowing individuals to locate themselves within larger structures, and to update their behavior in light of this information. This process would yield a bidirectional flow of information, which would allow groups of interacting individuals to search for the linked set of hypotheses that would make the most sense of the group's current situation.

If this analogy goes through, then collective computation in humans may reflect the imple-mentation of the same type of hierarchical information processing scheme that is found in the brain. If so, it may be possible to develop a unified theory of human collective computa-tion that is continuous with computational neuroscience. More research would be necessary to confirm this hypothesis; but no matter how the data turn out, we will gain a much clearer understanding of the computational structures that support patterns of stability, and patterns of variation in human sociality. Discovering a basic computational structure would have significant ramification for the design of effective social interventions, and for the development of efficient social institutions. Likewise, if no basic computational structure can be found, understanding the diversity inherent in human collective computation will have equally important consequences for good social design.

References

Anderson, M.L., Richardson, M.J., and Chemero, A. (2012) 'Eroding the Boundaries of Cognition: Implications of Embodiment', *Topics in Cognitive Science*, 4 (4), pp. 717–730.

Apicella, C.L. et al. (2012) 'Social Networks and Cooperation in Hunter-Gatherers', *Nature*, 481 (7382), pp. 497–501.

Barkoczi, D. and Galesic, M. (2016) 'Social Learning Strategies Modify the Effect of Network Structure on Group Performance', *Nature Communications*, 7, art. 13109. Available at: DOI: 10.1038/ncomms13109.

Berdahl, A. et al. (2013) 'Emergent Sensing of Complex Environments by Mobile Animal Groups', *Science*, 339 (6119), pp. 574–576.

Buck, J. et al. (1981) 'Control of Flashing in Fireflies', *Journal of Comparative Physiology*, 144 (3), pp. 287–298.

Clark, A. (2015) *Surfing Uncertainty: Prediction, Action, and the Embodied Mind*. Oxford: Oxford University Press.

Colombo, M. (2015) 'Bryce Huebner: *Macrocognition: A Theory of Distributed Minds and Collective Intentionality*'. Review of Macrocognition: A Theory of Distributed Minds and Collective Intentionality, by Bryce Huebner, *Minds and Machines*, 25 (1), pp. 103–109.

Couzin, I. (2007) 'Collective Minds', *Nature*, 445 (7129), p. 715.

Couzin, I. (2009) 'Collective Cognition in Animal Groups', *Trends in Cognitive Science*, 13 (1), pp. 36–43.

Dale, R. et al. (2013) 'The Self-organization of Human Interaction', *Psychology of Learning and Motivation*, 59, pp. 43–95.

DeDeo, S. (2013) 'Collective Phenomena and Non-finite State Computation in a Human', *PLoS ONE*, 8 (10), e75818.

Derex, M. and Boyd, R. (2015) 'The Foundations of the Human Cultural Niche', *Nature Communications*, 6, art. 9398. Available at: DOI:10.1038/ncomms9398.

Derex, M. and Boyd, R. (2016) 'Partial Connectivity Increases Cultural Accumulation within Groups', *Proceedings of the National Academy of Sciences*, 113, pp. 2982–2987.

Dikker, S. et al. (2017) 'Brain-to-Brain Synchrony Tracks Real-World Dynamic Group Interactions in the Classroom', *Current Biology*, 27, pp. 1375–1380.

Dyer, J.R. et al. (2008) 'Consensus Decision Making in Human Crowds', *Animal Behaviour*, 75 (2), pp. 461–470.

Flack, J.C. (2012) 'Multiple Time-Scales and the Developmental Dynamics of Social Systems', *Philosophical Transactions of the Royal Society of London B: Biological Sciences*, 367 (1597), pp. 1802–1810.

Flack, J.C. and Krakauer, D.C. (2006) 'Encoding Power in Communication Networks', *The American Naturalist*, 168 (3), pp. E87–E102.

Flack, J.C. et al. (2006) 'Policing Stabilizes Construction of Social Niches in Primates', *Nature*, 439 (7075), pp. 426–429.

Flack, J.C. et al. (2013) 'Timescales, Symmetry, and Uncertainty Reduction in the Origins of Hierarchy in Biological Systems', in Sterelny, K. et al. (eds.) *Cooperation and Its Evolution*. Cambridge, MA: MIT Press, pp. 45–74.

Friston, K. and Frith, C. (2015) 'A Duet for One', *Consciousness and Cognition*, 36, pp. 390–405.

Fuchs, B., Sornette, D., and Thurner, S. (2014) 'Fractal Multi-Level Organisation of Human Groups in a Virtual World', *Scientific Reports*, 4, pp. 1–6. Available at: DOI: 10.1038/srep06526.

Gallotti, M., Fairhurst, M., and Frith, C. (2017) 'Alignment in Social Interactions', *Consciousness and Cognition*, 48 (2017), pp. 253–261.

Goldstone, R. and Theiner, G. (2017) 'The Multiple, Interacting Levels of Cognitive Systems (MILCS) Perspective on Group Cognition', *Philosophical Psychology*, 30 (3), pp. 334–368.

Grofman, B. and Feld, S.L. (1988) 'Rousseau's General Will: A Condorcetian Perspective', *American Political Science Review*, 82 (2), pp. 567–576.

Hamilton, M.J. et al. (2007) 'The Complex Structure of Hunter-Gatherer Social Networks', *Proceedings of the Royal Society of London B: Biological Sciences*, 274 (1622), pp. 2195–2203.

Harris, C.B., Barnier, A.J., and Sutton, J. (2013) 'Shared Encoding and the Costs and Benefits of Collaborative Recall', *Journal of Experimental Psychology: Learning, Memory, and Cognition*, 39 (1), p. 183–195.

Harris, C.B. et al. (2011) 'We Remember, We Forget: Collaborative Remembering in Older Couples', *Discourse Processes*, 48 (4), pp. 267–303.

Harris, C.B. et al. (2014) 'Couples as Socially Distributed Cognitive Systems: Remembering in Everyday Social and Material Contexts', *Memory Studies*, 7 (3), pp. 285–297.

Hein, A.M. et al. (2015) 'The Evolution of Distributed Sensing and Collective Computation in Animal Populations', *eLife*, 4, e10955.

Hill, K.R. et al. (2011) 'Co-residence Patterns in Hunter-Gatherer Societies Show Unique Human Social Structure', *Science*, 331 (6022), pp. 1286–1289.

Huebner, B. (2014) *Macrocognition: A Theory of Distributed Minds and Collective Intentionality*. Oxford: Oxford University Press.

Hutchins, E. (1995a) *Cognition in the Wild*. Cambridge, MA: MIT Press.

Hutchins, E. (1995b) 'How a Cockpit Remembers Its Speed', *Cognitive Science*, 19 (3), pp. 265–288.

Jebari, J. and Huebner, B. (in press) 'From Objectivized Morality to Objective Morality. Commentary on P.K. Stanford, "The Difference between Ice Cream and Nazis: Moral Externalization and the Evolution of Human Cooperation"', *Behavioral and Brain Sciences*.

Kao, A. et al. (2014) 'Collective Learning and Optimal Consensus Decisions in Social Animal Groups', *PLoS Computational Biology*, 10 (8), e1003762.

Kelso, J.A.S. (2008) 'Haken-Kelso-Bunz Model', *Scholarpedia*, 3 (10), art. 1612.

Leonard, N.E. et al. (2012) 'Decision versus Compromise for Animal Groups in Motion', *Proceedings of the National Academy of Sciences*, 109 (1), pp. 227–232.

List, C., Elsholtz, C., and Seeley, T.D. (2008) 'Independence and Interdependence in Collective Decision Making: An Agent-based Model of Nest-Site Choice by Honeybee Swarms', *Philosophical Transactions of the Royal Society B*, 364, pp. 755–762.

Marshall, J.A.R. et al. (2011) 'On Optimal Decision-making in Brains and Social Insect Colonies', *Journal of the Royal Society Interface*, 6, pp. 1065–1074.

Michaelian, K. and Sutton, J. (2013) 'Distributed Cognition and Memory Research: History and Current Directions', *Review of Philosophy and Psychology*, 4 (1), pp. 1–24.

Mirollo, R.E. and Strogatz, S.H. (1990) 'Synchronization of Pulse-coupled Biological Oscillators', *SIAM Journal on Applied Mathematics*, 50 (6), pp. 1645–1662.

Moiseff, A. and Copeland, J. (1994) 'Mechanisms of Synchrony in the North American Firefly Photinus carolinus (Coleoptera: Lampyridae)', *Journal of Insect Behavior*, 8 (3), pp. 395–407.

Palermos, S.O. (2016) 'The Dynamics of Group Cognition', *Minds and Machines*, 26 (4), pp. 409–440.

Piccinini, G. (2008) 'Computation without Representation', *Philosophical Studies*, 137 (2), pp. 205–241.

Piccinini, G. and Bahar, S. (2013) 'Neural Computation and the Computational Theory of Cognition', *Cognitive Science*, 37 (3), pp. 453–488.

Piccinini, G. and Scarantino, A. (2011) 'Information Processing, Computation, and Cognition', *Journal of Biological Physics*, 37 (1), pp. 1–38.

Pratt, S.C. et al. (2002) 'Quorum Sensing, Recruitment, and Collective Decision-making during Colony Emigration by the Ant Leptothorax albipennis', *Behavioral Ecology and Sociobiology*, 52 (2), pp. 117–127.

Ramírez-Ávila, G., Guisset, J.L., and Deneubourg, J.L. (2003) 'Synchronization in Light-controlled Oscillators', *Physica D: Nonlinear Phenomena*, 182 (3), pp. 254–273.

Rand, D.G., Arbesman, S., and Christakis, N.A. (2011) 'Dynamic Social Networks Promote Cooperation in Experiments with Humans', *Proceedings of the National Academy of Sciences*, 108 (48), pp. 19193–19198.

Reid, C.R. et al. (2015) 'Army Ants Dynamically Adjust Living Bridges in Response to a Cost–Benefit Trade-off', *Proceedings of the National Academy of Sciences*, 112 (49), pp. 15113–15118.

Ren, Y. and Argote, L. (2011) 'Transactive Memory Systems 1985–2010: An Integrative Framework of Key Dimensions, Antecedents, and Consequences', *The Academy of Management Annals*, 5 (1), pp. 189–229.

Riesenhuber, M. and Poggio, T. (1999) 'Hierarchical Models of Object Recognition in Cortex', *Nature Neuroscience*, 2 (11), pp. 1019–1025.

Roepstorff, A. and Frith, C. (2004) 'What's at the Top in the Top-Down Control of Action? Script-sharing and 'Top-Top' Control of Action in Cognitive Experiments', *Psychological Research*, 68 (2–3), pp. 189–198.

Rosenthal, S. et al. (2015) 'Revealing the Hidden Networks of Interaction in Mobile Animal Groups Allows Prediction of Complex Behavioral Contagion', *Proceedings of the National Academy of Sciences*, 112 (15), pp. 4690–4695.

Salali, G.D. et al. (2016) 'Knowledge-Sharing Networks in Hunter-Gatherers and the Evolution of Cumulative Culture', *Current Biology*, 26 (18), pp. 2516–2521.

Sasaki, T. et al. (2013) 'Ant Colonies Outperform Individuals When a Sensory Discrimination Task Is Difficult but Not When It Is Easy', *Proceedings of the National Academy of Sciences*, 110 (34), pp. 13769–13773.

Schmidt, R.C. and Richardson, M.J. (2008) 'Dynamics of Interpersonal Coordination', in Fuchs, A. and Jirsa, V.K. (eds.) *Coordination: Neural, Behavioral and Social Dynamics*. Berlin: Springer, pp. 281–308.

Seeley, T. (1995) *The Wisdom of the Hive*. Cambridge, MA: Harvard University Press.

Seeley, T. (2010) *Honeybee Democracy*. Princeton, NJ: Princeton University Press.

Seeley, T. and Buhrman, S. (1999) 'Nest-Site Selection in Honey Bees: How Well do Swarms Implement the "Best-of-N" Decision Rule?', *Behavioral Ecology and Sociobiology*, 49, pp. 416–427.

Seeley, T. and Visscher, P. (2003) 'Choosing a Home: How the Scouts in a Honey Bee Swarm Perceive the Completion of Their Group Decision Making', *Behavioral Ecology and Sociobiology*, 54, pp. 511–520.

Seeley, T.D. et al. (2012) 'Stop Signals Provide Cross Inhibition in Collective Decision-making by Honeybee Swarms', *Science*, 335 (6064), pp. 108–111.

Strandburg-Peshkin, A. et al. (2015) 'Shared Decision-making Drives Collective Movement in Wild Baboons', *Science*, 348 (6241), pp. 1358–1361.

Sumpter, D.J. and Pratt, S.C. (2009) 'Quorum Responses and Consensus Decision Making', *Philosophical Transactions of the Royal Society of London B: Biological Sciences*, 364 (1518), pp. 743–753.

Sumpter, D.J. et al. (2008) 'Consensus Decision Making by Fish', *Current Biology*, 18 (22), pp. 1773–1777.

Surowiecki, J. (2005) *The Wisdom of Crowds*. Norwell, MA: Anchor Press.

Theiner, G. (2013) 'Transactive Memory Systems: A Mechanistic Analysis of Emergent Group Memory', *Review of Philosophy and Psychology*, 4 (1), pp. 65–89.

Theiner, G. (2014) 'A Beginner's Guide to Group Minds', in Sprevak, M. and Kallestrup, J. (eds.) *New Waves in Philosophy of Mind*. London: Palgrave Macmillan, pp. 301–322.

Torney, C.J. et al. (2015) 'Social Information Use and the Evolution of Unresponsiveness in Collective Systems', *Journal of the Royal Society Interface*, 12 (103), pp. 1–9.

Walton, A., Richardson, M.J., and Chemero, A. (2014) 'Self-Organization and Semiosis in Jazz Improvisation', *International Journal of Signs and Semiotic Systems (IJSSS)*, 3 (2), pp. 12–25.

Zhou, W.-X. et al. (2005) 'Discrete Hierarchical Organization of Social Group Sizes', *Proceedings of the Royal Society of London B: Biological Sciences*, 272 (1561), pp. 439–444.

INDEX